P. Michael McDermott, APR, Iona College

"It is clear, easy to read and understand, well written, us
global dimension other textbooks lack."

"I have found this book to be very readable, as have my students in several courses."

"In my opinion, the balance between theoretical and practical is good, as is its balance between providing direction while not being overly prescriptive."

"I will be delighted to adopt the new edition of this fine textbook when it is ready!"

Peter A. DeCaro, Ph.D., Buena Vista University

"It is a solid general PR text, delivering the major aspects of PR – from its historical context and contemporary implications, to its strategies and tactics."

"The Wilcox text is a good introductory text. For the most part it is well-balanced, not too demanding, and at most times, easily readable in narrative form. Fundamentally, it is coherent and cohesive in its pedagogical approach."

"The chapters are organized in a very logical and useful way."

"I find the approach the authors take to be appropriate for my course. They present public relations in a very logical, yet useful manner, with applications that are useful. Also, the authors' approach to some topics makes students aware of implications they would not, under many circumstances, become aware."

Public Relations:
Strategies and Tactics

seventh edition

Dennis L. Wilcox
San Jose State University

Glen T. Cameron
Missouri School of Journalism

Phillip H. Ault
Late, South Bend Tribune

Warren K. Agee
University of Georgia

Boston ■ New York ■ San Francisco
Mexico City ■ Montreal ■ Toronto ■ London ■ Madrid ■ Munich ■ Paris
Hong Kong ■ Singapore ■ Tokyo ■ Cape Town ■ Sydney

Series Editor: Molly Taylor
Editor-in-Chief: Karen Hanson
Series Editorial Assistant: Michael Kish
Marketing Manager: Mandee Eckersley
Composition and Prepress Buyer: Linda Cox
Manufacturing Manager: Megan Cochran
Text Designer: Glenna Collett
Photo Research: Helane Manditch-Prottas
Cover Administrator: Linda Knowles
Editorial-Production Coordinator: Mary Beth Finch
Editorial-Production Service: Heckman & Pinette
Electronic Composition: Monotype Composition

For related titles and support materials, visit our online catalog at www.ablongman.com

Between the time Website information is gathered and then published, it is not unusual for some sites to have closed. Also, the transcription of URLs can result in unintended typographical errors. The publisher would appreciate notification where these errors occur so that they may be corrected in subsequent editions.

Library of Congress Cataloging-in-Publication Data

Public relations: strategies and tactics/Dennis L. Wilcox . . . [et al.]. —7th ed.
p. cm.
Includes bibliographical references and index.

ISBN 0-205-36073-4 (alk. paper)

1. Public relations. 2. Public relations—United States. I. Wilcox, Dennis L.

HM1221 .P8 2003
659.2—dc21 2002021453

Printed in the United States of America
10 9 8 7 6 5 4 3 2 RRD-OH 07 06 05 04 03 02

In Remembrance
Phillip H. Ault
1914–2001
Friend, Colleague, and Coauthor

Brief Contents

Contents

The Audience and How to Reach It 235

The Internet and Other New Technologies 263

PART 5 TACTICS

Visual Tactics 527

Preface

This seventh edition of *Public Relations: Strategies and Tactics* is for students who want to understand the basic concepts of effective public relations and how they can prepare for the ethical practice of public relations in today's fast-changing world. The new millennium brings the challenge of working on a global scale, mastering the old and the new technologies of information dissemination, and meeting the public demand for accountability.

This edition, however, is published with a note of sadness. Our coauthor and good friend, Phillip H. Ault, passed away at the age of 87 in 2001 as we were beginning work on this edition. He was a vital, active participant since the inception of this textbook in 1984 and made numerous contributions to its success as a leading introductory book in the field. His counsel, advice, and dedication to meeting deadlines are sorely missed. Replacing Phil Ault as second primary author is Dr. Glen T. Cameron, University of Missouri, who became a coauthor in the sixth edition.

New in the Seventh Edition

The seventh edition continues with many of the innovations introduced in the sixth edition. Running through the chapters are four kinds of boxes, which are designed to give the student additional insights into the professional practice of public relations. One series, titled "Focus on Ethics," challenges students to make sound ethical decisions.

Another series of boxes, titled "Global Public Relations," illustrates public relations programs conducted in other nations and on a global scale. There are also "PR Insights" and "PR Casebook" boxes that focus on today's headlines and how individuals and organizations are using effective concepts of public relations. In some cases, as the text points out, there are major blunders.

Up-to-date Coverage

This textbook has always been known for its up-to-date coverage of current events. Students read and discuss issues that have been in the headlines and are familiar to them. This edition continues the tradition by adding new cases and discussion about:

- The Firestone recall of 6.5 million tires that also questioned the safety of the Ford Motor Company's popular Explorer SUV.
- How an Australian company motivated its employees to support the company's sponsorship of the Olympics in Sydney.
- Microsoft's introduction of the XP operating system.
- Oracle's use of "smashmouth" public relations to slam the competition.

- The advent of three or four major holding companies that control the majority of the public relations and advertising business.
- How Rep. Gary Condit of California flunked Persuasion 101.
- Can Carrie Bradshaw of "Sex and the City" sell mutual funds?
- Using public relations to reach a teenage audience.
- Selecting a new corporate name: What's an Accenture?
- SEC fines an individual for faking a financial news release.
- Starbucks responds to the murder of employees in one of its locations.
- Microsoft's lobbying pays off in an antitrust case.
- Coca-Cola bungles a product recall in Europe.
- Enron's lobbying efforts on Capitol Hill.
- Presidential campaigns: the public relations strategies of Gore and Bush.
- The war on terrorism: the government steps up propaganda efforts.
- Campaign finance reform: what it means to public relations practice.
- Public relations in the Bush White House.
- A U.S. Navy submarine sinks a Japanese fishing boat and adds new meaning to the term "damage control."
- Paying for publication: Russia's practice of "zakazukhi."
- Israel's concern for its image in the Palestinian conflict.
- How to conduct public relations in today's China.
- The travel industry's efforts to promote tourism in the wake of September 11.
- Michael Jackson's return to public life and the promotion of a new CD.

Organization of the Text

The basic structure of the book remains the same, but there have been two major changes in organization. First, the chapter on the Internet and Other New Technologies has been moved forward in the seventh edition to become Chapter 12, which follows the chapter on "The Audience and How to Reach It." The placement of the two chapters together recognizes the fact that the new technologies, particularly the Internet, are now commonly used to reach well-defined audiences.

The second major change is a new chapter in the seventh edition titled "Nonprofit Organizations" (Chapter 17) that combines two chapters in the previous editions of the book. The two merged chapters are "Membership Organizations" and "Social, Health, and Cultural Agencies." Reviewers recommended that the two chapters be combined so students could gain a more integrated understanding of how public relations is done in a variety of nonprofit and charitable organizations. As a result of merging these two chapters, the book now has 22 chapters.

The book remains divided into five parts:

Part One: Role
Part Two: Process
Part Three: Strategy
Part Four: Application
Part Five: Tactics

Part One: Role

The opening chapter, defining public relations, concludes with a detailed case study of how public relations was used in the high-stakes battle to save the reputation and credibility of Firestone Tire and Ford Motor Company. Both companies were involved in a massive crisis communications effort when it came to light that Firestone tires were defective and a large percent of blowouts occurred on Ford Explorers.

Chapter 2 describes the evolution of public relations, including a look at how instant information around the clock and on a global basis has significantly altered the work of public relations professionals. Because of extensive concern with the issue of ethical standards, the chapter on "Ethics and Professionalism" appears early in the textbook as Chapter 3. Here, the new code of ethics for the Public Relations Society of America (PRSA) is presented. "The Individual in Public Relations" and "Public Relations Departments and Firms" appear as Chapters 4 and 5. Again, as in all chapters, all data regarding entry-level salaries, rankings of global firms, and compensation for women are updated.

Under this arrangement, students are introduced in logical sequence to the public relations field—its purpose, its history and values, and the career opportunities for individuals wishing to pursue it. More importantly, however, the text emphasizes the increasingly important issue of diversity, both in public relations personnel and in the audiences public relations reaches. In Chapter 4, for example, we discuss the high percentage of women in the field and the growing number of them who hold top-level positions. We also note the expanding role of ethnic groups among practitioners.

Part Two: Process

The four chapters in this part form a unified whole, taking students in sequence through the basic steps involved in a public relations program—research, planning, communication, and evaluation. The use of the Internet and the World Wide Web in various stages of a public relations campaign is addressed.

To explain the process, the chapters follow the public relations programs of several organizations from conception to evaluation. Among these wide-ranging examples are the Mack Trucks campaign to increase market share, the Turkish government's promotion to attract tourists, and even a national product campaign by Levi Jeans. The challenge of crisis communications and risk communications in Chapter 8 receives extensive coverage, supported by discussion of numerous cases, both classic and new, and an examination of how various organizations respond to crises.

Part Three: Strategy

This part discusses the fundamental concepts of strategy. First, we explain how public opinion is formed (Chapter 10) and the ways practitioners can use persuasive techniques to accomplish their objectives. We explain the limitations of persuasive communication but also present the latest theory on how messages can affect attitudes and decision making.

Second, we look at the audience to which these programs are directed (Chapter 11). More precisely, this covers many target audiences—each with special qualities and interests—and describes the selection of media suitable for each program. This chapter, which tends to emphasize traditional media, is followed by more specific information (Chapter 12) about how to use the Internet and other new technologies to reach various audiences. Both Chapters 11 and 12 thoroughly discuss audiences defined by age, gender, race, and cultural background. We also present updated U.S. Census information on the growth of various ethnic populations in the United States.

Various laws and the policies of governmental regulatory agencies must also be considered when public relations strategy is devised. Chapter 13 gives students the latest information on copyright and trademark law, concepts of privacy and intellectual property in the Internet age, and how public relations professionals work with lawyers.

Part Four: Application

The next logical step is for students to learn the practical ways in which the process and strategies of public relations are applied in major areas of practice. Individual chapters are devoted to the corporation, politics and government, nonprofits, international public relations, education, and even entertainment, sports, and tourism.

Most public relations professionals work for a corporation, and this is the first topic that is discussed. Chapter 14 gives updated information on the objectives of corporate philanthropy, dealing with activist publics, and how various corporations have blundered in terms of effective public relations practice. Chapter 15, "Politics and Government," continues to discuss the activities of corporations (including Enron) and other groups who lobby Congress for favorable legislation. It also discusses the role of public relations in government and how various governmental entities, including the White House, have launched a number of informational efforts as part of the war on terrorism.

The expansion of international public relations practice, stimulated in part by the expansion of the World Trade Organization (WTO) and the Internet, is the focus of Chapter 16. It covers various aspects of conducting public relations on a global basis, and also discusses the rise of NGOs (nongovernmental organizations), which are increasingly influencing global public opinion on a host of social and economic issues.

Chapter 17 deals with nonprofit organizations, which include a wide range of membership groups, social agencies, and health care organizations. Fund-raising and development are essential parts of many such organizations, and there is a thorough discussion of fund-raising. Education, from grade school to college level, is the focus of Chapter 18. There is even a discussion of how schools should engage in crisis communication when a tragedy such as the shootings at Columbine High School in Colorado occurs. Many students, as they seek an exciting and rewarding career, are also attracted to sports and entertainment. Chapter 19 deals with the entertainment industry and conducting public relations on behalf of celebrities.

Part 5: Tactics

This final part describes the techniques of daily public relations practice. For the reader's convenience, we have grouped the techniques into three categories, with a chapter each on "Written Tactics" (Chapter 20), "Spoken Tactics" (Chapter 21), and "Visual Tactics" (Chapter 22). Although these topics may be covered in more intensive public relations writing courses, they are included here as an introduction to the student who is taking his or her first course in public relations.

Pedagogy

Every chapter includes several learning tools to (l) help students better understand and retain the principles of public relations and (2) give students the practice they need to apply those principles in real-life situations.

■ **Chapter opening previews.** The preview defines the objectives of the chapter and lists in concise form the major topics covered.

■ **End-of-chapter summaries.** The major themes and issues are summarized for the student at the end of each chapter.

■ **End-of-chapter case activities.** Fictionalized cases, based on actual situations, are presented for students to address.

■ **Questions for review and discussion.** There is a list of questions to test students on chapter concepts.

■ **Suggested readings.** End-of-chapter readings give students additional sources with which to further explore chapter topics.

Supplements

Instructors and students have a variety of ancillary tools available to them that help make teaching and learning with *Public Relations: Strategies and Tactics* easier.

■ **Website to accompany *Public Relations: Strategies and Tactics*** This exciting website contains an unparalled combination of resources for both students and instructors using *Public Relations: Strategies and Tactics*. The Web site's features complement the coverage and organization of the text, yet extend beyond the book to offer further study tools and enrichment. Features include chapter summaries, sample test questions, web links, and a variety of other rich resources to enhance your learning experience. Please visit us online at www.ablongman.com/wilcox7e.

■ **Instructor's Resource Manual/Test Bank with Transparency Masters** This manual includes chapter outlines, lecture topics, sample syllabi, class activities, multiple choice and essay questions, transparency masters, and a section on using media and software in the classroom. In addition, the manual helps professors incorporate PUBLICS: PR Research Software into their lesson plans. PUBLICS is also offered with this edition of the text. Details are provided in the Instructor's Resource Manual.

■ **Computerized Test Generator** The test bank portion of the Instructor's Resource Manual is available on our computerized testing system, TestGen-EQ 2.0. This fully networkable testing software is now available on a cross-platform CD-ROM. TestGen EQ's friendly graphical interface enables instructors to view, edit, and add questions; transfer questions to tests; and print tests in a variety of fonts and forms. Search-and-sort features help instructors locate questions quickly and arrange them in a preferred order. QuizMaster-EQ allows instructors to create and save tests to a network so that students can take them at any networked computer terminal. Instructors can set preferences for how and when tests are administered. QuizMaster-EQ automatically grades the exams and allows instructors to view or print a variety of reports for individual students or courses.

PowerPoint Presentation CD-ROM New to this edition, the transparency masters will now be available as PowerPoint presentation slides on CD-ROM.

Acknowledgments

We express our deep appreciation to many of our academic colleagues who reviewed the sixth edition and made many of the suggestions that we've incorporated into this new edition. Thank you: Walter Atkinson, Northern Illinois University; Anne Eastey, Normandale Community College; Peter DeCaro, Buena Vista University; Lisa Ferree, Eastern Kentucky University; Michael McDermott, Iona College; Mark McElreath, Towson University; Ruth Pate, Sam Houston University; and Holly Pieper, Ithaca College.

We also express our gratitude to those who reviewed drafts of the manuscript for previous editions: John M. Butler, University of Northern Iowa; Suzette Heiman, University of Missouri; E. Dennis Hinde, South Dakota State University; Linda Hon, University of Florida; John M. King, Louisiana State University; Maribeth Metzler, Miami University; Candace White, University of Tennessee-Knoxville; Erica Austin, Washington State University; Bill Dean, Texas Tech University; R. Brooks Garner, Oklahoma State University; Carroll Glynn, Cornell University; Diane Witmer Penkoff, Purdue University; Gayle Pohl, University of Northern Iowa; Tommy Smith, University of Southern Mississippi; Gail Baker Woods, University of Florida; Philip Adler, Jr., Georgia Tech University; Robert L. Bishop, University of Georgia; Glenn Butler, University of Florida; Jamie M. Byrne, Millersville University of Pennsylvania; Fred L. Casmir, Pepperdine University; Lois Conn, Grand Valley State College; Roberta L. Crisson, Kutztown University of Pennsylvania; Bill Day, University of Toledo; Thomas Healy, Endicott Junior College; Michael B. Hesse, University of Alabama; Jerry Hudson, Texas Tech University; Robert L. Kendall, University of Florida; Marilyn Kern-Foxworth, Texas A&M University; Carl Jensen, Sonoma State University; John T. Ludlum, Otterbein College; Norman R. Nager, California State University at Fullerton; Susan Pendleton, Mansfield University of Pennsylvania; Bruce Renfro, Southwest Texas State University; Maria Russell, Syracuse University; Walt Seifert, Ohio State University; Gene Sekeres, Youngstown State University; Tommy V. Smith, University of Southern Mississippi; John Spengler, Franklin University; Judy VanSlyke Turk, University of Southern California; and Albert Walker, Northern Illinois University.

Dennis L. Wilcox
Glen T. Cameron
Warren K. Agee

What Is Public Relations?

preview

The objective of this introductory chapter is to define public relations, explain its communication and counseling roles, and clarify the relationship of public relations to journalism, advertising, and marketing.

Topics covered in the chapter include:

- The challenge of public relations
- Definitions of public relations
- Public relations as a process
- The components of public relations
- How public relations differs from journalism, advertising, and marketing
- The integrated approach
- The Firestone vs. Ford controversy

The Challenge of Public Relations

It is 9 A.M. and Anne-Marie, an account executive in a San Francisco public relations firm, is at her computer working on a news release about a client's new software product. She finishes it, gives it a once-over, and e-mails it to the client for approval. She also attaches a note that an electronic news service can deliver it to newspapers across the country later in the day.

Her next activity is a brainstorming session with other staff members to generate creative ideas about a campaign to raise funds for the local AIDS foundation. When she gets back to her office, she finds a number of telephone messages. A reporter for a trade publication needs background information on a story he is writing; a graphic designer has finished a rough draft of a client's brochure; a catering manager has called about making final arrangements for a reception at an art gallery; and a video producer asks if she can attend the taping of a video news release next week.

Lunch is with a client who wants her counsel on how to announce the closing of a plant in another state. After lunch, Anne-Marie heads back to the office. She asks her assistant to check arrangements for a news conference next week in New York. She telephones a key editor to "pitch" a story about a client's new product. Anne-Marie also touches base with other members of her team, who are working on a 12-city media tour by an Olympic champion representing an athletic shoe manufacturer.

At 4 P.M., Anne-Marie checks several computer databases to gather information about the industry of a new client. She also checks online news updates to determine if anything is occurring that involves or affects her firm's clients. At 5 P.M., as she winds down from the day's hectic activities, she reviews news stories from a clipping service about her client, an association of strawberry producers. She is pleased to find that her feature story, which included recipes and color photos, appeared in 150 dailies.

As the previous scenario illustrates, the challenge of public relations is multifaceted. A public relations professional must have skills in written and interpersonal communication, research, negotiation, creativity, logistics, facilitation, and problem solving.

Indeed, those who want a challenging career with plenty of variety often choose the field of public relations. The U.S. Bureau of Labor Statistics estimates that the field already employs 200,000 nationwide, with public relations as one of the fastest-growing industries through 2006. In addition, a *Fortune* magazine survey ranks public relations No. 8 on a list of "where the best jobs will be."

Global Scope

It is difficult to estimate worldwide figures, but *Reed's Directory of Public Relations Organizations* lists 155 national and regional public relations associations with an aggregate membership of 137,000 people. Included are such groups as the Public Relations Institute of Southern Africa (PRISA), the Public Relations Association of Mauritius (PRAM), the Association of Public Relations Practitioners in Thailand, and the Public Relations Institute of Australia (PRIA).

Such memberships, however, are usually only a partial indication, because large numbers of public relations practitioners don't belong to professional organizations. The president of the China International Public Relations Association, for example, says that the country has more than 100,000 practitioners and that up to 500,000 are studying aspects of public relations in colleges and training institutes.

Large numbers of students around the world are studying public relations as a career field. In the United States, more than 250 colleges and universities offer programs in public relations, and about 80 European universities offer studies in the subject. Many Asian universities, particularly in Thailand, also offer public relations curricula.

In terms of economics, the public relations field is most extensively developed in the United States, where organizations spend an estimated $10 billion annually in such activity. The year 2000 was particularly good for public relations firms. The Council of Public Relations Firms surveyed its 316 members and found that global revenues topped $4.6 billion. Although statistics are scarce, European companies are estimated to spend $3 billion annually on public relations. This figure continues to increase through implementation of the European Community (EC) and the development of market economies in Eastern Europe and the new nations of the former Soviet Union. Areas with strong growth potential in Europe are public affairs, corporate relations, health care, and marketing communications.

The second area of major growth is Asia. Weber Shandwick Worldwide, the world's second largest firm, with revenues of $219 million in 2000, sees growth of 20 to 30 percent in such nations as Malaysia, Korea, Thailand, Singapore, Indonesia, and China. Increased privatization of national industries and expansion of free market economies are also fueling major growth in Latin America and southern Africa. A more detailed discussion of international public relations is found in Chapter 16.

In sum, public relations is a global activity with excellent prospects for growth. The challenge is to define and practice public relations in such a way that it fosters greater understanding and harmonious relationships among nations and organizations, in the public interest.

A Variety of Definitions

People often define public relations by some of its most visible techniques and tactics, such as publicity in a newspaper, a television interview with an organization's spokesperson, or the appearance of a celebrity at a special event.

What people fail to understand is that public relations is a process involving many subtle and far-reaching aspects. It includes research and analysis, policy formation, programming, communication, and feedback from numerous publics. Its practitioners operate on two distinct levels—as advisers to their clients or to an organization's top management and as technicians who produce and disseminate messages in multiple media channels.

A number of definitions have been formulated over the years. One of the early definitions that gained wide acceptance was formulated by the newsletter *PR News:* "Public relations is the management function which evaluates public attitudes, identifies the policies and procedures of an individual or an organization with the public interest, and plans and executes a program of action to earn public understanding and patience."

Rex Harlow, a pioneer public relations educator who founded what eventually became the Public Relations Society of America (PRSA), once compiled more than 500 definitions from almost as many sources. After mulling over them and talking with leaders in the field, Harlow came up with this definition:

> Public relations is a distinctive management function which helps establish and maintain mutual lines of communication, understanding, acceptance, and cooperation between an organization and its publics; involves the management of problems

> or issues; helps management keep informed on and responsive to public opinion; defines and emphasizes the responsibility of management to serve the public interest; helps management keep abreast of and effectively utilize change, serving as an early warning system to help anticipate trends; and uses research and sound ethical communication techniques as its principal tools.

More succinct definitions are provided by theorists and textbook authors. Scott M. Cutlip, Allen H. Center, and Glen M. Broom state in *Effective Public Relations* that "public relations is the management function that identifies, establishes, and maintains mutually beneficial relationships between an organization and the various publics on whom its success or failure depends." The management function is also emphasized in *Managing Public Relations* by James E. Grunig and Todd Hunt. They state that public relations is "the management of communication between an organization and its publics."

The best definition for today's modern practice is offered by Professors Lawrence W. Long and Vincent Hazelton, who describe public relations as "a communication function of management through which organizations adapt to, alter, or maintain their environment for the purpose of achieving organizational goals." Their approach represents the somewhat newer theory that public relations is more than persuasion. It should also foster open, two-way communication and mutual understanding with the idea that an organization also changes its attitudes and behaviors in the process—not just the target audience.

A company, for example, may modify its policies as a result of dialogue with environmental groups. McDonald's, after listening to such groups, decided to eliminate its "clamshell" boxes because they were not easily biodegradable.

National and international public relations organizations, including the Public Relations Society of America (PRSA), also have formulated definitions. Here is a sampling from around the world:

- "Public relations is the deliberate, planned, and sustained effort to establish and maintain mutual understanding between an organization and its publics."

global PR

A European View of Public Relations

Definitions of public relations coined by European theorists and practitioners—in a similar manner to their American counterparts—generally consist of aims and functions.

Karl Nessmann, a professor at the University of Klagenfurt (Austria) lists the following elements:

- Creating and reinforcing trust, comprehension, and sympathy
- Arousing attention, interest, and needs
- Creating and preserving communication and relationships
- Creating mutual understanding and agreement
- Articulating, representing, and adjusting interests
- Influencing public opinion
- Resolving conflicts (conflict resolution and negotiation)
- Creating consensus

Source: Public Relations Review, Summer 1995, p. 154.

(British Institute of Public Opinion, whose definition has also been adopted in a number of Commonwealth nations)

- "Public relations is the management, through communication, of perceptions and strategic relationships between an organization and its internal and external stakeholders." (Public Relations Institute of Southern Africa)
- "Public relations is the sustained and systematic managerial effort through which private and public organizations seek to establish understanding, sympathy, and support in those public circles with which they have or expect to obtain contact." (Dansk Public Relations Klub of Denmark, which also uses the English term)
- "Public relations practice is the art and social science of analyzing trends, predicting their consequences, counseling organization leaders, and implementing planned programs of action which serve both the organization's and the public's interest." (A definition approved at the World Assembly of Public Relations in Mexico City in 1978 and endorsed by 34 national public relations organizations)

Careful study of these explanations should enable anyone to formulate a definition of public relations; committing any single one to memory is unnecessary. The key words to remember in defining public relations follow:

- *Deliberate.* Public relations activity is intentional. It is designed to influence, gain understanding, provide information, and obtain *feedback* (reaction from those affected by the activity).
- *Planned.* Public relations activity is organized. Solutions to problems are discovered and logistics are thought out, with the activity taking place over a period of time. It is systematic, requiring research and analysis.
- *Performance.* Effective public relations is based on actual policies and performance. No amount of public relations will generate good will and support if the organization is unresponsive to community concerns. A Pacific Northwest timber company, despite a campaign with the theme "For Us, Every Day Is Earth Day," became known as the villain of Washington State because of its insistence on logging old-growth forests and bulldozing a logging road into a prime elk habitat.
- *Public interest.* Public relations activity should be mutually beneficial to the organization and the public; it is the alignment of the organization's self-interests with the public's concerns and interests. For example, the Mobil Corporation sponsors quality programming on public television because it enhances the company's image; by the same token, the public benefits from the availability of such programming.
- *Two-way communication.* Public relations is more than one-way dissemination of informational materials. It is equally important to solicit feedback. As Jim Osborne, former vice president of public affairs at Bell Canada, says, "The primary responsibility of the public relations counselor is to provide (management) a thorough grasp of public sentiment."
- *Management function.* Public relations is most effective when it is an integral part of decision making by top management. Public relations involves counseling and problem solving at high levels, not just the dissemination of information after a decision has been made.

PR insights

Public Relations Society of America Official Statement on Public Relations

Public relations helps our complex, pluralistic society to reach decisions and function more effectively by contributing to mutual understanding among groups and institutions. It serves to bring private and public policies into harmony.

Public relations serves a variety of institutions in society such as businesses, trade unions, government agencies, voluntary associations, foundations, hospitals, and educational and religious institutions. To achieve their goals, these institutions must develop effective relationships with many different audiences or publics such as employees, members, customers, local communities, shareholders, and other institutions, and with society at large.

The managements of institutions need to understand the attitudes and values of their publics in order to achieve institutional goals. The goals themselves are shaped by the external environment. The public relations practitioner acts as a counselor to management, and as a mediator, helping to translate private aims into reasonable, publicly acceptable policy and action.

As a management function, public relations encompasses the following:

- Anticipating, analyzing, and interpreting public opinion, attitudes, and issues which might impact, for good or ill, the operations and plans of the organization.
- Counseling management at all levels in the organization with regard to policy decisions, courses of action and communication, and taking into account their public ramifications and the organization's social or citizenship responsibilities.
- Researching, conducting, and evaluating, on a continuing basis, programs of action and communication to achieve informed public understanding necessary to the success of an organization's aims. These may include marketing, financial, fund-raising, employee, community or government relations, and other programs.
- Planning and implementing the organization's efforts to influence or change public policy.
- Setting objectives, planning, budgeting, recruiting and training staff, and developing facilities—in short, *managing* the resources needed to perform all of the above.
- Examples of the knowledge that may be required in the professional practice of public relations include communication arts, psychology, social psychology, sociology, political science, economics, and the principles of management and ethics. Technical knowledge and skills are required for opinion research, public issues analysis, media relations, direct mail, institutional advertising, publications, film/video productions, special events, speeches, and presentations.

In helping to define and implement policy, the public relations practitioner utilizes a variety of professional communication skills and plays an integrative role both within the organization and between the organization and the external environment.

To summarize, a person can grasp the essential elements of public relations by remembering the following words and phrases: *deliberate . . . planned . . . performance . . . public interest . . . two-way communication . . . management function.*

The elements of public relations just described are part of an interactive process that makes up what is called *public relations activity.* In the following section, public relations as a process is discussed.

Public Relations as a Process

Public relations is a *process*—that is, a series of actions, changes, or functions that bring about a result. One popular way to describe the process, and to remember its components, is to use the RACE acronym, first articulated by John Marston in his book

The Nature of Public Relations. Essentially, RACE means that public relations activity consists of four key elements:

- ***R**esearch.* What is the problem or situation?
- ***A**ction (program planning).* What is going to be done about it?
- ***C**ommunication (execution).* How will the public be told?
- ***E**valuation.* Was the audience reached and what was the effect?

Part Two of this text discusses this key four-step process.

Another approach is to think of the process as a never-ending cycle in which six components are links in a chain. Figure 1.1 shows the process.

The public relations process also may be conceptualized in several steps:

Level 1

a. Public relations personnel obtain insights into the problem from numerous sources.
b. Public relations personnel analyze these inputs and make recommendations to management.
c. Management makes policy and action decisions.

Level 2

d. Public relations personnel execute a program of action.
e. Public relations personnel evaluate the effectiveness of the action.

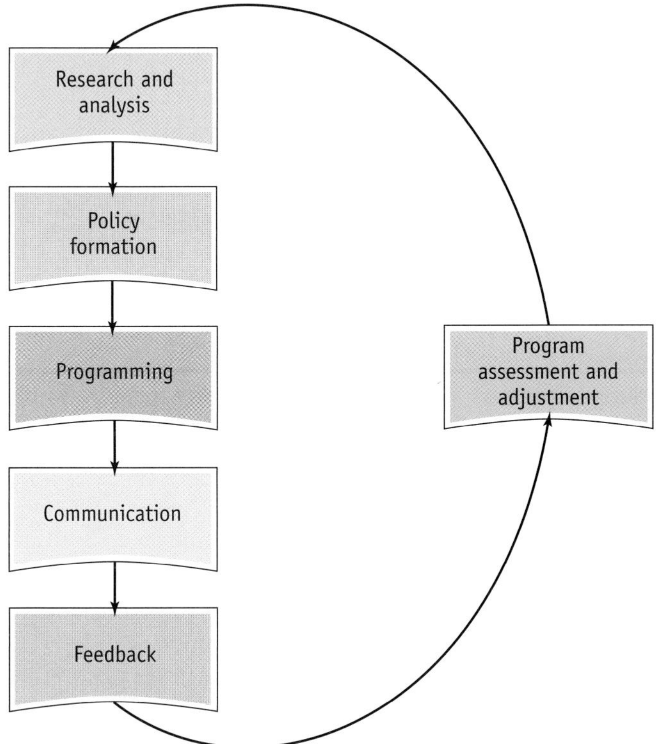

FIGURE 1.1

In the conceptualization of public relations as a cyclical process, feedback—or audience response—leads to assessment of the program, which becomes an essential element in the development of another public relations project.

Step A consists of inputs that determine the nature and extent of the public relations problem. These may include feedback from the public, media reporting and editorial comment, analysis of trend data, other forms of research, personal experience, and government pressures and regulations.

In Step B, public relations personnel assess these inputs, establish objectives and an agenda of activity, and convey their recommendations to management. As previously noted, this is the adviser role of public relations.

After management makes its decisions, in Step C, public relations personnel execute the action program in Step D through such means as news releases, publications, speeches, and community relations programs. In Step E, the effect of these efforts is measured by feedback from the same components that made up Step A. The cycle is then repeated to solve related aspects of the problem that may require additional decision making and action.

Note that public relations plays two distinct roles in this process, thus serving as a "middle ground" or "linking agent." On Level 1, public relations interacts directly with external sources of information, including the public, media, and government, and relays these inputs to management along with recommendations. On Level 2, public relations becomes the vehicle through which management reaches the public with assorted messages.

Diffusion-of-knowledge theorists call public relations people "linking agents." Sociologists refer to them as "boundary spanners" that act to transfer information between two systems. As the last lines of the official statement on public relations by the Public Relations Society of America note: "The public relations practitioner utilizes a variety of professional communication skills and plays an integrative role both within the organization and between the organization and the external environment."

The Components of Public Relations

The basic components of public relations, according to a monograph issued by the PRSA Foundation, include:

- *Counseling.* Providing advice to management concerning policies, relationships, and communications.
- *Research.* Determining attitudes and behaviors of publics in order to plan public relations strategies. Such research can be used to (1) generate mutual understanding or (2) influence and persuade publics.
- *Media relations.* Working with mass media in seeking publicity or responding to their interests in the organization.
- *Publicity.* Disseminating planned messages through selected media to further the organization's interests.
- *Employee/member relations.* Responding to concerns, informing, and motivating an organization's employees or members.
- *Community relations.* Planned activity with a community to maintain an environment that benefits both the organization and the community.
- *Public affairs.* Developing effective involvement in public policy and helping an organization adapt to public expectations. The term is also used by government agencies to describe their public relations activities and by many corporations as an umbrella term to describe multiple public relations activities.

- *Government affairs.* Relating directly with legislatures and regulatory agencies on behalf of the organization. *Lobbying* can be part of a government affairs program.
- *Issues management.* Identifying and addressing issues of public concern that affect the organization.
- *Financial relations.* Creating and maintaining investor confidence and building good relationships with the financial community. Also known as *investor relations* or *shareholder relations.*
- *Industry relations.* Relating with other firms in the industry of an organization and with trade associations.
- *Development/fund-raising.* Demonstrating the need for and encouraging the public to support an organization, primarily through financial contributions.
- *Multicultural relations/workplace diversity.* Relating with individuals and groups in various cultural groups.
- *Special events.* Stimulating an interest in a person, product, or organization by means of a focused "happening"; also, activities designed to interact with publics and listen to them.
- *Marketing communications.* Combination of activities designed to sell a product, service, or idea, including advertising, collateral materials, publicity, promotion, direct mail, trade shows, and special events.

These components, and how they function, constitute the substance of this textbook.

Other Terms for Public Relations

Public relations is used as an umbrella term on a worldwide basis. Sixty-four of the 69 national membership associations, from the Arab Public Relations Society to the Zimbabwe Institute of Public Relations, identify themselves with that term.

Some Positive Descriptive Terms

Individual companies and other groups, however, often use other terms to describe the public relations function. *O'Dwyer's PR Services Report* surveyed *Fortune* magazine's list of the largest 500 corporations and found that the most common name, used by 165 companies, is *corporate communications.* The term *public relations* is a distant second, with 64 companies using it. Other popular names, in descending order, were *public affairs, communication, corporate relations,* and *corporate public affairs.* Some companies link public relations with marketing. Chase Manhattan, for example, has a *corporate marketing and communications* unit.

Public information is the term most widely used by social service agencies, universities, and government agencies. The implication is that only information is being disseminated, in contrast to persuasive communication, generally perceived as the purpose of public relations. Social services agencies often use the term *community relations,* and the military is fond of *public affairs.*

In many cases it is clear that companies and organizations use *public information, public affairs,* or *corporate communications* as euphemisms for *public relations.* This, in part, is a reaction to the misuse of the original term by the public and the media. On occasion, a reporter or government official will use the term *public relations gimmick* or *ploy* to imply that the activities or statements of an organization are without substance or sincerity.

The popularity of *corporate communications* is also based on the idea that the term is broader than *public relations*, which is often incorrectly perceived as only *media relations*. Corporate communications, many contend, encompasses all communications of the company, including advertising, marketing communications, public affairs, community relations, and employee communications.

Other organizations use a term that better describes the primary activity of the department. It is clear, for example, that a department of investor relations deals primarily with stockholders, institutional investors, and the financial press. Likewise, a department of environmental affairs, community relations, or employee communications is self-explanatory. A department of marketing communications primarily emphasizes product publicity and promotion. The organization and functions of communications departments are discussed in Chapter 5.

Like departments, individuals specialize in subcategories of public relations. A person who deals exclusively with placement of stories in the media is, to be precise, a *publicist*. A *press agent* is also a specialist, operating within the subcategory of public relations that concentrates on finding unusual news angles and planning events or "happenings" that attract media attention—a stunt by an aspiring Hollywood actress, for example, or an attempt to be listed in the *Guinness Book of Records* by baking the world's largest apple pie.

global PR

Australian Company Motivates Employees to Support the Olympics

Telstra Corporation, Australia's telecommunications giant, had a problem. It was a major sponsor and provider of telecommunications services for the 2000 Olympics in Sydney, but research indicated that its employees needed more information and motivation to meet the challenge of serving the Olympic guests and the 25,000 media reporters covering the event.

Turnbull Porter Novelli, a public relations consultancy, was commissioned to accomplish the objective of increasing the staff's awareness of Telstra's involvement in the games and the benefits of such a sponsorship. The entire workforce and their managers were targeted for the campaign, and a variety of messages were defined. Some of the key messages were (1) the extent of Telstra's technical involvement, (2) its sponsorship of various athletes, (3) how integral the staff were to sponsorship success.

The major communication vehicle was a scripted 46-minute movie that incorporated historic footage and news coverage of Telstra-sponsored athletes. There was a teaser campaign for the special screenings organized at cinemas all over the country, and each staff member attending the movie received a show bag containing educational and inspirational materials about the Olympics, which at the time were still a year away. In addition, color posters, special e-news bulletins, and an incentive campaign assured that the 146 individual screenings were well attended.

Almost 40,000 Telstra employees attended the movie, well ahead of the projected target audience. Results from over 450 interviews showed that 56 percent of the employees now felt a sense of pride in the sponsorship, and two out of three felt they were important to its success. The campaign received a "Golden World Award" in employee relations from the International Public Relations Association (IPRA).

An important part of public relations is special events. Here, fireworks burst over the stadium during the opening ceremonies of the XIX Winter Games in Salt Lake City.

Some Less Flattering Terms

Unfortunately, the public and the press on occasion describe public relations people as "flacks" or "spin doctors."

A *flack* or *flak* is a derisive slang term that journalists often use for a press agent or anyone else working in public relations. Although in recent years most publications, including the *Wall Street Journal,* have refrained from using the "F" word in print, trade publications such as *Editor & Publisher* still use it on a regular basis.

The term has an interesting history. According to Wes Pedersen, director of communications for the Public Affairs Council, the term *flack* originated in 1939 in *Variety,* the show business publication. It began using flack as a synonym for press agent, he says, "in tribute to the skills of Gene Flack in publicizing motion pictures." Others say the word "flak" was used during World War I to describe heavy ground fire aimed at aircraft. At times, journalists consider the barrage of daily news releases they receive a form of flak that interferes with their mission of informing the public.

The term *spin doctor* is a more recent entry into the lexicon of public relations. It first appeared in 1984, according to *Safire's Political Dictionary* by William Safire, in a *New York Times* editorial about the activities of President Reagan's reelection campaign. In the beginning, the meaning of "spin" was restricted to what often were considered the unethical and misleading activities and tactics of political campaign consultants. By the mid-1990s, however, the media widely used the term to describe any effort by public relations personnel to put a positive slant on an event or issue.

Robert Dilenschneider, president of his own public relations firm in New York, wrote in a *Wall Street Journal* article: "I think the time has come for public relations professionals to condemn 'spin' and label 'spin doctors' for what they are: purveyors of deception, manipulation, and misinformation. Spin is antithetical to legitimate public relations, which aims to enhance the image of companies and individuals to generate public approval for the programs and policies they advance . . . Spin is to public relations what pornography is to art. . . ."

Not all public relations people, however, share Dilenschneider's views. Pat Jackson, publisher of *PR Reporter,* says: "We're all 'spinners'—because it simply means marshaling the data from your viewpoint, attempting to persuade others your viewpoint is legitimate." And Bill Patterson, vice president of reputation management at HMS Partners in Columbus, Ohio, in an article for *Public Relations Tactics* titled "Confessions of a Spin Doctor," wrote: "By 'spin,' I mean that I use all modern methods of communication to tell the most positive story I can about my clients. . . . I'm sorry that the term has taken on such a negative meaning, but national politics has a way of doing that to our actions and our language."

Indeed, *spin* seems to have well established itself as a popular slang term for any information with a point of view. It has even become popular as a title in books about public relations, as in *PR: A Social History of Spin,* by Stuart Ewan; *The Father of Spin: Edward L. Bernays & The Birth of Public Relations,* by Larry Tye; *Spin Man: The Topsy-Turvy World of Public Relations,* by Thomas Madden; *Spin Cycle: How the White House and the Media Manipulate the News,* by Howard Kurtz; and *Spin: How to Turn the Power of the Press to Your Advantage,* by Michael Sitrick.

Within the public relations community, feeling also exists that *PR* is a slang term that carries a somewhat denigrating connotation. The late Sam Black, a public relations consultant in the United Kingdom and author of several books on public relations, says, "The use of 'PR' was probably originated as a nickname for 'press relations,'" the primary activity of public relations in its early years (see Chapter 2).

Although PR is now more than press relations, the nickname is commonly used in daily conversation and is widely recognized around the world. A good compromise, which this book uses, is to adopt a style of spelling out "public relations" in the body of a text or article but to use the shorter term, "PR," in the accompanying boxed material.

How Public Relations Differs from Journalism

Writing is a common activity of both public relations professionals and journalists. Both also do their jobs in many of the same ways: They interview people, gather and synthesize large amounts of information, write in a journalistic style, and are trained to produce good copy on deadline. In fact, many reporters eventually change careers and become public relations practitioners.

This has led many people, including journalists, to the incorrect conclusion that little difference exists between public relations and journalism. For many, public relations is simply being a "journalist-in-residence" for a nonmedia organization.

However, despite the sharing of many techniques, the two fields are fundamentally different in scope, objectives, audiences, and channels.

Scope

Public relations, as stated earlier, has many components, ranging from counseling to issues management and special events. Journalistic writing and media relations, although important, are only two of these elements. In addition, effective practice of public relations requires strategic thinking, problem-solving capability, and other management skills.

Objectives

Journalists gather and select information for the primary purpose of providing the public with news and information. As Professors David Dozier and William Ehling explain, ". . . communication activities are an end in themselves." Public relations personnel also gather facts and information for the purpose of informing the public, but the objective is different. Communication activity is only a means to the end. In other words, the objective is not only to inform but to change people's attitudes and behaviors, in order to further an organization's goals and objectives.

Whereas journalists are objective observers, public relations personnel are advocates. Harold Burson, chairman of Burson-Marsteller public relations, makes the point:

> To be effective and credible, public relations messages must be based on facts. Nevertheless, we are advocates, and we need to remember that. We are advocates of a particular point of view—our client's or our employer's point of view. And while we recognize that serving the public interest best serves our client's interest, we are not journalists. That's not our job.

Audiences

Journalists write primarily for a mass audience—readers, listeners, or viewers of the medium for which they work. By definition, mass audiences are not well defined, and a journalist on a daily newspaper, for example, writes for the general public. A public relations professional, in contrast, carefully segments audiences into various demographic and psychological characteristics. Such research allows messages to be tailored to audience needs, concerns, and interests for maximum effect.

PR insights

Public Relations Takes More Than Writing . . .

You don't earn your right to sit at the public relations table just by being able to write well. I'll admit you probably won't be asked to pull up a chair without that skill. But keeping your seat requires more these days—a strategic contribution, big picture focus, broad-scale knowledge of the world within and outside your business, and the courage to be the reminding voice about ethical conduct, environmental impact, or the personal consequences of economic decisions.

—Robert Moulthrop
Scudder Stevens & Clark public relations
New York

Source: PR Reporter, April 29, 1996, p. 4.

Channels

Most journalists, by nature of their employment, reach audiences through one channel—the medium that publishes or broadcasts their work. Public relations professionals use a variety of channels to reach the audiences previously described. The channels employed may be a combination of mass media outlets—newspapers, magazines, radio, and television. Or they may include direct mail, pamphlets, posters, newsletters, trade journals, special events, and posting messages on the Internet.

How Public Relations Differs from Advertising

Just as many people mistakenly equate publicity with public relations, there is also some confusion about the distinction between *publicity* (one area of public relations) and advertising.

Although publicity and advertising both utilize mass media for dissemination of messages, the format and context are different. Publicity—information about an event, an individual or group, or a product—appears as a news item or feature story in the mass media. Material is prepared by public relations personnel and submitted to the news department for consideration. Editors, known as *gatekeepers,* determine whether the material will be used or simply thrown away.

Advertising, in contrast, is paid space and broadcast time. Organizations and individuals typically contract with the advertising department of a mass media outlet for a full-page ad or a one-minute commercial. An organization writes the advertisement, decides the type and graphics, and controls where and when the advertisement will be run. In other words, advertising is simply renting space in a mass medium. The lion's share of revenue for all mass media comes from the selling of advertising space.

Other differences between public relations activities and advertising include:

- Advertising works almost exclusively through mass media outlets; public relations relies on a number of communication tools—brochures, slide presentations, special events, speeches, news releases, feature stories, and so forth.
- Advertising is addressed to external audiences—primarily consumers of goods and services; public relations presents its message to specialized external audiences (stockholders, vendors, community leaders, environmental groups, and so on) and internal publics (employees).
- Advertising is readily identified as a specialized communication function; public relations is broader in scope, dealing with the policies and performance of the entire organization, from the morale of employees to the way telephone operators respond to calls.
- Advertising is often used as a communication tool in public relations, and public relations activity often supports advertising campaigns. Advertising's function is to sell goods and services; the public relations function is to create an environment in which the organization can thrive. The latter calls for dealing with economic, social, and political factors that can affect the organization.

The major disadvantage of advertising, of course, is the cost. Typically, a full-page ad in *Parade* magazine, distributed weekly in almost 350 dailies, costs $421,000. Advertising campaigns on network television can run into the millions of dollars. For example, advertisers paid an average of $2.3 million for a Super Bowl ad in 2002. Because of this, companies are increasingly using a tool of public relations—product publicity—that is more cost effective and often more credible because the message appears in a news context.

How Public Relations Differs from Marketing

Public relations is distinct from marketing in several ways, although their boundaries often overlap.

The functions overlap, for example, because both deal with an organization's relationships and employ similar communication tools to reach the public. Both have the ultimate purpose of assuring an organization's success and economic survival. Public relations and marketing, however, approach this task from somewhat different perspectives, or worldviews.

This difference is illustrated by the descriptions of each field that a distinguished panel of educators and practitioners in public relations and marketing developed during a colloquium at San Diego State University. After a day of debate, they formed this definition of public relations:

> Public relations is the management process whose goal is to attain and maintain accord and positive behaviors among social groupings on which an organization depends in order to achieve its mission. Its fundamental responsibility is to build and maintain a hospitable environment for an organization.

The group defined marketing's goal in different terms:

> Marketing is the management process whose goal is to attract and satisfy customers (or clients) on a long-term basis in order to achieve an organization's economic objectives. Its fundamental responsibility is to build and maintain markets for an organization's products or services.

In other words, public relations is concerned with building relationships and generating goodwill for the organization; marketing is concerned with customers and selling products and services.

James E. Grunig, editor of *Excellence in Public Relations and Communication Management,* put the differences between public relations and marketing in sharp contrast:

> . . . the marketing function should communicate with the markets for an organization's goods and services. Public relations should be concerned with all the publics of the organization. The major purpose of marketing is to make money for the organization by increasing the slope of the demand curve. The major purpose of public relations is to save money for the organization by building relationships with publics that constrain or enhance the ability of the organization to meet its mission.

In this passage, Grunig points out a fundamental difference between marketing and public relations in terms of how the public is described. Marketing and advertising professionals tend to speak of "target markets," "consumers," and "customers." Public relations professionals tend to talk of "publics," "audiences," and "stakeholders." These groups may be any publics that are affected by or can affect an organization. According to Grunig, "Publics can arise within stakeholder categories—such as employees, communities, stockholders, governments, members, students, suppliers, and donors, as well as consumers."

Public relations theorists point out another fundamental difference between public relations and marketing. In their view, "excellent" public relations is devoid of persuasion; its ideal purpose is to create mutual understanding and cooperation through two-way dialogue. Marketing, by definition, is persuasive in intent and purpose—to sell products and services. The four models of public relations are discussed in Chapter 2.

How Public Relations Supports Marketing

Philip Kotler, professor of marketing at Northwestern University and author of a leading marketing textbook, says public relations is the fifth "P" of marketing strategy, which includes four other Ps—Product, Price, Place, and Promotion. As he wrote in the *Harvard Business Review,* "Public relations takes longer to cultivate, but when energized, it can help pull the company into the market."

When public relations is used to support directly an organization's marketing objectives, it is called *marketing communications.* This was identified as a component of public relations earlier in the chapter. Another term, coined by Thomas Harris in his book *The Marketer's Guide to Public Relations,* is *marketing public relations.* He says:

> I make a clear distinction between those public relations functions which support marketing, which I call Marketing Public Relations (MPR) and the other public relations activities that define the corporation's relationships with its non-customer publics, which I label Corporate Public Relations (CPR).

Dennis L. Wilcox, in his text *Public Relations Writing and Media Techniques,* lists eight ways in which public relations activities contribute to fulfilling marketing objectives:

1. Developing new prospects for new markets, such as people who inquire after seeing or hearing a product release in the news media
2. Providing third-party endorsements—via newspapers, magazines, radio, and television—through news releases about a company's products or services, community involvement, inventions, and new plans
3. Generating sales leads, usually through articles in the trade press about new products and services
4. Paving the way for sales calls
5. Stretching the organization's advertising and promotional dollars through timely and supportive releases about it and its products
6. Providing inexpensive sales literature, because articles about the company and its products can be reprinted as informative pieces for prospective customers
7. Establishing the corporation as an authoritative source of information on a given product
8. Helping to sell minor products that don't have large advertising budgets

Harris summarizes:

> In its market-support function, public relations is used to achieve a number of objectives. The most important of these are to raise awareness, to inform and educate, to gain understanding, to build trust, to make friends, to give people reasons to buy and finally to create a climate of consumer acceptance.

Toward an Integrated Perspective

Although well-defined differences exist among the fields of advertising, marketing, and public relations, there is an increasing realization that an organization's goals and objectives can be best accomplished through an integrated approach.

The understanding gave rise in the 1990s to such terms as *integrated marketing communications, convergent communications,* and *integrated communications.* Don Schulz, Stanley Tannenbaum, and Robert Lauterborn, authors of *Integrated Marketing Communications,* explain the title of their book as follows:

> A concept of marketing communication planning that recognizes the added value of a comprehensive plan that evaluates the strategic roles of a variety of communication disciplines—e.g., General Advertising, Direct Response, Sales Promotion, and Public Relations—and combines these disciplines to provide clarity, consistency, and maximum communication impact.

Several factors have fueled the trend toward integration. One is the downsizing and reengineering of organizations. Many of them have consolidated departments and have also reduced staff dedicated to various communication disciplines. As a result, one department, with fewer employees, is expected to do a greater variety of communication tasks.

Second, there are tighter budgets for organizational marketing and communication. Many organizations, to avoid the high cost of advertising, look for alternative ways to deliver messages. These may include product publicity, direct mail, and sales promotion.

Third, a realization exists that the marketing of products and services can be affected by public and social policy issues. Environmental legislation influences packaging and content of products, a proposed luxury tax on expensive autos affects sales of those cars, and a company's support of Planned Parenthood or health benefits for same-sex partners may spur a product boycott.

The impact of such factors has led many professionals to believe that organizations should do a better job of integrating public relations and public affairs into overall marketing considerations. In fact, David Coronna, writing in the *Public Relations Journal,* suggests marketing's sixth "P" should be public policy.

Fourth, there is a rise of relationship marketing. As Ken Reich, a marketing communications expert, says, "The fundamental tenets of marketing have indeed shifted to a large degree, from the 1960s' four-Ps (product, price, place, and promotion) to today's four-Cs (customer needs, cost to meet those needs, convenience to purchase, and communication)—in other words, the building of solid, long-term customer loyalty through service and two-way communication."

The concept of integration, therefore, is the realization that an organization's communications should be consistent. As Michael Lissauer of *Business Wire* says, "It's essential that there be a consistency of message, that the communications effort project a singular voice. Business must deliver the right message in the right medium to elicit the right result."

This concept is less controversial than its implementation. It makes sense for an organization to coordinate its communications strategies, but considerable discord arises on exactly how to accomplish this.

In many organizations, marketing is the dominant voice. Public relations has historically been relegated to a marketing-support function, concentrating on techniques instead of strategy. This role often includes creating product publicity, planning

PR casebook

Microsoft Introduces XP

The headline in a major daily newspaper said it all: "XP hits street with plenty of hoopla." Microsoft's long-awaited XP operating system had its coming-out party during two days of special events in New York City, with the public relations objective of generating a great deal of media publicity.

Bill Gates, of course, was on hand to personally introduce and demonstrate his newest product at a Broadway theatre with 1500 guests in attendance. A white-robed gospel choir sang "God Bless America" in front of the Windows blue-sky banner. New York mayor Rudolph Giuliani strode on stage with Gates to personally thank him for deciding to keep the product's coming-out party in New York after the September 11 terrorist attack on the World Trade Center. And there was even a concert by the rock singer Sting.

Afterwards, TV host Regis Philbin held a live video chat with Gates as the software mogul roamed around Times Square. There were also plenty of photo opportunities for the press; one picture that appeared in many dailies was of Gates playing a video game with a teenager at a local arcade. Meanwhile, a 1200-pound cow lounged all day on a Manhattan street corner outside the Gateway Country retail shop, which just happened to be selling the new XP operating system.

Public relations techniques, such as events, are often used as part of a company's integrated marketing strategy to introduce a new product. The objective is to build awareness among the media, consumers, and the trade by generating excitement about the product. The XP introduction had a marketing budget of $200 million. The company, however, expected to sell 70 million copies of XP in the first year.

A public relations campaign is often the first step in launching a new product. Here, Bill Gates talks to TV host Regis Philbin about Microsoft's new XP operating system during a series of special events in New York City.

promotions, and arranging media interviews at a trade show. Problems also arise when advertising agencies attempt to do integrated programs. In many cases, 90 percent of the budget is spent on advertising and 10 percent or less on public relations.

Such examples make many public relations professionals wary of "integrated communications." They see it as a veiled attempt by marketing or advertising to reduce public relations to a product-publicity function. Thus, many public relations practi-

FIGURE 1.2

This illustration shows the interplay of messages and feedback in an integrated marketing communication campaign. The targeted database includes customers, media, and sales personnel. (*Source:* ©1996 Viacom & Partners)

tioners prefer to remain in separate departments and coordinate, not integrate, with other functions such as advertising, direct mail, and marketing. (See Figure 1.2.)

Turf battles no doubt will continue, but the concept of integrating, or coordinating, communications is here to stay. Paul Alvarez, former chairman of Ketchum Communications, says that if public relations people are going to have credibility with clients and employers, they must acknowledge the roles played by other communication disciplines such as advertising, direct marketing, and sales promotion. By the same token, other disciplines must realize the full potential of public relations.

All disciplines deserve an equal voice at the table when an organization considers its communication objectives and strategies. Integrated marketing communication is also discussed in Chapters 5, 7, and 14.

The Values of Public Relations

This chapter has placed public relations within the context of definitions, activities, and process. It has also attempted to explain how public relations differs from journalism, advertising, and marketing. And finally, the chapter has discussed the concept of an organization coordinating all its various communications to achieve maximum effectiveness.

More than ever, today the world needs not more information but sensitive communicators and facilitators who can explain the goals and methods of individuals, organizations, and governments to others in a socially responsible manner. Equally, these experts in communication and public opinion must provide their employers with knowledge of what others are thinking, to guide them in setting their policies wisely for the common good.

Patrick Jackson, a former president of the Public Relations Society of America (PRSA) and publisher of *PR Reporter*, makes the case for the important role of public relations in today's society. He once wrote:

> As soon as there was Eve with Adam, there were relationships, and in every society, no matter how small or primitive, public communication needs and problems inevitably emerge and must be resolved. Public relations is devoted to the essential function of building and improving human relationships.

PR insights

Nine Ways Public Relations Contributes to the Bottom Line

It is often said that public relations is a management process, not an event. Patrick Jackson, active in the top leadership of the Public Relations Society of America (PRSA) for many years and one of the best-known public relations counselors in the United States, formulated the following chart showing how public relations can contribute to the success of any organization.

Process	*Principal Activities*	*Outcomes*
1. Awareness and information	Publicity, promotion, audience targeting, publications	Pave the way for sales, fundraising, stock offerings, et al.
2. Organizational motivation	Internal relations and communications, OD interventions	Build morale, teamwork, productivity, corporate culture; work toward One Clear Voice Outreach
3. Issue anticipation	Research, liaison with all publics, issue anticipation teams	Early warning of issues, social/political change, constituency unrest
4. Opportunity identification	Interaction with internal and external audiences, "knowing the business"	Discover new markets, products, methods, allies, positive issues
5. Crisis management	Respond to or blanket issues, disasters, attacks; coalition building	Protect position, retain allies and constituents, keep normal operations going despite battles
6. Overcoming executive isolation	Counseling senior managers about what's really happening, research	Realistic, competitive, enlightened decisions
7. Change agentry	Corporate culture, similar techniques, research	Ease resistance to change, promote smooth transition, reassure affected constituencies
8. Social responsibility	Social accountancy, research, mount public interest projects and tie-ins, volunteerism, philanthropy	Create reputation, enhance economic success through "double bottom line," earn trust
9. Influencing public policy	Constituency relations, coalition building, lobbying, grassroots campaigns	Public consent to activities, products, policies; political barriers removed.

PR casebook

Firestone vs. Ford: An Epic Public Relations Battle

Joshua Miller is a 22-year-old college student, body builder, fitness trainer. Or he was until Aug. 15, when a Firestone tire lost its tread and sent his Ford Bronco II tumbling four times and crashing into traffic on Interstate Highway 40 near Conway, Ark. The violent turnover severed Miller's spinal cord, paralyzing him from the waist down. Doctors say there's only a 5% chance he will walk again.

This lead paragraph in a *USA Today* news story tells the human side of what the writer called "One of the biggest and deadliest auto safety problems in U.S. history," which seriously eroded the credibility and corporate reputation of two major companies, Bridgestone/Firestone and Ford Motor Company. Just six days before Miller's crash, Firestone had recalled 6.5 million tires, of which more than 60 percent were used on Ford vehicles, primarily the Ford Explorer.

The Second Largest Tire Recall in U.S. History

Firestone's tire recall came about in August 2000, three months after the government began investigating reports that treads peeled off its tires. The National Highway Traffic Safety Administration (NHTSA) was investigating reports that 46 deaths and more than 300 accidents were linked to the tires. Later, the number of deaths linked to the tires reached 148, with an additional 525 people injured.

Firestone's announcement followed basic public relations concepts. The company said it was working closely with regulatory agencies, apologized for the lack of information in previous weeks, and made assurances that "Nothing is more important to us than the safety of our customers." Ford, in the meantime, announced a separate public relations and advertising campaign notifying customers about possible tire problems with the Ford Explorer but assured them that the vehicles were completely safe. Ford's CEO, Jacques Nasser, was widely quoted saying, "This is a tire issue, without question. It is not a vehicle issue."

Ford's strategy was to distance itself as far as possible from Firestone's problems, but Congressional investigators and consumer activists were not convinced. Ford had already recalled Firestone tires in several nations prior to 1998, and Venezuelan investigators had accused Ford and Firestone of covering up problems with Explorers and Firestone tires. And consumer Web sites added fuel to the fire. One person emailed, "I feel ripped off by . . . Ford who continues to deny they have anything to do with this when it was their choice to use these tires. . . . And ultimately, it is their vehicles blowing tires, flipping over, and killing people." Indeed, according to the critics, Ford knew the Explorer was unstable and subject to rollover. The Firestone tires were not those best suited for the vehicle, but Ford continued to use them for cost reasons.

Recall Gets Mixed Reviews

Firestone, in the meantime, was receiving mixed reviews about its recall of 6.5 million tires. Some public relations experts faulted the company for being too slow in acknowledging the problem in the first place, because there was evidence there were complaints and lawsuits about tread problems as early as 1994. They also questioned the absence of senior management from the recall announcement and even the wisdom of a staged recall that would delay replacement tires to some consumers for many months.

Paul Hicks, head of corporate practice at Ogilvy Public Relations, said "I have yet to see a senior officer from the parent company quoted in any fashion. It's a grievous error in strategy that will cost them millions, if not hundreds of millions in the long run." Part of the problem, some experts say, was a difference in business culture. Bridgestone, the parent company of Firestone, is a Japanese company, and top executives in Japan normally don't make public statements when there is a major scandal or issue involving the company.

Regarding the staged recall, which favored consumers in hot-weather states where most of the tread peeling occurred, BSMG Worldwide president Harris Diamond didn't think consumers in other states would be very patient. He said, "If these tires are indeed dangerous, then consumers are understandably going to want to replace them immediately. Asking them to wait is simply not tolerable."

Firestone committed another public relations blunder before the voluntary recall because it tried to blame the consumer. Company spokespersons said the tires shredded or peeled because consumers didn't maintain proper inflation and drove on poor roads. However, as Paul Holmes of *Inside PR* pointed out, "By blaming the consumers, the company appeared to be shirking its own responsibility for the problem."

(continued)

A defective Firestone tire frames the head of Bridgestone Tires, the Japanese parent company, at a Congressional hearing about whether the company knowingly sold defective tires.

The expression of public opinion affects the corporate reputation of a company. Here, an owner of a Ford Explorer lets everyone know that the company hasn't replaced the tires on her vehicle.

Ford's Public Relations Strategy

Although Firestone seemed to come across as highly defensive, Ford decided on a more proactive public relations strategy. In addition to using Ford's CEO as a major spokesperson on the crisis, about 30 members of the company's internal public relations staff worked full-time on the automaker's crisis team. Ford PR chief Jason Vines was widely quoted, and Ford announced that new purchasers of Ford Explorers could choose what brand of tire they wanted.

The stakes for both Firestone and Ford were extremely high. Both companies saw a decline in sales of its products, and stock prices plunged as a result of both companies spending almost $1.3 billion on the recall. Bridgestone shareholders saw two-thirds of their stock value vanish practically overnight, while Ford experienced a $4 billion loss in shareholder stock value. Both companies also were highly vulnerable to multiple lawsuits and liability, and one newspaper headline put it bluntly, "Lawsuits against Firestone could total $50 billion." See Chapter 13 for a PR Insights on the relationship between lawyers and public relations staff during the tire recall.

Dealing with Multiple Issues

Firestone, in particular, had to deal with multiple public relations problems in an effort to save its corporate reputation and retain its title as the second-largest tire maker in the world after Michelin. Some publics that had to be reached included: (1) angry owners of Firestone tires; (2) other U.S. automakers, who had to be convinced that they should continue to use the brand; (3) about 8500 independent tire dealers who carried Firestone products; (4) large retailers, such as Sears, who had suspended sales of Firestone tires; (5) government regulators who wanted to enact new safety laws; (6) millions of consumers who were hesitant to buy a Firestone tire; (7) Wall Street analysts who were concerned that the company would go bankrupt; (8) trial lawyers who were eager to file class-action suits; and (9) employees in tire plants who were being laid off because of a 40 percent drop in sales.

Ford's public relations strategy was relatively simple and to the point. It understood that it was necessary to allay customers' concerns as well as those of Congressional investigators, so the legal department's apparent intent to paint Firestone as the responsible party was highly supported. Ford gave Congressional investigators internal memos noting that Firestone opposed Ford's Middle East recall of Explorers with Firestone tires. Ford was also the first to produce information about the failure rate of Firestone tires on its Explorers while, at the same time, affirming that the vehicle was completely blameless.

Firestone Attacks Ford

Firestone, on the defensive for six months and experiencing a major shredding of its 100-year-old brand name, finally took exception to Ford's strategy of projecting itself as the "good guy" in the situation. Firestone executives said they had compelling data that showed that the Explorer was twice as likely to roll over in a tire-related accident than any other SUV. They also claimed that Ford Explorers in Venezuela with Goodyear tires were also having rollover problems.

The stage was set for a major public relations battle between the two giants in the early months of 2001 as each company tried to take the high ground in convincing Congress and the public that the other one was at fault. The new CEO of Firestone, John Lampe, made the first strike in a news conference one day before Ford had scheduled a news conference. Lampe announced that Firestone was severing its 95-year-old relationship with Ford and would no longer do business with the automaker.

Lampe blamed Ford executives for not being completely truthful about design problems with the Ford Explorer and said that the company had given its customers incorrect information about the proper inflation for the tires. The next day in its own news conference, Ford announced that it would spend between $2 and $3 billion to replace 1.3 million Firestone tires on Ford vehicles in addition to the 6.5 million tires already recalled by Firestone. Ford again blamed Firestone for any problems but also had its own public relations problems trying to explain new design changes in the Explorer without admitting the older models were unsafe.

No Real Winner

Public relations experts thought that "finger pointing" and the "blame game" were not effective strategies for either company. One public relations veteran said, "This is a no-win for both sides. The more they fight, the more uncertain the public becomes." Indeed, public opinion polls seemed to indicate that Firestone made some headway in eroding consumer confidence in Ford, but public relations expert James Lukaszewski wondered about its value. He said, "Attacking Ford will not draw a single customer into a Firestone store."

A year after Firestone's voluntary recall, the pros and cons of each company's public relations strategy were still being hotly debated among public relations executives. A survey by the Council of Public Relations Firms found that 66 percent of its members disagreed with Firestone's decision to end its 95-year-old rela-

(continued)

tionship with Ford. The same percentage believe Ford made a good decision to replace all Firestone tires on its vehicles.

More important, perhaps, is the finding that 85 percent of the public relations executives believe Ford and Firestone could have avoided the damage to their credibility and consumer confidence if they had worked together rather than attacking each other publicly. There is also an ethical dimension of how Firestone and Ford handled the entire situation. See the "Focus on Ethics" box in Chapter 3.

Summary

The Challenge of Public Relations
A career in public relations is multifaceted; the practitioner will have a broad range of tasks in his or her daily work.

Global Scope
Although the public relations field is largest in the United States, it is developing worldwide, with growth especially strong in Europe and Asia.

A Variety of Definitions
Although it is often defined in terms of techniques and tactics, public relations is also an interactive process.

Public Relations as a Process
The public relations process can be described with the RACE acronym: Research, Action, Communication, Evaluation.

The Components of Public Relations
The basic components of public relations, as described in a monograph issued by the PRSA Foundation, constitute the substance of this text.

Other Terms for Public Relations
Public relations is an umbrella term; other terms used often include the words and phrases *communication, information, public affairs,* or *media relations.* Less flattering terms for public relations practitioners include *flack* or *spin doctor.*

How Public Relations Differs from Journalism
Although writing is a common activity of both public relations professionals and journalists, the two fields differ in scope, objectives, audiences, and channels.

How Public Relations Differs from Advertising
Publicity, one area of public relations, utilizes mass media for dissemination of messages, as does advertising; but the format and context are different, with advertising involving paid space or time.

How Public Relations Differs from Marketing
The functions of public relations can overlap with marketing, but public relations builds relationships and generates goodwill, while marketing is concerned with customers and selling products.

How Public Relations Supports Marketing
When public relations becomes part of a marketing strategy, it is often called *marketing communications.* Public relations can be used to create an environment in which a corporation can successfully sell its products.

Toward an Integrated Perspective
An organization's goals and objectives are best achieved by integrating the functions of advertising, marketing, and public relations. An organization's communications should be consistent.

The Values of Public Relations
Today we all need not more information but sensitive communication, with public relations practitioners who can explain goals and methods of their clients and provide them with guidance about their audiences.

Case Activity: What Would You Do?

The National Company plans to introduce a new line of its battery-powered notebooks and portable computers. The approach is an integrated marketing communications campaign that will incorporate public relations, direct mail, sales promotion, and advertising. The objectives are to:

- Generate awareness of the new product with business audiences.
- Position National as the technology leader in developing and manufacturing notebook/portable computers.
- Increase National's sales and market share.

Do some brainstorming. Can you think of any audience research that could be done before you plan the marketing communications program? What variety of techniques and activities could help accomplish National's objectives?

Do some brainstorming. Can you think of any audience research that could be done before you plan the marketing communications program? What variety of techniques and activities could help accomplish National's objectives?

Questions for Review and Discussion

1. How many people work in public relations? Is public relations a growing field around the world?
2. There are many definitions of public relations. Of those listed in Chapter 1, select the one you find most satisfying and discuss the reasons for your preference.
3. What ten words characterize the essential elements of public relations?
4. How would you summarize the official statement on public relations issued by the Public Relations Society of America?
5. The RACE acronym is a popular way of describing the public relations process. For what step does each initial stand?
6. Public relations is described as a *loop process.* What component makes it a loop process instead of just a linear process?
7. What are the basic components of public relations practice? Which one sounds the most interesting as a career specialty for you?
8. What other terms are used by organizations to describe the public relations function? Do you have a preference for any of them? Explain your reasons.
9. What is *spin*? To some, it has negative connotations that conjure up manipulation and dishonesty. To others, it's simply a slang term for telling an organization's perspective on an event or issue. What do you think?
10. The PR Casebook study on Firestone's tire recall and its subsequent public relations battle with Ford Motor Company raises some issues regarding the role of public relations in a crisis situation where corporate credibility and reputation are at stake. In your view, do you think Firestone or Ford "won" the public relations battle?
11. Do you consider *PR* a slang term that should be avoided? Why or why not?
12. How does public relations differ from journalism? Advertising? Marketing?
13. How can the techniques and activities of public relations support the marketing function?
14. What is marketing communications? What is the concept of integrated marketing communications?
15. What four reasons are given for an organization to establish an integrated approach to its communications strategy?

Suggested Readings

Burnett, John, and Moriarty, Sandra. *Introduction to Marketing Communications.* Upper Saddle River, NJ: Prentice-Hall, 1998.

Caywood, Clarke L., editor. *The Handbook of Strategic Public Relations & Integrated Communications.* New York: McGraw Hill, 1997.

Cowlett, Mary. "Using PR to Launch into New Markets." *Marketing,* February 24, 2000, pp. 35–38.

Curtis, James. "PR Takes Center Stage." *Campaigns,* March 10, 2000, pp. 32–35.

Dilenschneider, Robert L. "Spin Doctors Practice Public Relations Quackery." *Wall Street Journal,* June 1, 1998. Op-ed on editorial page.

Edmondson, Jan. "Come Together: Why Integrated Marketing Works." *Public Relations Tactics,* January 2000, p. 12.

"Firestone Gets Proactive, but Is PR War Working?" *PR Week,* June 18, 2001, p. 11.

Frank, John. "No Side Is Safe in Latest Ford/Firestone PR War." *PR Week,* May 28, 2001, p. 9.

Gordon, Joye C. "Interpreting Definitions of Public Relations: Self Assessment and a Symbolic Interactionism-Based Alternative." *Public Relations Review,* Spring 1997, pp. 57–66.

Harris, Thomas. *Value-Added Public Relations.* Lincolnwood, IL: NTC Books, 1998.

Heath, Robert L. "A Rhetorical Perspective on the Values of Public Relations: Crossroads and Pathways toward Concurrence." *Journal of Public Relations Research,* Vol. 12, No. 1, 2000, pp. 69–92.

Henderson, Julie K. "Negative Connotations in the Use of the Term 'Public Relations' in the Print Media." *Public Relations Review,* Spring 1998, pp. 45–54.

Seglin, Jeffrey L. "A Blame Game Hurts Both Ford and Firestone." *New York Times,* June 17, 2001, p. F3.

Stateman, Allison. "The Top PR Stories of 2000." *PR Tactics,* January 2001, pp. 15–20.

"Study Finds PR Is Essential for Success." *O'Dwyer's PR Services Report,* September 2001, pp. 1, 37.

The Evolution of Public Relations

preview

The objective of this chapter is to make students aware of the significant events and personalities that have helped shape today's public relations practices, to place these in context from ancient times, and to define current trends.

Topics covered in the chapter include:

- The roots of public relations
- The evolving functions of press agentry, publicity, and counseling
- Early leaders—Ivy Ledbetter Lee, Edward L. Bernays, Doris Fleischman, and others
- Trends during World Wars I and II
- Trends since World War II
- Major recent developments and predictions for the 21st century

The Roots of Public Relations

Public relations is a 20th-century phenomenon whose roots extend deep into history; in a sense it is as old as human communication itself. In preceeding civilizations, such as those of Babylonia, Greece, and Rome, people were persuaded to accept the authority of government and religion through techniques that are still used: interpersonal communication, speeches, art, literature, staged events, publicity, and other such devices. None of these endeavors was called public relations, of course, but their purpose and their effect were the same as those of similar activities today.

The following remarks of Peter G. Osgood, former president of Carl Byoir & Associates, provide a few examples of the early practice of the art of public relations:

> The art has many roots. For example, the practice of dispatching teams to prepare the way for a traveling dignitary or politician was not invented by Harry Truman or Richard Nixon. Their political ancestors in Babylonia, Greece, and Rome were quite adept at it.
>
> St. John the Baptist himself did superb advance work for Jesus of Nazareth.
>
> Publicity, community relations, speech writing, positioning, government relations, issues analysis, employee relations, even investor relations: when you think about these activities in terms of the skills needed to practice them, it's plain they have deep historical roots.
>
> Generating publicity for the Olympics in ancient Athens, for example, demanded the same skills as [it did in 1984] in Los Angeles.
>
> Speech writing in Plato's time meant the same thing as it does today at Byoir: you must know the composition of your audience, never talk down to them, and impart information that will enlighten their ignorance, change their opinion, or confirm their own good judgments.
>
> Businesses in the Republic of Venice in the latter half of the Fifteenth Century practiced as fine an art of investor relations as IBM does in the United States in the latter half of the Twentieth Century: perhaps even finer since it was practiced one-on-one, face-to-face, every day on the Rialto, just as it was under the spreading elm tree on Wall Street in the early days of the Stock Exchange.

Other examples abound. In the 11th century, throughout the far-flung hierarchy of the Roman Catholic Church, Pope Urban II persuaded thousands of followers to serve God and gain forgiveness of their sins by engaging in the Holy Crusades. Six centuries later, the church was among the first to use the word *propaganda,* with the establishment by Pope Gregory XV of the College of Propaganda to supervise foreign missions and train priests to propagate the faith. (See Chapter 10.)

The stories that Spanish explorers publicized of the never-discovered Seven Cities of Gold, and even the fabled Fountain of Youth, induced others to travel to the New World. Some of the explorers probably believed those stories themselves. Two more blatant deceptions—examples of actions unacceptable to public relations people today—occurred when Eric the Red, in A.D. 1000, discovered a land of ice and rock and, to attract settlers, named it Greenland, and when Sir Walter Raleigh sent back glowing accounts in 1584 of what was actually a swamp-filled Roanoke Island, to persuade other settlers to travel to America.

It is clear, then, that the idea of using all forms of human communication—drama and storytelling among them—to influence the behavior of other people is nothing new.

The Evolving Functions

An excellent way to understand what public relations is all about today is to examine the evolution of its principal functions—press agentry, publicity, and counseling—along with the methods used to carry out those functions.

Press Agentry

"Hyping"—the promotion of movie and television stars, books, magazines, and so on through shrewd use of the media and other devices—is an increasingly lively phenomenon in today's public relations world. At the center of hyping is the press agent, whom the *Webster's New World Dictionary* defines as "a person whose work is to get publicity for an individual, organization, etc."

Press agentry is simply an extension of the activities of those who, in ancient civilizations, promoted athletic events such as the Olympic games and built an aura of myth around emperors and heroes. Its modern expression may be found in the press agentry that, during the 19th century in America, promoted circuses and exhibitions; glorified Davy Crockett as a frontier hero in order to draw political support from Andrew Jackson; attracted thousands to the touring shows of Buffalo Bill and sharpshooter Annie Oakley; made a legend of frontiersman Daniel Boone; and promoted hundreds of other personalities.

The oldtime press agents and the show people they most often represented played on the credulity of the public in its longing to be entertained, whether deceived or not. Advertisements and press releases were exaggerated to the point of being outright lies. Doing advance work for an attraction, the press agent dropped a sheaf of tickets on the desk of a newspaper city editor along with the announcements. Voluminous publicity generally resulted, and reporters, editors, and their families flocked to their free entertainment with scant regard for the ethical constraints that largely prohibit such practices today.

Small wonder then that today's public relations practitioner, exercising the highly sophisticated skills of evaluation, counseling, communication, and influencing management policies, shudders at the suggestion that public relations grew out of press agentry. And yet some aspects of modern public relations have their roots in the practice.

Phineas T. Barnum, the great American showman of the 19th century, for example, was the master of the *pseudoevent,* the planned happening that occurs primarily for the purpose of being reported—a part of today's public relations activities. Some of the more fun and flamboyant aspects of public relations today trace their roots to the development of press agentry.

Barnum, who was born in Connecticut in 1810, was also a hardheaded businessman, devoted to his family, a generous contributor to charities, a nondrinker, an accumulator of property, imaginative and energetic, a man whose primary love in staging his circus performances was to make children smile. Beyond that, however, most of today's public relations people would like to part company—for Barnum, in his advertising and publicity, used extensive flowery language and exaggeration, very much the norm during that period in American life. Even so, a public hungry for entertainment accepted his exaggerations, perhaps because they were audacious. Spectators thrilled to the wonders that he presented:

- Tom Thumb became one of the sensations of the century. Barnum discovered Charles S. Stratton in Connecticut when Stratton was 5 years old, only an inch over 2 feet in stature and weighing 15 pounds. Barnum made a public relations event of "General" Tom Thumb's marriage to another midget. After triumphal tours of the United States, where Tom Thumb entertained audiences with singing, dancing, and comedy monologues, Barnum took his attraction to England. A tiny carriage and ponies helped to attract attention to the midget, but Barnum decided that the best way to get public acceptance was first to involve the opinion leaders. Consequently, he invited London society leaders to his townhouse, where they met the quick-witted Tom Thumb. This meeting resulted in an invitation to the palace. Having entertained royalty, Tom Thumb drew full houses every night. Barnum, even in his day, knew the value of third-party endorsement.

- Jenny Lind, the "Swedish Nightingale," was one of Europe's most famous singers but was virtually unknown in the United States. Consequently, Barnum launched an unprecedented press campaign to acquaint the American public with her well-loved voice. He obtained full houses on opening nights in each community by donating part of the proceeds to charity. As a civic activity, the event attracted many of the town's opinion leaders, whereupon the general public flocked to attend succeeding performances—a device still employed today.
- The Barnum & Bailey Circus, with its three rings, two stands, and 800 employees, was proclaimed "The Greatest Show on Earth." Neil Harris, in his book *Humbug: The Art of P. T. Barnum,* describes the circus as the showman's "one enduring monument to fame; the legacy lies in his name left for the future."

Barnum owed much of his success to a corps of press agents headed by Richard F. "Tody" Hamilton. A famous circus clown, "Uncle" Bob Sherwood, described Hamilton

Phineas T. Barnum, a master of "hype," created pseudo-events such as the beautiful baby show promoted by this poster. Notice how it appeals to two human instincts: the desire to win money and to look at a human oddity, quaterns (called quadruplets in modern usage).

as a verbal conjurer whose language was so polysyllabic that "an Oxford professor would have found it difficult to understand."

Upon Barnum's death in 1891, the London *Times* joined in almost universal acclaim of his life with the eulogy: "His death removes an almost classic figure, and his name is a proverb already, and a proverb it will continue until mankind has ceased to find pleasure in the comedy of the showman and his patrons—the comedy of the harmless deceiver and the willingly deceived."

Publicity

Early Development Publicity, which consists mainly of the issuing of news releases to the media about the activities of an organization or an individual, is one of the earliest forms of public relations. It has been used for virtually every purpose. Signs such as "Vote for Cicero. He is a good man." have been found by archaeologists in ruins of ancient civilizations. In 59 B.C. Julius Caesar ordered the posting of a news sheet, *Acta Diurna,* outside the Forum to inform citizens of actions of Roman legislators; Caesar's *Commentaries* were published largely to aggrandize the achievements of the emperor.

The Colonial Era In 1620, broadsides were distributed in Europe by the Virginia Company offering 50 acres of free land to those bringing settlers to America by 1625. In 1641, Harvard College published a fund-raising brochure, and in 1758, Kings College (now Columbia University) issued its first press release, announcing commencement exercises.

Mainly through the use of newspapers and pamphlets, a staged event (the Boston Tea Party), and wide publicity accorded the so-called Boston Massacre, fiery Samuel Adams and the Boston Radicals achieved a propaganda triumph in helping persuade the American colonists to revolt against Great Britain. According to David Hackett Fisher's *Paul Revere's Ride,* Revere was one of 255 members of seven patriot groups that Revere coalesced into the main participants in the revolt. Also highly instrumental in bringing lukewarm citizens into the Revolutionary movement was Tom Paine's *Common Sense;* more than 120,000 copies of the pamphlet were sold in three months. Influencing public opinion concerning the makeup of the new political system were the *Federalist Papers,* comprised of 85 letters written by Alexander Hamilton, James Madison, and John Jay, and a series of articles by John Dickinson titled "Letters from a Farmer in Pennsylvania." The most frequently cited female propagandists of the era included Mercy Otis Warren, Abigail Adams, and Sarah Bache, daughter of Benjamin Franklin.

Nineteenth Century Public affairs were controlled mainly by the aristocratic, propertied class until the revolt of the so-called common man placed rough-hewn Andrew Jackson in the White House in 1828. Amos Kendall, a former Kentucky newspaper editor, became an intimate member of Jackson's "kitchen cabinet" and probably the first presidential press secretary. The appointment demonstrated for the first time that public relations is integral to political policy-making and management.

Jackson's campaign and presidency represented the first attempt in American political life to gain broad-based support for a presidential candidate. Kendall sampled public opinion on issues, advised Jackson, and skillfully interpreted his rough ideas, putting

global PR

Public Relations Roots in Germany, Great Britain, and Australia

Germany

As the Industrial Revolution swept through Europe, few owners, as in the United States, sensed a need to communicate with the public about their operations. In Germany, however, railroad companies and at least one shareholding corporation began publicity efforts as far back as the mid-19th century. Alfred Krupp, founder of the Krupp Company, which became the premier industrial firm in Germany and the base of the Nazi war power, wrote to a financial adviser in 1866:

> We think . . . it is time that authoritative reports concerning factory matters in accordance with the facts should be propagated on a regular basis through newspaper reports which serve the enlightened public. We can supply the material for this purpose, and should qualified experts at times be unavailable, it is our wish to contact responsible newspaper editors ourselves.

Company documents reveal that Krupp was unable to find a qualified person to assist him in the effort. However, his son, Friedrich Alfred Krupp, hired Adolf Lauter in 1893 to establish a news bureau, and the department was integrated into the firm's operations in 1901.

As the Krupp public relations efforts expanded internationally, other major industries followed suit. Ivy Lee's involvement in 1933 with the I. G. Farben cartel, through its German Dye Trust, is mentioned later in the chapter.

Great Britain

The industrial and communication systems of Great Britain were already developed in 1910, when the Marconi Company established a department to distribute news releases about its achievements in wireless telegraphy.

Professional public relations counseling was introduced in the country in 1924, when Sir Basil Clarke, a former government press officer, established Editorial Services Ltd. in London. For his first client, a dairy group, he promoted the idea of milk pasteurization, an innovation that had met with some resistance from the public.

The first public relations officer so styled in Britain was Sir John Elliott, appointed in 1925 by the Southern Railway Company.

Beginning in the mid-19th century, the government enjoyed a close working relationship with the Reuters news agency for almost 100 years. Paul Julius Reuter, agency owner, was granted use of cables linking the empire's outposts; in return, agency dispatches did much to further the nation's commercial and political interests, and there is little doubt that the news service was careful to say at crucial points what the British government wished it to say. With such an arrangement, historians have noted, British government propaganda was particularly effective in bringing the United States to its side in World War I. Today, Reuters operates with scant if any government influence.

In 1911 the first government public relations campaign was carried out when, at the instigation of Prime Minister David Lloyd George, the Insurance Commission explained the benefits of the National Insurance Act, an unpopular measure that had attracted much adverse publicity. The Air Ministry appointed the first government press officer in 1919, and a year later the Ministry of Health selected Sir Basil Clarke, a former Reuters correspondent, as director of information.

Government public relations was substantially enlarged after World War II. The offices now are organized into three sections: press relations, publicity and inquiry, and intelligence. During recent extended freedom-of-information debates, however, the system was labeled the most secretive in the world (an obvious exaggeration), and demands were made that the service be disbanded and its work turned over to regular administrators.

Via shortwave, the British Broadcasting Company (BBC), chartered in 1922, carries a British point of view to an estimated 75 million adults around the world each week. In the early 1990s the BBC greatly expanded its World TV Service.

Australia

Public relations in Australia largely consisted of publicity efforts until after World War II. When U.S. General Douglas MacArthur arrived in Australia after his escape from Corregidor in 1942, he introduced the term *public relations* and, with a highly skilled staff, demonstrated numerous ways of promoting his image and war policy.

The industry grew steadily, and, in 1960, the Public Relations Institute of Australia (PRIA) was formed. It now includes more than 1500 practitioners. Women,

(continued)

today comprising about one-third of the nation's public relations specialists, were among its founders.

Notable practitioners include George Fitzpatrick, credited with being the first Australian to conduct public relations, and Eric White, who, a Hill and Knowlton official said, "virtually created the public relations industry" in Australia. As early as the 1960s White oversaw extensions of his firm in six Pacific Rim countries.

them into presentable form as speeches and news releases. He served as Jackson's advance agent on trips, wrote glowing articles that he sent to supportive newspapers, and was probably the first to use newspaper reprints in public relations; almost every complimentary news story or editorial about Jackson was reprinted and circulated.

After the Jacksonian era, American politicians increasingly used press releases, pamphlets, posters, and emblems to win favor. The effort reached a 19th-century crescendo during the presidential campaigns of William Jennings Bryan and William McKinley in 1896.

Throughout the century, publicity techniques helped populate western land. Newly sprung-up villages competed to attract printers, whose newspaper copies and pamphlets describing almost every community as "the garden spot of the West" were sent back East to induce increased settlement. Many settlers were lured to Illinois, for example, by gazettes that extolled the fertile land. Henry W. Ellsworth's *Valley of the Upper Wabash,* published in the 1830s, and another publication, *Illinois in 1837,* were subsidized by land speculators. One critic of the time called these gazettes downright puffery, "full of exaggerated statements, and high-wrought and false-colored descriptions." To promote rail travel, a daily newspaper called the *Trans-Continental* was published on a train carrying Easterners to western lands. Suggestive of current corporate press tour practice, the newspaper contained national and international news received by telegraph at various stops along the way.

In addition, the supporters of such causes as antislavery, antivivisectionism, women's rights, and prohibition employed publicity to maximum effect throughout the century. One of the most influential publicity ventures for the abolition of slavery was the publication of Harriet Beecher Stowe's *Uncle Tom's Cabin.* Stowe was among a number of women who, although they were not public relations people, extensively used some of the techniques of public relations to promote their causes. Sarah J. Hale,

Groups advocating the right of women to vote in the United States used a variety of public relations tactics to press their cause. Here, a group of suffragists participate in a 1914 parade in Washington, D.C. Through such parades and demonstrations, they received media coverage and also informed the public about their cause. Today, other groups representing various causes still continue to hold demonstrations, parades, and rallies.
Source: U.S. Library of Congress.

editor from 1836 to 1877 of *Godey's Ladies Book,* a best-selling magazine with 150,000 circulation, ardently promoted women's rights. After a women's rights convention in Seneca Falls, New York, in 1845, Amelia Bloomer became famous. Now associated with the loose-fitting trousers she wore in protest of the corset, she edited *The Lily,* a women's rights publication. Noted temperance crusader Carrie Nation got attention by invading saloons with an axe; in less dramatic fashion she served as business manager of *The Revolution,* which advocated a variety of radical causes. The American Woman Suffrage Association was formed in 1869 with Lucy Stone as editor of its weekly, *The Woman's Journal.* Adoption of the Nineteenth Amendment to the U.S. Constitution in 1920 finally gave women the right to vote.

Professor Carolyn M. Byerly of Ithaca College says that such campaigns for social reform qualify as public relations operations and deserve a place in the history of the field. She cites research by Genevieve Gardner McBride that points out that in Wisconsin the support for a constitutional amendment giving women the right to vote began with a few interested individuals and was carried out through carefully managed informational campaigns that included "publicity, press agentry, publications, petition drives, advertising, merchandising, lobbying, membership recruitment and training, special events, fund-raising . . . and issues management, or 'crisis PR.'"

A wave of industrialization, mechanization, and urbanization swept the nation after the Civil War. Concentrations of wealth developed throughout manufacturing and trade. Amid the questioning of business practices, the Mutual Life Insurance Company in 1888 hired journalist Charles J. Smith to write press releases designed to improve its image. In 1889 Westinghouse Corporation established what is said to be the first in-house publicity department, with former newspaper reporter E. H. Heinrichs as manager. In 1897 the term *public relations* was used by the Association of American Railroads in a company listing.

Twentieth Century As the use of publicity gained increased acceptance, the first publicity agency, known as the Publicity Bureau, was established in Boston in 1900. Harvard College was its most prestigious client. George F. Parker and Ivy Ledbetter Lee opened a publicity office in New York City in 1904. Parker remained in the publicity field, but Lee became an adviser to companies and individuals (as will be discussed in the section that follows). In Washington, D.C., William Wolf Smith established a firm to influence legislators through publicity.

A second Boston publicity business was opened in 1906 by James D. Ellsworth, who later joined the staff of the American Telephone & Telegraph Company. Theodore N. Vail greatly expanded the press and customer relations operations at AT&T after becoming its president in 1907. In 1909 another pioneer, Pendleton Dudley, established a public relations office in New York.

At the beginning of the 20th century, the Santa Fe Railway commissioned dozens of painters and photographers to depict scenes in the then little-known Southwest. The paintings unabashedly prettified the American Indian, and the photographs, colored by hand, showed the Indians weaving, grinding corn, and dancing. This corporate image making attracted hundreds of tourists and contributed to the romanticizing of the Indian and the West.

The Chicago Edison Company broke new ground in public relations techniques under the skillful leadership of its president, Samuel Insull. Well aware of the special need of a public utility to maintain a sound relationship with its customers, Insull created a variety of techniques—he established an external magazine, *Chicago, The*

A traditional form of publicity was the poster. This poster, publicizing the Franco-American Bicycle, was an early form of international advertising.

Electric City, in 1903; used press releases extensively; was the first in business to use films for public relations purposes, in 1909; and started the "bill stuffer" idea in 1912 by inserting company information into customer bills.

Henry Ford was probably the first major industrialist to utilize thoroughly two basic public relations concepts. The first was the notion of *positioning*—the idea that credit and publicity always go to those who do something first—and the second idea was ready accessibility to the press. Joseph Epstein, author of *Ambition,* says, "He may have been an even greater publicist than mechanic."

In 1900 Ford obtained coverage of the prototype Model T by demonstrating it to a reporter from the Detroit *Tribune.* By 1903 Ford achieved widespread publicity by racing his cars—a practice that is still carried out today by automakers. Ford hired Barney Oldfield, a champion bicycle racer and a popular personality, to drive a Ford car at a record speed of 1 minute and 6 seconds per mile, or a bit less than 60 miles per hour. The publicity from these speed runs gave Ford financial backing and a ready market.

Ford also positioned himself as the champion of the common person and was the first automaker to envision that a car should be affordable for everyone. He produced his first Model T in 1908 for $850 and, by 1915–1916, reduced its selling price to $360. Such price reductions made Ford dominant in the auto industry and on newspaper front pages. He garnered further publicity and became the hero of working men and women by being the first automaker to double his workers' wages to $5 per day.

Ford became a household word because he was willing to be interviewed by the press on almost any subject, including the gold standard, evolution, alcohol, foreign affairs, and even capital punishment. A populist by nature, he once said, "Business is a service, not a bonanza," an idea reiterated by many of today's top corporate executives who believe business has a social responsibility.

Although Ford was the first major industrialist to hire blacks in large numbers, he also wrote a number of anti-Semitic articles. In the 1930s, his earlier image as the champion of the working class was shattered by his resistance to organized labor, which led to several violent confrontations as the United Automobile Workers attempted to organize Ford workers.

In politics, President Theodore Roosevelt proved himself a master in generating publicity. Roosevelt was the first president to make extensive use of news conferences and interviews in drumming up support for his projects. He knew the value of the presidential tour for publicity purposes. For example, on a trip to what became Yosemite National Park, designed to publicize the idea of national parks, Roosevelt was accompanied by a bevy of reporters and photographers who wrote glowing articles about the need to preserve the area for public recreational use.

Not-for-profit organizations joined the publicity bandwagon in the century's first decade. The American Red Cross and the National Tuberculosis Association began extensive publicity programs soon after their formation in 1908. Two other nonprofit organizations, the Knights of Columbus and the National Lutheran Council, opened press offices in 1918.

Organized fund-raising for American higher education began in 1916 when John Price Jones, who later worked on the Liberty Loan campaign to help finance the U.S. war effort, directed a highly successful drive on behalf of Harvard University. The campaign exceeded its $10 million goal by $4 million. Scott M. Cutlip, in his 800-page book *The Unseen Power: Public Relations. A History,* reported that the campaign "not only made fund-raising history but changed the course of American higher education, for Harvard was dramatically telling the nation and sister colleges that the old methods of financing higher education in America were passé."

Standards for today's major health drives, Cutlip noted, were set by the creation of nationwide birthday balls in 1934 celebrating President Franklin D. Roosevelt's birthday and raising funds for infantile paralysis research. Leading to creation of the March of Dimes, the campaign by Carl Byoir & Associates orchestrated 6000 events in 3600 communities and raised more than $1 million.

Counseling

Industrialists and Muckrakers In the latter part of the 19th century, the United States was transformed by mighty economic and social forces. Industrialization moved forward on a major scale; cities swelled with even more immigrants; production was rapidly being mechanized; and business firms grew through the use of vastly improved transportation and communication facilities, along with new interlocking corporate structures and financing methods.

It was the era of the so-called robber barons, exploiters of natural resources and labor, known in less accusatory terms as founders of great American industries. Heavy concentrations of power were held by John D. Rockefeller, Sr., in oil; Andrew Carnegie in steel; J. Pierpont Morgan and Cornelius Vanderbilt in finance; and by other industrial leaders. Labor strife intensified, and the government, upon the urging of populist and progressive forces, began to challenge big business with the enactment of such measures as the Interstate Commerce Act and the Sherman Antitrust Act.

Within the dozen years after 1900, several magazines developed a literature of exposure that Theodore Roosevelt called the work of "muckrakers." He was comparing the more sensational writers to the Man with the Muckrake in the 17th-century work *Pilgrim's Progress*—a character who did not look up to see the celestial crown but continued to rake the filth. Led by Ida M. Tarbell, these writers posed a serious threat to business. Tarbell wrote a series of articles published by *McClure's* in 1903 titled "History of the Standard Oil Company," an attack on the corruption and unfair practices of the Rockefeller oil monopoly. Other noted muckrakers included Upton Sinclair, who exposed unsanitary and fraudulent practices of the meat packers in his 1906 book *The Jungle.*

■ **The First Public Relations Counsel** The combination of stubborn management attitudes and improper actions, labor strife, and widespread public criticism produced the first public relations counselor, Ivy Ledbetter Lee. Although, as previously noted, this Princeton graduate and former business reporter for the *New York World* began his private practice as a publicist, he shortly expanded that role to become the first public relations counsel.

The emergence of modern public relations can be dated from 1906, when Lee was hired by the anthracite coal industry, then embroiled in a strike. Lee discovered that, although the miners' leader, John Mitchell, was supplying reporters with all the facts they requested, by contrast the leader of the coal proprietors, George F. Baer, had refused to talk to the press or even to President Theodore Roosevelt, who was seeking to arbitrate the dispute. Lee persuaded Baer and his associates to change their policy. He issued a press notice signed by Baer and the other leading proprietors that began: "The anthracite coal operators, realizing the general public interest in conditions in the mining regions, have arranged to supply the press with all possible information. . . ."

Lee issued a "Declaration of Principles," which signaled the end of the "public-be-damned" attitude of business and the beginning of the "public-be-informed" era. Eric Goldman said the declaration "marks the emergence of a second stage of public relations. The public was no longer to be ignored, in the traditional manner of business, nor fooled, in the continuing manner of the press agent." The declaration reads:

> This is not a secret press bureau. All our work is done in the open. We aim to supply news. This is not an advertising agency; if you think any of our matter ought properly to go to your business office, do not use it. Our matter is accurate. Further details on any subject treated will be supplied promptly, and any editor will be assisted most cheerfully in verifying directly any statement of fact. . . . In brief, our plan is, frankly and openly, in behalf of business concerns and public institutions, to supply to the press and the public of the United States prompt and accurate information concerning subjects which it is of value and interest of the public to know about.

PR insights

Brightening Rockefeller's Public Image

Two New York writers helped John D. Rockefeller, Sr., shed much of his penchant for secrecy and resistance to press coverage, according to historian Ron Chernow, author of a 1997 book, *Titan: The Life of John D. Rockefeller, Sr.*

In 1906, the Standard Oil Company trust hired its first publicist, Joseph I. C. Clarke, an editor at the *New York Herald.* Jovial and outgoing, Clarke "greeted reporters with a quip and a cigar," to warm up the trust's image, Chernow relates. "Before long he was lining up reporters for breezy, lighthearted interviews with Rockefeller, featuring a game of golf with the mogul, who obligingly delivered pithy observations on topical subjects. Articles began to appear with titles like, 'The Human Side of John D. Rockefeller,' as if its existence wasn't taken for granted."

Soon thereafter, Rockefeller and friends sailed for France aboard the *Deutschland.* In an article for the *New York American,* reporter William Hoster speculated that Rockefeller needed to consult a European specialist because of ill health. He, too, boarded the *Deutschland,* spied on Rockefeller, and was surprised "to find . . . a tall, broad-shouldered robust man, with ruddy complexion, clear eyes, alert step and altogether vigorous manner."

At Cherbourg, Hoster confronted his subject. "Mr. Rockefeller, have you ever reflected that perhaps you yourself may be in measure responsible for the way that you have been treated by the newspapers?" For a time, writes Chernow, Rockefeller "gazed stonily at Hoster and dug his walking stick into the gravel path. Then his face relaxed and a faint smile crossed his lips. 'So it is my fault. I suppose there may be something in what you say, though I had never thought of it that way before.'"

Rockefeller invited Hoster to join his party. "After a lifetime spent escaping reporters," Chernow relates. "Rockefeller now converted William Hoster into his bosom companion. They rambled through the forest, golfed, and dined together in local hotels."

After that, perhaps also because of Clarke's influence, Rockefeller seemed to have lost his fear of the press and noticeably loosened up. "At the age of sixty-seven he is growing out of his chrysalis. For the first years of his life, he is beginning to enjoy himself. Two years ago, he dodged newspaper men. Now he courts them," Chernow says.

The continuance of Lee's policy of providing accurate information about corporate and institutional activities has saved American news media millions of dollars in reporter salaries during the intervening nine decades. Despite misleading information given out by some public relations people, news releases quickly became extremely valuable—even a necessity—to the media.

Railroads at the time also were seeking to operate secretly in their dealings with the press. Retained by the Pennsylvania Railroad Company to handle press relations after a major rail disaster, Lee persuaded the president to alter his policy. Lee provided press facilities, released all available information, and enabled reporters to view the disaster scene. Although such action appeared to the conservative railway directors to constitute reckless indiscretion, they later acknowledged that the company had received fairer press comment than on any previous such occasion.

In 1914, John D. Rockefeller, Jr., hired Lee in the wake of the vicious strike-breaking activities known as the Ludlow Massacre at the Rockefeller family's Colorado Fuel and Iron Company plant. Lee went to Colorado and talked to both sides. He also persuaded Rockefeller to talk with the miners and their families. Lee made sure that the press was there to record Rockefeller's eating in the workers' dining hall, swinging a pickax in the mine, and having a beer with the workers after hours. The press portrayed Rockefeller as seriously concerned about the plight of the workers, thus increasing his popularity with the striking miners. Meanwhile, Lee distributed a factsheet giving management's view of the strike and even convinced the governor of Colorado to write an article supporting the position taken by the company.

Rockefeller's visits with the miners led to policy changes and more worker benefits, but the company also prevented the United Mine Workers from gaining a foothold. George McGovern, former Democratic Party candidate for President, wrote his doctoral dissertation on the Ludlow Massacre: "It was the first time in any American labor struggle where you had an organized effort to use what has become modern public relations to sell one side of a strike to the American people."

Lee's success in transforming a labor dispute into a positive situation (and public image) for the Rockefeller family was based on the fact, according to Gordon M. Sears, president of T. J. Ross and Associates, that "Lee tried to solve the problem or at least establish the proper course toward solution before turning to communications." Lee's achievement led the Rockefeller family to hire him for a full-scale renovation of the Rockefeller name, badly damaged by the muckrakers who often pictured John D. Rockefeller, Sr., as an exploiter and the king of the greedy capitalists. Lee advised the Rockefellers to announce publicly the millions of dollars that they gave to charitable institutions. He also convinced John, Sr., to allow reporters and photographers to record his golf playing and socializing with family and friends. When John, Sr., died in 1937, he was mourned worldwide as a kindly old man and a great humanitarian and philanthropist.

Lee's public relations firm became Lee, Harris, and Lee in 1916. Three years later he was joined by Thomas J. Ross in the firm of Ivy Lee and T. J. Ross and Associates. Among other counseling activities, Lee advised the American Tobacco Company to initiate a profit-sharing plan, the Pennsylvania Railroad to beautify its stations, and the movie industry to stop inflated advertising and form a voluntary code of censorship.

Lee lost a measure of public trust by advocating diplomatic recognition and trade with the Bolsheviks in the 1920s. He argued that such action was necessary to resolve differences between the United States and the Soviet Union. His reputation was damaged more severely when a congressional hearing disclosed that he was working for the

Ivy Ledbetter Lee was recognized early in the 20th century as the first public relations counsel.

Hitler government while being paid by Germany's I. G. Farben chemical firm as a subterfuge in the early 1930s. Lee said he opposed Hitler and counseled the firm as a means of obtaining goodwill and product sales in the United States. The secret relationship caused Congress to pass the Foreign Agents Registration Act (see Chapter 16).

Lee died in 1934. He is remembered for four important contributions to public relations: (1) advancing the concept that business and industry should align themselves with the public interest, and not vice versa; (2) dealing with top executives and carrying out no program unless it had the active support and personal contribution of management; (3) maintaining open communication with the news media; and (4) emphasizing the necessity of humanizing business and bringing its public relations down to the community level of employees, customers, and neighbors.

Wartime Counsel to Government Both world wars saw a tremendous upsurge in the role of public relations on behalf of the government—especially the Creel Committee during World War I and the Office of War Information during World War II.

The Creel Committee "Literally public relations counselors to the United States Government" during World War I is the description given to members of the Committee on Public Information by James O. Mock and Cedric Larson in their book *Words That Won the War.* President Wilson called on George Creel, a former newspaper reporter, to organize a comprehensive public relations effort to advise him and his cabinet, to carry out programs, and to influence U.S. and world opinion. Wrote Mock and Larson:

> Mr. Creel assembled as brilliant and talented a group of journalists, scholars, press agents, editors, artists, and other manipulators of the symbols of public opinion as America had ever seen united for a single purpose. It was a gargantuan advertising agency, the like of which the country had never known, and the breathtaking scope of its activities was not to be equalled until the rise of the totalitarian dictatorship after the war. George Creel, Carl Byoir, Edgar Sisson, Harvey O'Higgins, Guy Stanton Ford, and their famous associates were literally public relations counselors to the United States Government, carrying first to the citizens of this country and then to those in distant lands, the ideas which gave motive power to the stupendous undertaking of 1917–1918.

Among numerous other activities, the committee persuaded newspapers and magazines to contribute volumes of news and advertising space to encourage Americans to save food and to invest heavily in Liberty Bonds, which more than 10 million people purchased. Thousands of businesses set up their own groups of publicity people to expand the effort. Wilson accepted Creel's advice that hatred of the Germans should be played down and loyalty and confidence in the government should be emphasized. The committee publicized the war aims and ideals of Woodrow Wilson—to make the world safe for democracy and to make World War I the war to end all wars. The American Red Cross, operating in cooperation with the committee, enrolled more than 19 million new members and received more than $400 million in contributions during the period.

The massive effort had a profound effect on the development of public relations by demonstrating the success of these full-blown techniques. It also awakened an awareness in Americans of the power of mediated information in changing public attitudes and behavior. This, coupled with postwar analysis of British propaganda devices alleged to have helped get the nation into the war, resulted in a number of scholarly books and college courses on the subject. Among the books was Walter Lippmann's classic *Public Opinion,* in which he pointed out how people are moved to action by "the pictures in our minds."

Another legacy was the training received by the noted practitioners Carl Byoir, associate chairman of the committee, and Edward L. Bernays. Byoir in 1930 founded a company that for more than 50 years was one of the largest public relations firms in the United States. In one of the early campaigns that established Byoir's reputation, he mobilized women's groups, along with business and labor groups, and directed a campaign that defeated a proposed New York State anti-chain-store tax. He employed the third-party endorsement technique described in Chapter 10. This and numerous other achievements have been described by George Hammond, a former Byoir chairman and chief executive officer, in a videotaped history interview.

Bernays's contributions to public relations will be discussed shortly.

Office of War Information (OWI) To head the vital war information operation during World War II, President Franklin Roosevelt turned to Elmer Davis, an Indiana-born journalist and a Rhodes Scholar. Davis had spent 15 years as a novelist and free-lance writer, 10 years as a *New York Times* reporter, and 3 years as a radio commentator for the Columbia Broadcasting System.

Profiting by knowledge of the techniques so successful in World War I, Davis orchestrated an even larger public relations effort during World War II. His job was exceptionally difficult because his office had to coordinate information from the military and numerous government agencies, wrestle for funds each year with a Congress suspicious that the OWI would become Roosevelt's personal propaganda vehicle, and overcome opposition from a large segment of the press that resented having to do business with an official spokesperson.

As in World War I, the OWI's campaigns were extremely successful in promoting the sale of war bonds and in obtaining press and broadcast support for other wartime necessities. These included food, clothing, and gasoline rationing; more

focus on ethics

Is Censorship Ever Justified?

During World War II all written and broadcast communications leaving the war zones, including Great Britain, were censored by the government. News stories, magazine articles, books, radio broadcasts, films, and letters had to be approved by military or civilian censors, who removed material they found objectionable.

Having a U.S. Army officer decide whether a news story could be sent to the United States was a clear violation of the freedom of speech principle guaranteed by the First Amendment to the Constitution. Yet this was accepted with relatively little protest. War correspondents did complain about the competence of some censors.

1. Why did the government impose, and the people accept, this restriction on their constitutional rights?
2. If World War II were being fought today, why would such total censorship be impossible to enforce?

See the answers at the bottom of the following page.

President Franklin D. Roosevelt's radio "fireside chats" from the White House strengthened public morale during the Great Depression of the 1930s and later during World War II.

"victory gardens"; higher productivity and less absenteeism; and secrecy regarding troop movements and weaponry development.

The Voice of America, established by the Department of State in 1942, carried news of the war to all parts of the world. The film industry provided support through such means as Frank Capra's documentary film for the U.S. Signal Corps, designed to build patriotism; bond-selling tours by film stars; and the production of commercial movies glorifying U.S. fighting forces.

The OWI was the forerunner of the U.S. Information Agency, established in 1953 under President Eisenhower to "tell America's story abroad." A number of the people who worked with Davis became public relations leaders during the ensuing decades.

Further Development of the Counseling Function The role of the public relations practitioner as an adviser to corporate and institutional managements grew in significance as the American economy expanded during the 1920s. The persons most responsible for defining this function and drawing public attention to it were Edward L. Bernays and his wife and partner Doris E. Fleischman. Fleischman was a talented writer, ardent feminist, and former assistant women's page and assistant Sunday editor of the *New York Tribune.* Married in 1922, they were equal partners in the firm of Edward L. Bernays, Counsel on Public Relations, until Fleischman died in 1980.

The answers on censorship questions:

1. Keeping military information such as troop movements, battlefront positions, and ship convoy sailings from the enemy was essential for victory. The censorship saved many lives.
2. Strict censorship succeeded because the governments controlled the transmission lines, broadcast facilities, and postal service in the war zones. Television, satellite transmission, and the Internet did not exist during that time. Today, the Internet operates virtually uncontrolled, satellite spying can detect troop and ship movements, and satellite transmission makes it easy to bypass traditional transmission lines.

Fleischman, indeed, was an equal partner in the work of the firm, interviewing clients, writing news releases, editing the company's newsletter, and writing and editing books and magazine articles, among other duties. Historian Susan Henry, a professor of journalism at California State University, Northridge, and contributor to a 1989 book, *Women in Mass Communication: Challenging Gender Values,* edited by Pamela J. Creedon, says that Bernays called Fleischman "the brightest woman I'd ever met in my life" and "the balance wheel of our operation."

The gender value system of the time, however, did not allow Fleischman to represent the firm to its clients or even to be included in the firm's title. Other historians have credited to Bernays both his own and their shared public relations achievements, included in the list of early examples of counseling that follows shortly.

■ The Public Relations Function Explained "In writing this book I have tried to set down the broad principles that govern the new profession of public relations counsel." With this opening sentence of *Crystallizing Public Opinion,* published in 1923, Bernays coined a term to describe a function that was to become the core of public relations. He illuminated the scope and function, methods and techniques, and social responsibilities of public relations. Following by a year Walter Lippmann's insightful treatise on public opinion, the book attracted much attention, and Bernays was invited by New York University to offer the first public relations course in the nation.

This poster urging women to join the home front workforce during World War II was an extremely effective recruiting tool. It was issued by the War Production Coordinating Committee.

Edward L. Bernays, a legendary figure in public relations with a career spanning about three-quarters of a century, died at age 103 in 1995. On his 100th birthday he was honored at a dinner by the Boston chapter of the Public Relations Society of America.

Even so, the name and definition that Bernays gave to the scope and function of public relations failed for years to gain acceptance by editors and scholars, most of whom equated the new business with press agentry. Following World War I, the newspaper industry, led by the American Society of Newspaper Publishers, conducted a campaign against "spacegrabbers," identified as press agents who demanded free publicity instead of buying advertising space. Later, Stanley Walker, city editor of the *New York Herald Tribune,* leveled his scorn at Bernays:

> Bernays has taken the sideshow barker and given him a philosophy and a new and awesome language. . . . He is no primitive drum-beater. . . . He is devoid of swank and does not visit newspaper offices [as did the circus advance agents]; and yet, the more thoughtful newspaper editors, who have their own moments of worry about the mass mind and commercialism, regard Bernays as a possible menace, and warn their colleagues of his machinations.

This antipathy toward public relations still lingers among many journalists.

In 1955 Bernays refined his approach to public relations and, in a book titled *The Engineering of Consent,* he gave the field a new description. To many people, the word *engineering* implied manipulation through propaganda and other devices. Bernays, who himself later railed at use of the word *image* to mean reputation-building, defended his terminology and concept:

> The term *engineering* was used advisedly. In our society, with its myriad of group interests, interest groups, and media, only an engineering approach to the problems of adjustment, information, and persuasion could bring effective results. . . .
>
> Public relations practiced as a profession is an art applied to a science, in which the public interest and not pecuniary motivation is the primary consideration. The engineering of consent in this sense assumes a constructive social role. Regrettably,

public relations, like other professions, can be abused and used for anti-social purposes. I have tried to make the profession socially responsible as well as economically viable.

Early Examples of Counseling The following examples illustrate how effectively Bernays performed his public relations work:

- When, in the 1910s, the actor Richard Bennett wanted to produce *Damaged Goods,* a play about sex education, Bernays blunted the anticipated criticism of moralists, and possibly avoided a police raid, by organizing the Sociological Fund of the *Medical Review of Reviews* journal, with contributors paying $4 each to attend the play as an educational event.
- To help Procter & Gamble sell Ivory soap, Bernays attracted the attention of children and their parents to cleanliness by developing a nationwide interest in soap sculpture.
- At a time when public opinion and some legislation kept women from smoking in public, Bernays was hired by George Washington Hill, president of the American Tobacco Company, to expand sales of Lucky Strike cigarettes. Bernays consulted a psychoanalyst, who told him that cigarettes might be perceived as "torches of freedom" by women seeking equality with men. Bernays helped break the barrier by inducing ten debutantes to "light up" while strolling in New York's Easter parade.

Doris Fleischman was the wife of Edward L. Bernays and his partner in their pioneer public relations counseling firm.

- Later, when research showed that sales of Lucky Strike cigarettes to women were down because many felt that the green package clashed with their clothes, Bernays tried to persuade Hill to change the color. Unsuccessful in the effort, Bernays made green fashionable by arranging a prestigious socialites' ball with that color scheme; getting makers of accessories to promote green shoes, hosiery, and gloves; and arranging for green fashion displays on the covers of *Harper's Bazaar* and *Vogue* on the date of the ball. (Only during World War II, when an ingredient in the color became an industrial scarcity, did Hill relent, nevertheless reaping continued sales with the slogan, "Lucky Strike Green Has Gone to War.")

Perhaps the most spectacular example of Bernays's skill took place in 1929. To celebrate the 50th anniversary of Thomas Edison's invention of the electric light bulb, Bernays arranged the worldwide-attention-getting Light's Golden Jubilee. On October 21, many of the world's utilities shut off their power all at one time, for one minute, in honor of Edison. President Herbert Hoover and many other dignitaries attended a banquet climaxing the celebration. The event achieved such fame that the U.S. Post Office, on its own, issued a commemorative two-cent postage stamp.

Sociologist Leonard W. Doob described the jubilee as "one of the most lavish pieces of propaganda ever engineered in this country during peace time." Bernays, wrote Doob, was working "not for Edison or for Henry Ford, but for very important interests [General Electric had hired Bernays] which saw this historic anniversary as an opportunity to publicize the uses of the electric light."

Light's Golden Jubilee is considered one of Bernays's major accomplishments. It showed, in 1929, the potential of effective public relations. And when television commentator Bill Moyers interviewed Bernays in 1984 on a Public Broadcasting Service program about the early beginnings of public relations, Moyers said: "You know, you got Thomas Edison, Henry Ford, Herbert Hoover, and masses of Americans to do what you wanted them to do. You got the whole world to turn off its lights at the same time. You got American women to smoke in public. That's not influence. That's power."

Replied Bernays: "But you see, I never thought of it as power. I never treated it as power. People want to go where they want to be led."

Bernays is widely acknowledged as the founder of modern public relations; one historian has even described him as "the first and doubtless the leading ideologist of public relations." Sigmund Freud, founder of psychoanalysis, must have been proud of his nephew. In 1990 *Life* magazine cited Bernays as one of the 100 most important Americans of the twentieth century.

After Bernays's death in 1995 at the age of 103, journalist Larry Tye searched more than 800 boxes of material that Bernays bequeathed to the Library of Congress and interviewed more than 100 people who knew him. His 1998 book *The Father of Spin: Edward L. Bernays & the Birth of Public Relations* offers a sometimes unflattering portrait of Bernays as an egotistical person who often practiced deception, for example by not revealing the sponsorship of his "Torches of Freedom" parade of female cigarette smokers on New York's Fifth Avenue. Tye maintains that Ivy Lee and other pre-World War I practitioners could lay greater claim than Bernays to having fathered the profession.

Other Public Relations Pioneers Benjamin Sonnenberg, Rex Harlow, Leone Baxter, and Henry C. Rogers loom large in the list of other early, influential public relations counselors.

Benjamin Sonnenberg It was Sonnenberg who suggested that the Texaco Company sponsor performances of the Metropolitan Opera Company on national radio. Sponsorship of the Saturday afternoon series, which began in 1940, still continues. Sonnenberg, who believed that a brief mention of a client in the right context is better than a long-winded piece of flattery, proposed Texaco's sponsorship after some segments of the American public criticized the company for negotiating with Adolf Hitler on an oil deal in the mid-1930s. With time, Texaco emerged as a patron of the arts, and critics forgot about the dealings with Hitler before the outbreak of World War II.

Rex Harlow Harlow, known as "the father of public relations research," was probably the first full-time public relations educator. As a professor in Stanford University's School of Education, Harlow began teaching a public relations course on a regular basis in 1939. In that same year he founded the American Council on Public Relations (which eventually became the Public Relations Society of America), serving as its president for eight years. He crisscrossed the country giving workshops and seminars for practitioners for about 20 years. It is estimated that 10,000 people received their first formal instruction in public relations from this educator.

In 1952, Harlow founded the *Social Science Reporter,* one of the first newsletters in the field. In it he actively sought to show practitioners and top management how social science research findings benefit the practice of public relations. Harlow produced many articles and seven books on public relations. He died in 1993 at age 100.

Leone Baxter A partner for more than 25 years with Clem Whitaker in the firms of Whitaker & Baxter, Campaigns Incorporated, W&B Advertising, and California Feature Service, Leone Baxter counseled clients in the United States and abroad.

The firm is credited with being the first professional political campaign management organization in the United States, setting the pace for many that followed.

Some Whitaker & Baxter guidelines became standard political campaign tenets:

- Attempt to create actual news instead of merely sending out publicity.
- More Americans like corn than caviar.
- "The average American doesn't want to be educated, doesn't want to improve his mind, doesn't want to work, consciously, at being a good citizen. But most every American likes to be entertained. . . . So, if you can't fight, *put on a show!*"
- Never wage a campaign defensively! "The only successful defense is a spectacular, hard-hitting, crushing offensive."

Henry C. Rogers In the mid-1930s Rogers, with Warren Cowan, established the public relations firm of Rogers & Cowan, the largest and by most measures the most successful Hollywood image-making operation.

In a *New York Times Magazine* article, Neal Gabler relates that Rogers achieved his breakthrough in 1939 "when he met a beautiful but unknown starlet named Rita Hayworth, then a contract player at Columbia Pictures who feared being dropped without some new publicity.

"Rogers went to an editor at *Look* magazine, told him that Hayworth spent every cent she made on clothes and produced a telegram from the Fashion Couturiers Association of America (a fictitious organization) that declared Hayworth the best-dressed off-screen actress.

"Taking the bait, *Look* provided a photographer. Rogers persuaded clothiers to provide the wardrobe. Hayworth struck a seductive pose that made the magazine's cover and her career as well as Rogers's was on its way."

Rogers later became a corporate counsel. Of his image-building years, Rogers said: "Dog food and movie stars are much alike because they are both products in need of exposure."

Among the most widely known advocates of social causes in the 20th century who effectively used some of the techniques of public relations were Margaret Sanger, founder of the Planned Parenthood Federation of America; singer Kate Smith, who sold thousands of dollars in U.S. bonds during World War II while making Irving Berlin's "God Bless America" almost the national anthem; Dorothy Day, founder of the widely respected *Catholic Worker* magazine in 1933 and its editor until 1980, an active pacifist and worker for the nonviolent achievement of social justice; Gloria Steinem, cofounder with Patricia Carbine of *Ms.* magazine, chronicler of the feminist movement for more than two decades; and Betty Friedan, originator of the National Organization for Women (NOW) in 1966, who promoted numerous women's causes and whose accomplishments included the adoption of a pro-choice plank at the NOW convention in 1967.

Serving on the Management Team Public relations counseling is at its best when it functions at the very top level of management. American corporate executives have increasingly adopted this viewpoint. Its recognition in recent years has resulted mostly from the experiences of companies whose leaders understood much of what public relations is all about.

PR insights

Principles of Public Relations Management

Noted counselor Arthur W. Page practiced six principles of public relations management as a means of implementing his philosophy:

1. *Tell the truth.* Let the public know what's happening and provide an accurate picture of the company's character, ideals, and practices.
2. *Prove it with action.* Public perception of an organization is determined 90 percent by doing and 10 percent by talking.
3. *Listen to the customer.* To serve the company well, understand what the public wants and needs. Keep top decision-makers and other employees informed about public reaction to company products, policies, and practices.
4. *Manage for tomorrow.* Anticipate public reaction and eliminate practices that create difficulties. Generate goodwill.
5. *Conduct public relations as if the whole company depends on it.* Corporate relations is a management function. No corporate strategy should be implemented without considering its impact on the public. The public relations professional is a policy maker capable of handling a wide range of corporate communications activities.
6. *Remain calm, patient, and good-humored.* Lay the groundwork for public relations miracles with consistent, calm, and reasoned attention to information and contacts. When a crisis arises, remember that cool heads communicate best.

Page recognized an additional truth: A company's true character is expressed by its people. This makes every active and retired employee a part of the public relations organization. So it is the responsibility of the public relations function to support each employee's capacity to be an honest, knowledgeable ambassador to customers, friends, and public officials.

Source: Membership Directory, The Arthur W. Page Society, New York.

Arthur W. Page, who became vice president of the American Telephone & Telegraph Company in 1927, helped shape today's practice by advocating the philosophy that public relations is a management function and that it should have an active voice in management. He also expressed the belief that a company's performance, not press agentry, comprises its basis for public approval.

More than any other individual, Page is credited with laying the foundation for the field of corporate public relations. He served on the boards of numerous corporations, charitable groups, universities, and civic groups. After his death in 1960, at the age of 77, he became the only public relations leader to be honored with a membership society named after him. The Arthur W. Page Society, comprised of about 300 members, mostly senior-level communication executives from large companies and major public relations firms, conducts a seminar and a conference each year.

Alfred P. Sloan, then president of General Motors Corporation, also was among the first executives to place great trust in public relations. In 1931, during the early years of the Great Depression when business was attacked widely for its failures, Sloan hired Paul W. Garrett as his first public relations employee.

Garrett was charged with ascertaining public attitudes and executing a program to bring the company full public approval. For one thing, the board of directors felt that favor might be gained by making the billion-dollar corporation appear small. Garrett considered that approach neither reasonable nor possible. Instead, he informed management that it must interpret itself by words and deeds that had meaning to those outside the company, that it must put the broad interests of the public first, that it must develop sound internal relationships with its employees, and that it must be frank and honest and explain the company's policies clearly through every possible medium.

Garrett's program proved highly effective, and his speechmaking and other activities during a 25-year career with General Motors broadened the understanding of leaders of many other major organizations about the full-fledged public relations function. *Fortune* magazine, in a series of articles in 1938 and 1939, praised the GM program, along with those of Chrysler, Ford, and AT&T, and also lauded public relations itself.

Public Relations Comes of Age

During the second half of the 20th century, public relations became firmly established as indispensable to America's economic, political, and social development. And by the turn of the century, it was well integrated into the total communication programs of companies and institutions both nationally and globally.

After World War II

The booming economy after World War II produced rapid growth in all areas of public relations. Companies opened public relations departments or expanded existing ones. Government staffs increased in size, as did those of nonprofit organizations such as educational institutions and health and welfare agencies. Television emerged in the late 1940s as a new challenge for public relations expertise. New firms sprang up nationwide. Many were required not only to sell their own services to potential clients but first to educate many managers on the value of public relations itself.

PR insights

Four Models of Public Relations

To aid in understanding the history of formal public relations as well as its practice today, Professors James E. Grunig of the University of Maryland and Todd Hunt of Rutgers: The State University of New Jersey have constructed four models of public relations. All four models are practiced today, but the "ideal" one that is in increasing use is the two-way symmetric model. They explain the models as follows in their 1984 book *Managing Public Relations.*

Press Agentry/Publicity

Propaganda is the purpose, sought through one-way communication that is often incomplete, distorted, or only partially true. The model is source → receiver. Communication is viewed as telling, not listening, and little if any research is undertaken. P. T. Barnum was the leading historical figure during this model's heyday from 1850 to 1900. Sports, theater, and product promotion are the main fields of practice today.

Public Information

Dissemination of information, not necessarily with a persuasive intent, is the purpose. The model is source → receiver. Research, if any, is likely to be confined to readability tests or readership studies. Ivy Lee is the leading historical figure during this model's early development period from about 1900 into the 1920s. Government, nonprofit associations, and business are primary fields of practice today.

Two-Way Asymmetric

Scientific persuasion is the purpose, and communication is two-way, with imbalanced effects. The model is source → receiver, with feedback (←) to the source. Research is both formative, helping to plan an activity and to choose objectives, and evaluative, finding if the objective has been met. Edward Bernays is the leading historical figure during the model's period beginning in the 1920s. Competitive business and public relations firms are the primary places of practice today.

Two-Way Symmetric

Gaining mutual understanding is the purpose, and communication is two-way with balanced effects. The model is group → group with feedback (←). Formative research is used mainly both to learn how the public perceives the organization and to determine what consequences the organization has for the public, resulting in the counseling of management about policies. Evaluative research is used to measure whether a public relations effort has improved both the understanding publics have of the organization and that which management has of its publics.

Edward L. Bernays, educators, and professional leaders have been the main historical figures of the two-way symmetric model, followed by some organizations since the 1960s and 1970s.

(continued)

Public Relations in the 1950s By 1950 an estimated 17,000 men and 2000 women were employed as practitioners in public relations and publicity. Typical of the public relations programs of large corporations at midcentury was that of the Aluminum Company of America. Heading the operation was a vice president for public relations–advertising, aided by an assistant public relations director and an advertising manager. Departments included community relations, product publicity, motion pictures and exhibits, employee publications, news bureau, and industrial economics (speechwriting and educational relations). *Alcoa News* magazine was published for all employees, as well as separate publications for those in 20 plants. The main broadcast effort was sponsorship of Edward R. Murrow's *See It Now* television program.

	Characteristics of Four Models of Public Relations			
	Model			
	One-Way		Two-Way	
	Press Agentry/ Publicity	*Public Information*	*Two-Way Asymmetrical*	*Two-Way Symmetrical*
Purpose	Propaganda	Dissemination of information	Scientific persuasion	Mutual understanding
Organizational contribution	Advocacy	Dissemination of information	Advocacy	Mediation
Nature of communication	One-way; complete truth not essential	One-way; truth important	Two-way; imbalanced effects	Two-way; balanced effects
Communication model	Source → Rec.*	Source → Rec.	Source → Rec. feedback	Group → Group feedback
Nature of research	Little; "counting house"	Little; readability, readership	Formative; evaluative of attitudes	Formative; evaluative of understanding

* "Rec." is abbreviation for "Receiver."

Source: Adapted from Grunig and Hunt, *Managing Public Relations,* 1984, p. 22.

A British scholar, J. A. R. Pimlott, wrote in 1951: "Public relations is not a peculiarly American phenomenon, but it has nowhere flourished as in the United States. Nowhere else is it so widely practiced, so lucrative, so pretentious, so respectable and disreputable, so widely suspected and so extravagantly extolled."

Census-takers in 1960 counted 23,870 men and 7271 women engaged in public relations, although some observers put the total figure at approximately 35,000. Since 1960, the number of public relations practitioners has dramatically increased, as stated in Chapter 4. Since 1986, women have comprised more than 50 percent of public relations personnel. Recent surveys show that four out of five large companies and trade organizations now have public relations departments. Additionally, there are more than 6000 public relations firms.

Journalism and mass communications schools also have felt the impact of public relations majors. In 1999 an estimated 185 colleges and universities offered degrees or sequences in public relations—about 50 percent of the total number of institutions offering journalism and mass communications programs.

The popularity of public relations as a major field of study is reflected in annual statistics gathered by the Association for Education in Journalism and Mass Communication (AEJMC). As early as 1987, Professor Paul Peterson of Ohio State University, who conducted the annual AEJMC survey for many years, declared, "Indications are clear that the areas of advertising and public relations are the leaders in attracting student interests." Reports from Australia, Singapore, England, and Germany also show major increases in public relations enrollments.

The Public Relations Student Society of America, founded in 1968, provides important professional training on campus (see Chapter 4). The International Association of Business Communicators (IABC) also has individual student members and some student chapters, but no national student organization.

Public Relations and Social Growth Public relations has become essential in modern life because of a multiplicity of reasons, including the following: heavy, continuing population growth, especially in cities where individual citizens have scant direct contact with Big Business, Big Labor, Big Government, Big Institutions, and other powerful organizations influencing their lives; scientific and technological advances, including automation and computerization; the communications revolution; mergers and consolidations, with bottom-line financial considerations often replacing the more personalized decision making of previous, more genteel times; and the increased interdependence of a complex world society.

The globalization of business and communications has been accompanied by a parallel increase in public relations activity around the world (see Chapter 16). At home, government regulation has brought about the employment of thousands of government public information people and a corresponding increase in the number of public relations people helping those regulated to comply with or oppose the regulations.

Many citizens feel alienated, bewildered by such rapid change, cut off from the sense of community that characterized the lives of previous generations. They seek power through innumerable pressure groups, focusing on causes such as environmentalism, human rights, and antinuclear campaigns. Public opinion, registered through continual polling, has become increasingly powerful in opposing or effecting change.

Both physically and psychologically separated from their publics, American business and industry have turned increasingly to public relations specialists for audience

PR insights

Why Public Relations Is Growing

Ronald B. Millman, a partner of the Financial Relations Board, Inc., of Chicago and president of that city's PRSA chapter, says public relations "came of age" during the 1980s. Citing the increasing number of practitioners and the rise in billings by the top ten U.S. public relations firms (to more than $910 million in 1990, more than seven times that of 1980), Millman offers seven reasons for the growth:

- *PR is cost-efficient.* An annual public relations campaign costs less than the production of most television commercials.
- *PR has won over management.* With issues such as ecology, civil rights, equal rights, and consumerism commanding increased attention, management has come to realize the value of its public relations operation.
- *The penalties of poor PR are viewed each night on the 10 o'clock news.* With the Exxon oil disaster as an example, good managers realize they must prepare for crises as though they were part of the year's business plan.
- *PR is no longer measured by the ink (or time) it produces.* Measurement tools are now far more sophisticated.
- *PR is becoming more specialized.* Many public relations firms now concentrate their efforts solely in one area, such as finance, consumer marketing, crisis communications, employee communications, and politics.
- *PR tools are becoming more complex.* For example, video news releases are a basic ingredient of almost every marketing public relations program, and faxing releases is an accepted means of distributing news not only to the media but also to the business community.
- *Markets are going international.* The stakes of competing in the global marketplace have increased along with the obstacles, such as different languages, cultures, and approaches. Public relations is the technique of choice as a global communication tool.

analysis, strategic planning, and issues management, among other functions. Corporate social responsibility has become the norm and the expectation. One of the most important tasks of these specialists is that of environmental surveillance—serving, in effect, much like the periscope of a submarine. The continued growth of companies, if not survival itself, depends in large part on the skills of public relations people.

Research has assumed an importance never before known. Back in 1883, Theodore N. Vail sensed its importance, sending letters to AT&T customers seeking their opinions. In 1912, public relations–wise Henry Ford had asked 1000 customers why they had purchased his Model T car. These were among the forerunners of the social science research techniques that were developed after World War I. In the 1930s, George Gallup, Elmo Roper, Claude Robinson, and others began to conduct modern public opinion and marketing surveys. With these, public relations specialists and others could evaluate public attitudes quantitatively and obtain objective measurements to supplement personal estimates.

Major Developments in Today's World

Technological and societal changes continued to transform aspects of public relations during the 1990s. As largely foreseen by communications leaders and management executives, the major developments included those pertaining to the global economy, quality of the environment, an increased management role for public relations, and other areas of practice.

A Global Economy Every national economy and every business is part of an integrated global economy, analysts declare. The internationalization of business means that companies and public relations people must learn foreign cultures, business practices, and languages. The rise of the World Wide Web has accelerated the need to relate an organization's messages to a wide array of audiences in different countries and subcultures.

Quality of the Environment Concern for the environment is now a widespread issue; people in many countries believe that protecting it is so important that no requirements and standards can be too high. Environmental issues also translate as a "quality of life" issue: People are concerned about their health and perceive a direct self-interest in such issues as the "greenhouse effect," acid rain, pollution, toxic wastes, and the spread of AIDS. Because such issues are transnational in scope, international dialogue and cooperation are prerequisites for effective solutions.

Corporations must be more sensitive to environmental concerns than in the past and show diverse publics that they are part of the solution, not the problem. At the same time, according to C. J. Silas, chairman of Phillips Petroleum Company, the challenge for industry and government is "to balance the two good, but seemingly paradoxical, objectives of environmental protection and economic growth and development."

Increased Management Role for Business Impediments to sales success such as environmental concerns have required that public relations play a major role in the strategic planning and policy formulation of companies. John L. Clendenin, chairman of BellSouth Corporation, says, "I can't imagine any institution being able to operate successfully in today's environment without effective and proactive public relations management."

■ **New Emphasis on Issues Management** Many companies are seeking to cope with a flood of public policy issues. Governments as well as corporations are turning to experts skilled in problem analysis and conflict resolution to deal with the tough problems facing society and the planet Earth. (See Chapter 14.)

■ **Proliferation of Publics** The splintering of mass markets into hundreds of smaller markets, begun mainly in the 1980s, continued in the 1990s. Public relations personnel used microdemographics (closely defining target audiences by age, sex, educational level, and the like) to reach multiple publics with tailored information. In addition to traditional publics such as consumers and stockholders, audiences increasingly were fragmented into special-interest groups.

■ **Decline of Mass Media** The fragmentation of publics has meant the decline of mass media as vehicles with which to reach audiences. Technology is providing many avenues for transmitting messages to specific audiences; the key terms are *niche programming* and *narrowcasting.*

Cynthia Pharr, president of Tracy-Locke-Pharr Public Relations, put it this way: "With mass media rapidly giving way to specialized vehicles of communication, it is essential to tailor messages to narrow, well-defined audiences." This means identifying and understanding particular interest groups, working effectively with the media those groups trust, and developing a variety of messages to reach different audiences. The "one size-fits-all" news release, she contends, is dead.

■ **Rapid Spread of New Media Technologies** During the 1990s, the number of World Wide Web sites increased from 4 million to more than 20 million. By mid-1998, according to *Nielsen Media Research,* 78 million people were using the Web, with 20 million of them making online purchases. Public relations people are increasingly using the electronic media as their principal method of communication. The *Public Relations Journal* forecasted: "Partly what is pushing the electronic public relations frontier is the accessibility of electronic technology and the merging of telephone, cable, and computer companies, as well as the increasing utilization of e-mail and the Internet by journalists, cumulatively creating the information superhighway."

■ **More One-to-One Communication** Public relations people are communicating much more on a one-to-one basis rather than seeking a mass audience. Says John Beardsley, past president of the Public Relations Society of America and CEO of Padilla, Speer, Beardsley Public Relations: "You're dealing with many audiences, many constituencies. The technology makes it possible to subdivide and subdivide—until you get to the point where you're almost talking one-to-one. The people are still there . . . but the way to reach them has absolutely demolished the concept of a mass audience."

■ **International Media Relations** Press conferences and simultaneous briefings by teams of public relations professionals in various countries are being transmitted by satellite. Corporations are maintaining decentralized public relations offices on several continents and publishing newsletters in a variety of languages.

■ **Higher Priority on Employee Communication** The employee ranks of many corporations were severely downsized (reduced) during the 1990s to satisfy the demands

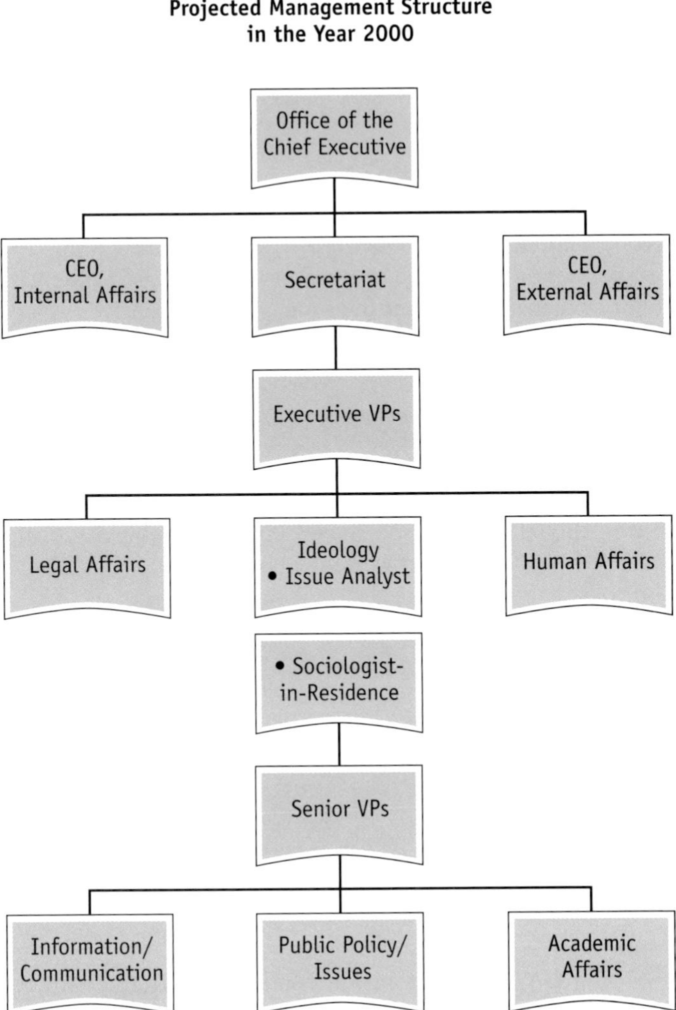

FIGURE 2.1

The organizational chart of a public relations structure for the new century, designed by veteran counselor John F. Budd, Jr. (Copyright 1989, John Budd, Jr.)

of the global marketplace and company stakeholders. At the same time, employees noted huge increases in salaries of chief executive officers of major corporations. Vastly diminished employee loyalty often resulted, causing management to place high priority on using public relations communications to restore or hold employee trust.

■ **The Managerial Trajectory** Public relations personnel of many global corporations increased their training and professional experience in marketing, international business, finance, and government during the 1990s. In the new century, they are charged with performing like other senior-level managers: thinking, visualizing, and implementing strategies. They are increasingly expected to integrate their total communications, with fewer freestanding fiefdoms of public relations, advertising, and marketing. Public relations will be less a process of persuasion and more one of negotiation between an organization and its publics with the mutual goal being a "win-win" solution.

Summary

The Roots of Public Relations

Although *public relations* is a 20th-century term, the roots of its practice extend back to our early history.

The Evolving Functions

The three main functions of public relations are press agentry, publicity, and counseling. Press agentry involves promotion of people and events. Publicity, one of the earliest forms of public relations, involves the issuing of news releases, and has been with us in various forms since ancient times. Counseling evolved in the early 20th century.

Public Relations Comes of Age

Public relations became firmly established by the second half of the 20th century. Technological and social changes contribute to its ongoing evolution.

Case Activity: What Would You Do?

The latter part of this chapter lists a number of national and global trends taking place in public relations. Select one of these issues and do some additional research. Write a short paper from the standpoint of what a public relations person should know about this issue and how it may affect working in public relations.

Questions for Review and Discussion

1. The roots of public relations extend deep into history. What are some of the early antecedents of today's public relations practice?
2. What is meant by "hyping"?
3. Which practices of press agent Phineas T. Barnum should modern practitioners use? Which should they reject?
4. Describe briefly the publicity practices used by Henry Ford and by Theodore Roosevelt.
5. Ivy Lee made four important contributions to public relations. Can you identify them?
6. What effect did the Creel Committee of World War I have on the development of public relations?
7. Who was Doris E. Fleischman? Name at least three other women who used public relations techniques in pursuit of their causes.
8. Identify three of the successful public relations campaigns conducted by Edward L. Bernays.
9. What are some of the aspects of current American social and business life that make public relations essential?
10. What major national and global issues confront public relations practitioners today?

Suggested Readings

Celente, Balog. *Trends 2000: How to Prepare for and Profit from Changes of the 21st Century.* New York: Warner Books, 1997.

Chernow, Ron. *Titan: The Life of John D. Rockefeller, Sr.* New York: Random House, 1997.

Cutlip, Scott M. *The Unseen Power: A History of Public Relations.* Hillsdale, NJ: Lawrence Erlbaum, 1994.

Feldman, Robert. "Keys to the Golden Age." *Public Relations Strategist,* Fall 1997, pp. 24–26.

Gabler, Neal. "The Fathers of P.R." *New York Times Magazine,* December 31, 1995, pp. 28–29.

Goldman, Elaine. "21st-Century Sea Change in Public Relations Careers." *Public Relations Strategist,* Spring 1998, pp. 43–45.

Grates, Gary F. "Seeing through New Eyes . . . A View on Optimizing the Future." *Public Relations Strategist,* Summer 1998, pp. 7–11.

Henry, Susan. "Dissonant Notes of a Retiring Feminist: Doris E. Fleischman's Last Years." *Journal of Public Relations Research,* Vol. 10, No. 1, 1998.

Leahigh, Alan K. "The History of—Quote, Unquote—Public Relations." *Public Relations Quarterly,* Fall 1993, pp. 24–25.

Nessmann, Karl. "Public Relations in Europe: A Comparison with the United States." *Public Relations Review,* Summer 1995, pp. 151–160.

Pinkleton, Bruce. "The Campaign of the Committee on Public Information: Its Contributions to the History and Evolution of Public Relations." *Journal of Public Relations Research,* Vol. 6, No. 4, 1994, pp. 229–240.

Ponder, Stephen. "Popular Propaganda: The Food Administration in World War I." *Journalism & Mass Communication Quarterly,* Autumn 1995, pp. 539–550.

Strenski, James B. "Public Relations in the New Millenium." *Public Relations Quarterly,* Fall 1998, pp. 24–25.

Tye, Larry. *The Father of Spin: Edward L. Bernays & the Birth of Public Relations.* New York: Crown Publishers, 1998.

Ethics and Professionalism

preview

The goal of this chapter is to give students an understanding of the ethical standards and professionalism required of public relations practitioners today, and to help them identify their own standards as public relations professionals.

The topics covered in this chapter include:

- What is ethics?
- Codes of ethics
- Professionalism, licensing, and accreditation
- Ethics in individual practice
- Ethical dealings with news media
- "Front groups"

What Is Ethics?

Ethics refers to the value system by which a person determines what is right or wrong, fair or unfair, just or unjust. It is expressed through moral behavior in specific situations. An individual's conduct is measured not only against his or her conscience but also against some norm of acceptability that has been societally, professionally, or organizationally determined. The difficulty in ascertaining whether an act is ethical lies in the fact that individuals have different standards and perceptions of what is "right" and "wrong." Often the situation is not black or white but falls into the gray area.

A person's philosophical orientation can also determine how he or she acts in a specific situation. Philosophers say the three basic value orientations are (1) absolutist, (2) existentialist, and (3) situationalist. The absolutist believes every decision is either "right" or "wrong," regardless of the consequences. The existentialist, whose choices are made without a prescribed value system, decides on the basis of immediate rational choice. The situationalist's decisions are based on what would cause the least harm or most good.

Most people, depending on the actual situation, probably choose a course of action somewhere along the continuum of the three types. They make decisions on the building blocks of truth telling, promise keeping, loyalty, and commitment.

Public relations professionals have the added dilemma of making decisions that satisfy (1) the public interest, (2) the employer, (3) the professional organization's code of ethics, and (4) their personal values. In the ideal world, the four would not conflict. In reality, however, they often do.

Codes of Ethics

Most professional organizations and many businesses have codes of ethics. These documents, also called *codes of professional conduct,* are supposed to set acceptable norms of behavior for working professionals and employees. The Public Relations Society of America (PRSA) and the International Association of Business Communicators (IABC) both have such codes for their members, to be discussed in the following pages. The PRSA code is emphasized because of its age (dating back to 1950) and its comprehensive approach, unique among communications organizations.

The New PRSA Member Code of Ethics

In 2000 PRSA abandoned its 50-year-old *Code of Professional Standards for the Practice of Public Relations* in favor of a greatly different *Member Code of Ethics.* The move followed several years of intensive debate amid realization that the former code had ceased to work satisfactorily. The PRSA Board of Ethics and Professional Standards declared that, "What used to be clear violations of the code now go unresolved due to numerous loopholes in the way the code is written, administered and supported by the organization's leadership and members as well."

Emphasis on enforcement of the code was eliminated. The PRSA board of directors, however, retained the right to bar from membership or expel from the society any person who has been or is sanctioned by a government agency or convicted in a court of law of an action that is in violation of the code.

The core principles of the new code follow.

PRSA Member Statement of Professional Values

This statement presents the core values of PRSA members and, more broadly, of the public relations profession. These values provide the foundation for the *Member Code of Ethics* and set the industry standard for the professional practice of public relations. These values are the fundamental beliefs that guide our behaviors and decision-making process. We believe our professional values are vital to the integrity of the profession as a whole.

ADVOCACY

- We serve the public interest by acting as responsible advocates for those we represent.
- We provide a voice in the marketplace of ideas, facts, and viewpoints to aid informed public debate.

HONESTY

- We adhere to the highest standards of accuracy and truth in advancing the interests of those we represent and in communicating with the public.

EXPERTISE

- We acquire and responsibly use specialized knowledge and experience.
- We advance the profession through continued professional development, research, and education.
- We build mutual understanding, credibility, and relationships among a wide array of institutions and audiences.

INDEPENDENCE

- We provide objective counsel to those we represent.
- We are accountable for our actions.

LOYALTY

- We are faithful to those we represent, while honoring our obligation to serve the public interest.

FAIRNESS

- We deal fairly with clients, employers, competitors, peers, vendors, the media, and the general public.
- We respect all opinions and support the right of free expression.

Examples of improper conduct are contained in six provisions that amplify the code.

PRSA Code Provisions

FREE FLOW OF INFORMATION

Core Principle

Protecting and advancing the free flow of accurate and truthful information is essential to serving the public interest and contributing to informed decision making in a democratic society.

Intent

- To maintain the integrity of relationships with the media, government officials, and the public.
- To aid informed decision making.

Guidelines

A member shall:

- Preserve the integrity of the process of communication.
- Be honest and accurate in all communications.
- Act promptly to correct erroneous communications for which the practitioner is responsible.
- Preserve the free flow of unprejudiced information when giving or receiving gifts by ensuring that gifts are nominal, legal, and infrequent.

Examples of Improper Conduct Under This Provision:

- A member representing a ski manufacturer gives a pair of expensive racing skis to a sports magazine columnist, to influence the columnist to write favorable articles about the product.
- A member entertains a government official beyond legal limits and/or in violation of government reporting requirements.

COMPETITION

Core Principle

Promoting healthy and fair competition among professionals preserves an ethical climate while fostering a robust business environment.

Intent

- To promote respect and fair competition among public relations professionals.
- To serve the public interest by providing the widest choice of practitioner options.

Guidelines

A member shall:

- Follow ethical hiring practices designed to respect free and open competition without deliberately undermining a competitor.
- Preserve intellectual property rights in the marketplace.

Examples of Improper Conduct Under This Provision:

- A member employed by a "client organization" shares helpful information with a counseling firm that is competing with others for the organization's business.
- A member spreads malicious and unfounded rumors about a competitor in order to alienate the competitor's clients and employees in a ploy to recruit people and business.

DISCLOSURE OF INFORMATION

Core Principle

Open communication fosters informed decision making in a democratic society.

Intent

- To build trust with the public by revealing all information needed for responsible decision making.

Guidelines

A member shall:

- Be homest and accurate in all communications.

- Act promptly to correct erroneous communications for which the member is responsible.
- Investigate the truthfulness and accuracy of information released on behalf of those represented.
- Reveal the sponsors for causes and interests represented.
- Disclose financial interest (such as stock ownership) in a client's organization.
- Avoid deceptive practices.

Examples of Improper Conduct Under This Provision:

- Front groups: a member implements "grass roots" campaigns or letter-writing campaigns to legislators on behalf of undisclosed interest groups.
- Lying by omission: A practitioner for a corporation knowingly fails to release financial information, giving a misleading impression of the corporation's performance.
- A member discovers inaccurate information disseminated via a web site or media kit and does not correct the information.
- A member deceives the public by employing people to pose as volunteers to speak at public hearings and participate in "grass roots" campaigns.

SAFEGUARDING CONFIDENCES

Core Principle

Client trust requires appropriate protection of confidential and private information.

Intent

- To protect the privacy rights of clients, organizations, and individuals by safeguarding confidential information.

Guidelines

A member shall:

- Safeguard the confidences and privacy rights of present, former, and prospective clients and employees.
- Protect privileged, confidential, or insider information gained from a client or organization.
- Immediately advise an appropriate authority if a member discovers that confidential information is being divulged by an employee of a client company or organization.

Examples of Improper Conduct Under This Provision:

- A member changes jobs, takes confidential information, and uses that information in the new position to the detriment of the former employer.
- A member intentionally leaks proprietary information to the detriment of some other party.

CONFLICTS OF INTEREST

Core Principle

Avoiding real, potential or perceived conflicts of interest builds the trust of clients, employers, and the publics.

Intent

- To earn trust and mutual respect with clients or employers.

- To build trust with the public by avoiding or ending situations that put one's personal or professional interests in conflict with society's interests.

Guidelines

A member shall:

- Act in the best interests of the client or employer, even subordinating the member's personal interests.
- Avoid actions and circumstances that may appear to compromise good business judgment or create a conflict between personal and professional interests.
- Disclose promptly any existing or potential conflict of interest to affected clients or organizations.
- Encourage clients and customers to determine if a conflict exists after notifying all affected parties.

Examples of Improper Conduct Under This Provision:

- The member fails to disclose that he or she has a strong financial interest in a client's chief competitor.
- The member represents a "competitor company" or a "conflicting interest" without informing a prospective client.

ENHANCING THE PROFESSION

Core Principle

Public relations professionals work constantly to strengthen the public's trust in the profession.

Intent

- To build respect and credibility with the public for the profession of public relations.
- To improve, adapt and expand professional practices.

Guidelines

A member shall:

- Acknowledge that there is an obligation to protect and enhance the profession.
- Keep informed and educated about practices in the profession to ensure ethical conduct.
- Actively pursue personal professional development.
- Decline representation of clients or organizations that urge or require actions contrary to this Code.
- Accurately define what public relations activities can accomplish.
- Counsel subordinates in proper ethical decision making.
- Require that subordinates adhere to the ethical requirements of the Code.
- Report ethical violations, whether committed by PRSA members or not, to the appropriate authority.

Examples of Improper Conduct Under This Provision:

- A PRSA member declares publicly that a product the client sells is safe, without disclosing evidence to the contrary.
- A member initially assigns some questionable client work to a non-member practioner to avoid the ethical obligation of PRSA membership.

focus on ethics

Ford/Firestone Tire Recall

Can public relations gloss over a lack of corporate responsibility? The Firestone/Ford tire recall controversy, detailed in Chapter 1, raises serious ethical questions about each company's failure to take action until the glare of publicity apparently forced them to admit there was a problem.

For nearly two years before the recall, for example, Ford had received complaints from overseas about possible problems with Firestone tires on its Explorers in such nations as Venezuela and Saudi Arabia. Yet, Ford continued to sell Explorers with Firestone tires in the U.S. market. Firestone also had indications that the tread was separating from some of its models as early as 1994, because there already was a pattern of lawsuits.

Even when the National Highway Traffic Safety Administration (NHTSA) launched an investigation in May of 2000 after receiving numerous reports of accidents and fatalities, it took another three months before Firestone voluntarily recalled 6.5 million tires. This has led many critics to charge that both Firestone and Ford were more interested in preserving their image and corporate reputation than in saving lives.

But hiding information, or refusing to act swiftly in the public interest, is no doubt the worst public relations strategy. Both Firestone and Ford saw their reputations and credibility plummet in the wake of disclosures about what they knew and when. Corporate credibility also declined when both companies actively blamed each other for the problem. Kirk O. Hanson, a senior lecturer in business ethics at the Stanford Business School, wrote "In the long run, sound ethical behavior makes good business sense, allowing companies to protect their reputations and their bottom line. Acting ethically is also the right thing to do."

Other Codes

Practically every national public relations organization has a code of ethics, and such organizations as the Canadian Public Relations Society (CPRS), the Public Relations Institute of Southern Africa (PRISA), and the Public Relations Institute of Australia (PRIA) have codes similar to the PRSA one.

These national organizations also exercise the right to censure or expel members who violate the code, but PRSA, despite flaws in enforcement, was unique in having a highly structured grievance procedure in place. Indeed, during the first 33 years of the code's life, at least 10 members were disciplined by PRSA.

Critics often complain that such codes of ethics "have no teeth," and one cynic, quoted by *Ragan's PR Intelligence Report,* says, "Watching the public relations industry discuss ethics is a little like watching tourists from a foreign country attempting to speak a language they barely understand. They seem enthusiastic and sincere, and many of the right words come out of their mouths, but they just don't quite manage to make sense."

Problems in code enforcement, however, are not unique to public relations groups. Professional organizations in which membership is voluntary are often reluctant to discipline members for several reasons, including lawsuits and the First Amendment guarantee of free speech.

Consequently, most professional membership groups believe that the primary purpose of establishing codes of ethics is not enforcement, but education and information—enunciating standards of conduct that will guide members in their professional lives. The International Association of Business Communicators (IABC) takes this approach.

IABC's Code of Ethics

The International Association of Business Communicators, with members in 52 nations, updated its code of ethics in 1995 to 1996. The new code, which has 12 articles, represents little change in content from the 1985 version, but the major points are more streamlined. It continues to be based on the principles that professional communication not only is legal and ethical but also is in good taste and sensitive to cultural values and beliefs. Members also are encouraged to be truthful, accurate, and fair in all their communications.

According to the *Worldbook of IABC Communicators,* "IABC fosters compliance with its code by engaging in global communication campaigns rather than through negative sanctions." The code is published in several languages, and IABC bylaws require that articles on ethics and professional conduct be published in the organization's monthly publication *IABC: Communication World.* In addition, the organization includes sessions on ethics at its annual meetings, conducts workshops on ethics, and encourages chapters to include ethics discussions in their local programs. New and renewing members of IABC also must sign the following statement as part of their application: "I have reviewed and understand the IABC Code of Ethics for Professional Communicators."

IABC's ethics board, consisting of three accredited members, also answers inquiries about ethics. An IABC spokesperson, however, reports that "very few inquiries" have been received during the past several years, and that the organization has never taken the formal action of suspending or expelling a member. Instead, if a member is conducting his or her professional activities contrary to the code, the usual procedure is to have an informal conversation with the offender and point out the areas of the code being violated. This is usually enough for the offender to amend his or her ways.

Since 1990, at least two IABC members have voluntarily resigned because they had violated Article 6, which deals with a member who has been found guilty by a

focus on ethics

Smashmouth PR

Is it ethical for a company to trash the competition? Oracle and its public relations firm, Applied Communications, thinks it is. Alan Kelly, president and CEO of Allied, was quoted in *Forbes ASAP* saying, "It's not so much a question of how we can position our client, but how we can de-position their competitors."

Oracle, for example, posted a steady stream of provocative news releases needling popular software makers Siebel Systems, i2 Technologies, and PeopleSoft. The statements, according to Shelley Pannill of *Forbes,* "focused on alleged deficiencies in their products and the perceived advantage of Oracle's software suite."

PeopleSoft was also targeted by Oracle and its public relations firm hours before the company reported strong fourth-quarter earnings. An Oracle media alert urged journalists and investors to "remain skeptical of the difference between the company's claims and the reality behind them." Another news release charged that i2 Technologies "is trying to cobble together a multi-application 'suite' story" but failing miserably compared to Oracle.

What do you think? Is the concept of "Smashmouth" public relations and "de-positioning" the competition an ethical public relations practice?

government body or judicial body of violating laws governing professional activities. In one case, a member resigned after being charged with embezzling funds from a chapter treasury.

The code of professional conduct of the International Public Relations Association (IPRA), based on the charter of the United Nations, is discussed in Chapter 16.

Video News Release Code of Good Practice

Are video news releases (VNRs) fake news? A survey published in *TV Guide* disclosed that almost half of TV station news directors failed to identify the source of VNRs on their news programs. *TV Guide,* in a cover story, labeled such reports "fake news."

"Don't blame the makers of the VNRs," said Bob Kimmel, senior vice president of the News/Broadcast Network. "We are doing everything we can by putting the source of the material on the VNR. We can't control what happens at the news level, however." Many stations pass off the VNRs as products of their own staffs. (See Chapter 22.)

Six video news producers, members of the Public Relations Service Council in New York, drew up a Code of Good Practice and pointed out that a seal bearing the code's insignia would reassure news directors that the release contained accurate information and was clearly labeled as coming from a corporate sponsor. The code:

> The objective of a VNR is to present information, pictures, and sound that television journalists can use and rely on for quality, accuracy, and perspective.
>
> Information contained in a VNR must be accurate and reliable. Intentionally false and misleading information must be avoided.
>
> A video news release must be clearly identified as such, both on the video's opening slate and on any advisory material and scripts that precede or accompany tape distribution.
>
> The sponsor of the video news release must be clearly identified on a video slate and on the VNR tape. Name and phone number of a responsible party must be provided on the video for journalists to contact for further information.
>
> Persons interviewed in the VNR must be accurately identified by name, title, and affiliation on the video.

Professionalism, Licensing, and Accreditation

Is public relations a profession? Should its practitioners be licensed? Does the accreditation of practitioners constitute a sufficient guarantee of their talents and integrity? These and other such questions are addressed in the section that follows.

Professionalism

Among public relations practitioners there are considerable differences of opinion about whether public relations is a craft, a skill, or a developing profession. Certainly, at its present level, public relations does not qualify as a profession in the same sense that medicine and law do. Public relations does not have prescribed standards of educational preparation, a mandatory period of apprenticeship, or state laws that govern admission.

Adding to the confusion about professionalism is the difficulty of ascertaining what constitutes public relations practice. John F. Budd, Jr., a veteran counselor, wrote

PR insights

Ethical Dilemmas in Public Relations Practice

How would you respond to the following situations? Consider your answers. Then, see how your responses correspond with the PRSA and IABC codes.

1. The company president asks you to write a news release claiming that a new product is four times better than the competition and that it represents a "revolutionary" breakthrough in technology.
2. You're a student intern at a public relations firm. One of your assignments is to call corporations and say you're a student doing a class project. You would like to know what kinds of outside public relations services would be most helpful to the company.
3. An American company wants to increase its visibility and market share in Eastern Europe. As director of public relations, you invite a group of Hungarian business editors to visit the firm's headquarters with all expenses paid.
4. Your company, in order to improve the quality and media acceptance of news releases, hires the local daily's business editor on a retainer fee for periodic advice and counsel.
5. Your company, as part of its holiday tradition, gives journalists who regularly cover it an expensive gift. Last year, it was a weekend at a local resort.
6. You are asked by your employer to establish a "citizens' task force" for the purpose of writing state legislators opposing an environmental bill that negatively affects the company.
7. Your public relations firm is competing for an account with two other firms. As a sales point, you say, "We can get you coverage in the *Wall Street Journal*."
8. You're looking for a job in public relations, and a tobacco company offers you the highest salary.
9. You work for a public relations firm. A printing company representative contacts you with the following proposal: If you refer clients that result in new business, the representative will pay you a $250 "finder's fee."

in *Public Relations Quarterly:* "We *act* as publicists, yet we *talk* of counseling. We *perform* as technologists in communication but we *aspire* to be decision-makers dealing in policy."

On the other hand, there is an increasing body of literature about public relations—including this text and many others in the field. PRSA has compiled a Body of Knowledge abstract that contains more than 1000 references, available on computer disk or hard copy. Substantial progress also is being made in developing theories of public relations, conducting research, and publishing scholarly journals.

There is also the idea, advanced by many professionals and PRSA itself, that the most important thing is for the individual to *act like a professional* in the field. This means that a practitioner should have:

- A sense of independence
- A sense of responsibility to society and the public interest
- Manifest concern for the competence and honor of the profession as a whole
- A higher loyalty to the standards of the profession and fellow professionals than to the employer of the moment. The reference point in all public relations activity must be the standards of the profession and not those of the client or the employer.

PR insights

IABC's Code of Ethics for Professional Communicators

Preface

Because hundreds of thousands of business communicators worldwide engage in activities that affect the lives of millions of people, and because this power carries with it significant social responsibilities, the International Association of Business Communicators developed the Code of Ethics for Professional Communicators. The Code is based on three different yet interrelated principles of professional communication that apply throughout the world.

These principles assume that just societies are governed by a profound respect for human rights and the rule of law; that the ethics—the criteria for determining what is right and wrong—can be agreed upon by members of an organization; and, that understanding matters of taste requires sensitivity to cultural norms.

These principles are essential:

- Professional communication is legal.
- Professional communication is ethical.
- Professional communication is in good taste.

Recognizing these principles, members of IABC will:

- Engage in communication that is not only legal but also ethical and sensitive to cultural values and beliefs
- Engage in truthful, accurate and fair communication that facilitates respect and mutual understanding
- Adhere to the following articles of the IABC Code of Ethics for Professional Communicators

Because conditions in the world are constantly changing, members of IABC will work to improve their individual competence and to increase the body of knowledge in the field with research and education.

Articles

1. Professional communicators uphold the credibility and dignity of their profession by practicing honest, candid and timely communication and by fostering the free flow of essential information in accord with the public interest.
2. Professional communicators disseminate accurate information and promptly correct any erroneous communication for which they may be responsible.
3. Professional communicators understand and support the principles of free speech, freedom of assembly, and access to an open marketplace of ideas and act accordingly.
4. Professional communicators are sensitive to cultural values and beliefs and engage in fair and balanced communication activities that foster and encourage mutual understanding.
5. Professional communicators refrain from taking part in any undertaking which the communicator considers to be unethical.
6. Professional communicators obey laws and public policies governing their professional activities and are sensitive to the spirit of all laws and regulations and, should any law or public policy be violated, for whatever reason, act promptly to correct the situation.
7. Professional communicators give credit for unique expressions borrowed from others and identify the sources and purposes of all information disseminated to the public.
8. Professional communicators protect confidential information and, at the same time, comply with all legal requirements for the disclosure of information affecting the welfare of others.
9. Professional communicators do not use confidential information gained as a result of professional activities for personal benefit and do not represent conflicting or competing interests without written consent of those involved.
10. Professional communicators do not accept undisclosed gifts or payments for professional services from anyone other than a client or employer.
11. Professional communicators do not guarantee results that are beyond the power of the practitioner to deliver.
12. Professional communicators are honest not only with others but also, and most importantly, with themselves as individuals; for a professional communicator seeks the truth and speaks the truth first to the self.

Unfortunately, a major barrier to professionalism is the attitude that many practitioners themselves have toward their work. As James Grunig and Todd Hunt state in their text *Managing Public Relations,* practitioners tend to hold more "careerist" values than professional values. In other words, they place higher importance on job security, prestige in the organization, salary level, and recognition from superiors than on the values listed above. For example, 47 percent of the respondents in a survey of IABC members gave a neutral or highly negative answer when asked if they would quit their jobs rather than act against their ethical values. And 55 percent considered it "somewhat ethical" to present oneself misleadingly as the only means of achieving an objective. Almost all agreed, however, that ethics is an important matter, worthy of further study.

On another level, many practitioners are limited in their professionalism by what might be termed a "technician mentality." These people narrowly define professionalism as the ability to do a competent job of executing the mechanics of communicating (preparing news releases, brochures, newsletters, and so on) even if the information provided by management or a client is in bad taste, is misleading, lacks documentation, or is just plain wrong.

The *Wall Street Journal* once highlighted the pitfalls of the technician mentality. The story described how Jartran, Inc., used the services of the Daniel J. Edelman, Inc., public relations firm to distribute a press packet to the media. The packet included a letter offering information about wheels falling off trucks owned by U-Haul, its archrival. When the newspaper reporter asked about the ethics of this approach, an Edelman junior account executive was quoted as saying, "It was their idea. We're merely the PR firm that represents them."

In other words, readers may get the impression that the public relations expertise of a firm is available to the highest bidder, regardless of professional values, fair play, and ultimately, the public interest. When public relations firms and departments take no responsibility for what is communicated—only *how* it is communicated in terms of techniques—they reinforce the perception that public relations is more flackery than profession.

Some practitioners defend the technician mentality, however, arguing that public relations people are like lawyers in the court of public opinion. Everyone is entitled to his or her viewpoint and, whether the public relations person agrees or not, the client or employer has a right to be heard. Thus a public relations representative is a paid advocate, just as a lawyer is. The only flaw in this argument is that public relations people are not lawyers, nor are they in a court of law where judicial concepts determine the roles of defendant and plaintiff. In addition, lawyers have been known to turn down clients or resign from a case because they doubted the client's story.

In Chapter 13, which concerns legal aspects of public relations, it is pointed out that courts are increasingly holding public relations firms accountable for information disseminated on behalf of a client. Thus it is no longer acceptable to say, "The client told me to do it."

Licensing

Proposals that public relations practitioners be licensed were discussed before PRSA was founded. One proponent, Edward L. Bernays, who was instrumental in formulating the modern concept of public relations (see Chapter 2), believed that licensing would protect the profession and the public from incompetent, shoddy opportunists who do not have the knowledge, talent, or ethics required.

The problem is stated by PRSA's task force on demonstrating professionalism:

> Pick up any metropolitan newspaper and scan the employment ads. Under the "public relations" classification, you are likely to find opportunities for door-to-door salespersons, receptionists, used-car salesmen, singles bar hostesses and others of less savory reputation. The front pages of the newspapers are full of stories about former government employees peddling influence and calling it public relations.

Thus, under the licensing approach, only those individuals who pass rigid examinations and tests of personal integrity could call themselves "public relations" counselors. Those not licensed would have to call themselves "publicists" or adopt some other designation.

Several arguments for mandatory licensing and registration with legal sanctions exist:

- It would define the practice of public relations.
- It would establish uniform educational curricula.
- It would set uniform ethical and professional standards.
- It would provide for decertification of violators of ethical standards.
- It would protect the consumer of public relations services (clients and employers) from impostors and charlatans.
- It would protect qualified practitioners from unfair competition from the unethical and unqualified.
- It would raise the credibility of public relations practitioners.
- Because licensing would not control anyone's right to deal with the media, government, or public, or to speak out in any way, no infringement of First Amendment rights would be involved.

Several arguments against licensing and in favor of continued reliance on a voluntary approach to public relations ethics also exist:

- Any licensing in the communications field is an infringement on the First Amendment.
- It is difficult to define public relations.
- Too much emphasis would be placed on education.
- Voluntary accreditation is sufficient to establish standards.
- Civil and criminal laws already exist to deal with malpractice.
- Legislatures show little or no interest in licensing public relations because the health and welfare of the general public are not at stake.
- Licensing would be a state function, and public relations people often work on a national and international basis.
- Licensing assures only minimum competence and professional standards; it doesn't necessarily assure high ethical behavior.
- The credibility and status of an occupation are not necessarily assured through licensing. Attorneys, for example, don't enjoy particularly high public status and prestige because they are licensed. Nor do licensed practical nurses.
- The machinery required for government to license and police all public relations practitioners in this country would be elaborate and very costly to the American taxpayer.

PR insights

Guidelines for Fair Dealing

Ketchum Communications has established guidelines for its employees on how to deal fairly with clients.

The code deals with (1) truth and accuracy in communications, (2) confidential information, (3) purchasing, (4) gifts and excessive entertainment and other payments, (5) industry groups, (6) union agreements, (7) suppliers to the agency and clients, (8) services for competitors, (9) use of inside information, and (10) misuse of business opportunities.

"We will deal with clients in a fair and businesslike fashion, providing unbiased, professional recommendations to move their business ahead," the code promises.

"We will safeguard their proprietary information and help protect their financial assets."

Many other public relations firms have similar codes.

A PRSA study group on licensing and registration bluntly reported:

> There is an almost universal disdain for licensing and a sharp dislike for any type of government oversight of public relations practice. It is our judgment . . . that the ethical code and sense of public and professional morality that must be maintained by public relations professionals cannot be delegated to government. The process of morality, while personal, is democratic and cannot be legislated. It can best be sustained through peer-imposed discipline based on a common code of ethics and consistently maintained levels of professional excellence in practice.

In sum, the licensing of public relations professionals is not likely to be initiated. Although many, including Edward L. Bernays, thought it would be a good solution to getting the charlatans out of the field and enforcing ethical practice, the field (unlike medicine or law) is so broad that it's difficult to define. Licensing also raises serious questions about possible violation of First Amendment rights in the United States and even the considerable expense of administering such a system on a state-by-state basis. In addition, neither the public, governmental agencies, nor even the public relations industry, is actively lobbying for any form of licensing.

An alternative to licensing is accreditation, which many national public relations groups actively endorse and promote.

Accreditation

The major effort to improve standards and professionalism in public relations around the world has been related to establishing accreditation programs. PRSA, for example, began its accreditation program in 1965. Since then, other national groups such as IABC, the Canadian Public Relations Society (CPRS), the British Institute of Public Relations (BIPR), the Public Relations Institute of Australia (PRIA), and the Public Relations Institute of Southern Africa (PRISA)—to name a few—have established accreditation programs.

In all cases, public relations practitioners are accredited if they have achieved a high level of experience, competence, and ethical conduct. Accreditation, ideally, is a "seal of approval."

PR insights

Use of "Front Groups" Poses Ethical Concerns

The proliferation of so-called "front groups" waging purported "grassroots" campaigns to achieve public relations goals has created much debate in the field in recent years.

The establishment of dozens of such groups evoked a strongly worded statement from the board of directors of the Public Relations Society of America.

> PRSA specifically condemns the efforts of those organizations, sometimes known as "front groups," that seek to influence the public policy process by disguising or obscuring the true identity of their members or by implying representation of a much more broadly based group than exists.

Almost every "save the environment" organization has spawned a counter group. For example, the Forest Alliance of British Columbia posed as a grassroots movement opposing the International Coalition to Save British Columbia's Rainforests, composed of 25 "green" groups. It was later revealed that the Canadian timber industry paid Burson-Marsteller $1 million to create the alliance, whose aim was to convince the public that environmental destruction has been exaggerated and to persuade lawmakers to abolish unprofitable environmental regulations.

Names given to many of the organizations are confusing, if not downright deceptive. Northwesterners for More Fish was the name chosen for a "grassroots" coalition of utilities and other companies in the Northwest under attack by environmental groups for depleting the fish population.

In California's Riverside County, a public relations firm organized Friends of Eagle Mountain on behalf of a mining company that wanted to create the world's largest landfill in an abandoned iron ore pit.

A prohunting group that works to convince people that wildlife is already so plentiful there is no reason not to kill some of it is known as the Abundant Wildlife Society of North America.

A Gallup Poll once showed that the majority of Americans considered themselves environmentalists. In the face of such findings, "People sometimes create groups that try to fudge a little bit about what their goals are," said Hal Dash, president of Cerrell Associates, a Los Angeles public relations firm that has represented clients with environmental problems.

Questioned about the tactics used in so-called grassroots campaigns, more than half of professionals surveyed by *PR News* said that it is unethical for parties to fail to mention that their impetus for contacting a government official or other organization is due to a vested interest or membership in another organization sponsoring the campaign.

PRSA Accreditation PRSA's approach is somewhat typical. To become an accredited member of the society, with the designation APR, a person must have at least five years' full-time experience in public relations or teaching and pass a written and oral exam. The written exam consists of "textbook knowledge" (key terms, theories, and history), interpretation of the code of ethics, and a case problem that tests the candidate's ability to develop public relations plans to deal with a specific situation. To date, about a fourth of PRSA's 19,000 members have earned the APR designation.

In 1998, PRSA set up a "Universal Accreditation Program" in an effort to make its accreditation available to non-PRSA members who belong to other groups—such as the Agricultural Relations Counsel and the Florida Public Relations Association.

Other national groups have developed written and oral exams; but, unlike PRSA, they also require the candidate to submit a portfolio of work samples. IABC, which uses the designation of ABC (Accredited Business Communicator), places a heavy emphasis on a person's professional work samples. The candidate must document the objectives and the overall communication strategy and provide evaluation of the results. The national public relations groups in Australia, Canada, and South Africa also require candidates to submit a portfolio of work samples and require a written and oral presentation. About 650 of IABC's 12,500 members have ABC designation.

Various national groups also take different approaches to assuring that accredited members are knowledgeable about the history and general concepts of effective public relations practice. PRSA, in a somewhat controversial decision in 1998, decided that all candidates should read one, officially designated, undergraduate textbook. This was a move that Mel Sharpe, chair of the PRSA Educators' Academy, criticized as ". . . a vocational, one-course, one-book entry-level attitude about PR." Other educators also questioned whether accreditation should be based on the concept of reading just one book and having five years' experience. The Canadian Public Relations Society (CPRS) offers a list of readings, while the IABC doesn't recommend any specific articles or books. South Africa's PRISA, on the other hand, assures some knowledge of the field by requiring that each candidate first complete a Certificate in Public Relations Management course before taking the exam.

In the United Kingdom, persons wishing to join the 4000 full members of the Institute of Public Relations must have four years of experience at an executive level and hold a public relations degree from one of seven recognized university programs or from the Communications, Advertising and Marketing Foundation.

■ **Continuing Education** PRSA in 1989 adopted a requirement that all accredited members must accumulate 10 points every three years to maintain accreditation. Points could be earned by taking university courses, attending professional workshops, writing articles, or even serving on PRSA committees. The implementation has been somewhat less than successful. By 1996, a large number of APRs had failed to complete the reaccreditation process, so PRSA excused 2782 members who had earned the APR status before 1993 from the requirement.

The Public Relations Institute of Australia (PRIA) has also begun a mandatory system of CPE (Continuing Professional Education). All members are obligated to earn Certified Practitioner (CP) status by completing 40 hours of continuing education each year, but most national groups of professional practitioners don't require continuing education for their members.

Other Steps toward Professionalism

PRSA, IABC, and other national groups have various programs designed to advance the profession of public relations. They include (1) working with universities to standardize curricula, (2) establishing research activities, (3) recognizing outstanding senior practitioners, (4) organizing professional development workshops, and (5) establishing international standards for the conduct of business.

■ **Education** PRSA, IABC, and other organizations such as the National Communication Association (NCA) have worked with the public relations division of the Association for Education in Journalism and Mass Communication (AEJMC) to improve and standardize the curricula of public relations at the bachelor's and master's degree levels.

One result of this cooperation was the 1999 Commission on Pubic Relations Education, which consisted of leading educators and practitioners representing a number of professional communication groups. This commission examined the role and function of public relations education for the new century and concluded, as did a previous commission report in 1987, that a strong background in liberal arts and social sciences is a necessary foundation for public relations majors. In addition, coursework in a public relations major should comprise 25 to 40 percent of all undergraduate credit hours. Of those, at least half would be clearly identified as public relations courses in such topics as (1) principles, (2) case studies, (3) research and evaluation, (4) writing and production, (5) planning and management, (6) campaigns, and (7) supervised internships. The commission also recommended a minor or double major in another discipline such as business or the behavioral sciences.

PRSA also has a certification program for colleges and universities that offer public relations majors and degree programs. This was started in 1989, and only six universities have been certified in the voluntary program. One reason for the low number is that the vast majority of journalism units, in which most public relations programs are housed, are accredited by the American Council on Education in Journalism and Mass Communication (ACEJMC). Many public relations educators, as well as unit administrators, feel this is sufficient. The Australian PRIA and the South African PRISA also work closely with universities in their respective nations.

Sponsorship of student chapters also is common. PRSA sponsors the Public Relations Student Society of America (PRSSA), which has about 210 chapters and 6000 members nationally. IABC currently has chapters at 45 college and universities.

Research The IABC Foundation and the Institute for Public Relations Research and Education regularly fund research projects that advance the body of knowledge in public relations. Both also sponsor symposiums, fund graduate student research projects, and commission a variety of research studies.

Recognition of Senior Professionals Several national groups, including PRSA and IABC, have established "Fellow" programs that recognize career achievement and contributions to the profession. PRSA, for example, in 1990 established a College of Fellows, which has grown to about 400 members. In addition, annual awards by both PRSA and IABC honor outstanding individuals.

PR casebook

Would You Take This Client?

Here's a hypothetical situation. A well-known professional basketball player is charged with cocaine possession and the rape of a contestant in a local beauty contest. His attorney asks you to advise and assist him in handling the intense media interest in the case. He wants you to try to place favorable stories about the athlete in the media and create a positive pretrial environment for him. If convicted, it would mean the end of his professional basketball career.

You are not asked to do anything unethical. The money is quite good, and you know the publicity from working on the case will probably help your public relations consulting career, especially if the athlete is found innocent. Would you take the account? The lawyer tells you confidentially that the athlete has admitted that he snorted cocaine and raped the woman, but the plea will be "not guilty." Does this information affect your decision? What are the ethics of the situation as you see them?

Professional Development The primary purpose of most public relations groups is to advance the profession through education and information. Monthly membership publications, such as PRSA's *Tactics* and *IABC: Communication World,* are one form of education and information. In addition, most national groups usually have a professional practice center that offers everything from one-day seminars and workshops to videocassettes, topical information packets, certificate programs, audiocassettes, home study programs, and books. PRSA's catalog of resources, for example, is a 34-page booklet. IABC has a similar array of offerings.

Business Standards A number of organizations, including the International Public Relations Association (IPRA), have supported a European-based ISO 9000 system of management controls, suitable for all businesses and also applicable to public relations firms. The process was created in 1987 by the International Organization for Standardization.

Ethics in Individual Practice

Despite codes of professional practice and formalized accreditation, ethics in public relations boils down to deeply troubling questions for the individual practitioner: Will I lie for my employer? Will I rig a doorprize drawing so a favorite client can win? Will I deceive in order to gain information about another agency's clients? Will I cover up a hazardous condition? Will I issue a news release presenting only half the truth? Will I seek to bribe a reporter or a legislator? Will I withhold some information in a news conference and provide it only if a reporter asks a specific question? Will I quit my job rather than cooperate in a questionable activity? In other words, to what extent, if any, will I compromise my personal beliefs?

These and similar questions plague the lives of many public relations people, although a number hold such strong personal beliefs and/or work for such highly principled employers that they seldom need to compromise their personal values. If employers make a suggestion that involves questionable ethics, the public relations person often can talk them out of the idea by citing the possible consequences of such an action—adverse media publicity, for example.

"To thine own self be true," advised New York public relations executive Chester Burger at an IABC conference. A fellow panelist, Canadian politician and radio commentator Stephen Lewis, commented: "There is a tremendous jaundice on the part of the public about the way things are communicated. People have elevated superficiality to an art form. Look at the substance of what you have to convey, and the honesty used in conveying it." With the audience contributing suggestions, the panelists formulated the following list of commendable practices:

- Be honest at all times.
- Convey a sense of business ethics based on your own standards and those of society.
- Respect the integrity and position of your opponents and audiences.
- Develop trust by emphasizing substance over triviality.
- Present all sides of an issue.
- Strive for a balance between loyalty to the organization and duty to the public.
- Don't sacrifice long-term objectives for short-term gains.

Adherence to professional standards of conduct—being truly independent—is the chief measure of a public relations person. Faced with such personal problems as a mortgage and children to educate, practitioners may be strongly tempted to become yes men (or yes women) and decline to express their views forcefully to an employer, or to resign. J. Kenneth Clark, vice president of corporate communications, Duke Power Company, Charlotte, North Carolina, once gave the following advice to an IABC audience:

> If the boss says newspapers are no damn good, the yes man agrees.
>
> If the boss says to tell a reporter "no comment," the yes man agrees.
>
> If the boss says the company's employees get a paycheck and don't really need to be informed about anything else, the yes man agrees.
>
> If the boss says the public has no right to pry into what's going on inside a company—even though that company is publicly held and is dependent upon public support and public sales—the yes man nods his head agreeably and starts work on the corporate version of a Berlin Wall.
>
> The fate of the yes man is as inevitable as it is painful. Although your boss may think you're the greatest guy in the world for a while, you're going to lose your internal credibility because you never really state your professional opinions. And you're talking to a person who dotes on strong opinions and does not think highly of people who fail to offer them.

Allen H. Center, professor emeritus at San Diego State University and a long-time corporate public relations executive, has written: "Public relations has emerged more as an echo of an employer's standards and interests than that of a professional discipline applied to the employer's problems." Yet many a practitioner has resigned rather than submit to a compromising situation.

In some cases practitioners have been arbitrarily fired for refusing to write news releases that are false and misleading. This happened to an accredited PRSA member in the San Francisco Bay area. The company president wanted him, among other things, to write and send a news release giving a list of company clients when, in fact, none of the companies had signed a contract for services. When the practitioner refused, on the grounds that the PRSA code would be violated, he was fired. In turn, the practitioner sued the company for unlawful dismissal and received almost $100,000 in an out-of-court settlement.

Tommy Ross, pioneer public relations practitioner and partner of Ivy Lee before founding T. J. Ross and Associates, once told a *Fortune* magazine interviewer: "Unless you are willing to resign an account or a job over a matter of principle, it is no use to call yourself a member of the world's newest profession—for you are already a member of the world's oldest."

Thus, it can be readily seen that ethics in public relations really begins with the individual—and is directly related to his or her own value system as well as to the good of society. Although it is important to show loyalty to an employer, practitioners must never allow a client or an employer to rob them of their self-esteem.

Ethical Dealings with News Media

The most practical consideration facing a public relations specialist in his or her dealings with the news media is that anything less than total honesty will destroy credibility and, with it, the practitioner's usefulness to an employer.

Trust is maintained even when practitioners say "no comment" and refuse to answer questions that go beyond information reported in the news releases, according to a study by Professors Michael Ryan and David L. Hartinson, published in *Journalism Quarterly*. Practitioners and journalists tend to agree on how they define lying; both, for example, believe that giving evasive answers to reporters' questions constitutes lying.

Gifts

Achieving trust is the aim of all practitioners, and it can be achieved only through highly professional and ethical performance. It is for this reason that providing junkets with doubtful news value, extravagant parties, expensive gifts, and personal favors for media representatives should never be done.

Newspeople and public relations executives alike questioned the propriety of Coca-Cola USA's sending sample cans of Coke Classic stuffed with $5 bills to 200 consumer and trade reporters and editors. The attention-getting gimmick was once part of the company's "Magic Summer" promotion in which 750,000 cans of the soft drink were to be distributed nationwide containing up to $200 cash and prize vouchers for trips and tickets to vacation and entertainment destinations. The cans were devised so that the cash or a voucher would pop up when what looked like an ordinary container was opened.

The public relations newsletter *Bulldog Reporter* quoted a number of newspeople and public relations executives who, for the most part, pointed out that the sending of cash to news sources raised the question of a conflict of interest whether a bribe was intended or not.

Autos: Shades of Gray

The most difficult ethical situations are those that are neither black nor white, but differing shades of gray. Relationships between automotive journalists and car manufacturers are questionable, according to an article in the *Wall Street Journal*. It is not unusual, for example, for an editor at *Car and Driver* to write reviews for autos made by a manufacturing firm that also employs the journalist as a consultant. As the article writer says, "Welcome to the world of automotive enthusiast journalism where the barriers that separate advertisers from journalists are porous enough for paychecks to pass through."

PRSA's code forbids "corrupting the channels of communication" by placing journalists on the payroll, but this stricture doesn't seem to mean much in the world of "buff" magazines such as *Car and Driver, Motor Trend,* and *Road & Track*. The journalists say they are professionals and would never let their consulting relationships interfere with their writing independence, but the public is left wondering about the integrity of such statements. At the same time, if hiring editors to be consultants is standard operating procedure, how does the public relations person for an auto company reconcile this "reality" with the standards of his or her profession? Ethical issues in the travel industry are discussed in Chapter 19. Some other aspects of public relations and news media ethical relationships are examined in "The Press Party" section of Chapter 21. The special legal and ethical obligations involved in the handling of financial information are discussed in Chapter 13.

PR insights

Reporters Also Have Codes of Ethics

Should someone working in public relations offer a reporter free tickets or even a free meal? Al Rothstein, owner of his own public relations firm, says it's not a good idea. He publishes a newsletter titled *Media E-Tips* and the following is an excerpt from it:

> More news organizations are adopting codes of ethics today. Most newspapers base their guidelines on the code developed by the Society of Professional Journalists (www.spj.org). Television stations usually derive theirs from the Radio Television News Director's Association's code (www.rtnda.com). A relatively new organization for Internet journalists, the Online News Association (www.onlinenewsassociation.org) has adopted a set of principles for its members.
>
> Once a year the Florida Times Union in Jacksonville, Florida publishes a summary of its code of ethics. Reader Advocate Mike Clark has granted permission for us to reprint his Q&A summary in this newsletter. It will give you an idea of the tone of professionalism reporters set for themselves.
>
> Q. Do your reporters accept free tickets?
> A. No free tickets are accepted other than working press credentials that give assigned reporters and photographers access to restricted areas. If editors decide that regular-seat tickets are needed for staff members, the tickets are purchased by the newspaper. Reviewers of movies, restaurants, concerts and the like often purchase tickets and are reimbursed by the paper. Free trips are banned, too. The newspapers pay the cost of travel for news coverage.
>
> Q. What do you do with gifts?
> A. News coverage cannot be bought. Gifts, no matter how well-intentioned, are returned to the donor. If that is not possible, the gifts are turned over to the editor, whose office holds an auction among newspaper staff. The proceeds are donated to charities. Reviewers of books, CDs and computer software, for instance, may keep the items they review. The rest are used in the company library or donated to schools.
>
> Q. Are reporters allowed to go undercover for a story?
> A. Reporters and photographers should identify themselves, except in very rare circumstances that are approved by the editor.
>
> Q. What are some of the main conflict of interest rules?
> A. Staffers are not allowed to profit or obtain business advantages from information obtained as a result of their employment. Business staff must disclose all of their securities ownership. Free or reduced memberships in clubs are not accepted. Staffers are not allowed to provide publicity services for outside agencies or political causes. Outside work may not conflict with the staffer's work with the newspaper.

Al's advice:

1. It is not a good idea to offer a reporter free tickets or even a free meal.
2. Reporters are not allowed to profit from the information they obtain.
3. Responsible reporters will not publish names of certain victims of crimes.
4. If you believe a reporter has violated his/her code of ethics, point it out to them.
5. If you get nowhere complaining to the reporter, contact his/her immediate supervisor and ask that any mistakes be corrected.

Summary

What Is Ethics?

The word *ethics* refers to a person's value system and how he or she determines right or wrong, with a personal philosophy that is either absolutist, existentialist, or situationalist.

Codes of Ethics

Most professional organizations have codes of ethics, including the Public Relations Society of America (PRSA) and the International Association of Business Communicators (IABC). These codes cover such areas as competition, confidentiality, conflicts of interest, and the like.

Professionalism, Licensing, and Accreditation

Although public relations is not a "profession" like those with standards in educational preparation or admission governed by law, practitioners should act like professionals in the sense of having a higher loyalty to the standards of the field than to those of a current employer. The issues of licensing and registration of public relations practitioners remain controversial, while several national groups actively endorse and promote accreditation.

Ethics in Individual Practice

Because so many practitioners work independently, the ethical bottom line comes down to each person's personal approach to the professional codes of ethics and to his or her own standards.

Ethical Dealings with News Media

Honesty is essential in all dealings with the news media to maintain trust, even if the practitioner must limit responses to "no comment." Gifts of any sort to the news media can raise the question of conflict of interest.

Case Activity: What Would You Do?

Prism Computer Corporation, a manufacturer of personal computers, has developed a new laser printer that is cheaper and more efficient than those produced by competitors. Although prototype models have been built, actual production of the new printer has been stalled up to three months by manufacturing problems.

Despite these difficulties, Prism's top management believes it is important from a marketing standpoint to announce that the new laser printer is now available. Consequently, you are asked as the product information specialist to write and distribute a new product release about the laser printer and its features.

You are told that no mention should be made in the news release that the product won't be available for another three months. What would you do in this situation? Does the situation violate professional ethics in any way? Why or why not?

Questions for Review and Discussion

1. Sound ethical practice is essential in public relations work. What is meant by *ethics,* and how is it that two individuals can disagree about what constitutes an ethical dilemma?
2. What do you consider the most important points in the PRSA and IABC codes? How do the standards serve the interest of (1) the organizations' members and (2) the public? Can you find any loopholes that might hinder full-fledged enforcement?
3. What are some of the principal problems involved in enforcing the codes?
4. What does the PRSA code say about giving gifts and free trips to representatives of the media? Is it all right to buy drinks or dinner for a news reporter?
5. To what four standards should a practitioner adhere in acting like a professional?
6. Should TV news directors identify the source of video news releases (VNRs) carried on their programs? Why?
7. Should public relations practitioners be licensed? What are some of the reasons pro and con?
8. Is the primary goal of the PRSA code of ethics enforcement or education?
9. In your opinion, should a PRSA member be held responsible for the ethical misconduct of a non-PRSA member whom he or she is supervising?
10. Is the use of a "front" organization deceptive?

Suggested Readings

Budd, John F. "The Incredible Credibility Dilemma." *Public Relations Quarterly,* Fall 2000, pp. 22–26.

Kelley, Alan. "Know the Power of De-Positioning." *Public Relations Quarterly,* Summer 2001, pp. 27–28.

Kemper, Cynthia L. "Living in Spin: Have 21st Century Communicators Stopped Telling the Truth?" *Communication World,* April/May 2001, pp. 6–9.

Kruckeberg, Dean. "The Public Relations Practitioner's Role in Practicing Strategic Ethics." *Public Relations Quarterly,* Fall 2000, pp. 35–39.

Martinson, David L. "Ethical Decision Making in Public Relations: What Would Aristotle Say?" *Public Relations Quarterly,* Fall 2000, pp. 18–21.

Mindszenthy, Bart J. "Ten Rules for the Practice of Public Relations in the New Century." *Public Relations Tactics,* January 2000, p. 29.

Seib, Phillip, and Fitzpatrick, Kathy. *Public Relations Ethics,* Fort Worth, TX: Harcourt Brace College Publishers, 1995.

Stauber, John, and Rampton, Sheldon. *Toxic Sludge Is Good for You: Lies, Damn Lies and the Public Relations Industry.* Monroe, ME: Common Courage Press, 1995.

Sung, Jessica. "Shandwick Accused of Ethical Violations." *PR Week,* September 18, 2000, p. 1.

Weiss, William S. "When Is the Truth the Whole Truth?" *Public Relations Tactics,* April 2000, p. 29.

The Individual in Public Relations

preview

The objective of this chapter is to give the student a personal perspective on public relations work—how the individual fits into public relations practice and the rewards and challenges for a practitioner.

Topics covered in the chapter include:

- Changing focus in public relations
- The range of public relations work
- Personal qualifications and attitudes
- Professional organizations providing support
- Internships
- Women and ethnic groups in a diversified workforce
- Salaries in public relations

The Public Relations Role

A person entering public relations may develop a career in numerous areas of this increasingly diverse field. Similarly, the variety of personal traits and skills that bring success is wide. While certain abilities are basic for all, such as writing well, public relations practitioners, as their experience grows, may develop special skills and find personally gratifying niches.

This chapter explains the job opportunities and requirements and discusses the individual attributes most likely to bring success.

A Changing Focus in Public Relations

Traditionally, it was widely held that public relations practitioners should if possible have experience as reporters, to polish their writing skills and to learn firsthand how the media function. In an earlier era, a large percentage of public relations people did have newspaper or broadcast experience. This is no longer true for several reasons, however.

The field of public relations has broadened far beyond working with the mass media. Much writing today in public relations is done for controlled media such as company publications, direct mail campaigns to key audiences, and membership newsletters, requiring no media relations savvy or contacts. Writing skill and knowledge of the media are vital, but so is training in management, logistics, and planning. A *PR Reporter* survey showed that there are now just as many practitioners in the field without newspaper experience as there are with such experience.

More universities than in the past are now offering joint public relations/advertising programs, in part because of growing interest in integrated marketing communications.

An annual study by Billy I. Ross of Louisiana State University and Keith F. Johnson of Texas Tech University, published in 2000, reported that public relations enrollment was 16,959 students in undergraduate and graduate programs. In the 1999–2000 academic year, public relations programs graduated 4,622 undergraduates. Details can be found on the World Wide Web at www.mcom.ttu.edu/wsig/?/.

Fortunately the number of public relations jobs continues to increase as the field expands. According to the Federal Bureau of Labor Statistics, employment of public relations managers will increase faster than the average for all occupations through the year 2005, placing public relations in the top ten growth industries. The spring 2000 issue of *Occupational Outlook Quarterly* forecasted a 24 percent increase in public relations jobs from 1998 to 2008. Job growth projections are particularly strong in health care and technology sectors, as well as the crisis communications specialty. The strong demand for public relations majors is also reflected in current employment rates of college graduates. According to the 1999 Annual Surveys of Journalism and Mass Communication conducted by Lee B. Becker of the University of Georgia and Gerald Kosicki of Ohio State University, advertising and public relations majors have the greatest success among all majors in obtaining full-time employment. Details can be found on the World Wide Web at www.grady.uga.edu/annualsurveys.

The Range of Public Relations Work

Women and men entering public relations may work in company departments, public relations firms that serve clients, or a wide range of organizations that require public relations services. The major areas of public relations work they will find include:

- *Corporations.* Departments seek to protect and enhance a company's reputation. They provide information to the public as well as to special audiences such as stockholders, financial analysts, and employees. Their work also includes community relations and often marketing communications.

PR insights

Qualities for a Successful Career

Art Stevens, CEO of Publicis Dialog in New York City and author of *The Persuasion Explosion,* has formulated what it takes to become successful in public relations. The individual:

1. Must be an excellent writer capable of writing client reports, effective article themes to editors, news releases, captions, annual reports, feature stories, and the like. His or her writing must require little editing and supervision.
2. Must be able to do short- and long-range planning, conceive and execute a full public relations plan for each account, and adhere strictly to deadlines.
3. Must be innovative and imaginative, not bound by trite, traditional ideas. Must be willing to keep an open mind to new ideas and to researching better ways.
4. Must be well informed about a client's business and continue to keep abreast of all developments in business and government that have an effect on the client's or company's business. Must function as a counselor as well as a communicator.
5. Must be results oriented, whether the task is the placement of major stories about a client in important publications or the successful execution of a special event. Must be a doer and a self-starter. Must know what follow-up means and have a solid respect for timetables and deadlines.
6. Must be thorough "pro," skilled in all the techniques used in the practice of public relations: writing and distribution of news releases, producing press kits, running press conferences, and so on. Must be familiar with feature writers, magazine contributors, and hot current subjects being written about.
7. Must know how to create publicity by conceiving a meaningful idea and carrying it through to its conclusion. Must know how to create sundry ideas where none are evident and must know where to take them.
8. Must know what it takes to establish and maintain acquaintanceship with key media people, since editorial contact is one of the primary functions of the public relations professional. The public relations professional must know how to deal with the media and understand their need for quick and responsive answers.
9. Must be able to learn and grow as new situations and client needs arise. Must draw upon prior experiences in the public relations field to move into new situations effortlessly and effectively.
10. Must be a good manager, capable of organizing and arranging his or her workload for maximum results. Must be capable of carrying many assignments at the same time and be in control of each one.
11. Finally, the public relations professional must not be a "yes-man/woman." Public relations has outgrown the caricature of second-class professionalism by producing individuals who speak their minds confidently to top management of major corporations and make valuable recommendations to these executives. So long as the public relations professional earns the respect and confidence of the chief executive officer, public relations will grow as a profession and will contribute to the broad communications goal of companies and institutions across the United States.

Source: Newsletter of the PRSA Counselors Academy.

- *Nonprofit organizations.* These range from membership organizations, such as trade and environmental associations, to social and cultural groups, hospitals, and other health agencies. Fund-raising often is involved.
- *Entertainment, sports, and travel.* Practitioners in these areas often are concerned with publicity for individuals and promotion of events ranging from football games to motion pictures.
- *Government and the military.* This area includes promotion of political issues, sometimes through lobbying, work with politicians, dissemination of information about government activities to citizens, and distribution of information about the armed forces.
- *Education.* At the college level, public relations people work primarily with alumni, faculty and administration, students, and the public to promote the school's image, recruit students, and raise funds. Secondary schools frequently have specialists to handle community relations.
- *International public relations.* The immense expansion of almost instantaneous global communications has opened an intriguing new area, especially for practitioners with language skills and familiarity with other cultures.

Detailed discussion of these areas appears in later chapters.

Personal Qualifications and Attitudes

Any attempt to define a single public relations type of personality is pointless, because the field is so diverse that it needs people of differing personalities. Some practitioners deal with clients and the public in person on a frequent basis; others work primarily at desks, planning, writing, and researching. Many do both.

Basic Personal Attributes

A few basic personal attributes are evident in all successful practitioners, no matter what their specific assignments. These include:

1. Ability with words, written or spoken
2. Analytical skill, to identify and define problems
3. Creative ability, to develop fresh, effective solutions to problems
4. An instinct for persuasion
5. Ability to make compelling and polished presentations

Bill Cantor, writing in the Public Relations Student Society of America's *Forum,* emphasizes the importance of curiosity and persistence:

> The public relations professional should have an inquiring mind, should want to learn everything possible about the product, service, client or organization, and the competition.
>
> Because public relations is not an exact science, frequently the public relations person must try a number of approaches in order to solve a problem, . . . Problems are solved by persistence and intelligence.

PR insights

Job Levels in Public Relations

- ***Entry-Level Technician*** Use of technical "craft" skills to disseminate information, persuade, gather data, or solicit feedback
- ***Supervisor*** Supervises projects, including planning, scheduling, budgeting, organizing, leading, controlling, and problem solving
- ***Manager*** Constituency and issue-trend analysis; departmental management, including organizing, budgeting, leading, controlling, evaluating, and problem solving
- ***Director*** Constituency and issue-trend analysis; communication and operational planning at departmental level, including planning, organizing, leading, controlling, evaluating, and problem solving
- ***Executive*** Organizational leadership and management skills, including developing the organizational vision, corporate mission, strategic objectives, annual goals, businesses, broad strategies, policies, and systems

Source: Adapted from the *Public Relations Professional Career Guide,* Public Relations Society of America, 33 Irving Place, New York, NY 10003.

Veteran public relations executives responsible for hiring staff members emphasize that people with normal personalities possessing the required skills are better suited for most public relations jobs than the brash "glad-hand" type.

Four Essential Abilities

Those who plan careers in public relations should develop four basic abilities, no matter what area of work they enter. These are writing skill, research ability, planning expertise, and problem-solving ability.

1. *Writing skill.* The ability to put information and ideas onto paper clearly and concisely is essential. Good grammar and good spelling are vital. Misspelled words and sloppy sentence structure look amateurish. The importance of writing skill is emphasized in a career advice column in *Working Woman:* "I changed careers, choosing public relations as having the best potential, but found it difficult to persuade employers that my *writing and interpersonal skills* were sufficient for an entry-level job in the profession."
2. *Research ability.* Arguments for causes must have factual support instead of generalities. A person must have the persistence and ability to gather information from a variety of sources, as well as to conduct original research by designing and implementing opinion polls or audits. Too many public relations programs fail because the organization does not assess audience needs and perceptions. Skillful use of the Internet and computer databases is an important element of research work.
3. *Planning expertise.* A public relations program involves a number of communication tools and activities that must be carefully planned and coordinated. A

PR insights

Public Relations Personality Checklist

This checklist, based on careful evaluation, can measure the effectiveness of your personality in terms of the public relations profession.

Rate each item "yes" or "no." Each "yes" counts for 4 points. A "no" doesn't count. Anything below 60 is a poor score. A score between 60 and 80 suggests you should analyze your weak areas and take steps to correct them. Scores above 80 indicate an effective public relations personality.

____ Good sense of humor
____ Positive and optimistic
____ Friendly, meet people easily
____ Can keep a conversation going with anybody
____ Take frustration and rejection in stride
____ Able to persuade others easily
____ Well-groomed, businesslike appearance
____ Flair for showmanship
____ Strong creative urge
____ Considerate and tactful
____ Adept in use of words
____ Able to gain management's confidence
____ Enjoy being with people
____ Enjoy listening
____ Enjoy helping other people resolve problems
____ Curious about many things
____ Enjoy reading in diverse areas
____ Determined to complete projects
____ High energy level
____ Can cope with sudden emergencies
____ See mistakes as learning experiences
____ Factual and objective
____ Respect other people's viewpoints
____ Perceptive and sensitive
____ Quickly absorb and retain information

Source: PRSSA Forum, Spring 1990.

person needs to be a good planner to make certain that materials are distributed in a timely manner, events occur without problems, and budgets are not exceeded. Public relations people must be highly organized, detail-oriented, and able to see the big picture.

4. *Problem-solving ability.* Innovative ideas and fresh approaches are needed to solve complex problems or to make a public relations program unique and

Counselors at a Public Relations Society of America conference discuss ways to use the "New Media" in their work. Gil Bashe, Executive Vice President of Hill and Knowlton, New York, describes the swiftly expanding electronic techniques.

memorable. Increased salaries and promotions go to people who show top management how to solve problems creatively.

The following three typical help-wanted advertisements illustrate how a public relations career may develop. The first is for an entry-level position of a routine nature, the second for a job with more responsibility, and the third for a high-level director who does strategic planning, directs a staff, and serves as the institution's spokesperson.

Staff Aide

Credit union seeks public relations aide to write and edit monthly newsletter, design and write brochure, and plan a variety of promotions for each quarter. Successful applicant must maintain rapport with members through publications as well as telephone and personal contact and assist various departments with public relations/promotion activities. Degree in public relations or journalism required. Candidate should be a self-starter with initiative to work independently, be able to work under pressure to meet deadlines, and accept constructive criticism without being offended.

Public Relations Account Coordinator

Public Relations Account Coordinator at fast-growing high-tech public relations agency. Four-year degree preferably in business/public relations. Position involves providing support to account team members and assisting in the implementation of PR programs for our clients. Includes use of strong writing/proofing skills, understanding of AP style, familiarity with Macintosh, strong multitasking capabilities, ability to deal with publications by phone, and ability to be a team player. Familiarity with the Internet, FileMaker Pro, and MS Word a plus.

University Director of Public Affairs

The university seeks an individual to create, direct, and manage a comprehensive and integrated public affairs program in support of the university's mission and goals on a national, regional, and community level. This entails developing communication and public affairs strategies and programs in conjunction with the president and other officers and academic leaders.

Serving as the principal spokesperson for the university, specific responsibilities include directing the dissemination of information within the university itself, to the media and to the many publics involved with the university, promoting special events, enhancing the university's visibility, and identifying areas within the community that could benefit from university resources and facilities.

Systematic research shows that there is a hierarchy of roles in public relations practice. In several studies, Professors Glen Broom and David Dozier of San Diego State University have found four empirically grounded organizational roles. They describe the roles as follows:

1. *Communication managers.* Practitioners playing this role are perceived by others as the organization's public relations experts. They make communication policy decisions and are held accountable by others and themselves for the success or failure of communication programs. They follow a systematic planning process.
2. *Communication liaisons.* Practitioners playing this role represent the organization at public meetings and create opportunities for management to hear the views of priority publics. Predominantly communication facilitators, these

practitioners also identify alternative solutions to organizational problems. Similar to communication managers in many respects, communication liaisons do not make policy decisions and are not held accountable for program success or failure.

3. *Media relations specialists.* Practitioners playing this role actively seek to place messages about the organization in the mass media. At the same time, they keep others in the organization informed of what is being said about the organization (and about issues important to the organization) in the media. They do not make policy, nor are they accountable for program outcomes.
4. *Communication technicians.* Practitioners playing this role are responsible for producing communication products and implementing decisions made by others. They take photographs and assemble graphics; write brochures, pamphlets, and news releases; and handle all aspects of production. They do not participate in policy decision making, nor are they responsible for outcomes.

The communication manager usually stands at the top of the hierarchy. Many practitioners continue to play lower-level organizational roles—even after years of professional experience.

Some evidence suggests that women in public relations tend to fulfill the technician role, resulting in lower pay and less power in organizations. In some studies, however, those in technician roles report higher job satisfaction. This may result from the intrinsic rewards of writing and graphic design. The higher satisfaction may also derive from avoiding some of the responsibility and time demands shouldered by managers.

Needed: An Understanding of Economics

In preparing themselves for public relations careers, students should obtain a solid grounding in economics and business, through course electives, internships, and other work experience. Once they are employed as professionals, they should study the financial aspects and the business model of their employers or clients. This advice also holds true for students intending to work in the fiscally restrained and competitive world of nonprofit public relations. More and more, public relations involves distribution and interpretation of financial information. To handle this material well, the practitioner first must understand it. Investor relations, which requires detailed financial knowledge, is the highest-paid specialty area in public relations work.

After a few years of work, some public relations people return to the classroom to earn advanced degrees. The Master of Business Administration degree, commonly called the MBA, probably is the most frequently sought, but the list of master's and PhD degrees held by public relations specialists ranges over many fields. According to professors Katherine Kinnick of Kennesaw State University and Glen T. Cameron of the Missouri School of Journalism, public relations students should be exposed to business-style training in their major coursework. The increasing emphasis on public relations as a management function calls for public relations students to learn the "nuts and bolts" of business. Students who plan to do corporate public relations work should remember the fundamental fact about American business: Every company was created to earn a profit for those who risked their money to start it. Businesses can continue to exist only as long as they are profitable. The task of public relations in the business world is to help companies prosper. Unfortunately, many college students believe that American business makes excessive profits. This belief arises from a lack of comprehension of free enterprise economics.

Many progressive companies use a *triangle* concept, representing three basic elements in their business. Customers, shareholders, and employees form the three sides. The management goal is to keep the sides of the triangle in balance, satisfying all three. Public relations has an important role in achieving this balance through effective communication with the three groups and by providing responsible counsel to top management.

Professional Support Services

Talking with other public relations people about their successes and failures and exchanging ideas are important activities in building a career. Reading professional literature as well as attending workshops and seminars also are beneficial activities. Public relations organizations provide many opportunities of this nature.

There are multiple resources on the World Wide Web to find a job in public relations and its related fields. One source is Workinpr.com.

Organizations and Societies

Public relations groups at the local, state, national, and international levels provide an important channel of communication for practitioners in all areas of the profession. Some of the better-known organizations include the Council for the Advancement and Support of Education (CASE), the National Investor Relations Institute (NIRI), and the International Public Relations Association (IPRA).

The largest national group is the Public Relations Society of America, with 19,000 members and more than 100 chapters. The society has 14 special interest sections, a national professional development and awards program, and publishes the monthly *Public Relations Tactics* and a quarterly named *The Strategist.* PRSA also operates a professional practice center, which provides answers to members' research requests from its extensive library and from the Nexis and Dialog databases. The society distributes issue papers that help recipients plan strategies. It is the parent organization of the Public Relations Student Society of America (discussed in the next section).

The second largest organization of communication and public relations professionals is the International Association of Business Communicators (IABC), with 13,500 members in 56 countries. Most members live in the United States (72 percent), with Canada, the United Kingdom, and Hong Kong having significant numbers. Although its membership has diversified somewhat in recent years, a large percentage of IABC members are involved in employee communications. The organization publishes the monthly magazine *Communication World.*

Internships

Internships are extremely popular in the communications industry, and a student whose résumé includes practical work experience along with an academic record has an important advantage. Obtaining an internship offered by a public relations firm, company department, or charitable agency is among the best ways to get this desired experience. The intern, in most cases, earns academic credit and gets firsthand knowledge of work in the professional field.

Although internships offer an advantage in getting a first job, the practice by some companies of using unpaid interns has drawn increasing criticism because it puts downward pressure on wages in fields where internships proliferate. The contention is that when students or recent graduates work for nothing, aspiring professionals will accept low beginning salaries. A trend is growing among colleges and universities, and employers as well, to advocate paid internships. Former Fortune 50 executive Tom Hagley argued in *Public Relations Tactics* that paying interns well enables the student to focus effort and maintain high performance standards, resulting in an excellent return on the salary investment by the company.

Another way for students to get exposure and experience is through membership in the Public Relations Student Society of America (PRSSA). The society has chapters at about 200 universities and a national membership of 6000. Members can participate in a national case study competition or carry out projects on local campuses as part of a corporate collegiate program. Many chapters also have student-run firms that implement programs for local and campus organizations. A university must offer five courses in public relations before a PRSSA chapter can be established on its campus.

A Diversified Workforce

More than half the public relations practitioners in the United States are women, an increasing number of whom hold high-level management positions. Thus the public relations industry provides a healthy diversity of gender perspective as it prepares and delivers its messages.

Public relations falls seriously short, however, in developing a workforce rich in racial diversity. As the U.S. industry faces the challenge of addressing the abundance of target audiences in the increasingly multiracial, multicultural American population, its composition remains overwhelmingly white.

Ethnic Groups

According to the Census Bureau, more than 20 percent of the U.S. population in 2000 consisted of racial minorities—primarily African Americans, Hispanics, Asians and Pacific Islanders, and Native Americans—and the percentage is growing (find details on the Web at http://www.census.gov/prod/cen2000/dpl/2kh00.pdf). The number of minority workers in public relations falls far short of equaling that population percentage. Nevertheless, some progress is being made toward a more diverse workforce in public relations.

The membership profile for the Public Relations Society of America in 1997 showed that 93 percent of respondents were white, 3 percent black, 2 percent Hispanic, and 1 percent Asian. In a survey reported in *PR Week*, the public relations industry in 2001 was still predominantly white (89.4 percent in public relations versus 82.2 percent of the population); while blacks (4.5 percent versus 12.8 percent), Hispanics (2.8 percent versus 11.8 percent) and Asians (2.1 percent versus 4.1 percent) are all underrepresented. A U.S. Department of Labor report in 2001 presents a somewhat more inclusive workforce with 8.3 percent African American workers and 3.1 percent Hispanic for a total of 11.4 percent. Asians and other ethnic groups were not listed separately. (Details are available at http://stats.bls.gov/news.release/empsit.t02.htm.)

Some public relations firms say that they have difficulty hiring minority staff members because they receive so few applications from minority aspirants. Seeking to improve the situation, PRSA has taken several significant steps to stimulate recruitment of minorities. It has a national task force to promote minorities in public relations, a program of seminars and a speakers bureau to identify and encourage candidates, a list of minority candidates available, and a scholarship fund to place minority students in intern programs.

The public relations industry should do more to address various explanations offered for the shortage of minorities in public relations. Among them are inadequate school counseling to steer minority students toward public relations careers, a fear among some young people—usually unfounded—that they will not be accepted by coworkers; a dislike of being paraded as "token" minorities and assigned only to minority clients; and, in some instances, actual discrimination by public relations offices and/or clients.

Some men and women from ethnic groups take the route into "mainstream" departments and firms. Others join local and regional minority-owned firms. These firms, usually small, earn much of their income by representing minority clients or working in the minority marketplace on behalf of large general firms.

African American Kim Hunter, president of Lagrant Communications in Los Angeles, pointed out at a PRSA meeting that a "minority market" as such does not exist, because the diverse and segmented audiences within the spectrum of minority populations respond to different messages.

As public relations practice becomes more and more internationalized, firms entering the world market have an especially strong need for diversified ethnic staffs. With constant communication between their U.S. offices and firms abroad, they need staff members with language skills, personal knowledge of other countries, and sensibility to the customs and attitudes of others. Knowledge of Spanish and the Asian languages is especially valuable.

Women

As more and more young women entered the public relations field during the 1980s, the percentage of female workers rose swiftly. In February 1987, the U.S. Bureau of Labor Statistics for the first time showed women in the majority, at 51.7 percent. In 2000, labor statistics indicated that the percentage of women in the public relations field was approaching 70 percent. Membership in the International Association of Business Communicators (IABC) consists of 70 percent women, with PRSA figures nearly as high. A *USA Today* article reported that in spite of this vast majority of women practitioners, only 37 percent of the top 100 public relations firms are headed by women.

Womens' Career Tracks The proportion of women in public relations is growing rapidly because nearly 80 percent of the candidates for entry-level jobs are women. But rapid change is not occurring in the career track taken by women. A 1989 study by DeAnna DeRosa of Menlo College and Dennis L. Wilcox of San Jose State has been replicated twice with similar conclusions. All three studies of majors in public relations suggest that women are very well equipped for business life. They display self confidence, assertiveness, risk-taking attitudes, and accountability necessary for business success but are less career oriented, fully expecting to take family leaves, to limit work hours, and to interrupt their careers for family duties. Apparently the public relations major appeals to many women because it blends creativity and business. More important, it is a field that lends itself to interrupted careers and freelancing for the sake of child rearing. Although female undergraduates were strong in aptitudes needed for advancement along the management track, the disinclination to management positions and the stereotyping of women as technicians may pose a problem for the field in general.

Martha Lauzen has found that when women are disinclined to handle management duties, preferring to focus on writing and other technical roles, encroachment occurs. Encroachment takes place when top management puts people from outside public relations in charge of public relations. As a result, the definition of public relations is further muddled or diluted. Lauzen concluded that being a woman in public relations did not lead to encroachment, but being a technician did.

Although women are still concentrated in lower- and middle-level jobs, times are changing, as evidenced by the success of many women in the field. Marilyn Castaldi, a senior vice president of the Fleishman-Hillard public relations firm, said, "Women are now ascending en masse into top positions in corporations, major agencies, and firms of their own."

A 70 to 30 percent female-to-male ratio in fields that virtually demand a college education is exceptionally high. For comparison, women on average held less than one-third of U.S. radio news positions. The ratio in television, however, is more favorable to women. The Federal Communications Commission reported in 1996 that females constituted 40.7 percent of full-time broadcast employees and 41.9 percent of cable industry employees.

Gender discrimination in public relations is less than in some of the traditional mass media, with discrimination least likely in public relations firms. Firms are driven financially by billable hours charged to clients and by the generation of new business

focus on ethics

The Debate about Salary Disparities in Public Relations

Pr reporter (1998, Oct) documented that female practitioners in the United States and Canada made 78 cents for every dollar male practitioners earned in 1998. A more recent survey conducted by *PR Week* (2001, March 26) reported that female practitioners earned 72 cents for every dollar earned by male practitioners. However, neither report adjusted annual income for age, experience, or position of responsibility in the organization. According to both surveys, men in the field tend to be older and have more experience than women. It's possible that age and experience factors account for much of the disparity.

PR Week found that segregation of women in lower-paid jobs contributes to salary differences. Male practitioners tend to work in the best-paid specialties such as investor relations and financial services, whereas female practitioners are found more often in lower-paid specialties such as community relations and internal communications. The largest income disparities were found at the top management level, including president, CEO, and vice president positions ($100,000 for male versus $75,000 for female in the *pr reporter* survey, $134,000 for male versus $105,000 for female in the *PR Week* survey). The gender-based disparity among entry level practitioners is much smaller. The survey conducted by *pr reporter* (1998) showed that entry-level male practitioners made $40,000, while their female counterparts earned $32,000. *PR Week* found much greater parity: Male practitioners at the entry-level earned $36,000 while their female peers earned $35,000.

These results suggest that the pay gap between male and female practitioners at the entry level has become small to insignificant in recent years. The disparity may be further diminished when controlling for specialty, except at the highest managerial levels. Nevertheless, many scholars argue an unjust disparity still exists.

According to O'Dwyer's *PR Services Report* (March 2001), other scholars such as James Hutton consider the salary disparity to be entirely unproven. They say that the original Velvet Ghetto study of salary disparities concluded that men are more serious about their careers than are women, so perhaps the entire disparity is self-inflicted rather than blatant sexism! Factors such as higher male salary expectations and stronger careerist orientation, along with a male inclination to harder-nosed salary negotiation tactics and willingness to move to better jobs may account for much of the disparity. A study by LeAna S. Bui in *PR Quarterly* (Summer 1999) adds to this argument of self-imposed salary penalties for women. Bui's study found that women stay in lower-level, technician roles and make career-sacrificing decisions for the sake of their maternal roles in families.

In addition to the question of justice, the salary disparity holds another consequence. Harold Burson, public relations pioneer and principal of Burson-Marsteller, admires the performance of women executives in public relations but worries that a profession too closely identified as a female occupation with low salaries will become marginalized and under-compensated.

What do you think?

for the firm. In such an analytical reward system, the individual's productivity counts far more than favoritism in earning raises and promotions. Women appear to fare very well on such a level playing field, arguably because they show strength in building personal relationships and offer a fresh perspective toward social problems.

Women Receive Lower Pay Despite the numerical superiority of women in public relations, studies show that men earn more than women do. The longtime gap in male versus female salary scales remains substantial at many levels but is diminishing.

A survey published by the Public Relations Society of America in 1996 reported that on average men's salaries were 45 percent higher than women's—$59,460 against $41,110.

The IABC survey in 1995, in which 4679 members participated, showed that salaries of U.S. female members amounted to 79 percent of men's salaries. For IABC women members in Canada, the 1995 percentage was 87, compared to 86 in 1989.

The salary advantage for men over women is widespread in most of American business, according to a survey of 28 fields of endeavor conducted in 1996 by *Working Woman* magazine. It found that typically women earned 5 to 15 percent less than men. A fact influencing the salary gap is that corporate/industrial public relations work, traditionally dominated by men, pays the highest salaries, while the public sector and nonprofit organizations, in which women dominate, are among the lowest.

Other explanations for this discrepancy involve conflicting pressures on a woman's time by job demands and family needs. Family concerns diminish a woman's earning power, according to analysts for the Independent Women's Forum. Diana Furchtgott-Roth and Christina Stolba found that childless young career women's salaries were 98 percent of comparable men's salaries. Some pessimists worry that the large number of women in the field will result in a "velvet ghetto" in public relations with lower prestige and pay than in fields requiring comparable education and skill. Optimists believe that equality in pay will be achieved eventually as women gain more professional experience and perhaps as family responsibilities become increasingly shared by men.

What Kinds of Salaries?

Public relations work pays relatively well. This is true from the entry level to the top. The prospect of steady advancement in income as practitioners gain experience and take on more responsibility is attractive.

Salary Statistics

According to the 2001 *PR Week* survey, salaries in corporate PR ($64,000) remain higher than in agencies ($59,000). But agencies saw the biggest salary gains, up 18.9% as opposed to 15.8% in corporate PR from 2000 to 2001. Positions in government ($51,000) and nonprofit ($46,000) trail, while the best pay of all is for solo practitioners and freelance consultants ($73,000). This is up from the IABC survey in 1995, stating that its members had reached the $50,000 median. The upward trend in salaries suggests a continued strong need in the marketplace for public relations professionals. This demand partly accounts for the 17 percent average annual salary increase found by *PR Week* in the 2001 salary survey.

PR insights

Public Relations: High in Job Satisfaction

The components of job satisfaction, according to sociologists, are (1) income, (2) power, (3) prestige, (4) autonomy, and (5) creativity.

Margaret DeFleur used these components to survey 3000 college graduates in various media industries about the level of their job satisfaction. The rankings of combined job satisfaction scores were as shown in the accompanying table.

A Harris/Impulse Research survey offers support for the favorable depiction of the public relations profession. An almost unanimous 98 percent of the 3162 public relations staffers felt challenged and personally rewarded by their work. And according to *pr reporter,* "A whopping 94% say they have sufficient time for personal or family life and 91% feel appreciated."

Source: DeFleur, Margaret H. "Foundations of Job Satisfaction in the Media Industries." *Journalism Educator,* Spring 1992, pp. 3–15.

Rank	*Career Category*
1	Photography
2	Public relations
3	Magazine
4	Advertising
5	Broadcast journalism
6	Film
7	Television
8	Radio
9	Newspaper journalism
10	Other careers

Median salaries, of course, include those for employees at both ends of the pay ladder, from entry-level beginners to the heads of public relations firms and major corporate departments. Pay for top-level executives reaches $300,000 in salary, bonuses, and stock options—even higher in some instances.

Entering the Field

College graduates entering the job market can expect a median annual salary of $28,964 in public relations, according to the "2000 Annual Survey of Journalism and Mass Communications Graduates" by the Association for Education in Journalism and Mass Communications (AEJMC). This is somewhat higher than the $26,162 reported for graduates joining daily newspapers and the $26,988 reported for those going into advertising. Graduates in radio received $23,400, and those in television received a median salary of $21,840.

Starting salaries in public relations vary by type of organization. One PRSA survey indicated that the top pay went to those who joined corporations. Although public relations firms offered somewhat lower entry-level pay, individuals do earn more salary with some experience. For example, according to the *PR Week* annual survey in 2001, the relatively junior position of assistant account executive at a firm earned a salary in the mid-30s.

According to the Annual Surveys of Journalism and Mass Communication conducted by Lee B. Becker and Gerald Kosicki, more public relations graduates took full-time work in firms than in departments. The degree provides the most general preparation of all sequences in journalism programs, with public relations majors entering a wide range of communication jobs. The public relations major also enjoyed among the highest earnings upon graduation from journalism and mass communication programs.

Two factors spur upward mobility once that first job is obtained. Those who are willing to change jobs, called "job jumpers" by executive search specialist Dennis Spring, can expect 12 to 20 percent increases in salary. Changing jobs and locations can be stressful but does often accelerate salary increases over a career. The sacrifice necessary to earn a graduate degree also reaps rewards. Becker and Kosicki found a $10,000 boost in starting salary for 2000 among those graduating with a master's degree in any journalism or mass communication major.

This group of high-ranking executives exemplifies the rise of women to senior positions in public relations at large corporations. From left to right, top row: Elizabeth Board, vice president of global communications, The Reader's Digest Association; and Diane B. Dixon, senior vice president of worldwide communications, Avery Dennison Corporation. Second row, Mary Ellen Kating, senior vice president of corporate communications, Barnes & Noble Booksellers; and Mary Linder, senior vice president of corporate communications, Northwest Airlines. Third row: Anne M. McCarthy, vice president of corporate communications, Polaroid Corporation; and Judith Muhlberg, vice president of communications, The Boeing Company.

Summary

The Public Relations Role
Those entering public relations traditionally came from journalism backgrounds, and writing skills are still important. Public relations positions exist in corporations; nonprofit organizations; entertainment, sports, and travel; government and the military; education; or international public relations.

Personal Qualifications and Attitudes
To succeed in public relations, one needs verbal ability, analytical skill, creativity, the ability to persuade, and the ability to make presentations. Anyone planning such a career should be able to write, do research, plan effectively, and solve problems.

Needed: An Understanding of Economics
A solid grounding in economics and business is essential for the successful public relations practitioner.

Professional Support Services
Those entering this field will benefit from reading professional literature, attending workshops and seminars, membership in professional organizations, and internships.

A Diversified Workforce
Although more than half of public relations professionals are now women, the profession has fallen short in the area of racial diversity.

What Kinds of Salaries?
Public relations work is well paid, with the prospect of steady advancement. Corporate salaries are higher than those in agencies.

Case Activity: What Would You Do?

The local Public Relations Society of America (PRSA) chapter is sponsoring an essay contest to select a winner who will receive a $2500 scholarship. The topic is "Why I have what it takes to have a successful career in public relations." Write a 1000-word essay on this topic.

Questions for Review and Discussion

1. What additional skills do former newspaper reporters need to work in public relations?
2. Can you name four major areas of public relations work?
3. What are the basic job levels in public relations?
4. Those who plan careers in public relations should develop four fundamental abilities. What are they?
5. What essential economic fact should students who enter corporate public relations work always keep in mind?
6. Glen Broom and David Dozier say that there is a hierarchy of roles in public relations. What are these roles?
7. What is the largest national organization of public relations professionals? What is another major one?
8. Why is it important for a student to complete an internship while in college?
9. What is the ratio of female-to-male practitioners in the public relations field? Why do you think women find the public relations field so attractive?
10. How do you explain the fact that women in public relations are paid less than men?

Suggested Readings

Aldoory, Linda. "The Language of Leadership for Female Public Relations Professionals." *Journal of Public Relations Research,* Vol. 10, No. 2, 1998, pp. 73–101.

Farmer, Betty, and Waugh, Lisa. "Gender Differences in Public Relations Students' Career Attitudes: A Benchmark Study." *Public Relations Review, 25*(2), Summer, 1999, pp. 235–249.

Goldman, Elaine. "21st-Century Sea Change in Public Relations Careers." *The Strategist,* Spring, 1998, pp. 43–44.

Grunig, Larissa A., Toth, Elizabeth L., and Hon, L. C. *Women in Public Relations: How Gender Influences Practice.* New York: Guilford Press, 2001.

Hon, Linda. "Toward a Feminist Theory of Public Relations." *Journal of Public Relations Research,* Vol. 7, No. 1, 1995, pp. 27–88.

Lauzen, M. "Effects of Gender on Professional Encroachment in Public Relations." *Journalism Quarterly, 69* (1), 1992, pp. 173–180.

Leichty, Greg, and Springston, Jeff. "Elaborating on Public Relations Roles." *Journalism and Mass Communication Quarterly,* Summer 1996, pp. 467–477.

Mitrook, Michael A., Wilkes, Kimberly V., and Cameron, Glen T. "Dealing with the Feminization of the Field: Attitudes and Aptitudes of College Women in Public Relations." Public Relations Division, Association for Education in Journalism and Mass Communication, Baltimore, 1998.

Redeker, Lauren. "Internships Provide Invaluable Job Preparation." *Public Relations Journal,* September 1992, pp. 20–21.

Serini, Shirley A., Toth, Elizabeth, Wright, Donald K., Emig, Arthur G. "Watch for Falling Glass . . . Women, Men, and Job Satisfaction in Public Relations: A Preliminary Analysis." *Journal of Public Relations Research,* Vol. 9, No. 2, 1997, pp. 99–118.

Tam, Shuk Yin, Dozier, David, Lauzen, Martha, and Real, Michael. "The Impact of Superior–Subordinate Gender on the Career Advancement of Public Relations Practitioners." *Journal of Public Relations Research,* Vol. 7, No. 4, 1995, pp. 259–272.

Public Relations Departments and Firms

preview

The objective of this chapter is to explain what top management expects from its public relations department and to give students an understanding of how departments and public relations firms operate.

Topics covered in the chapter include:

- The role of public relations departments
- Organization of departments
- Line and staff functions
- Public relations firms
- Advertising and public relations mergers
- Work in a public relations firm
- Fees and charges

Public Relations Departments

Public relations departments serve various roles and functions within companies and organizations. The following sections discuss the public relations function in organizational structures, names of departments, line and staff functions, sources of friction with other departments, and the pros and cons of working in a department

Role in Various Organizational Structures

For over a century, public relations departments have served companies and organizations. George Westinghouse is reported to have created the first corporate department in 1889 when he hired two men to publicize his pet project, alternating current (AC) electricity. Their work was relatively simple when compared to the mélange of physical, sociological, and psychological elements that contemporary departments employ. Eventually Westinghouse won out over Thomas A. Edison's direct current (DC) system, and his method became the standard in the United States. Westinghouse's public relations department concept has also grown into a basic part of today's electronic world.

Today, public relations is expanding from its traditional functions, enlarged over the years as explained in Chapter 2, to exercise its influence in the highest levels of management.

Importance in Today's World In a changing environment, and faced with the variety of pressures previously described, executives increasingly see public relations not as publicity and one-way communication, but as a process of negotiation and compromise with a number of key publics. James Grunig, professor of public relations at the University of Maryland, calls the new approach "building good relationships with strategic publics," which will require public relations executives to be "strategic communication managers rather than communication technicians."

Grunig, head of a six-year IABC Foundation research study on *Excellence in Public Relations and Communications Management,* continues:

> When public relations helps that organization build relationships, it saves the organization money by reducing the costs of litigation, regulation, legislation, pressure campaign boycotts, or lost revenue that result from bad relationships with publics—publics that become activist groups when relationships are bad. It also helps the organization make money by cultivating relationships with donors, customers, shareholders and legislators.

The results of the IABC study seem to indicate that chief executive officers (CEOs) consider public relations a good investment. A survey of 200 organizations showed that CEOs gave public relations operations a 184 percent return on investment (ROI), a figure just below that of customer service and sales/marketing.

Professional public relations people, ideally, assist top management in developing policy and communicating with various groups. Indeed, the IABC study emphasizes that CEOs want communication that is strategic, based on research, and involves two-way communication with key publics.

Dudley H. Hafner, executive vice president of the American Heart Association (AHA), echoed these thoughts:

> In the non-profit business sector, as well as in the for-profit business of America, leadership needs to pay close attention to what our audiences (supporters or customers as well as the

general public) want, what they need, what their attitudes are, and what is happening in organizations similar to ours. Seeking, interpreting, and communicating this type of critical information is the role of the communications professional.

Importance of Organizational Structure Research indicates, however, that the role of public relations in an organization often depends on the type of organization, the perceptions of top management, and even the capabilities of the public relations executive.

Research studies by Professor Larissa Grunig at the University of Maryland and Mark McElreath at Towson State University, among others, show that large, complex organizations have a greater tendency than do smaller firms to include public relations in the policy-making process. Companies such as IBM and General Motors, which operate in a highly competitive environment, are more sensitive than many others to policy issues and public attitudes and to establishing a solid corporate identity. Consequently, they place more emphasis on news conferences, formal contact with the media, writing executive speeches, and counseling management about issues that could potentially affect the corporate bottom line.

In such organizations, classified as mixed organic/mechanical by management theorists, the authority and power of the public relations department are quite high. Public relations is part of what is called the "dominant coalition" and has a great deal of autonomy.

In contrast, a small-scale organization of low complexity, with a standardized product or service, feels few public pressures and little governmental regulatory interest. It has scant public relations activity, and staff members are relegated to such technician roles as producing the company newsletter and issuing routine news releases. Public relations in what is called the traditional organization has little or no input into management decisions and policy formation.

Research also indicates that the type of organization involved may be less significant in predicting the role of its public relations department than are the perceptions and expectations of its top management. In many organizations, top-level management perceives public relations as primarily a journalistic and technical function—media relations and publicity. In large-scale mechanical organizations of low complexity, there is also a tendency to think of public relations as only a support function of the marketing department.

Such perceptions by top management severely limit the role of the public relations department as well as its power to take part in management decision making and solve problems. Instead, public relations staff members are relegated to being technicians who simply prepare messages without input on what should be communicated.

A third dimension influencing the role and function of a public relations department is the background and capabilities of its staff. As the IABC Foundation research has pointed out, CEOs want strategic communication managers; yet a large number of public relations managers, many of them journalists by training, self-select technician roles because they lack a knowledge base in research, environmental scanning, problem solving, and managing total communication strategies.

Instead, they continue to be preoccupied with one-way communication to the mass media even though, as the IABC research points out, the mass media "generally are not the most effective way of communicating with strategic publics—especially at the stage of building relationships rather than responding to issues."

According to Dena Winokur and Robert Kinkead, writing in the *Public Relations Journal*, CEOs increasingly view public relations as a strategic management tool. They write:

> CEOs . . . demand communication counselors who can analyze corporate cultures and understand how to influence their evolution. These counselors must be as comfortable in the board room as they are at the computer keyboard. They must be able to handle a crisis, write a speech, and devise a corporate strategy with equal ease.

Names of Departments

A public relations department in an organization goes by many names. And most often it is not "public relations." In the largest corporations (the Fortune 500), the terms *corporate communications* or *communications* outnumber *public relations* by almost four to one.

O'Dwyer's PR Services Report, in a survey of the Fortune 500 companies, found 200 such departments and only 48 public relations departments. Among those switching from "public relations" to "corporate communications" in recent years are Procter & Gamble and Hershey Candies. In both cases, the companies say that the switch occurred because the department had expanded beyond "public relations" to include such activities as employee communications, shareholder communications, annual reports, consumer relations, and corporate philanthropy.

Such activities, however, are considered subcategories of modern public relations, so consultant Alfred Geduldig has offered another reason. He told *O'Dwyer's PR Services*

PR insights

Expertise Required in a Department

The *Excellence in Public Relations and Communication Management* study, funded by IABC, identified 15 areas of specialized expertise that should be present in a public relations department:

Strategic and Operational Management Knowledge

- Develop strategies for solving problems
- Manage organizational response to issues
- Develop goals and objectives for department
- Prepare budgets
- Manage people

Research Knowledge

- Perform environmental scanning
- Determine public reactions to your organization
- Use research to segment publics
- Conduct evaluation research

Negotiation Knowledge

- Negotiate with activist publics
- Help management understand opinions of publics
- Use conflict resolution theories with publics

Persuasion Knowledge

- Persuade a public that your organization is right
- Use attitude theory in a campaign
- Get publics to behave as your organization wants

Source: Dozier, David, with Grunig, James, and Larissa. *The Manager's Guide to Excellence in Public Relations and Communication Management.* Mahwah, NJ: Lawrence Erlbaum Publishers, 1995, p. 64.

Report that the term *public relations* had suffered from repeated derogatory usage, causing companies to move away from the term. He also thought that the term *corporate communications* was a sign that public relations people were doing many more things in a company than in the past, reflecting an integration of communications services.

Echoing this thought is Linda Ambrose, director of corporate affairs for Tenneco. She says that the company changed from "public relations" to "elevate the function of the department." The unit now handles internal relations, speech writing, and community affairs. It is headed by a vice president who reports to the chairman of the company. "So corporate affairs is precisely what it is," Ambrose told *O'Dwyer's PR Services Report.*

Other names used for public relations departments in the corporate world include *corporate relations, investor relations, public affairs, marketing communications, public and community relations,* and *external affairs.*

Government agencies, educational institutions, and charitable organizations use such terms as *public affairs, community relations, public information,* and even *market services.*

Organization of Departments

The head executive of a public relations or similarly named department usually has one of three titles—manager, director, or vice president. A vice president of corporate communications may have direct responsibility for the additional activities of advertising and marketing communications.

A department usually is divided into specialized sections that have a coordinator or manager. Common sections found in a large corporation are media relations, investor relations, consumer affairs, governmental relations, community relations, marketing communications, and employee communications.

The organizational chart of IBM's corporate communications department is shown in Figure 5.1.

One of the world's largest corporations, General Motors, has more than 300 public relations personnel and a wide range of job titles based on geography and operating divisions. Each division, such as Buick or the Saginaw Steering Gear Division, has its own director of public relations. General Electric, another corporate giant, has several hundred persons in various public relations functions.

These examples should not mislead the reader about the size and budget of public relations departments. Multimillion-dollar corporations often have small departments. A Conference Board survey of 150 major U.S. corporations found that the typical department has nine professionals. The typical department budget, the survey noted, was about $3.5 million.

Public relations personnel may also be dispersed throughout an organization in such a manner that an observer has difficulty in ascertaining the extent of public relations activity. Some may be housed under marketing communications in the marketing department. Others may be assigned to the personnel department as communication specialists producing newsletters and brochures. Still others may be in marketing, working exclusively on product publicity. Decentralization of the public relations function, and the frictions it causes, will be discussed later in this chapter.

Line and Staff Functions

Traditional management theory divides an organization into *line* and *staff* functions. A line manager, such as a vice president of manufacturing, can delegate authority, set production goals, hire employees, and directly influence the work of others. Staff

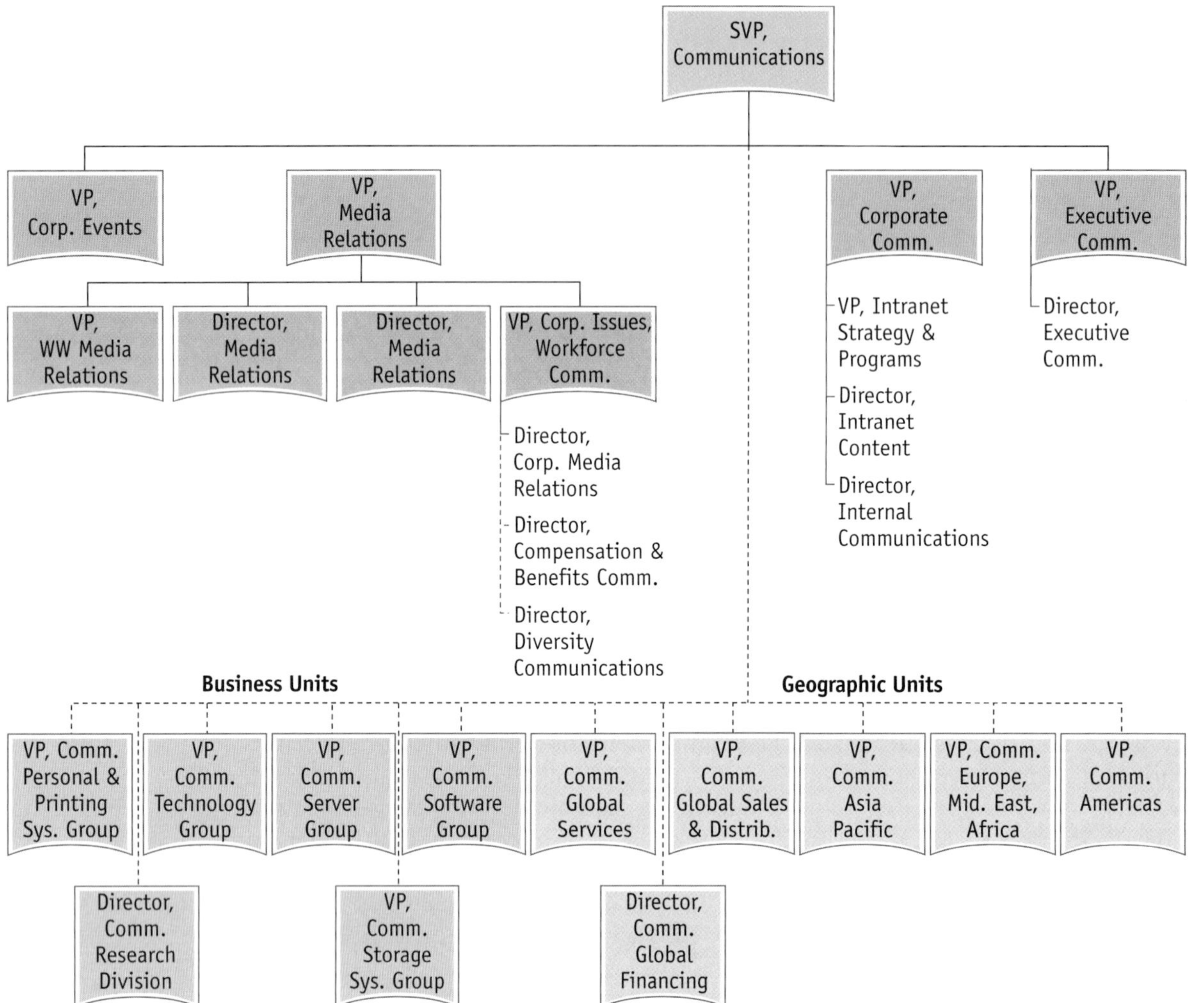

FIGURE 5.1

This chart shows the overall organization of IBM's global communications team. It shows delegation of responsibilities by function, business unit, and geography under a senior vice president of communications. Courtesy of IBM Corporation.

people, in contrast, have little or no direct authority. Instead, they indirectly influence the work of others through suggestions, recommendations, and advice.

According to accepted management theory, public relations is a staff function. Public relations people are experts in communication; line managers, including the chief executive officer, rely on them to use their skills in preparing and processing data, making recommendations, and executing communication programs to implement the organization's policies.

Public relations staff members, for example, may find through a community survey that people have only a vague understanding of what the company manufactures. In order to improve community comprehension and create greater rapport, the public relations department may recommend to top management that a community open house be held at which product demonstrations, tours, and entertainment would be featured.

PR insights

A Snapshot of Corporate Public Relations

PR Week conducted a national survey of 1405 companies and issued a report titled "Corporate Benchmarking Survey 2001." It found that the average number of professionals on a corporate staff was eight, although corporations with more than $5 billion in revenues averaged 24 full-time public relations professionals on staff. Other findings are summmarized below:

Who Does the Head of Communications Report to in Your Company?

Chairman/CEO/president	42%	Chief financial officer (CFO)	3%
Head of marketing	28%	Head of human resources	2%
Chief operations officer (COO)	4%	Other	18%
General counsel	4%		

Breakdown of Average Communications/PR Budgets

Media relations	23.8%	Financial/investor relations	6.7%
Issues advertising	4.4%	Community relations	7.4%
Crisis management	4.8%	Special events	8.6%
Annual/quarterly reports	5.3%	Product/brand communications	17.1%
Public affairs/government relations	5.6%	Employee/internal communications	9.9%
Reputation management	6.4%		

Percent of In-House Departments Responsible for the Following PR Functions

Media relations	97%	Annual/quarterly reports	48%
Crisis management	83%	Public affairs/government relations	37%
Special events	70%	Product/brand communications	35%
Employee/internal communications	69%	Marketing	35%
Reputation management	69%	Issues advertising	31%
Community relations	63%	Financial/investor relations	23%
Product/brand communications	60%		

Source: PR Week, February 26, 2001, pp. 1, 18–22.

Notice that the department *recommends* this action. It would have no direct authority to decide arbitrarily on an open house and to order various departments within the company to cooperate. If top management approves the proposal, the department may take responsibility for organizing the event. Top management, as line managers, has the authority to direct all departments to cooperate in the activity.

Although public relations departments can function only with the approval of top management, there are varying levels of influence that departments may exert. These levels will be discussed shortly.

Access to Management The power and influence of a public relations department usually result from access to top management, which uses advice and recommendations to formulate policy. That is why public relations, as well as other staff functions, is located high in the organizational chart and is called upon by top management to make reports and recommendations on issues affecting the entire company. In today's environment, public acceptance or nonacceptance of a proposed policy is an important factor in decision making—as important as costing and technological ability. This is why the former president of RJR Nabisco, F. Ross Johnson, told the *Wall Street Journal* in an interview that his senior public relations aide was "Numero Uno" and quipped, "He is the only one who has an unlimited budget and exceeds it every year."

Levels of Influence Management experts state that staff functions in an organization operate at various levels of influence and authority. On the lowest level, the staff function may be only *advisory:* Line management has no obligation to take recommendations or even request them.

When public relations is purely advisory, it is often not effective. A good example is the Alaska oil-spill crisis (see Chapter 8). Exxon generated a great deal of public, legislative, and media criticism because public relations was relegated to a low level and was, for all practical purposes, nonexistent.

Johnson & Johnson, on the other hand, gives its public relations staff function higher status. The Tylenol crisis, in which seven persons died after taking capsules containing cyanide, clearly showed that the company based much of its reaction and quick recall of the product on the advice of public relations staff. In this case, public relations was in a *compulsory-advisory* position.

Under the compulsory-advisory concept, organization policy requires that line managers (top management) at least listen to the appropriate staff experts before deciding on a strategy. Don Hellriegel and John Slocum, authors of the textbook *Management,* state: "Although such a procedure does not limit the manager's decision-making discretion, it ensures that the manager has made use of the specialized talents of the appropriate staff agency."

Another level of advisory relationship within an organization is called *concurring authority.* For instance, an operating division wishing to publish a brochure cannot do so unless the public relations department approves the copy and layout. If differences arise, the parties must agree before work can proceed. Many firms use this mode to prevent departments and divisions from disseminating materials not in conformity with company standards. In addition, the company must ascertain that its trademarks are used correctly to ensure continued protection (see Chapter 13).

Concurring authority, however, may also limit the freedom of the public relations department. Some companies have a policy that all employee magazine articles and external news releases must be reviewed by the legal staff before publication. The material cannot be disseminated until legal and public relations personnel have agreed upon what will be said. The situation is even more limiting on public relations when the legal department has *command authority* to change a news release with or without the consent of public relations. This is one reason that newspaper editors find some news releases so filled with "legalese" as to be almost unreadable.

Sources of Friction

Ideally, public relations is part of the managerial subsystem. It is, say professors James and Larissa Grunig at the University of Maryland, "the management of communication between an organization and its publics." However, other staff functions also are involved in the communication process with internal and external publics. And, almost invariably, friction occurs. The four areas of possible friction are legal, human resources, advertising, and marketing.

Legal The legal staff is concerned about the possible effect of any public statement on current or potential litigation. Consequently, lawyers often frustrate public relations personnel by taking the attitude that any public statement can potentially be used against the organization in a lawsuit. Conflicts over what to release and when often have a paralyzing effect on decision making, causing the organization to seem unresponsive to public concerns. This is particularly true in a crisis, when the public demands information immediately.

Human Resources The traditional personnel department has now evolved into the expanded role of "human resources," and there are often turf battles over who is responsible for employee communications. Human resources personnel believe they should control the flow of information. Public relations administrators counter that satisfactory external communications cannot be achieved unless effective employee

PR insights

Attributes for Job Success

Top management expects a number of qualities in a public relations person. Robert L. Woodrum, vice president of Korn/Ferry International, lists some of these attributes:

- *Solid communication skills.* A person should be able to articulate and get ideas across, both orally and in writing.
- *Analytical ability.* A person must be able to examine every problem and opportunity from a business perspective: identify the issue, determine the options and consequences, and provide a recommended course of action.
- *Results orientation.* A practitioner must set an objective and achieve it. Be realistic; don't make the mistake of overpromising and then not delivering. A high energy level is mandatory. Keep producing.
- *Ability to be a team player.* A person must recognize that teamwork is critical to the success of the company, particularly in such high-growth industries as telecommunications, where change is rapid. A "Lone Ranger" will be less effective and will lack the support of other executives, a formula for short tenure.
- *Personality.* An individual must be personable, confident, intelligent, energetic, and cooperative. The senior public relations executive must be trustworthy, maintain confidentiality, and possess an extraordinary amount of common sense and perspective for setting priorities and managing crisis. The public relations executive should always be a calm, quiet voice of reason.

Source: Woodrum, Robert L. "How to Please the CEO and Keep Your Job." *Public Relations Strategist,* Fall 1995, pp. 7–12.

relations are conducted simultaneously. Layoffs, for example, affect not only employees but community and investor relations.

Advertising Advertising and public relations departments often collide because they compete for funds to communicate with external audiences. Philosophical differences also arise. Advertising's approach to communications is, "Will it increase sales?" Public relations asks, "Will it make friends?" These differing orientations frequently cause breakdowns in coordination of overall strategy.

Marketing Marketing, like advertising, tends to think only of customers or potential buyers as key publics. Public relations, on the other hand, defines "publics" in a broader way—any group that can have an impact on the operations of the organization. These publics include governmental agencies, environmental groups, neighborhood groups, and a host of other "publics" that marketing would not consider "customers."

The friction between marketing and public relations people reached a new height in the early 1990s when marketing departments began to advocate the concept of "integrated marketing communications."

Some public relations people thought this new trend would mean a loss of autonomy for them and that public relations would lose its counseling role to top management. Others were concerned that marketing-directed public relations would reduce professionals to the role of technicians working to support marketing objectives and functions. Historically, this work has been to handle product publicity.

Another argument was that public relations should do more than get people to buy goods and services. Marketing, by definition, is persuasive in intent. On the other hand, IABC's excellence study concludes that the ideal of public relations is symmetrical communication—the building of mutual understanding and communication between the organization and its various publics.

All this has led James Grunig, editor of the IABC study, to conclude, "We believe, then, that public relations must emerge as a discipline distinct from marketing and that it must be practiced separately from marketing in the organization." Logic dictates, however, that an organization needs a coordinated and integrated approach to communications strategy. Indeed, the Conference Board also found in its survey that CEOs increasingly want "business-related results," and all departments need to align their activities with their organization's overall strategic goals.

The following suggestions may help achieve this goal:

- Representatives of departments should serve together on key committees to exchange information on how various programs can complement each other to achieve overall organizational objectives.
- Heads of departments should be equals in job title. In this way, the autonomy of one department is not subverted by another.
- All department heads should report to the same superior, so that all viewpoints can be considered before an appropriate strategy is formulated.
- Informal, regular contacts with representatives of other departments help dispel mind-sets and create understanding and respect for each other's viewpoint.
- Written policies should be established to spell out the responsibilities of each department. Such policies are helpful in settling disputes over which department has authority to communicate with employees or alter a news release.

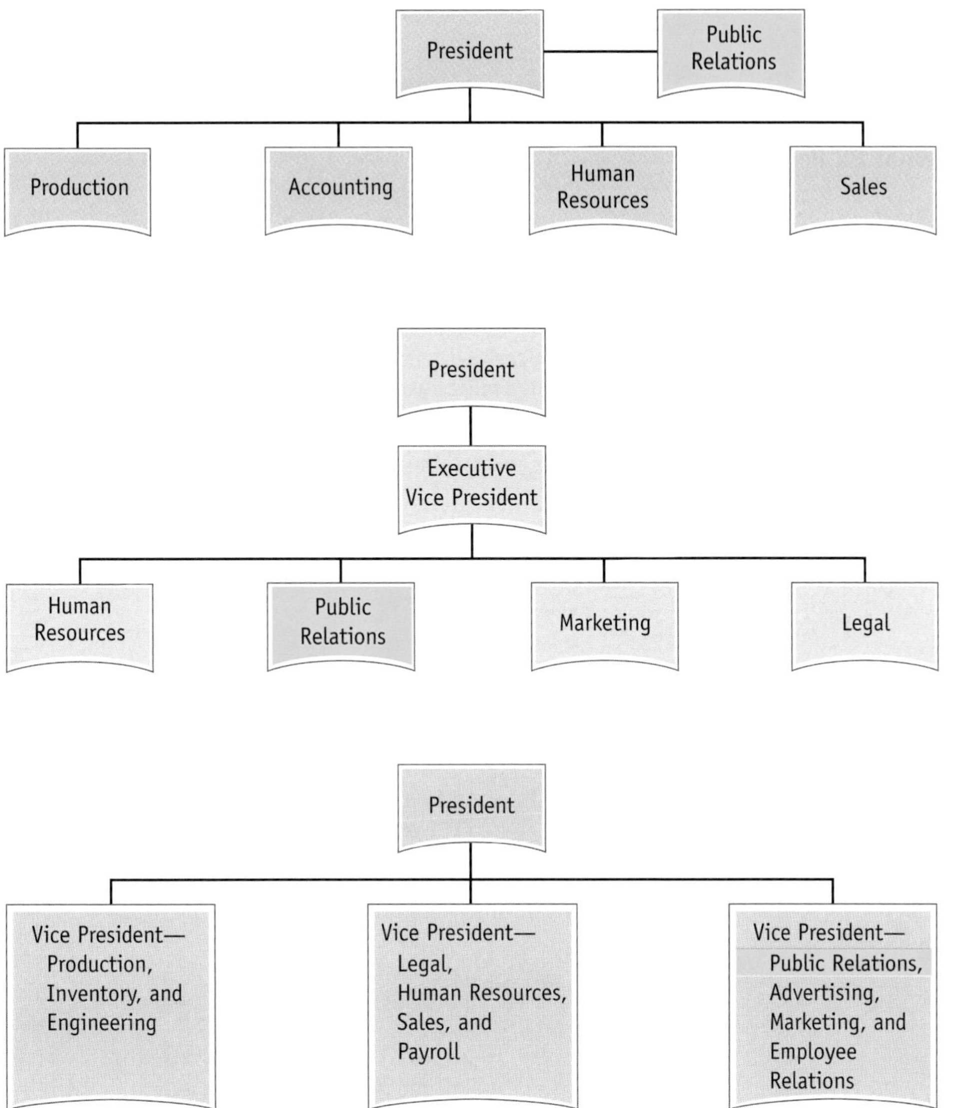

FIGURE 5.2

This chart depicts three examples of corporate management organization, showing the important position of public relations.

Some organizational charts for public relations and other departments are shown in Figure 5.2.

The Trend toward Outsourcing

Although one survey of Fortune 500 companies shows that 47 percent increased their public relations staffs between 1995 and 2000, there is also evidence that organizations are increasingly "outsourcing" their communication activities to public relations firms and outside contractors. Indeed, a survey by Bisbee & Co. and Leone Marketing Research found that 73 percent of respondents who work within corporate public relations departments said their organizations currently outsource activities.

PR insights

What PR People Do

A survey of 3500 public relations professionals indicates that they are spending an increasing amount of time on strategic planning. According to *PR Week,* "The strategic planning focus is there no matter where PR people work. The study found that 78 percent of those who work for agencies, 60 percent of those who work for corporations and 46 percent of those who work for nonprofits spend time on strategic planning."

The Gary Siegel Organization, which conducted the survey on behalf of PRSA's Universal Accreditation Board (UAB), asked professionals how much time they spent on various functions. The results:

Function	*Spend a Great Deal of Time*	*Spend Some Time*	*Total*
Strategic planning	58%	31%	89%
PR program planning	57%	31%	88%
Project management	60%	26%	86%
Media relations	50%	28%	78%
Account/client management	47%	20%	67%
Special events/conferences	32%	34%	66%
Internal relations	34%	31%	65%
Community relations	29%	31%	60%
Issues management	23%	32%	55%
Relations with special audiences	20%	34%	54%
Crisis management	18%	27%	45%

Source: PR Week, November 6, 2000, p. 9

One indication of this is how the budgets of corporate public relations departments are divided. An annual survey by Thomas Harris & Company and Impulse Research in 2000, for example, found that 41 percent of all public relations work is now assigned to public relations firms. The greatest increases in assigned work were in online communications (11 percent), public affairs (7 percent), media training (5 percent), and reputation management (3 percent).

Another national survey by *PR Week* in 2001 found that companies spent an average of 43.3 percent of their public relations budget on the services of external public relations firms. In high-technology firms, the percentage was even larger—a whopping 66.3 percent of the corporate budget. In contrast, nonprofits allocated an average of 38.6 percent of their budgets for external public relations services.

The opportunity to bring resources to the company that are not available internally was the most popular motivation for outsourcing (70 percent), followed by the need to supplement staff during peak work periods (67 percent). The most frequently outsourced activity, according to the Bisbee study, was in the descending order of (1) writing and communications, (2) media relations, (3) publicity, (4) strategy and planning, and (5) event planning.

Public relations firms with global reach offer prospective clients a variety of services. This advertisement for a major public relations firm appeared in an issue of *PRWeek,* a major trade publication.

Public relations firms are often commissioned to organize press tours, news conferences, and photo opportunities for celebrities. Here, Britney Spears smiles during a "photo op" in Toronto after a news conference to promote a new album. (AP Photo/Canadian Press, Frank Gunn.)

The trend toward outsourcing, say some experts, follows what has occurred in advertising. Today, about 90 percent of corporate and institutional advertising is handled by advertising agencies instead of in-house departments. As a new century dawns, it appears that the major beneficiary of this trend will be public relations firms, which are discussed next.

Public Relations Firms

Public relations firms are found in every industrialized nation and most of the developing world.

In size, public relations firms range from one- or two-person operations to global giants such as Burson-Marsteller, which employs almost 2000 professionals in 35 nations (*www.bm.com*). The scope of services provided to clients varies, but there are common denominators. Big or small, each firm gives counsel and performs technical services required to carry out an agreed-upon program. The firm may operate as an adjunct to an organization's public relations department or, if no department exists,

TABLE 5.1

The Top 20 Global Public Relations Firms

Rank	*Name*	*Worldwide Revenues (in millions)*	*Employees*
1	Weber-Shandwick	$426.57	2832
2	Fleishman-Hillard	$345.09	2288
3	Hill & Knowlton	$325.11	1117
4	Incepta (Citigate)	$266.01	2236
5	Burson-Marsteller	$259.11	1613
6	Edelman Worldwide	$223.70	1973
7	Ketchum	$185.22	1066
8	Porter Novelli	$179.29	1553
9	GCI Group/APCO	$151.08	1282
10	Ogilvy PR	$145.94	1110
11	Euro RSCG	$124.15	942
12	MS&L	$116.02	885
13	Golin/Harris	$113.24	655
14	Cordiant	$90.65	633
15	Ruder Finn Group	$80.34	543
16	Brodeur	$70.00	671
17	Waggener Edstrom	$59.89	469
18	Cohn & Wolfe	$57.79	379
19	Rowland	$42.66	125
20	Text 100	$33.67	405

Source: Council of Public Relations Firms. *PR Week* Agency Rankings 2002. May 13, 2002, p. 11.

conduct the entire effort. Examples of work done by firms in other nations are given in Chapter 16.

The United States, because of its large population and economic base, has the world's most public relations firms (about 9000, according to one count) and generates the most fee income. In fact, the international committee of the Public Relations Consultancies Association reported in a worldwide study that the fee income of U.S. firms "plainly dwarfs those in all other regions."

A survey by the Council of Public Relations Firms in 2000, for example, found that U.S. industry revenues grew 33% over 1999 to $3 billion. Worldwide revenues were $4.6 billion. About 50 percent of the U.S. revenues were generated by the ten largest firms (see Table 5.1). The major sectors of growth in 2000, according to the survey, were technology, 46 percent; financial products and services, 37 percent; industry, 36 percent; government and nonprofit, 36 percent; health care, 30 percent; and consumer and retail, 22 percent. Fueling all this growth, as already mentioned, was the increased outsourcing of work by corporations.

American public relations firms have proliferated in proportion to the growth of the global economy. As American companies expanded after World War II into booming domestic and worldwide markets, many corporations felt a need for public relations firms that could provide them with professional expertise in communications.

Also stimulating the growth of public relations firms were increased urbanization, expansion of government bureaucracy and regulation, more sophisticated mass media systems, the rise of consumerism, international trade, and the demand for more information. Professionals were needed to maintain lines of communication in an increasingly complicated world and to provide much of the material to be distributed. Executives of public relations firms predict future growth as more countries adopt free market economies and more international outlets such as CNN are established. In addition, the skyrocketing use of the Internet has fueled the global reach of public relations firms. Also expected is an increasing demand for public relations in the high-technology, health care, financial, sports, and entertainment fields.

Services They Provide

Counseling firms today offer services far more extensive than those provided by the nation's first firm, the Publicity Bureau, founded in 1900 in Boston. Today, public relations firms provide a variety of services:

- *Marketing communications.* This involves promotion of products and services through such tools as news releases, feature stories, special events, brochures, and media tours.
- *Executive speech training.* Top executives are coached on public affairs activities, including personal appearances.
- *Research and evaluation.* Scientific surveys are conducted to measure public attitudes and perceptions.
- *Crisis communication.* Management is counseled on what to say and do in an emergency such as an oil spill or recall of an unsafe product.
- *Media analysis.* Appropriate media are examined for targeting specific messages to key audiences.

global PR

Firms Win Golden World Awards

Public relations firms around the world handle a variety of assignments. Here are some that have received a Golden World award from the International Public Relations Association (IPRA):

- *Alpha Beta Ltd. (Denmark).* Conducted a program to establish Canal Digital as the leading independent provider of pay TV in the country and to pass a law (enacted) to ban piracy of television programs.
- *Edelman Public Relations Worldwide (Germany).* Conducted a public information campaign to make German citizens more aware of Parkinson's disease and the need for early diagnosis and treatment to improve a patient's quality of life.
- *Vulindlela Marketing & Public Relations (South Africa).* Conducted a campaign on behalf of the Inner West City Council in Durban to educate black homeowners on the value of paying their utility bills and tax assessments in order to finance public services in their neighborhoods.
- *Green Active PR (Turkey).* Conducted a campaign on behalf of Unilever, the market leader in bath and kitchen cleaners, to increase brand awareness in 26 smaller Turkish cities through a program that included the cleaning of local landmarks and monuments.
- *Media In (Slovakia).* Helped Slovnaft, the nation's largest petrochemical complex, position itself as ecologically concerned through grants to fund local "green" projects.
- *Japan Counselors, Inc. (Japan).* Organized a national information campaign for the Japan Allergy Association to give citizens a better understanding of the actual number of sufferers and to inform doctors on the latest treatments and studies.

- *Community relations.* Management is counseled on ways to achieve official and public support for such projects as building or expanding a factory.
- *Events management.* News conferences, anniversary celebrations, rallies, symposiums, and national conferences are planned and conducted.
- *Public affairs.* Materials and testimony are prepared for government hearings and regulatory bodies, and background briefings are prepared.
- *Branding and corporate reputation.* Advice is given on programs that establish a company brand and its reputation for quality.
- *Financial relations.* Management is counseled on ways to avoid takeover by another firm and effectively communicate with stockholders, security analysts, and institutional investors.

Increasingly, public relations firms emphasize the counseling aspect of their services. This transition to counseling is best expressed by Harold Burson, chairman of Burson-Marsteller, who once told an audience, "In the beginning, top management used to say to us, 'Here's the message, deliver it.' Then it became, 'What should we say?' Now, in smart organizations, it's 'What should we do?'"

Because of the counseling function, we use the term "public relations firm" rather than "public relations agency" throughout the book. Advertising firms, in contrast, are properly called agencies because they serve as agents, buying time or space on behalf of a client.

Global Reach

Public relations firms, large and small, usually are found in major metropolitan areas. On an international level, the firms and their offices or affiliates are situated in most major world cities. Edelman Public Relations Worldwide, for example, has 35 offices in the United States, Canada, Mexico, Europe, and Asia-Pacific and more than 50 affiliates worldwide. Other large U.S. firms have firmly planted their flags from Moscow to Bangkok.

The importance in international operations is reflected in the fact that most of the top 20 firms (Table 5.1) have generated substantial revenues from international operations. Hill & Knowlton and Burson-Marsteller, for example, generate about 40 percent of their fee income from international accounts. Weber Shandwick and Porter Novelli receive about 35 percent of their income from international clients. Incepta/Citigate, which is one of the few firms on the top 20 based outside the United States (in London), generates almost 70 percent of its income from international operations.

International work isn't only for the large firms. Small and medium-sized firms around the world have formed working partnerships with each other. The largest group is WORLDCOM, with 100 firms on six continents. And Pinnacle Worldwide is a network of 10 independent firms in 33 nations. Other groups include Public Relations Organization International (PROI) and IPREX. These four groups recently formed a Council of PR Networks, marketing the collective expertise of the 240 firms as superior to the "one voice" campaigns that are the hallmarks of large international public relations firms such as Burson-Marsteller.

Essentially, firms in an affiliation cooperate with each other to service clients with international needs. A firm in India may call its affiliate in Los Angeles to handle the details of a news conference for a visiting trade delegation from India. This approach gives small firms with limited resources an opportunity to offer the same kinds of services as the largest firms.

The large international firms, as well as various affiliated groups, have been well established in Western Europe for several years. A new area of expansion is the major cities of Eastern Europe and the former Soviet Union. Another area of new business is Latin America, as free market economies become the rule rather than the exception. Asia, particularly China and India with their large populations, also present new opportunities. To date, however, international firms have not significantly expanded their operations on the African continent. (See Chapter 16.)

Public Relations and Advertising Mergers

Until the 1970s, the largest public relations firms were independently owned by their principal officers or, in some cases, by employee stockholders. A significant change began in 1973 when Carl Byoir & Associates, then the third largest U.S. public relations firm, was purchased by the advertising firm of Foote, Cone & Belding.

Today, both public relations firms and advertising agencies have become part of large, diversified holding companies with global reach. Foote, Cone & Belding, for example, is now FCB Worldwide and is just one of several major advertising agencies now owned by Interpublic Group (IPG). The holding company also owns McCann-Erickson, another major advertising agency, and several major public relations firms. They include Weber Shandwick Worldwide, Golin/Harris International, and BSMG. All three are among the world's top 20 public relations firms in terms of fee income. In fact, after the rankings were released (see Table 5.1), Weber Shandwick Worldwide claimed it became the world's largest public relations firm when BSMG was folded into it in mid-2001. The combined fee revenues of both firms was about $525 million.

IPG, despite its total revenues of $5.63 billion in 2000, is only the third largest holding company. The largest one is Omnicom with revenues in 2000 of $6.1 billion. It owns the major advertising agencies of BBDO Worldwide, DDB Worldwide, and TBWA Worldwide. It also owns seven major public relations firms, four of which are among the top 20 in global fees. They are Porter Novelli, Fleishman-Hillard, Ketchum, and Brodeur Worldwide.

WPP, which is London-based, is the second largest holding company with total revenues of $5.66 billion in 2000. It owns three major advertising agencies: J. Walter Thompson, Ogilvy & Mather, and Y&R Advertising. It also owns six major public relations firms, four of which are in the top 20 in terms of global revenues. They are Hill & Knowlton, Ogilvy, Burson-Marsteller, and Cohn & Wolfe.

In sum, about 75 percent of the top 20 public relations firms listed in Table 5.1 are owned by multimedia conglomerates. Only four firms remain independently owned. They are Edelman Worldwide, Ruder Finn, Waggener Edstrom, and Text 100 (London-based).

There are several reasons for the acquisition of public relations firms by large advertising conglomerates. One is the natural evolutionary step of integrating various communication disciplines into "total communication networks." Supporters say no single-function agency is equipped with the personnel and resources to handle complex, often global, marketing functions efficiently for a client. In other words, the synergy between advertising and public relations under one corporate banner can more efficiently deliver a consistent message in a multifaceted campaign. In addition, joint public relations and advertising endeavors can increase the pool of potential new clients, generate more referrals, and expand the number of geographical locations.

A second reason is pure business. Advertising firms and their holding companies find public relations firms an attractive investment. According to *PR Week*, revenues from advertising clients have remained somewhat static over the past five years,

focus on ethics

Should We Represent This Client?

Public relations firms often work for a variety of clients, and the question is often raised whether any client who is willing to pay should be entitled to service.

Should a public relations firm, for example, work for a government that tramples human rights? What about a mining company that claims that it has discovered the world's richest gold deposit but can't provide much verifiable evidence except the assurances of the company's president? What about working for the tobacco industry?

Do public relations firms have the obligation to do proper background checks on new clients before signing them onto their rosters? On what basis should a public relations firm accept or turn down a client?

focus on ethics

Codes of Ethics Recommended for Public Relations Firms

Public relations firms work for a number of clients, and it is necessary to establish some ethical guidelines regarding what a firm will or won't do for a client. Liese L. Hutchison, writing in *PR Tactics,* has some suggestions to help account executives deal with sticky predicaments.

- *The firm should establish a code of ethics.* Such a code provides a guideline for all employees.
- *Ask all employees, including interns, to sign the code.* This reinforces the firm's commitment to ethical behavior and lets employees know it is an important part of the firm's culture.
- *Insert the code into all client proposals.* This will let the client know that the public relations firm has a set of principles.
- *Display the code in the office.* The code should be posted in the firm's office for clients and employees to read.
- *Set up an ethics committee.* The firm should set up a committee to regularly discuss possible ethical dilemmas so there is an understanding of how the code of ethics is applied to real-world situations.
- *Set ethical guidelines.* The firm should set guidelines on what behavior and activities are appropriate.
- *Discuss ethical situations the firm has recently faced.* This will help educate employees and keep the ethics code fresh in their minds.
- *Senior management must set the standard.* They need to set the example and lead by example, not platitudes.

Source: PR Tactics, May 2000, p. 13.

whereas public relations firms have experienced double-digit growth in the same time frame. Increasingly, public relations firms are becoming the "glittering jewels" in holding company portfolios, according to *PR Week.*

Although earlier efforts to create "total communication networks" often met with limited success, there is now increasing evidence that public relations firms and advertising agencies owned by the same corporate entity are achieving some success in the marketplace. One area is joint pitches for business. Interpublic's McCann-Erickson and Shandwick, for example, got a multimillion-dollar advertising and public relations account from Aon Insurance Company after making a joint pitch. Considerable new business is also generated from units of the same company making referrals to each other.

One development that has fueled more cooperation between advertising agencies and public relations firms is a more sophisticated understanding of public relations by advertising agencies. Traditionally, advertising firms considered public relations as simply a nice add-on to an extensive advertising campaign. Consequently, many advertising firms applied the 90–10 rule: advertising received 90 percent of the budget and public relations got 10 percent. Today, Michael Petruzzello, CEO of Shandwick American, says, "Advertising and PR are developing a mutual respect of each other's disciplines."

Consequently, a better appreciation now exists of how each specialty—advertising, public relations, direct mail, sales promotion—can complement others in the marketing communications mix. And although there is a strong trend toward "integrated" campaigns, clients who use this method often contract with separate agencies to execute various parts of the plan. When Microsoft introduced Windows 95, it used separate public relations and advertising agencies. Public relations firms, even if owned by an advertising agency, continue to do business under their own names and maintain their own client lists.

Structure of a Counseling Firm

A small public relations firm may consist only of the owner (president) and an assistant (vice president), supported by a secretary. Larger firms have a more extended hierarchy.

The organization of Ketchum Public Relations/San Francisco is fairly typical. The president is based in the New York office of Ketchum Public Relations, so the executive vice president is the on-site director in San Francisco. A senior vice president is associate director of operations. Next in line are several vice presidents who primarily do account supervision or special projects.

An *account supervisor* is in charge of one major account or several smaller ones. An *account executive,* who reports to the supervisor, is in direct contact with the client and handles most of the day-to-day activity. At the bottom of the list is the *assistant account executive,* who does routine maintenance work compiling media lists, gathering information, and writing rough drafts of news releases.

Recent college graduates usually start as assistant account executives. Once they learn the firm's procedures and show ability, promotion to account executive may occur within 6 to 18 months. After two or three years, it is not uncommon for an account executive to become an account supervisor.

Executives at or above the vice-presidential level usually are heavily involved in selling their firm's services. In order to prosper, a firm must continually seek new business and sell additional services to current clients. Consequently, the upper management of the firm calls on prospective clients, prepares proposals, and makes new business presentations. In this very competitive field, a firm not adept at selling itself frequently fails.

Firms frequently organize account teams, especially to serve a client whose program is multifaceted. One member of the team, for example, may set up a nationwide media tour in which an organization representative is booked on television talk shows. Another may supervise all materials going to the print media, including news stories, feature articles, background kits, and artwork. A third may concentrate on the trade press or perhaps arrange special events.

Pros and Cons of Using a Public Relations Firm

Because public relations is a service industry, a firm's major asset is the quality of its people. Potential clients thinking about hiring a public relations firm usually base their decisions on that fact, according to a survey of Fortune 500 corporate vice presidents.

Thomas L. Harris, a consultant who conducted a survey of corporate communication directors, found that clients believe meeting deadlines and keeping promises are the most important criteria for evaluating firms. Other important considerations were, in descending order: (1) client services; (2) honest, accurate billing; (3) creativity; and (4) knowledge of the client's industry.

Advantages Public relations firms offer:

- *Objectivity.* The firm can analyze a client's needs or problems from a new perspective and offer fresh insights.
- *A variety of skills and expertise.* The firm has specialists, whether in speechwriting, trade magazine placement, or helping with proxy battles.
- *Extensive resources.* The firm has abundant media contacts and works regularly with numerous suppliers of products and services. It has research materials, including data information banks, and experience in similar fields.
- *Offices throughout the country.* A national public relations program requires coordination in major cities. Large firms have on-site staffs or affiliate firms in many cities and even around the world.
- *Special problem-solving.* A firm may have extensive experience and a solid reputation in desired areas. For example, Burson-Marsteller is well known for expertise in crisis communications, health and medical issues, and international coordination of special projects. Hill & Knowlton is known for expertise in public affairs, and Ketchum Public Relations is the expert in consumer marketing.
- *Credibility.* A successful public relations firm has a solid reputation for professional, ethical work. If represented by such a firm, a client is likely to get more attention among opinion leaders in mass media, government, and the financial community.

On the Minus Side Despite many successes, not everything always goes smoothly between a firm and its client. There are several drawbacks to using public relations firms:

- *Superficial grasp of a client's unique problems.* While objectivity is gained from an outsider's perspective, there is often a disadvantage in the public relations firm's not thoroughly understanding the client's business or needs.
- *Lack of full-time commitment.* A public relations firm has many clients to service. Therefore, no single client can monopolize its personnel and other resources.
- *Need for prolonged briefing period.* Some companies become frustrated because time and money are needed for a public relations firm to research the organization and make recommendations. Consequently, the actual start of a public relations program may take weeks or months.
- *Resentment by internal staff.* The public relations staff members of a client organization may resent the use of outside counsel because they think it implies that they lack the ability to do the job.
- *Need for strong direction by top management.* High-level executives must take the time to brief outside counsel on specific objectives sought.
- *Need for full information and confidence.* A client must be willing to share its information, including the skeletons in the closet, with outside counsel.
- *Costs.* Outside counsel is expensive. In many situations, routine public relations work can be handled at lower cost by internal staff.

Fees and Charges

A public relations firm charges for its services in several ways. The three most common methods, also used by law firms and management consultants, are:

1. *Basic hourly fee, plus out-of-pocket expenses.* The number of hours spent on a client's account is tabulated each month and billed to the client. Work by personnel in the counseling firm is billed at various hourly rates. Out-of-pocket expenses, such as cab fares, car rentals, airline tickets, and meals, are also billed to the client. In a typical $100,000 campaign, about 70 percent of the budget is spent on staff salaries.
2. *Retainer fee.* A basic monthly charge billed to the client covers ordinary administrative and overhead expenses for maintaining the account and being "on call." Many retainer fees also specify the number of hours the counseling firm will spend on the account each month. Additional work is billed at normal hourly rates. Out-of-pocket expenses are normally billed separately.
3. *Fixed project fee.* The public relations firm agrees to do a specific project, such as an annual report, a newsletter, or a special event, for a fixed fee. For example, a counseling firm may write and produce a quarterly newsletter for $30,000 annually. The fixed fee is the least popular among public relations firms because it is difficult to predict all work and expenses in advance. Many clients, however, like fixed fees for a specific project because it is easier to budget and there are no "surprises."

The primary basis for all three methods is to estimate the number of hours that a particular project will take to plan, execute, and evaluate. The first method—the basic hourly fee—is the most flexible and most widely used among large firms. It is preferred by public relations people because they are paid for the exact number of hours spent on a project and because it is the only sound way that a fee can be determined intelligently. The retainer fee and the fixed project fee are based on an estimate of how many hours it will take to counsel a client.

A number of variables are considered when a public relations firm estimates the cost of a program. These may include the size and duration, geographical locations involved, the number of personnel assigned to the project, and the type of client. A major variable, of course, is billing the use of the firm's personnel to a client at the proper hourly rate.

An account supervisor, for example, may earn $60,000 annually and receive benefits (health insurance, pension plan, and so on) that cost the firm an additional $13,000. Thus the annual cost of the employee to the firm totals $73,000. Using 1600 billable hours in a year (after deducting vacation time and holidays), the account executive makes $45.63 per hour.

The standard industry practice, however, is to bill clients at least three times a person's salary. This multiple allows the firm to pay for office space, equipment, insurance, supplies, and try to operate at a profit level of about 10 to 20 percent before taxes. Thus the billing rate of the account supervisor (3 × $45.63) rounds off at $137 per hour. The principals of a counseling firm, because of their much higher salaries, often command $175 to $500 per hour depending on the size and capabilities of the firm. On the other hand, an assistant account executive may be billed out at only $85 per hour.

The primary income of a public relations firm comes from the selling of staff time, but some additional income results from markups on photocopying, telephone, fax, and artwork the firm supervises. The standard markup in the trade is between 15 and 20 percent.

PR insights

A Job at a Corporation or a PR Firm?

Recent college graduates often ponder the pros and cons of joining a corporate department or going to work for a PR firm. The following summarizes some of the pluses and minuses:

PR Firm: Breadth of Experience	*Corporate PR: Depth of Experience*
Experience gained quickly; tip—find a mentor you can learn from.	Jobs more difficult to find without experience; duties more narrowly focused.
Variety. Usually work on several clients and projects at same time. Possibility of rapid advancement.	Sometimes little variety at entry level.
Fast-paced, exciting.	Growth sometimes limited unless you are willing to switch employers.
Seldom see the impact of your work for a client; removed from "action."	Can be slower paced.
Abilities get honed and polished. (This is where a mentor really helps.)	Heavy involvement with executive staff; see impact almost instantly. You are an important component in the "big picture."
Networking with other professionals leads to better job opportunities.	Strength in all areas expected. Not a lot of time for coaching by peers.
Learn other skills, such as how to do presentations and budgets and establish deadlines.	Sometimes so involved in your work, you don't have time for networking.
Intense daily pressure on billable hours, high productivity. Some firms are real "sweat-shops."	Same "client" all the time. Advantage: get to know organization really well. Disadvantage: can become boring.
Somewhat high employment turnover.	Less intense daily pressure; more emphasis on accomplishing longer-term results.
Budgets and resources can be limited.	Less turnover.
Salary traditionally low at entry level.	More resources usually available.
Insurance, medical benefits can be minimal.	Salaries tend to be higher.
Little opportunity for profit-sharing, stock options.	Benefits usually good, sometimes excellent.
High emphasis on tactical skills, production of materials.	More opportunities available.
	Can be more managerial and involved in strategic planning.

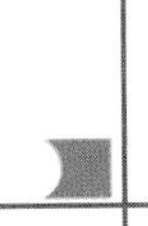

Summary

Public Relations Departments

Public relations departments work within companies and organizations. They can have different roles and names in different organizations, as well as various internal structures.

Public Relations Firms

Public relations firms come in all sizes and are found worldwide, providing a variety of services. In recent decades, many public relations firms have either merged with advertising agencies or become subsidiaries of diversified holding companies. Advantages of using outside firms include versatility and extensive resources, among other considerations; but they can also lack the full-time commitment of an in-house department, need a lot of direction, and are often more expensive.

Case Activity: What Would You Do?

You will graduate from college in several months and plan a career in public relations. After several interviews, you receive two job offers.

One is with a high-technology company that makes inkjet printers and scanners for the consumer market. The corporate communications department has about 20 professionals, and it is customary for beginners to start in employee publications or product publicity. Later, with more experience, you might be assigned to do marketing communications for a product group or work in a specialized area such as investor relations, governmental affairs, or even community relations.

The second job offer is from a local office of a large, national public relations firm. You would begin as an assistant account executive and work on several accounts, including a chain of fast-food restaurants and an insurance company. The jobs pay about the same, but the corporation offers better insurance and medical plans. Taking into consideration the pros and cons of working for public relations firms versus corporations, what job would best fit your abilities and preferences? Explain your reasons.

Questions for Review and Discussion

1. How have the role and function of public relations departments changed in recent years?
2. In what ways do the structure and culture of an organization affect the role and influence of the public relations department?
3. What kinds of knowledge does a manager of a public relations department need today?
4. Many departments are now called "corporate communications" instead of "public relations." Do you think the first term is more appropriate? Why or why not?
5. What is the difference between a line and staff function? To which function does public relations belong, and why?
6. Why is a compulsory-advisory role within an organization a good one for a public relations department to have?
7. What four areas of the organization cause the most potential for friction with public relations? Explain.
8. In your opinion, should public relations or human resources be responsible for employee communications?
9. Public relations people express a fear that they will lose influence and be relegated to purely technical functions if they are controlled by the marketing department. Do you think their fears are justified? Why or why not?
10. Name at least seven services that a public relations firm offers clients.
11. What are the three largest public relations firms in the world?
12. How important is international business to American public relations firms?
13. Why do large advertising agencies and holding companies find the acquisition of public relations firms so attractive?
14. What are the pros and cons of using a public relations firm?
15. What are the standard methods used by a public relations firm to charge for its services?

Suggested Readings

Barnett, Chris. "After the Honeymoon: The Rush of Global Agency Networks Whipping Out Their Checkbooks to Boost Agency Line-ups Shows No Sign of Letting Up." *PR Week,* November 13, 2000, pp. 16–17.

Bourne, James S. "From Retainers to Stock: The New World of PR Billing." *PR Week,* August 7, 2000, p. 20.

Bourne, James. "The Cost of PR." *PR Week,* December 18, 2000, pp. 20–27. A survey of corporations and expenditures for public relations.

Boyle Matthew. "Most Admired Companies Are Biggest PR Spenders." *PR Week,* June 21, 1999, p. 1.

Dozier, David M. *Manager's Guide to Excellence in Public Relations and Communication Management.* Mahwah, NJ: Lawrence Erlbaum Associates, 1995.

Grove, Aimee. "How to Choose the Right PR Agency." *PR Week,* July 31, 2000, pp. 20–29.

Kim, Yungwook. "Measuring the Economic Value of Public Relations." *Journal of Public Relations Research,* Vol. 13, No. 1 (2001), pp. 3–26.

Leyland, Adam. "PR Budgets Rise by 9%, In-house Spending Up." *PR Week,* February 26, 2001, p. 1, 18–22.

Leyland, Adam. "U.S. Firms Grew 32% in 2000; Fleishman Now World No. 1." *PR Week,* April 23, 2001, p. 1.

Miller, Karen S. *The Voice of Business: H&K and Post-War PR.* Chapel Hill: University of North Carolina Press, 1998.

Research

preview

The objective of this chapter is to demonstrate the necessity for research as a basic element in public relations programs and to give students an understanding of techniques and applications in informal and formal research.

Topics covered in the chapter include:

- The importance and use of research
- Informal research methods
- Use of online databases and the Internet
- Formal research: random sampling
- Questionnaire design
- Ways of reaching respondents

The Importance of Research

Effective public relations is a process, and the essential first step is research. Today, research is widely accepted by public relations professionals as an integral part of the planning, program development, and evaluation process.

Defining the Research Role

In basic terms, research is a form of listening. Professors Glen Broom and David Dozier of San Diego State University, in their book *Using Research in Public Relations,* say simply, "Research is the controlled, objective, and systematic gathering of information for the purpose of describing and understanding."

Before any public relations program can be undertaken, information must be gathered, data collected, and interpretation done. Only by performing this first step can an organization begin to make policy decisions and map out strategies for effective communication programs.

Broom and Dozier quote a number of public relations executives on the importance of research. Among them is Blair C. Jackson, senior vice president of Rogers & Cowan, Inc., in New York:

> The most compelling reason for using research is to make sure that your program is the best it can be—that what you are doing is as "right on" as it can be. You will be confident that you are addressing the right audience, that you are using the right messages, and that you are focusing on the right perceptions or attitudes. Evaluation research will tell you whether or not it works.

Various kinds of research can be used to accomplish an organization's objectives and meet its need for information. The choice really depends on the subject and situation. Time and budget are important considerations, as is the perceived importance of the situation. Consequently, many questions should be asked before formulating a research design, such as:

- What is the problem?
- What kind of information is needed?
- How will the results of the research be used?
- What specific public (or publics) should be researched?
- Should the organization do the research or hire an outside consultant?
- How will the research data be analyzed, reported, or applied?
- How soon are the results needed?
- How much will the research cost?

These questions will help the public relations person determine the extent and nature of the research needed. Only informal research, for example, may be required because of its lower cost and the need for immediate information. Or a random scientific survey may be selected, despite its cost and time, because a political candidate wants to know exactly how he or she stands in the polls. The pros and cons of each method will be discussed later in the chapter.

Using Research

Research is a multipronged tool that is involved in virtually every phase of a communications program. In general, studies show that public relations departments spend about 3 to 5 percent of their budget on research. Some experts contend that it should be 10 percent. These are ways that public relations professionals use research.

Achieve Credibility with Management Executives want facts, not guesses and hunches. The inclusion of public relations personnel in an organization's policy and decision making, according to the findings of IABC's exhaustive research on excellence in communication management, is strongly correlated with their ability to do research and relate their findings to the organization's objectives.

Define Audiences and Segment Publics Detailed information about the demographics, lifestyles, characteristics, and consumption patterns of audiences helps to assure that messages reach the proper audiences. A successful children's immunization information campaign in California was based on State Health Department statistics that showed first, that past immunization programs had not reached rural children and second, that Hispanic and Vietnamese children were not being immunized in the same proportion as other ethnic groups.

Formulate Strategy Much money can be spent pursuing the wrong strategies. Officials of the New Hampshire paper industry, given the bad press about logging and waterway pollution, thought a campaign was needed to tell the public what it was doing to reduce pollution. An opinion survey of 800 state residents by a public relations firm, however, indicated that the public was already generally satisfied with the industry's efforts. Consequently, the new strategy focused on reinforcing positive themes such as worker safety, employment, and environmental responsibility.

Test Messages Research is often used to determine what particular message is most salient with the target audience. A campaign to encourage carpooling, according to one focus group study, found that the message most significant with commuters was saving time and money, not air quality or environmental concern. Consequently, the campaign emphasized how many minutes could be cut from an average commute by using car pool lanes and the annual savings in gasoline, insurance, and car maintenance.

Help Management Keep in Touch In a mass society, top management increasingly is isolated from the concerns of employees, customers, and other important publics. Research helps bridge the gap by periodically surveying key publics about problems and concerns. This feedback is a "reality check" for top executives and often leads to better policies and communication strategies.

Prevent Crises An estimated 90 percent of organizational crises are caused by internal operational problems rather than unexpected natural disasters. Research can often uncover trouble spots and public concerns before they become page-one news. (See the section on issues management in the next chapter.) Analyzing complaints on a toll-free number or monitoring chat rooms on the Internet often can tip off an organization that it should act before the problem attracts media attention.

PR insights

Rules for Publicizing Surveys and Polls

The Council of American Survey Research Organizations (CASRO), a nonprofit national trade organization for more than 150 survey research companies, says survey findings released to the public should contain the following information:

- Sponsorship of the study
- Name of the research company conducting the study
- Description of the study's objectives
- Description of the sample, including the size and the population to which the results are intended to generalize
- Dates of data collection
- Exact wording of the questions asked
- Any information the researcher believes is relevant to help the public make a fair assessment of the results

In addition, CASRO recommends that other information should be readily available if anyone asks. This includes (1) the type of survey conducted, (2) methods for selecting the survey sample, (3) how respondents were screened, and (4) the procedure for data coding and analysis.

■ **Monitor the Competition** Savvy organizations keep track of what the competition is doing. This is done through surveys asking consumers to comment on competing products, content analysis of the competition's media coverage, and reviews of industry reports in trade journals. Such research often helps an organization shape its marketing and communications strategy to counter a competitor's strengths and capitalize on any weaknesses.

■ **Sway Public Opinion** Facts and figures, compiled from a variety of primary and secondary sources, can change public opinion. Shortly before an election in Ohio, 90 percent of the voters supported a state ballot measure that would require cancer warnings on thousands of products from plywood to peanut butter. A coalition called Ohioans for Responsible Health Information, opposing the bill, commissioned universities and other credible outside sources to research the economic impact of such legislation on consumers and major industries. The research, used as the basis of the grassroots campaign, caused the defeat of the ballot measure with 78 percent of the voters voting "no."

■ **Generate Publicity** Polls and surveys can generate publicity for an organization. Indeed, many surveys seem to be primarily designed with publicity in mind. Simmons Mattress once polled people to find out if they slept in the nude. And Kiwi Brands, a shoe polish company, obtained extensive media coverage about a survey it commissioned that showed a high correlation between ambition and shiny shoes. The study found that 97 percent of self-described "ambitious" young men believe polished shoes are important.

■ **Measure Success** The bottom line of any public relations program is whether the time and money spent accomplished the stated objective. As one of its many programs to boost brand awareness, Miller Genuine Draft sponsored a "reunion ride" on Harley Davidson Corporation's 90th anniversary. Ketchum Public Relations, Chicago, generated extensive media publicity about the "ride" and Miller's sponsorship that was

98 percent positive. Perhaps more importantly, sales increased in all but two of the cities included in the event. Evaluation, the last step of the public relations process, is discussed in Chapter 9. The next sections will discuss ways of doing research.

Research Techniques

When the word *research* is used, people tend to think only of scientific surveys and complex statistical tabulations. In public relations, however, research techniques also are used to gather data and information.

In fact, a survey of practitioners by Walter K. Lindenmann, senior vice president and director of research for Ketchum Public Relations, found that three-fourths of the respondents described their research techniques as casual and informal, rather than scientific and precise. The technique cited most often was literature searches and database information retrieval.

This technique is called *secondary research* because existing information in books, magazine articles, electronic databases, and so on is used. This contrasts with *primary research* in which "new" and "original" information is generated through a research design that is specific and directed to answer a specific need. Some examples are in-depth interviews, focus groups, surveys, and polls.

Another way of categorizing types of research is by using the terms *qualitative* and *quantitative.* Lindenmann contrasts the basic differences between the two in the table in Table 6.1.

The following sections describe briefly the most common research techniques.

TABLE 6.1

Differences Between Qualitative and Quantitative Research

QUALITATIVE	*QUANTITATIVE*
"Soft" data	"Hard" data
Usually open-ended free response, unstructured	Usually closed-ended, forced choice, highly structured
"Exploratory," probing, fishing-expedition type of research	"Descriptive" or "explanatory" type of research
Usually "valid," but not reliable	Usually "valid" and reliable
Rarely "projectable" to larger audiences	Usually very "projectable" to larger audiences
Generally uses nonrandom samples	Generally uses random samples
Examples	*Examples*
Focus groups	Telephone polls
One-on-one, depth interviews	Mail surveys
Observation, participation, role-playing studies	Mall intercept studies
Convenience polling	Face-to-face interview studies
	Shared cost or omnibus studies
	Panel studies

Organizational Materials

Robert Kendall, in his book *Public Relations Campaign Strategies,* calls organizational materials *archival* research. The material may include the organization's policy statements, speeches by key executives, past issues of employee newsletters and magazines, reports on past public relations and marketing efforts, and news clippings. Marketing statistics, in particular, often provide the baseline data for public relations firms that are hired to launch a new product or boost awareness and sales for an existing product or service.

Kendall observes, "archives provide the resources for background research, which is the essential first step in most other research techniques." Archival research also is a major component in most audits intended to determine how the organization communicates to its internal and external publics. (See Chapter 9 for more information on audits.)

Library Methods

Reference books, academic journals, and trade publications are found in every library. In many cases, these materials are on CD-ROMs. Two such services are *Proquest,* which indexes more than 300 business journals, and *INFOTRAC,* which indexes 960 periodicals, journals, and major newspapers.

Some common reference sources for public relations professionals are the *Statistical Abstract of the United States,* which summarizes census information; the *Gallup Poll* and the *Gallup Index,* which give an index of public opinion on a variety of issues; *American Demographics,* which reports on population shifts and lifestyle trends; and *Simmons' Media and Markets,* an extensive annual survey of households in terms of product usage by brand and exposure to various media.

Online Resources

Although the library offers numerous sources of information, the information revolution has made it possible for working professionals to do much of this research in their offices through online databases.

Literature searches, the most often used form of informal research in public relations, can be done by using a computer and a modem to extract information from an estimated 1500 electronic databases that store an enormous amount of current and historical information.

Public relations departments and firms use online databases in a number of ways:

- Researching facts and figures to support a proposed project or campaign that requires top management approval
- Keeping up-to-date with news about clients and their competitors
- Tracking the media campaigns of an organization and the press announcements of its competitors
- Finding a special quotation or impressive statistic for a speech or report
- Tracking the press and business reaction to an organization's latest actions
- Finding an expert for advice on an issue or a possible strategy
- Keeping top management apprised of current business trends and issues
- Learning the demographics and attitudes of target publics

global PR

Database Research Can Track Media Coverage

What sports events generate the most news coverage? The use of search engines to access electronic databases that store thousands of print and broadcast stories can answer such a question.

Delahaye Medialink, a measurement and evaluation firm, used the names of several major sporting events around the world as key words and came up with the following number of news stories:

The British Open	5237
Women's World Cup soccer	4635
The French Open	3598
NBA draft	3218
Stanley Cup finals	2996
WNBA All-Star Game	1474
Tour de France	1296
NBA Championships	720

Online databases are available on a subscription basis and usually charge by the minute in the same way that a telephone company charges for long-distance calls.

Here are some of the online databases commonly used in public relations:

- *Burrelle's Broadcast Database.* This contains the full-text transcripts of radio and television programs within 24 hours after they are transmitted. Sources include ABC, NBC, CBS, CNN, National Public Radio, and selected syndicated programs.
- *Dialog.* This Knight-Ridder service provides more than 45 databases with 2500 magazines, journals, and newsletters.
- *Dow Jones News/Retrieval.* This massive business library, with more than 45 million documents drawn from nearly 3000 key business and financial publications, includes the *Wall Street Journal* and the *New York Times.*
- *Lexis/Nexis.* Including 8 million full-text articles from more than 125 magazines, newspapers, and news services, this online database contains the full text of the *New York Times* and the *Washington Post.* Abstracts also are available from leading international publications.

Online Networks

The use of online networks has skyrocketed in recent years. They not only have many of the same services that commercial online databases provide, but they enable users to send e-mail, participate in chat groups on specific subjects, post notes on computer bulletin boards, and fully access millions of documents on the Internet, including the

World Wide Web containing thousands of home pages for various individuals and organizations.

The largest of the online networks is America Online, with about 31 million subscribers and about 40 percent of the market. The next largest service is the Microsoft Network (MSN) with about 7 million subscribers.

The Internet and World Wide Web

The Internet provides a powerful research tool for the public relations practitioner. Any number of corporations, nonprofits, trade groups, special interest groups, foundations, universities, think tanks, and government agencies post reams of data on the Internet, usually in the form of home pages on the World Wide Web.

Online search engines are the essential key to finding information about virtually any subject on the Internet and the World Wide Web. With literally millions of possible Web sites, search engines make it possible for the researcher simply to type in a keyword or two, click "Go," and receive in a few seconds all the links that the search engine has found relating to the topic.

Jupiter Media Metrix and Netratings are companies that survey the Web's top domains. One of the more popular search engines is Yahoo, which in one month alone had 36.2 million visitors. Other popular engines are Google, Go.com, MSN Search, AOL Search, and Ask Jeeves. Specialized search engines can find audio and video content or content of topical interest, such as sports or business news. Reviews and directories of search engines are available at www.searchenginewatch.com. Public relations professionals should visit such sites from time to time to keep current on search capabilities as well as changes in policy such as payment for high placement in search results.

PR insights

Surfing the Internet

Public relations requires research and fact-finding. Here's a sample of sites on the Internet helpful to public relations professionals and how to access them:

- *Statistical Abstract of the US*
  http://www.census.gov/stat_abstract
- Bureau of Labor Statistics
  http://stats.bis.gov/blshome.html
- Environmental News Network
  http://www.enn/com/
- Public Relations firms (list of home pages)
  http://www.yahoo.com/Business.
  Corporations/Corpor
- International Association of Business Communicators (IABC)
  http://www.iabc.com
- Public Relations Society of America (PRSA)
  http://www.prsa.org
- Business Wire (hyperlinked to corporate home pages)
  http://www.hnt.com/bizwire
- Electronic Newsstand (magazines and newspapers)
  http://enews.com

PRFORUM, a news group dedicated to communications, is a place where researchers can request information; people who know something about the subject then respond by sending the researcher an e-mail message. One public relations professional, for example, asked for information on how to develop a communication strategy for a client. Within a day, several replies offered valuable tips, including (1) linking the communication strategy to the organization's goals, (2) segmenting publics with particular techniques, and (3) learning about what the audience wants.

An extensive discussion of the Internet's development and operation appears in Chapter 12.

Content Analysis

This research method can be relatively informal or quite scientific in terms of random sampling and establishing specific subject categories. It is often applied to news stories about an organization. At a basic level, a researcher can assemble news clips in a scrapbook and count the number of column inches.

In general, Robert Kendall says content analysis involves:

> . . . systematic analysis of any of several aspects of what a communication contains, from key words or concept references, such as company name or product; to topics, such as issues confronting the organization; to reading ease of company publications; or to all elements of a company video production.

A good example of content analysis is the way a company evaluated press coverage of its publicity campaign to celebrate its 100th anniversary. According to Lindenmann: "A low-budget content analysis was carried out on 427 newspaper, magazine, radio, and television placements referring both to the client and its product. The research found that the client's principal themes and copy points were referred to in most of the media coverage the company had received."

Another use of content analysis is to determine if a need exists for additional public relations efforts. Faneuil Hall Marketplace in Boston stepped up its public relations activities after it was found that the number of travel articles about it had decreased. An anniversary celebration of the Marketplace helped generate increased coverage.

Content analysis can be applied also to letters and phone calls. They provide good feedback about problems with the organization's policies and services. A pattern of letters and phone calls pointing out a problem is evidence that something should be done.

Interviewing

As in content analysis, there are several levels of interviewing. Almost everyone, on a daily basis, talks to colleagues and calls other organizations to gather information. Public relations personnel, faced with solving a particular problem, often "interview" other public relations professionals for ideas and suggestions.

If research is needed on public opinion and attitudes, many public relations firms conduct short interviews with people in a shopping mall or at a meeting. This kind of research is called *intercept* interviews, because people literally are intercepted in public places and asked their opinion.

The intercept interview is not scientific in terms of sampling method, but it does give an organization a sense of current thinking or exposure to certain key messages. A health group wanted to find out if the public was actually receiving its message and

Surveys of public opinion, often taken by researchers on the street or in shopping malls, help public relations practitioners target audiences they wish to reach and to shape their messages.

retaining crucial aspects of the message. To gather such information, shopping center or mall intercept interviews were conducted with 300 adults at six malls. Both unaided and aided recall questions were asked to assess overall publicity impact.

In another example, intercept interviews helped a fast-food restaurant chain determine customer attitudes about a city law regarding the recycling of the packaging in retail food establishments. Interviewers intercepted patrons at ten different fast-food restaurants and got useful information about consumer perceptions and behavior patterns relating to the issue.

Intercept interviews last only two to five minutes. At other times, the best approach is to do in-depth interviews to get more comprehensive information. Major fund-raising projects by charitable groups, for example, often require in-depth interviewing of community and business opinion leaders. The success of any major fund drive seeking $500,000 or more depends on the support of key leaders and wealthy individuals.

This approach is called *purposive interviewing* because the interviewees are carefully selected for their expertise, influence, or leadership. The Greater Durham, North Carolina, Chamber of Commerce interviewed 50 "movers and shakers" to determine support for an extensive image-building and economic development program.

Focus Groups

A good alternative to individual interviewing is the focus group. The technique is widely used in advertising, marketing, and public relations to help identify attitudes and motivations of important publics. Another purpose of focus groups is to formulate or pretest message themes and communications strategies before launching a full campaign.

The Paging Services Council used six focus groups in three cities to plan a campaign that would help consumers understand that beepers were more than little black boxes worn only by doctors and drug dealers. The groups helped the council and its public relations firm (1) define target audiences, (2) test program messages, (3) explore consumer attitudes about paging, and (4) evaluate product positioning statements.

Focus groups usually consist of 8 to 12 people representing the characteristics of the target audience, such as employees, consumers, or community residents. The Paging Services Council used baby boomers and users of pagers.

A trained facilitator uses nondirective interviewing techniques that encourage group members to talk freely about a topic or give candid reactions to suggested message themes. The setting is usually a conference room and the discussion is informal. A focus group may last one or two hours, depending on interaction and subject matter.

A focus group, by definition, is an informal research procedure that develops qualitative information instead of hard data. Results cannot be summarized by percentages or even projected onto an entire population. Nevertheless, focus groups are useful in identifying the range of attitudes and opinions in the participants. Such insights can help an organization structure its messages or, on another level, formulate hypotheses and questions in a quantitative research survey.

Copy Testing

All too often, organizations fail to communicate effectively because they produce and distribute materials that the target audience can't understand. In many cases, the material is written above the educational level of the audience.

Consequently, representatives of the target audience should be asked to read or view the material in draft form before it is mass-produced and distributed. This can be done on a one-to-one basis or in a small group setting.

A brochure about employee medical benefits or pension plans, for example, should be pretested with rank-and-file employees for readability and comprehension. Executives and lawyers who must approve the copy may understand the material, but a worker with a high school education might find it difficult to follow.

Another approach is to determine the degree of difficulty by applying a readability formula to the draft copy. Fog, Flesch, and similar techniques have formulas that relate the number of words and syllables per sentence or passage to reading level. Highly complex sentences and multisyllabic words require an audience with a college education.

Scientific Sampling

The research techniques discussed so far can provide good insights to public relations staff and help them formulate effective programs. Increasingly, however, there is a need to conduct polls and surveys using highly precise scientific sampling methods. Such sampling is based on two important factors—randomness and large numbers of respondents.

Random Sampling Procedures For best results, a random sample is taken. In statistics, this means that everyone in the targeted audience (as defined by the researcher) has an equal chance of being selected for the survey. This is also called a *probability* sample.

In contrast, a *nonprobability* survey is not random at all. Mall-intercept interviews, for example, are usually restricted only to shoppers in the mall at the time interviewers are working. A number of factors affect exactly who is interviewed, including the time of day and the location of the intercept interviews. Researchers doing interviews in the morning may have a disproportionate number of homemakers, while interviews after 5 P.M. may include more high school students and office workers. Also, if the researcher stands outside a record store or athletic shoe outlet, the age of those interviewed may be much younger than that of the general population.

A random sampling could be accomplished much better if researchers were present at all hours and conducted interviews throughout the mall. This would ensure a more representative sampling of mall shoppers, particularly if large numbers were interviewed.

Researchers must be careful, however, about projecting results to represent an entire city's population. Market surveys show that the demographic characteristics of shoppers vary from mall to mall. In other words, the selection of malls for random intercept interviewing often depends on how the researcher defines the target audience.

A survey sponsored by the International Franchise Association shows how selection of a sample can distort results. The organization touted the findings that "92 percent of franchise owners were successful." The survey, however, involved only franchises still operating and not those that had failed.

The most precise random sampling is usually done from lists that give the name of everyone in the targeted audience. This is relatively simple when doing a random survey of an organization's employees or members because the researcher can randomly select, for example, every 25th name on a list. Care must be taken to avoid patterns in the lists based on rank or employee category, for example. It is always advisable to

focus on ethics

Is This News Release Misleading?

Organizations often publicize the favorable findings of survey research, and the International Franchise Association (IFA) is no exception. It sent out a news release quoting a Gallup survey, with the headline, "Gallup Survey: 92 Percent Franchise Owners Successful." The text continued, "Whether you're serving burgers or bagels, tending to taxes or helping the bereaved select a casket, franchise owners consider themselves successful . . . ."

The news release didn't include the fact that the survey involved only those still operating and not those who failed. It also didn't specify how the sample was derived and whether bagel or even casket franchise owners were sampled. The IFA also grouped two categories of the survey results together—those who said "very successful"—and those who said "somewhat successful" to come up with the 92 percent.

If you were the public relations director for IFA, would you have allowed this news release to be distributed? Why or why not?

choose large intervals between selected names so that the researcher makes numerous passes through the list. Computerized lists may enable a random selection of a specified number of names.

Another common method to ensure representation is to draw a random sample that matches the characteristics of the audience. This is called *quota sampling.* Human resource departments usually have breakdowns of employees by job classification, and it is relatively easy to proportion a sample accordingly. If 42 percent of the employees work on the assembly line, for instance, then 42 percent of the sample should be assembly-line workers. A quota sample can be drawn on any number of demographic factors—age, sex, religion, race, income—depending on the purpose of the survey.

Random sampling becomes more difficult when there are no comprehensive lists. In that case, researchers surveying the general population often use telephone directories or customer lists to select respondents at random.

A travel company used a nationwide telephone survey of 1000 adult Americans to determine if the hurricane that devastated the island of Kauai affected vacation plans to visit the other Hawaiian islands not struck by the hurricane. On the basis of the results, the travel company restructured its advertising and public relations messages to emphasize that resorts on the other islands were open for business as usual.

The Size of the Sample In any probability study, there is always the question of sample size. National polling firms usually sample 1000 to 1500 persons and get a highly accurate idea of what the U.S. adult population is thinking. The average national poll samples 1500 people, and the margin of error is within three percentage points 95 percent of the time. In other words, 19 out of 20 times that the same questionnaire is administered, the results should be within the same three percentage points and reflect the whole population accurately.

In public relations the primary purpose of poll data is to get indications of attitudes and opinions, not to predict elections. Therefore, it is not usually necessary or practical to do a scientific sampling of 1500 people. A sample of 250 to 500 will give relatively accurate data—with a 5 or 6 percent variance—that will help determine general public attitudes and opinions. A sample of about 100 people, accurately drawn according to probability guidelines, will include about a 10 percent margin of error.

This percentage of error would be acceptable if a public relations person, for example, asked employees what they want to read in the company magazine. Sixty percent may indicate that they would like to see more news about opportunities for promotion. If only 100 employees were properly surveyed, it really doesn't matter if the actual percentage is 50 or 70 percent. The large percentage, in either case, would be sufficient to justify an increase in news stories about advancement opportunities.

This is also true in ascertaining community attitudes. If a survey of 100 or fewer citizens indicates that only 25 percent believe the organization is a good community citizen, it really doesn't matter whether the result is 15 or 40 percent. The main point is that the organization must take immediate steps to improve its image.

Questionnaire Design

Although correct sampling is important in gaining accurate results, pollsters generally acknowledge that sampling error may be far less important than the errors that result from the wording and order of questions and even the timing of the survey.

The Problem of Semantics

The wording of questions on a questionnaire is a time-consuming process, and it is not unusual for a questionnaire to go through multiple drafts in order to achieve maximum clarity. There is a difference between one question, "Is it a good idea to limit handguns?" and another, "Do you think registration of handguns will curtail crime?" On first glance, they seem to be asking the same thing. On closer examination, however, one can realize that a respondent could easily answer "yes" to the first question and "no" to the second.

The first question asks if the limiting of handguns is a good idea. The second asks if people think it will curtail crime. A third question that might elicit a different response would be, "Do you think laws curtailing the use of handguns would work?" Thus, the questions emphasize three different aspects of the problem. The first stresses the value of an idea, the second explores a possible effect, and the third examines the practicality of a proposed solution. Research shows that people often think something is a good idea, but do not think it would work. Another related problem is how respondents might interpret the words *limit* and *curtail.* To some, they may refer to a total ban on handguns, while others may think the words suggest that all guns should be kept away from people with criminal records.

Avoid Biased Wording

Questionnaires should avoid questions that use highly charged words to elicit a particular response. Such a question was used by Republican Party pollsters who asked respondents whether they agreed or disagreed that "We should stop *excessive* legal claims, *frivolous* lawsuits, and *overzealous* lawyers." Not surprisingly, an overwhelming majority of the respondents agreed. Another example of a loaded question is one by U.S. English, Inc., a group advocating English as the official language. It asked, "Do you think American taxpayers should be *forced* to pay for special voter registration drives for those who *insist* on or want to vote in a language other than English?"

Such statements and questions, in a survey, are indications that "advocacy research" is being conducted. That is, the questionnaire is intentionally skewed to promote a cause or product. Such studies tarnish the reputation of legitimate research and make the public increasingly skeptical of any survey results.

Timing and Context

Responses to survey questions are influenced by events, and this should be taken into consideration when reviewing the results of a survey. The public's esteem for an airline, for example, will get lower marks if a survey is conducted just after a plane crash. Intel's corporate reputation took a dip in company surveys just after major news coverage about a flaw in its Pentium microchip.

On the positive side, surveys by Coca-Cola about its reputation and corporate citizenship showed very favorable public attitudes just after its massive investment in the Atlanta Olympic Games.

Consequently, polls and surveys should be conducted when the organization isn't in the news or connected to a significant event that may influence public opinion. In such a neutral context, a more valid survey can be conducted about an organization's reputation, products, or services.

Large organizations such as Exxon/Mobil, General Electric, and AT&T counterbalance the effects of one-time events by conducting quarterly surveys. Called *benchmarking,* this is discussed in Chapter 9.

Political Correctness

Another problem with questionnaire design involves questions that tend to elicit the "correct" response. This is also called a *courtesy bias.* Respondents choose answers that won't offend the interviewer and reflect mainstream thinking. Surveys, for example, show that 80 percent of Americans consider themselves "environmentalists." As skeptics point out, however, would anyone admit that he or she was not concerned about the environment?

Surveys of public relations practitioners about the value of research also show a degree of courtesy bias in choosing the politically correct answer. Almost 90 percent agree that research is a necessary and integral part of public relations work. Almost the same percentage, however, agree that research is talked about more than it is done.

Those conducting employee surveys also fall into the "courtesy" trap by posing such questions as "How much of each newsletter do you read?" or "How well do you like the column by the president?" Employees may never read the newsletter and think the column is ridiculous, but they know the "correct" answer should be that they read the "entire issue" and the column is "excellent."

Researchers try to avoid the "politically correct" answers by making questionnaires confidential and promising anonymity to people who are interviewed. Because employees often perceive the public relations department to be part of management, it is often best to employ an outside research firm to conduct employee surveys.

The Answer Categories

Answer categories can skew a questionnaire. It is important that answer choices are provided to cover a range of opinions. A national polling organization several years ago asked the question "How much confidence do you have in business corporations?" but provided only the following answer categories: (a) a great deal, (b) only some, and (c) none at all. A large gap exists between "a great deal" and the next category, "only some." Such categories invariably skew the results to show very little confidence in business. A better list of answers might have been (a) a great deal, (b) quite a lot, (c) some, (d) very little, and (e) none. Perhaps an even better approach would be to provide the answer categories (a) above average, (b) average, and (c) below average. The psychological distance between the three choices is equal, and there is less room for respondent interpretation of what "quite a lot" means.

In general, "yes-or-no" questions are not very good for examining respondents' perceptions and attitudes. A "yes" or "no" answer provides little feedback on the strength or weakness of a respondent's opinion. A question such as "Do you agree with the company's policy of requiring drug testing for all new employees?" can be answered by "yes" or "no," but more useful information would be obtained by setting up a Likert-type scale—(a) strongly agree, (b) agree, (c) undecided, (d) disagree, and (e) strongly disagree. These types of answers enable the surveyor to probe the depth of feeling among respondents and may serve as guidelines for management in making major changes or just fine-tuning the existing policy.

Another way of designing a numerical scale in order to pinpoint a respondent's beliefs or attitudes is to use, for example, a 5-point scale. Such a scale might look like this.

> **Question:** How would you evaluate the company's efforts to keep you informed about job benefits? Please circle one of the following numbers ("1" being a low rating and "5" being a high rating).
>
> **Answer:** 1 2 3 4 5

The advantage of numerical scales is that medians and means can be easily calculated. In the previous example, the average from all respondents might be 4.25, which indicates that employees think the company does keep them informed about job benefits but that there is still room for communication improvement.

Questionnaire Guidelines

Here are some general guidelines for the construction of questionnaires:

- Decide what kinds of information are needed and in what detail.
- State the objectives of the survey in writing.
- Decide which group will receive the questionnaire.
- Decide on the size of the sample.
- State the purpose of the survey and guarantee anonymity.
- Use closed-end (multiple-choice) answers as much as possible. Respondents find it easier and less time-consuming to check answers than compose them in an open-end (essay) questionnaire.
- Design the questionnaire in such a way that answers can be easily coded for statistical analysis.
- Strive to make the questionnaire no more than 25 questions. Long questionnaires put people off and reduce the number of responses, particularly in print questionnaires where it is easy to see how long the survey will take to complete.
- Use categories when asking questions about education, age, and income. People are more willing to answer when a category or range is used. For example, what category best describes your age? (a) Under 25, (b) 26 to 40, and so on.
- Use simple, familiar words. Readability should be appropriate for the group being sampled. At the same time, don't talk down to respondents.
- Avoid ambiguous words and phrases that may confuse the respondent.
- Edit out leading questions that suggest a specific response or bias an answer.
- Remember context and placement of questions. One question close to another can influence response to the later question.
- Provide space at the end of the questionnaire for respondents' comments and observations. This allows them to provide additional information or elaboration that may not have been covered in the main body of the questionnaire.
- Pretest the questions for understanding and possible bias. Representatives of the proposed sampling group should read the questionnaire and make comments for possible improvement.

Designing a questionnaire and analyzing the results can be time-consuming, but there is a software program that can make the task much easier. It is *Publics PR Research Software,* developed by Prof. Glen T. Cameron at the University of Missouri and Tim Herzog of Kno Technology. The software helps the user to create questionnaires by providing ready-made questions that can be tailored to fit any situation. In addition, the program also helps with data analysis.

Ways of Reaching Respondents

A questionnaire is only as good as the delivery system that gets it to respondents. The following sections discuss the pros and cons of (1) mail questionnaires, (2) telephone surveys, (3) personal interviews, and (4) piggyback or omnibus surveys.

Mail Questionnaires

Questionnaires may be used in a variety of settings. They may be handed out at a manufacturing plant, at a county fair, or even in a bank lobby. Most survey questionnaires, however, are mailed to respondents. There are several reasons for this:

- Because the researchers have better control as to who receives the questionnaire, they can make sure the survey is representative.
- Large geographical areas can be covered economically.
- It is less expensive to administer them than to hire an interviewer to conduct personal interviews.
- Large numbers of people can be included at minimal cost.

Mail questionnaires have some disadvantages. The biggest is a low response rate. A mail questionnaire by a commercial firm to the general public usually produces a response rate of 1 to 2 percent. If the survey concerns issues affecting the general public, the response rate might be 5 to 20 percent. A much better response rate would be generated, however, if the questionnaire were mailed by an organization to its members. In this case, the response rate may be 30 to 80 percent. The more closely people identify with the organization and the questions, the better the response.

The response rate to a mail questionnaire can be increased, say the experts, if all the guidelines of questionnaire construction are followed. In addition, a researcher should keep the following suggestions in mind:

- Include a stamped, self-addressed return envelope and a personally signed letter explaining the importance of participation.
- Provide an incentive. Commercial firms often encourage people to fill out questionnaires by including a token amount of money or a discount coupon. Other researchers promise to share the results of the survey with the respondent.
- Mail questionnaires by first-class mail. Some research shows that placing special issue stamps on the envelope attracts greater interest than simply using a postage meter.
- Mail a reminder postcard three or four days later.
- Do a second mailing (either to nonrespondents or to the entire sample) two or three weeks after the first mailing. Again, enclose a stamped, self-addressed

return envelope and a cover letter explaining the crucial need for the recipient's participation.

Telephone Surveys

Surveys by telephone, particularly if the survey is locally based, are extensively used by research firms. The telephone survey has several advantages:

- There is an immediate response or nonresponse. A researcher doesn't have to wait several weeks for responses to arrive by mail.
- A telephone call is personal. It is effective communication, and it is much cheaper than a personal interview.
- A phone call is less intrusive than going door-to-door and interviewing people. Surveys show that many people are willing to talk on the phone for up to 45 minutes but will not stand at a door for more than 5 or 10 minutes and are unwilling to admit strangers to their homes.
- The response rate, if the survey is properly composed and phone interviewers trained, can reach 80 to 90 percent.

The major disadvantage of phone interviews is the difficulty in getting access to everyone's phone number. In many urban areas, a third to half of the numbers are unlisted. Although researchers can let a computer program pick numbers through random digit dialing, this method is not as effective as actually knowing who is being called. Another barrier is convincing respondents that a legitimate poll or survey is being taken. Far too many salespeople have attempted to sell goods by posing as researchers.

Personal Interviews

The personal interview is the most expensive form of research because it requires trained staff and travel. If travel within a city is involved, a trained interviewer often can interview only eight or ten people a day, and salaries and transportation costs make it expensive. There is also the need for considerable advance work in arranging interviews and appointments and, as previously pointed out, researchers encounter reluctance by residents to admit strangers to their homes.

Personal interviews, on the other hand, can be cost-effective and can generate a wealth of information if the setting is controlled. Many research firms conduct personal interviews at national conventions or trade shows, where there is a concentration of people with similar interests. An equipment company, for example, may hire a research firm to interview potential customers at a national trade show.

The Piggyback Survey

An alternative method of reaching respondents is the *piggyback survey,* also known as the *omnibus survey.* In basic terms, an organization "buys" a question in a national survey conducted by a survey organization such as Gallup or Harris.

For example, General Mills may place one or two questions in a national poll asking respondents what professional athlete they most admire, as a way to find new endorsers for its breakfast foods. In the same survey, the American Cancer Society may place a question asking how the public feels about sporting events sponsored by tobacco companies.

The method is attractive to public relations people for two reasons. One is cost. An organization pays much less to participate in a piggyback poll than to conduct its own survey. A second reason is expertise. Firms such as Gallup or Harris have the skill and organization to do a survey properly and efficiently; few public relations departments or firms do.

Piggyback surveys, however, have limitations. An organization can only get a small snapshot of public opinion with one or two questions, and the subject matter must be relevant to the general public.

Web and E-Mail Surveys

The newest way to reach respondents is through electronic communication. One way is to post the questionnaire on the organization's Web site and ask visitors to answer it online. The advantage is instant reply, with a running tabulation of the results instantly available.

Researchers use several methods to attract respondents to the Web site, including (1) banner ads announcing the survey on other Web sites or online networks, (2) e-mailing invitations to a target audience, (3) telephoning individuals with an invitation to participate, and (4) sending a postal card. The major disadvantage of a Web survey is how to control the exact characteristics of the respondents, since a Web site is accessible to virtually anyone with a computer and a modem. It is also very important to control repeated participation by the same respondent by identifying the unique identifying number for a computer (called the IP Address) and only allowing one submission. Of course those using a public terminal, such as are available in libraries, might be blocked from participating if that terminal has already been used to complete the survey. One of the biggest problems for online surveys is the low response rate due to the impersonal nature of the survey when compared to telephone and the ease of leaving a survey with a single mouse click. For this reason, many online surveys begin with the most crucial questions to be asked and the key demographics needed for analysis.

If reaching the exact audience is important, another approach is the e-mailed survey, sent to a list of known respondents. Organizations can compile e-mail lists of clients or customers, but it's also now possible to purchase e-mail address lists from a variety of sources.

Summary

The Importance of Research

Research is the basic groundwork of any public relations program, involving the gathering and interpretation of information. Research is used in every phase of a communications program.

Research Techniques

Secondary research uses information from library sources, and, increasingly, online and Internet sources. Primary research involves gathering new information through interviews or sampling procedures.

Questionnaire Design

The design of a questionnaire—wording and order of the questions—is probably even more important than correct sampling. The timing and context will also affect the response.

Ways of Reaching Respondents

Survey respondents may be reached by mail, telephone, personal interviews, or in piggyback or omnibus surveys.

Case Activity: What Would You Do?

Universal Manufacturing Corporation is located in a midwestern city of 500,000 people. Its 6000 employees make it one of the largest employers in the country, and the company has been in its present location for the past 50 years. Despite this record, management believes that the company doesn't have a strong identity and visibility in the community.

The director of public relations is asked to prepare a new public relations plan for the coming fiscal year. She recommends that the company first do research to determine exactly what its image is in the community.

If you were the public relations director, what informal methods of research would you use? What more formal research methods could be used? What kinds of information about the company's image should be researched?

Questions for Review and Discussion

1. Why is research important in public relations work?
2. What kinds of questions should a person ask before formulating a research design?
3. Name at least five ways to use research in public relations.
4. How can survey research be used as a publicity tool?
5. Name at least five informal research methods.
6. What are online databases and how are they used?
7. How can the Internet and World Wide Web be used as research tools?
8. What is the procedure for organizing and conducting a focus group? What are the pros and cons of using focus groups?
9. What is an intercept interview?
10. What is the difference between probability (random) and nonprobability samples?
11. What guidelines should be followed when releasing the results of a survey to the media and the public?
12. What percentage margin of error is associated with various sample sizes? What size samples are usually adequate for public relations work?
13. Name at least five guidelines that should be followed when preparing a survey questionnaire.
14. What are the pros and cons of mail questionnaires, telephone surveys, personal interviews, and piggyback surveys?

Suggested Readings

Broom, Glen, and Dozier, David. *Using Public Relations Research.* Englewood Cliffs, NJ: Prentice Hall, 1990.

Brody, E. W., and Stone, Gerald. *Public Relations Research.* New York: Praeger, 1989.

Geddie, Tom. "Surveys Are a Waste of Time and Money . . . Until You Use Them." *Communication World,* April 1996, pp. 24–26.

"How to Measure Relationships? Grunig/Hon Study for Institute Measurement Commission Lays Groundwork." *pr reporter,* Vol. 42, No. 40, October 11, 1999, pp. 1–3.

Grunig, Larissa A. "Using Focus Group Research in Public Relations." *Public Relations Review,* Summer 1990, pp. 36–49.

Kendall, Robert. *Public Relations Campaign Strategies.* New York: HarperCollins, 1996.

"When Conventional Wisdom Meets Research: The Myth of Implied Third-Party Endorsement." *jim & lauri grunig's research, a supplement of pr reporter,* No. 8, May 22, 2000, pp. 1–4.

Stempel, Guido, and Westley, Bruce. *Research Methods in Mass Communications.* Englewood Cliffs, NJ: Prentice Hall, 1995.

7 Program Planning

preview

This chapter describes how to organize a well-planned public relations campaign, step-by-step, and how planning applies to issues management.

Topics covered in the chapter include:

- The value of planning
- Systematic approaches to planning
- Elements of a program plan
    - Situation
    - Objectives
    - Audience
    - Strategy
    - Tactics
    - Calendar/timetable
    - Budget
    - Evaluation
- Issues management planning

The Value of Planning

The second step in the public relations process, after research, is program planning. Before any public relations activity can be implemented, it is essential that considerable thought be given to what should be done and in what sequence to accomplish an organization's objectives.

A good public relations program should be an effective tool to support an organization's business, marketing, and communications objectives. As Larry Werner, executive vice president of Ketchum Public Relations, points out, "No longer are we simply in the business of putting press releases out; we're in the business of solving business problems through communications."

In other words, public relations planning should be strategic. As Glen Broom and David Dozier say in their text, *Using Public Relations Research,* "Strategic planning is deciding where you want to be in the future (the goal) and how to get there (the strategies). It sets the organization's direction proactively, avoiding 'drift' and routine repetition of activities." A practitioner must think about a situation, analyze what can be done about it, creatively conceptualize the appropriate strategies and tactics, and determine how the results will be measured. Planning also involves the coordination of multiple methods—news releases, special events, press kits, news conferences, media interviews, brochures, newsletters, speeches, and so on—to achieve specific results.

Paying attention to systematic planning prevents haphazard, ineffective communication. Having a blueprint of what is to be done and how it will be executed makes programs more effective and public relations more valuable to the organization.

Approaches to Planning

Planning is like putting together a jigsaw puzzle. Research, discussed in Chapter 6, provides the various pieces. Next, it is necessary to arrange the pieces so that a coherent design, or picture, emerges. The best planning is systematic, the process of gathering information, analyzing it, and creatively applying it for the specific purpose of attaining an objective.

Two approaches are discussed here. In both cases, the emphasis is on asking, and answering, many questions.

Management by Objective (MBO)

One popular approach is a process called *management by objective (MBO).* In other words, the idea is to formulate a strategy that will accomplish an organization's specific objective. MBO provides focus and direction for this type of thinking. According to Robert E. Simmons, author of *Communication Campaign Management,* the use of MBO in planning ensures the "... production of relevant messages and establishes criteria against which campaign results can be measured."

Norman R. Nager and T. Harrell Allen, in their book *Public Relations Management by Objectives,* discuss nine basic MBO steps that can help a practitioner conceptualize everything from a simple news release to a multifaceted communications program. The steps, adapted from their book, are as follows:

1. *Client/employer objectives.* What is the purpose of the communication, and how does it promote or achieve the objectives of the organization? Specific objectives

such as "to make consumers aware of the product's high quality" are more meaningful than "to make people aware of the product."

2. *Audience/publics.* Who exactly should be reached with the message, and how can that audience help achieve the organization's objectives? What are the characteristics of the audience, and how can demographic information be used to structure the message? The primary audience for a campaign to encourage carpooling consists of people who regularly drive to work, not the general public.
3. *Audience objectives.* What is it that the audience wants to know, and how can the message be tailored to audience self-interest? Consumers are more interested in how a new computer will increase their productivity than in how it works.
4. *Media channels.* What is the appropriate channel for reaching the audience, and how can multiple channels (news media, brochures, special events, and direct mail) reinforce the message among key publics? An ad may be best for making consumers aware of a new product, but a news release may be better for conveying consumer information about the product.
5. *Media channel objectives.* What is the media gatekeeper looking for in a news angle, and why would a particular publication be interested in the information? A community newspaper is primarily interested in a story with a local angle.
6. *Sources and questions.* What primary and secondary sources of information are required to provide a factual base for the message? What experts should be interviewed? What database researches should be conducted? A quote from a project engineer about a new technology is better than a quote from the marketing vice president.
7. *Communication strategies.* What environmental factors will affect the dissemination and acceptance of the message? Are the target publics hostile or favorably disposed to the message? What other events or pieces of information negate or reinforce the message? A campaign to conserve water is more salient if there has been a recent drought.
8. *Essence of the message.* What is the planned communication impact on the audience? Is the message designed merely to inform, or is it designed to change attitudes and behavior? Telling people about the values of physical fitness is different from telling them how to achieve it.
9. *Nonverbal support.* How can photographs, graphs, films, and artwork clarify and visually enhance the written message? Bar graphs or pie charts are easier to understand than columns of numbers.

A Strategic Planning Model

A similar approach is taken by Ketchum Communications, which has developed a "Strategic Planning Model for Public Relations." The Ketchum approach is:

Facts

- *Category facts.* Summarize recent industry trends.
- *Product/service issues.* What are significant characteristics of product, service, or issue?
- *Competitive facts.* Who are the competitors, and what are their competitive strengths, similarities, and differences?
- *Customer facts.* Who uses the product and why?

Observance of the 100th anniversary of the automobile was an event created by the automobile industry and the Detroit Convention & Visitors Bureau to promote American-made automobiles and attract visitors to Detroit, "the Motor City." Display of early automobiles, such as this Packard, attracted crowds. Note the hand crank, small tires, and steering wheel on the right-hand side.

Goals

- *Business objectives.* What are the company's business objectives and in what timeframe?
- *Role of public relations.* How does public relations fit into the marketing mix?
- *Sources of new business.* What sectors will produce growth?

Audience

- *Target audiences.* Define audiences and their "hot" buttons.
- *Current mindset.* How do audiences feel about the product, service, or issue?
- *Desired mindset.* How do we want them to feel?

Key Message

- *Main point.* What one key message must be conveyed to change or reinforce mindsets?

These two approaches to planning, MBO and the Ketchum model, lead to the next important step—the writing of a strategic public relations plan. The next section explains the elements of such a plan.

Elements of a Program Plan

Writing a plan for a public relations program is nothing more than preparing a document identifying what is to be done and how to accomplish it. By preparing such a plan, either as a brief outline or an extensive document, the practitioner can make certain that all the elements have been properly considered and that everyone involved understands the "big picture."

It is common practice for public relations firms to prepare a program plan for client approval and possible modification before implementing it. At that time, both the public relations firm and the client reach a mutual understanding of the objectives and how to accomplish them. Public relations departments of organizations also map out a particular campaign or show the department's plans for the coming year.

Although there can be some variation, public relations plans include eight basic elements:

1. Situation
2. Objectives
3. Audience
4. Strategy
5. Tactics
6. Calendar/timetable
7. Budget
8. Evaluation

The following sections will elaborate on these elements and give examples from campaigns that received PRSA Silver Anvil Awards for excellence.

Situation

Valid objectives cannot be set without a clear understanding of the situation that led to the conclusion that a public relations program was needed.

Three kinds of situations often dictate the conduct of a public relations program. They are: (1) The organization must conduct a remedial program to overcome a problem or situation that negatively affects the organization; (2) the organization needs to conduct a specific one-time project; and (3) the organization wants to reinforce an ongoing effort to preserve reputation and public support.

Loss of market share and declining sales often require a remedial program. Mack Trucks, for example, initiated an extensive public relations campaign after seeing its share of market decline from 21 percent in the 1980s to less than 9 percent in the 1990s. Other organizations launch such campaigns to change public perceptions. The Turkish government conducted an extensive tourism campaign designed to combat negative public perceptions that the country was "uncivilized" and an "underdeveloped, Third-World Middle Eastern country."

One-time, specific events often lead to public relations programs. One such campaign was for the grand opening of San Antonio's new public library. It was important to plan a celebration that showcased the facility as an educational, cultural, and entertainment resource for everyone. The introduction of Microsoft's *Windows 95* computer program was also a one-time event; it required a program plan that covered 20 months of prelaunch activities.

In the third situation program plans are initiated to preserve and develop customer or public support. Department 56, a leading designer and manufacturer of miniature lighted village collectibles, already had a successful business but wanted new customers. Its public relations program to accomplish this included distribution of

PR casebook

The 100th Anniversary of Jell-O

A public relations plan contains eight basic elements. The following is an outline of a plan that Kraft Foods and its public relations firm, Hunter & Associates, developed for Jell-O's 100th anniversary celebration.

Situation

- Sales of this famous dessert were flat. Brand research shows Jell-O, on the eve of its 100th anniversary celebration, was not top-of-mind with consumers, who were moving to "newer" desserts. Research in company archives provided extensive historical information and graphics about the use and promotion of Jell-O through the years.

Objectives

- Increase brand awareness in order to increase sales.
- Generate widespread awareness of Jell-O's 100th anniversary in high-profile media.

Target Audience

- Current and lapsed Jell-O consumers; women, aged 25–44, with families.

Strategies

- Use the nostalgic appeal of this brand to capture major media interest.
- Develop many story angles around three key messages for a broad range of media.
- Introduce a new Jell-O product to convey the idea that the brand is still in sync with the times.
- Involve LeRoy, NY, where Jell-O was invented, in the anniversary celebration.
- Involve Kraft Food employees with anniversary celebrations at each plant and corporate location.
- Generate stories emphasizing three key messages: (1) Jell-O is fun, (2) Jell-O is contemporary, and (3) Jell-O is an American and Canadian icon.

Tactics

- Host gala event with Bill Cosby, Jell-O spokesperson, as master of ceremonies.
- Introduce new flavor—Champagne.
- Publish new cookbook.
- Open new museum and tour exhibits around the country.
- Use Jell-O's hometown, LeRoy (NY), to host a Jell-O Jubilee.
- Establish a new Web site.
- Provide print and broadcast media with press kits that include historical backgrounders and artwork.

Calendar

- 18 months for entire campaign.
- Three months for research, planning.
- Four months for preparing press kits, media lists, etc.
- 11 months of scheduled events and news releases at quarterly intervals.

First Quarter—Jell-O celebrates its 100th anniversary.

Second Quarter—Champagne flavor introduced, cookbook promoted.

Third Quarter—Jell-O museum opens and begins touring the nation.

Fourth Quarter—Jell-O builds new float for Macy's Thanksgiving Parade.

Budget

- $450,000 for 18 months.

Evaluation

- Brand awareness was established through extensive media coverage. Research showed 6617 positive stories, 7893 minutes of TV time, 101 minutes of radio time. This included extensive stories in the *New York Times,* inclusion of Jell-O in a Jay Leno monologue, and Jell-O featured on Oprah Winfrey's Mother's Day Special.
- Survey research showed 48 percent of respondents heard about the anniversary from television, while another 37 percent found out about it from newspapers or magazines.
- Sales of Jell-O increased more than 5 percent from the previous year.

brochures on home decoration for the Christmas holidays and participation by its dealers in local efforts to decorate Ronald McDonald houses. In another example, BayBank in Boston maintained its community visibility by annually sponsoring the Head of the Charles Regatta, the world's largest rowing event.

In a program plan, relevant research often is included as part of the situation. In the case of Department 56, consumer market analysis revealed a strong link between consumers interested in home decorating and those involved in collecting. Microsoft found in focus groups that consumers would respond favorably to messages about a "faster and easier" computing experience. In the Turkish campaign, research showed little public awareness of Turkey as a European travel destination, and a content analysis of press clippings disclosed a large percentage of negative stereotypes. Other research portrayed the typical American traveler to Turkey as sophisticated, 40-plus years old, with an income of at least $50,000. For the repositioning of Levi jeans for the college market, media use patterns of students were analyzed using secondary research, including data collection about college student use of computers.

Such research provides the foundation for setting program objectives and shaping other elements of the program plan.

Objectives

Once the situation or problem is understood, the next step is to establish objectives for the program. A stated objective should be evaluated by asking: (1) Does it really address the situation? (2) is it realistic and achievable? and (3) can success be measured in meaningful terms?

An objective is usually stated in terms of program outcomes instead of inputs. Or, put another way, objectives should not be the "means" but the "end." A poor objective, for example, is "generate publicity for a new product." Publicity is not an "end" in itself. The actual objective is to "create consumer awareness about a new product." This is accomplished by such tactics as news releases, special events, and brochures.

It is particularly important that public relations objectives complement and reinforce the organization's objectives. Professor David Dozier of San Diego State University expressed the point well in a *Public Relations Review* article: "The prudent and strategic selection of public relations goals and objectives linked to organizational survival and growth serves to justify the public relations program as a viable management activity."

Basically there are two kinds of objectives: informational and motivational.

Informational Objectives A large percentage of public relations plans is designed primarily to expose audiences to information and to increase awareness of an issue, an event, or a product. The five objectives of public relations activity will be discussed in Chapter 8. The first two of these—message exposure and accurate dissemination of messages—are the most common. Many communication and marketing professionals believe the major criteria for public relations effectiveness are (1) an increase in public awareness and (2) delivery of key messages.

Some examples of informational objectives are:

- *Mack Trucks:* "Increase awareness and understanding of Mack highway vehicles and engine technology."
- *Levi Jeans:* "Double teen traffic to Levi.com."

- *National Association of Manufacturers (NAM):* "Educate target audiences on the fundamental importance of manufacturing to our nation's current competitiveness and future prosperity."

One difficulty with an informational objective is in measuring how well the objective has been achieved. Public awareness and the extent of education that takes place are somewhat abstract and difficult to quantify. Survey research often is required, as will be explained in Chapter 9; many organizations, however, infer "awareness" by counting the number of media placements. In reality, message exposure doesn't necessarily mean increased public awareness.

■ **Motivational Objectives** Although changing attitudes and influencing behavior are more difficult to accomplish in a public relations campaign, motivational objectives are easier to measure. That's because they are bottom-line oriented and are based on clearly measurable results that can be quantified. This is true whether the goal is an increase in product sales, a sellout crowd for a theatrical performance, or expanded donations to a charitable agency.

Some examples of motivational objectives are:

- *Mack Trucks:* "Increase Mack's market share and support Mack's drive to become a dominant player in the highway truck market."
- *San Antonio Library:* "Increase the number of people visiting the Central Library by 25 percent and the number of materials circulated by at least 50 percent."
- *M&M's Chocolate Candies:* "Build consumer sales and market category share."
- *Turkish Government Tourism Campaign:* "Increase the number of U.S. visitors to Turkey."
- *Levi Jeans:* "Reverse Levi's stodgy image with young consumers by generating upbeat media coverage."

A public relations program will often have both informational and motivational objectives. A good example is the Fighting Hunger in Wisconsin campaign. Its objectives were to (1) increase public awareness of hunger in Wisconsin, (2) enlist additional volunteers, and (3) raise more money than in the previous year to support hunger-relief programs around the state.

Objectives, and how to measure the accomplishment of them, will be discussed in Chapter 9 on evaluation.

Audience

Public relations programs should be directed toward specific and defined audiences or publics. Although some campaigns are directed to a "general public," such instances are the exception. Even the M&M's Chocolate Candies national "election" campaign to select a new color (blue) for its famous mix was designed to reach consumers 24 years of age or under.

In other words, public relations practitioners target specific publics within a "general public." This is done through market research that can identify key publics by such demographics as age, income, social strata, education, existing ownership or consumption of specific products, and where people live. Market research, for example, told M&M's Candies that young people were the primary consumers of its product. On a more basic level, a water conservation campaign defines its target audience by geography—people living in a particular city or area.

In many cases, common sense is all that is needed to define adequately a specific public. Take, for example, the Ohio vaccination program for children under the age of 2. The primary audience for the message is parents with young children. Other audiences are pregnant women and medical professionals who treat young children. Perhaps a more complex situation involves a company that wants to increase the sale of a CD-ROM program on home improvement for do-it-yourselfers. Again, the primary audience is not the "general public" but those persons who actually have CD-ROM players and enjoy working around the house. Such criteria exclude a large percentage of the American population.

The following are examples of how organizations already mentioned defined target audiences:

- *Mack Trucks:* "Licensed Class 6, 7, and 8 truck drivers, truck fleet owners, and 600 Mack dealers."
- *San Antonio Library:* "Citizens of San Antonio."
- *Turkish Government Tourism Campaign:* "Seasoned travelers (40-plus years old, with an income of at least $50,000), consumer travel magazines, tour agents, and travel agents in the primary markets of New York, Chicago, and Los Angeles."
- *Levi Jeans:* "(1) College-age consumers; (2) Youth-focused media."

As previously noted, some organizations identify the media as a "public." On occasion, in programs that seek media endorsements or try to change how the media report on an organization or an issue, editors and reporters can become a legitimate "public." In general, however, mass media outlets fall in the category of a means to an end. They are channels to reach defined audiences that need to be informed, persuaded, and motivated.

A thorough understanding of the primary and secondary publics is essential if a program's objectives are to be accomplished. Such knowledge also provides guidance on the selection of appropriate strategies and tactics that would reach these defined audiences.

The manufacturer of the CD-ROM on home improvement, for example, might completely bypass the general press and concentrate on specialized publications in the home improvement and CD-ROM fields. Cost is a driving factor; spending large sums to reach members of the general public on matters in which they have no stake or interest is nonproductive and a waste of money.

Strategy

A strategy statement describes how, in concept, an objective is to be achieved, providing guidelines and themes for the overall program. One general strategy may be outlined, or a program may have several strategies, depending on the objectives and the designated audiences.

The public relations programs for Mack Trucks and Levi Jeans illustrate the basic concept of formulating and writing a strategy. Note that the strategies listed below are broad statements; specific activities are part of tactics, to be covered in the next section.

Mack Trucks summarized its strategies as follows: "(1) build a dominant share-of-voice in the trucking trade media; (2) use proprietary media to reach current and prospective Mack customers and dealers; (3) stimulate product trial through the Bulldog National Test Drive Tour; and (4) further the Mack brand identity through cause-related marketing."

Levi Jeans's strategies were: "(1) Build an online community for college-age kids *about* college-age kids that's entertaining and interactive; (2) creatively capitalize on the e-commerce explosion to engage target media; (3) stimulate ongoing coverage via newsworthy moments-in-time." The anchor for these three strategies was the Levi's Online Challenge—select three college students who would purchase everything needed to live online for one semester.

Key Messages/Themes The strategy element of a program plan should state key themes and messages to be reiterated throughout the campaign on all publicity materials. The Ohio immunization program, for example, was based on the concept that parents love their children and want them to be healthy. Thus, a key message was to tell parents how important vaccinations were to keep their children out of danger. Carrying out this message was the theme of the campaign, "Project L.O.V.E" with the subhead "Love Our Kids Vaccination Project."

In the Turkish tourism campaign, the strategy of combating "negative stereotypes and lack of knowledge about Turkey . . ." included key messages designed to reinforce historical/cultural sites, natural beauty, upscale accommodations, great shopping, excellent cuisine, ideal weather, and friendly people. In an effort to position Turkey as part of Europe instead of the Middle East, the themes of "Center of World History" and "Where Europe Becomes Exotic" were used.

Tactics

The issue of tactics is the nuts-and-bolts part of the plan that describes, in sequence, the specific activities that put the strategies into operation and help to achieve the stated objectives. Tactics involves using the tools of communication to reach primary and secondary audiences with key messages. Chapters 20 through 22 discuss communication tools in greater detail.

The Tactics of Mack Trucks In many cases, each strategy is supported by specific tactics. In the Mack Truck campaign, the first strategy to build a dominant share-of-voice in the trucking trade media was supported by the following tactics:

- A toll-free number facilitated product literature requests generated through publicity efforts.
- New models of Mack trucks were driven to key trucking publications in various cities for demonstrations and background briefings.
- A press conference for trucking trade editors was held at a major trade show to introduce a new Mack engine.
- A press kit featuring news and features about the company's 95-year history was sent to the trade press.
- News releases were sent regularly to the trade press that promoted new products, major customer orders, and awards earned by the company for product quality.

The second strategy—use proprietary media—was supported by these tactics:

- A 24-page quarterly magazine, *The Bulldog,* was sent to more than 15,000 Mack customers and dealers.
- More than 100 customer testimonials were collected and installed on software for use by Mack sales representatives.

Planning a public relations program requires conferences like this one, at which participants weigh information on such diverse topics as objectives, graphics, media selection, demographics, and timing.

The third strategy—stimulate product trial through the Bulldog National Test Drive Tour—was accomplished by having two fully loaded Mack trucks crisscross the continent visiting truck stops, Mack dealerships, and key prospective customers.

The fourth strategy—enhance the Mack brand through cause-related marketing—arranged with the U.S. Forest Service to haul America's Christmas tree from California to Washington, D.C. Along the way, the truck stopped at dealerships and distributed toy Bulldogs (the company's trademark) to local Toys for Tots programs. This tactic generated considerable local print and broadcast coverage.

The Tactics of Levi Jeans Levi also used a number of tactics to support the objectives and strategies in the program to reposition Levi jeans in the college-age market as a hip brand. The Levi's Online Challenge was kicked off through a contest to select three "point and click pioneers" who would make all necessary purchases online for a semester. Contestants answered questions such as: "What was the wackiest online purchase you ever made?" and "If you named your computer and mouse, what would you call them?" Other tactics included:

- Announcement of winners and "freshman orientation" for publicity
- The semester of online shopping, including Levi outfits, documented on the personal Web pages of the three shoppers with digital photos, virtual diaries, and personal anecdotes
- Creation of a weekly Web show using Webcams and headsets to broadcast online shopping experiences as well as chat on issues from cars to safe sex with thousands of teens logged on to Levi.com
- A $1 donation to the brand's ongoing beneficiary, the music industry's cause against AIDS called LIFEbeat, was made by Levi Jeans for every viewer who logged on to the final show

Calendar/Timetable

The three aspects of timing in a program plan are: (1) deciding when a campaign should be conducted, (2) determining the proper sequence of activities, and (3) compiling a list of steps that must be completed to produce a finished product. All three aspects are important to achieve maximum effectiveness.

The Timing of a Campaign Program planning should take into account the environmental context of a situation and the time when key messages are most meaningful to the intended audience. A campaign to encourage carpooling, for example, might be more successful if it follows a major price rise in gasoline or a government report that traffic congestion has reached gridlock proportions.

Some subjects are seasonal. Department 56, the designer and manufacturer of miniature lighted village collectibles and other holiday giftware, timed the major bulk of its campaign in November to take advantage of the Christmas holidays, when there was major interest in its product lines. Charitable agencies such as the Wisconsin Project on Hunger also gear their campaigns around Christmas when there is increased interest in helping the unfortunate.

By the same token, strawberry producers increase public relations efforts in May and June, when a crop comes to market and the stores have large supplies of the fruit. Similarly, a software program on income tax preparation attracts the most audience interest in February and March, just before the April 15 filing deadline. In another situation, a vendor of a software program designed to handle personal finances launched a public relations/marketing program in January. The timing was based on research indicating that people put "getting control of personal finances" high on their list of New Year's resolutions.

Other kinds of campaigns depend less on environmental or seasonal context. The Mack Truck and Levi Jeans campaigns, for example, could be conducted at almost any time.

focus on ethics
Should Public Relations Writers Join In?

Microsoft, under attack from the U.S. Department of Justice and its major competitors for monopolistic business practices, asked a public relations firm for a plan to tell its side of the story and influence public opinion. One suggestion from the firm was for Microsoft to ask influential supporters to write op-ed pieces and letters to the editor in states whose regulators were also considering possible antitrust violations.

A copy of this memo was leaked to the *Los Angeles Times,* and an article appeared accusing Microsoft of secretly trying to place articles or editorials. A *Washington Post* columnist also called it, "a phony grass-roots campaign" in the same leagues as the tactics used by "Big Tobacco." Other critics accused Microsoft of unethical behavior. On the other side, others wondered what the big fuss is about. They say it's standard practice for PR firms to solicit articles from opinion leaders and even assist in the writing of them.

What do you think? Should such an idea be a legitimate part of a public relations plan? Why or why not?

Scheduling of Tactics The second aspect of timing is the scheduling and sequencing of various tactics or activities. A typical pattern is to concentrate effort at the beginning of a campaign, when a number of tactics are implemented. This launch phase of a campaign, much like that of a rocket, takes a burst of activity just to break the awareness barrier. After the campaign has achieved orbit, however, less energy and fewer activities are required to maintain momentum.

To further the rocket analogy, public relations campaigns often are the first stage of an integrated marketing communications program. Once public relations has created awareness and customer anticipation of a new product, the second stage may be an advertising and direct mail campaign.

Compiling a Calendar An integral part of timing is advance planning. A video news release, a press kit, or a brochure often take weeks and months of work to prepare. Arrangements for a special event also take considerable time. Practitioners must take into account the deadlines of publications. Monthly periodicals, for example, frequently need information at least six to eight weeks before publication. A popular talk show may book guests three or four months in advance.

In other words, the public relations professional must think ahead to make things happen in the right sequence, at the right time. One way to achieve this goal is to compile time lines and charts that list the necessary steps and their required completion dates.

Calendars and time lines take various forms. One simple method is to post activities for each day in a large-size monthly calendar. The public relations manager of Kendall-Jackson Winery used this method to plan a luxury wine tasting and dinner. Figure 7.1 shows an excerpt from one day on the April calendar (initials in the left column indicate person responsible for the activity).

Gantt Charts are also used for planning purposes. Essentially, the format is a column matrix that has two sides. The left side has a vertical list of activities that must be accomplished, and the top has a horizontal line of days, weeks, or months. Figure 7.2 is a simplified example.

global PR

An Indian View of Public Relations

A public relations plan, to be strategic, must be tied to the organization's overall business plan and organizational objectives. This is how Aarohan Communications of Bombay, India, expresses it:

> A PR program contributes toward achieving corporate objectives by using various communication tools. A professional develops and manages such a program. The effectiveness of the professional depends on whether he/she is able to analyze the situation, understand the issues involved, properly identify the target audiences, and use the correct communication tools that would support the accomplishment of corporate objectives. The results must be measured to assure that all of the above have been done effectively.

Wednesday, April 12

M	Begin development of invitation, RSVP, envelopes, tickets, program, nametags, placards, etc.
J/M	Review printing costs and options
T	Investigate possibility of having palette tasting trays
T	Reserve Stars' Grill Room for evening of event (asking Jess)
T	Determine RSVP voice mail #
ALL	**2 p.m. Committee Meeting at SF War Memorial and Performing Arts Center**

FIGURE 7.1

A page from the April calendar used to plan an event.

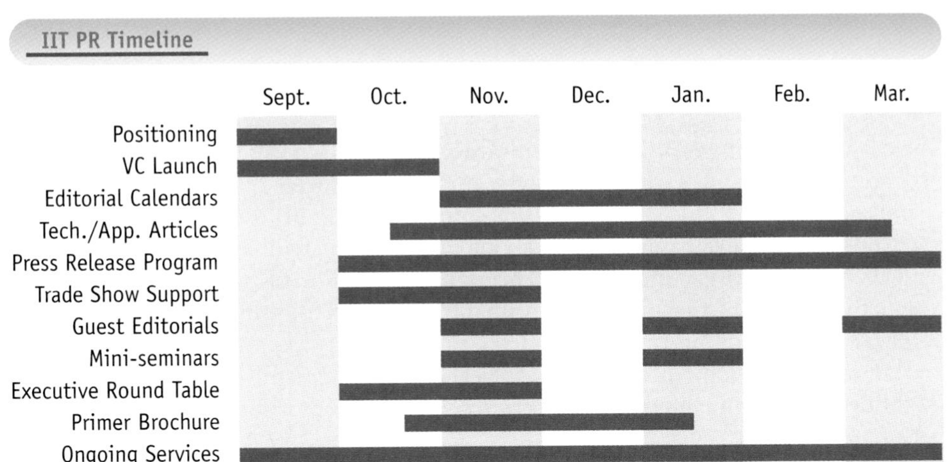

FIGURE 7.2

A typical Gantt Chart.

Budget

No program plan is complete without a budget. Both clients and employers ask, "How much will this program cost?" In many cases, the reverse approach is taken. Organizations establish an amount they can afford, then ask the public relations staff or firm to write a program plan that reflects the amount allocated.

Some budgets of campaigns already discussed were as follows:

- *Mack Trucks:* $204,000 annually, plus expenses
- *M&M's Chocolate Candies:* $555,000

- *Department 56:* $160,000 for 500,000 brochures, $85,000 for a video seminar, and $24,250 for a satellite tour; fees for event planning and media relations activities by public relations firm, $100,000
- *Turkish Government Tourism:* $650,000 for 15-month program: $450,000 in public relations firm fees and $200,000 in expenses
- *Levi Jeans:* $600,000: $460,000 in public relations firm fees and $140,000 in out-of-pocket expenses

A budget, as shown above, can be divided into two categories: staff time and out-of-pocket (OOP) expenses. Staff and administrative time usually takes the lion's share of any public relations budget. In a $100,000 campaign done by a public relations firm, for example, it is not unusual for 70 percent to be salaries and administrative fees. Information about how public relations firms charge fees is in Chapter 5.

One method of budgeting is to use two columns. The left column will list the staff cost for writing a pamphlet or compiling a press kit. The right column will list the actual OOP for having the pamphlet or press kit designed, printed, and delivered. Internal public relations staffs, whose members are on the payroll, often complete only the OOP expenses. It is good practice to allocate about 10 percent of the budget for contingencies, or unexpected costs.

Budgets, in a program plan, are usually estimated on the basis of experience and requests from vendors for estimates. After the program is completed, part of the evaluation (see Chapter 9) is to compile a form that shows estimated expenses versus actual expenses.

Evaluation

The evaluation element of a plan relates directly back to the stated objectives for the program. As discussed earlier, objectives must be measurable in some way to show clients and employers that the program accomplished its purpose.

Consequently, evaluation criteria should be realistic, credible, specific, and in line with client or employer expectations. The evaluation section of a program plan should restate the objectives, then name the evaluation methods to be used.

Evaluation of an informational objective often entails a compilation of news clips and an analysis of how often key message points were mentioned. Other methods might be to determine how many brochures were distributed, or the estimated number of viewers who saw a video news release. Motivational objectives often are measured and evaluated by increases in sales or market share, the number of people who called an 800 number for more information, or by benchmark surveys that measure people's perceptions before and after a campaign.

Chapter 9 discusses evaluation techniques and refers to many of the campaigns mentioned here.

Planning in Issues Management

We have been discussing the step-by-step progression of planning for all types of public relations programs. Now we will see how planning can be applied in an area of practice called *issues management.*

PR insights

An Issues Management Matrix

Issues management involves an assessment of an issue and its importance to the organization.

The Milwaukee-based firm of Bader Rutter & Associates uses the following matrix to rate issues on their potential to affect a client's business. For example, if an issue gets a 10 on its potential impact on the business and an 8 on the client's ability to influence the outcome, it will fall into the upper-right-hand quadrant of the matrix, meaning it should be high priority.

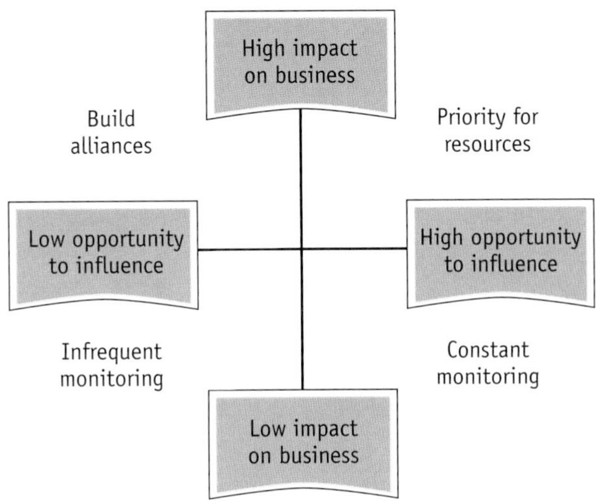

The interaction of organizations with various elements of society has led to the emergence of issues management as an important part of effective public relations and strategic planning. Essentially, issues management is a proactive and systematic approach to (1) predict problems, (2) anticipate threats, (3) minimize surprises, (4) resolve issues, and (5) prevent crises. Martha Lauzen, a professor at San Diego State University, says effective issues management requires two-way communications, formal environmental scanning, and active sense-making strategies.

Another definition of issues management has been formulated by Coates, Coates, Jarratt, and Heinz in their book *Issues Management: How You Can Plan, Organize, and Manage for the Future.* They say, "Issues management is the organized activity of identifying emerging trends, concerns, or issues likely to affect an organization in the next few years and developing a wider and more positive range of organizational responses toward the future."

The basic concept of issues management is proactive planning. Philip Gaunt and Jeff Ollenburger, writing in *Public Relations Review,* say, "Issues management is proactive in that it tries to identify issues and influence decisions regarding them before they have a detrimental effect on a corporation."

Gaunt and Ollenburger contrast this approach with crisis management (see Chapter 8) that is essentially reactive in nature. They note, "Crisis management tends to be more reactive dealing with an issue after it becomes public knowledge and affects the company." In other words, active planning and prevention through issues management can often mean the difference between a noncrisis and a crisis. Or, as one practitioner put it, the difference between little or no news coverage and a page-one headline. This point is particularly relevant because studies show (see Chapter 8) that the majority of organizational crises are self-inflicted because management ignored early warning signs.

The issue about the exploitation of women and children in Third-World sweatshops to make clothes for American companies, for example, simmered for several years before it finally broke into headlines after a worker activist group finally accused television celebrity Kathie Lee Gifford of using "sweatshop" labor to make her clothing line for Wal-Mart Stores. (See Chapter 19.)

Such revelations put the entire U.S. garment industry on the defensive. David Birenbaum, a consultant to the garment industry, wrote in the *Wall Street Journal* that the issue of using cheap Third-World labor was not really new, but the public reaction to such practices was different. He wrote, in an op-ed article, "What's changed is that for the first time human rights concerns could become a major marketing issue. . . . More and more importers are now considering safety and other conditions in Asian factories. Few can afford not to, because all it takes is one disaster to damage a label's reputation."

All the publicity and public outrage, however, might have been avoided if the various clothing and athletic shoe manufacturers had paid attention to the concepts of issues management.

Public relations counselors W. Howard Chase and Barrie L. Jones were among the first practitioners to specialize in issues management. They defined the process as five basic steps: (1) issue identification, (2) issue analysis, (3) strategy options, (4) action plan, and (5) evaluation of results. The following is an illustration of how these steps could have been used by the garment industry.

Issue Identification

Organizations should track the alternative press, mainstream media, online chat groups, and the newsletters of activist groups to learn what issues and concerns are being discussed. Of particular importance is establishing a trend line of coverage. Concern about the working conditions of women and children in the garment industry began showing up as an emerging issue several years before the Kathie Lee Gifford exposé.

Issue Analysis

Once an emerging issue is identified, the next step is assessment of its potential impact on the organization. Another consideration is whether the organization is vulnerable on the issue. Are its policies exploitative? Is the company being ethical and socially responsible by turning a blind eye to violations of human rights in the interest of high profit margins? Can revelations about sweatshop conditions affect sales or damage the label's reputation?

Strategy Options

If the company decides that the emerging issue is potentially damaging, the next step is to consider what to do about it. One option might be to set higher standards for foreign contractors seeking the company's business. Another option: Work with human rights groups to monitor possible violations in foreign factories that produce the company's products. A third option might be to establish a new policy that would assure Third-World workers decent pay and health benefits. The pros and cons of each option are weighed against what is most practical and economical for the company.

Action Plan

Once a policy is decided, the fourth step is to communicate it to all interested publics. These may include consumers, the U.S. Department of Labor, labor unions and worker activist groups, company employees, and the financial community. The action may be an opportunity to use the new policy as a marketing tool among consumers who make buying decisions based on a company's level of social responsibility.

Evaluation

With the new policy in place and communicated, the final step is to evaluate the results. Has news coverage been positive and favorable? Have activist groups called off boycotts of your product? Have the working conditions for women and children in the factories improved? Is the company being positioned as an industry leader? Have public perceptions of the company and the industry improved? If the company has acted soon enough, perhaps the greatest measurement of success is avoiding the media coverage that occurs when the problem eventually becomes a crisis.

How issues and situations become crises is discussed further in Chapter 8.

Summary

The Value of Planning

After research, the next step is program planning. Such planning must be strategic.

Approaches to Planning

Two approaches to planning are management by objective (MBO) and Ketchum's strategic planning model. Both involve asking and answering many questions.

Elements of a Program Plan

A program plan is either a brief outline or an extensive document identifying what is to be done and how. Firms prepare these for client approval. They usually include the eight elements of situation, objectives, audience, strategy, tactics, a calendar or timetable, budget, and evaluation.

Planning in Issues Management

Issues management is a proactive and systematic approach to predict problems, anticipate threats, minimize surprises, resolve issues, and prevent crises. The five steps in the issues management process are issue identification, issue analysis, strategy options, an action plan, and evaluation of results.

Case Activity: What Would You Do?

Sunshine Cafe, a chain of coffee houses, did some market research and found that college students would be an excellent audience to reach. To this end, Sunshine Cafe has contacted your public relations firm and asked that you develop a comprehensive plan to (1) create brand awareness among college students and (2) increase walk-in business at their local stores in college towns.

Using the eight-point planning outline described in this chapter, write a public relations program for Sunshine Cafe. You should consider a variety of communication tools, including events on a campus. However, no money is allocated for advertising.

Questions for Review and Discussion

1. Why is planning so important in the public relations process?
2. What is MBO, and how can it be applied to public relations planning?
3. Name the eight elements of a program plan.
4. Name the three situations that often require a public relations campaign.
5. Explain the difference between an "informational" objective and a "motivational" objective.
6. Should a practitioner define an audience as "general public"? Why or why not?
7. What is the difference between a "strategy" and an "objective"?
8. Review the Levis Jeans company's strategies and tactics for reversing Levi's stodgy image. Do you think it was a well-conceived campaign?
9. Why are timing and scheduling so important in a public relations campaign?
10. What is the largest expense in a campaign conducted by a public relations firm?
11. What are the five steps in the issues management process?
12. How can effective issues management prevent organizational crises?

Suggested Readings

Austin, Erica, and Pinkleton, Bruce. *Strategic Communication Management: Planning and Managing Effective Communication Programs.* Mahwah, NJ: Lawrence Erlbaum Associates, 2001.

Bounds, Wendy, and Stout, Hilary. "Sweatshop Pact: Good Fit or Threadbare? Industry Could Get a PR Boon, but Activists Worry." *Wall Street Journal,* April 10, 1997, p A2.

Gaunt, Philip, and Ollenburger, Jeff. "Issues Management Revisited: A Tool That Deserves Another Look." *Public Relations Review,* Fall 1995, pp. 199–210.

Gibbs, Nancy. "Cause Celeb." *Time,* June 17, 1996, pp. 28–30.

Heath, Robert L., and Nelson, Richard. *Issues Management.* Newbury Park, CA: Sage Publications, 1986.

Kendall, Robert. *Public Relations Campaign Strategies.* New York: HarperCollins, 1996.

Lauzen, Martha M. "Public Relations Manager Involvement in Strategic Issue Diagnosis." *Public Relations Review,* Winter 1995, pp. 287–303.

McElreath, Mark P. *Managing Systematic and Ethical Public Relations Campaigns.* Madison, WI: Brown & Benchmark, 1996.

Nager, Norman R., and Allen, T. Harrell. *Public Relations Management by Objectives.* New York: Longman, 1983.

Thomsen, Steven R. "Using Online Databases in Corporate Issues Management." *Public Relations Review,* Fall 1995, pp. 103–121.

Tucker, Kerry, and Broom, Glen. "Managing Issues: A Bridge to Strategic Planning." *Public Relations Journal,* November 1993, pp. 38–40.

Communication

preview

In this chapter, the objective is to explain the basic process of communication, the theories that underlie it, and its techniques, in order to help students formulate and disseminate effective messages.

Topics covered in this chapter include:

- A public relations perspective
- Paying attention to the message
- Understanding the message
- Believing the message
- Remembering the message
- Acting on the message
- Crisis communication, with case studies
- Risk communication

The Goals of Communication

The third step in the public relations process, after research and planning, is communication. This step, also called *execution,* is the most visible part of public relations work.

Implementing the Plan

In a public relations program, as pointed out in Chapter 7, *communication is the implementation of a decision,* the process and the means by which *objectives* are achieved. A program's *strategies and tactics* may take the form of news releases, news conferences, special events, brochures, speeches, bumper stickers, newsletters, rallies, posters, and the like.

The goals of the communication process are to inform, persuade, motivate, or achieve mutual understanding. To be an effective communicator, a person must have basic knowledge of (1) what constitutes communication and how people receive messages, (2) how people process information and change their perceptions, and (3) what kinds of media and communication tools are most appropriate for a particular message.

Concerning the last point, Kirk Hallahan of Colorado State University makes the point that today's communication revolution has given public relations professionals a full range of communication tools and media, and the traditional approach of simply obtaining publicity in the mass media—newspapers, magazines, radio, and television—is no longer sufficient, if it ever was. He writes:

> PR program planners need to reexamine their traditional approaches to the practice and think about media *broadly* and *strategically.* PR media planners must now address some of the same questions that confront advisers. What media best meet a program's objectives? How can media be combined to enhance program effectiveness? What media are most efficient to reach key audience?

Hallahan's concept of an integrated public relations media model, which outlines five categories of media, is shown in Table 8.1. Many of these media are discussed in Part 5, Tactics, at the end of this book.

A Public Relations Perspective

A number of variables must be considered when planning a message on behalf of an employer or client.

Patrick Jackson, editor of *pr reporter* and a senior counselor, believed the communicator should ask whether the proposed message is (1) appropriate, (2) meaningful, (3) memorable, (4) understandable, and (5) believable to the prospective recipient. "Many a wrongly directed or unnecessary communication has been corrected or dropped by using a screen like this," Jackson says.

In addition to examining the proposed content, a communicator should determine exactly what objective is sought through the communication. James Grunig, professor of public relations at the University of Maryland, lists five possible objectives for a communicator:

1. *Message exposure.* Public relations personnel provide materials to the mass media and disseminate other messages through controlled media such as newsletters and brochures. Intended audiences are exposed to the message in various forms.

TABLE 8.1

An Integrated Public Relations Media Model. The variety and scope of media and communication tools available to public relations professionals runs the spectrum from mass media (public media) to one-on-one communication (interpersonal communication). Here, in chart form, is a concept developed by Professor Kirk Hallahan at Colorado State University.

CHARACTERISTIC	*PUBLIC MEDIA*	*INTERACTIVE MEDIA*	*CONTROLLED MEDIA*	*EVENTS/GROUPS*	*ONE-ON-ONE*
Key use	Build awareness	Respond to queries; Exchange information	Promotion; provide Detailed information	Motivate attendees; Reinforce attitudes	Obtain commitments; Resolve problems
Examples	Newspapers, magazines, radio, television	Computer-based World Wide Web, databases, e-mail listservs, newsgroups, chat rooms, bulletin boards	Brochures, newsletters, sponsored magazines, annual reports, books, direct mail, point of purchase displays, videobrochures	Speeches, trade shows, exhibits, meetings/conferences, demonstrations, rallies, sponsorships, anniversaries	Personal visits, lobbying, personal letters, telephone calls, telemarketing
Nature of communication	Nonpersonal	Nonpersonal	Nonpersonal	Quasi-personal	Personal
Direction of communication	One-way	Quasi-two-way	One-way	Quasi-two-way	Two-way
Technological sophistication	High	High	Moderate	Moderate	Low
Channel ownership	Media organizations	Common carrier or institution	Sponsor	Sponsor or other organization	None
Messages chosen by	Third parties and producers	Receiver	Sponsor	Sponsor or joint organization	Producer and audience
Audience involvement	Low	High	Moderate	Moderate	High
Reach	High	Moderate-low	Moderate-low	Low	Low
Cost per impression	Extremely low	Low	Moderate	Moderate	High
Key challenges to effectiveness	Competition; media clutter	Availability, accessibility	Design, distribution	Attendence, atmosphere	Empowerment, personal dynamics

2. *Accurate dissemination of the message.* The basic information, often filtered by media gatekeepers, remains intact as it is transmitted through various media.
3. *Acceptance of the message.* Based on its view of reality, the audience not only retains the message but accepts it as valid.
4. *Attitude change.* The audience not only believes the message but makes a verbal or mental commitment to change behavior as a result of the message.
5. *Change in overt behavior.* Members of the audience actually change their current behavior or purchase the product and use it.

PR insights

A Behavioral Communication Model

The behavioral communication model, suggests *PR Reporter,* is better than traditional communication models because it forces practitioners to think in terms of what behaviors they are trying to motivate in target publics, rather than what information is being communicated. The process is described as follows:

1. *Awareness.* Salience or relevance is the key to reaching awareness. The purpose of communication here is to create awareness, which is the start of any behavioral process.
2. *Latent readiness.* Either positive or negative readiness to behave in a certain way starts to form, often subconsciously (latently). People get ready to act by accumulating and developing experience, information, word-of-mouth, beliefs, opinions, and emotions.
3. *Triggering event.* The triggering event step gives people a chance to act on their latent readiness. Triggering events may be an election day, a store sale, distribution of a company's annual report, or even a major event announcing a new product or service. Public relations people should build triggering events into their planning: This moves the emphasis from communication to behavior motivation.
4. *Behavior.* Although the ultimate goal is to motivate people to buy something or act in a certain way, they may adopt intermediate behaviors such as requesting more literature, visiting a showroom, or trying the product or idea experimentally.

Grunig says that most public relations experts usually aim at the first two objectives, exposure to the message and accurate dissemination. The last three objectives depend in large part on a mix of variables—predisposition to the message, peer reinforcement, feasibility of the suggested action, and environmental context, to name a few. The first two objectives are easier to evaluate than attitude change (see Chapter 10).

Although the communicator cannot always control the outcome of a message, researchers recognize that effective dissemination is the beginning of the process that leads to opinion change and adoption of products or services. Therefore, it is important to review all components of the communication process.

David Therkelsen, director of marketing for the American Red Cross in St. Paul, Minnesota, succinctly outlines the process:

> To be successful, a message must be *received* by the intended individual or audience. It must get the audience's *attention.* It must be *understood.* It must be *believed.* It must be *remembered.* And ultimately, in some fashion, it must be *acted upon.* Failure to accomplish *any* of these tasks means the entire message fails.

Therkelsen appropriately places the emphasis on the audience and what it does with the message. The following sections elaborate on the six elements he enumerates.

Receiving the Message

Several communication models explain how a message moves from the sender to the recipient. Some are quite complex, attempting to incorporate an almost infinite number of events, ideas, objects, and people that interact among the message, channel, and receiver.

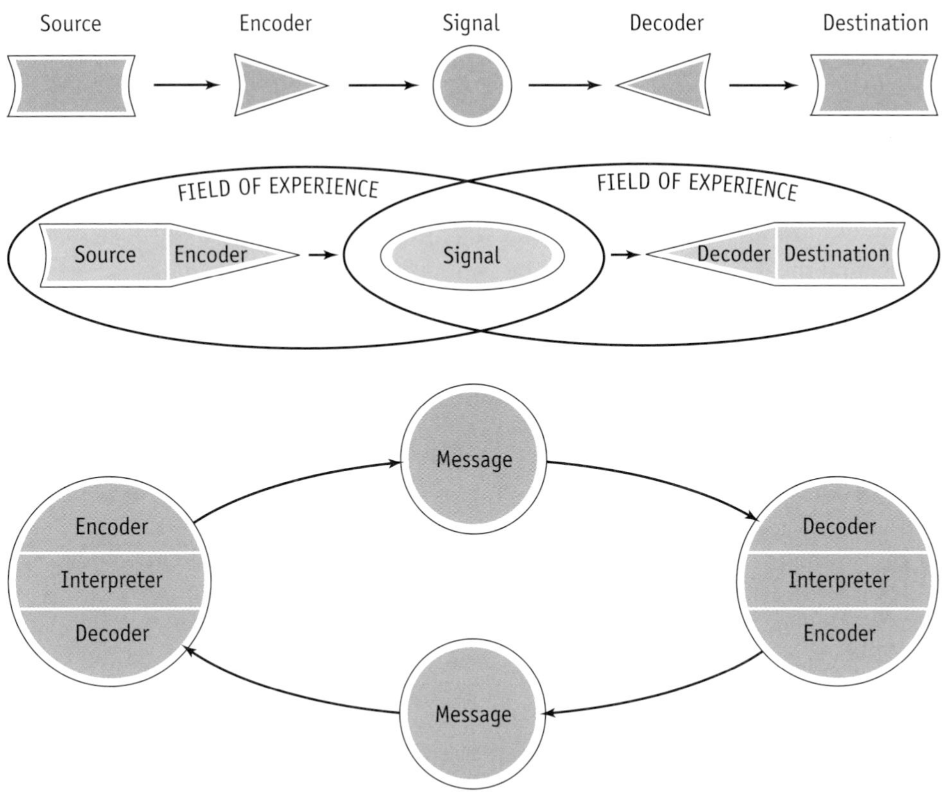

FIGURE 8.1

These three models, formulated by Wilbur Schramm, show the evolution of portraying communication as an interactive process between a sender and a receiver. Effective communication takes place within a sphere of "shared experience."

Five Communication Elements

Most communication models, however, incorporate four basic elements. David K. Berlo's model is an example. It has *sender/source (encoder), message, channel,* and *receiver (decoder).* A fifth element, *feedback* from the receiver to the sender, is now incorporated in modern models of communication.

Mass media researcher Wilbur Schramm's early models (see Figure 8.1) started with a simple communication model (top), but he later expanded the process to include the concept of "shared experience" (middle diagram). In other words, little or no communication is achieved unless the sender and the receiver share a common language and even an overlapping cultural or educational background. The importance of "shared experience" becomes apparent when a highly technical news release about a new computer system causes a local business editor to shake his or her head in bewilderment.

Schramm's third model (bottom) incorporates the idea of continuous feedback. Both the sender and the receiver continually encode, interpret, decode, transmit, and receive information. The loop process also is integral to all models showing the public relations process of research, planning, communication, and evaluation. This concept was illustrated in Chapter 1, which showed public relations as a cyclical process. Communication to internal and external audiences produces feedback that is taken into consideration during research, the first step, and evaluation, the fourth step. In this way, the structure and dissemination of messages are continuously refined for maximum effectiveness.

The Importance of Two-Way Communication

Another way to think of feedback is two-way communication. One-way communication, from sender to receiver, only disseminates information. Such a monologue is less effective than two-way communication, which establishes a dialogue between sender and receiver.

Grunig goes even further to postulate that the ideal public relations model is two-way symmetrical communication. That is, communication is balanced between the sender and the receiver. He says: "In the symmetric model, understanding is the principal objective of public relations, rather than persuasion."

In reality, research shows most organizations have mixed motives when they engage in two-way communication with targeted audiences. Although they may employ dialogue to obtain a better sense of how they can adjust to the needs of an audience, their motive often is asymmetrical—to convince the audience of their point of view through dialogue.

The most effective two-way communication, of course, is two people talking to each other. Small-group discussion is also effective. In both forms the message is fortified by gestures, facial expressions, intimacy, tone of voice, and the opportunity for instant feedback. If the listener asks a question or appears puzzled, the speaker has an instant cue and can rephrase the information or amplify a point.

Barriers to communication tend to mount as one advances to large-group meetings and, ultimately, to the mass media. Organizational materials can reach thousands and, through the mass media, even millions of people at the same time, but the psychological and physical distance between sender and receiver is considerably lengthened. Communication is less effective because the audience no longer is involved with the source. No immediate feedback is possible, and the message may undergo distortion as it passes through mass-media gatekeepers.

Models of communication emphasize the importance of feedback as an integral component of the process. As they implement communication strategies, public relations personnel need to give it careful attention.

Paying Attention to the Message

Sociologist Harold Lasswell has defined the act of communication as "Who, says what, in which channel, to whom, with what effect?"

Although in public relations much emphasis is given to the formation and dissemination of messages, this effort is wasted if the audience pays no attention. It is therefore important to remember the axiom of Walt Seifert, professor emeritus of public relations at Ohio State University. He says: "Dissemination does not equal publication, and publication does not equal absorption and action." In other words, "All who receive it won't publish it, and all who read or hear won't understand or act upon it."

Some Theoretical Perspectives

Seifert and social psychologists recognize that the majority of an audience at any given time is not particularly interested in a message or in adopting an idea. This doesn't mean, however, that audiences are merely passive receivers of information. Werner

Severin and James Tankard, in their text *Communication Theories,* quote one researcher as saying:

> The communicator's audience is not a passive recipient—it cannot be regarded as a lump of clay to be molded by the master propagandist. Rather, the audience is made up of individuals who demand something from the communication to which they are exposed, and who select those that are likely to be useful to them.

This is called the *media uses and gratification theory* of communication. Its basic premise is that the communication process is interactive. The communicator wants to inform and even persuade; the recipient wants to be entertained, informed, or alerted to opportunities that can fulfill individual needs.

In other words, audiences come to messages for very different reasons. People use mass media for such purposes as: (1) surveillance of the environment to find out what is happening, locally or even globally, that has some impact on them; (2) entertainment and diversion; (3) reinforcement of their opinions and predispositions; and (4) decision making about buying a product or service.

Uses and gratification theory assumes that people make highly intelligent choices about which messages require their attention and fulfill their needs. If this is true, as research indicates it is, the public relations communicator must tailor messages that focus on getting the audience's attention.

One approach is to understand the mental state of the intended audience. Grunig and Hunt, in *Managing Public Relations,* suggest that communication strategies be designed to attract the attention of two kinds of audiences, those who actively seek information and those who passively process information.

Passive audiences may initially pay attention to a message only because it is entertaining and offers a diversion. They can be made aware of the message through brief encounters—with a billboard glimpsed on the way to work, a radio announcement heard in the car, a television advertisement broadcast before a show begins, and information available in a doctor's waiting room. In other words, passive audiences use communication channels that can be utilized while they are doing little else.

For this reason, passive audiences need messages that have style and creativity. The person must be lured by photos, illustrations, and catchy slogans into processing information. Press agentry, the dramatic picture, the use of celebrities, radio and television announcements, and events featuring entertainment can make passive audiences aware of a message. The objectives of a communication, therefore, are simply exposure to and accurate dissemination of a message. In most public relations campaigns, communications are designed to reach primarily passive audiences.

A communicator's approach to audiences that actively seek information is different. These people are already at the *interest* stage of the adoption process (discussed later) and seek more sophisticated supplemental information. The tools may include brochures, in-depth newspaper and magazine articles, slide presentations, videotape presentations, symposiums and conferences, major speeches before key groups, and demonstrations at trade shows.

At any given time, of course, the intended audience has both passive and active information-seekers in it. It is important, therefore, that multiple messages and a variety of communication tools be used in a full-fledged information campaign.

Public relations personnel have two ways by which to determine strategies. First, research into audience attitudes can give insight into the extent of group interest in, or apathy toward, a new product or idea. Second, more efficient communication can be achieved if the intended audience is segmented as much as possible. After dividing an audience into segments, a practitioner can select the appropriate communication tools.

Other Attention-Getting Concepts

Communicators should think in terms of the five senses—sight, hearing, smell, touch, and taste. Television and film or videotape are the most effective methods of communication because they engage an audience's senses of sight and hearing. In addition are their attractions of color and movement. Radio, on the other hand, relies on only the sense of hearing. Print media, although capable of communicating a large amount of information in great detail, rely only on sight.

Individuals learn through all five senses, but psychologists estimate that 83 percent of learning is accomplished through sight. Hearing accounts for 11 percent. Fifty percent of what individuals retain consists of what they see and hear. For this reason speakers often use visual aids.

These figures have obvious implications for the public relations practitioner. Any communication strategy should, if possible, include vehicles of communication designed to tap the senses of sight or hearing, or a combination of the two. In other words, a variety of communication tools is needed, including news releases, publicity photos, slide presentations, videotapes, billboards, newsletters, radio announcements, video news releases, media interviews, and news conferences. This multiple approach not only assists learning and retention, discussed later, but provides repetition of a message in a variety of forms that accommodate audience needs.

Other research suggests that audience attention can be generated if the communicator raises a "need" level first. The idea is to "hook" an audience's attention by beginning the message with something that will make its members' lives easier or benefit them in some way. An example is a message from the Internal Revenue Service. It could begin with a reminder about the necessity of filing tax returns on time, but it would get far more audience attention if it opened by urging people to take all the exemptions for which they were eligible. The prospect of paying less tax would be alluring to most people.

Public relations writers also should be aware that audience attention is highest at the beginning of a message. Thus it is wise to state the major point at the beginning, give details in the middle, and end with a summary of the message.

Another technique to garner audience attention is to begin a message with a statement that reflects audience values and predispositions. This is called *channeling*. (See Chapter 10.) According to social science research, people pay attention to messages that reinforce their predispositions.

Prior knowledge and interest also make people pay more attention to messages. If a message taps current events or issues of public concern already in the news, there is an increased chance that the audience will pay attention.

Understanding the Message

Communication is the act of transmitting information, ideas, and attitudes from one person to another. Communication can take place, however, only if the sender and receiver have a common understanding of the symbols being used.

Effective Use of Language

Words are the most common symbols. The degree to which two people understand each other is heavily dependent on their common knowledge of word symbols. Anyone who has traveled abroad can readily attest that very little communication occurs between two people who speak different languages. Even signs translated into English for tourists often lead to some confusing and amusing messages. A brochure for a Japanese hotel, for example, said, "In our hotel, you will be well fed and agreeably drunk. In every room there is a large window offering delightful prospects."

Even if the sender and receiver speak the same language and live in the same country, the effectiveness of their communication depends on such factors as education, social class, regional differences, nationality, and cultural background.

Employee communication specialists are particularly aware of such differences as a multicultural workforce becomes the norm for most organizations. One major factor is the impact of a global economy in which organizations have operations and employees in many countries. A second factor is the increasing multicultural composition of the American workforce. One study says that 85 percent of new entries in the workforce early in the new century will be white women, immigrants, African Americans, Hispanics, and Asians. For many of these workers, English will be a second language.

These statistical trends will require communicators to be better informed about cultural differences and conflicting values in order to find common ground and build bridges between various groups. At the same time, a major task will be to communicate in clear and simple terms. A national survey by the Educational Testing Service found that 42 million American adults fall within the lowest category of literacy. Other studies show that one in eight employees reads at no better than fourth-grade level.

Writing for Clarity

The nature of the audience and its literacy level are important considerations for any communicator. The key is to produce messages that match, in content and structure, the characteristics of the audience.

global PR

Different Worlds of Value Systems

Many theories that explain the communication process are applicable around the world. The application of communication theory, however, is closely tied to the values of a particular culture. A.H. Tobaccowala of Voltas Limited in India makes this observation:

> While galloping modernization and the impact of global value systems will accelerate, as of now the idols and heroes of most people in Asia are not the highly successful wealthy industrialists or the stars of the entertainment world or the record breakers in sports. Those who are most honored, admired, and almost worshipped are the Gandhis, the Mandelas, the Mother Theresas, the monks, and the ascetics. This is a world of very different value systems that the western PR person must deal with.

The Illinois Public Health Department had the right idea when it commissioned a song in rap-music style as one way to inform low-income, poorly educated groups about the dangers of AIDS. The words and music of the "Condom Rag," however, were offensive to elected officials, who cancelled the song.

This example poses the classic dilemma for the expert communicator. Should the message be produced for supervisors, who may be totally different in background and education from the intended audience, or should it be produced with the audience in mind? The obvious answer is the latter, but it is often difficult to convince management of this. One solution is to copy-test all public relations materials on a target audience. This helps convince management—and communicators—that what they like isn't necessarily what the audience wants, needs, or understands.

Another approach is to apply readability and comprehension formulas to materials before they are produced and disseminated. Learning theory makes the case: The simpler the piece of writing, the easier it will be for audiences to understand.

The most widely known readability formula is by Rudolph Flesch. Another is by Barr, Jenkins, and Peterson. Both are based on average sentence length and the number of one-syllable words per 100 words. If a randomly selected sample of 100 words contains 4.2 sentences and 142 syllables, it is ranked at about ninth-grade level. This is the level for which most news releases and daily newspapers strive. In other words, long, complex sentences (more than 19 words) and multisyllabic words ("compensation" instead of "pay") reduce comprehension for the average reader.

The *Cloze* procedure, developed by William Taylor, also tests comprehension. The concept comes from the idea of closure, the human tendency to complete a familiar but incomplete pattern. In the *Cloze* procedure, copy is tested for comprehension and redundancy by having test subjects read passages in which every fifth or ninth word is removed. Their ability to fill in the missing words determines whether the pattern of words is familiar and people can understand the message.

Audience understanding and comprehension can also be increased by following some of the following concepts.

Use Symbols, Acronyms, and Slogans Clarity and simplicity of message are enhanced by these devices. Each is a form of shorthand that quickly conceptualizes ideas and travels through extended lines of communication.

The world is full of symbols, such as the Christian cross, the Star of David, and the crusading sword of the American Cancer Society. Corporate symbols such as the Mercedes Benz star, the Nike swoosh, and the multicolored apple of Apple Computer are known throughout the world. The concept is called branding, and corporations invest considerable time and money to make their names and logos become a symbol for quality and service.

A symbol should be unique, memorable, widely recognized, and appropriate. Organizations spend considerable time and energy searching for unique symbols that convey the essence of what they are or hope to be. Considerable amounts of money are then spent on publicizing the symbols and creating meanings for them.

Acronyms also are shorthand for conveying information. An acronym is a word formed from the initial letters of other words. The Group Against Smokers' Pollution goes by the acronym GASP; Juvenile Opportunities in Business becomes JOB. The National Organization for Women has the acronym NOW, which says a great deal about its political priorities.

In many cases, the acronym—because it is short and simple—becomes the common name. The mass media continually use the term AIDS instead of "acquired immune deficiency syndrome." And "UNESCO" is easier to write and say than United Nations Educational, Scientific, and Cultural Organization.

Slogans help condense a concept. Massive advertising and promotion have made "Don't Leave Home without It" readily identified with American Express. "The Ultimate Driving Machine" is strongly identified with BMW, an acronym for Bavarian Motor Works.

Avoid Jargon One source of blocked communication is technical and bureaucratic jargon. When delivered to a general audience, it is called *semantic noise* by social scientists. Jargon interferes with the message and impedes the receiver's ability to understand it. An example of a useless news release is the following, which was actually sent to business editors of daily newspapers. This is how it began:

> Versatec, a Xerox Company, has introduced the Graphics Network Processor-SNA (Model 451). The processor, operating as a 377x RJE station, sends and receives EBCDIC or binary data in IMB System Network Architecture (SNA) networks using Synchronous Data Link Control (SDLC) protocol. . . .

This news release may be perfectly appropriate for an engineering publication serving a particular industry, but the information must be written in simple terms for the readers of a daily newspaper. A failure to understand the audience means a failure in communication.

Make the Campfire Right Before You Light

Smokey is counting on you to build a safe campfire.

1. Dig a small pit away from overhanging branches.
2. Circle the pit with rocks.
3. Clear a five-foot area around the pit down to the soil.
4. Keep a bucket of water and shovel nearby.
5. Stack extra wood upwind and away from the fire.
6. After lighting, do not discard match until it is cold.
7. Never leave a campfire unattended, even for a minute.

REMEMBER, ONLY YOU CAN PREVENT FOREST FIRES.

A Public Service of the USDA Forest Service and Your State Forester.

Ad Council

Smokey Bear is a familiar symbol in the campaign to prevent forest fires. Some advertisements for Smokey merely carry the slogan "Only You," while others like this one include a detailed list of prevention measures. The Advertising Council prepares the campaign.

■ **Avoid Clichés and Hype Words** Highly charged words with connotative meanings can pose problems, and overuse of clichés and hype words can seriously undermine the credibility of the message.

The *Wall Street Journal,* for example, mocked the business of high-technology public relations with a story titled, "High-Tech Hype Reaches New Heights." A reporter analyzed 201 news releases and compiled a "Hype Hit Parade" which included the 11 most overused and ineffective words. They were *leading, enhanced, unique, significant, solution, integrated, powerful, innovative, advanced, high performance,* and *sophisticated.*

Similar surveys have uncovered overused words in business and public relations. A New York firm, John Rost Associates, compiled a list of words and phrases used excessively in business letters and reports. The list includes: *agenda, proactive, interface, networking, finalize, done deals, impact, bottom-line, vis-à-vis, world class, state-of-the-art, user-friendly, competitive edge, know-how, win–win, breakthrough, fast track, hands-on, input, dialogue,* and *no-brainer.*

A survey of corporate annual reports also reveals the constant use of certain words. Robert K. Otterbourg, president of a company that does annual reports for corporations, says the most overused words include *challenge, opportunity, fundamental achievements, pioneering efforts,* and *state-of-the-art.*

■ **Avoid Euphemisms** A euphemism, according to Frank Grazian, founding editor of *Communication Briefings,* is "an inoffensive word or phrase that is less direct and less distasteful than the one that represents reality."

Public relations personnel should use positive, favorable words to convey a message, but they have an ethical responsibility not to use words that hide information or mislead. Probably little danger exists in substituting positive words such as saying a person has a "disability" rather than using the word "handicapped." Some euphemisms can even cause amusement when car mechanics become "automotive internists" and luxury cars are called "pre-owned" on the used car lot.

More dangerous are euphemisms that actually alter the meaning or impact of a word or concept. Writers call this *doublespeak*—words that pretend to communicate but really do not. Governments are famous for doublespeak. In the Persian Gulf War, U.S. military briefing officers described civilian casualties and destruction as "collateral damage." And Serbian authorities used the term "ethnic cleansing" to sanitize the murder of thousands in Kosovo. A government economist once called a recession "a meaningful downturn in aggregate output."

Corporations also use euphemisms and doublespeak to hide unfavorable news. Reducing the number of employees, for example, is often called "right-sizing," "skill mix adjustment," or "career assignment and relocation." An airline once called the crash of a plane "the involuntary conversion of a 727."

Use of euphemisms to hide or mislead obviously is contrary to professional public relations standards and the public interest. As William Lutz writes in *Public Relations Quarterly,* "Such language breeds suspicion, cynicism, distrust, and, ultimately, hostility."

■ **Avoid Discriminatory Language** In today's world, effective communication also means *nondiscriminatory* communication. Public relations personnel should double-check every message to eliminate undesirable gender, racial, and ethnic connotations.

In regard to gender, it is unnecessary to write about something as being *man-made* when a word like *synthetic* or *artificial* is just as good. Companies no longer have *man-*

power but *employees, personnel,* and *workers.* Most civic organizations have *chairpersons* now, and cities have *firefighters* instead of *firemen* and *police officers* instead of *policemen.* Airlines, of course, have *flight attendants* instead of *stewardesses.*

Writers also should be careful about descriptive phrases for women. *Bulldog Reporter,* a West Coast public relations newsletter, once criticized a Chicago public relations firm for describing a female company president as "a tall, attractive blonde who could easily turn heads on Main Street [but] is instead turning heads on Wall Street."

Nor is it appropriate in professional settings to say that a woman is the wife of someone also well known. A female vice president of a public relations firm cried foul when a local newsletter described her as the wife of a prominent journalist. The newsletter editor apologized in the next issue.

Messages should not identify any individual by ethnic designation, but it may be necessary in some situations to designate a particular ethnic or racial group. Although fashions and preferences change, today's writers use *Asian American* instead of the now pejorative *Oriental.* And the term *Hispanic* is now more acceptable than the politically charged *Spanish-speaking.* The term *Latino,* however, raises some controversy; some women say that it is sexist because the "o" in Spanish is male.

The term *black* seems to be making a comeback, according to the U.S. Department of Labor that surveyed 60,000 households in 1995 about the names of race and ethnic categories to use in job statistics. Forty-four percent of the blacks preferred this designation, while another 28 percent preferred *African American* and 12 percent chose *Afro-American.* As a matter of policy, many newspapers use *African American* on first reference and *black* on second reference. Headlines almost always use *black* because it is short.

Believing the Message

One key variable in the communication process, discussed further in Chapter 10, is *source credibility.* Do members of the audience perceive the source as knowledgeable and expert on the subject? Do they perceive the source as honest and objective or just representing a special interest? Audiences, for example, ascribe lower credibility to statements in an advertisement than to the same information contained in a news article because news articles are selected by media gatekeepers.

Source credibility is a problem for any organizational spokesperson because the public already has a bias. In one study conducted for the GCI Group, Opinion Research Corporation found that more than half of the Americans surveyed are likely to believe a large company is probably guilty of some wrongdoing if it is being investigated by a government agency or if a major lawsuit is filed against the company. At the same time, only one-third would trust the statements of a large company.

The problem of source credibility is the main reason that organizations, whenever possible, use respected outside experts or celebrities as representatives to convey their messages.

The *sleeper effect* also influences source credibility. This concept was developed by Carl Hovland, who stated: "There is decreased tendency over time to reject the material presented by an untrustworthy source."

In other words, even if organizations are perceived initially as not being very credible sources, people may retain the information and eventually separate the source from the opinion. On the other hand, studies show that audiences register more constant opinion change if they perceive the source to be highly credible in the first place.

focus on ethics

How Do You Write This News Release?

You work in public relations for a large medical center, and one of your duties is publicizing major research studies by the staff.

One study that comes across your desk shows that postmenopausal women taking estrogen experience a 30-percent increase in the risk of breast cancer. You talk with the head of the research study, and she says that this percentage—when you consider other factors—actually means that a woman who doesn't take estrogen increases her odds of avoiding cancer by only about 1 percent—to 96 percent from 95 percent.

You know the media won't be very much interested in the latter figure because there is no psychological effect of an impressive number. So what do you do? Would you just go ahead and use the 30-percent figure, which is technically correct, or would you write a news release emphasizing the minimal difference?

A second variable in believability is the *context* of the message. Action (performance) speaks louder than a stack of news releases. A bank may spend thousands of dollars on a promotion campaign with the slogan, "Your Friendly Bank—Where Service Counts," but the effort is wasted if employees are not trained to be friendly and courteous.

Incompatible rhetoric and actions can be somewhat amusing at times. At a press briefing about the importance of "buying American," the U.S. Chamber of Commerce passed out commemorative coffee mugs marked in small print on the bottom, "Made in China."

Another barrier to the believability of messages is the audience's predispositions. This problem brings to mind the old saying, "Don't confuse me with the facts, my mind is already made up."

In this case, Leon Festinger's theory of *cognitive dissonance* should be understood. In essence, it says that people will not believe a message contrary to their predispositions unless the communicator can introduce information that causes them to question their beliefs.

Creating dissonance can be done in at least three ways. First, make the target audience aware that circumstances have changed. "In other words," says Patrick Jackson of *PR Reporter,* "they needn't rationalize any longer; it's safe and OK to change because the situation has changed." Second, give information about new developments or discoveries. This is an unthreatening way to break through a person's opinions. Third, use an unexpected spokesperson. Chevron, for example, sought to overcome opposition to some of its oil exploration policies by getting endorsements from several respected leaders in the conservation movement.

Involvement is another important predisposition that impacts how messages are processed by audience members. Involvement can be described in simple terms as interest or concern for an issue or a product. Those with higher involvement often process persuasive messages with greater attention to detail and to logical argument (central processing), while those with low involvement for the topic are impressed more by incidental cues such as an attractive spokesperson, humor, or the number of arguments given. The public relations professional can use the involvement concept to devise messages that focus more on "what is said" for high involvement audiences, with more attention to "who says it" for low involvement audiences.

Remembering the Message

Many messages prepared by public relations personnel are repeated extensively, for several reasons:

- Repetition is necessary because all members of a target audience don't see or hear the message at the same time. Not everyone reads the newspaper on a particular day or watches the same television news program.
- Repetition reminds the audience, so there is less chance of a failure to remember the message. If a source has high credibility, repetition prevents erosion of opinion change.
- Repetition helps the audience remember the message itself. Studies have shown that advertising is quickly forgotten if not repeated constantly.
- Repetition can lead to improved learning and increase the chance of penetrating audience indifference or resistance.

Researchers say that repetition, or redundancy, also is necessary to offset the "noise" surrounding a message. People often hear or see messages in an environment filled with distractions—a baby crying, the conversations of family members or office staff, a barking dog—or even while daydreaming or thinking of other things.

Consequently, communicators often build repetition into a message. Key points may be mentioned at the beginning and then summarized at the end. If the source is asking the receiver to call for more information or write for a brochure, the telephone number or address is repeated several times. Such precautions also fight *entropy,* which means that messages continually lose information as media channels and people process the information and pass it on to others. In one study about employee communications, for example, it was found that rank-and-file workers got only 20 percent of a message that had passed through four levels of managers.

The key to effective communication and retention of the message is to convey information in a variety of ways, using multiple communication channels. This helps people remember the message as they receive it through different media and extends the message to both passive and active audiences.

A good example of using multiple communication tools is a campaign to get a bond issue passed for Macomb Community College in Michigan. The message was quite simple: Vote "Yes." A nonprofit citizens group used 13 communication tools to put the message across: *news releases, media interviews, news conferences, rallies, debates, campaign buttons, speaker's bureau, posters, direct mail, flyers, newsletters, phone calls to registered voters,* and *an essay contest.* The bond issue passed.

Acting on the Message

The ultimate purpose of any message is to have an effect on the recipient. Public relations personnel communicate messages on behalf of organizations to change perceptions, attitudes, opinions, or behavior in some way. Marketing communications, in particular, has the objective of convincing people to buy goods and services.

The Five-Stage Adoption Process

Getting people to act on a message is not a simple process. In fact, research shows that it can be a somewhat lengthy and complex procedure that depends on a number of intervening influences. One key to understanding how people accept new ideas or products is to analyze the adoption process. The five stages, shown in Figure 8.2, are summarized as follows:

1. *Awareness.* A person becomes aware of an idea or a new product, often by means of an advertisement or a news story.
2. *Interest.* The individual seeks more information about the idea or the product, perhaps by ordering a brochure, picking up a pamphlet, or reading an in-depth article in a newspaper or magazine.
3. *Evaluation.* The person evaluates the idea or the product on the basis of how it meets specific needs and wants. Feedback from friends and family is part of this process.
4. *Trial.* Next, the person tries the product or the idea on an experimental basis, by using a sample, witnessing a demonstration, or making qualifying statements such as, "I read . . ."
5. *Adoption.* The individual begins to use the product on a regular basis or integrates the idea into his or her belief system. The "I read . . . " becomes "I think . . ." if peers provide support and reinforcement of the idea.

It is important to realize that a person does not necessarily go through all five stages with any given idea or product. The process may be terminated after any step. In fact, the process is like a large funnel. Although many are made aware of an idea or a product, only a few will ultimately adopt it.

FIGURE 8.2

This graph shows the steps through which an individual or other decision-making unit goes in the innovation-decision process from first knowledge of an innovation to decision to adopt it, followed by implementation of the new idea and confirmation of the decision.

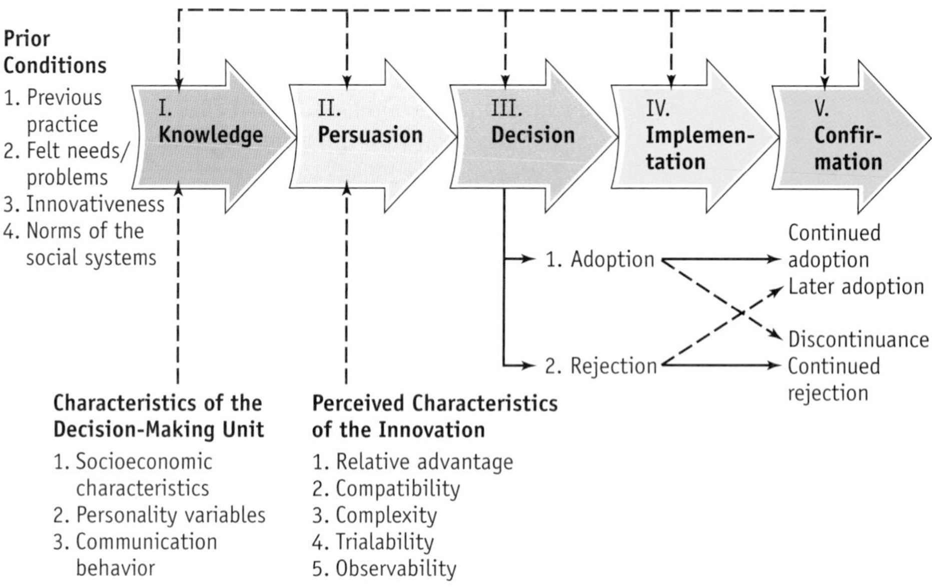

This is because a number of factors affect the adoption process. Everett Rogers, author of *Diffusion of Innovation,* lists at least five:

1. *Relative advantage.* The degree to which an innovation is perceived as better than the idea it replaces
2. *Compatibility.* The degree to which an innovation is perceived as being consistent with the existing values, experiences, and needs of potential adopters
3. *Complexity.* The degree to which an innovation is perceived as difficult to understand and use
4. *Trialability.* The degree to which an innovation may be experienced on a limited basis
5. *Observability.* The degree to which the results of an innovation are visible to others

The communicator should be aware of these factors and attempt to implement communication strategies that will overcome as many of them as possible. Repeating a message in various ways, reducing its complexity, taking into account competing messages, and structuring the message to meet the needs of the audience are ways to do this.

The Time Factor

Another aspect that confuses people is the amount of time needed to adopt a new idea or product. Depending on the individual and situation, the entire adoption process can take place almost instantly if the result is of minor consequence or requires low-level commitment. Buying a new brand of soft drink or a bar of soap is relatively inexpensive and often done on impulse. On the other hand, deciding to buy a new car or vote for a particular candidate may involve an adoption process that takes several weeks or months.

Rogers's research shows that people approach innovation in different ways, depending on their personality traits and the risk involved. "Innovators" are venturesome and eager to try new ideas, while "Laggards" are traditional and the last to adopt anything. Between the two extremes are "Early Adopters," who are opinion leaders; "Early Majority," who take the deliberate approach; and "Late Majority," who are often skeptical but bow to peer pressure.

Psychographics, discussed in Chapter 10, can often help communicators segment audiences that have "Innovator" or "Early Adopter" characteristics and would be predisposed to adopting new ideas.

How Decisions Are Influenced

Of particular interest to public relations people is the primary source of information at each step in the adoption process. Mass media vehicles such as advertising, short news articles, feature stories, and radio and television news announcements are most influential at the *awareness* stage of the adoption process. A news article or a television announcement makes people aware of an idea, event, or new product. They also are made aware through such vehicles as direct mail, office memos, and simple brochures.

Individuals at the *interest stage* also rely on mass media vehicles, but they are actively seeking information and pay attention to longer, in-depth articles. They rely more on detailed brochures, specialized publications, small-group seminars, and meetings to provide details. At the *evaluation, trial,* and *adoption* stages, group norms and opinions are the most influential. Feedback, negative or positive, from friends and peers may determine adoption. If a person's friends generally disapprove of the candidate, the movie, or the automobile brand, it is unlikely that the individual will complete the adoption process even if he or she is highly sold on the idea. If a person does make a commitment, mass media vehicles become reinforcing mechanisms. Studies show, for example, that owners of a new car are the most avid readers of that car's advertising. The complexities of the adoption process show that public relations communicators need to think about the entire communication process—from the formulation of the message to the ways in which receivers ultimately process the information and make decisions. By doing so, communicators can form more effective message strategies and develop realistic objectives for what can actually be accomplished.

A special kind of communication problem comes up when an organization faces a crisis. The following section gives some tips and case studies on how to communicate in such a situation.

Crisis Communications

The communication process, difficult in the best of times, is severely tested in crisis situations when a high degree of uncertainty exists. At such times verifiable information about what is happening or has happened may be lacking.

This causes people to become more active seekers of information and, as research suggests, more dependent on the media for information to satisfy the human desire for closure. A crisis situation, in other words, puts a great deal of pressure on organizations to respond with accurate, complete information as quickly as possible. How an organization responds in the first 24 hours, experts say, often determines whether the situation remains an "incident" or becomes a full-blown crisis.

What Is a Crisis?

Academics cite many dimensions of what constitutes a crisis for an organization. Ole R. Holsti, author of several articles on crisis theory, defines crises as "situations characterized by surprise, high threat to important values, and a short decision time." Thierry C. Pauchant and Ian J. Mitroff, authors of *Transforming the Crisis-Prone Organization,* use this definition: "A disruption that physically affects a system as a whole and threatens its basic assumptions, its subjective sense of self, its existential core." Steven Fink, author of *Crisis Management: Planning for the Inevitable,* states, "Crises are forewarning situations that run the risk of escalating in intensity, falling under close media or government scrutiny, interfering with normal operations, jeopardizing organizational image and damaging a company's bottom line."

Perhaps the best definition, however, is provided by Pacific Telesis, the parent company of Pacific Bell. Its manual on crisis communication says a crisis is "An extraordinary event or series of events that adversely affects the integrity of the product, the reputation or financial stability of the organization; or the health or well-being of employees, the community, or the public at large."

In other words, an organizational crisis can constitute any number of situations. A *PR Week* article makes the point: "Imagine one of these scenarios happening to your

PR casebook

West Point Averts a Crisis

Charges of sexual harassment can seriously damage an organization's reputation and diminish public support.

Officials at West Point knew they had a potential crisis on their hands when a group of women cadets on a "spirit run" were groped as they ran through a cordon of football players at a practice session.

After the women complained, the Academy triggered its crisis communications plan. Four objectives were established: (1) The Academy's investigation would be conducted swiftly, fairly, and openly; (2) the incident was an exception; (3) the complaint should not be equated with the infamous Tailhook scandal; and (4) West Point had a zero tolerance of sexual harassment.

The Academy's superintendent, as the spokesperson, reported the incident at a scheduled meeting with the *New York Times*. The Academy also communicated with the cadets, faculty, employees, alumni, parents, admission officers, the Pentagon, and members of Congress. The public relations staff coordinated media interviews with cadets and officials at the Academy.

Two weeks after the incident, the Academy issued a news release announcing final results of the investigation and the punishment awarded to the guilty cadets. Media reports were uniformly positive about how West Point handled the problem.

By being open, forthright, and candid, and by effectively communicating its policy that sexual harassment would not be tolerated, West Point got its key messages across and emerged from the incident with an enhanced reputation. In fact, acceptance of admission offers from women increased 50 percent from the previous year.

company: a product recall; a plane crash; a very public sexual harassment suit; a gunman holding hostages in your office; an *E. coli* bacteria contamination scare; a market crash, along with the worth of your company stock; a labor union strike; a hospital malpractice suit . . ."

Nor are crises always unexpected. One study by the Institute for Crisis Management found that only 14 percent of business crises are unexpected. The remaining 86 percent are what the Institute called "smoldering" crises in which an organization is aware of a potential business disruption long before the public finds out about it. The study also found that management—or in some cases, mismanagement—caused 78 percent of the crises. "Most organizations have a crisis plan to deal with sudden crises, like accidents," says Robert B. Irvine, president of the Institute. "However, our data indicates many businesses are denying or ducking serious problems that eventually will ignite and cost them millions of dollars and lost management time."

A Lack of Crisis Planning

Echoing Irvine's thought, another study by Steven Fink found that 89 percent of the chief executive officers of Fortune 500 companies reported that a business crisis was almost inevitable; however, 50 percent admitted that they did not have a crisis management plan.

This situation has caused Kenneth Myers, a crisis consultant, to write, "If economics is the dismal science, then contingency planning is the abysmal science." As academics Donald Chisholm and Martin Landry have noted, "When people believe

PR casebook

Flight Disasters Teach Valuable Lessons in Crisis Communications

The night sky framed a fireball plunging into the Atlantic Ocean, and TWA had a crisis on its hands. Flight 800, from New York to Paris, had crashed, killing all 230 persons on board. In such a disaster, it is essential to initiate a crisis communications plan within minutes. TWA, however, was not prepared. Among the mistakes made were the following:

- Calls from the media went unanswered, partly because the airline had no plan in place to handle the heavy volume of inquiries.
- The airline took 16 hours to confirm a passenger list and start notifying relatives.
- The TWA president didn't make a public statement or appearance until the day after the crash, then cut short a news conference, refusing to take questions.
- The airline failed to convey heartfelt sympathy for the victims and their families and to convince the public that it was doing everything possible to deal with the disaster.
- TWA took several days to establish a crisis communications center and provide information on a regular, ongoing basis.

By contrast with the TWA experience, Air Force and Coast Guard officers who handled media relations during John Kennedy Jr.'s tragic plane crash reflect improvements in crisis management. According to *pr reporter* (August 23, 1999), seven valuable lessons were displayed:

1. Don't leave a vacuum—a spokesperson was dispatched immediately.
2. Use a trained spokesperson and stick to the script of what is known.
3. Keep it tight and stay on your turf—refer questions to authoritative sources.
4. Control the agenda, but be generous—cut off questioning on schedule, but let reporters know the time frame.
5. Don't answer hypotheticals or speculate.
6. Consider the audience—avoid acronyms, jargon, and complicated explanations.
7. Skip transparently noncredible statements.

Public relations counselor Jeffrey Geibel summarized the handling of the crisis: "The net result is a better informed public and increased confidence in government agencies and their effectiveness in emergency operations."

that because nothing has gone wrong, nothing will go wrong, they court disaster. There is noise in every system and every design. If this fact is ignored, nature soon reminds us of our folly."

Here is a sampling of major crises that have hit various organizations:

- Nike became the archetype of a company lacking social consciousness about the exploitation of workers in foreign plants. The value of the company stock went down, media wrote numerous unflattering stories, and human rights activists had a field day.
- Microsoft, caught in a battle with the U.S. Department of Justice and its competitors about monopolistic policies, received mostly unfavorable publicity throughout 1998 and 1999.
- Odwalla, the natural juice maker, had to recall about 70 percent of its product line after several cases of *E. coli* poisoning—including one death—were linked to its unpasteurized apple juice. The company pleaded guilty to criminal charges and agreed to pay a $1.5 million fine.

- McDonald's got negative publicity when an 81-year-old woman won a multi-million-dollar lawsuit against the company because she suffered third-degree burns from a scalding cup of coffee.
- Intel, the leading manufacturer of computer chips, faced a major problem in credibility when flaws were found in its Pentium chip.

Each of these examples, as Irvine suggests, started as a "smoldering" crisis that management could have prevented if it had used more environmental scanning and issues management. Instead, it left the issue to fester and ultimately ignite in national headlines. In the McDonald's case, the company had received at least 700 complaints of coffee burns during the last decade and had settled claims from scalding injuries for more than $500,000.

Intel worsened its problem by treating the Pentium flaw as a trivial matter and failing to offer customers an explanation or a replacement. Indeed, the Intel crisis finally got national attention when IBM announced its decision to halt the sale of Pentium-based personal computers. This decision was made six weeks after Intel knew there was a problem but failed to take corrective action. Alfonso Gonzalez-Herrero and Cornelius B. Pratt, writing about the Intel situation, said, "Intel possibly forgot two key principles of modern corporate communications: (a) image is perceptual reality, and (b) passiveness is a transitory state that can change when publics feel outraged."

How to Communicate during a Crisis

There are many lists giving advice on what to do during a crisis. Here's a compilation of good suggestions:

- *Put the public first.*
- *Take responsibility.* An organization should take responsibility for solving the problem.
- *Be honest.* Don't obscure facts and try to mislead the public.
- *Never say, "No comment."* A Porter/Novelli survey found that nearly two-thirds of the public feel that "no comment" almost always means that the organization is guilty of wrongdoing.
- *Designate a single spokesperson.*
- *Set up a central information center.*
- *Provide a constant flow of information.* When information is withheld, the cover-up becomes the story.
- *Be familiar with media needs and deadlines.*
- *Be accessible.*
- *Monitor news coverage and telephone inquiries.*
- *Communicate with key publics.*

How Various Organizations Respond to Crises

The above list offers sound, practical advice, but recent research has shown that organizations don't all respond to a crisis in the same way. Indeed, W. Timothy Coombs postulates that an organization's response may vary on a continuum from *defensive* to *accommodative.* Here is a list of crisis communication strategies that an organization may use:

- *Attack the accuser.* The party that claims a crisis exists is confronted and its logic and facts are faulted. Sometimes a lawsuit is threatened.
- *Denial.* The organization explains that there is no crisis.
- *Excuse.* The organization minimizes its responsibility for the crisis. Any intention to do harm is denied, and the organization says it had no control over the events that led to the crisis. This strategy is often used when there is a natural disaster or product tampering.
- *Justification.* Crisis is minimized with a statement that there is no serious damage or injuries. Sometimes, the blame is shifted to the victims, as in the case of the Firestone recall outlined in Chapter 1. This is often done when a consumer misuses a product or there is an industrial accident.
- *Ingratiation.* Actions are taken to appease the publics involved. Consumers who complain are given coupons or the organization makes a donation to a charitable organization. Burlington Industries, for example, gave a large donation to the Humane Society after the discovery that it had imported coats from China with fur collars containing dog fur instead of "coyote" fur.
- *Corrective action.* Steps are taken to repair the damage from the crisis and to prevent a repetition.
- *Full apology.* Organization takes responsibility and asks forgiveness. Some compensation of money or aid is often included.

The Coombs typology gives the list prices for crisis communication management depending on the situation. However, he notes that organizations do have to consider more accommodative strategies (ingratiation, corrective action, full apology) if defensive strategies (attack accuser, denial, excuse) are not effective in repairing an organization's reputation or restoring previous sales levels. He says, "Accommodative strategies emphasize each repair, which is what is needed as image damage worsens. Defensive strategies, such as denial or minimizing, logically become less effective as organizations are viewed as more responsible for the crisis."

Often, however, an organization doesn't adopt an accommodative strategy because of corporate culture and other constraints. Glen T. Cameron at the University of Missouri has developed a contingency theory of conflict management in public relations that seeks to explain why agencies don't always engage in two-way communication and accommodative strategies when confronted with a crisis or conflict with some publics.

Some variables proscribing the organization, according to Cameron, might be: (1) management's moral conviction that the public is wrong; (2) moral neutrality when two contending publics want the organization to take sides on a policy issued; (3) legal constraints; (4) regulatory constraints such as the FTC or SEC; (5) prohibition by senior management against an accommodative stance; and (6) possible conflict between departments of the organization on what strategies to adopt.

In some cases, Cameron contends that Grunig's ideal goal of symmetrical communication to achieve mutual understanding and accommodation doesn't occur because both sides have staked out highly rigid positions and are not willing to compromise their strong moral positions. For example, it is unlikely that the prolife and prochoice forces will ever achieve mutual understanding and accommodation.

How Some Organizations Have Handled a Crisis

The crisis communication strategies outlined by Coombs are useful when evaluating how organizations handled a crisis. Intel, for example, first denied there was a problem with its Pentium chip. As the crisis deepened and was covered in the mainstream press, Intel then tried the strategy of *justification* by saying the problem wasn't serious enough to warrant replacing the chips. It minimized the concerns of end-users such as engineers and computer programmers. Only after considerable damage had been done to Intel's reputation and IBM had suspended orders for the chip did Intel take corrective action to replace the chips, and Andy Grove, Intel's president, issued a full apology.

Exxon, still highly identified with a major oil spill in Prince William Sound, Alaska, also chose a defensive strategy when one of its ships, the *Exxon Valdez,* hit a reef in 1989 and spilled nearly 240,000 barrels of oil into a pristine environment. The disaster, one of history's worst environmental accidents, was badly mismanaged from the beginning.

Exxon management started its crisis communication strategy by making excuses. Management claimed that Exxon, as a corporation, wasn't at fault because (1) the weather wasn't ideal, (2) the charts provided by the U.S. Coast Guard were out of date, and (3) the captain of the ship was derelict in his duties by drinking while on duty. As cleanup efforts began, Exxon also tried to shift the blame by maintaining that government bureaucracy and prohibitions against the use of certain chemicals hampered the company's efforts.

Exxon also used the strategy of justification to minimize the damage, saying that environmentalists in the government were exaggerating the ill effects on bird and animal life. Meanwhile, negative press coverage was intense and public outrage continued to rise. William J. Small of Fordham University, who researched the press coverage, wrote, "Probably no other company ever got a more damaging portrayal in the mass media." More than 18,000 customers tore up their Exxon credit cards, late-night talk show hosts ridiculed the company, and congressional committees started hearings. Exxon dropped from eight to 110th on *Fortune's* list of most admired companies.

Exxon's response to all these developments was somewhat ineffective. It did try the strategy of ingratiation by running full-page advertisements stating that the company was sorry for the oil spill—but didn't take responsibility for it. Instead of calming the storm, that approach only further enraged the public.

Exxon also took corrective action and cleaned up the oil spill, spending about $3 billion in its efforts. The company received little credit for this action, however, because most of the public believed it was done only under government pressure. And by the time the cleanup was finished, public attitudes about Exxon had already been formed.

In the cases of Intel and Exxon, Cameron's ideas also come into play. Neither company first initiated an accommodative strategy, perhaps because (1) management thought that the public was morally wrong, or (2) the companies were concerned about possible liability lawsuits.

Odwalla and Pepsi provide examples of more successful crisis communication strategies.

Odwalla didn't bother with a defensive strategy when they got a phone call from Washington State health officials that the company's apple juice was implicated in several cases of *E. coli* poisoning. Only 20 minutes later, Odwalla at a press conference announced its recall of all products containing unpasteurized apple juice.

Within 72 hours, the company set up a crisis-related Web site with the aid of its public relations firm, Daniel Edelman worldwide. The company's Web site, widely publicized, contained links to the Food and Drug Administration (FDA) and the Centers for Disease Control and Prevention so consumers could get additional information about *E. coli* contamination.

Company management, from the very beginning, initiated an accommodative strategy. The press conference and the Web site were an ingratiation strategy to retain consumer confidence; corrective action was taken immediately by recalling the product and taking steps to change the production process. The company president, early on, also issued a full apology and garnered much public support by announcing that the company would pay any medical bills of the approximately 70 people poisoned. The company also offered to replace any bottles of apple juice on consumer shelves. The result was widespread public approval, and in one survey almost 90 percent of consumers said they would continue to buy the product.

It is important to note, however, that not all successful crisis communication strategies need to be accommodative. Pepsi-Cola was able to mount an effective defensive crisis communication strategy and avoid recall when a hoax of nationwide proportions created an intense but short-lived crisis for the soft-drink company.

The crisis began when the media reported that a man in Tacoma, Washington, claimed that he had found a syringe inside a can of Diet Pepsi. As the news spread, men and women across the country made similar claims of finding a broken sewing needle, a screw, a bullet, and even a narcotics vial in their Pepsi cans. As a consequence, demands for a recall of all Pepsi products arose, an action that would have major economic consequences for the company.

Company officials were confident that insertion of foreign objects into cans on the high-speed, closely controlled bottling lines was virtually impossible, so they chose to defend their product. The urgent problem, then, was to convince the public that the product was safe, and any foreign objects found had been inserted after the cans were opened.

In their ultimately successful public relations campaign, they used some of the methods the makers of Tylenol found so helpful.

The company officials and their public relations staff set about doing this with several strategies. One approach was to attack the accuser. Pepsi officials said the foreign objects probably got into the cans after they were opened, and even explained that many people make such claims just to collect compensation from the company. The company also announced that it would pursue legal action against anyone making false claims about the integrity of the company's products.

Pepsi also took the strategy of denial, saying that no crisis actually existed. Pepsi president Craig E. Weatherup immediately made appearances on national television programs and gave newspaper interviews to state the company's case that its bottling lines were secure. Helping convince the public was U.S. Food and Drug Administration Commissioner David Kessler, who said that a recall was not necessary.

These quick actions deflated the public's concern and polls showed considerable acceptance of Pepsi's contention that the problem was a hoax. A week after the scare began, Pepsi ran full-page advertisements with the headline, "Pepsi is pleased to announce . . . Nothing." It stated, "As America now knows, those stories about Diet Pepsi were a hoax. . . ."

In sum, no one crisis communication strategy is appropriate for all situations, as the above examples indicate. Therefore, as Coombs indicates, "It is only by understanding the crisis situation that the crisis manager can select the appropriate response for the crisis." Corporate culture and management mindsets also influence how an organization responds to a developing crisis.

Risk Communication

Closely associated with crisis communication is *risk communication*. In essence, this is defined as any verbal or written exchange that attempts to communicate information regarding risk to public health and safety and the environment.

Organizations, including large corporations, increasingly engage in risk communication to inform the public of such risks as those involving the content of food products, chemical spills, the disposal of radioactive wastes, and the placement of drug-abuse treatment centers or halfway houses in neighborhoods. These issues are subject to expensive lawsuits, legislation, consumer boycotts, and public debate if organizations fail to disclose potential hazards.

An example of somewhat unsuccessful risk communication was the 1996 "mad cow scare" in Great Britain. Despite assurances by health officials and the beef industry that a fatal cow disease posed an "extremely small" risk to consumers, the British public stopped buying beef and the European Community (EC) banned the import of British beef.

This example illustrates the point that the dissemination of accurate information is insufficient in risk communication. Complicating the process is the problem of scientific studies that often contradict each other, leaving the public somewhat uncertain about the amount of risk. Another problem is distortion of scientific findings by a portion of the mass media, where headlines imply a "cure" despite the qualifying details in the story.

As Marcia Angell, executive editor of the *New England Journal of Medicine,* wrote in the *New York Times Magazine,* "Most Americans are not very good at distinguishing big risks from little ones, or risks based on solid evidence from those that aren't. We are likely to react to all reported risks in the same way, or choose which to respond to, on the basis of irrational fears or the prominence given them on the 6 o'clock news."

Such a situation poses considerable challenges to public relations personnel as they attempt to ascertain how the public perceives a risk. In the "mad cow" scare, the public perceived the risk as greater than the statistical probability indicated because the disease could be fatal.

Risk communication researchers have identified several variables that affect public perceptions:

- Risks voluntarily taken tend to be accepted better than those over which individuals have little or no control. Smokers have more control over their health situation, for example, than airline passengers do over their safety.
- The more complex a situation, the higher the perception of risk. Disposal of radioactive wastes is more difficult to understand than the danger of cigarette smoking.
- Familiarity breeds confidence. If the public understands the problem and its factors, it perceives less risk. In one study done by Robert Heath, Shaila Seshadri, and Jaesub Lee at the University of Houston, they found communities living close to chemical plants had more favorable views of the industry, probably because of the economic benefit to the community.

- Perception of risk increases when the messages of experts conflict.
- The severity of consequences affects risk perceptions. There is a difference between having a stomachache and getting cancer.

Suzanne Zoda, writing on risk communication in *Communication World,* gives some suggestions to communicators:

- Begin early and initiate a dialogue with publics that might be affected. Do not wait until the opposition marshals its forces. Vital to establishing trust is early contact with anyone who may be concerned or affected.
- Actively solicit and identify people's concerns. Informal discussions, surveys, interviews, and focus groups are effective in evaluating issues and identifying outrage factors.
- Recognize the public as a legitimate partner in the process. Engage interested groups in two-way communication and involve key opinion leaders.
- Address issues of concern, even if they do not directly pertain to the project.
- Anticipate and prepare for hostility. To defuse a situation, use a conflict-resolution approach. Identify areas of agreement and work toward common ground.
- Understand the needs of the news media. Provide accurate, timely information and respond promptly to requests.
- Always be honest, even when it hurts.

Summary

The Goals of Communication

Communication, also called *execution,* is the third step in the public relations process. Five possible objectives at this stage are message exposure, accurate dissemination of the message, acceptance of the message, attitude change, and change in overt behavior.

Receiving the Message

Successful communication involves interaction, or shared experience, because the message must be not only sent but received. The larger the audience, the greater the number of barriers to communication.

Paying Attention to the Message

Because audiences have different approaches to receiving messages, communicators must tailor the message to get the recipient's attention. They need to understand the audience's mental state. Messages for passive audiences must have style and creativity, while messages for an audience actively seeking information must have more sophisticated content. In either case, the effective message will raise the audience's "need" level by providing some obvious benefit.

Understanding the Message

The most basic element of understanding between communicator and audience is a common language. This is becoming a greater issue with the emphasis on multiculturalism. Public relations practitioners must consider their audiences and style their language appropriately, taking into consideration literacy levels, clarity and simplicity of language, and avoidance of discriminatory language.

Believing the Message

Key variables in believability include source credibility, context, and the audience's predispositions, especially their level of involvement.

Remembering the Message

Messages are often repeated extensively to reach all members of the target audience and to help them remember and enhance their learning. One way to do this is to convey information in several ways, through a variety of channels.

Acting on the Message

The success of a message is in its effect on the recipient. Five steps in acceptance of new ideas or products are awareness, interest, evaluation, trial, and adoption. The adoption process is affected by relative advantage, compatibility, complexity, trialability, and observability. The time needed to adopt a new idea or product can be affected by the importance of the decision as well as the personality of the person receiving the message. The primary source of information varies at each step of the adoption process.

Crisis Communications

The communications process is severely tested in crisis situations, which can take on many forms. A common problem is the lack of crisis management plans, even when a "smoldering" crisis is building. Organizations' responses may vary from defensive to accommodative. Corporate culture and other constraints may prevent adoption of an appropriate strategy. Examples of successful handling of crises include Odwalla's response to the revelation that some of their apple juice had bacterial contamination, Pepsi's response to hoax claims of foreign objects in soft-drink cans, and the Tylenol product-tampering case.

Risk Communication

Risk communication attempts to convey information regarding risk to public health and safety and the environment, such as food contamination, chemical spills, or the placement of a substance-abuse treatment facility in a neighborhood. This involves more than the dissemination of accurate information. The communicator must begin early, identify and address the public's concerns, recognize the public as a legitimate partner, anticipate hostility, respond to the needs of the news media, and always be honest.

Case Activity: What Would You Do?

Extensive information campaigns are being mounted throughout the world to inform people about the dangers of acquired immune deficiency syndrome (AIDS). Information specialists must utilize a variety of communication strategies and tactics to create public awareness and cause changes in individual behavior patterns.

At the same time, the communication process is very complex because a number of variables must be considered. Using this chapter as a guide, how would you apply the various communication concepts and theories to the task of informing people about AIDS?

Questions for Review and Discussion

1. Kirk Hallahan lists five categories of media and communication tools. What are they, and what are some of the pros and cons of each?
2. James Grunig says there are at least five possible objectives for a communicator. What are they? What two objectives do most public relations campaigns try to achieve?
3. What are the five basic elements of a communication model?
4. Why is two-way communication (feedback) an important aspect of effective communication?
5. What are the advantages and disadvantages, from a communication standpoint, of reaching the audience through mass media channels?
6. Explain the behavioral communication model. What is the importance of the "triggering event"?
7. What is the premise of the media uses and gratification theory?
8. What kinds of messages and communication channels would you use for a passive audience? An active information-seeking audience?
9. Why is it necessary to use a variety of messages and communication channels in a public relations program?
10. Why is it important to write with clarity and simplicity? How can symbols, acronyms, and slogans help?
11. Explain the concept behind readability formulas.

12. Why is it important to build repetition into a message?
13. Explain the five steps in the adoption process. What are some of the factors that affect the adoption of an idea or product?
14. Both Exxon and Pepsi used *defensive* crisis communication strategies. However, one succeeded and the other failed. What factors do you think made the difference?
15. What is *risk communication?*

Suggested Readings

Angell, Maria. "Overdosing on Health Risks," *New York Times Magazine,* May 14, 1998, pp. 44–45.

Benoit, William L. "Image Repair Discourse and Crisis Communication." *Public Relations Review,* Summer 1997, pp. 176–186.

Budd, John F. "The Downside of Crisis Management." *The Strategist,* Fall 1998, pp. 36–37.

Coombs, Timothy W. "An Analytic Framework for Crisis Situations: Better Response from a Better Understanding of the Situation." *Journal of Public Relations Research,* Vol. 8, No. 2, 1996, pp. 79–106.

Gonzalez-Herrero, Alfonso, and Pratt, Cornelius B. "An Integrated Symmetrical Model for Crisis-Communication Management." *Journal of Public Relations Research,* Vol. 8, No. 2, 1996, pp. 79–106.

Hallahan, Kirk. "Strategic Media Planning: Toward an Integrated Public Relations Media Model." *Handbook of Public Relations,* edited by Robert Heath. Thousand Oaks, CA: Sage Publications, 2000.

Heath, Robert L., Seshardi, Shaila, and Lee, Jaesub. "Risk Communication: A Two-Way Community Analysis of Proximity, Dread, Trust, Involvement, Uncertainty, Openness/Accessibility, and Knowledge on Support/Opposition toward Chemical Companies." *Journal of Public Relations Research,* Vol. 10, No. 1, 1998, pp. 35–56.

Irvine, Robert B. "What's a Crisis, Anyway?" *Communication World,* July 1997, pp. 36–40.

Perloff, Richard M. *The Dynamics of Persuasion.* Hillsdale, NJ: Lawrence Erlbaum Associates, 1993.

"Response to Kennedy Crash Shows Some Lessons Learned." *Pr reporter,* August 23, 1999, pp. 3–4.

Stossel, John. "Overcoming Junk Science." *Wall Street Journal,* January 9, 1997, p. A10.

Wylie, Frank W. "Anticipation: Key to Crisis Management." *Communication World,* July 1997, pp. 34–35.

Yarbrough, C. Richard, Cameron, Glen T., Sallot, Lynne M., and McWilliams, Allison. "Tough Calls to Make: Contingency Theory and the Centennial Olympic Games." *Journal of Communication Management,* Vol. 3, No. 1, 1998, pp. 39–56.

Evaluation

preview

In this chapter the objectives are to explain the critical role of evaluation in public relations, to describe the advantages and disadvantages of various evaluation methods, and to help students select the ones most suitable for specific programs.

Topics covered in the chapter include:

- The purpose of evaluation
- Objectives: A prerequisite for evaluation
- The current status of measurement and evaluation
- The measurement of production
- Message exposure
- Audience comprehension
- Audience change and action
- Supplemental activities

The Purpose of Evaluation

The fourth step of the public relations process is evaluation. It is the measurement of results against established objectives set during the planning process discussed in Chapter 7.

Evaluation is well described by Professor James Bissland of Bowling Green State University. He defines it as "the systematic assessment of a program and its results. It is a means for practitioners to offer accountability to clients—and to themselves."

Results and accountability also are themes of Professors Glen Broom and David Dozier of San Diego State University. In their text *Using Research in Public Relations,* they state, "Your program is intended to cause observable impact—to change or maintain something about a situation. So, after the program, you use research to measure and document program effects."

Professor Frank Wylie, emeritus professor at California State University in Long Beach, summarizes:

> We are talking about an orderly evaluation of our progress in attaining the specific objectives of our public relations plan. We are learning what we did right, what we did wrong, how much progress we've made and, most importantly, how we can do it better next time.

The desire to do a better job next time is a major reason for evaluating public relations efforts, but another equally important reason is the widespread adoption of the management-by-objectives system by clients and employers of public relations personnel. They want to know if the money, time, and effort expended on public relations are well spent and contribute to the realization of an organizational objective, such as attendance at an open house, product sales, or increased awareness of ways to prevent the spread of AIDS.

Objectives: A Prerequisite for Evaluation

Before any public relations program can be properly evaluated, it is important to have a clearly established set of measurable objectives. These should be part of the program plan (discussed in Chapter 7), but some points need reviewing.

First, public relations personnel and management should agree on the criteria that will be used to evaluate success in attaining objectives. A Ketchum public relations monograph simply states, "Write the most precise, most results-oriented objectives you can that are realistic, credible, measurable, and compatible with the client's demands on public relations."

Second, don't wait until the end of the public relations program to determine how it will be evaluated. Albert L. Schweitzer at Fleishman-Hillard public relations in St. Louis makes the point: "Evaluating impact/results starts in the planning stage. You break down the problem into measurable goals and objectives, then after implementing the program, you measure the results against goals."

If an objective is informational, measurement techniques must show how successfully information was communicated to target audiences. Such techniques fall under the rubric of "message dissemination" and "audience exposure," but they do not measure the effect on attitudes or overt behavior and action.

Motivational objectives are more difficult to accomplish. If the objective is to increase sales or market share, it is important to show that public relations efforts caused the increase rather than advertising or other marketing strategies. Or, if the objective is to change attitudes or opinions, research should be done before and after the public relations activity to measure the percentage of change.

Although objectives may vary, the following checklist contains the basic evaluation questions that any practitioner should ask:

- Was the activity or program adequately planned?
- Did recipients of the message understand it?
- How could the program strategy have been more effective?
- Were all primary and secondary audiences reached?
- Was the desired organizational objective achieved?
- What unforeseen circumstances affected the success of the program or activity?
- Did the program or activity fall within the budget set for it?
- What steps can be taken to improve the success of similar future activities?

Current Status of Measurement and Evaluation

During the past decade, public relations professionals have made considerable progress in evaluation research and the ability to tell clients and employers exactly what has been accomplished. More sophisticated techniques than previously are being used, including computerized news clip analysis, survey sampling, and attempts to correlate efforts directly with sales.

Today, the trend toward more systematic evaluation is well established. Katherine Delahaye Paine, founder of her own public relations measurement firm, says that the percentage of a public relations budget devoted to measurement and evaluation was about 1 percent a decade ago, but is now closer to 5 percent. In this decade, it is projected that the amount will increase to 10 percent. One reason: There is increasing pressure on all parts of the organization—including public relations—to prove their value to the "bottom line."

There are, however, still those who say public relations is not an exact science and is extremely difficult to measure. Walter K. Lindenmann, a former senior vice president and director of research of Ketchum Public Relations, takes a more optimistic view. He wrote in *Public Relations Quarterly:* "Let's get something straight right off the bat. First, it is possible to measure public relations effectiveness. . . . Second, measuring public relations effectiveness does not have to be either unbelievably expensive or laboriously time-consuming."

Lindenmann suggests that public relations personnel use a mix of evaluation techniques, many borrowed from advertising and marketing, to provide more complete evaluation. In addition, he notes that there are at least three levels of measurement and evaluation (see Figure 9.1).

On the most basic level are compilations of message distribution and media placements. The second level, which requires more sophisticated techniques, deals with the measurement of audience awareness, comprehension, and retention of the message. The most advanced level is the measurement of change in attitudes, opinions, and behavior.

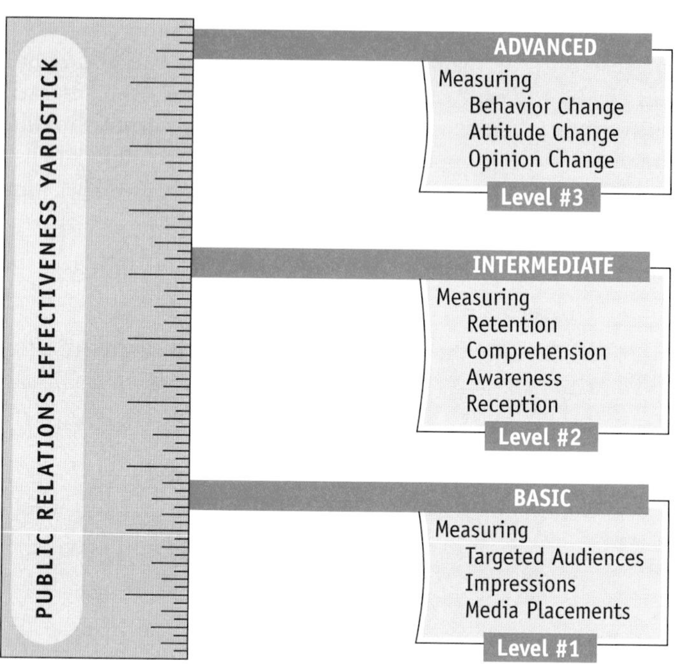

FIGURE 9.1

Evaluation goals for public programs can be grouped at three levels of measurement, as shown in this chart. (*Source:* Ketchum public relations, New York, published in *Public Relations Quarterly*.)

The following sections outline the most widely used methods for evaluating public relations efforts. These include: measurement of production, message exposure, audience awareness, audience attitudes, and audience action. Supplemental activities such as communication audits, readability tests, event evaluation, and split messages also are discussed. In most cases, a skilled practitioner will use a combination of methods to evaluate the effectiveness of a program.

Measurement of Production

One elementary form of evaluation is simply to count how many news releases, feature stories, photos, letters, and the like are produced in a given period of time.

This kind of evaluation is supposed to give management an idea of a staff's productivity and output. Public relations professionals, however, do not believe that this evaluation is very meaningful because it emphasizes quantity instead of quality. It may be more cost-effective to write fewer news releases and spend more time on the few that really are newsworthy. It may, for example, be more important for a staff person to spend five weeks working on an article for the *Wall Street Journal* or *Fortune* than to write 29 routine personnel releases.

Another side of the production approach is to specify what the public relations person should accomplish in obtaining media coverage. One state trade association evaluated its director of media relations on the expectation that (1) four feature stories would be run in any of the 11 largest newspapers in the state and (2) news releases would be used by at least 20 newspapers, including 5 or more among the 50 largest.

Such evaluation criteria not only are unrealistic but almost impossible to guarantee because media gatekeepers—not the public relations person—make such decisions. Management may argue, however, that such placement goals provide incentive to the public relations staff and are tangible criteria in employee performance evaluation.

Closely allied to the production of publicity materials is their distribution. Thus a public relations department might report, for instance, that a total of 756 news releases were sent to 819 daily newspapers, 250 weeklies, and 137 trade magazines within one year, or that 110,000 copies of the annual report were distributed to stockholders, security analysts, and business editors.

Measurement of Message Exposure

The most widely practiced form of evaluating public relations programs is the compilation of press clippings and radio–television mentions. Public relations firms and company departments working primarily on a local basis often have a secretary or intern clip the area newspapers. Large companies with regional, national, or even international outreach usually hire clipping services to scan large numbers of publications. It also is possible to have electronic clipping services monitor and tape major radio and television programs on a contractual basis. Burrelle's, for example, monitors nearly 400 local TV stations in 150 cities. Web tracking systems and firms are discussed in Chapter 12.

Strategic research by Hallmark Cards with its public relations firm, Fleishman-Hillard, identified the need for a line of less expensive cards to compete with deep discount card companies and to increase occasions for sending a card to a friend, colleague, or relative. Hallmark used media clips as one measure of its Warm Wishes campaign. According to Fleishman-Hillard's report, which was the basis for the firm's receipt of a Silver Anvil award from PRSA:

global PR

Airline's Employees Spread the Word

British Airways (BA), a decade after it was privatized, had become one of the world's leading airlines. It was decided, however, to reinforce its mission "To Be the Undisputed Leader in World Travel" by launching a new corporate identity program on a worldwide basis.

The objective was to reach 70 percent of the 55,000 staff members worldwide prior to the public launch of a new corporate identity program. It was reasoned that if the employees were aware of the key messages behind the campaign, they could also convey the key messages to various publics, including customers. British Airways used 13 satellites to link 30,000 guests and employees at 126 locations in 63 countries for a simultaneous, all-time-zone launch.

This is how the airline evaluated the results:

> An average of 89 percent of overseas employees, ahead of the 70 percent target, saw the new BA prior to June 10. Almost 80 percent of 444 articles from 49 countries were positive, and 48 percent used visuals. Key messages were conveyed in 78 percent of the articles.

> The public relations strategies and tactics generated nearly 107 million trackable impressions.
>
> The television outreach resulted in 71 known placements and 12.8 million impressions nationwide, with many stations showing footage of the BigBox Color production process, furthering the quality message. Warm Wishes was even included in the Tonight Show monologue by Jay Leno. The story proved to be an "evergreen," with hits in March, April, May, and June.

The agency not only noted the total impressions but alluded to the importance of the key message remaining as part of the coverage. Similar analysis was provided for print coverage. Such a compilation measures media acceptance of the story and shows that Hallmark received massive coverage. Clearly, the publicity effort accomplished the first stage of the adoption process by making people aware of the Warm Wishes line of cards.

Media Impressions

In addition to the number of media placements, public relations departments and firms report how many people may have been exposed to the message. These numbers are described as *media impressions,* the potential audience reached by a periodical or a broadcast program.

If, for example, a story about an organization appears in the local daily with a circulation of 130,000, the media impressions are 130,000. If another story is published the next day, this counts for 130,000 more impressions. Estimated audiences for radio and television programs, certified by auditing organizations, also are used to compile media impressions.

A regional or national news story can generate millions of impressions by simple multiplication of each placement times the circulation or audience of each medium. Two examples:

- The American College of Obstetricians and Gynecologists organized a public relations campaign to celebrate the 35th anniversary of the birth control pill. According to its report, total media impressions were almost 61 million from print, radio, and television stories.
- M&M's Chocolate Candies conducted a national contest to name a new color for M&M's candies. Public relations activities generated 1.06 billion impressions from 10,000 TV, radio, and print placements; these included 36,000 print column inches, 12 hours of television news coverage, and 74 hours of radio broadcast time.

Media impressions are commonly used in advertising to document the breadth of penetration of a particular message. Such figures give a rough estimate of how many people are exposed to a message. They don't, however, disclose how many people actually read or heard the stories and, more important, how many absorbed or acted on the information. Other techniques needed for this kind of evaluation are discussed later in this chapter.

Hits on the Internet

A cyberspace version of media impressions is the number of people reached via an organization's World Wide Web site or home page. Each instance of a person accessing a site is called a "hit" or a "visit."

BayBank of Boston, for example, established a Web site as part of its sponsorship of the Head of the Charles Regatta. In evaluating its public relations program, the bank also noted that 10,000 visits were recorded at its Web site in the two weeks prior to the event. Another 33,000 visits were recorded in the month after the regatta, to review results and see cyberspace re-creations of the races.

Purple Moon, a software developer of girls' interactive entertainment, used a Web site to promote its latest CD-ROM product, "friendship adventures." According to the company and its public relations firm, Ketchum public relations, "Media relations and grassroots online programs helped drive traffic resulting in 700,000 visitors in the first six months and an average of 6 million impressions per month, equaling or surpassing those of top kids' sites including *Disney.com* and *Sports Illustrated for Kids.*"

A third example is MCI, which included a Web site to make consumers aware of its Internet services. The Web site provided information and also included a test that visitors could take to measure their Internet skills. According to the company and its public relations firm, Ruberry Communications, "More than 2.3 million hits were recorded for the Web test site. More than 16,500 people actually completed the test and recorded a score. The test was taken by people from 12 countries."

Advertising Equivalency

Another approach is to calculate the value of message exposure. This is done by converting stories in the regular news columns or on the air into equivalent advertising costs. In other words, a 5-inch article in a trade magazine that charges $100 per column inch for advertising would be worth $500 in publicity value.

Mack Trucks, for example, evaluated its public relations campaign to improve its image in the trucking industry by using advertising equivalency. It reported, "The program generated more than 9000 inches of editorial coverage with an advertising equivalency of more than $1.2 million—more than five times the company's investment in the program."

Some practitioners even take the approach of calculating the cost of advertising for the same amount of space and then multiplying that total three to six times to reflect a number of research studies that show a news story has higher credibility than an advertisement. Consequently, if Mack Trucks multiplied the equivalent advertising space by three, it could say that the editorial space was worth $3.6 million in publicity.

Although such dollar amounts apparently impress some top managements, the technique of calculating advertising equivalency is really comparing apples and oranges. In fact, Ron Levy, president of North American Precis Syndicate, told *Jack O'Dwyer's Public Relations Newsletter* that he thought the technique was "blatantly ridiculous."

One reason is the fundamental difference between advertising and publicity. Advertising copy is directly controlled by the organization and can be oriented to specific objectives. The organization also controls the size and placement of the message. News mentions, on the other hand, are determined by media gatekeepers and can be negative, neutral, or positive. In addition, a news release can be edited to the point that key corporate messages are deleted. In other words, the organization can't control size, placement, or content.

It becomes a question of what is being measured. Should an article be counted as equivalent advertising space if it is negative? It also is questionable whether a 15-inch article that mentions the organization only once among six other organizations is comparable to 15 column-inches of advertising space. And the numbers game doesn't take into account that a 4-inch article in the *Wall Street Journal* may be more valuable in reaching key publics than a 20-inch article in the *Denver Post.*

In summary, the dollar-value approach to measuring publicity effectiveness is somewhat suspect, and there has been a rapid decline of such statistics in PRSA award entries. The equating of publicity with advertising rates for comparable space also does not engender good media relations. The technique reinforces the opinion of many media gatekeepers that all news releases are just attempts to get "free advertising."

Systematic Tracking

As noted earlier, message exposure traditionally has been measured by sheer bulk. New advances in computer software and databases, however, now make it possible to track media placements in a more sophisticated way.

Computer databases can be used to analyze the content of media placements by such variables as market penetration, type of publication, tone of coverage, sources quoted, and mention of key copy points. Ketchum public relations, for example, can build up to 40 variables into its computer program, including the tracking of reporter bylines to determine if a journalist is predisposed negatively or positively to the client's key messages. Other firms, such as Carma International and Delahaye MediaLink, do extensive analysis for clients using databases such as NEXIS/LEXIS.

Table 9.1, prepared by Delahaye MediaLink for a client, illustrates the type of analysis that can be done.

The value of systematic tracking is manifested in several ways. One is continuing, regular feedback during a campaign to determine if an organization's publicity efforts are paying off in terms of placements and mention of key messages. Tracking coverage and comparing it over a period of time is called *benchmarking.*

An example is the campaign that Capitoline/MS&L public relations conducted on behalf of the Turkish government to make Americans more aware of Turkey as a travel destination. By comparing the number of stories before and after the campaign was

TABLE 9.1

Total Coverage

	TOTAL
Total impressions	89,641,378
Percent of positive impressions	26.98%
Percent of negative impressions	19.85%
Total articles	1049
Percent of positive articles	35.65%
Percent of negative articles	16.02%
Percent of articles containing one or more positive messages	52.43%
Percent of articles containing one or more negative messages	18.78%

launched, Carma International found that articles with Turkey as the primary destination increased 400 percent. Favorable articles on Turkey increased 90 percent from the previous year.

At other times, an organization may wish to do a systematic analysis comparing its media coverage with the competition's. Is a major competitor getting more favorable publicity? Is the company being portrayed as an innovative leader, or is its size the only major message being mentioned? Such evaluation allows an organization to fine-tune its public relations efforts and concentrate on problem areas.

Another form of analysis is comparing the number of news releases sent with the number actually published and in what kinds of periodicals. Such analysis often helps a public relations department determine what kinds of publicity are most effective and earn the most return on investment (ROI).

As Katharine Paine, president of Delahaye MediaLink, says, "The world doesn't need more data. What it needs is analyzed data."

Requests and 800 Numbers

Another measure of media exposure is to compile the number of requests for more information. A story in a newspaper or an appearance of a company spokesperson on a broadcast often provides information as to where people can get more information about a subject.

In many cases, a toll-free 800 number is provided. Dayton Hudson Corporation, owner of several department store chains, used a toll-free hotline number as part of its "Child Care Aware" program to help educate parents about quality child care and how to get it. In a six-month period, 19,000 calls were received seeking advice and copies of a brochure. Dole Food Company, through its toll-free 800 number, got requests for more than 100,000 copies of its brochure titled, "Fun with Fruits and Vegetables: Kid's Cookbook."

Requests for materials also can show the effectiveness of a public relations program. An information program by the U.S. Centers for Disease Control on AIDS prevention, for example, received nearly 2000 phone calls on its information hotline after its "Safe Sex" program on the Public Broadcasting Service (PBS). In addition, the program and resulting publicity generated 260 requests for videotapes and 400 requests for "Smart Sex" organization kits.

Cost per Person

Another way to evaluate exposure to the message is to determine the cost of reaching each member of the audience.

The technique is commonly used in advertising in order to place costs in perspective. Although a 30-second commercial during the 2002 Super Bowl telecast cost approximately $2 million, advertisers believed it was well worth the price because an audience of more than 130 million would be reached for less than a half-cent each. This was a relatively good bargain, even if several million viewers probably visited the refrigerator while the commercial played. Professor Dean Krugman at the University of Georgia conducts viewer behavior research that suggests that television ratings used in advertising offer a false precision. His findings indicate that public relations professionals should use caution in adapting such ratings to estimates of media coverage.

Cost-effectiveness, as this technique is known, also is used in public relations. *Cost-per-thousand* (CPM) is calculated by taking the cost of the publicity program and dividing it by the total media impressions (discussed earlier). SkyTel, for example, spent $400,000 to publicize its new two-way paging and messaging system and obtained 52 million impressions, about seven-tenths of a cent per impression. According to counselor Ford Kanzler, "CPMs for print publicity programs usually fall well below media space advertising and about 100 percent above direct mail promotions."

In another example, a campaign by the Virginia Department of Tourism to attract Canadian visitors cost $5500 but generated 90,000 consumer inquiries. This made the cost per inquiry only six cents. The same approach can be done with events, brochures, and newsletters. Nike produced a sports video for $50,000 but reached 150,000 high school students for a per-person cost of 33 cents.

Audience Attendance

Counting attendance at events is a relatively simple way of evaluating the effectiveness of pre-event publicity.

The New York Public Library centennial day celebration, for example, attracted a crowd of 10,000 for a sound and laser show and speeches. In addition, 20,000 visitors came to the library on the designated centennial day and more than 200,000 people from around the world visited the library's exhibitions during the year.

Poor attendance at a meeting or event can indicate inadequate publicity and promotion. Another major cause is lack of public interest, even when people are aware that a meeting or event is taking place. Low attendance usually results in considerable finger-pointing; thus an objective evaluation of exactly what happened—or didn't happen—is a good policy.

Measurement of Audience Awareness

So far, techniques of measuring audience exposure and accurate dissemination have been discussed. A higher level of evaluation is to determine whether the audience actually became aware of the message and understood it.

Walter Lindenmann calls this the second level of public relations evaluation. He notes:

focus on ethics

Measuring Use of a Client's Name

You've been hired as an intern at a public relations firm for the summer. One of your duties is to go through recent issues of trade magazines and clip any article in which the name of a client appears. You are then asked to look up advertising rates for these publications and calculate what the comparable space in advertising would cost. The idea, says the account supervisor, is to count entire articles even if the client's name is only mentioned once. "The client is impressed with big numbers," she says, "so count anything you can find." Does this approach raise any ethical concerns on your part? Why or why not?

> At this level, public relations practitioners measure whether target audience groups actually *received* the messages directed at them: whether they paid *attention* to those messages, whether they *understood* the messages, and whether they have *retained* those messages in any shape or form.

The tools of survey research are needed to answer such questions. Members of the target audience must be asked about the message and what they remember about it. Such research, for example, found that Microsoft achieved a phenomenal 99 percent public awareness that Windows 95 was coming and available for purchase.

Public awareness of what organization sponsors an event also is important. BayBank found that only 59 percent of the spectators recognized the bank as sponsor of the Head of the Charles Regatta. Through various innovations, increased publicity efforts, and more signage at the following year's regatta, BayBank raised public awareness to 90 percent.

Another way of measuring audience awareness and comprehension is the day-after recall. Under this method, participants are asked to view a specific television program or read a particular news story; then they are interviewed to learn which messages they remembered.

Ketchum public relations, on behalf of the California Prune Board, used this technique to determine if a 15-city media tour was conveying the key message that prunes are a high-fiber food source. Forty women in Detroit considered likely to watch daytime television shows were asked to view a program on which a Prune Board spokesperson would appear. The day after the program, Ketchum asked the women questions about the show, including their knowledge of the fiber content of prunes. Ninety-three percent remembered the Prune Board spokesperson, and 65 percent, on an unaided basis, named prunes as a source of high fiber.

Measurement of Audience Attitudes

Closely related to audience awareness and understanding of a message are changes in an audience's perceptions and attitudes.

A major technique to determine such changes is the *baseline study*. Basically, it is a measurement of audience attitudes and opinions before, during, and after a public relations campaign. Baseline studies, also called *benchmark studies*, graphically show the percentage difference in attitudes and opinions as a result of increased information and publicity. A number of intervening variables may account for changes in attitude, of course, but statistical analysis of variance can help pinpoint how much the change is attributable to public relations efforts.

The Prudential, the insurance company, regularly conducts baseline studies. One survey found that the company scored high in respondent familiarity, but achieved only a 29 percent favorable rating in fulfilling its corporate social responsibilities.

As a result, the company launched "The Prudential Helping Hearts Program." This provided $2 million in matching grants to volunteer emergency medical squads (EMS) to help purchase portable cardiac arrest equipment used to treat heart attack victims before they reach the hospital. After a year of publicizing the program and making grants, The Prudential found that its overall corporate image rose 29 percent.

The American Iron and Steel Institute also did a baseline study to determine the effectiveness of its campaign to inform the public about the industry's recycling efforts. Before the program, only 52 percent of the respondents in Columbus, Ohio, were aware that steel cans are recyclable. After the campaign, the percentage had risen to 64 percent.

The value of the baseline survey is underscored by Frank R. Stansberry, manager of guest affairs for Coca-Cola. He told the *Public Relations Journal:* "The only way to determine if communications are making an impact is by pre- and posttest research. The first survey measures the status quo. The second one will demonstrate any change and the direction of that change."

Measurement of Audience Action

The ultimate objective of any public relations effort, as has been pointed out, is to accomplish organizational objectives. As David Dozier of San Diego State University aptly points out, "The outcome of a successful public relations program is not a hefty stack of news stories. . . . Communication is important only in the effects it achieves among publics."

The objective of the amateur theater group is not to get media publicity; the objective is to sell tickets. The objective of an environmental organization such as Greenpeace is not to get editorials written in favor of whales, but to motivate the public to (1) write elected officials, (2) send donations for its preservation efforts, and (3) get protective legislation passed. The objective of a company is to sell its products and services, not get 200 million media impressions. In all cases, the tools and activities of public relations are a means, not an end.

Thus it can be seen that public relations efforts are ultimately evaluated on how they help an organization achieve its objectives. Here are some bottom-line examples:

- The M&M's Chocolate Candies color contest campaign caused a 6.5 percent increase in sales.
- The Mack Truck image and customer service campaign increased the company's market share from 9.2 to 12 percent, lifting Mack Trucks from sixth to third place in the large truck market.
- The campaign to promote Turkish tourism caused a 10 percent increase in the number of U.S. travelers to Turkey.
- BayBank saw a 10 percent increase in the number of student bank accounts during the Head of the Charles Regatta it sponsored.
- During its centennial year celebration, the National Association of Manufacturers (NAM) had a growth of 800 members; membership retention set a new record.
- Government agencies in Orange County, California, approved a plan to restore a degraded wetlands area after a campaign to organize public support.
- A public information campaign on behalf of Fighting Hunger in Wisconsin raised $170,000—$70,000 more than the previous year.

Measurement of Supplemental Activities

Other forms of measurement can be used in public relations activities. The following sections discuss (1) communication audits, (2) pilot tests and split messages, (3) meeting and event attendance, and (4) newsletter readership.

Communication Audits

The entire communication activity of an organization should be evaluated at least once a year to make sure that every primary and secondary public is receiving appropriate messages.

David Hilton-Barber, past president of the Public Relations Institute of South Africa, has written:

> The most important reasons for an audit are to help establish communication goals and objectives, to evaluate long-term programs, to identify strengths and weaknesses, and to point up any areas which require increased activity.

A communication audit, as an assessment of an organization's entire communication program, could include the following:

- Analysis of all communication activities—newsletters, memos, policy statements, brochures, annual reports, position papers, mailing lists, media contacts, personnel forms, graphics, logos, advertising, receptionist contacts, waiting lounges for visitors, and so on
- Informal interviews with rank-and-file employees and middle management and top executives
- Informal interviews with community leaders, media gatekeepers, consumers, distributors, and other influential persons in the industry

A number of research techniques, as outlined in Chapter 6, can be utilized during a communication audit, including mail and telephone surveys, focus groups, and so forth. The important point is that the communications of an organization should be analyzed from every possible angle, with the input of as many publics as possible. Security analysts may have something to say about the quality of the company's financial information; municipal leaders are best qualified to evaluate the company's efforts in community relations. Consumers, if given a chance, will make suggestions about quality of sales personnel and product instruction booklets.

Pilot Tests, Split Messages, Perception Analyzers, and Think-Aloud Techniques

Evaluation is important even before a public relations effort is launched. If exposure to a message is to be maximized, it is wise to pretest it with a sample group from the targeted audience. Do its members easily understand the message? Do they accept the message? Does the message motivate them to adopt a new idea or product?

A variation of pretesting is the *pilot test.* Before going national with a public relations message, companies often test the message and key copy points in selected cities to learn how the media accept the message and how the public reacts. This approach is quite common in product marketing because it limits the costs and enables the company to revamp or fine-tune the message for maximum exposure. It also allows the company to switch channels of dissemination if original media channels are not exposing the message to the proper audiences.

The *split-message approach* is common in direct mail campaigns. Two or three different appeals may be prepared by a charitable organization and sent to different audiences. The response rate is then monitored (perhaps the amount of donations is totaled) to learn what message and graphics seemed to be the most effective.

Perception analyzer systems, sometimes also called theater systems, allow selected subjects to view speeches, public service announcements, or video news releases while turning a dial up or down to offer their ratings of favorability as the television message is presented. This dynamic system enables the public relations firm to identify which passages of a tape are working best or which message strategies are most effective.

Increasingly, professionals in Web development are seeking to refine the content of organizational Web sites. Among Web publishers, the refrain often heard is: "Content is king." This means that it is insufficient for public relations professionals to simply be satisfied with having a Web site at all or rely on bells and whistles such as flashing elements and animation to jazz up a site. The content needs to be compelling and effective in meeting organizational objectives. A relatively new research technique, called the *think-aloud method,* can be used to assess Web content in a similar fashion to the perception analyzers. By encouraging expression of every thought that occurs to a Web user, comments are collected as the subject browses the various pages of a Web site. Practice sessions occur first to help the subject become accustomed to vocalizing every thought about the content and to become comfortable with audio- and videotaping equipment. After sufficient numbers of subjects are recorded, audio- and videotape are coded and systematically content analyzed to provide an empirical assessment of the Web pages.

Meeting and Event Attendance

It has already been pointed out that meetings can be evaluated to some degree by the level of attendance. Such data provide information about the number of people exposed to a message but still don't answer the more crucial question of what they thought about the meeting.

Public relations people often get an informal sense of an audience's attitudes by its behavior. A standing ovation, spontaneous applause, complimentary remarks as people leave, and even the expressions on people's faces provide clues as to how a meeting was received. On the other hand, if people are not responsive, if they ask questions about subjects supposedly explained, if they express doubts or antagonism, the meeting can be considered only partly successful.

Public relations practitioners use a number of information methods to evaluate the success of a meeting, but they also employ more systematic methods. The most common technique is an evaluation sheet that participants fill out at the end of the meeting.

A simple form asking people to rate such items as location, costs, facilities, and program on a 1-to-5 scale (1 being the best) can be used. Other forms may ask people to rate aspects of a conference or meeting as (1) excellent, (2) good, (3) average, (4) poor, and (5) very poor.

Evaluation forms also can ask how people heard about the program and what suggestions they would make for future meetings.

Newsletter Readership

Editors of newsletters should evaluate readership annually. Such an evaluation can help ascertain (1) reader perceptions, (2) the degree to which stories are balanced, (3) kinds of stories that have high reader interest, (4) additional topics that should be covered, (5) credibility of the publication, and (6) the extent to which it is meeting organizational objectives.

Systematic evaluation, it should be emphasized, is not based on whether all the copies are distributed or picked up. This information doesn't tell the editor what the audience actually read, retained, or acted upon. A newsletter, newspaper, or even a brochure can be evaluated in a number of ways. The methods include (1) content analysis, (2) readership interest surveys, (3) readership recall of articles actually read, (4) application of readability formulas, and (5) use of advisory boards.

Content Analysis From a representative sample of past issues, stories may be categorized under general headings such as (1) management announcements, (2) new product developments, (3) new personnel and retirements, (4) features about employees, (5) corporate finances, (6) news of departments and divisions, and (7) job-related information.

Such a systematic analysis will show what percentage of the publication is devoted to each category. It may be found that one division rarely is covered in the employee newsletter or that management pronouncements tend to dominate the entire publication. Given the content-analysis findings, editors may wish to shift the content somewhat.

Readership Interest Surveys The purpose of these surveys is to get feedback about the types of stories employees are most interested in reading.

The most common method is simply to provide a long list of generic story topics and have employees rate each as (1) important, (2) somewhat important, or (3) not important. The International Association of Business Communicators (IABC) conducted such a survey on behalf of several dozen companies and found that readers were not very interested in "personals" about other employees (birthdays, anniversaries, and the like).

A readership interest survey becomes even more valuable when it is compared with the content analysis of a publication. Substantial differences signal a possible need for changes in the editorial content.

Article Recall The best kind of readership survey occurs when trained interviewers ask a sampling of employees what they have read in the latest issue of the publication.

Employees are shown the publication page by page and asked to indicate which articles they have read. As a check on the tendency of employees to report that they have read everything, interviewers also ask them (1) how much of each article they have read and (2) what the articles were about. The results are then content-analyzed to determine which kinds of articles have the most readership.

A variation of the readership recall technique involves individual evaluation of selected articles for accuracy and clarity. For example, an article about a new production process may be sent before or after publication to the head of production for evaluation. On a form with a rating scale of excellent, good, fair, and deficient, the person may be asked to evaluate the article on the basis of such factors as (1) technical data provided, (2) organization, (3) length, (4) clarity of technical points, and (5) quality of illustrations.

Advisory Boards Periodic feedback and evaluation can be provided by organizing an employee advisory board that meets several times a year to discuss the direction and content of the publication. This is a useful technique because it expands the editor's feedback network and elicits comments that employees might be hesitant to tell the editor face-to-face.

A variation of the advisory board method is periodically to invite a sampling of employees to meet to discuss the publication. This approach is more systematic than just soliciting comments from employees in the hallway or cafeteria.

Summary

The Purpose of Evaluation

Evaluation is the measurement of results against objectives. This can both enhance future performance and also establish whether the goals of management by objective have been met.

Objectives: A Prerequisite for Evaluation

Objectives should be part of any program plan. There must be agreed-upon criteria used to evaluate success in obtaining these objectives.

Current Status of Measurement and Evaluation

The proportion of public relations budgets devoted to measurement and evaluation has grown in the past decade to about 5 percent. On the most basic level, practitioners can measure message distribution and media placements. The second level would be measurement of audience awareness, comprehension, and retention. The most advanced level is the measurement of changes in attitudes, opinions, and behavior.

Measurement of Production

Measurement of production gives management an idea of a staff's productivity and output.

Measurement of Message Exposure

Message exposure can be measured using several criteria, including the compilation of: press clippings and radio–television mentions; the media impressions, or potential audience reached; Internet hits on a Web site; advertising equivalency, calculated by converting news stories to the cost of a comparable amount of paid space; systematic tracking by use of computer databases; requests for additional information, often through a toll-free telephone number; and audience attendance at special events. Sometimes exposure is evaluated by determining the cost to reach each member of the target audience.

Measurement of Audience Awareness

The next level of evaluation is whether the audience became aware of and understood the message. Audience awareness can be measured with survey research.

Measurement of Audience Attitudes

Changes in audience attitudes can be evaluated through a baseline or benchmark study, measuring awareness and opinions before, during, and after a public relations campaign.

Measurement of Audience Action

Ultimately, public relations campaigns are evaluated by how they help the organization achieve its objectives through change in audience behavior, whether this involves sales, fund-raising, or the election of a candidate.

Measurement of Supplemental Activities

A yearly communication audit is necessary to ensure that all publics are receiving appropriate messages. Pretesting a public relations effort can be done with a pilot test, a split-message approach, a perception analyzer system, or the think-aloud method. Meeting and event attendance can be measured both by the number of attendees and by their behavior, which is an indicator of their acceptance of a message. Newsletter readership can be evaluated by content analysis, interest surveys, and article recall.

Case Activity: What Would You Do?

The Ohio Department of Transportation, with 17 rideshare groups, is planning a Rideshare Week. The objective is to increase participation in carpooling and use of mass transit during this special week. A long-term objective, of course, is to increase the number of people who use car pools or mass transit on a regular basis.

Your public relations firm is retained to promote Ohio Rideshare Week. Your campaign will include a news conference with the governor encouraging participation, press kits, news releases, interviews on broadcast talk shows, special events, and distribution of Rideshare information booklets at major businesses.

What methods would you use to evaluate the effectiveness of your public relations efforts on behalf of Ohio Rideshare Week?

Questions for Review and Discussion

1. What is the role of stated objectives in evaluating public relations programs?
2. What primary method of evaluation do public relations people use? Is there any evidence that other methods are increasingly being used?
3. What are some general types of evaluation questions that a person should ask about a program?
4. Name four ways by which publicity activity is evaluated. What, if any, are the drawbacks to each one?
5. Do you think news stories about a product or service should be evaluated in terms of comparable advertising costs? Why or why not?
6. What are the advantages of systematic tracking and content analysis of news clippings?
7. How are pilot tests and split messages used to determine the suitability of a message?
8. How does measurement of message exposure differ from measurement of audience comprehension of the message?
9. How are benchmark studies used in evaluation of public relations programs?
10. What is a communication audit?
11. What methods of evaluation can be done for a company newsletter or magazine?

Suggested Readings

Austin, Erica, and Pinkleton, Bruce. *Strategic Communication Management: Planning and Managing Effective Communication Programs.* Mahwah, NJ: Lawrence Erlbaum Associates, 2001.

Baron, Ayelet. "It's Time for Communicators to Integrate Evaluation into Strategic Planning." *Communication World,* April/May 1997, pp. 32–34.

Cameron, Glen T. "Does Publicity Outperform Advertising? An Experimental Test of the Third-Party Endorsement." *Journal of Public Relations Research,* Vol. 6, No. 3, 1994, pp. 185–207.

Elsasser, John. "Escape From 'Measure-Not Land'." *Public Relations Tactics,* July 1997, pp. 30–31.

Eveland, W. P., Jr., and Dunwoody, S. "Examining Information Processing on the World Wide Web Using Think Aloud Protocols. *Media Psychology,* No. 2, 2000, pp. 219–244.

Freitag, Alan R. "How to Measure What We Do." *Public Relations Quarterly,* Summer 1998, pp. 42–47.

Grunig, James, and Grunig, Lauri. "Does Evaluation of PR Measure the Real Value of PR?" *pr reporter,* September 7, 1998, four-page supplement.

Hon, Linda Childers. "Demonstrating Effectiveness in Public Relations: Goals, Objectives, and Evaluation." *Journal of Public Relations Research,* Vol. 10, No. 2, 1998, pp. 103–135.

Hon, Linda Childers. "What Have You Done for Me Lately? Exploring Effectiveness in Public Relations." *Journal of Public Relations Research,* Vol. 9, No. 1, 1997, pp. 1–30.

Kanzler, Ford. "Making Sense of News Clippings." *PR Tactics,* April 1996, pp. 5, 26.

Krugman, D. M., Cameron, G. T., and White, C. M. "Visual Attention to Programming and Commercials: The Use of In-Home Observations." *Journal of Advertising,* No. 14, 1995, pp. 1–12.

Lindenmann, Walter K. "Setting Minimum Standards for Measuring Public Relations Effectiveness." *Public Relations Review,* Winter 1997, pp. 391–401.

Lindenmann, Walter K., editor. *Guidelines and Standards for Measuring and Evaluating PR Effectiveness,* Gainesville, FL: Institute for Public Relations Research, University of Florida, P.O. Box 118400, Gainesville, FL 32611-8400. (www.jou.ufl.edu/iprre/homepage.htm)

"Publicity Has More Impact Than Mag Ads." *O'Dwyer's PR Services Report,* September 1994, pp. 1, 40.

Whitney, Pamela. "News Content Analysis Is Cost-Efficient PR Tool." *O'Dwyer's PR Services Report,* July 1997, pp. 46–47.

Public Opinion and Persuasion

preview

The objectives of this chapter are to explain what constitutes public opinion and how it is formed, and to guide students in selecting the appropriate techniques for public relations situations.

Topics covered in the chapter include:

- What is public opinion?
- Opinion leaders as catalysts
- The media's role
- Persuasion: pervasive in our lives
- Factors in persuasive communication
- Propaganda
- Persuasion and manipulation
- The ethics of persuasion

What Is Public Opinion?

Americans talk about public opinion as if it were a monolithic entity overshadowing the entire landscape. Editorial cartoonists, in contrast, humanize it in the form of John or Jane Q. Public, characters who symbolize what people think about any given issue. The reality is that public opinion is somewhat elusive and extremely difficult to measure at any given moment.

In fact, to continue the metaphor, public opinion is a number of monoliths and John and Jane Q. Publics all existing at the same time. Few issues create unanimity of thought among the population, and public opinion on any issue is split in several directions. It may also come as a surprise to note that only a small number of people at any given time take part in public opinion formation on a specific issue.

There are two reasons for this. First, psychologists have found that the public tends to be passive. Few issues generate an opinion or feeling on the part of an entire citizenry. It is often assumed that a small, vocal group represents the attitude of the public when, in reality, it is more accurate to say that the majority of the people are apathetic because the issue doesn't interest or affect them. Thus "public" opposition to such issues as nuclear power, gay rights, abortion, and gun control may really be the view of a small but significant number of concerned people.

Second, one issue may engage the attention of one part of the population, while another arouses the interest of another segment. Parents, for example, may form public opinion on the need for improved secondary education, while senior citizens constitute the bulk of public opinion on the need for increased Social Security benefits.

These two examples illustrate the most common definition of public opinion: "Public opinion is the sum of individual opinions on an issue *affecting* those individuals." Another popular definition states: "Public opinion is a collection of views held by persons *interested* in the subject." Thus a person unaffected by or uninterested in (and perhaps unaware of) an issue does not contribute to public opinion on the subject.

Inherent in these definitions is the concept of *self-interest.* The following statements appear in public opinion research:

- Public opinion is the collective expression of opinion of many individuals bound into a group by common aims, aspirations, needs, and ideals.
- People who are interested or who have a vested or *self-interest* in an issue—or who can be affected by the outcome of the issue—form public opinion on that particular item.
- Psychologically, opinion basically is determined by *self-interest.* Events, words, or any other stimuli affect opinion only insofar as their relationship to *self-interest* or a general concern is apparent.
- Opinion does not remain aroused for any long period of time unless people feel their *self-interest* is acutely involved or unless opinion—aroused by words—is sustained by events.
- Once *self-interest* is involved, opinion is not easily changed.

How practitioners utilize the concept of self-interest in focusing their message to fit the audience is discussed under "Appeal to Self-Interest," later in this chapter.

Research studies also emphasize the importance of *events* in the formation of public opinion. Social scientists, for example, have made the following generalizations:

Demonstrations and rallies play a major role in creating public awareness and persuading individuals that their viewpoint is valid. Here, supporters of George W. Bush rally in Florida after allegations on both sides that certain groups of people didn't have their votes properly counted. The Florida recount kept the presidential election of 2000 in limbo for several weeks.

- Opinion is highly sensitive to *events* that have an impact on the public at large or a particular segment of the public.
- By and large, public opinion does not anticipate *events*. It only reacts to them.
- *Events* trigger formation of public opinion. Unless people are aware of an issue, they are not likely to be concerned or have an opinion. Awareness and discussion lead to crystallizing of opinions and often a consensus among the public.
- *Events* of unusual magnitude are likely to swing public opinion temporarily from one extreme to another. Opinion does not stabilize until the implication of the event is seen with some perspective.

An event that triggered formation of public opinion, causing people to swing from apathy to outrage, was the French government's decision to conduct nuclear bomb tests on Mururoa Atoll in the South Pacific. After President Jacques Chirac announced the tests, an outpouring of public condemnation resounded around the world. Nations in the South Pacific, among them Australia and New Zealand, announced a boycott of French goods. The French Polynesian Independence Movement conducted massive demonstrations in Tahiti and motivated thousands of Polynesians to sign petitions. Greenpeace gained thousands of new members. Nevertheless, the French conducted the tests. A year later, public outrage was no longer a subject of media attention.

People also have more opinions and are able to form them more easily with respect to goals than with the methods necessary to reach those goals. Fairly strong public opinion, according to polls, favors improving the quality of the nation's schools. There is little agreement, however, on how to do this. One group advocates higher salaries for "master" teachers, another endorses substantial tax increases for school operations. A third group urges more rigorous standards. All three groups, plus assorted other ones with still other solutions, make up public opinion on the subject.

Opinion Leaders as Catalysts

Public opinion on an issue may have its roots in self-interest or in events, but the primary catalyst is public discussion. Only in this way does opinion begin to crystallize, and pollsters can measure it.

Serving as catalysts for the formation of public opinion are people who are knowledgeable and articulate about specific issues. They are called *opinion leaders.* Sociologists describe them as (1) highly interested in the subject or issue, (2) better informed on the issue than the average person, (3) avid consumers of mass media, (4) early adopters of new ideas, and (5) good organizers who can get other people to take action.

Types of Leaders

Sociologists traditionally have defined two types of leaders. First are the *formal opinion leaders,* so called because of their positions as elected officials, presidents of companies, or heads of membership groups. Often news reporters ask them for statements when a specific issue relates to their areas of responsibility or concern. People in formal leadership positions are also called *power leaders.*

Second are the *informal opinion leaders,* who have clout with peers because of some special characteristic. They may be *role models* who are admired and emulated or opinion leaders because they can exert peer pressure on others to go along with something. In general, informal opinion leaders exert considerable influence on their peer groups by being highly informed, articulate, and credible on particular issues.

A survey of 20,000 Americans by the Roper Organization found that only 10 to 12 percent of the general public are opinion leaders. These "influentials," those whom other people seek out for advice, fit the profile of (1) being active in the community, (2) having a college degree, (3) earning relatively high incomes, (4) regularly reading newspapers and magazines, (5) actively participating in recreational activities, and (6) showing environmental concern by recycling.

Regis McKenna, a marketing communications expert responsible for the original launch of the Apple Macintosh, likes to think of opinion leaders as *luminaries* because, "There are about 20 to 30 key people in every industry who have major influence on trends, standards, and an organization's reputation." He also knows that journalists seek quotes from key opinion leaders in an industry whenever a new product is introduced.

Microsoft, for example, used the McKenna formula in the introduction of its Windows 95 program. Long before the product hit the shop shelves, Microsoft sent Windows 95 to key opinion leaders in the industry and the trade media. Their positive statements to the press, obtained in advance, provided important credibility and built public excitement about the forthcoming product. This is a form of two-step information flow, discussed next.

The Flow of Opinion

Many public relations campaigns, particularly those in the public affairs area, concentrate on identifying and reaching key opinion leaders who are pivotal to the success or failure of an idea or project. Sociologists Elihu Katz and Paul Lazarsfeld in the 1940s discovered the importance of opinion leaders during a study of how people chose candidates in an election. They found that the mass media had minimal influence on electoral choices, but voters did rely on person-to-person communication with formal and informal opinion leaders.

These findings became known as the *two-step flow theory of communication.* Although later research confirmed that it really was a multiple-step flow, the basic idea remained intact. Public opinion is really formed by the views of people who have taken the time to sift information, evaluate it, and form an opinion that is expressed to others.

PR insights

The Life Cycle of Public Opinion

Public opinion and persuasion are important catalysts in the formation of a public issue and its ultimate resolution. The natural evolution of an issue involves five stages:

1. *Definition of the issue.* Activist and special interest groups raise an issue, perhaps a protest against scenic areas being threatened by logging or strip mining. These groups have no formal power but serve as "agenda stimuli" for the media that cover controversy and conflict. Visual opportunities for television coverage occur when activists hold rallies and demonstrations.
2. *Involvement of opinion leaders.* Through media coverage, the issue is put on the public agenda and people become aware of it. Opinion leaders begin to discuss the issue and perhaps see it as symbolic of broader environmental issues.
3. *Public awareness.* As public awareness grows, the issue becomes a matter of public discussion and debate, with extensive media coverage. The issue is simplified by the media into "them versus us." Suggested solutions tend to be at either end of the spectrum.
4. *Government/regulatory involvement.* Public consensus begins to build for a resolution as government/regulatory involvement occurs. Large groups identify with some side of the issue. Demand grows for government to act.
5. *Resolution.* The resolution stage begins as people with authority (elected officials) draft legislation or interpret existing rules and regulations to make a statement. A decision is made to protect the scenic areas or to reach a compromise with advocates of development. If some groups remain unhappy, however, the cycle may repeat itself.

The *multiple-step flow model* is graphically illustrated by a series of concentric circles. In the epicenter of action are opinion makers. They derive large amounts of information from the mass media and other sources and share that information with people in the adjoining concentric circle, who are labeled the "attentive public." These latter are interested in the issue but rely on opinion leaders to provide synthesized information and interpretation. The outer ring consists of the "inattentive public." They are unaware of or uninterested in the issue and remain outside the opinion-formation process. The multiple-step flow theory, however, means that some will eventually become interested in, or at least aware of, the issue.

The Role of Mass Media

One traditional way that public relations personnel reach opinion leaders and other key publics is via the mass media—radio, television, newspapers, and magazines. *Mass media,* as the term implies, means that information from a public relations source can be efficiently and rapidly disseminated to literally millions of people.

Although journalists often argue that they rarely use public relations materials, one has only to look at the daily newspaper to see the quote from the press officer at the sheriff's department, the article on a new computer product, the statistics from the local real estate board, or even the after-game interview with the winning quarterback. In almost all cases, a public relations source at the organization provided the information or arranged the interview. Indeed, Oscar H. Gandy, Jr., of the University of Pennsylvania says that up to 50 percent of what the media carry comes from public relations sources in the form of "information subsidies."

Gandy and other theorists have concluded, therefore, that public relations people—via the mass media—are major players in forming public opinion because they often provide the mass media with the information in the first place. This opinion is also echoed by Elizabeth L. Toth and Richard L. Heath, authors of *Rhetorical and Critical Approaches to Public Relations.* They say, "Few professions have so many skilled and talented individuals contributing to the thoughts, actions, and policies of our nation."

In order to better understand how public relations people strive to inform the public and shape public opinion via the mass media, it is necessary to review briefly several theories about mass media effects.

■ Agenda Setting Theory One of the early theories, developed by Paul Lazarsfeld and Elihu Katz, contends that media content sets the agenda for public discussion. People tend to talk about what they see or hear on the 6 o'clock news or read on the front page of the newspaper. Media, by the selection of stories and headlines, tell the public what to think about but not necessarily what to think. The Clinton/Lewinsky sex scandal, for example, was high on the media agenda for many months, but public opinion polls indicated a variety of viewpoints on the subject.

Social scientist Joseph Klapper calls this the "limited effects" model of mass media. He postulates, "Mass media ordinarily does not serve as a necessary and sufficient cause for audience effects, but rather functions among and through a nexus of mediating factors and influence." Such factors may include the way that opinion leaders analyze and interpret the information provided by the mass media.

From a public relations standpoint, even getting a subject on the media agenda is an accomplishment that advances organizational goals. Sales of Apple's iMac rose as the media reported its success and the public became aware of this "hot" item.

■ Media Dependency Theory Although the agenda-setting function of the media is generally valid, other research indicates that mass media can have a "moderate" or even "powerful" effect on the formation of opinions and attitudes. When people have no prior information or attitude disposition regarding a subject, the mass media play a role in telling people what to think.

Mass media effects are also increased when people cannot verify information through personal experience and knowledge. They are highly dependent on the media for information. Therefore, if much of this information comes from official spokespersons of organizations, it's an opportunity for public relations to shape the tone and content of a story—or, as was noted in Chapter 1, put a particular spin on the story. Mass communications and public relations researchers Debbie Steele and Kirk Hallahan analysed a crisis situation for a blood bank and found, "Official sources enjoy an advantage in the early phases of a crisis or issue, particularly when media and others are still in the discovery phase of coverage and the primary emphasis is merely to identify the extent of the problem."

■ Framing Theory The term *framing* has a long history in mass media research. Traditionally, framing was related to journalists and how they selected certain facts, themes, treatments, and even words to "frame" a story. According to researchers Julie L. Andsager at Washington State University and Angela Powers at Northern Illinois University, "Mass media scholars have long argued that it is important to understand the ways in which journalistic framing of issues occurs because such framing impacts public understanding and, consequently, policy formation." For example, how media frame the debate over health care and the role of HMOs often plays a major role in public perceptions of the problem.

Increasingly, however, scholars are also applying framing theory to public relations efforts. One research paper, by James Tankard and Bill Israel of the University of Texas, was titled, "PR Goes to War: The Effects of Public Relations Campaigns on Media Framing of the Kuwait and Bosnian Crises." Their basic contention was that the governments involved used public relations professionals to help frame the issues involved, which were then picked up by the press.

In the case of Kuwait, Hill and Knowlton used the theme of Iraqi atrocities to frame the issue in support of Kuwait. In Bosnia, Ruder-Finn framed the issue as Serb genocide against Bosnian Muslims. Almost overnight, the media were also equating the Serbs with the Nazis in the public mind by using highly emotional phrases such as "ethnic cleansing" and "concentration camps."

Tankard and Israel point out that the media dependency of most Americans—who have little direct knowledge of these places and the complex issues involved—means that they accept the media's version of reality—which originally came from what the two researchers describe as "special interest groups or other groups with particular causes."

Most public relations personnel rarely find themselves framing the issues of an international conflict, but they do exercise framing or positioning strategies on any number of products and services. When Edelman Worldwide, for example, was considering strategy for the launch of Apple's iMac computer, one of the strong themes (or frames) was that Apple was on the way back to prosperity after several years of massive losses and erosion of customer support. Indeed, one headline in a daily newspaper proclaimed, "Apple Regains Its Stride." Such framing obviously bolsters investor and consumer confidence in the company.

Cultivation Theory Communication researchers like to call the news content of mass media "mediated reality" because events are repackaged to be more succinct, logical, and interesting to a reader or viewer. This mediated reality, however, can influence beliefs and even conduct if repeated often enough. George Gerbner, of the University of Pennsylvania, conducted decades of research on the topic of violence on television and how it affects people. He and his associates found that constant violence portrayed in TV shows eventually cultivated viewers to the idea that crime was rampant, and their fears about violence in their own neighborhoods became highly exaggerated.

Again, from a public relations perspective, does that mean that public relations professionals are able, via the media, to cultivate viewers into the mediated reality to perceive that a company is a solid citizen or that the brand name does mean quality? Or does a corporate advertising campaign, repeated often enough, really cultivate consumers to accept the image of the organization portrayed? The vote is still out.

Persuasion: Pervasive in Our Lives

Persuasion has been around since the dawn of human history. It was formalized as a concept more than 2000 years ago by the Greeks, who made *rhetoric,* the art of using language effectively and persuasively, part of their educational system. Aristotle was the first to set down the ideas of *ethos, logos,* and *pathos,* which roughly translate as "source credibility," "logical argument," and "emotional appeal."

More recent scholars, such as Richard Perloff, author of *The Dynamics of Persuasion,* say "Persuasion is an activity or process in which a communicator attempts to induce a change in the belief, attitude, or behavior of another person or group of persons through the transmission of a message in a context in which the persuadee has some degree of free choice."

Such a definition is consistent with the role of public relations professionals in today's society. Indeed, Professor Richard Heath says:

> . . . public relations professionals are influential rhetors. They design, place, and repeat messages on behalf of sponsors on an array of topics that shape views of government, charitable organizations, institutions of public education, products and consumerism, capitalism, labor, health, and leisure. These professionals speak, write, and use visual images to discuss topics and take stances on public policies at the local, state, and federal levels.

The Dominant View of Public Relations

The dominant public view of public relations, in fact, is one of persuasive communication actions performed on behalf of clients, according to Professors Dean Kruckeberg at the University of Northern Iowa and Ken Starck at the University of Iowa. Gandy adds that ". . . the primary role of public relations is one of purposeful, self-interested communications." And Edward Bernays even called public relations the "engineering" of consent to create "a favorable and positive climate of opinion toward the individual, product, institution or idea which is represented." See Chapter 2 for definitions by Edward L. Bernays.

To accomplish this goal, public relations personnel use a variety of techniques to reach and influence their audiences. At the same time, persuasion or rhetoric should

PR insights

A Sampler on Persuasion

A number of research studies have contributed to a basic understanding of persuasion concepts. Here are some basic ideas from the text *Public Communication Campaigns,* edited by Ronald E. Rice and William J. Paisley:

- Positive appeals are generally more effective than negative appeals for retention of the message and actual compliance.
- Radio and television messages tend to be more persuasive than print, but if the message is complex, better comprehension is achieved through print media.
- Strong emotional appeals and fear arousal are most effective when the audience has minimal concern about or interest in the topic.
- High fear appeals are effective only when a readily available action can be taken to eliminate the threat.
- Logical appeals, using facts and figures, are better for highly educated, sophisticated audiences than strong emotional appeals.
- Altruistic need, like self-interest, can be a strong motivator. Men are more willing to get a physical checkup to protect their families than to protect themselves.
- A celebrity or an attractive model is most effective when the audience has low involvement, the theme is simple, and broadcast channels are used. An exciting spokesperson attracts attention to a message that would otherwise be ignored.

be considered more than a one-way flow of information, argument, and influence. In the best sense, Toth and Heath in their book say persuasion should be a dialogue between points of view in the marketplace of public opinion, where any number of persuaders are hawking their wares.

Indeed, persuasion is an integral part of democratic society. It is the freedom of speech used by every individual and organization to influence opinion, understanding, judgment, and action.

Uses of Persuasion

Persuasion is used to (1) change or neutralize hostile opinions, (2) crystallize latent opinions and positive attitudes, and (3) conserve favorable opinions.

The most difficult persuasive task is to turn hostile opinions into favorable ones. There is much truth to the adage "Don't confuse me with the facts; my mind is made up." Once people have decided, for instance, that HMOs are making excessive profits or that a nonprofit agency is wasting public donations, they tend to ignore or disbelieve any contradictory information. Everyone, as Walter Lippmann has described, has pictures in his or her head based on an individual perception of reality. People generalize from personal experience and what peers tell them. For example, if a person has an encounter with a rude clerk, the inclination is to generalize that the entire department store chain is not very good.

Persuasion is much easier if the message is compatible with a person's general disposition toward a subject. If a person tends to identify Toyota as a company with a good reputation, he or she may express this feeling by purchasing one of its cars. Nonprofit agencies usually crystallize the public's latent inclination to aid the less fortunate by asking for a donation. Both examples illustrate the reason that organizations strive to have a good reputation—it is translated into sales and donations. The concept of message channeling will be discussed in more detail later in the chapter.

The easiest form of persuasion is communication that reinforces favorable opinions. Public relations people, by providing a steady stream of reinforcing messages, keep the reservoir of goodwill in sound condition. More than one organization has survived a major problem because public esteem for it tended to minimize current difficulties. Continual efforts to maintain the reservoir of goodwill is called *preventive public relations*—the most effective of all.

Factors in Persuasive Communication

A number of factors are involved in persuasive communication, and the public relations practitioner should be knowledgeable about each one. The following is a brief discussion of (1) audience analysis, (2) source credibility, (3) appeal to self-interest, (4) clarity of message, (5) timing and context, (6) audience participation, (7) suggestions for action, (8) content and structure of messages, and (9) persuasive speaking.

Audience Analysis

Knowledge of audience characteristics such as beliefs, attitudes, concerns, and lifestyles is an essential part of persuasion. It helps the communicator tailor messages that are salient, answer a felt need, and provide a logical course of action.

PR insights

Appeals That Move People to Act

Persuasive messages often include information that appeals to an audience's self-interest. Here is a list of persuasive message themes:

- Make money
- Save money
- Save time
- Avoid effort
- More comfort
- Better health
- Cleaner
- Escape pain
- Gain praise
- Be popular
- Be loved/accepted
- Keep possessions
- More enjoyment
- Satisfy curiosity
- Protect family
- Be stylish
- Have beautiful things
- Satisfy appetite
- Be like others
- Avoid trouble
- Avoid criticism
- Be individual
- Protect reputation
- Be safe
- Make work easier
- Be secure

Source: Marsh, Charles, "Fly Too Close to the Sun." *Communication World,* September 1992, p. 24.

Basic demographic information, readily available through census data, can help determine an audience's gender, income level, education, ethnic background, and age groupings. Other data, often prepared for marketing departments, give information on a group's buying habits, disposable income, and ways of spending leisure time.

Polling and surveys, discussed in Chapter 6, tap a target audience's attitudes, opinions, and concerns. Such research tells about the public's resistance to some ideas, as well as its predisposition to support other ideas. Recycling programs, for example, made a slow start in the early 1990s because the public resisted changing its habit of throwing everything into the same garbage container. Yet surveys showed that although the public was concerned about the environment, "convenience" was king. The only way to change habits was to make it easy for homeowners to recycle by providing sorting bins that, in turn, were regularly picked up. Many cities also opened neighborhood recycling centers that paid people for bottles and cans. Today, recycling is the norm. The concepts of making suggestions for action and self-interest will be discussed shortly.

Another tool of audience analysis is use of *psychographics.* This method attempts to classify people by lifestyle, attitudes, and beliefs. The Values and Lifestyle Program, popularly known as VALS, was developed by SRI International, a research organization in Menlo Park, California, about 30 years ago.

VALS is now routinely used in public relations to help communicators structure persuasive messages to different elements of the population. A good illustration is the way Burson-Marsteller used VALS for its client, the National Turkey Foundation. The problem was simple: how to encourage turkey consumption throughout the year, not just at Thanksgiving and Christmas.

One element of the public was called Sustainers and Survivors; VALS identifies them as low-income, poorly educated, often elderly people who ate at erratic hours, consumed inexpensive foods, and seldom ate out. Another element was the Belongers, who were highly family oriented and served foods in traditional ways. The Achievers, on the other hand, were more innovative and willing to try new foods.

Burson-Marsteller tailored a strategy for each group. For Survivors and Sustainers, the message stressed bargain cuts of turkey that could be stretched into a full meal. The message for Belongers focused on cuts that signaled turkey, such as drumsticks. Achievers, better educated and at higher income levels, received the message about gourmet cuts and new, innovative recipes.

This segmentation of the consumer public into various VALS lifestyles enabled Burson-Marsteller to select appropriate media for specific story ideas. An article placed in *True Experience,* a publication reaching the demographic characteristics of Survivors and Sustainers, was headlined "A Terrific Budget-Stretching Meal." *Better Homes and Gardens* was used to reach Belongers with such titles as "Streamlined Summer Classics" and stories about barbecued turkey on the Fourth of July. Articles for Achievers in *Food and Wine* magazine and *Gourmet* included recipes for turkey salad and turkey tetrazzini.

Such audience analysis, coupled with suitably tailored messages in the appropriate media outlets, is the technique of *channeling.* Persuasive messages are more effective when they take into account the audience's lifestyles, beliefs, and concerns.

Source Credibility

A message is more believable to the intended audience if the source has *credibility.* This was Aristotle's concept of *ethos,* mentioned earlier, and it explains why organizations use a variety of spokespeople, depending upon the message and the audience.

The California Strawberry Advisory Board, for example, arranges for a home economist to appear on television talk shows to discuss nutrition and to demonstrate easy-to-follow strawberry recipes. The viewers, primarily homemakers, identified with the representative and found her highly credible. By the same token, a manufacturer of sunscreen lotion uses a professor of pharmacology and a past president of the State Pharmacy Board to discuss the scientific merits of sunscreen versus suntan lotions.

The Three Factors Source credibility is based on three factors. One is *expertise.* Does the audience perceive the person as an expert on the subject? Companies, for example, use engineers and scientists to answer news conference questions about how an engineering process works or whether an ingredient in the manufacturing process of a product presents a potential hazard.

The second component is *sincerity.* Does the person come across as believing what he or she is saying? Robin Williams may not be an expert on all the products he endorses, but he does get high ratings for sincerity.

The third component, even more elusive, is *charisma.* Is the individual attractive, self-assured, and articulate, projecting an image of competence and leadership?

Ideally, a source will exhibit all three attributes. Steve Jobs, president of Apple, is a good example. He is highly credible as an expert on Apple products because he is one of the company's founders and also a "geek" in his own right. In countless media interviews and trade show presentations, he comes across as a candid, open individual who really believes in the company's products. Jobs also has charisma; he is self-assured, confident, and articulate. His standard uniform—the open-neck shirt, the vest, and the designer jeans—gives him additional aura as a legendary figure in the computer industry.

Not every organization, however, has a Steve Jobs for its president. Depending on the message and the audience, various spokespersons can be used and quoted for source credibility. A news release for a new product, for example, might quote the director of research and development (R&D) for the company. If the information is about an organization's financial picture, the most credible person would be the chief executive officer (CEO) or the vice president of finance, primarily because of perceived expertise.

Expertise is less important than sincerity and charisma if celebrities are used as spokespersons. Their primary purpose is to call attention to the product or service. Another purpose is to associate the celebrity's popularity with the product. This technique is called *transfer,* mentioned later in this chapter as a propaganda device.

PR casebook

Can Sex Sell Mutual Funds?

Financial surveys are not exactly stimulating reading, but adding a little sex appeal helps. Oppenheimer Funds used the allure of *Sex and the City's* Carrie Bradshaw to enliven the results of a survey on the financial planning attitudes of Generation X women.

According to the financial firm, many women are showing signs of "Carrie Bradshaw Syndrome" when it comes to their finances. The survey, for example, revealed that 54 percent of the single women surveyed are likely to acquire 30 pairs of shoes before saving $30,000 toward their retirement. Another 50 percent said at this time in life, money is for spending, not for saving.

Oppenheimer sent out a news release and a complete copy of the survey results to the media. One major result: the *New York Times* ran a feature story on the "Carrie Bradshaw Syndrome." Apparently, Carrie truly represents women.

Even fictional figures such as Carrie Bradshaw can become endorsers of products.

Basketball legend Michael Jordan lends credibility and visibility to a host of products and services that he endorses. Here, Jordan appears at a press conference to announce that he's signed a five-year deal to become a spokesperson and endorser of AMF bowling products. (AP Photo/Matt Ferguson).

Problems with Celebrities Using celebrities has its problems, however. One is the increasing number of endorsements to the point that the public sometimes can't remember who endorses what. Candice Bergen endorses Sprint, but a third of the Video Storyboard respondents thought she endorsed AT&T or MCI. A second problem can be overexposure of a celebrity such as Michael Jordan, who still earns about $35 million annually for endorsing more than a dozen products.

The third problem occurs when an endorser's actions undercut the product or service. Singer Britney Spears, for example, has a $108 million contract to exclusively promote Pepsi, but British tabloids photographed her twice in one month swigging a Coca-Cola. The German unit of America Online also had a problem after signing up tennis legend Boris Becker for a series of commercials portraying him as a "family man" who discovers how easy it is to get hooked up with AOL. However, shortly after the campaign started, Becker divorced his wife. Another German company hired a famous soccer coach as a celebrity endorser, but then he flunked a drug test and was fired from the national team. "Anytime an advertiser pins its image to a star, whether an athlete or an actor, it takes a chance that reality won't live up to the storyboard," says Christina White, a reporter for the *Wall Street Journal.*

In summary, the use of various sources for credibility depends, in large part, on the type of audience being reached. That is why audience analysis is the first step in formulating persuasive messages.

PR casebook

Gary Condit Flunks Persuasion 101

Rep. Gary Condit of California found himself the focus of national media attention during much of 2001 after a student intern in Washington, D.C., who was intimately involved with the married man disappeared.

Condit, at the beginning, said he had only met Chandra Levy in a social setting. Then, as Washington police gathered more information and the Levy family hired a detective (as well as a public relations firm to keep their daughter in the news), Condit decided to stonewall and not answer any media questions. The media had a field day; the story was a great circulation builder: a politician, a coed, an affair, and mystery (what happened to Chandra?).

After some weeks, Condit's advisors (including lawyers and public relations professionals who were experts in damage control) finally convinced Condit that he should explain himself by doing a national interview on ABC's *PrimeTime* with a highly credible reporter, Connie Chung. The two questions on everyone's mind, including Chung's, were: (1) Did you have an affair with Chandra Levy? and (2) did you kill her?

Condit, within a few minutes, lost all credibility. He refused to answer the first question, nor did he express much sympathy or even remorse that she was missing. In terms of the second question, he insisted that he was not involved in her disappearance but didn't offer much believable information. In sum, Condit was castigated by viewers for being evasive, robotic in his answers, and totally lacking in credibility.

Jeffrey Graubard, president of his own firm in New York, summed it up best in a letter to *PR Week*. He said, "Condit should have affected a more informal and empathic pose, admitted adultery, and reminded Chung that philandering is a deeply troubling private issue, but not criminal. He could have apologized for withholding information, concluding that he'd seen his miscalculation and is now fully cooperating."

Sandra Sokoloff, senior vice president of Magnet Communications in New York, added, "While Condit's media trainers certainly hammered some key messages into his head, what they failed to realize is that messages are a means to help frame answers to questions, not a tactic to avoid them. . . . Condit's messages did not achieve any of this. Rather than reaching out and appeasing, his messages just raised another level of suspicion and negativity."

Voters in Condit's Congressional district apparently agreed. He lost the Democratic primary election in March 2002 by a wide margin to a former aide after a 30-year record of never losing an election.

Rep. Gary Condit faces tough questioning from the press about the disappearance of a Washington intern, Chandra Levy, after he admits having a romantic relationship with her.

Appeal to Self-Interest

Self-interest was described during an earlier discussion about the formation of public opinion. Publics become involved in issues or pay attention to messages that appeal to their psychic or economic needs.

Publicity for a personal computer can serve as an example. A news release to the trade press serving the computer industry might focus on the technical proficiency of the equipment. The audience, of course, consists of engineers and computer programmers. A brochure prepared for the public, however, may emphasize how the computer can (1) help people keep track of personal finances, (2) assist youngsters in becoming better students, (3) fit into a small space, and (4) offer good value. Consumers are interested in how the personal computer can make life easier for them.

Charitable organizations don't sell products, but they do need volunteers and donations. This is accomplished by careful structuring of messages that appeal to self-interest. This is not to say that altruism is dead. Thousands of people give freely of their time and money to charitable organizations, but they do receive something in return, or they would not do it. The "something in return" may be (1) self-esteem, (2) the opportunity to make a contribution to society, (3) recognition from peers and the community, (4) a sense of belonging, (5) ego gratification, or even (6) a tax deduction. Public relations people understand psychic needs and rewards, and that is why there is constant recognition of volunteers in newsletters and at award banquets. (Further discussion of volunteerism appears in Chapter 17.)

Sociologist Harold Lasswell says people are motivated by eight basic appeals. They are power, respect, well-being, affection, wealth, skill, enlightenment, and physical and mental vitality. Psychologist Abraham Maslow, in turn, says any appeal to self-interest must be based on a *hierarchy of needs.* The first and lowest level involves basic needs such as food, water, shelter, and even transportation to and from work. The second level consists of security needs. People need to feel secure in their jobs, safe in their homes, and confident about their retirement. At the third level are "belonging" needs—people seek association with others. This is why individuals join organizations.

"Love" needs comprise the fourth level in the hierarchy. Humans have a need to be wanted and loved—fulfilling the desire for self-esteem. At the fifth and highest level in Maslow's hierarchy are self-actualization needs. Once the first four needs are met, Maslow says, people are free to achieve maximum personal potential; for example, through traveling extensively or perhaps becoming experts on orchids.

Maslow's hierarchy helps explain why some public information campaigns have difficulty getting the message across to people classified in the VALS lifestyle categories as "survivors" and "sustainers." Efforts to inform minorities and low-income groups about AIDS provide an example of this problem. For these groups, the potential danger of AIDS is less compelling than the day-to-day problems of poverty and satisfying the basic needs of food and shelter.

The challenge for public relations personnel, as creators of persuasive messages, is to tailor information to fill or reduce a need. Social scientists have said that success in persuasion largely depends on accurate assessment of audience needs and self-interests.

Clarity of Message

Many messages fail because the audience finds the message unnecessarily complex in content or language. The most persuasive messages are direct, are simply expressed, and contain only one primary idea. Peter Drucker, a management expert, once said, "An innovation, to be effective, has to be simple and it has to be focused. It should do only one thing, otherwise it confuses." The same can be said for the content of any message.

Public relations personnel should always ask two questions: "What do I want the audience to do with the message?" and "Will the audience understand the message?" Although persuasion theory says people retain information better and form stronger opinions when they are asked to draw their own conclusions, this doesn't negate the importance of explicitly stating what action an audience should take. Is it to buy the product, visit a showroom, write a member of Congress, make a $10 donation, or what?

If an explicit request for action is not part of the message, members of the audience may not understand what is expected of them. Public relations firms, when making a presentation to a potential client, always ask for the account at the end of the presentation.

Timing and Context

A message is more persuasive if environmental factors support the message or if the message is received within the context of other messages and situations with which the individual is familiar. These factors are called timing and context.

Information from a utility on how to conserve energy is more salient if the consumer has just received the January heating bill. A pamphlet on a new stock offering is more effective if it accompanies an investor's dividend check. A citizens' group lobbying for a stoplight gets more attention if a major accident has just occurred at the intersection.

Political candidates are aware of public concerns and avidly read polls to learn what issues are most salient with voters. If the polls indicate that crime and unemployment are key issues, the candidate begins to use these issues—and to offer his or her proposals—in the campaign.

Timing and context also play an important role in achieving publicity in the mass media. Public relations personnel, as pointed out earlier, should read newspapers and watch television news programs to find out what media gatekeepers consider newsworthy. A manufacturer of a locking device for computer files got extensive media coverage about its product simply because its release followed a rash of news stories about thieves' gaining access to bank accounts through computers. Media gatekeepers found the product newsworthy within the context of actual news events.

The value of information and its newsworthiness are based on timing and context. Public relations professionals disseminate information at the time it is most highly valued.

Audience Participation

A change in attitude or reinforcement of beliefs is enhanced by *audience involvement and participation.*

An organization, for example, may have employees discuss productivity in a quality-control circle. Management may already have figured out what is needed, but if workers are involved in the problem solving, they often come up with the same solution or even a better one. And, from a persuasion standpoint, the employees are more committed to making the solution work because it came from them—not as a policy or order handed down by higher management.

Participation can also take the form of samples. Many companies distribute product samples so the consumer can conveniently try them without expense. A consumer who samples the product and makes a judgment about its quality is more likely to purchase it.

Activist groups use participation as a way of helping people actualize their beliefs. Not only do rallies and demonstrations give people a sense of belonging, but the act of participation reinforces their beliefs. Asking people to do something—conserve energy, collect donations, or picket—activates a form of self-persuasion and commitment.

Suggestions for Action

A principle of persuasion is that people endorse ideas only if they are accompanied by a proposed action from the sponsor.

Recommendations for action must be clear. Public relations practitioners must not only ask people to conserve energy, for instance, but also furnish detailed data and ideas on how to do it.

A campaign conducted by Pacific Gas & Electric Company provides an example. The utility inaugurated a Zero Interest Program (ZIP) to offer customers a way to implement energy-saving ideas. The program involved several components:

- *Energy kit.* A telephone hotline was established and widely publicized so interested customers could order an energy kit detailing what the average homeowner could do to reduce energy use.
- *Service bureau.* The company, at no charge, sent representatives to homes to check the efficiency of water heaters and furnaces, measure the amount of insulation, and check doors and windows for drafts.
- *ZIP.* The cost of making a home more energy efficient was funded by zero-interest loans to any qualified customer.

Content and Structure of Messages

A number of techniques can make a message more persuasive. Writers throughout history have emphasized some information while downplaying or omitting other pieces of information. Thus they addressed both the *content* and *structure of messages.*

Expert communicators continue to use a number of devices, including (1) drama, (2) statistics, (3) surveys and polls, (4) examples, (5) testimonials, (6) mass media endorsements, and (7) emotional appeals.

Drama Because everyone likes a good story, the first task of a communicator is to get audience attention. This is often accomplished by graphically illustrating an event or situation. Newspapers often dramatize a story to get reader interest in an issue. Thus we read about the family evicted from its home in a story on the increase in bankruptcies; the old man who is starving because of welfare red tape; or the worker disabled because of toxic waste. In newsrooms, this is called *humanizing an issue.*

Dramatizing is also used in public relations. Relief organizations, in particular, attempt to galvanize public concern and donations through stock black-and-white photographs and emotionally charged descriptions of suffering and disease.

A more mundane use of dramatizing is the so-called *application story,* sent to the trade press. This is sometimes called the *case study technique,* in which a manufacturer prepares an article on how an individual or a company is using the product. IBM, for example, provides a number of application stories about the unique ways in which its products are being used.

Snowflake

Dear Friend,

For polar bear cubs like Snowflake, life starts out as a nearly impossible challenge.

Born with her sister Aurora in the frigid darkness of the Arctic winter, Snowflake weighed only about a pound at birth, the size of a cell phone. For months, she and her sister didn't leave the den where they were born, a small cave that their mother had dug in a snow bank. Helpless, they depended on their mother for the essentials of life — her body warmth and her nutrient-rich milk.

Snowflake and her sister will stay with their mother for more than two years. She will feed them, teach them to hunt, and protect them from predators.

With the fierce maternal protection of her mother, cuddly little Snowflake will grow up to become one of the most awesome animals on Earth.

But now, a looming new threat could cut short the lives of precious little polar bear cubs like Snowflake.

You see, the powerful oil lobby and its political allies in Congress are pushing to open Snowflake's home — the Arctic National Wildlife Refuge — to environmentally destructive oil and gas drilling. The Refuge's coastal plain is America's most important on-shore polar bear nursery, and scientist warn that the habitat destruction, pollution and other impacts of the plan could be deadly to the bears.

That's why I'm asking you to please "adopt" a polar bear cub like Snowflake by joining Defenders of Wildlife today with a contribution of $15 or more.

Defenders of Wildlife is helping lead the fight to save America's greatest wildlife sanctuary for Snowflake and the other wild animals that call it home. But to succeed, we urgently need the help of concerned individuals like you to overcome the enormous money and political clout of the oil lobby.

And we must act now — because politicians are already moving to hand over this unique natural treasure to Big Oil. Congressman Don Young (R-Alaska) — who decorates his office with animal skins — has already introduced legislation to allow drilling. The pristine 19 million-acre Arctic Refuge is the last place in North America where Arctic wildlife is fully protected. And the Refuge's coastal plain, often referred to as "America's Serengeti," is the biological heart of this

(over, please)

Defenders of Wildlife • 1101 Fourteenth Street, N.W. • Room 1400 • Washington, D.C. 20005
www.defenders.org • www.kidsplanet.org

Your continued activism is important. Please call your representatives in Washington to let them know you support the preservation of wildlife and its habitat. You can contact them at 202-224-3121. Thank you.

Successful persuasion by direct mail depends heavily on an eye-catching opening that persuades the recipient to read on rather than toss the letter aside. Letters such as this have an emotional appeal and often stir the reader's high concern for a particular situation.

■ **Statistics** People are impressed by statistics. Use of numbers can convey objectivity, size, and importance in a credible way that can influence public opinion. Caterpillar, for example, got considerable media publicity for its new 797 mining dump truck by combining statistics and some humor. In the news release for the largest truck in the world, it announced that the bed of the truck was so large that it could haul the following payloads: four blue whales, 217 taxicabs, 1200 grand pianos, and 23,490 Furbies.

Surveys and Polls Airlines and auto manufacturers, in particular, use the results of *surveys* and *polls* to show that they are first in "customer satisfaction," "service," and even "leg room" or "cargo space." The most credible surveys are those conducted by independent research organizations, but readers still should read the fine print to see what is being compared and rated. Is an American-made auto, for example, being compared only with other U.S. cars or with foreign cars as well?

Examples A statement of opinion can be more persuasive if some *examples* are given. A school board can often get support for a bond issue by citing examples of how the present facilities are inadequate for student needs. Environmental groups tell how other communities have successfully established greenbelts when requesting a city council to do the same. Automakers promote the durability of their vehicles by citing their performance on a test track or in a road race.

Testimonials A form of source credibility, *testimonials* can be either explicit or implied. A campaign to curtail alcohol and drug abuse may feature a pop singer as a spokesperson, or have a young woman talk about being paralyzed and disfigured as the victim of a drunk driver. Implied testimonials also can be effective. Proclamations by mayors and governors establishing Red Cross Day or Library Week are implied testimonials. The testimonial as a propaganda device is discussed later in the chapter.

Endorsements In addition to those by paid celebrities, products and services benefit from favorable statements by experts in what is called a *third-party endorsement.* A well-known medical specialist may publicly state that a particular brand of exercise equipment is best for general conditioning. Organizations such as the American Dental Association and the National Safety Council also endorse products and services.

Media endorsements, usually unpaid, can come through editorials, reviews, surveys, and news stories. A daily newspaper may endorse a political candidate, review restaurants and entertainment events, and even compile a survey ranking the best coffeehouses. The media also produce news stories about new products and services which, because of their perceived objectivity, are considered a form of *third-party endorsement.* The idea is that media coverage bestows legitimacy and newsworthiness on a product or service. When the *Washington Post* reported that President Clinton's favorite burger was a soybean-based vegetarian product made by Boca Burger Company, sales of the product immediately boomed.

Emotional Appeals Fund-raising letters from nonprofit groups, in particular, use this persuasive device. Amnesty International, an organization dedicated to human rights and fighting state terrorism, began one direct-mail letter with the following message in large red type:

> "We Are God in Here . . ."
>
> . . . That's what the guards taunted the prisoner with as they applied electrical shocks to her body while she lay handcuffed to the springs of a metal bed. Her cries were echoed by the screams of other victims and the laughter of their torturers.

Such emotional appeals can do much to galvanize the public into action, but they also can backfire. Such appeals raise ego defenses, and people don't like to be told that in some way they are responsible. A description of suffering makes many people uncomfortable, and, rather than take action, they may tune out the message. A relief

PR insights

Motivation-Ability-Opportunity Model for Enhancing Message Processing

The chart below summarizes the various communication strategies that can be used to reach publics who have little knowledge or interest in a particular issue, product, or service. The object, of course, is to structure persuasive messages that attract their attention.

Enhance Motivation	*Enhance Ability*	*Enhance Opportunity*
Attract and encourage audiences to commence, continue processing	*Make it easier to process the message by tapping cognitive resources*	*Structure messages to optimize processing*
Create attractive, likable messages (create affect)	Include background, definitions, explanations	Expend sufficient effort to provide information
Appeal to hedonistic needs (sex, appetite, safety)	Be simple, clear	Repeat messages frequently
Use novel stimuli • Photos • Typography • Oversized formats • Large number of scenes, elements • Changes in voice, silence, movement	Use advance organizers, e.g. headlines	Repeat key points within text—in headlines, text, captions, illustrations, etc.
Make the most of formal features • Format size • Music • Color • Include key points in headlines	Include synopses	Use longer messages
Use moderately complex messages	Combine graphics, text, and narration (dual coding of memory traces)	Include multiple arguments
Use sources who are credible, attractive, or similar to audience	Use congruent memory cues (same format as original)	Feature "interactive" illustrations, photos
Involve celebrities	Label graphics (helps identify which attributes to focus on)	Avoid distractions • Annoying music • Excessively attractive spokespersons • Complex arguments • Disorganized layouts
Enhance relevance to audience—ask them to think about a question	Use specific, concrete (versus abstract) words and images	Allow audiences to control pace of processing
Use stories, anecdotes, or drama to draw into action	Include exemplars, models	Provide sufficient time
Stimulate curiosity: Use humor, metaphors, questions	Make comparison with analogies	Keep pace lively and avoid audience boredom
Vary language, format, source	Show actions, train audience skills through demonstrations	
Use multiple, ostensibly independent sources	Include marks (logos, logotypes, trademarks), slogans, and symbols as continuity devices	
	Appeal to self-schemas (roles, what's important to audience's identity)	
	Enhance perceptions of self-efficacy to perform tasks	
	Place messages in conducive environment (priming effects)	
	Frame stories using culturally resonating themes, catchphrases	

Source: Kirk Hallahan, "Enhancing Motivation, Ability, and Opportunity to Process Public Relations Messages." *Public Relations Review,* Vol. 26, No. 4, pp. 463–480.

organization once ran full-page advertisements in magazines with the headline "You Can Help Maria Get Enough to Eat . . . Or You Can Turn the Page." Researchers say that most people, their ego defenses raised, turn the page and mentally refuse to acknowledge that they even saw the ad. In sum, emotional appeals that attempt to lay a guilt trip on the audience are not very successful.

Strong fear arousals also can cause people to tune out, especially if they feel that they can't do anything about the problem anyway. Research indicates, however, that a moderate fear arousal, accompanied by a relatively easy solution, is effective. A moderate fear arousal is: "What would happen if your child were thrown through the windshield in an accident?" The message concludes with the suggestion that a baby, for protection and safety, should be placed in a secured infant seat.

Psychologists say the most effective emotional appeal is one coupled with facts and figures. The emotional appeal attracts audience interest, but logical arguments are also needed.

Persuasive Speaking

Psychologists have found that successful speakers (and salespeople) use several persuasion techniques:

- *Yes–yes.* Start with points with which the audience agrees, to develop a pattern of "yes" answers. Getting agreement to a basic premise often means that the receiver will agree to the logically developed conclusion.
- *Offer structured choice.* Give choices that force the audience to choose between A and B. College officials may ask audiences, "Do you want to raise taxes or raise tuition?" Political candidates ask, "Do you want more free enterprise or government telling you what to do?"
- *Seek partial commitment.* Get a commitment for some action on the part of the receiver. This leaves the door open for commitment to other parts of the proposal at a later date. "You don't need to decide on the new insurance plan now, but please attend the employee orientation program on Thursday."
- *Ask for more/settle for less.* Submit a complete public relations program to management, but be prepared to compromise by dropping certain parts of the program. It has become almost a cliché that a department asks for a larger budget than it expects to receive.

A persuasive speech can either be one-sided or give several sides of an issue, depending on the audience. A series of studies by Hovland and his associates determined that one-sided speeches were most effective with persons favorable to the message, while two-sided speeches were most effective with audiences that might be opposed to the message.

By mentioning all sides of the argument, the speaker accomplishes three objectives. First, he or she is perceived as having objectivity. This translates into increased credibility and makes the audience less suspicious of motives. Second, the speaker is treating the audience as mature, intelligent adults. Third, including counterarguments allows the speaker to control how these arguments are structured. It also deflates opponents who might challenge the speaker by saying, "But you didn't consider . . ."

Panel discussions and debates present other problems. Psychologists say the last person on a panel to talk will probably be most effective in changing audience attitudes—

or at least be longer remembered by the audience. But it has also been shown that the first speaker sets the standard and tone for the remainder of the discussion. Being first or last is better positioning than being between two presentations.

Propaganda

No discussion of persuasion would be complete without mentioning propaganda and the techniques associated with it.

Garth S. Jowett and Victoria O'Donnell in their book, *Propaganda and Persuasion,* say "Propaganda is the deliberate and systematic attempt to shape perceptions, manipulate cognitions, and direct behavior to achieve a response that furthers the desired intent of the propagandist." Its roots go back to the 17th century, when the Roman Catholic Church set up the *congregatio de propaganda* (congregation for propagating the faith). The word took on extremely negative connotations in the 20th century.

In World Wars I and II, propaganda was associated with the information activities of the enemy. Germany and Japan were sending out "propaganda" while the United States and its allies were disseminating "truth." Today, propaganda connotes falsehood, lies, deceit, disinformation, and duplicity—practices that opposing groups and governments accuse each other of employing.

Some have even argued that propaganda, in the broadest sense of the word, also includes the advertising and public relations activity of such diverse entities as Exxon and the Sierra Club. Social scientists, however, say that the word *propaganda* should be used only to denote activity that sells a belief system or constitutes political or ideological dogma.

Advertising and public relations messages for commercial purposes, however, do use several techniques commonly associated with propaganda. The most common are the following:

- *Plain folks.* An approach often used by individuals to show humble beginnings and empathy with the average citizen. Political candidates, in particular, are quite fond of telling about their "humble" beginnings.

focus on ethics

Is Framing an Issue OK?

The chapter includes information about the efforts of public relations firms to frame issues that would, in turn, be reflected by media coverage. Others might call this kind of effort positioning or even putting a spin on a particular event. The objective, of course, is to define the issues involved for the media and subsequently for the public. Hill and Knowlton, for example, helped frame the invasion of Kuwait by Iraq, using the theme of atrocity stories to generate anti-Iraq sentiment in the American people. Is framing a legitimate and ethical aspect of today's public relations practice? Why or why not?

- *Testimonial.* A frequently used device to achieve credibility, as discussed earlier. A well-known expert, popular celebrity, or average citizen gives testimony about the value of a product or the wisdom of a decision.
- *Bandwagon.* The implication or direct statement that everyone wants the product or that the idea has overwhelming support. "Millions of Americans support a ban on abortion" or "Every leading expert believes . . ."
- *Card stacking.* The selection of facts and data to build an overwhelming case on one side of the issue, while concealing the other side. The advertising industry says a ban on beer advertising would lead to enormous reductions in network sports programming, and a ban on cigarette advertising would kill many magazines.
- *Transfer.* The technique of associating the person, product, or organization with something that has high status, visibility, or credibility. Many corporations, for example, paid millions to be official sponsors of the 2000 Olympic Games, hoping that the public would associate their products with excellence.
- *Glittering generalities.* The technique of associating a cause, product, or idea with favorable abstractions such as freedom, justice, democracy, and the American way. Las Vegas bills itself as "The American Way to Play," and American oil companies argue for offshore drilling to keep "America energy-independent."

A student of public relations should be aware of these techniques, if only to make certain that he or she doesn't intentionally use them to deceive and mislead the public. Ethical responsibilities exist in every form of persuasive communication; guidelines are discussed at the end of the chapter.

Persuasion and Manipulation

The discussion on previous pages examined ways in which an individual can formulate persuasive messages. The ability to use these often leads to charges that public relations practitioners have great power to influence and manipulate people.

In reality, the effectiveness of persuasive techniques is greatly exaggerated. Persuasion is not an exact science, and no surefire way exists to predict that people or media gatekeepers will be persuaded to believe a message or act on it. If persuasive techniques were as refined as the critics say, all people might be driving the same make of automobile, using the same soap, and voting for the same political candidate.

This doesn't happen because several variables intervene in the flow of persuasive messages. Katz says the two major intervening variables are selectivity and interpersonal relations; these are consistent with the "limited effects" model of mass communications.

For purposes of discussion, the limitations on effective persuasive messages can be listed as (1) lack of message penetration, (2) competing messages, (3) self-selection, and (4) self-perception.

Lack of Message Penetration

The diffusion of messages, despite modern communication technologies, is not pervasive. Not everyone, of course, watches the same television program or reads the same newspapers and magazines. Not everyone receives the same mail or attends the same meetings. Not everyone the communicator wants to reach will be in the audience eventually reached, despite advances in audience segmentation techniques. There is also the problem of messages being distorted as they pass through media gatekeepers. Key message points often are left out, or the context of the message is changed.

Competing Messages

In the 1930s, before much was known about the complex process of communication, it was believed that people received information directly without any intervening variable. This was called the *bullet theory* or the *hypodermic needle theory* of communication.

Today communication experts realize that no message is received in a vacuum. Messages are filtered through a receiver's entire social structure and belief system. Nationality, race, religion, gender, cultural patterns, family, and friends are among the variables that filter and dilute persuasive messages. In addition, people receive countless competing and conflicting messages daily. Social scientists say a person usually conforms to the standards of his or her family and friends. Consequently, most people do not believe or act on messages that are contrary to group norms.

Self-Selection

The people most wanted in an audience are often the least likely to be there. As any minister attests, sinners don't go to church on a regular basis. Vehement supporters or loyalists frequently ignore information from the other side. They do so by being selective in the messages that they want to hear. They read books, newspaper editorials, and magazine articles and view television programs that support their predispositions. This is why social scientists say that the media are more effective in reinforcing existing attitudes than in changing them.

Self-Perception

Self-perception is the channel through which messages are interpreted. People will perceive the same information differently, depending on predispositions and already formulated opinions. *Inside PR* newsletter describes how people react to news stories: "If they believe something to be true and see a story affirming that belief, their belief is strengthened. If they believe something to be true and see a story challenging that belief, they assume the story is biased or just plain wrong."

Thus, depending on a person's views, an action by an organization may be considered a "great contribution to the community" or a "self-serving gimmick."

The Ethics of Persuasion

Public relations people, by definition, are advocates of clients and employers. The emphasis is on persuasive communication to influence a particular public in some way. At the same time, as Chapter 3 points out, public relations practitioners must conduct their activities in an ethical manner.

The use of persuasive techniques, therefore, calls for some additional guidelines. Professor Richard L. Johannesen of Northern Illinois University, writing in *Persuasion, Reception and Responsibility,* a text by Charles Larson, lists the following ethical criteria for using persuasive devices that should be kept in mind by every public relations professional:

- Do not use false, fabricated, misrepresented, distorted, or irrelevant evidence to support arguments or claims.
- Do not intentionally use specious, unsupported, or illogical reasoning.
- Do not represent yourself as informed or as an "expert" on a subject when you are not.
- Do not use irrelevant appeals to divert attention or scrutiny from the issue at hand. Among the appeals that commonly serve such a purpose are smear attacks on an opponent's character, appeals to hatred and bigotry, innuendo, and "God" or "devil" terms that cause intense but unreflective positive or negative reactions.
- Do not ask your audience to link your idea or proposal to emotion-laden values, motives, or goals to which it actually is not related.
- Do not deceive your audience by concealing your real purpose, your self-interest, the group you represent, or your position as an advocate of a viewpoint.
- Do not distort, hide, or misrepresent the number, scope, intensity, or undesirable features of consequences.
- Do not use emotional appeals that lack a supporting basis of evidence or reasoning or that would not be accepted if the audience had time and opportunity to examine the subject itself.
- Do not oversimplify complex situations into simplistic, two-valued, either/or, polar views or choices.
- Do not pretend certainty when tentativeness and degrees of probability would be more accurate.
- Do not advocate something in which you do not believe yourself.

It is clear from the preceding list that a public relations professional should be more than a technician or a "hired gun." This raises the issue that public relations personnel often lack the technical and legal expertise to know whether information provided to them by the client or employer is accurate.

Richard Heath makes it clear that this doesn't excuse public relations professionals from ethical responsibility. He writes:

> The problem of reporting information that they cannot personally verify does not excuse them from being responsible communicators. Their responsibility is to demand that the most accurate information be provided and the evaluation be the best available.

Persuasive messages require truth, honesty, and candor for two practical reasons. First, Heath says that a message is already suspect because it is advanced on behalf of a client or organization. Second, half-truths and misleading information do not serve the best interests of the public or the organization.

Summary

What Is Public Opinion?

Public opinion can be difficult to measure; there are few if any issues on which the public (which is in fact many publics) can be said to have a unanimous opinion. In fact, only a small number of people will have opinions on any given issue. Engaging the interest of a public will involve affecting its self-interest. Publics also react strongly to events.

Opinion Leaders as Catalysts

The primary catalyst in the formation of public opinion is public discussion. People who are knowledgeable and articulate on specific issues can be either formal opinion leaders (power leaders) or informal opinion leaders (role models). Opinion "flows" from these leaders to the public, often through the mass media.

Persuasion: Pervasive in Our Lives

The concept of persuasion has been around at least since the time of the ancient Greeks. The dominant view of public relations is of persuasive communications on behalf of clients. Persuasion can be used to change or neutralize hostile opinions, crystallize latent opinions and positive attitudes, and conserve favorable opinions.

Factors in Persuasive Communication

Factors involved in persuasion include audience analysis, source credibility, appeal to self-interest, message clarity, timing and context, audience participation, suggestions for action, content and structure of messages, and persuasive speaking.

Propaganda

Although the roots of the word *propaganda* go back to the 17th century, during the 20th century the word took on extremely negative connotations. During the world wars, it was associated with the enemies' information activities. It is now used to refer to political or ideological persuasion, with emphasis on deceit and duplicity. Propaganda techniques can be the same as those used in advertising and other public relations messages.

Persuasion and Manipulation

Limitations on effective persuasion include lack of message penetration, competing messages, self-selection, and self-perception.

The Ethics of Persuasion

There are two practical reasons for an ethical approach to persuasive messages. First, publics will automatically have a level of suspicion because they know the communicator is promoting a client or organization; and secondly, the interests of that client or organization will not be well served by false or misleading communications.

Case Activity: What Would You Do?

The school system of a major city wants to draw attention to the need for more volunteer adult tutors in the city's 200 public schools. Budget cutbacks in teaching staff and other resources have made it a vital necessity to recruit volunteers who would work with students on an individual basis to improve reading and math skills.

Your public relations firm has volunteered to organize a public information campaign. Explain what you would do in each of the following categories that relate to the structure and content of persuasive messages: drama, statistics, examples, testimonials, endorsements, and emotional appeals.

Questions for Review and Discussion

1. Public opinion is highly influenced by self-interest and events. What are these concepts?
2. What is the importance of opinion leaders in the formation of public opinion?
3. What theories about mass media effects have relevance for public relations?
4. What are the stages of public opinion in the life cycle of an issue?
5. Name the three objectives of persuasion in public relations work. What objective is the most difficult to accomplish?
6. Can you name and describe the nine factors involved in persuasive communication?
7. What are three factors involved in source credibility?
8. What are the pros and cons of using celebrities for product endorsements?
9. What are the levels of Maslow's hierarchy of needs? Why is it important for public relations people to understand the basic needs of people?
10. Why is audience involvement and participation important in persuasion?
11. What kinds of techniques can a person use to write persuasive messages?
12. Name several propaganda techniques. Should they be used by public relations people?
13. What are some ethical responsibilities of a person who uses persuasion techniques to influence others?

Suggested Readings

Callison, Coy. "Do PR Practitioners Have a PR Problem? The Effect of Associating a Source with Public Relations and Client-Negative News on Audience Perception of Credibility." *Journal of Public Relations Research,* Vol. 13, No. 3, 2001, pp. 219–234.

Dobrow, Larry. "Keeping Tabs on the Talent." *PR Week,* September 3, 2001, p. 25.

Glasser, Theodore L., and Salmon, Charles T., editors. *Public Opinion and the Communication of Consent.* New York: The Guilford Press, 1995.

Green, Deatherage. "So, You Want (Your Spokesperson) to Be Famous?" *PR Week,* September 4, 2000, p. 28.

Hallahan, Kirk. "Enhancing Motivation, Ability, and Opportunity to Process Public Relations Messages." *Public Relations Review,* Vol. 26, No. 4, 2000, pp. 463–480.

Hallahan, Kirk. "Inactive Publics: The Forgotten Publics in Public Relations." *Public Relations Review,* Vol. 26, No. 4, 2000, pp. 499–515.

Hallahan, Kirk. "No, Virginia, It's Not True What They Say about Publicity's 'Implied Third-Party Endorsement' Effect." *Public Relations Review,* Vol. 25, No. 3, 1999, pp. 331–350.

Newman, Kelli B. "The Power of Emotion." *Public Relations Tactics,* July 2001, p. 27.

"PR Pros Are among the Least Believable Public Figures." *O'Dwyer's PR Services Report,* August 1999, pp. 1, 24.

11 The Audience and How to Reach It

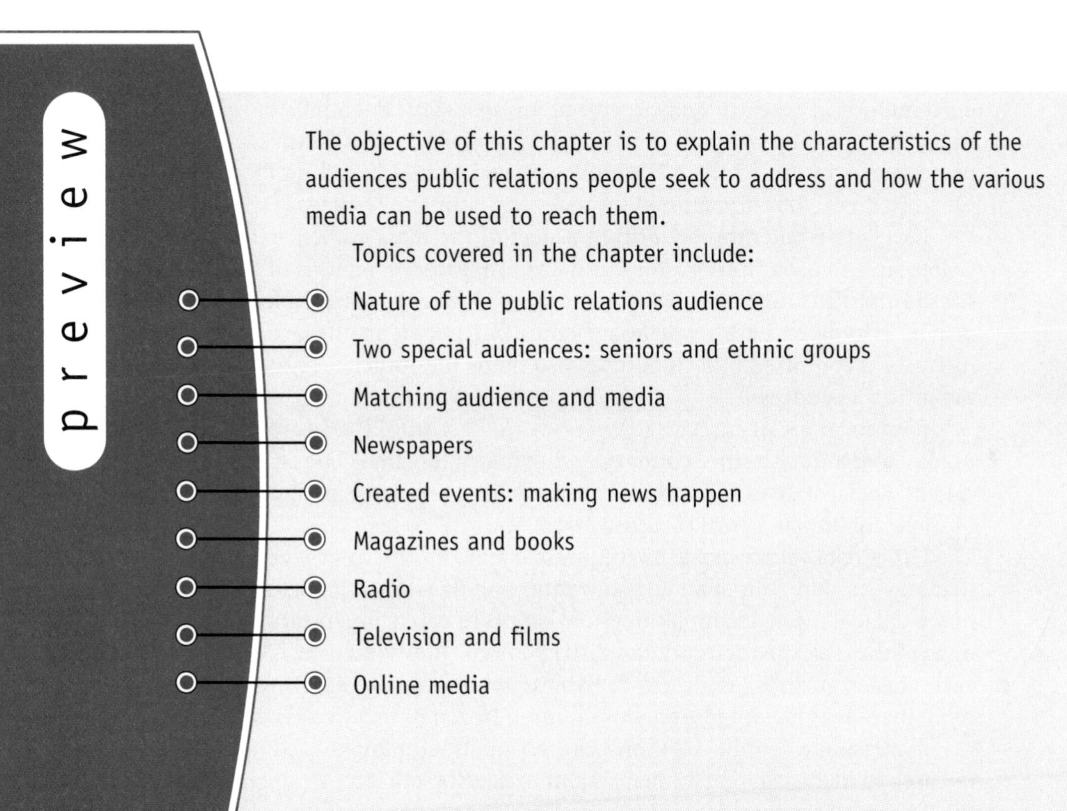

The objective of this chapter is to explain the characteristics of the audiences public relations people seek to address and how the various media can be used to reach them.

Topics covered in the chapter include:

- Nature of the public relations audience
- Two special audiences: seniors and ethnic groups
- Matching audience and media
- Newspapers
- Created events: making news happen
- Magazines and books
- Radio
- Television and films
- Online media

The Nature of the Public Relations Audience

If the audience on which public relations practitioners focus their messages were a monolithic whole, their work would be far easier—and far less stimulating. The audience, in fact, is just the opposite: a complex intermingling of groups with diverse cultural, ethnic, religious, and economic attributes whose interests coincide at times and conflict at others.

For the public relations professional, knowledge of these shifting audience dynamics is essential. A successful campaign must be aimed at those segments of the mass audience that are most desirable for its particular purpose and must employ those media most effective in reaching them. Some of these segments are easily identifiable and reachable, a category that Zoe McCathrin of Kent State University calls "prepackaged publics." These are well-organized groups whose members have banded together in a common interest; they constitute ready-made targets for practitioners who have projects of concern to them. Examples of such prepackaged publics are businesspeople in Rotary Clubs and animal lovers in the Humane Society.

Diversity is the most significant aspect of the mass audience in the United States. Differences in geography, history, and economy among regions of the sprawling country are marked; ranchers in Montana have different attitudes from residents in the heavily populated Eastern seaboard cities. Yet people in the two areas have national interests in common. Ethnic cultures also shape the audience segments public relations practitioners address.

Identification of target audiences can be accomplished through computer technology to conduct both secondary and primary research. The rich lode of geographical and social statistics found in Census Bureau reports provides a foundation. Many of these are broken down by census tract and ZIP code.

Other data sources, such as automobile registration, voter registration, sales figures, mailing lists, and church and organization memberships, can be merged into the computer database. For example, one marketing research organization, Claritas Inc., has divided the Chicago metropolitan district into 62 lifestyle clusters. It assigned a name to each cluster, such as "Boomers & Babies," whose buying habits, it says, include "rent more than five videos a month, buy children frozen dinners, read parenting magazines."

Increasingly, public relations professionals employ the computer for primary research to identify target audiences and to develop effective strategies for each. Publics PR Research Software™ was developed specifically to identify target publics using the situational theory created by University of Maryland professor James E. Grunig. The theory posits that groups define themselves as active publics when they identify an issue as a problem (problem recognition component) that affects them personally (involvement component) and that they feel empowered to address in some way (constraint recognition component).

Active publics merit attention by organizations dealing with an issue because their members seek information about the issue and will likely play a role in the outcome of the issue. (Chapter 6 provides details about the research process and additional information about Publics PR Research Software™.)

Public relations has become more strategic in practice with audiences precisely targeted and messages customized in some instances to the individual level. In health care settings, messages can be tailored for e-mail delivery to the individual patient based on his or her most recent examination. Not only can the practitioner target a precise public, but in many cases the professional can actually bypass the media and communicate directly with the target audience. The use of communication channels that reach directly to the audience is called controlled media. Using a database developed by the organization, letters can be sent directly to key decision makers such as stockholders. The same technique can be used by directing e-mail or a broadcast fax to key constituents.

Publications directed at employees and customers serve as examples of controlled media. Two of the most effective and popular controlled media are sponsored films and videotape and online media.

Senior and Ethnic Markets

As the demographic makeup changes dramatically in the United States, two major target audiences have emerged that deserve special attention. One is the *seniors.* This group frequently is defined as men and women 65 years or older, although some sociologists and marketing experts include everyone over age 50. The other group consists of *ethnic minorities.*

Similar audiences are developing to various degrees in other countries.

Seniors

Medical advances have improved life expectancy so much that today almost 35 million Americans are 65 or older, according to the U.S. Bureau of the Census. A heavy upsurge in the senior population will peak at 50 million by 2010, when the post–World War II "baby boomers" begin to reach the age of 65. These older citizens form an important opinion group and a consumer market with special interests.

When appealing to seniors, public relations people should try to ignore the stereotypes of "old folks" so often depicted in the movies and television. Some 80-year-old women sit in rocking chairs, knitting or snoozing, but others cheer and boo ardently while watching professional basketball on TV. Nor are all grandfathers crotchety complainers with quavering voices or kindly patriarchs who fly kites with their grandsons. As many differences in personality, interest, financial status, and living styles exist in the older audience as among their young-adult grandchildren.

Public relations practitioners should remember these characteristics of seniors:

- With the perspective of long experience, they are often less easily convinced than young adults, demand value in the things they buy, and pay little attention to fads.
- They vote in greater numbers than their juniors and are more intense readers of newspapers and magazines. Retirees also watch television heavily.
- They form an excellent source of volunteers for social, health, and cultural organizations because they have time and often are looking for something to do.
- They are extremely health conscious, out of self-interest, and want to know about medical developments. A Census Bureau study showed that most people past 65 say they are in good health; not until their mid-80s do they frequently need assistance in daily living.

Financially, the elderly are better off than the stereotypes suggest. The poverty rate among older Americans is slightly below that of the population at large. The Census Bureau found that people aged 65 to 74 have more discretionary income than any other group. In many instances their homes are completely paid for, and they hold 70 percent of the country's assets. While they are poor customers for household goods, they eat out frequently and do much gift buying. They travel frequently. In fact, seniors account for about 80 percent of commercial vacation travel, especially cruises.

Ethnic Groups

Historically, the United States has welcomed millions of immigrants and assimilated them into the cultural mainstream. They bring a bubbling mixture of personal values, habits, and perceptions that are absorbed slowly, sometimes reluctantly. The questions of assimilation—how much, how little?—also exist with two longtime indigenous minorities, African Americans and Native Americans. This diversity is a great strength of the United States but also a source of friction and misunderstandings. Communication campaigns have been employed in Malaysia and the Mideast to build understanding and interaction among diverse ethnic groups. Called nation-building, this important public relations work will become invaluable in building a relevant new definition of nationhood in the United States as it embraces growing diversity.

Recently the easily identifiable ethnic groups—primarily Hispanics, African Americans, Asian Americans, and Native Americans—as a whole have been growing five times faster than the general population with nonwhite ethnic groups now comprising a majority in some states. The U.S. Census Bureau predicted that by the year 2010 Hispanics and African Americans will make up 14.6 and 12.5 percent, respectively, of the U.S. population, a total of 27.1 percent, while Anglos will be 67.3 percent. Asian Americans and Native Americans will provide the remaining percentage. Even greater changes will occur by 2050, the Census Bureau predicted. Notably, Hispanics will form nearly one fourth of the U.S. population. (See Figure 11.1.)

A basic point to remember is that the minority population forms *many* target audiences, not a massive monolithic group whose interests are identical. Asians in San Francisco have different cultures and concerns from Hispanics in Miami. To be more precise, even the common terms for minority groups, such as Asian American, miss the cultural diversity among that racial group. For example, the lifestyles, values and interests of fourth-generation Japanese Americans in Los Angeles are dramatically different from what is found among recent immigrants from Vietnam or the Philippines. Thus the practitioner must define the audience with particular care and sensitivity.

Expanding populations have been accompanied by an increase in the number and strength of the minority media through which messages can be delivered. The 2001 *Gale Directory of Publications and Broadcast Media* lists 162 Hispanic publications and 245 black publications; Spanish and African American radio stations have increased correspondingly. Two Spanish-language TV networks, Univision and Telemundo, serve millions of viewers. The Black Entertainment Television Network has a large national audience. Thus a substantial number of outlets exist for public relations messages, provided news releases and story pitches are translated and culturally appropriate.

The swift expansion of the Hispanic population is a challenge for public relations practitioners. Merely translating their messages into Spanish is not enough. They must shape communications to the Hispanic culture, in particular the group's family ties. According to the U.S. Census Bureau, 12 million Hispanic children lived in the United States in 1996, up from 9.8 million six years earlier. This compares to 50.8 million Anglo children and 11.4 million non-Hispanic blacks. According to New America Strategies and DemoGraph Corporation, this family-oriented culture is why Hispanic

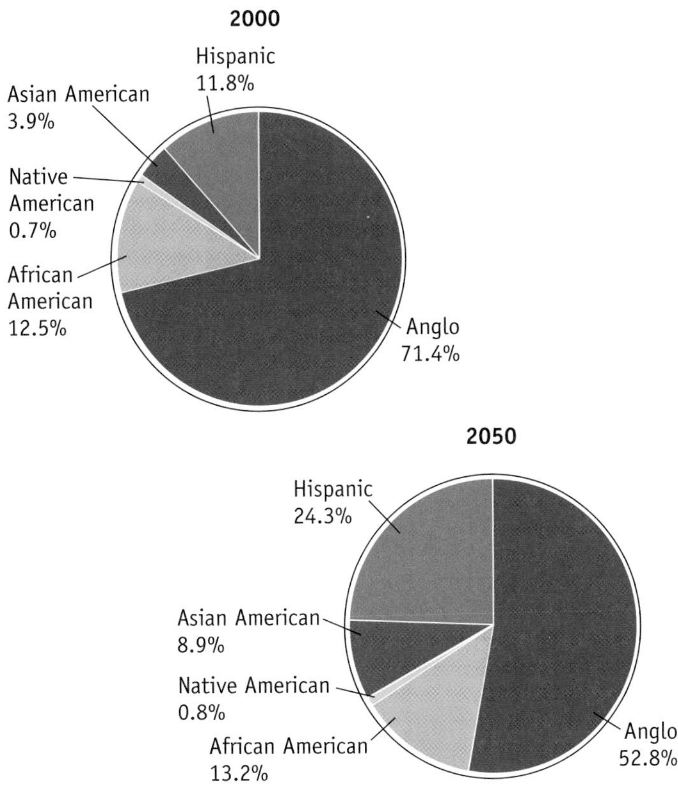

FIGURE 11.1

Predicted changes in U.S. population groups.

(*Source:* U.S. Census Bureau 2000)

spending on health care and entertainment will be more than three times greater than white household expenditures.

Radio is an especially important way to reach this ethnic group. Surveys show that the average Hispanic person listens to radio 26 to 30 hours a week, about 13 percent more than the general population. Hispanic station KLVE-FM has the largest audience in Los Angeles, more than any English-language station.

Television also has a large, rapidly expanding Hispanic audience. The Nielsen rating service in 2001 estimated the number of Hispanic households in the United States with television sets at 8,940,000. Such households are defined as those in which the head of the household is of Hispanic descent. Univision, the predominant Spanish-language TV network, claims to reach three-fourths of Hispanic viewers.

Hispanic-owned businesses are multiplying in the United States. These offer new client possibilities, not only for Hispanic-owned firms but for general public relations firms that adapt their services to Hispanic needs. A Census Bureau report in 2001 showed an 83.7-percent increase in the number of Hispanic companies in the United States during the five-year period from 1992 to 1997. In 1997, Hispanics owned the largest number of minority businesses, with the largest share of minority business revenue earned by Asian and Pacific Islander owners.

Business Wire, a major distributor of public relations messages, recognizes diversity of interest among the minority groups by operating separate Hispanic, African American, and Asian American media circuits within the United States. As further

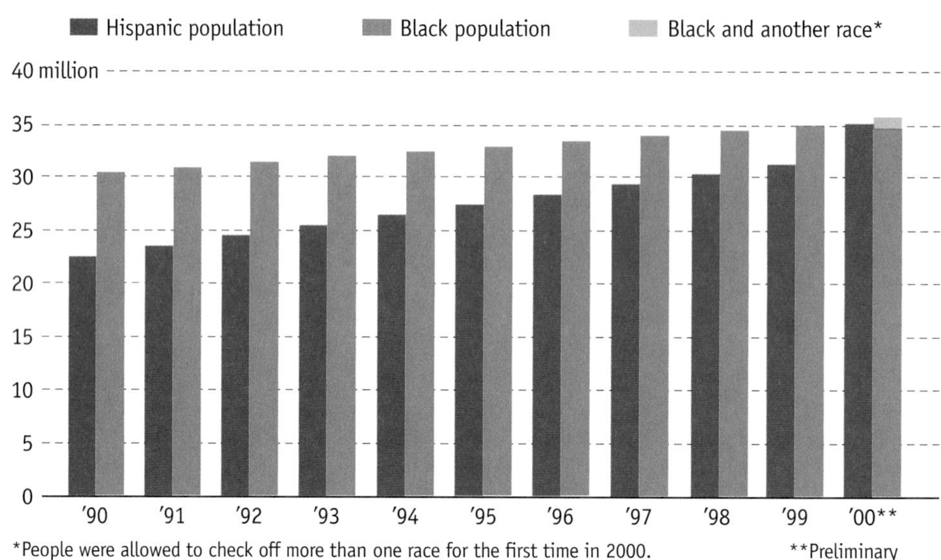

FIGURE 11.2

The Hispanic population is the fastest-growing minority group in the United States. Many public information campaigns now include brochures and radio spots in Spanish to reach this population.

indication of diversity, the *Gale Directory* lists ethnic publications in 48 languages other than English.

Public relations people should give particular attention to the sensitivities of minority audiences. For example, the familiar figure of Aunt Jemima on packages of Quaker Oats food products was widely regarded in the black community as a patronizing stereotype. To change this perception, Quaker Oats cooperated with the National Council of Negro Women to honor outstanding African-American women in local communities, who then competed for a national award. At the local award breakfasts, all food served was Aunt Jemima brands, and Quaker Oats officials participated in the programs. The project generated an atmosphere of mutual understanding.

Characteristics of the Audience

Human drives have changed little over the centuries. As we move deeper into the 21st century, we continue to love, hate, worship, work for food and shelter, protect our families, and respond to our neighbors' needs much as our forefathers did 300 years ago. Knowing how to appeal to these basic emotions is essential.

Even with these drives constant, specific aspects and attitudes of the audience change. In numerous respects, audience trends of the 1990s differed from those of the 1930s, for example, in ways significant to the public relations practitioner:

- *The public became increasingly visually oriented.* The enormous impact of television on daily life was largely responsible for an increased visual orientation. Many people obtained virtually all their news from the TV screen. Several studies indicated local television as the most credible and frequently used news source, supplanting the local newspaper. Television news was told primarily in pictures presented briefly, at a swiftly changing pace. Such exposure led to a shortened attention span so that, for example, political leaders' policies reached the public largely in ten-second "sound bites." Television also served as a potent communicator of manners and mores.

Never had a country had as much information available to its citizens as the United States had in the 1990s—yet the rate of illiteracy remained disgracefully high. Nevertheless, those who could not read or write, or who did so at a child's level, were part of the public relations audience.

- *Fervent support was generated for single issues.* Many individuals became so zealously involved in promoting or opposing a single favorite issue that they lost the social and political balance so needed in a country. Such vehement behavior may create severe public relations problems for the objects of their attacks.
- *Heavy emphasis was placed on personality and celebrity.* Sports stars, television and movie actors, and rock music performers were virtually worshipped by some fans. When stars embraced causes, many people blindly followed them. More and more, they were used as spokespersons and fund-raisers, even though their expertise as performers did not necessarily qualify them as experts or opinion leaders for complex issues such as the environment or world trade.
- *Strong distrust of authority and suspicion of conspiracy arose.* People were so inundated with exaggerated political promises, saw so much financial chicanery, and were exposed to so many misleading television advertisements that many of them distrusted what they read and heard. They suspected evil motives and tended to believe rumors. The need for public relations programs to develop an atmosphere of justifiable, rational trust became obvious.
- *The international audience for public relations expanded swiftly.* Growth of global corporations and expanded foreign marketing by smaller firms opened new public relations situations, as did increased foreign ownership of U.S. companies.

Many of these trends have continued into the 2000s, creating an ongoing need for flexibility and growth among public relations practitioners.

Matching Audience and Media

This chapter explains each of the major media—how each one functions and ways in which it can be used for public relations purposes. With such an array of printed, spoken, visual, and computer communication methods available, practitioners must make choices in order to use their time and budgets efficiently.

Before we look at each of the media in more detail, some general guidelines can be given for matching audience and media:

- Print media are the most effective for delivering a message that requires absorption of details and contemplation by the receiver. Printed matter can be read repeatedly and kept for reference. The Internet, perhaps more like traditional print sources than like the broadcast media, is the fastest to deliver breaking news. Newspapers are also fast, with the most widespread impact. Magazines, while slower, are better directed to special-interest audiences. Books take even longer but can generate strong impact over time.
- Television has the strongest emotional impact of all media. Its visual power makes situations seem close to the viewer. The personality of the TV communicator creates an influence that print media cannot match.

- Radio's greatest advantages are flexibility and the ability to reach specific target audiences. Messages can be prepared for and broadcast on radio more rapidly than on television, at much lower cost. Because there are nine times as many radio stations as TV stations, audience exposure is easier to obtain, but the audiences reached are smaller.
- The online media are usually used as a supplemental method of reaching a generally well-educated, relatively affluent audience interested in new ideas and fresh approaches. However, usage patterns are changing almost weekly, and major breaking news stories now reach a large audience online. The most striking recent example was the enormous attention by audiences to the release of the report by independent counsel Kenneth Starr about President Clinton's relationship with Monica Lewinsky.

In some campaigns the most cost-effective results come from use of a single medium. Other campaigns work best when several types of media are used. Wise selection of media, based on the audience sought and the money available, is an important skill for public relations practitioners to develop.

Media Relations

Before examining the print, electronic, and film media individually, we need to look at the relationship between the media and public relations practitioners, who need to understand this sometimes sensitive interplay.

Editors and reporters on the one hand, and public relations people on the other, need each other. The media must have material and ideas from public relations sources, and practitioners must have the media as a place to tell their stories.

Public relations people should remember several things about editors and reporters:

- They are busy. When you approach them with a story idea, either verbally or on paper, make your sales pitch succinctly and objectively.
- Editors pride themselves on making their own decisions about what stories to run and how to run them. That is their job. Excessive hype of a story often turns them against it. An urgent demand that editors *must* run a story may lead to rejection.
- Stories submitted by nonprofits are better received by editors than are corporate news releases, which are perceived as attempts to obtain free advertising.
- Able editors and competent public relations people respect each other and work well together. A review of studies for *Communication Yearbook 20* found that over the decades, media respect for public relations has increased. The reviewers also noted that editorial distrust of the public relations profession in general coexisted with trust of individual public relations sources. If editors discover, however, that they have been misled or fed false information, they will never again fully trust the offending practitioner.

Practitioners also need to remember several things about themselves when dealing with the media:

- Your job is important in keeping the public informed. You are performing a service, not asking a favor, when you submit a story idea or a news release.

- You should assume that your story will be judged on its merits as seen by the editor, and should not demean yourself by begging an editor to use it.
- Your role continues after the story or idea has been accepted. You cannot control the tone of the story that appears, but you can influence it by providing favorable story angles and additional information. A public relations person's helpful, pleasant personality does influence most writers, at least subtly.

The Print Media

Printed words can be kept indefinitely and can be reread. Messages delivered in that form through newspapers, magazines, and books are a fundamental element in public relations work.

Newspapers

Every edition of a newspaper contains hundreds of news stories and pieces of information, in much greater number than the largest news staff can gather by itself. More than most readers realize, and many editors care to admit, newspapers depend upon information brought to them voluntarily.

The *Columbia Journalism Review* noted, for example, that in one edition the *Wall Street Journal* had obtained 45 percent of its 188 news items from news releases. Because of its specialized nature, the *Journal*'s use of news releases may be higher than that of general-interest daily newspapers. Public relations generates about 50 percent of the stories in New York City newspapers, according to Albert Scardino, press secretary for former Mayor David L. Dinkins.

Approximately 1500 daily newspapers and 7200 weekly newspapers are published in the United States. Most cities today have only one daily newspaper, resulting in little competition between newspapers. Television, direct mail, and the Internet are now the main challenges to newspapers. While some metropolitan newspapers have circulations of more than a million copies a day, approximately two-thirds of the daily newspapers have circulations of 20,000 or less.

Newspapers published for distribution in the late afternoon, called evening or P.M. papers, outnumber morning (A.M.) papers approximately three to one. Especially in larger cities, however, a substantial trend toward morning publication is in progress. Knowledge of a newspaper's hours of publication and the deadlines it enforces for submission of copy is essential for everyone who supplies material to the paper.

Approximately three-quarters of American daily newspapers are owned by newspaper groups. The publishers and editors of a group-owned newspaper have broad local autonomy but must follow operating standards laid down by group headquarters.

A Commercial Institution In dealing with a newspaper, public relations people should remember that it is a commercial institution, created to earn a profit as a purveyor of news and advertising. Although newspapers often are so deeply rooted in a community that they seem like public institutions, they are not. Their publishers and editors as a whole seek to serve the public interest and often succeed admirably in doing so. Like any other business, however, a newspaper that loses money soon disappears. Therefore, in the long run and sometimes in the short run as well, management decisions about what appears in a newspaper must be made with the balance sheet in mind.

Newspapers receive nearly 80 percent of their income from advertising and about 20 percent from selling papers to readers. They cannot afford to publish press releases that are nothing more than commercial advertising; to do so would cut into their largest source of income. To be published, a release submitted to a newspaper must contain information that an editor regards as news of interest to a substantial number of readers.

Because newspapers are protected by the First Amendment to the Constitution, they cannot be forced to publish any material, including news releases, nor need they receive permission from the government or anyone else to publish whatever they desire. Editors resist pressure on them to suppress material they consider to be newsworthy and, conversely, to print material they do not believe to be newsworthy. However, the definitions of newsworthiness are abstract and fluctuating. What one newspaper considers to be news, another will not.

Nevertheless, editors do not enjoy the unfettered privilege of publishing whatever they desire. Two severe limitations hang over their decisions:

1. *The laws of libel and invasion of privacy.* Publication of material that, if challenged in court, is ruled to be libelous or an unreasonable invasion of privacy can cost a newspaper extremely heavy judgments and legal expenses. The newspaper management is legally responsible for everything a newspaper publishes, including material submitted by outsiders, even letters to the editor.
2. *The interests and desires of their readers.* If a newspaper fails to publish news and features that readers find to be valuable or entertaining, its circulation will dwindle, and it will perish. Alert editors, therefore, are receptive to fresh ideas. Their doors are open to public relations representatives who can supply useful information.

Organization of a Newspaper Public relations professionals should know how a newspaper staff is organized, so they can take story ideas or policy problems to the proper person. In the usual table of organization, the publisher is the director of all financial, mechanical, and administrative operations. Frequently the publisher also has ultimate responsibility for news and editorial matters.

PR insights

Three Cardinal Rules for News Releases to Newspapers

A news release submitted to a newspaper should:

- Contain information that is newsworthy in that newspaper's circulation area
- Be addressed to the city editor if it is of general interest or to the appropriate section editor if it contains special-interest material such as sports news
- Be delivered to the newspaper well in advance of the desired publication date to provide time for processing.

The editor heads the news and editorial department. The associate editor conducts the editorial and commentary pages and deals with the public concerning their content. The managing editor is the head of news operations to whom the city editor and the editors of sections such as sports, business, entertainment, and family living answer. The city editor directs the local news staff of reporters. Some members of the city staff cover beats such as police and city hall; others are on general assignment, meaning that they are sent to cover any type of story the city editor deems to be potentially newsworthy. (Submission of news releases to editors is discussed in Chapter 20.)

Weekly newspapers have a different focus from that of daily newspapers and much smaller staffs. The weekly concentrates exclusively on its own community. Weekly editors need the help of much volunteered material. Although weekly newspapers often are overlooked in public relations programs, they can be effective outlets for those who study how to meet their needs.

Large daily newspapers, to demonstrate editorial independence, often have a rule against publishing a news release exactly as received.

Current, updated mailing lists of contacts in the media are essential in public relations work, including editors in the print media and news editors, assignment editors, and producers in the electronic media. Media directories that supply such information are listed in the bibliography at the end of this textbook.

Public Relations Opportunities in Newspapers

Material for a newspaper should be submitted either as a news release ready for publication or as a fact sheet from which a reporter can develop a feature story or interview. When an invitation to a news conference is sent to a newspaper, it should include a fact sheet containing basic information. Frequently, the reporter to whom an editor assigns a news release for processing rewrites and expands it, developing additional story angles and background. When a public relations representative presents an important story idea in fact sheet form rather than as a news release for publication, a personal conversation with the appropriate editor, if it can be arranged, helps to sell the concept and expand its potential. *Such personal calls on editors should last no longer than is necessary to explain the idea adequately.* Although some practitioners make a follow-up phone call shortly after the fact sheet has arrived, this practice irritates many editors. They dislike being interrupted. (Preparations of news releases and fact sheets is discussed in Chapter 20.)

Public relations representatives never should assume that editors and reporters are all-knowing about projects being planned in a community. A basic rule: When you have news to announce, tell the media; don't wait for them to come to you.

For large-scale projects such as a communitywide fund drive, make an appointment with the managing editor or city editor after the deadline hour has passed. A newspaper is more likely to give a major project sympathetic treatment if its editors receive background information before the first stories break. This allows them time to plan coverage.

At times, an organization's representative or other individual needs to discuss a policy issue with the newspaper management—a complaint against perceived mistreatment by the newspaper, for example, or an attempt to obtain editorial support. Usually this is done by appointment with the editor or associate editor or, in the case of a news story, with the managing editor.

Created Events: Making News Happen

Some news stories *happen*. Other stories must be *created*. Successful public relations practitioners must do more than produce competent, accurate news releases about routine occurrences in the affairs of their clients or employers. They must use ingenuity and organizing ability to create events that attract coverage in the news media. Historian Daniel Boorstin calls these projects "pseudoevents." This extra dimension of creativity is the difference between acting to make news and merely reacting to news that happens. We are not speaking here of feeding phony stories to the media or doing anything else unethical. We are talking about causing something to occur.

Such created events vary in scope from the huge antiabortion and prochoice marches in Washington, staged by ardent advocates of opposite positions, to small, clever publicity promotions that draw media coverage because they are unusual, involve prominent people, or are just plain fun.

According to Jarol B. Manheim at Northwestern University, created events play an important role in corporate campaigns, which are the organized assault on a company centered around the media where the activists attempt to redefine the image and reputation of the target company.

The 100th anniversary of the invention of Jell-O gelatin dessert posed a challenge to Kraft Foods' public relations firm, Hunter and Associates: celebrate the traditions of Jell-O in American life without contributing to a consumer perception in the 1990s that Jell-O was old-fashioned (see Chapter 7).

Every one of the events listed later in this chapter represents a legitimate news story that the local newspaper and other media might cover. But these stories exist only because a public relations adviser convinced the company to sponsor or conduct them. Once this decision is made, the practitioner must produce a flow of news releases with fresh angles, as well as use other techniques to build public interest.

Openings of stores and shopping centers, as well as groundbreakings, happen so frequently that the ingenuity of public relations representatives is challenged. Editors dislike pictures of the traditional, rigidly posed group of men in dark business suits and incongruous hard hats lined up behind one man with a shovel.

Magazines

Magazines differ markedly from newspapers in content, time frame, and methods of operation. Therefore they present different opportunities and problems to the public relations practitioner. In contrast to the daily newspaper, with its hurry-up deadlines, magazines are published weekly, monthly, or sometimes quarterly. Because these publications usually deal with subjects in greater depth than newspapers do, magazine editors may allot months for the development of an article. Those who seek to supply subject ideas or ready-to-publish material to them must plan much further ahead than is necessary with newspapers.

A newspaper is designed for family reading, with something for men, women, and children; its material is aimed at an audience of varying educational and economic levels. Its editors fire buckshot, to hit the reading interests of as many persons as possible. Magazine editors, on the other hand, in most instances aim carefully at special-interest audiences. They fire rifle bullets at limited, well-defined readership groups.

The more than 75,000 periodicals published in the United States may be classified in several ways. For purposes of this discussion, periodicals are grouped into two broad

focus on ethics

Information Pollution in Trade Publications?

It is not uncommon in the trade press for an editor to make a subtle demand on a public relations person who wants to place a story in the magazine or newsletter. There is a "linkage" between getting the story published and buying advertising space in the trade publication. If a company wants a good editorial spread, it must help "pay the freight" through an advertising buy. Some trade press publishers defend this "linkage," saying that the publication cannot survive without advertising—so it is only fair for the companies that want coverage to contribute to the financial stability of the publication. From another perspective, editors simply give preference to advertisers when selecting stories to cover. Either view violates the Public Relations Society of America code of ethics, which says that the exchange of advertising for "good" copy is one form of "corrupting the media."

Imagine that you pitch a story by telephone to the editor of a trade publication. The editor knows that you really want coverage for your client and she implies that you need to buy ad space to assure your story will be run. What would you do?

Do you think that advertiser influence on stories diminishes the value of public relations?

In your mind, is there a qualitative difference between trade publications that require advertising and more independent publications such as newspapers? Which has more value for the practice of public relations?

categories, those for the public at large and those for specific audiences. Each is in turn broken down into several subdivisions.

Periodicals for the Public at Large Among the types in this category are:

- *General interest.* Only a few national magazines with across-the-board appeal exist today. Prominent among them are *Reader's Digest,* enormously successful worldwide; *People,* which capitalizes on the contemporary interest in personalities; and *National Geographic.*
- *News magazines.* High-circulation weekly newsmagazines report and interpret the news, adding background that daily newspapers lack time to develop. The biggest periodicals of this type are *Time, Newsweek, U.S. News & World Report,* and the *Economist.*
- *Women's interest.* Magazines designed for women have a very large audience. They publish articles about fashions and beauty, cooking, home decorating, self-improvement, work and leisure, and personal relationships. Prominent in this group are *Ladies' Home Journal, Cosmopolitan, Working Woman, Better Homes and Gardens, Good Housekeeping,* and *Family Circle.*
- *Men's interest.* Growing participation of women in athletics has increased female readership of traditionally male sports magazines. *Sports Illustrated* and *Field and Stream* are perhaps the best known of these magazines. With their emphasis on sex, *Playboy* and *Penthouse* aim primarily at the male audience but also draw substantial female readership.

- *The senior market. Modern Maturity,* published by the American Association of Retired Persons (AARP), has the largest magazine circulation in the United States, more than 22.8 million.

The categories of magazines just listed offer tremendous public relations opportunities. They are difficult markets to hit, however, except by highly experienced specialists well acquainted with the magazines' operating methods. Far more abundant opportunities for placing public relations material exist with the other periodicals, those aimed at more specific audiences.

Periodicals for Specific Audiences The specific-interest group includes a wide array of publications, including:

Special-Audience Magazines Hundreds of these prosper because they are carefully edited on single themes. Each attracts an audience with strong interest in its particular topic; this audience in turn draws advertisers whose products are especially relevant to these readers. A glance at the magazine rack in a supermarket gives an indication of the diversity of special-interest magazines—only an indication, however, because such periodicals are distributed primarily by subscription.

A few examples include *Dog World, Backpacker, Stereo Review, Car Craft, Skin Diver, Surfing, Ski, International Photographer,* and *World Oil.* Broader in appeal than many of these are magazines about business, including *Fortune, Business Week, Forbes,* and *Barron's.*

Trade Journals Trade journals are designed for the business and professional audience, not a recreational one. While virtually unknown to the public, these periodicals are vital channels of communication within various industries and professions. In their pages, readers learn about the activities of their competitors, new products and trends in their field of work, and the movement of individuals from one job to another. Often trade journals have the same intimacy in their respective fields as weekly newspapers do in their communities.

The following small sampling of trade journals indicates the extremely specialized nature of their contents: *American Christmas Tree Journal, Mini-Micro Systems, Fleet Owner, The Indian Trader, Insulation Outlook, Progressive Grocer,* and *Wire Journal International.*

Placement of material in trade journals is an essential assignment for many public relations representatives. A story about a new product published in an appropriate trade journal may be more valuable to the manufacturer of that product than a story about it in a large newspaper, because the information reaches a target audience containing potential purchasers. Products and specialized services offered by companies are often not publicized to a general audience. If a manufacturer of coin-operated machines has a new product ready for release, for example, its public relations representative should concentrate on placing stories in such journals as *American Coin-Op, Play Meter Magazine,* and *Vending Times.*

Company and Organizational Magazines There are two types of company and organizational magazines:

1. *Internal,* designed for and distributed primarily to employees, retirees, influential outsiders who may have some interest in the organization, and often stockholders of the firm. (These are discussed in Chapter 20.)

2. *External,* distributed to selected portions of the public. Published by companies and organizations to promote public appreciation of the sponsor and to form a psychological tie between sponsor and recipient, these are usually circulated among customers, stockholders, and users of the sponsor's services. The editorial content has general appeal. The magazines that airline travelers find in the seat pockets in front of them, such as *American Way* (American Airlines), are prime examples of this group.

Public Relations Opportunities in Magazines

A study of the monthly periodical *Writer's Digest* will provide abundant information about individual magazines and the kind of material each publishes. Every magazine has its special formula.

Operating with much smaller staffs than newspapers have, magazines are heavily dependent on material submitted from outside their offices. Some, especially the smaller ones, are almost entirely staff written. The staffs create ideas and cover some stories; they also process public relations material submitted to them. The more carefully the submitted material is tailored to the particular periodical's audience and written in a style preferred by the editor, the more likely it is to be published, with or without rewriting by the staff. Many magazines purchase part, or almost all, of their material from freelance writers on a fee basis. An editor may buy a submitted article for publication if it fits the magazine's formula, or the editor may commission a writer to develop an idea into an article along specified lines.

Editors are always looking for ideas. Many magazine articles have their origins in suggestions submitted by public relations practitioners. An article in a women's magazine on preventing sunburn, for example, may have resulted from a letter and a press kit sent to an editor by a sunscreen manufacturer or its public relations firm.

A public relations practitioner has four principal approaches for getting material into a periodical:

1. Submit a story idea that would promote the practitioner's cause, either directly or subtly, and urge the editor to have a writer, freelance or staff, develop the story on assignment.
2. Send a written query to the editor outlining an article idea and offering to submit the article in publishable form if the editor approves the idea.
3. Submit a completed article, written either by the practitioner or by an independent writer under contract, and hope that the editor will accept it for publication. In this and the two previously mentioned instances, however, the editor should be made fully aware of the source of the suggestion or article. As pointed out in Chapter 3, allowing a freelance writer to place what presumably is an "independent" article is a violation of the PRSA Code of Professional Standards, which forbids using third parties who are purported to be independent but serve the special interests of the employer or client.
4. For trade journals and other periodicals that use such material, submit news releases in ready-to-publish form.

The size and nature of each magazine determines its content. Most common is a formula of several major articles, one or two short articles, and special departments. These may be personal commentary, a compilation of news items in a specific category (short items about new products in a trade journal, for example), or chitchat about personalities. Special departments offer excellent public relations opportunities.

Books

Because their writing and publication is a time-consuming process, often involving years from the conception of an idea until appearance of the volume, books are not popularly recognized as public relations tools. Yet they can be. A book, especially a hardcover one, has stature in the minds of readers. They read it with respect and give attention to the message it carries.

Books are promulgators of ideas. As channels of communication, they reach thoughtful audiences, including opinion leaders. Often publication of a book starts a trend or focuses national discussion on an issue.

The standard method of book publishing is for an author and publisher to sign a contract describing the material the author will deliver to the publisher and the conditions under which the publisher will issue and sell the book. The publisher pays the cost of production and marketing. The author receives a royalty fee on each copy sold, perhaps 10 to 15 percent of the retail price. Publishers often make advance payments to authors against the royalties their books are expected to earn.

PR insights

32 Ways to Create News for Your Organization

1. Tie in with news events of the day.
2. Work with another publicity person.
3. Tie in with a newspaper or other medium on a mutual project.
4. Conduct a poll or survey.
5. Issue a report.
6. Arrange an interview with a celebrity.
7. Take part in a controversy.
8. Arrange for a testimonial.
9. Arrange for a speech.
10. Make an analysis or prediction.
11. Form and announce names for committees.
12. Hold an election.
13. Announce an appointment.
14. Celebrate an anniversary.
15. Issue a summary of facts.
16. Tie in with a holiday.
17. Make a trip.
18. Make an award.
19. Hold a contest.
20. Pass a resolution.
21. Appear before public bodies.
22. Stage a special event.
23. Write a letter.
24. Release a letter you have received.
25. Adapt national reports and surveys for local use.
26. Stage a debate.
27. Tie into a well-known week or day.
28. Honor an institution.
29. Organize a tour.
30. Inspect a project.
31. Issue a commendation.
32. Issue a protest.

A book published in hardcover often requires a year from acceptance of the manuscript to publication. Thus, a public relations effort made through publication of a hardcover book must be long range in nature and aimed at the broad-stroke influencing of public opinion.

The tremendous growth of paperback publishing has opened new avenues for use of books as public relations vehicles. Hundreds of titles, ranging from classical literature to how-to-do-it books on gardening, plumbing, and sex, are on sale. An examination of nonfiction titles on the paperback shelves will show the range of opportunity that exists to promote products, ideological movements, personalities, and fads.

Unless he or she knows the publishing industry well, a public relations representative seeking to publicize a client's cause through publication of a book is well advised to work through an agent.

Although the fact is seldom mentioned publicly, companies and nonprofit organizations sometimes pay subsidies to both hardcover and paperback publishers to help defray production costs of a book they wish to see published. The subsidy may take the form of a guarantee to purchase a specific number of copies.

The idea for a beautifully illustrated book on New England, to cite an example, might come from a state travel agency, which approaches the publisher either directly or through an author. The state agency pays part of the publisher's cost, knowing that the book will draw visitors to the area.

Public Relations Opportunities in Books

As indicated previously, books as public relations tools, both hardcover and paperback, usually are best suited to promote ideas and create a favorable state of mind. For example, the autobiography of Conrad Hilton, placed in hotel rooms, helps establish the character and tradition of Hilton Hotels. Political movements often are publicized through books by proponents. On a more mundane level, every book published about gardening indirectly helps the sale of garden tools. Although a specific brand of tools may not be mentioned in such a book, it benefits from the book's existence. The manufacturer's public relations representative can help the company's cause by assisting the author in assembling material. Public relations efforts need not be overt to be effective. *The Complete Dairy Foods Cookbook,* by E. Annie Proues and Lew Nichols, inevitably helped promote use of dairy products, while *The Joy of Chocolate,* by Judith Olney, must have made chocolate manufacturers happy.

From the point of view of publishers, publicity for books and their authors is an important public relations function. The public relations departments of publishing houses use news releases, prepublication endorsements, interviews, and other standard techniques to create awareness of a forthcoming book. A writer may be taken on a tour of major cities for interviews and autograph parties or speak to reviewers nationwide by satellite.

The Spoken and Visual Media

Radio, television, motion pictures, and video have strong impact on virtually everyone. The messages they contain usually are delivered by individuals whose personality, expressed through voice and/or visual manner, adds emphasis to the words.

Radio

Speed and mobility are the special attributes that make radio unique among the major media of communication. If urgency justifies such action, messages can be placed on the air by radio almost instantly upon their receipt at a radio station. They need not be delayed by the time-consuming production processes of print. Because radio pro-

PR casebook

Teen Audience Offers Novel Challenges to Public Relations Pros

Generalizing is always dangerous, especially for large segments of the population just emerging from childhood to independent living. Nevertheless, today's teens and young adults, conveniently grouped by some media under the rubric Generation Y (GY) or Generation.com, comprise an interesting and powerful force in modern life. Accounting for over $150 billion in annual purchases, the youth market represents significant disposable income. In a *pr reporter* article, Marianne Friese of Ketchum public relations succinctly stated the importance of the youth audience: "They rival the baby boom in sheer size and their global purchasing power is enormous." Like every new generation before them, they cause adults to fret about their character but show signs that they too will rise to the challenges that come with maturity.

Generation Y (GY) Might Better Be Labeled the E-Generation

The Fortino Group (Pittsburgh) projects GY will spend 23 years online. Spending one-third of their lives online will have interesting impacts:

- GY will spend equal time interacting with friends online and in person.
- Initial interaction online will precede most dating and marriages.
- GY time online will exceed interaction with parents tenfold.
- GY will be more reserved in social skills.
- GY will be savvy and skeptical about online identities such as chat participants.
- Print forms, slow application processes, and archaic systems will not be tolerated by GY.

GY will share this propensity to online pastime with retired seniors. Their world will be diverse and global in perspective, and, like no previous generation, they will understand world cultures and markets.

Generation Y Values Relationships and Trust

In a survey of 1200 teens worldwide, Ketchum's Global Brand Marketing Practice found:

- Parents still rule when it comes to advice about careers and drugs, and even for product decisions.
- Trust in information is derived from relationships.
- The top 5 sources of advice are parents, doctors, clergy, friends, and teachers.
- As avid and skilled Internet users, GY remains savvy about unfiltered and unpoliced content.
- Teens also recognize the credibility of editorial content compared to ads and even public service announcements, with television being the most trusted medium for them.
- Garnering publicity for products and issues will impact GY, whether directed at them or at those to whom they look for advice.

This active consumer market instills trust in cause-oriented companies and rewards companies that do what is perceived as right. Work such as Liz Claiborne's activism against dating violence serves as a good example (www.lizclaiborne.com) of corporate responsibility that is appreciated by GY.

Music pervades their waking hours, accompanying other media use such as Web surfing or gaming. Although 64 percent of respondents in an Ogilvy PR survey would rather go a day without food than without music, the message effects of music are subtle.

Sources:
pr reporter, May 21, 2001
pr reporter, Nov. 13 and Feb. 7, 2000
pr reporter, Nov. 22, 1999

gramming is more loosely structured than television programming, interruption of a program for an urgent announcement can be done with less internal decision making. Although most public relations material does not involve such urgency, moments of crisis do occur when quick on-the-air action helps a company or other organization get information to the public swiftly.

Radio benefits, too, from its ability to go almost anywhere. Reporters working from mobile trucks can be broadcasting from the scene of a large fire within minutes after it has been discovered. They can hurry from a press conference to a luncheon speech, carrying only a small amount of equipment. A disc jockey can broadcast an afternoon program from a table in a neighborhood shopping center. Flexibility is ever-present.

So is flexibility among listeners. Radios in automobiles reach captive audiences, enhancing the popularity of drive-time disc jockeys. The tiny transistor or mini earphone-type radio brings programs to mail carriers on their routes, carpenters on construction sites, and homeowners pulling weeds in their gardens.

More than 12,000 radio stations reach over 150 million Americans each day, with listenership at all-time highs according to *pr reporter*. In many markets, the media company will own a group of stations, including both AM and FM formats, with perhaps one news director and one weathercaster serving all the stations in the market. Both AM and FM stations in the group attempt to develop distinctive "sounds" by specializing in one kind of music or talk format. A public relations practitioner should study each station's format and submit material suitable to it. Don't send information about senior citizen recreational programs to the news director of a hard-rock station with an audience primarily of teenagers.

Public Relations Opportunities in Radio

Commercial radio is highly promotional in nature and provides innumerable opportunities for public relations specialists to further their causes. Radio programs may be divided into two general categories: news-talk and entertainment. The news director for a station or station group is responsible for the former, the program director for the latter. At least eight possible targets exist in radio:

1. *Newscasts.* Many stations have frequent newscasts, of which the five-minute variety is the most common. If the station has a network affiliation, some newscasts it carries are national in content. Of much more interest to the public relations practitioner are the local newscasts. News releases sent to a radio station should cover the same newsworthy topics as those sent to a newspaper; they should follow identical rules of accuracy and timeliness. Brevity is fundamental on radio. A story that runs 400 words in a newspaper may be told in 50 words or fewer on radio. Lengthy news releases for radio stations are unnecessary, indeed unwise.
2. *Community calendars.* Many stations broadcast a daily program called the "Community Bulletin Board," or a similar title. This listing of coming events is an excellent place to circulate information about a program the practitioner is handling.
3. *Actualities.* Radio news directors brighten their newscasts by including *actualities.* These are brief reports from scenes of action, either live or on tape. Public relations representatives may supply stations with actualities from events or speeches to be used on newscasts.

4. *Talk shows.* Placement of a client on a talk show provides exposure for the individual and for the cause being espoused while avoiding the filtering of information by news staff. Talk shows may be news oriented, such as a discussion of a controversial issue, and produced by the news director; or they may be entertainment oriented, controlled by the program director and handled by a staff producer. Midmorning homemaker hours have numerous spots for guest appearances.

   Call-in talk shows on current events are an important factor in forming public opinion, although the verbal excesses of certain hosts and their callers weaken their influence with some people. According to Michael Pfau at the University of Wisconsin, the Rush Limbaugh show is syndicated with about 650 of 1000 daily talk shows nationwide, reaching nearly 20 million listeners. Pfau's research suggests that such radio programs have increased negative perceptions of the presidency, the court system, public schools, and the news media. Only Congress has avoided the negative treatment directed at U.S. institutions.
5. *Editorials.* Powerful radio stations often broadcast editorials, comparable to newspaper editorials, usually delivered by the station manager. Public relations specialists may be able to persuade a station to carry an editorial of endorsement for their cause. They should stay alert, too, for editorials that condemn a cause they espouse. The representative should request equal time on the air for a rebuttal, usually given by a leading executive of the organization or cause under attack. Hundreds of smaller stations, however, do not carry editorials.
6. *Disc jockey shows.* On the entertainment side, disc jockeys in their programs of music and chitchat frequently air material provided by public relations sources. The DJs conduct on-the-air contests and promotions, give away tickets to shows, discuss coming local events, offer trivia quizzes—whatever they can think of to make their programs distinctive and lively. A disc jockey on the air several hours a day devours large amounts of material. After studying a program's style, an able practitioner can supply material that the DJ welcomes.
7. *Community events.* At times, radio stations sponsor community events such as outdoor concerts or long-distance runs. Repeated mention of such an event on the air for days or weeks usually turns out large crowds. Here, too, is an opportunity for the public relations person to convince a station either to sponsor such an event or to develop tie-ins with it.
8. *Public service announcements (PSAs).* These commercials promoting public causes such as health care and civic programs are run free of charge by stations, usually in unsold time slots during scheduled commercial breaks. PSA scripts should be written to run 20, 30, or 60 seconds. Use of celebrity voices is common.

A close relationship exists between radio stations and the recording industry. Recording companies depend on the stations to play their new releases; the stations in turn use those companies as the primary source for the music they play. This relationship has created a highly specialized form of public relations work by representatives of the record companies.

Television

Our lives feel the impact of television more than that of any other communications medium. More than 1600 television stations are in operation, projecting over-the-air visual programming. According to estimates provided by the A. C. Nielsen Company, the major rating firm for national programming, more than 102 million American households own television sets. According to Nielsen statistics, the average American family watches television about seven hours a day.

Little wonder that public relations specialists look upon television as an enormous arena in which to tell their stories!

The fundamental factor that differentiates television from the other media and gives it such pervasive impact is the visual element. Producers of entertainment shows, newscasts, and commercials regard movement on the screen as essential. Something must happen to hold the viewer's attention. Persons talking on the screen for more than a brief time without movement, or at least a change of camera angle, are belittled as "talking heads."

Because of this visual impact, television emphasizes personality. Entertainment programs are built around stars. Only on television do news reporters achieve "star quality." When public relations people plan material for television, they should remember the importance of visual impact and personality.

Television shows live and die by their ratings. A scorecard mentality dominates the selection of programs and program content, especially on the networks. The viewing habits of a few thousand Americans, recorded by the Nielsen, Arbitron, and other rating services, determine what programs all TV watchers can see. The explanation is money. Networks and local stations determine the prices they charge to show commercials by the estimated size of the audience watching a program when the commercial is shown. Thus the larger the audience, the higher the price for commercial time and the higher the profit. Even nonprofit television stations keep a close watch on the size of their audiences, because their income in part comes from the grants that corporations give them to show certain programs.

A tremendous battle for admission to the home viewer's screen has developed among satellite dish, cable TV, video, and the traditional over-the-air stations and networks. In the mid-1970s, the three basic commercial networks were viewed by 92 percent of the audience during prime-time evening hours. This figure was projected to fall to 31.3 percent in 2002 according to PricewaterhouseCoopers as the total television audience was fragmented.

This turmoil opened enormous new programming potential and a consequent increase in public relations opportunities. When a cable system offers 100 or more channels, as many are capable of doing, the need for program material is voracious.

Although most television stations are on the air for 18 hours or more a day, only a few hours of programming originate in their studios—mostly newscasts, local talk shows, and midmorning homemaker programs. Much of the day's programming consists of network "feeds," if the station has a network affiliation. Development of satellite transmission (discussed in Chapter 12) has created numerous smaller networks that provide entertainment, news, and sports shows for independent stations.

■ Cable Television Because television networks and individual stations, especially those in major cities, gear their programming to large audiences, public relations practitioners have difficulty in obtaining airtime for projects lacking mass appeal. Cable television, however, often presents valuable opportunities.

More than 69 million U.S. households were wired for cable TV by 2001. However, the number of viewers for a cable channel is usually relatively small, because the total TV audience is fragmented among the numerous competing channels. On the plus side, the public relations specialist faces fewer editing and management barriers in getting a program or short segment broadcast.

Municipal authorities have the right to demand that cable systems to which they grant operating franchises include an *access channel* for public, educational, or government programming, without advertising. Public relations directors for cultural, social, and other nonprofit agencies—and even for commercial interests—can use these so-called PEG channels effectively to promote public-service causes by creating interesting programs.

Some cable systems also produce *local origination* (LO) programming. LO programs may carry advertising. They offer an outlet for public relations material that provides substantial information without being obviously commercial in tone.

Public Relations Opportunities in Television

The possibilities for the public relations specialist to use television are so numerous that they are worth examining on two levels: network and local.

The Network Level There are six principal methods commonly used:

1. *Guest appearances on news and talk shows.* Placement of clients on such programs as the *Tonight* and *Today* shows allows them to give plugs to new products, books, films, and plays, and to advocate their causes. For entertainment personalities in particular, these interviews provide a setting in which to display their skills. National leaders are interviewed in depth on the Sunday discussion panel shows such as *Meet the Press.* Guests on network interview shows must be articulate and poised, so they won't freeze up before the camera. Consequently they are carefully screened by show production staffs before being granted an appearance. Nationally syndicated talk programs such as the *Oprah Winfrey Show* and the *Rosie O'Donnell Show,* which are sold to individual stations, pro-

Late-night television talk shows are often a string of promotional appearances by various celebrities. Randy Johnson, the winning pitcher in the World Series, shares his 15 minutes of fame by appearing on the Jay Leno show. Such appearances on the late-night interview programs are much sought after by publicists for their clients—who just happen to be promoting a book, a new movie, or even a new diet fad.

vide excellent showcases. Public relations people wishing to place guests on these programs should apply to the producers of the shows.

2. *News releases and story proposals to network news departments.* This process is identical to that followed with radio stations. If a story or an idea is accepted, the assignment editor gives it to a reporter for visual development. Letters are often sent directly to popular TV personalities, suggesting stories for them to do. When a client is criticized in a controversial news situation or editorial, a representative should submit the client's response and urge that it be used on the air. If the response is submitted in concise videotape form, the likelihood of a quick airing is increased.
3. *Video news releases, commonly called VNRs.* These are ready-to-broadcast tapes or background footage for use in news programs. News programs will use VNRs in some form if they are well done and avoid delivering an obvious commercial message. (VNRs are discussed in Chapter 22.)
4. *Program ideas.* The representative of an important cause may propose to a network that it build an episode in a dramatic or situation comedy series around this cause. The public relations person can assist the program producer by supplying technical information. Such programs do not make overt sales pitches for the treatment organizations, but the message is inherent in the story line.

   Activist groups apply considerable pressure on television producers and the networks to include social issues such as environmental cleanups, drunk driving, and AIDS in their program scripts. Characters in situation comedies or dramas quite frequently take strong advocacy positions in the plotline, thus delivering a message to viewers.
5. *Silent publicity.* There are almost subliminal impacts in entertainment programs that quietly publicize a representative's cause. In a private detective show, for example, the star may be shown chasing the villain through an airport terminal past a Delta sign. Or the automobiles used by the lead characters may be Ford products exclusively. Sometimes a program's credits include a mention such as, "Transportation provided by American Airlines." Another way to generate silent publicity, especially valuable for the tourist industry, is to convince network show producers to shoot their programs in a client's city or region, showing the scenery there. The network series *Chicago Hope, NYPD Blue* and *Seinfeld,* all set in New York, and *Wings,* based in Nantucket, provided those localities with publicity.
6. *Public service announcements.* Stations nationwide run about one in three of the spots they receive as public relations gestures. The Advertising Council prepares material for national nonprofit organizations as a public service. To optimize use of the public service announcement, limit the total reading length to 30 seconds and provide the local contact. Whenever possible, enhance the relevance of the announcement for the local audience.

■ **The Local Station Level** The methods listed for network public relations apply just as effectively on the local level—indeed, even more so in some instances, because competition for time on local stations often is less intense. The more intimate nature of local programming increases public relations opportunities. Even a diaper-changing contest at a shopping mall can gain airtime.

PR insights

How to Place a Client on a TV Talk Show

Television stations are looking for interesting, articulate guests for their talk shows. The larger the station, the more stringent are its requirements for accepting a guest. This summary of needs and procedures for *AM/San Francisco,* the morning show on KGO-TV, the ABC network outlet in San Francisco, is typical of those for metropolitan stations. The information is from an article published in *Bulldog,* a West Coast public relations newsletter.

The station wants guests "who will provide information that will help our viewers to save money and save time, helpful hints around the house, consumer-type things." The station also uses guests from the business community who can comment on money, taxes, the stock market, and similar topics.

KGO-TV defines the audience for this show as primarily nonworking women, 18 to 49, married, with at least one child. The show also attracts working viewers before they leave for their jobs.

Segments on the one-hour show run from six to ten minutes. The usual pattern is to open with a celebrity-entertainer, then offer two segments on consumer topics. Segments 4, 5, and 6 cover "more serious subjects."

The production staff will normally consider for appearance only those who have appeared on television previously. Usually it asks to see a video clip of a prior TV appearance; an effective clip is an important way to gain acceptance.

"TV is a visual medium and a lot of our audience isn't just sitting there watching. They're folding clothes or ironing, so we need a voice that will grab their attention."

The public relations practitioner should submit a brief written query to the show's producer—"a 1-page letter getting straight to the basics: whom you're offering, what their experience is, exactly what their topic would be, what shows they've been on previously, a bio (biographical statement) and all other information available on the person, as well as clippings, copies of articles on the person or topic."

Staff members try to answer queries in about a week, perhaps sooner. The show is booked at least a week in advance but sometimes has last-minute openings.

There are four most frequently used techniques:

1. *Guest appearances on local talk shows.* Visiting experts in such fields as homemaking crafts, sponsored by companies and trade associations, demonstrate their skills for moderator and audience. National public relations firms send such clients around well-established circuits of local television and radio shows in each city they visit. The North American Precis Syndicate, Inc. (NAPS) claims great results for a service that edits and reuses an organizations's VNR material in pitches to local talk shows.
2. *Protest demonstrations.* Filmed demonstrations are such a staple on some television stations in large cities as to be a visual cliché. A group supporting or opposing a cause notifies a station that it will march at a certain time and place. Carrying placards, the marchers parade before the camera, and a representative is shown explaining their cause. Although, for fairness, stations should put on an advocate for the other side in the same sequence, some stations neglect this responsibility, and so the marching group's point of view dominates. Many group demonstrations are so much alike, however, that their impact is minimized. Stations use them primarily because they involve movement.

3. *Videotapes for news shows.* Smaller TV stations, in particular, lack enough staff to cover all potentially newsworthy events in their areas. Practitioners can fill the gaps by delivering videotapes of events they handle, for inclusion in newscasts. Excerpts from a local speech by a prominent client may be incorporated in an evening news show. Arrival or departure at the local airport of a client in the news might be used, too, if the person says something newsworthy on camera.
4. *General-interest films.* Local cable channels sometimes will show films of 15- or 20-minute duration produced by corporations in which the direct commercial message is nonexistent or muted. The purpose of such films is to strengthen a company's image as a good community citizen. Films explaining large civic programs by nonprofit organizations also may be used.

Motion Pictures

Mention of motion pictures brings to mind, first and inevitably, the commercial entertainment film turned out by that nebulous place called Hollywood. From a public relations point of view, possibilities for influencing the content of commercial motion pictures for client purposes are relatively limited. Practitioners who know their way through the labyrinth of Hollywood financing and production can make deals for silent publicity through use of brand-name merchandise, negotiating how the product will be used and whether there will be a fee. Firms such as Pepsi and Coca-Cola make deals to show their products in a movie, often tied in with an off screen promotion of the item. In the 2001 summer movie season, they spent about $250 million on such deals.

Public relations counselors and corporate departments occasionally serve as advisers on films that involve their areas of expertise. Filmmakers seek this advice to prevent embarrassing technical errors on the screen and to protect themselves from inadvertently angering a group that might retaliate by denouncing the picture. In terms of specific public relations results similar to those obtainable from the other mass media, however, commercial films are a minor channel.

Sponsored Films and Videotape

In other forms, the motion picture is an important public relations tool.

Corporations and nonprofit organizations use motion pictures and videotapes for internal purposes as part of audiovisual programs to train and inform their employees, or for external purposes to inform and influence the public and the financial community.

When, for example, Levi Strauss & Co. needed to explain to its employees a new personnel management program called Teamwork, it prepared a video for them. Like some other corporations, San Diego Gas & Electric Company produces a periodic Employee Video News Magazine. The topics covered range from the company's annual meeting to an employees' campaign against graffiti.

A significant use of the motion picture or video in public relations is directly promotional. Although avoiding frontal-attack sales messages such as those in television commercials, these films seek to whet the interest of audience members who are potential purchasers of the sponsor's product or contributors to the sponsor's cause. For example, a travel agency shows members of an invited audience a film about a Caribbean cruise. Colorful photography with voice-over narration depicts beautiful scenery, shipboard activities, luxurious accommodations and the enormous buffet tables from which travelers select their meals (no passenger ever is seasick in such films, of course).

Similarly, a university president at a dinner meeting of alumni shows a video of the campus as it is today. The videotape is a carefully contrived balance of nostalgia and progress, with scenes of football games and students at work in the new science building. Having rekindled alumni interest in the old school, the video closes with a recital of the university's plans and aspirations. Usually these include the need for a new building, the funds for which the alumni are invited to contribute.

A discussion of filmmaking appears in Chapter 22.

Online Media

The personal computer is a significant, swiftly expanding tool for public relations practitioners. Its ability to deliver information about client projects, establish contacts with reporters, and exchange ideas through the commercial online services and the global Internet is fascinating and not yet fully realized.

The World Wide Web portion of the Internet, which provides on-screen graphics, photographs, audio, and video clips along with text, is an especially effective form of cyberspace public relations.

Companies, public relations firms, nonprofit organizations, newspapers, and broadcasters, even individuals, maintain *home pages* about themselves on the Web. By calling up a desired home page on their computer screens, viewers can obtain information from the sponsor. As one example from thousands on the Web, the San Francisco Giants baseball team's home page carries game schedules, ticket information, photographs of players, and Giants merchandise. It also contains an e-mail form that viewers can use to request additional information. (See Chapter 12, "The Internet and Other New Technologies," for a detailed discussion.)

Home pages on the World Wide Web offer an unusual opportunity to reach an audience with a message in the exact form a public relations practitioner conceives it, because the Web is not subject to editing by any media gatekeeper. Tens of thousands of companies, nonprofit organizations, and individuals maintain sites on the World Wide Web, on which they explain and promote their services. Specific examples of how the Web is used in public relations appear in Chapter 12. By participating in online discussion groups and similar online interchanges, public relations people often reach opinion leaders in specific fields with facts and opinions favorable to their cause. Among these key online contacts are reporters and editors of Web-based publications that increasingly offer breaking news more immediately than print or broadcast outlets. The pace of media relations has increased as public relations professionals monitor online news, striving for what Professor Stephen Thomsen of Brigham Young University calls real-time response. The public relations person hopes to catch errors or offer balancing comments for stories as they break online and before they pick up momentum through print and broadcast dispersion.

Summary

The Nature of the Public Relations Audience

The public relations practitioner must reach a diverse and constantly changing audience. One of the most important aspects of the job will be identifying the target audience in order to customize communications appropriately.

Senior and Ethnic Markets

Two increasingly important publics are seniors and ethnic minorities. The senior group has grown in number as life span has increased, as well as growing in affluence. The population of ethnic groups is increasing at five times the rate of the general population, and they constitute many target audiences. Language is only one of the challenges in reaching them. The public relations practitioner must be sensitive to the special issues of different ethnic audiences.

Characteristics of the Audience

Current trends include an increase in the publics' visual orientation; fervent support for single issues; emphasis on personality and celebrity; a strong distrust of authority; and an expanding international audience.

Matching Audience and Media

Each of the media has different strengths for different types of communications; the practitioner must be careful to use the appropriate media (or, sometimes, single medium) for each campaign.

Media Relations

While public relations practitioners and editors need one another, public relations people can be more effective by remembering that media people can be busy and resistant to hype. At the same time, public relations practitioners are providing a service by keeping the public informed.

The Print Media

Print media—newspapers, magazines and other periodicals, and books—are appropriate for communications that should be kept over time and reread. Both newspapers and magazines are commercial institutions that depend heavily on advertising for their income, but magazines are published less frequently and often deal with subjects at greater length and depth than is possible in a daily newspaper. Magazines are also more likely to be targeted at a special-interest audience. Books are published on much longer schedules than either magazines or newspapers, but can still be useful as public relations tools.

The Spoken and Visual Media

Radio is one of the quickest and most flexible means of communicating a message, reaching a variety of audiences through such types of programming as newscasts, community calendars, talk shows, and public service announcements. The visual element of television and its pervasiveness in our society give it tremendous impact with the public. The growth of cable television has provided new venues for public relations with access channels and local origination programming. Public relations opportunities exist in television on both the network and the local level. Product placement is an example of public relations at work in the motion-picture industry. Sponsored films and videotapes can also be important public relations tools.

Online Media

Internet home pages provide an opportunity for the public relations practitioner to communicate directly with an audience without the filter of editors and journalists.

Case Activity: What Would You Do?

Cygna Labs, a medium-sized pharmaceutical firm located in Salt Lake City, has developed a sunscreen lotion. The product, Sun-Cure, joins a number of similar products on store shelves. Independent laboratory testing shows that Sun-Cure is particularly effective in blocking UVB rays, which cause burning and even premature aging of the skin. It is a good product and gets high ratings from dermatologists.

Unfortunately, the public still shows confusion about the differences between sunscreens and suntan lotions, as well as the merits of competing brands. Your public relations firm is retained to develop a product publicity program for Sun-Cure that would reach daily newspapers, selected magazines, radio, and television. What communication strategies would you develop for getting coverage in each medium?

Questions for Review and Discussion

1. Why is the senior audience so important in the United States, and what are some of its characteristics?
2. On what basis do newspaper editors select the news releases they publish?
3. A good public relations person knows how to create news events. Why is this important?
4. What significant differences between magazines and newspapers must a public relations practitioner keep in mind when submitting material to them?

5. Why are special-audience magazines and trade journals such important targets for many public relations people?
6. What are the three factors in Professor James Grunig's situational theory that help identify active publics for an issue?
7. What two special attributes make radio distinctive among the major media of mass communication?
8. Do local radio newscasts have a good potential as an outlet for news releases? If so, why?
9. Ratings determine which television programs survive and which die. Why do ratings have such power?
10. How should public relations representatives go about trying to place their clients on television interview shows?
11. Can you describe three ways in which public relations practitioners use online media?

Suggested Readings

Atkinson, Claire. "Radio Ga Ga." *PR Week,* March 1, 1999, pp. 18–19.

Atkinson, Claire. "How Do You Complain to the Press?" *PR Week,* July 12, 1999, p. 29.

Cameron, Glen T., Sallot, Lynne, and Curtin, Patricia A. "Public Relations and the Production of News: A Critical Review and a Theoretical Framework." *Communication Yearbook 20,* 1997, pp. 111–155.

Caruthers, Dewey. "'Media Placement: An Art That Gets No Respect." *PR Tactics,* October 1998, p. 23.

Durham, Deborah. "How to Get the Biggest Bang Out of Your Next Spokesperson Campaign." *Public Relations Quarterly,* Spring 1997, pp. 38–41.

Lubove, Seth. "Get Smart: A Reporter's Take on Good PR Practices." *PR Tactics,* October 1998, p. 20.

Manheim, Jarol B. *The Death of a Thousand Cuts: Corporate Campaigns and the Attack on the Corporation.* Mahwah, NJ: Lawrence Erlbaum Associates, 2001.

Montaigne, Fen. "Name That Chintz! How Shelter Magazines Boost Brands." *Wall Street Journal,* March 14, 1997, pp. B1, 8.

Morton, Linda P. "Targeting Minority Publics." *Public Relations Quarterly,* Summer 1997, pp. 23–27.

Pfau, Michael, Moy, Patricia, Holbert, R. Lance, Szabo, Erin A., Lin, Wei-Kuo, and Zhang, Weiwu. "The Influence of Political Talk Radio on Confidence in Democratic Institutions." *Journalism and Mass Communication Quarterly,* Vol. 75, Winter 1998, pp. 730–745.

Rabin, Phil. "How to Create a Top-Notch PSA." *PR Week,* July 26, 1999, p. 21.

Wartzman, Rick. "When You Translate 'Got Milk' for Latinos, What Do You Get?" *Wall Street Journal,* June 3, 1999, pp. 1, 10.

The Internet and Other New Technologies

preview

The objective of this chapter is to give students an understanding of the global communications explosion caused by development of new technologies and to describe how these can be used in public relations.

Topics covered in the chapter include:

- The Internet and World Wide Web
- Uses of the computer
- Facsimile transmission
- Satellite transmission
- Teleconferencing
- Software and other electronic tools
- A peek at the future of communication technology

The Communications Explosion

The explosive growth of the Internet during the 1990s has created a form of mass communication unlike all others. In 1990 the Internet merely exchanged scientific information. Today the Internet has become a household word as a global communications tool for millions of people. According to a study commissioned by *pr reporter* in 1998, use of the new technology is the leading trend in public relations.

Internet users exchange messages around the world electronically. They "surf" the World Wide Web, tapping the masses of information and entertainment the interlocking system of computer networks offers, virtually unconstrained by time and space. Through the Internet's World Wide Web, thousands of companies, organizations, other media, and individuals tell the world about themselves, sell their wares, and promote their ideas. By posting *pages* of printed words, graphics, photographs, and sounds, these cyberspace hosts communicate with millions of "netizens" worldwide. Nielsen Media Research reported that 254 million people used the World Wide Web globally in the latter half of 2001, with 20 million of them making online purchases.

The Internet is the most intriguing of the new electronic methods that are changing mass communications in general and providing public relations practice with innovative tools. According to the Middleberg/Ross Survey of journalists nationwide, the Internet is a rapidly growing means of receiving news releases, story ideas, and even audio and photo files from public relations sources.

Three familiar methods of communication—telephone, television, and the computer—are blended together in new forms of transmission such as the much-publicized *information superhighway.* A fundamental fact is that a large portion of the emerging services is interactive; that is, it affords the two-way communication that is so vital in professional public relations. Instead of depending on the programs television networks and cable systems provide, for example, viewers can order pay-per-view

Much of the world's communication today flashes upward through satellite dishes like these. Messages are bounced from transponders on satellites and caught by dishes at homes and offices.

movies onto their computer screens or move seamlessly between TV programming and high-speed Internet access on their television sets.

Two key factors in this electronic outburst are:

1. Use of fiber optic cable—multiple strands of glass thinner than hairs—in place of the traditional copper cable. This tremendously increases transmission volume and speed. The GTE Corporation reports that one of its fiberglass cables can transmit a 500-page novel in slightly more than two seconds.
2. Digital transmission of sounds and pictures; that is, transmission of messages in code numbers that are reconstructed at the receiving end into words and pictures. Digitalization will vastly improve TV reception through development of high-definition television (HDTV), now emerging from the experimental stage.

The enormous cost of development and construction has delayed general use of some electronic applications, but each year additional ones reach consumers.

In this chapter we explain how the principal new technologies can be applied to accomplish public relations objectives. Table 12.1 compares traditional mass media with the new media.

TABLE 12.1

Pros and Cons of New Media in Public Relations

TRADITIONAL MASS MEDIA	*NEW MEDIA*
Geographically constrained: *local or regional targets*	Distance insensitive: *topic, need or interest targeting worldwide*
Hierarchical: *series of gatekeepers/editors*	Flattened: *one to many and many to many*
Unidirectional: *one-way dissemination*	Interactive: *feedback, discussion, debate, response to requests by person or machine*
Space/time constraints: *limited pages and airtime*	Less space/time constraints: *large, layered capacity for information*
Professional communicators: *highly trained to pro standards*	Nonprofessional: *anyone with limited training or professional values may participate*
High access costs: *startup and production costs prohibitive*	Low access costs: *more affordable, but expensive talent required*
General interest: *large audiences and broad coverage*	Customized: *narrowcasts, even individually tailored*
Linearity of content: *news hierarchy*	Nonlinearity of content: *hypertext links enable nonlinear navigation*
Feedback: *slow, effortful, and limited*	Feedback: *e-mail and online chat are immediate and easy*
Ad-driven: *big audiences and revenue*	Diverse funding sources: *varied but limited revenue*
Institution-bound: *corporate ownership*	Decentralized: *grassroots efforts*
Fixed format: *predictable in format, time and place*	Flexible format: *emerging but fluid formats; multimedia*
News, values, journalistic standards: *conventional*	Formative standards: *currently obscure*

Source: Adapted from *pr reporter,* May 17, 1999.

The Computer

For public relations practitioners, the computer serves many purposes. It handles office procedures faster and more extensively than the old do-it-by-hand methods. As a research tool it makes an immense amount of information easily accessible. Through electronic mail and chat forums it provides a stimulating exchange of ideas. Project management, time billing, and digital presentations are just three of many functions made more efficient and flexible using computers.

Even more intriguing, the personal computer is the vehicle that can carry the practitioner into the maze of the Internet.

The standard way to enter the Internet at first was by subscribing to a commercial online computer service such as America Online or Microsoft Network and obtaining entry to the Internet through that source. Then the giant AT&T long-distance telephone company offered direct entry, as did numerous independent providers.

Each commercial online service contains masses of stored information: news reports, complete texts of major newspapers and magazines for years back, encyclopedias, government records, texts of books, and more. They provide rich sources for public relations researchers. (See Chapter 6, Research.)

The step beyond these services is the Internet itself. We shall examine the Internet first, then describe the other less glamorous but basic uses of the computer in public relations.

The Internet

Created in the late 1960s by researchers who found how to link computers in separate cities, the Internet first functioned as an academic–government tool. It came into public use in the early 1990s; tie-ins developed between the American system and those in more than 150 other countries.

An upsurge in Internet usage developed with the creation of graphics and sound on what was named the World Wide Web. Aware of the Web's commercial possibilities but not quite sure how to exploit them, tens of thousands of companies established *sites* on the Web. A site consists of one or more pages, the first of which is the home page. A searcher enters the home page by using its code name of letters, figures, and punctuation marks. An effective home page is a colorful mixture of text and graphics on which the sponsoring organization introduces itself.

The Internet has no official central control headquarters, so obtaining valid statistics on use of the global system is difficult. The number of hits for each page can be determined; that is, the number of times users enter the page. Because many hits are by "surfers" hunting around to see what they can find, this figure is of limited commercial value. Figures for hits can be wildly inflated because complex Web pages may generate hits for each major component of the page rather than one hit per page. Furthermore, each time a user returns to a page during a visit, another hit is recorded. Several organizations, including the Audit Bureau of Circulation (ABC), are working on more sophisticated tracking methods that count number of visitors to a site.

The worldwide total of computer owners having access to the Internet, and using it, can only be estimated. A Nielsen Media Research 2002 study estimated approximately 115 million Internet users in the United States and Canada. The Nielsen figure for Internet use nearly doubled from its 1998 figure of 58 million.

Ford's site on the World Wide Web, intended for the news media, enables the corporation to deliver information and photographs about its activities 24 hours a day.

In its sample of 6000 households, Nielsen found Internet users to be well educated. Sixty percent were male, and 53 percent were between the ages of 16 and 34. These surveys depict a youthful, affluent, well-educated audience.

The Internet and Public Relations

The Internet gives public relations practitioners a many-faceted form of worldwide communication, primarily involving message exchange by e-mail, information delivery and persuasion by its World Wide Web, and research opportunities.

These are the primary Internet uses:

- *E-mail distribution.* Electronic mail includes messages to individuals, newsletters to staff members, transmission of news releases, photos, and pitch letters to media offices, and dispatch and receipt of copy between public relations firms and clients, including fully formatted documents using software such as Adobe Acrobat. Most e-mail systems now accept hypertext e-mail that presents images in full color when the e-mail is opened. Professional Training Associates, a newsletter publisher, was able to send its direct mail postcard on the Internet to selected editors and reporters. The postcard announced a new Web site entitled Hard@Work with a whimsical shot of the publisher and editor perched on a rock in the middle of a stream.
- *World Wide Web sites.* These sites provide a way for organizations to tell Internet users what they do, publicize projects, and advocate policies. Edelman Public Relations Worldwide, for example, gives information about its clients. Ketchum public relations offers recipes from its food product clients.

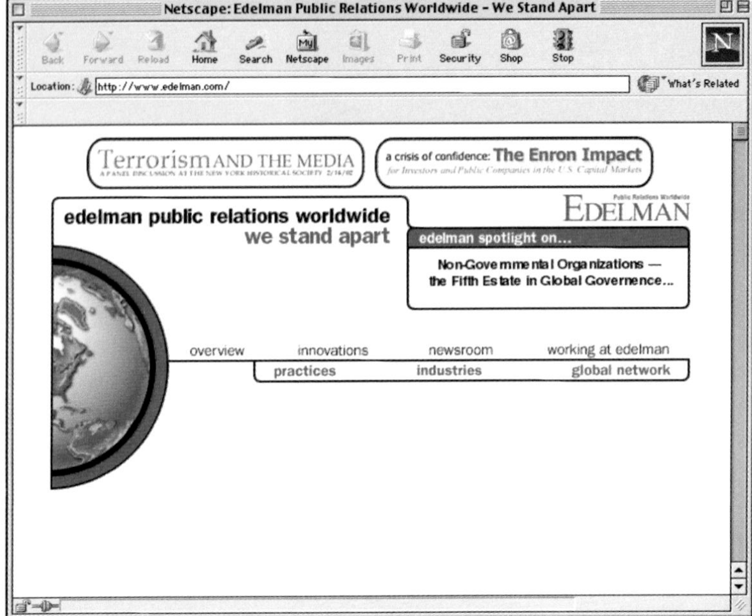

An example of how public relations firms use the Internet is this home page of Edelman Public Relations Worldwide, offering a variety of information.

Greenpeace, the activist environmentalist organization, uses its Web site to publicize its confrontations at sea with vessels whose work it opposes. Here, a Greenpeace ship tries to block passage of a Norwegian whaling vessel. The Web site carries news reports and background information from the Greenpeace point of view.

PR insights

Creating Winning Web Sites

Web sites can serve as a controlled, yet credible, tool for organizations to disseminate messages. National surveys indicate that audiences hold Web-based information in high regard. Internet information, according to one survey of over 1000 respondents by professors at the University of California at Santa Barbara, was as credible as TV, radio, and magazines but less credible than newspapers. Researchers say high credibility perhaps explains why Web information is seldom double-checked with other sources by the audience.

Web sites also enable strategic targeting of messages to audiences. Responsible practitioners can get the word out to key publics using links to customized Web pages tailored to the particular public. However, according to Stuart Esrock and Greg Leichty (*Public Relations Reporter*, Fall 2000), most corporate Web sites are used to service investors, customers, and, to a lesser extent, media. Consequently, the communication potential of Web sites has not yet been fully tapped.

To date, according to Candace White and colleagues at the University of Tennessee, most Web site planning has been done by trial and error, with little formal research and evaluation. Practitioners report Web site development as a low priority on to-do lists because of skepticism about effectiveness, inefficient evaluation methods, and lack of control over the site. Opportunities for a broader range of publics should be developed as support for Web sites increases and public relations practitioners become more assertive in taking control of Web sites. Given the enormous and burgeoning audience for Web sites, as well as key target audiences, creating more effective Web sites will be essential for public relations departments.

Louis Falk, of Florida International University, offers some no-nonsense advice for Web site development.

- *Make it fast.* Be sure pages load in eight seconds.
- *Use a functional, balanced design.* Make the site work on all major Web browsers, such as Explorer and Netscape. Place the most important information to the left. Use standard colors that work consistently on many different browsers and machines. Offer an easy and logical interaction, making good use of internal search engines.
- *Make sure there are no dead links.*
- *Include contact information.*
- *Identify your purpose(s).* Public information differs dramatically from e-commerce, for instance.
- *Keep it fresh.* Not only should information be current, but your most recent personal visit to check performance should never become dated either.
- *Register with major search engines.* This assures that you can be found.

- *Brochureware.* Although this term is used ironically by those who envision Web sites as a unique new channel, much of the content on Web sites is little more than an online version of the brochures and collateral materials that organizations provide to stakeholders. Public relations professionals should increasingly capitalize on the interactive and multimedia characteristics that distinguish Web communication from traditional print materials. Over time, interactivity and video clips will distinguish brochureware from its print predecessor, adding to the mix of communication tools available to the public relations professional.
- *Usenet discussion groups.* Individuals concerned with a certain issue discuss it by making comments and reading the responses of other participants. Sometimes this exchange is called an *electronic bulletin board.* Usenet groups also are used for audience research, in which a participant requests opinions and facts. An estimated 10,000 such groups operate.

PR insights

Getting Reporters to Use Your Web Site

According to the Nielsen Norman Group, professionals should conduct usability studies of their Web sites, especially to understand the problems and concerns of ordinary users and journalists. Nielsen Norman says that journalists frequently go to company Web sites as they start to work on a story. Reporters look to:

- Find a PR contact
- Check basic facts about a company
- Discover a company's perspective on events
- Check financial information
- Download images to illustrate stories

Typical steps taken by reporters include:

1. *Getting to your site.*

- Tip: Submit site to major search engines, such as Google.
- Tip: Avoid Flash or Shockwave features that may not work or may bog down the reporter's research.

2. *Finding the news.*

- Tip: Don't lose reporters in the forest.
- Tip: Clearly and prominently label information meant for reporters (Media; Press; News).

3. *Looking for contact information.*

- Tip: Reporters in the Nielsen Norman Group study had the lowest success rate in finding the phone number for the public relations contact.
- Tip: Put contact information on every page of your site, especially the phone number, to help journalists get answers in a short time.

4. *Researching a product, event or person.*

- Tip: Dedicate an easy-to-find link to press releases.
- Tip: Make releases searchable and sortable by topic or date.
- Tip: Avoid popup windows for press releases because they imply skimpy information.
- Tip: Link to third-party resources that provide credible supplements to the company's story.

5. *Fact checking.*

- Tip: Provide fact sheets, executive biographies, financial data, and product information.

6. *Looking at pictures.*

- Tip: Reporters like graphics, and they convey much about a company.
- Tip: Don't overdo it; make sure the images are useful and not just "eye candy."

- *Listservs.* PRFORUM and other listservs offer a similar interactive and dynamic opportunity for public relations professionals to query members of the discussion list. A participant must enroll with the list manager, thereby gaining access to the discussions. All messages submitted to the list appear in the participant's e-mail in-box, sometimes several score per day! To reduce e-mail traffic, a digest of the list can be specified so that only one e-mail summarizing the day's discussion is received.

Here are specific examples of how the Internet is used in public relations practice:

- Firms not only pitch stories to journalists via e-mail, but also rapidly respond to stories. Geoworks produces a smart cellular phone—a pager, an office organizer, a Web browser, and an e-mail tool all in one. Whenever palm-sized computers were covered in a national magazine, Geoworks contacted the publication to tout its product as the next-generation device. Ensuing online dialogue with editors at *Newsweek, Business Week, ComputerWorld,* and *Time Digital* were crucial in raising awareness of smart phones.

- Organizations increasingly set up Web sites to serve informational needs of reporters, especially during a crisis or a breaking news situation. The Starr Report investigation of President Clinton's affair with Monica Lewinsky was released to the Web for wide and immediate dissemination. News organizations then made it available on their own Web sites, where an estimated 24.7 million people read parts of it in a matter of days.
- Xerox's public relations Web site offers answers to any question—any question at all. In response to an online question, the offbeat site reported its calculation that it would take 33,661 years to vacuum the state of Ohio! *People* magazine and various TV news features resulted.
- LifeSavers, like many Web sites, offers free online games that attract users to the Web site, where they are exposed to the LifeSaver brand. Sweepstakes serve a similar role of attracting traffic to Web sites.
- Companies like Boeing and Compaq have used Webcasting to increase coverage of important news conferences by broadcasting video footage over the Web via Medialink's Web site, NewStream.com.
- At least 400 health care organizations and companies use their Web sites to distribute medical information. Two examples are: (1) The American Medical Association, which provides information for physicians and patients about treatments, medical developments, and other health care news; and (2) The National Alliance of Breast Cancer Organizations (NABCO), which provides current information about breast cancer research and treatment, events, and links to Internet sites.
- The United Nations High Commissioner for Refugees provides a Web site to increase public awareness of the global refugee problem. It includes maps, photographs, and news about people who have left their homes to escape war and persecution. On a positive note, international sponsors are helping local newspapers mount Web versions so that refugees can assess when conditions are favorable for a return to their homelands.
- The governor of Hawaii used a Webcast to address critics and field questions from concerned citizens regarding a teachers' strike and lockout. At a minimal direct cost of $100, an enormous audience, estimated at 30,000, was reached. Facing a crisis in the schools, Governor Cayetano communicated directly to the audience, generating both advanced and follow-up coverage and ongoing access to the archived Webcast online.

Key Aspects of the Internet

Public relations professionals should keep in mind these important facts about the Internet:

- Its reach is worldwide. A message intended for local or regional use may draw reactions, good or bad, from unexpected places.
- The content of the Internet is virtually uncontrolled. Anyone can say or show anything without passing it through "gatekeepers," the editors and producers

who approve the material that reaches the public through traditional media channels. Lack of editorial control permits unfettered freedom of speech but also permits distribution of unconfirmed, slanted, or even potentially libelous material.

The potential for damage resulting from unconfirmed information on the Internet was demonstrated by Pierre Salinger, press secretary for President John F. Kennedy and retired ABC television correspondent. He received worldwide attention with an announcement in France that he had obtained a security document confirming that TWA Flight 800, which exploded off Long Island with 230 deaths in 1996, had been shot down accidentally by a U.S. Navy missile. In fact his source was a bogus story, previously discredited, that someone had circulated on the Internet.

Public Relations Tactics, published by the Public Relations Society of America, welcomes this freedom from editorial control. It asserts, "PR pros can now get messages out without passing them through the filter of editors and journalists. Traditional media gatekeepers have lost their power in today's print-and-click world."

- Issue tracking can be more thorough using the Internet and far more immediate. Services such as NewsEdge monitor Web-based news and wire services and alert users when relevant topics appear in Internet news sources. By monitoring the Internet, practitioners can keep track of what competitors, opponents, and the general audience are saying. Thus informed, practitioners can better shape their own tactics and messages as well as respond in real time to forestall erroneous or unbalanced stories from gaining momentum without correction. A PRNewswire executive recalled how a story released by his service at 7:30 A.M. prompted an e-mail response by a public relations person. The result was a factually corrected release on PRNewswire by 7:35.

Internet Problems

The global spiderweb of interlocking computer networks has problems, as well as its manifest benefits. The following should be kept in mind as users plan Internet communication programs:

- The difficulty in finding information they desire through the complexities of the system frustrates some users. Increasingly search engines prioritize sites based on fee payment, making the search more biased.
- Controversial problems of security and legal questions of copyright infringement, libel, invasion of privacy, and pornography remain unsolved.
- Time-consuming procedures for online transactions or registration of products can be terminated by an error message that the procedure was not successful, generating skepticism about the efficiency of the Web and its reliability as a communication tool. The claim that online public relations builds positive relationships with key constituents can be seriously eroded by such events.

In sum, the Internet is an evolving form of mass communication that fascinates participants but must pass through a trial-and-error period before its effectiveness as a public relations tool can be fully realized.

Other Computer Uses

Because a computer can store, codify, analyze, and search out information at speeds far beyond human capability, its applications are enormous. When we add its ability to transmit information over long distances at fantastically high speeds, its potential becomes even greater. Ease of revision, updating, and modeling makes computers powerful tools for text editing. Still more astounding is the anticipated development of the "thinking" computer, a machine designed to diagnose and solve problems in addition to calculating and processing data as present computers do. The highly publicized chess match between Garry Kasparov and IBM Corporation's Deep Blue dramatically displayed the growing ability of computers to emulate human intelligence. Deep Blue won the match. The well-known physicist and thinker Stephen Hawking predicts that artificial intelligence will one day universally supercede human brainpower. Some of the new technologies being used by public relations practitioners are listed in Table 12.2.

TABLE 12.2

Selected New-Technology Tools in Public Relations Practice

A wide range of technologies serve important functions of modern public relations, often directed at particular audiences. Some of these technologies are just emerging, others are more commonly used.

NEW TECH TOOL	PR FUNCTION	TYPICAL AUDIENCE	TECHNIQUES/FEATURES
Internet	Media relations	Media contacts	Pitching stories and sending digital media kits
	Activism	Media	Evens the resource playing field for activist groups
	Crisis management	Media and internal audiences	Pre-emptive tool against investigative hatchet job
	Event or product promotion	Widespread, often teens or trendsetters	Guerrilla (subtle) and viral (self-generating) dissemination
Intranet	Internal communication	Employees and password access outsiders	Enables confidential communication and rumor research
Online newswires, (e.g., Newstream.com)	Investor relations	Investors and financial media in 6000 online newsrooms	Submit to Business Wire and index with Yahoo company news
Webcasting services such as Medialink	Meetings and media relations	Varied	Enables vast and widespread audience to participate online
Web searching	Issues tracking	Management	Search client or industry name

(continued)

NEW TECH TOOL	*PR FUNCTION*	*TYPICAL AUDIENCE*	*TECHNIQUES/FEATURES*
Web site development	E-commerce and public information	Customers and constituents	Offer products and services
Online monitoring services, (e.g., Newsedge, E-Watch.Com and Briefme.Com)	Issues and crisis management	Practitioner receives news alerts	Enables monitoring of both slow boil and breaking news about own organization
CD-ROM	Media relations	Media	Digital media kit or reporter's resource
	Employee communication	Employees	Interactive, audio-visual training and notification
Satellite and radio media tours	Publicity	Viewers and listeners	Overcomes distance barriers in media appearances
Web research	Audience analysis and message testing	Colleagues and clients	Online surveys, focus groups, secondary research, and usability studies
Media database software (e.g., Prpowerbase)	Release distribution/tracking	Media	Access and use Bacon's and other major databases
Research software (e.g., Publics, SPSS)	Formative and evaluative research	Client	Enables targeted audiences and tailored messages
Presentation software (e.g., Powerpoint, Flash)	Briefings	Varied	Multimedia features and last minute changes
Calendar software (e.g., Sidekick, Outlook)	Project and event coordination	Varied	Set up team meetings and recurring appointments
Project management software (e.g., MS Project)	Production and campaign planning/tracking	Colleagues and clients	Enables control of complex projects
Time tracking and billing software (e.g., Timeslips)	Management	Colleagues and clients	Track time for productivity analysis and billing of services
Media management software (e.g., Vocus, Spinware)	Media relations	Media	Track media contacts and coverage, online press center
Creativity tools (e.g., Visio, Photoshop, Quark)	Materials production	Readers and viewers	Design and layout of materials
Netbusiness card	Firm visibility and marketing	Clients	Registered users appear in all major online Yellow Pages

Dictation and Voice Generation

Most computers being sold today have the memory and processing speed needed to recognize human speech. Software called Dragon Naturally Speaking not only recognizes the user's speech but improves its recognition accuracy by taking into account corrections the user makes in the dictated text on the computer screen. The program becomes more accurate in converting speech to word processing, presentation, Web, database, or spreadsheet content. Computer commands may also be spoken, including the command "Read Text," which prompts the computer to generate speech by reading the written text to the user. One of the important boons of this new technology may well be a reduction in painful repetitive motion syndrome injuries in public relations due to hours of keyboarding.

Expert Systems

One modest form of artificial intelligence, called expert system programming, has made its mark in the business world. Expert systems identify a limited domain of expertise and then emulate the decision making that an expert would undertake. In public relations, the expertise of a research expert is embodied in Publics PR Research Software™. The software not only streamlines the process of making a questionnaire but converts statistical results into plain language. (See Chapter 6 for details about research in public relations and the use of Publics PR Research Software™). Expert systems will some day also assist public relations professionals with special-event planning, issue evaluation, and other domains of expertise in the field.

Public Relations Management Tools

Project scheduling software such as Microsoft Project and MacProject enable Gantt charts to be quickly created and modified while tracking resources and progress toward completion of projects. (See Figure 12.1 for a sample Gantt chart.) Special software such as Timeslips streamlines the time-billing process and allows professionals to use the computer as a timer and recorder of billable hours. Software such as Spin Control is used in public relations to manage the media relations process. The program helps the public relations professional develop media contact databases, track mail and phone pitches to those contacts, and record news coverage obtained from the media relations effort.

Processing of News Releases

Word processing is valuable in preparation of news releases that can be reworded by computer for different types of publications, such as trade magazines, daily newspapers, and the business press. A draft document can be attached to e-mail for delivery to the client or supervisor. Changes made by others can be automatically highlighted in the text with the editor identified. Using a mail merge function, professionals are increasingly adept at customizing or even localizing releases to increase news value for individual editors in a distribution list.

Electronic Mail

When a writer creates copy for a brochure, the edited text can be recorded on a disk for delivery to the printing company. Increasingly, the printing company will have suitable

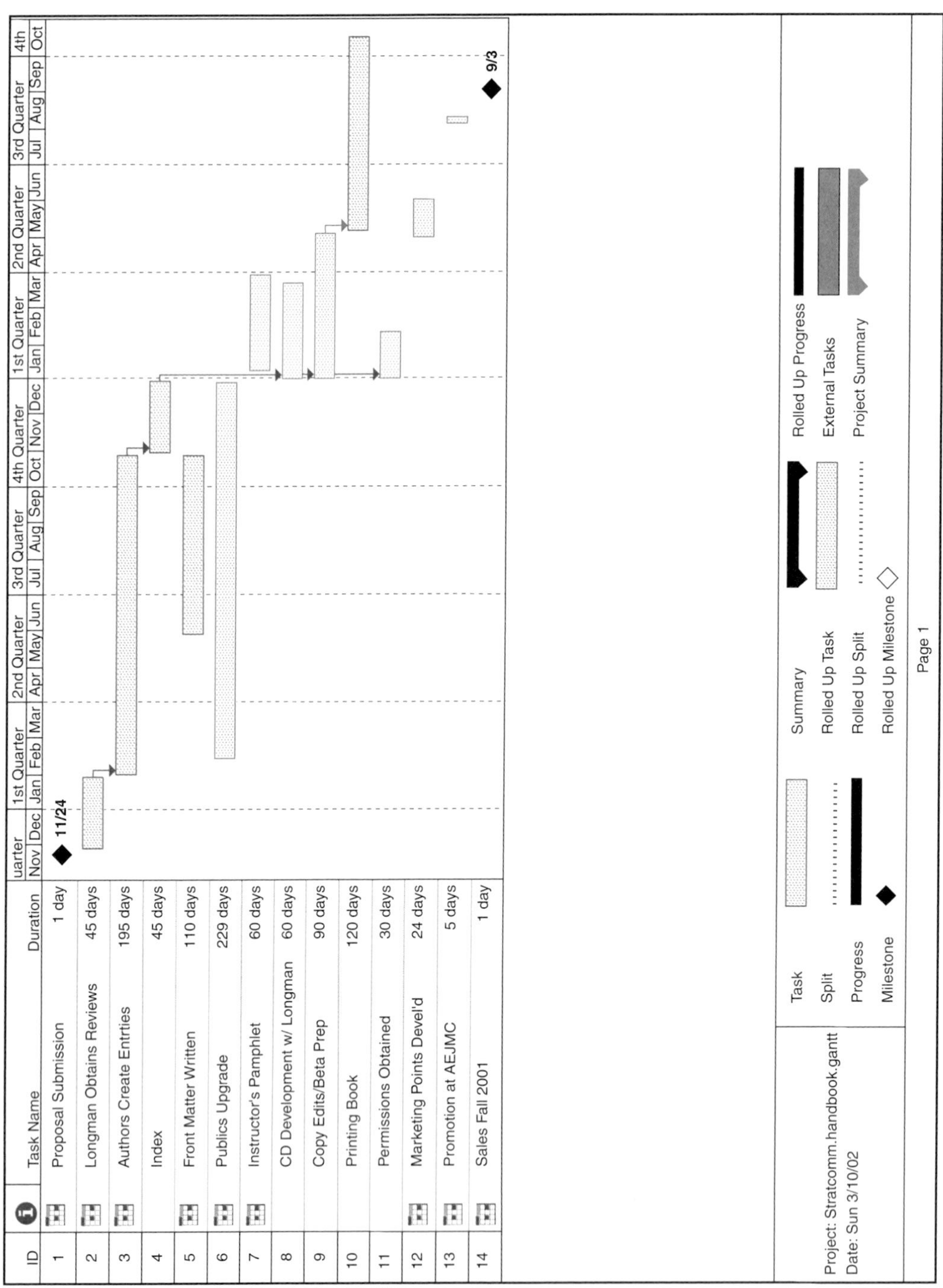

FIGURE 12.1

Software such as Microsoft Project makes creation of Gantt charts easy and flexible. These charts provide a visual and linear depiction of project tasks. For tracking progress, these charts can include deadlines and identify resources required for each task. The Gantt chart can also indicate percent complete as well as a comparison of the proposed timeline with the actual time each task took.

computer connections, enabling brochure copy to be transmitted electronically from the writer's computer into the printing company's computer. No paper is used. That computer in turn can feed the copy into a phototypesetting system, from which it will emerge as type on paper ready to be reproduced, with headlines included. The frequent collaboration of public relations professionals with clients and colleagues has been greatly enhanced through the sharing of draft documents via e-mail. When compatible word processing, graphics, or desktop publishing software is used by both parties, documents attached to e-mail can be opened, edited, and returned, even when one person uses a Mac and the other is on a Windows machine. Even incompatible systems can communicate using software such as Adobe Acrobat to view documents and attach the equivalent of sticky notes to the document without actually being able to open and change the document.

Desktop Publishing

Recent advances in computer techniques make possible the creation of professional-looking newsletters and graphically illustrated material on a personal computer right in the office. This is known as desktop publishing.

Desktop publishing allows the public relations writer and editor to design and lay out reports, newsletters, brochures, and presentations by manipulating copy and graphics right on a computer screen instead of on a drawing board. It produces pages ready for offset printing, but often high-quality printers produce materials in small batches in-house. For example, a professionally published press kit may include space for fact sheets or other inserts. This "just-in-time" printing enables a sense of immediacy in content without sacrificing appearance.

Desktop publishing saves cost and time. Less than $5,000 will buy all the components necessary for producing high-quality newsletters and graphics: a personal computer, a word-processing program, a graphics program, page-making software, and a laser printer. Producing materials in-house reduces the fuss and expense of involving a commercial printer. Apple Computer estimates that a 16-page newsletter can be produced by the desktop method in eight hours, compared with 16 hours by the traditional commercial printing method.

Mailing Lists

Up-to-date mailing lists are vital in public relations work. Lists of names are typed into database programs such as Microsoft Works or ACT! contact management software and stored in computer memory. Changes of address or other alterations can be made by calling up a name and using a few keystrokes. When a mailing is to be made, the desired names on the master list can be activated and printed on adhesive labels or on the individual envelopes.

The capability to select groups of names from the master list assists the practitioner in reaching target audiences. For example, when introducing its new models, Ford sought to generate ample publicity for more than 2000 of its dealers located in primarily rural areas. As reported in *Public Relations Journal,* the automaker created a computer file on each dealer including address, phone number, and name of local spokesperson. By combining this file with its standard news release, Ford created 9600 customized releases. Every release mentioned a local dealer by name. These were sent to carefully culled mailing lists within the dealer's territory.

Public relations departments and firms may compile their own computer lists of media contacts or purchase CD-ROM databases from press-directory companies such as *Bacon's Media Source Software* that list mail, e-mail, and phone data for nearly 30,000 editors.

Online Conferences

Online conferences, essentially a series of typed messages exchanged among a group, are increasingly valuable in public relations work. Practitioners use their computers to "converse" with clients and suppliers, or they participate in forums on professional matters with groups of their peers. The transcript of the exchange of messages can be retained for the record in computer storage or typed out by a hard-copy printer.

As the number of personal computers reaches the saturation point, online conferences are becoming commonplace. Mobile computing with laptop, mini-notebook, and palm-sized personal digital assistants (PDAs) makes out-of-office conferences during business travel an important part of the business communication landscape. Free software such as Netmeeting is available for online conferencing. For more sophisticated applications involving numerous participants, companies offer services and software to meet advanced needs.

Graphics

Use of computers to design for publications eye-catching colored graphics—drawings, graphs and charts, and text—has emerged as a stellar new technology in public relations practice. Recent developments in computer software make such graphics possible.

PR casebook

Hewlett-Packard Leads in Video Communication

Hewlett-Packard, headquartered in Palo Alto, California, spends more than $20 million annually on video communications and produces some of the nation's most sophisticated business television.

The company began live, interactive broadcasts in 1981, using a transmitter to reach more than 80 plant and sales sites nationwide. This enabled an executive to address many audiences simultaneously. By 1996, HP had 127 sites linked to its video communications network, including several in Canada, South America, and Europe.

HP also has 48 teleconference rooms at 44 locations in the United States, Europe, and Asia. These facilities allow participants to hold meetings with people in as many as eight locations. Two-way audio and video allow a truly interactive meeting format; participants can also share information, including files and graphics, on personal computers.

HP is developing a desktop interactive multimedia network so that employees eventually will be able to view live videos on their personal computers, including the company president's semiannual address. "Until the majority of employees can view video on their PCs or workstations, I don't think business television is going to advance much," said Mary Anne Easley, manager of HP's employee communications.

To communicate with employees, HP also produces a high-quality video magazine. Released four times a year at a cost of $50,000 an issue, it is formatted after television's "Evening Magazine." According to Easley, "Television is an effective medium for reaching the baby boomers, the production and clerical workers."

Attractive graphics give visual impact to annual reports and employee publications, as well as to video programs and slide presentations. Imaginative visual effects may be obtained with only a modest investment of time and money. Slide presentations in particular can be enhanced dramatically with computer-generated graphics. Representations of people, designs, and charts add visual zest that stimulates audiences. Increasingly, public relations departments and firms employ such graphics to dress up transparencies used in presentations to gain management approval for their ideas. (Presentation software is discussed in Chapter 22.)

Facsimile Transmission

An invaluable tool in public relations practice is facsimile transmission, commonly called *fax*. Such frequently heard remarks as "I'll fax it to you" have added a new verb to the language.

Facsimile transmission moves an exact copy of printed matter and graphics by telephone circuit from a machine or computer in one office to one in another office, across town, or on the other side of the world. A news release, a draft of a client's newsletter, instructions from headquarters to a branch office—these are merely three among scores of ways in which practitioners use fax. Office workers even fax their lunch orders to nearby restaurants.

By using *broadcast fax*, a sender can transmit a single document to hundreds of recipients simultaneously. A corporation, for example, can distribute a news release swiftly and equally to competing news media. In another application, a customer can call a major vendor such as PR Newswire and Business Wire by a toll-free 800 number, request a piece of information, and receive it by fax within minutes.

A word of caution: Discretion should be used in faxing news releases to editors. Send only those you consider to be truly important and urgent. Editors complain, often quite sharply, about the amount of "junk fax" they receive. They say that the inpouring of materials useless to them, including advertisements and irrelevant announcements, ties up their machines and may delay delivery of important news material. Some states have enacted laws restricting distribution of unsolicited fax items.

Increasingly, the lines between fax and e-mail have blurred. It is now possible to use services that will convert an e-mail message into a broadcast fax delivered to the physical fax machines of the target public. Similarly, incoming faxes to a professional's phone number can be received and forwarded as e-mail to the traveling public relations person.

Satellite Transmission

Text messages and pictures can be flashed around the world in seconds using satellite transmission. Information is dispatched by computer through a ground "uplink" station to a transponder pad on a satellite, then bounced back to a receiving dish on the ground and into a receiving computer. Enormous amounts of material can be transmitted at rates about 160 times faster than can be done over land lines, and at much lower cost.

The *Wall Street Journal, New York Times,* and *USA Today* use satellites to transmit entire page layouts to regional printing plants. The Associated Press, United Press International, and other news services transmit their stories and pictures by satellite. The television and radio networks deliver programs in the same manner.

PR insights

Building Relationships Online

Many definitions of public relations embrace the concept of relationship management, often emphasizing mutual benefit in the relationship between an organization and its publics. These definitions also take a longer-term perspective that stresses loyalty built upon trust and loyalty between parties. The unique features of new media, particularly the interactivity and decentralization of communication, afford public relations practitioners special opportunities to build beneficial relationships for the organization.

In a study funded by the Institute for Public Relations, Maria Len-Rios found that stronger relationships can result from more extensive use of an organization's Web site. Minor mistakes in content or online service are more likely to be forgiven, and loyal users will accept a more assertive program of e-mail offers and messages. These so-called "push" strategies include everything from requests for assistance with a charitable cause, to online sales offers, to e-mail reminders for employees or members.

In precision public relations, we seek to target key publics. Online channels facilitate this narrow targeting through the creation of messages based on the individual's characteristics. Provided permission is granted, e-mail and customized Web content can be tailored to the individual. As the relationship between an organization and an individual matures, more personalized or tailored messaging can be directed to that individual without violating the rules for appropriate online communication.

The interactive element of the Internet is particularly relevant to public relations. Building relationships through an interactive Web site will ultimately serve to improve the corporate image and align corporate policy with public opinion. This two-way symmetrical communication reflects change on the part of the organization to accommodate the public.

Some examples of such two-way communication include:

- Personal satellite radio is available in luxury cars. It enables programming to personal tastes and will soon include personalized news and current affairs.
- Naturally spreading movements of ideas, often called viral marketing, and tactics to spur social movements work well when push e-mail and tailored messages are directed to "e-fluentials," according to Burson Marsteller public relations. (See www.efluentials.com for details.)
- The personal greeting at log in on Amazon.com with customized information such as offers of new books by favorite authors is based on the user profile built upon previous activity by the customer at the Amazon Web site. For a regular and loyal user, this is likely to be viewed as a convenience, not an imposition.

News Release Delivery

More than a dozen American companies deliver news releases electronically to large newspapers and other major news media offices. In the receiving newsrooms these releases are fed into computers, to be examined by editors on video display terminals.

The difference between news release delivery firms and the traditional news services such as the Associated Press is this: Newspapers, radio, and television stations pay large fees to receive the reports of the news services, which maintain staffs of editors and reporters to gather, analyze, select, and write the news in a neutral style. On the other hand, the news release delivery companies are paid by creators of news releases to distribute those releases to the media, which pay nothing to receive them. These delivery services are prepaid transmission belts, not selectors of material. They do enforce editing standards and occasionally reject releases as unsuitable.

One of the largest news release companies is Business Wire. Using electronic circuits and satellite communications, the company can simultaneously reach more than

1600 media points in the United States and Canada and more than 500 in Europe, Latin America, East Asia, and Australia. In addition, Business Wire provides rapid dissemination of financial news releases to more than 600 securities and investment firms worldwide. The company sends an average of 175 news releases daily for a roster of more than 9000 clients.

Electronically delivered news releases have an advantage over the conventional variety. Releases transmitted by satellite tend to receive closer, faster attention from media editors than those arriving by mail.

Another large news release delivery company, PR Newswire, was the first to distribute its releases by satellite. PR Newswire's computers distribute releases and official statements from more than 7500 organizations directly into the newsroom computers of the media. Each day PR Newswire transmits approximately 150 such releases. The releases by PR Newswire go into several commercial databases.

Video and Audio News Release Distribution

Transmission by satellite also makes possible fast distribution of video news releases (VNRs). The picture-and-voice releases are sent primarily to cable television networks, local cable systems, and local television stations. Nearly 30 companies produce and distribute hundreds of video news releases for clients. Only relatively few of the most newsworthy, technically superior VNRs succeed in obtaining airtime. (See Chapter 22 for a discussion of video news releases.) Successful VNRs usually feature video footage that would be difficult for a station to obtain, as in these examples:

- A VNR sponsored by OshKosh B'Gosh bib overalls quotes the winner of its Search for the Oldest Bib Overall contest, 89-year-old Claude Mehder, who owns a pair of circa-1901 bibs: "We'll keep having kids, as long as the bib overalls hold up."
- Ringling Brothers & Barnum & Bailey circus clowns helped *PC Computing* magazine conduct the Notebook Torture Test of laptop computers.
- "The Car of the Future," a VNR distributed by D. S. Simon Productions, included DVD video screens, on-board message systems, global positioning, and a home security monitor.

Voice-and-sound news releases for use on radio also are distributed by satellite.

Teleconferencing

The most spectacular use of satellite transmission for public relations purposes is *teleconferencing,* also called *videoconferencing.* A public relations professional can easily arrange a teleconference by employing a firm that specializes in this form of communication. Through it, groups of conferees separated by thousands of miles can interact instantaneously with strong visual impact.

Use of this technique is growing rapidly. Around the United States some 20,000 sites are equipped to handle such events. A traditional conference consists of a group of men and women assembled at a central location for discussion, exchange of information, and inspiration. Participants frequently come from distant points. Their travel costs and hotel bills are often high, they may be plagued by the nuisances of flight reservations and connections, and they may be away from their offices for days.

Satellite-relayed television has changed this concept radically. Now the conferees can remain at their home offices, or gather in groups in nearby cities, and hold their conferences by television. Travel time and cost are reduced or eliminated. In one five-year period, the Boeing Company used teleconferencing for 5699 meetings and eliminated the need for more than 1.5 million miles of travel.

Long-distance discussions among widely separated groups began in the 1930s when the telephone company created conference calls that enabled three or more parties to talk among themselves. The American Telephone & Telegraph Company had videoconferencing in mind when it introduced the ill-fated Picturephone in 1964, but the high cost kept the idea from taking hold. Now the 3G cell phones in Japan enable videophone as a standard feature.

The most widely used form of teleconferencing blends one-way video and two-way audio. This one-way video technology, a form of direct broadcast satellite (DBS), broadcasts a live presentation to many locations simultaneously. DBS is the least expensive method because cameras, transmitters, and other expensive equipment are needed only at one end. The video signal can be received by small, relatively inexpensive antennas at locations around the world via satellite. Figure 12.2 shows, in schematic form, how the satellite transmission works.

Guests at receiving locations view the presentation on large screens. Regular telephone circuits back to the point of origin enable the guests to ask follow-up questions. Teleconferencing also has great potential for employee relations. Ford Motor Company, for example, has installed a $10 million system connecting more than 200 Ford locations in North America. Other companies have similar systems.

Here are examples of teleconferencing in operation:

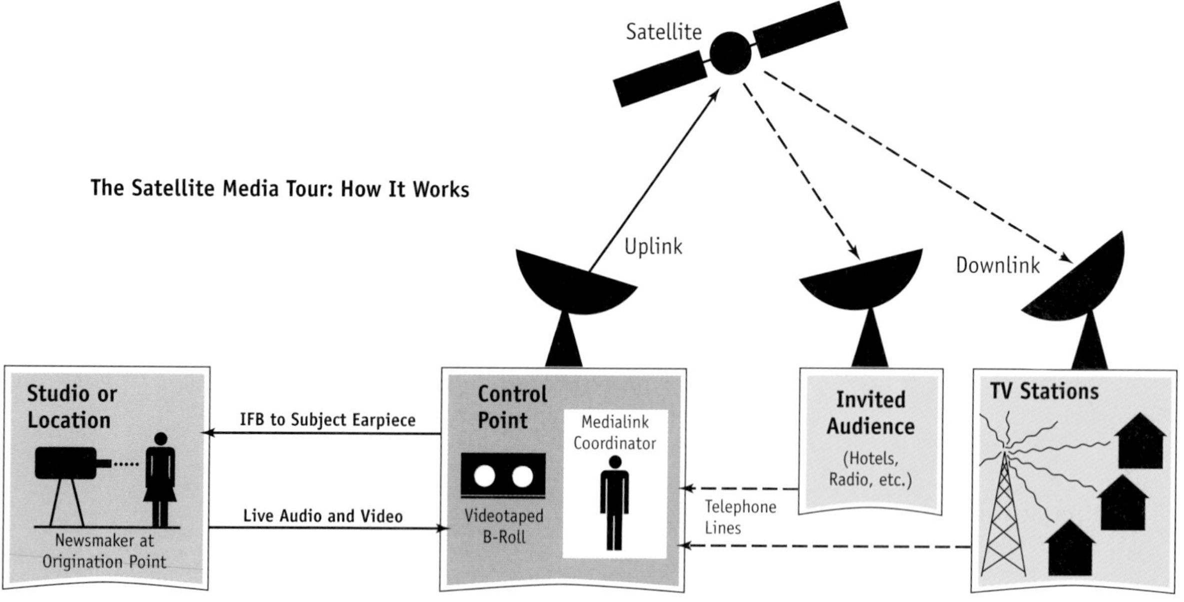

FIGURE 12.2

This diagram explains how a satellite media tour is conducted, enabling the person being interviewed to remain in one place while appearing on screens in other cities. (*Source:* Media Link, Inc.©)

- A midwestern magazine company incurred major costs for expensive executive travel on short notice to its parent company in New York, with as many as five midweek flights. The costs for installation of a Picturetel system were recovered in a matter of months. The system's robotic camera can switch from a wide angle shot of all participants at a large conference table to a full-screen shot of each speaker. The speaker's microphone activates the camera to "zero-in" on him or her while speaking, providing a fairly naturalistic meeting environment in all locations.
- The Whirlpool Corporation in the United States and an N. V. Philips division in the Netherlands needed to explain their new $2 billion joint-venture agreement. So they held an international teleconference for their respective stockholders and employees, the media, and financial analysts.
- Hill and Knowlton, on behalf of several government agencies, arranged a two-hour conference between Cairo, Egypt, and five U.S. cities that permitted several hundred U.S. investors to talk directly with high-ranking Egyptian officials about private investment in that nation.
- To introduce a newly developed hepatitis B vaccine, Merck Sharp & Dohme used a teleconference beamed to more than 400 locations where doctors, health care workers, and reporters had gathered. After watching the presentation, the invited guests telephoned questions to a panel of experts.

A more economical system is the "slow scan" conference. This provides for transmission of still pictures or slides over a telephone circuit between conference points, with voice transmission over a separate line.

To decide whether a teleconference will be cost effective, a potential user should obtain quotations on all expenses involved and then compare these figures to the price of travel, lodging, and entertainment if all employees or invited guests were brought to a central conference location.

Those who use teleconferencing emphasize that it is most effective for reaching large audiences for such purposes as introduction of a product, sales meetings, and announcement of new corporate policies. It lacks the personal warmth that comes from a handshake and a face-to-face conversation.

Webconferencing

Although in its infancy, the Web has become a less expensive alternative for videoconferencing. Called "see-you-see-me" technology, cameras and microphones mounted on the computer monitors of two users enable them to engage in an Internet version of videophone. One of the authors of this text participated in a student's defense of his master's thesis using Microsoft Netshow. Audio was carried by telephone with video displayed on the computer screen via the Web. A 15-second delay in video feed and the student's preference for the comfort and support of a human presence suggest that such conferencing requires further development.

Satellite Media Tours

Instead of having a personality—an actor or author, for example—crisscross the country on an expensive, time-consuming promotional tour, public relations sponsors increasingly use the so-called "satellite tour."

The personality is stationed in a television studio, and TV reporters interview him or her by satellite from their home studios. Two-way television is used, permitting a visual dialogue. Each station's reporter is put through to the personality at a specified time; thus a series of interviews, 5 to 10 minutes each, can be done in sequence. Corporations also employ satellite media tours to promote their products or services, using a well-known performer or other "name" figure as spokesperson. See Figure 12.2.

Before his paralyzing spinal injury, actor Christopher Reeve set an endurance record by doing 45 consecutive interviews at one sitting. Tiresome mentally and physically, no doubt, but much faster and cheaper than visiting all those cities!

Other Tools

Numerous other tools created through electronic technology also are used regularly in public relations practice. New instruments based on digital transmission appear frequently.

Cellular Phones

While driving, a public relations practitioner can conduct business by using a cellular telephone, but does so at risk of personal injury. A cellular system has interlocking low-power transmitters; as a motorist moves from one zone to another, calls from the car are switched by computer into the next zone, permitting continuous nonfading conversations. Interviews on talk radio shows by clients calling from a practitioner's moving car are one attention-getting device. But in one instance, a state representative was recorded on air as he rear-ended a car in stop-and-go traffic. Safety and etiquette are increasingly important objectives in public service announcements from cell phone companies. Safety considerations aside, all phones enable practitioners to be in touch no matter where they go in their busy days.

Personal Digital Assistants (PDAs)

The almost ubiquitous Palm Pilot and other devices such as smart cellphones and pagers provide portable management of traditional information such as calendars and contacts, but also striking new business functions such as the electronic exchange of business cards by infrared beam between Palm Pilots. Web browsing and instant Internet messaging are also increasingly common. Advanced wristwatches can download data from a personal computer, such as the day's meeting schedule or a database of reporters with phone numbers.

The CD-ROM and CD-RW

The CD-ROM (Compact Disc–Read Only Memory), the multimedia version of the familiar compact disc that plays music, contains video, audio, and text on the same surface. With an enormous capacity, the CD-ROM can display up to 300,000 pages of text, color pictures, and graphics.

Although material can be accessed digitally, either on the Web or on CD, many people prefer a tangible product that meets many human needs in ways that virtual information does not yet accomplish. The *Akron Beacon Journal* is selling a CD version of its paper at newsstands in Akron, Ohio, even though it is available on the Web. The offline version loads quickly, looks like the print version, and allows typesize changes. Public relations practitioners should keep the apparent need for tangible communication products in mind when deciding how much information to provide exclusively in digital form.

As an example of the CD-ROM's potential, Yale University Press issued a disc called Perseus for use in teaching Greek language and history. The disc has 25 volumes of Greek text with English translation, a 35,000-word Greek dictionary, and 6000 photos and drawings of architectural sites and artifacts. In Norway, a public health effort to enhance appropriate interaction and respect between boys and girls was modeled in a computer game distributed on CD-ROM. In the United States, alcohol, tobacco, and other drugs are discussed constructively by experts and former addicts in a television talk show format reminiscent of Sally Jesse Raphael's or Jerry Springer's. The difference is that these talk show segments appear on CD-ROM through a program sponsored by the Missouri Institute of Mental Health, enabling repeated viewing and convenient selection of segments. One digital form of the informational brochure is the computer disk, which a person "reads" on a personal computer. Buick, for example, mailed 20,000 disks to users of Apple personal computers to tell them about its new models.

Breakthroughs in software design made it possible for recipients of the Buick disk to "interact" with the information presented. By pushing a few buttons, computer users could load the trunk with luggage and ask questions about mileage, standard equipment, and how the Buick compared with other auto makes.

A "press disk," the computer disk version of a press kit, is being used, but reporters make little use of the novelty. A more efficient use of the disk technique is distribution to targeted audiences that seek information, such as stockholders in corporations that distribute their annual reports on diskettes. As these reports grow in graphic splendor, memory demands outstrip disk drive capacity. Super disks enable multimedia presentation of extensive content. The Zip Disk has become common "coinage" in public relations firms for the transfer of Web pages, graphics, and entire publications among account or project team members.

CD-RWs that allow data to be read and written to the CD much like a computer diskette for data storage are becoming common. Creation of backups of data and delivery to colleagues or clients of very large files such as multimedia presentations are feasible using the CD-RW medium. In addition, small production-runs of CDs, either for distribution to a targeted group or for internal use, facilitate sharing of vast amounts of information with revision of the CD-RW at any time. CD-RWs enable updating and even interaction between the recipient and the creator when the recipient opens files, makes changes or comments, and then returns the CD-RW or replies over the Web.

CD Business Cards enable up to 600 megabytes of information on a CD cut down to business card size that fits in the small circle in the tray of the computer's CD-ROM drive. An agency can present all of its collateral materials about the firm as well as sample campaigns, including video and audio clips, on one business 25 megabyte card (www.avo-card.com).

Electronic Blackboards

Blackboards with chalk now belong to the past as companies use "whiteboards" that serve the same function as facsimile machines. A person can write on a whiteboard with a liquid marker during a presentation, and the image is electronically scanned to allow a printer rapidly to produce multiple copies of the image for future reference.

The electronic whiteboard image can also be transmitted to Webconference participants immediately or after a presentation is complete.

A Peek at the Future of New Technologies

Although it is unwise to predict the future in general, it is even more questionable in a fast-changing world of new media technologies. Nevertheless, it can be useful to anticipate in general what may be coming and what technological advances may mean for public relations professionals.

- *Think digital, but not necessarily online.* Many public relations tools will involve specialized digital devices or media that are not online or are used more frequently offline. For example, digital tablets and digital ink enable online content to be downloaded overnight so that the user can carry the lighweight device on a commuter train. Page loads are instantaneous because there is no download delay, and voice recognition/generation features enable commands and replies. News and other content can be read to the user by the tablet, making better use of professional travel time.
- *Broadband.* Cable and other high-capacity services such as satellite and special telephone lines called DSL service are often called broadband services. Broadband will enable online public relations professionals to meet the eight-second rule for loading time while offering broadcast-quality video and unlimited information stores to media, investors, and other publics.
- *Virtual presence.* Increased online capacity through broadband services will help public relations professionals and Webmasters create virtual environments and emulate the bricks-and-mortar presence of their organizations. Special boxes are becoming commercially available that will generate scents to accompany other elements of virtual reality to give users a sense of presence in a world created by the organization. Activist groups could convey pollution conditions. E-commerce sites could offer a restaurant aura to help users decide what take-out food to order.
- *Processing speed and memory capacity.* Without belaboring the ongoing quest for faster computer chips and larger storage media, it is important to expect that public relations professionals will enjoy digital tools unimagined now. According to a National Public Radio program entitled *Talk of the Nation, Science Friday,* computer processors will be 25 times faster within five years. Quantum computing researchers are manipulating the spin of electrons in atoms to compute and record data at rates 1000 times what we know today. Artificial intelligence to assist with crises, issues management, complex event management, and visual design will become commonplace. Multimedia and unusual hybrid media will meet public relations objectives such as on-demand information and virtual presence, which are currently constrained by machine limitations.
- *Managerial judgment and people skills.* The future holds many changes and advances in communication tools and channels. However, each tool requires an "operator" with good managerial judgment and excellent people skills. In the midst of a new age of electronic wonders, most public relations triumphs will continue to hinge on human creativity.

Summary

The Communications Explosion

In the 1990s, the Internet grew from a means of exchanging scientific information in a relatively small community to become a global communications tool for the masses, blending telephone, television, and the computer into an information superhighway. Two key factors have been the use of fiber optic cable and digital transmission of sound and pictures.

The Computer

The computer has become not just a tool to handle office procedures but also a vehicle into the Internet.

The Internet

One use of the Internet is for communication, both in the form of e-mail and in information delivery and research opportunities. Its reach is worldwide, but it must be kept in mind that Internet content is virtually uncontrolled. There also can be a high level of frustration in research, as well as potential for problems with security and copyright infringement.

Other Computer Uses

Computers can be used by public relations practitioners for dictation and voice generation, expert system programming, management tools such as Gantt charts, processing news releases, e-mail, desktop publishing of newsletters and brochures, mailing lists, online conferencing, the creation of graphics, and facsimile transmission.

Satellite Transmission

Major newspapers are now using satellites to transmit material to regional printing plants. A number of companies are now delivering news releases electronically, including audio and video releases. Teleconferencing is a rapidly growing application of satellite transmission, with about 20,000 U.S. sites equipped to use this technology, saving time and money on business travel.

Other Tools

Other electronic tools include cell phones, personal digital assistants, the CD-ROM and CD-RW, and electronic blackboards.

A Peek at the Future of New Technologies

When anticipating evolving electronic technologies, some trends may include the use of offline digital devices, the growth of broadband services, the development of "virtual presence" capabilities, and expanded processing speed and memory capacity. All these wonders will still require traditional managerial judgment and people skills.

Case Activity: What Would You Do?

Ashland Community Hospital is deeply involved in health education as part of its approach to preventive care. In the past, the hospital has distributed leaflets about various diseases and conducted community seminars on such topics as how to stop smoking, the importance of physical fitness, and how to detect early signs of cancer.

The new technologies, however, now enable the hospital to expand its potential in health education. Write a proposal on how the hospital would use the Internet, the World Wide Web, e-mail, CD-ROM, fax, and diskettes to disseminate health care information to the community.

Questions for Review and Discussion

1. What part of the Internet has "home pages," and what does that term mean?
2. What is the Internet, and what are some of its most promising uses in public relations?
3. Define such terms as broadband, virtual presence, brochureware, listservs, Webcasting, and artificial intelligence.
4. How do you think public relations professionals should address the tangibility factor when pitching stories to reporters?
5. What is the difference between a news release delivery system such as Business Wire and a news service such as the Associated Press?

6. Teleconferencing is growing in popularity. Explain how it operates. How does it differ from Webconferencing? How do you think the two will merge as a result of broadband Internet service?
7. Authors frequently make satellite media tours. How do they work, and why do many authors prefer them to traditional book promotion tours?
8. What impact do you think the tailoring of messages to individual audience members will have on public relations? Will it make our work more difficult? Noticeably more effective? Less ethically sound?
9. As a public relations practitioner, how might you use online computer conference calls?
10. Do you think that new technologies will facilitate or hamper creativity in public relations?

Suggested Readings

"Basic Training: The Internet, A Useful Public Relations Tool." *PR Reporter,* May 13, 1996.

Cameron, Glen T. "The Advisory Board of the Future: Expert Systems in Public Relations." In W. Brody (Ed.), *New Technology and Public Relations.* Sarasota, FL: Institute for Public Relations Research and Education, 1991.

Cooley, Tracy. "Interactive Communication—Public Relations on the Web." *Public Relations Quarterly,* Summer 1999, pp. 41–42.

Coombs, W. Timothy. "The Internet as Potential Equalizer: New Leverage for Confronting Social Irresponsibility." *Public Relations Review,* Fall 1998, pp. 289–304.

Esrock, Stuart L., and Leichty, Greg B. "Social Responsibility and Corporate Web Pages." *Public Relations Review,* Fall 1998, pp. 305–320.

Gordon, Gloria. "Why Go Online? The Real Experience." *Communication World,* February/March, 1997, pp. 14–20.

Howard, Carole M. "Technology and Tabloids: How the New Media World Is Changing Our Jobs," *Public Relations Quarterly,* Spring 2000, pp. 8–12.

"Industry Report on Technology." *Public Relations Journal,* May 1995, p. 235.

Kent, Michael L., and Taylor, Maureen. "Building Dialogic Relationships through the World Wide Web," *Public Relations Review,* Fall 1998, pp. 321–334.

Mickey, Thomas J. "Selling the Internet: A Cultural Studies Approach to Public Relations." *Public Relations Review,* Fall 1998, pp. 335–350.

Rescigno, Jeanne. "Whither the Internet?" *Communication World,* October 1995, pp. 24–27.

Ryan, James. "Hollywood Puts Out a Welcome Mat in Cyberspace." *New York Times,* November 10, 1996, pp. HM20–21.

Weber, Thomas, E. "The Web Is a Dark Horse in Campaign News Race." *Wall Street Journal,* August 29, 1996, pp. B1 and 10.

"The Wild, Wild Web." *Public Relations Tactics,* March 1996, pp. 1, 7–8, 10, 12–15, and 18–22.

Public Relations and the Law

preview

In this chapter the objective is to provide a general understanding of legal considerations involved in public relations and to show students specifically how laws on defamation, copyright, and trademarks, as well as government agency regulations, affect the distribution of messages.

Topics covered in this chapter include:

- A sampling of legal problems
- Libel and defamation
- Invasion of privacy
- Copyright law and trademark law
- Regulations of government agencies, including the Federal Trade Commission and Securities and Exchange Commission
- Corporate/employee free speech
- Liability for sponsored events
- Working with lawyers

A Sampling of Legal Problems

The law and its many ramifications are somewhat abstract to the average person. Many people may have difficulty imagining exactly how public relations personnel can run afoul of the law or generate a suit, simply by communicating information.

To bring things down to earth and to make this chapter more meaningful, we provide here a sampling of recent government regulatory agency cases and lawsuits that involved public relations materials and the work of practitioners:

- The Princeton Dental Resource Center paid a $25,000 settlement after the New York attorney general's office charged the organization with making false and misleading claims in its newsletter.
- Labtest International, a New Jersey firm, was ordered by a U.S. District Court to pay $111,000 to Washington Business Information, Inc., for copyright infringement. It had illegally photocopied the company's weekly *Product Safety Letter.*
- The Securities and Exchange Commission (SEC) stopped the mailing of 45,000 prospectuses from Krupp Securities of Boston because the company had attached a sales brochure to the prospectus, a violation of SEC guidelines.
- The estate of the late children's author, Dr. Seuss, won a $1.5 million judgment against a Los Angeles T-shirt maker for infringement of copyright. The manufacturer portrayed a parody of Dr. Seuss's Cat in the Hat character smoking marijuana and giving the peace sign.
- The owner of a Detroit public relations firm, asked to write a news release about an impending corporate merger, ran afoul of SEC regulations when he used the confidential information to purchase stock before the merger became public.
- The Rock and Roll Hall of Fame, in Cleveland, filed a trademark infringement suit against a photographer who snapped a picture of the unique building at sunset and sold posters of his work.
- A Kentucky couple filed a $240,000 complaint against Merrill Lynch for invasion of privacy, claiming that they were in the background of a photograph used in an advertisement.
- The Federal Trade Commission filed false advertising charges against three national diet firms after they failed to provide factual evidence that clients actually achieved weight-loss goals or maintained the loss.

These examples provide some idea of the legal pitfalls that a public relations person may encounter. Many of the charges were eventually dismissed or settled out of court, but the organizations paid dearly for the adverse publicity and the expense of defending themselves.

Public relations personnel must be aware that they can be held legally liable if they provide advice or tacitly support an illegal activity of a client or employer. This area of liability is called *conspiracy.* A public relations person can be named as a coconspirator with other organizational officials if he or she:

- participates in an illegal action such as bribing a government official or covering up information of vital interest to the public health and safety

- counsels and guides the policy behind an illegal action
- takes a major personal part in the illegal action
- helps establish a "front group" whereby the connection to the public relations firm or its clients is kept hidden
- cooperates in any other way to further an illegal action

These five concepts, it is emphasized, also apply to public relations firms that create, produce, and distribute materials on behalf of clients. The courts have ruled on more than one occasion that public relations firms cannot hide behind the defense of "the client told me to do it." Public relations firms have a legal responsibility to practice "due diligence" in the type of information and documentation supplied by a client. Regulatory agencies such as the Federal Trade Commission (discussed shortly) have the power under the Lanham Act to file charges against public relations firms that distribute false and misleading information.

Libel and Defamation

Public relations professionals should be thoroughly familiar with the concepts of libel and slander. Such knowledge is crucial if an organization's internal and external communications are to meet legal and regulatory standards with a minimum of legal complications.

Traditionally, *libel* was a printed falsehood and *slander* was an oral statement that was false. Today, as a practical matter, there is little difference in the two, and the courts often use *defamation* as a collective term.

Essentially, defamation is any false statement about a person (or organization) that creates public hatred, contempt, ridicule, or inflicts injury on reputation. A person filing a libel suit usually must prove that: (1) the false statement was communicated to others through print, broadcast, or electronic means; (2) the person was identified or is

global PR

In China, Product Liability Depends on News Coverage

Public relations professionals, when operating in any nation, must be familiar with local laws that can affect their activities. In China, for example, press reports can be introduced as evidence to prove claims of product liability.

So, if a person wants to sue a company for a faulty product, one common strategy is to get the story in the press. Defendants in such cases have no choice but also to get press coverage or convince Chinese editors not to run a story.

A *Wall Street Journal* article on product liability in China notes: "Building good relations with the press is one way to head off potential lawsuits. When a Shanghai fast-food customer took a fly in his fish fillet to the newspaper because the U.S. restaurant chain refused to compensate him, the restaurant's manager called local editors to explain his side of the story. No article ran and no suit was filed."

identifiable; (3) there is actual injury in the form of money losses, loss of reputation, or mental suffering; and (4) the person making the statement was malicious or negligent.

In general, private citizens have more success winning defamation suits than public figures or corporations. With public figures—government officials, entertainers, political candidates, and other newsworthy personalities—there is the extra test of whether the libelous statements were made with actual malice (*New York Times* v. *Sullivan*).

Corporations, to some degree, are also considered "public figures" by the courts for several reasons: (1) They engage in advertising and promotion offering products and services to the public, (2) they are often involved in matters of public controversy and public policy, and (3) they have some degree of access to the media—through regular advertising and news releases—that enables them to respond and rebut defamatory charges made against them.

This is not to say that corporations don't win lawsuits regarding defamation. A good example is General Motors, which filed a multimillion-dollar defamation suit against NBC after the network's *Dateline* news program carried a story about gas tanks on GM pickup trucks exploding in side-impact collisions.

GM's general counsel, in a news conference, meticulously provided evidence that NBC had inserted toy rocket "igniters" in the gas tanks, understated the vehicle speed at the moment of impact, and wrongly claimed that the fuel tanks could be easily ruptured. Within 24 hours after the suit was filed, NBC caved in. It agreed to air a nine-minute apology on the news program and pay GM $2 million to cover the cost of its investigation.

Increasingly, corporations are using fraud and contract law to sue news organizations, instead of pursuing harder-to-prove libel claims. In *Food Lion* v. *Capital Cities/ABC* (1995), for example, the grocery chain was awarded $315,000 after it sued ABC News for fraud and trespassing; two TV producers had lied on job applications and hidden cameras in their wigs to report an expose on alleged health violations at several stores. In another case, a federal judge in Cincinnati ruled that a *Business Week* reporter lied and breached a contract with a credit-reporting agency while writing a cover story on privacy.

Avoiding Libel Suits

There is little investigative reporting in public relations, but libel suits can be filed against organizational officials who make libelous accusations during a media interview, send out news releases that make false statements, or injure someone's reputation.

Some executives have been sorry that they lost control during a news conference and called the leaders of a labor union "a bunch of crooks and compulsive liars." Suits have been filed for calling a news reporter "a pimp for all environmental groups." Such language, while highly quotable and colorful, can provoke legal retaliation, merited or not.

Accurate information, and a delicate choice of words, must be used in news releases. For example, a former employee of J. Walter Thompson advertising agency claimed she was libeled in an agency news release that stated she had been dismissed because of financial irregularities in the department she headed. Eventually, the $20 million lawsuit was dismissed because she couldn't prove that the agency acted in a "grossly irresponsible manner."

In situations involving personnel, organizations often try to avoid lawsuits by saying that an employee left "for personal reasons" or to "pursue other interests," even if the real reason was incompetence or a record of sexual harassment. News releases and product publicity should also be written in accordance with FTC and SEC regulations, to be discussed shortly.

Another potentially dangerous practice is making unflattering comments about the competition's products. Although comparative advertising is the norm in the United States, a company must walk a narrow line between comparison and "trade libel," or "product disparagement." Statements should be truthful, with factual evidence and scientific demonstration available to substantiate them. Companies often charge competitors with overstepping the boundary between "puffery" and "factual representation."

An organization can offer the opinion that a particular product or service is the "best" or "a revolutionary development" if the context clearly shows that the communication is a statement of opinion attributed to someone. Then it is classified as "puffery" and doesn't require factual evidence.

Along the same line, a statement of opinion also has a degree of legal protection through the First Amendment guarantee of freedom of speech. In one case, the owner of the New York Yankees was sued for libel by a baseball umpire when a team news release called him a "scab" who "has had it in" for the Yankees. A lower court awarded damages, but the New York Supreme Court overturned the judgment, ruling that the comments in the new release constituted protected statements of opinion under the fair comment concept.

Don Sneed, Tim Wulfemeyer, and Harry Stonecipher, in a *Public Relations Review* article, say that a news release should be written to indicate clearly statements of opinion and statements of fact. They suggest that (1) opinion statements be accompanied by the facts upon which the opinions are based, (2) statements of opinion be clearly labeled as such, and (3) the context of the language surrounding the expression of opinion be reviewed for possible legal implications.

The Fair Comment Defense

Organizations can do much to assure that their communications avoid materials that could lead to potential lawsuits. By the same token, organizations are somewhat limited in their ability to use legal measures to defend themselves against criticism.

Executives are often incensed when an environmental group includes their corporation on its annual "dirty dozen" polluters or similar lists. Executives are also unhappy when a broadcast consumer affairs reporter flatly calls the product a "rip-off."

A corporate reputation may be damaged and product sales may go down, but a defamation case is difficult to win because, as previously mentioned, the accuser must prove actual malice. Also operating is the concept of fair comment and criticism.

This defense is used by theater and music critics when they lambaste a play or concert. Fair comment also means that when companies and individuals voluntarily display their wares to the public for sale or consumption, they have no real recourse against criticism done with honest purpose and lack of malicious intent.

A utility company in Indiana, for example, once tried to sue a citizen who wrote a letter to a newspaper criticizing it for seeking a rate hike. The judge threw the suit out of court, stating that the rate increase was a "matter of public interest and concern" even if the letter writer didn't have all the facts straight.

Invasion of Privacy

An area of law that particularly applies to employees of an organization is *invasion of privacy*. Public relations staff must be particularly sensitive to the issue of privacy in at least four areas: (1) employee newsletters, (2) photo releases, (3) product publicity and advertising, and (4) media inquiries about employees.

Employee Newsletters

It is no longer true, if it ever was, that an organization has an unlimited right to publicize the activities of its employees. In fact, Morton J. Simon, a Philadelphia lawyer and author of *Public Relations Law*, wrote, "It should not be assumed that a person's status as an employee waives his right to privacy." Simon correctly points out that a company newsletter or magazine does not enjoy the same First Amendment protection that the news media enjoy when they claim "newsworthiness" and "public interest." A number of court cases, he says, show that company newsletters are considered commercial tools of trade.

PR insights

Litigation PR: The New Game in Town

One of the newer specialties in public relations practice is *litigation public relations* (LPR). According to Mary Gottschall, a legal affairs correspondent for the *New York Times*, "This has emerged as an increasing trend, especially where major litigation is involved. The idea is that the case might be tried in the court of public opinion as well as before the jury."

Dirk Gibson, a professor at the University of New Mexico, says four types of legal proceedings are likely to elicit significant publicity: tabloid-type titillating cases; shocking, heinous crimes; cases with celebrity victims; and cases with celebrity defendants. The O. J. Simpson murder trial, for example, involved considerable LPR as lawyers on both sides continually held news conferences and leaked information to the media. In the JonBenet Ramsey murder case, the parents of the murdered child hired not only lawyers but also a public relations counselor to defend themselves against leaks by the district attorney's office that they were under suspicion.

More recently, the year-long sparring between Independent Counsel Kenneth Starr and President Clinton (see Chapter 15) involved considerable public relations activity as each side tried to bolster its case in the court of public opinion. William Ginsburg, a trial attorney who first represented Monica Lewinsky, gave so many press interviews that he suffered from overexposure and was eventually replaced.

Corporations have also realized the value of LPR when litigation attracts extensive media coverage. Microsoft and its chairman, Bill Gates, not only hired a platoon of lawyers to do battle with the U.S. Justice Department about monopoly and antitrust but also hired several public relations firms to present the company's case to the public. Good public relations is needed, experts say, because surveys show that nearly one-third of the public believes an organization is automatically guilty after being accused of wrongdoing.

Hill and Knowlton, responding to the trend toward more publicized and potentially damaging lawsuits, has even created an LPR specialty group to help clients sway public opinion. Jim Cox, head of the new group, told *PR Tactics*: "Litigation communications is something whose time has come. More people are willing to sue and when they do they are more likely to sue big corporations. Big Business needs to defend itself and not naively believe they will have their day in court."

This distinction does not impede the effectiveness of newsletters, but it does indicate editors should try to keep employee stories organization-oriented. Indeed, most lawsuits and complaints are generated by "personals columns" that may invade the privacy of employees. Although a mention that Joe Doaks honeymooned in Hawaii or that Mary Worth is now a great-grandmother may sound completely innocent, the individuals involved—for any number of reasons—may consider the information a violation of their privacy. The situation may be further compounded into possible defamation by "cutesy" editorial asides in poor taste.

In sum, one should avoid anything that might embarrass or subject an employee to ridicule by fellow employees. Here are some guidelines to remember when writing about employee activities:

- Keep the focus on organization-related activities.
- Have employees submit "personals" in writing.
- Double-check all information for accuracy.
- Ask: "Will this embarrass anyone or cause someone to be the butt of jokes?"
- Don't rely on secondhand information; confirm the facts with the person involved.
- Don't include racial or ethnic designations of employees in any articles.

Photo Releases

Ordinarily, a public relations practitioner doesn't need a signed release if a person gives "implied consent" by posing for a picture and is told how it will be used. This is particularly true for "news" photographs published in internal newsletters.

Public relations departments, however, should take the precaution of (1) filing all photographs, (2) dating them, and (3) giving the context of the situation. This precludes the use of old photos that could embarrass employees or subject them to ridicule. In other cases, it precludes using photographs of persons who are no longer employed or have died. This method also helps to make certain that a photo taken for the employee newsletter isn't used in an advertisement.

If a photo of an employee or customer is used in product publicity, sales brochures, or advertisements, the standard practice is to obtain a signed release. Here is a simplified release used by Hewlett-Packard Company:

> I grant to Hewlett-Packard Company ("HP"), its representatives and employees the right to take photographs of me and my property in connection with the above identified subject and I authorize HP, its assigns and transferees to copyright, use, and publish the same in print and/or electronically.
>
> I agree that HP may use such photographs of me with or without my name and for any lawful purpose, including for example, such purposes as publicity, illustration, and advertising.

Next we discuss the use of photographs and testimonials in an advertising context.

Product Publicity and Advertising

As already noted, an organization must have a signed release on file if it wants to use the photographs or comments of employees and other individuals in product publicity, sales brochures, and advertising. An added precaution is to give some financial compensation to make a more binding contract.

Chemical Bank of New York unfortunately learned this lesson the hard way. The bank used pictures of 39 employees in various advertisements designed to "humanize" the bank's image, but the employees maintained that no one had requested permission to use their photos in advertisements. Another problem was that the pictures had been taken up to five years before they began appearing in the series of advertisements.

An attorney for the employees, who sued for $600,000 in damages, said, "The bank took the individuality of these employees and used that individuality to make a profit." The judge agreed and ruled that the bank had violated New York's privacy law. The action is called *misappropriation of personality,* which is discussed later in this chapter. Jerry Della Femina, an advertising executive, succinctly makes the point: Get permission. "If I used my mother in an ad," he said, "I'd get her permission—and I almost trust her 100 percent."

Written permission also should be obtained if the employee's photograph is to appear in sales brochures or even in the corporate annual report. This rule also applies to other situations. A graduate of Lafayette College sued the college for using a photo of his mother and him at graduation ceremonies, without their permission, in a financial aid brochure.

Media Inquiries about Employees

Because press inquiries have the potential of invading an employee's right of privacy, public relations personnel should follow basic guidelines as to what information will be provided on the employee's behalf.

In general, employers should give a news reporter only basic information. This may include (1) confirmation that the person is an employee, (2) the person's title and job description, and (3) date of beginning employment, or, if applicable, date of termination.

Unless it is specified by law or permission is given by the employee, a public relations person should avoid providing information about an employee's (1) salary, (2) home address, (3) marital status, (4) number of children, (5) organizational memberships, and (6) job performance.

If a reporter does seek any of this information, because of the nature of the story, several methods may be followed.

First, a public relations person can volunteer to contact the employee and have the person speak directly with the reporter. What the employee chooses to tell the reporter is not then a company's responsibility. Second, many organizations do provide additional information to a reporter if it is included on an optional biographical sheet that the employee has filled out. In most cases, the form clearly states that the organization may use any of the information in answering press inquiries or writing its own news releases. A typical biographical form may have sections in which the employee can list his or her (1) honors and awards, (2) professional memberships, (3) marital status and names of any children, (4) previous employers, (5) educational background, and (6) hobbies or interests. This sheet should not be confused with the person's official employment application, which must remain confidential.

If an organization uses biographical sheets, it is important that they be dated and kept current. A sheet compiled by an employee five years previously may be hopelessly out of date. This is also true of *file photographs* taken at the time of a person's employment.

PR insights

Ford/Firestone: Lawyers vs. PR

The situation is typical. The company is in trouble about the safety of its product. The lawyers, fearful of liability and lawsuits, say admitting any mistakes or apologizing for them can be a handicap in a court of law. Crisis communications experts, on the other hand, argue that management should publicly take responsibility, apologize to its customers, and fix the problem.

This tug-of-war between lawyers and public relations professionals is common, and the legal department often prevails. This was evident in the Firestone/Ford tire recall case. Both companies faced potential lawsuits totaling billions of dollars that could ultimately bankrupt them. At the same time, they were losing sales and stock value because the public thought they were hiding something and pointing the finger of blame at each other. As Larry Kamer, principal of the GCI Kamer-Singer, told *PRWeek*, "The public can smell communication that sounds like it was driven by lawyers."

Indeed, many crisis communication experts say Firestone got a black eye early on because the company was slow to accept responsibility; it even blamed tire failures on consumers because they under-inflated the tires. Later on, Firestone shifted the blame to Ford and accused the automaker of making unsafe vehicles that easily rolled over when a tire failed. Indeed, the vice president of public affairs for Firestone during this time was a lawyer who previously was chief counsel for the company.

Ford's public relations strategy, however, was also shaped by the legal department. From the very beginning, Ford made every effort to distance itself from Firestone's problem by having the CEO issue statements like, "This is a tire issue, not a vehicle issue," and telling the press that Firestone was not being forthright about tire failure data.

The experts say, however, that an organization's credibility is much broader than a point of law. As John Frank of *PRWeek* notes, "Some crisis experts say corporate PR people have to get senior management to think beyond the short-term costs of lawsuits to the long-term public-image damage a crisis can produce."

Copyright Law

Should a news release be copyrighted? How about a corporate annual report? Can a *New Yorker* cartoon be used in the company magazine without permission? What about reprinting an article from *Fortune* magazine and distributing it to the company's sales staff? Are government reports copyrighted? What constitutes copyright infringement?

These are some of the bothersome questions that a public relations professional should be able to answer. Knowledge of copyright law is important from two perspectives: (1) what organizational materials should be copyrighted and (2) how correctly to utilize the copyrighted materials of others.

Before going into these areas, however, it is important to know what copyright means. In very simple terms, *copyright* means protection of a creative work from unauthorized use. A section of the U.S. copyright law of 1978 states: "Copyright protection subsists . . . in the original works of authorship fixed in any tangible medium of expression now known or later developed." The word *authorship* is defined in seven categories: (1) literary works; (2) musical works; (3) dramatic works; (4) pantomimes and choreographic works; (5) pictorial, graphic, or sculptural works; (6) motion pictures; and (7) sound recordings. The word *fixed* means that the work is sufficiently permanent or stable to permit it to be perceived, reproduced, or otherwise communicated.

The shield of copyright protection was reduced somewhat in 1991 when the Supreme Court ruled unanimously that directories, computer databases, and other compilations of facts may be copied and republished unless they display "some minimum degree of creativity." The court stated, "Raw facts may be copied at will."

Thus a copyright does not protect ideas, but only the specific ways in which those ideas are expressed. An idea for promoting a product, for example, cannot be copyrighted—but brochures, drawings, news features, animated cartoons, display booths, photographs, recordings, videotapes, corporate symbols, slogans, and the like that express a particular idea can be copyrighted.

Because much money, effort, time, and creative talent are spent on organizational materials, copyright protection is important. By copyrighting materials, a company can prevent competitors from capitalizing on its creative work or producing a facsimile brochure that tends to mislead the public. A manufacturer of personal computers would be in serious legal difficulties if it began distributing sales brochures that tended to look just like ones from Apple Computer. (The concept of trademark infringement [such as copying the Apple logo with slight changes] will be discussed in the section titled "Trademark Law.")

The 1978 law presumes that material produced in some tangible form is copyrighted from the moment it is created. This is particularly true if the material bears a copyright notice. One of the following methods may be employed:

- Using the letter "c" in a circle (©), followed by the word *copyright.*
- Citing the year of copyright and the name of the owner.

This presumption of copyright is often sufficient to discourage unauthorized use, and the writer or creator of the material has some legal protection if he or she can prove that the material was created before another person claims it.

A more formal step, providing full legal protection, is official registration of the copyrighted work within three months after creation. This is done by depositing two copies of the manuscript (it is not necessary that it has been published), recording, or artwork with the Copyright Office, Library of Congress, Washington, DC 20559. Copyright registration forms are available from U.S. post offices. Registration is not a condition of copyright protection, but it is a prerequisite to an infringement action against unauthorized use by others.

Copyright protection of a work lasts for the life of the author plus 50 years, and no longer. Material copyrighted by a business or organization is protected for 75 years from the time the material is published. In 1998, Congress passed and the President signed the Copyright Term Extension Act, which extends the period of copyright protection on existing copyrightable material by another 20 years. The Disney organization, in particular, lobbied hard for the extension because it kept Mickey Mouse and all his friends out of the public domain. The legislation, complains law professor Richard Epstein, was " . . . a gift of billions of dollars in future revenues" to a "grateful Disney."

In early 2002, however, the U.S. Supreme Court decided to hear a case (*Eldred* v. *Ashcraft*) challenging the 20-year extension rule on existing material. According to the *New York Times,* "At issue is whether Congress overstepped its authority to grant copyrights 'for limited times' to 'promote the progress of science and useful arts.'" The case pits publishers and media companies, who support extension of copyright, against libraries and other organizations who believe material should be more widely available for public use. As one academic told the *New York Times,* " . . . copyright is supposed to work for the public and not a small set of corporations."

Fair Use versus Infringement

Public relations people are in the business of gathering information from a variety of sources, so it is important to know where *fair use* ends and *infringement* begins.

Fair use means that part of a copyrighted article may be quoted directly, but the quoted material must be brief in relation to the length of the original work. It may be, for example, only one paragraph in a 750-word article and up to 300 words in a long article or book chapter. Complete attribution of the source must be given regardless of the length of the quotation. If the passage is quoted verbatim, quote marks must be used.

It is important to note, however, that the concept of fair use has distinct limitations if part of the copyrighted material is to be used in advertisements and promotional brochures. In this case, permission is required. It also is important for the original source to approve the context in which the quote is used. A quote out of context often runs into legal trouble if it implies endorsement of a product or service.

The copyright law does allow limited copying of a work for fair use such as criticism, comment, or research. However, in recent years, the courts have considerably narrowed the concept of "fair use" when multiple copies of a copyrighted work are involved.

A landmark case was a successful lawsuit in 1991 by book publishers against Kinko's, a national chain of photocopying stores. The chain was charged with copyright infringement because it reproduced excerpts from books without permission and sold them in anthologies to college students. Although Kinko's argued "fair use" for educational purposes, the court rejected this defense. The court settlement cost Kinko's $500,000 in damages and almost $1.5 million in legal fees.

Even the unauthorized photocopying of newsletters and published articles can cost the organization large sums of money. Texaco, for example, lost a lawsuit filed by publishers of scientific journals, who claimed that the company violated the copyright law by permitting employees to photocopy articles for their files.

Organizations that have a single subscription to a newsletter, then circulate it via in-house e-mail, also violate the law. Atlas Telecom paid a $100,000 settlement after admitting that it electronically distributed about a dozen telecommunications newsletters to its employees. According to the suit filed by Phillips Publishing, Inc., the company made hundreds of copies by reproducing the newsletters on the in-house database.

Such lawsuits can be avoided if an organization orders quantity reprints from the publisher or pays a licensing fee permitting it to make paper or electronic copies.

The same concept applies to videotaping television shows or news programs. The Supreme Court has ruled that it is "fair use" to make a videotape of a television show for later personal viewing, but a public relations staff must get permission from the television producer if widespread use of the videotape is planned. Adolph A. Coors Company paid $40,000 to CBS-TV for the right to show a videotape throughout the country of a *60 Minutes* segment about the company.

Government documents (city, county, state, and federal) are in the public domain and cannot be copyrighted. Public relations personnel, under the fair use doctrine, can freely use quotations and statistics from a government document, but care must be exercised to ensure that the material is in context and not misleading. The most common problem occurs when an organization uses a government report as a form of endorsement for its services or products. An airline, for example, might cite a government study showing that it provides the most service to customers, but neglect to state the basis of comparison or other factors.

Photography and Artwork

The copyright law makes it clear that freelance and commercial photographers retain ownership of their work. In other words, a customer who buys a copyrighted photo owns the item itself, but not the right to make additional copies. That right remains with the photographer unless transferred in writing.

In a further extension of this right, the duplication of copyrighted photos is also illegal. This was established in a 1990 U.S. Federal District Court case in which the Professional Photographers of America (PP of A) sued a nationwide photofinishing firm for ignoring copyright notices on pictures sent for additional copies.

Freelance photographers generally charge for a picture on the basis of its use. If it is used only once, perhaps for an employee newsletter, the fee is low. If, however, the company wants to use the picture in the corporate annual report or on the company calendar, the fee may be considerably higher. Consequently it is important for a public relations person to tell the photographer exactly how the picture will be used. Arrangements and fees then can be determined for (1) one-time use, (2) unlimited use, or (3) the payment of royalties every time the picture is used.

Computer manipulation of original artwork can also violate copyright. One photographer's picture of a racing yacht was used on a poster after the art director electronically changed the numbers on the sail and made the water a deeper blue. In another case, a photo distribution agency successfully sued *Newsday* for unauthorized use of a color image after the newspaper reconstructed the agency's picture using a computer scanner, then failed to credit the photographer. FPG International was awarded $20,000 in damages, ten times the initial licensing fee of $2000. In sum, slightly changing a copyrighted photo or a piece of artwork can be considered a violation of copyright if the intent is to capitalize on widespread recognition of the original art.

A less clear-cut issue is the use of art masterpieces that are considered to be in the public domain. Is it all right to use a reproduction of Grant Wood's "American Gothic" in an advertisement or a brochure? Or, is it acceptable to insert a Hershey candy bar in the hand of a van Gogh self-portrait?

Although art museums normally don't have copyright claims on art masterpieces in their collections, they do try to control the commercial use of color transparencies. These provide much higher-quality reproduction in an art book than would a postcard or a photograph. In many cases, if a museum approves the intended use, it charges a licensing fee for the use of original color transparencies. Public relations personnel who decide to use art masterpieces in organizational materials should also consider what is appropriate and in good taste.

The Rights of Freelance Writers

Although the rights of freelance photographers have been established for some years, it was only recently that freelance writers gained more control over the ownership of their work.

In the now famous Reid Case (*Community for Creative Nonviolence* v. *Reid*), the U.S. Supreme Court in 1989 ruled that writers retained ownership of their work and that purchasers of it simply gained a "license" to reproduce the copyrighted work.

Prior to this ruling, the common practice was to assume that commissioned articles were "work for hire" and the purchaser owned the copyright. In other words, a magazine could reproduce the article in any number of ways and even sell it to another publication without the writer's permission.

Under the new interpretation, ownership of a writer's work is subject to negotiation and contractual agreement. Writers may agree to assign all copyright rights to the work they have been hired to do, or they may give permission only for a specific one-time use.

In a related matter, freelance writers are pressing for additional compensation if an organization puts their work on CD-ROM, online databases, or the Internet's World Wide Web. They won a major victory in 2001 when the Supreme Court (*New York Times* v. *Tasni*) ruled that publishers, by making articles accessible through electronic databases, infringed the copyrights of freelance contributors.

Public relations firms and corporate public relations departments are responsible for ensuring compliance with the copyright law. This means that all agreements with a freelance writer must be in writing, and the use of the material must be clearly stated. Ideally, public relations personnel should negotiate multiple rights and even complete ownership of the copyright.

Copyright Issues on the Internet

The emergence of the information superhighway, particularly the Internet and World Wide Web, has raised new issues about the protection of intellectual property. Three issues regarding copyright are: (1) the downloading of copyrighted material, (2) the unauthorized uploading of such material, and (3) the responsibilities of online carriers to police copyright violations.

The Downloading of Material In general, the same rules apply to cyberspace as to more earthbound methods of expressing and disseminating ideas. Original materials in digital form are still protected by copyright. The fair-use limits for materials found on the Internet are essentially the same as the fair use of materials disseminated by any other means.

Related to this is the use of news articles and features that are sent via e-mail or the Web to the clients of clipping services. An organization may use such clips to track its publicity efforts, but it can't distribute the article on its own Web site or intranet without permission and a royalty payment to the publication where the article appeared. One national clipping service, Burrelle's, has already made an agreement with more than 300 newspapers to have their customers pay a small royalty fee in exchange for being able to make photocopies of clippings and make greater use of them.

The Uploading of Material In many cases, owners of copyrighted material have uploaded various kinds of information with the intention of making it freely available. Some examples are software, games, and even the entire text of *The Hitchhiker's Guide to the Galaxy*. The problem comes, however, when third parties upload copyrighted material without permission. Consequently, copyright holders are increasingly patrolling the Internet and World Wide Web to stop the unauthorized use of material. Some examples:

- Dutton Children's Books threatened a lawsuit against a New Mexico State University student for using Winnie the Pooh illustrations on his home page.
- Paramount Pictures sent warning notes to *Star Trek* fans against using the Internet to disseminate photos from the TV series.
- Elvis Presley Enterprises ordered the removal of sound clips of "Blue Suede Shoes" and "Hound Dog" from a home page that also displayed images from Graceland postcards.

The unauthorized use of copyrighted material on the Internet has led to calls for Congress to update the existing law to cover online information. One measure considered by the Senate would make it illegal to evade copyright protections built into electronically distributed material.

The Liability of Online Services An even stickier problem is the liability of online services if a subscriber violates copyright law by uploading material owned by others. The issue has not yet been fully tested in the courts. One federal judge in California, however, ruled that Netcom On-Line Communication Services, Inc. could be held liable for "contributory copyright infringement" because it failed to stop a subscriber from posting the Church of Scientology's copyrighted texts on the Internet.

Advocates of computer users' civil rights, such as the Electronic Frontier Foundation, assert that holding online service companies responsible for content would cause a chilling effect on free speech and stifle the vast potential of the Internet as a communication medium. The arguments, pro and con, promise to keep the courts busy for several years.

Copyright Guidelines

A number of points have been discussed about copyright. A public relations person should keep the following in mind:

- Ideas cannot be copyrighted, but the expression of those ideas can be.
- Major public relations materials (brochures, annual reports, videotapes, motion pictures, position papers, and the like) should be copyrighted, if only to prevent unauthorized use by competitors.
- Although there is a concept of *fair use,* any copyrighted material intended directly to advance the sales and profits of an organization should not be used unless permission is given.
- Copyrighted material should not be taken out of context, particularly if it implies endorsement of the organization's services or products.
- Quantity reprints of an article should be ordered from the publisher.
- Permission is required to use segments of television programs or motion pictures.
- Permission must be obtained to use segments of popular songs (written verses or sound recordings) from a recording company.
- Photographers and freelance writers retain the rights to their works. Permission and fees must be negotiated to use works for other purposes than originally agreed upon.
- Photographs of current celebrities or those who are now deceased cannot be used for promotion and publicity purposes without permission.
- Permission is required to reprint cartoon characters, such as Snoopy or Garfield. In addition, cartoons and other artwork or illustrations in a publication are copyrighted.
- Government documents are not copyrighted, but caution is necessary if the material is used in a way that implies endorsement of products or services.
- Private letters, or excerpts from them, cannot be published or used in sales and publicity materials without the permission of the letter writer.

- Original material posted on the Internet and the World Wide Web has copyright protection.
- The copyrighted material of others should not be posted on the Internet unless specific permission is granted.

Trademark Law

What do the names Coca-Cola, Marlboro, and IBM, the Olympic rings, and the logo of the Dallas Cowboys have in common? They are all registered trademarks protected by law.

A trademark is a word, symbol, or slogan, used singly or in combination, that identifies a product's origin. According to Susan L. Cohen, writing in *Editor & Publisher's* annual trademark supplement, "It also serves as an indicator of quality, a kind of shorthand for consumers to use in recognizing goods in a complex marketplace." Research indicates, for example, that 53 percent of Americans say brand quality takes precedence over price considerations.

The concept of a trademark is nothing new. The ancient Egyptians carved marks into the stones of the pyramids, and the craftsmen of the Middle Ages used guild marks to identify the source and quality of products.

What is new, however, is the proliferation of trademarks and service marks in modern society. Coca-Cola may be the world's most recognized trademark, according to some studies, but it is only one of almost one million active trademarks registered with the federal Patent and Trademark Office. And, according to the International Trademark Association, the number keeps going up at a rapid rate.

The Protection of Trademarks

Trademarks are always capitalized and never used as nouns. They are always used as adjectives modifying nouns. For example, the proper terms are Kleenex tissues, Xerox copies, and Rollerblade skates. A person who "uses a Kleenex," "makes a Xerox," or "goes Rollerblading" is violating trademark law.

PR casebook

Use the Logo, Pay the Fee

Sports logos are registered trademarks, and a licensing fee must be paid before anyone can use logos for commercial products and promotions.

Teams in the National Football League and the National Basketball Association earn more than $3 billion annually just selling licensed merchandise, and the sale of college and university trademarked goods is rapidly approaching that mark. Schools such as Notre Dame, Michigan, and Ohio State rake in more than $3 million a year in royalties from licensing their logos to be placed on everything from beer mugs to T-shirts.

The penalty for not paying a licensing fee is steep. The NFL, during Super Bowl week, typically confiscates about $1 million in bogus goods and files criminal charges against the offending vendors.

In addition, organizations take the step of designating brand names and slogans with various marks. The registered trademark symbol is a superscript, small capital "R" in a circle—®. "Registered in U.S. Patent and Trademark Office" and "Reg. U.S. Pat. Off" may also be used. A "TM" in small capital letters indicates a trademark that isn't registered. It represents a company's common-law claim to a right of trademark, or a trademark for which registration is pending.

A service mark is like a trademark, but it designates a service rather than a product, or is a logo. An "SM" in small capitals in a circle— ℠ —is the symbol for a registered service mark. If registration is pending, the "SM" should be used without the circle.

These symbols are used in advertising, product labeling, news releases, company brochures, and so on to let the public and competitors know that a name, slogan, or symbol is protected by law. See the ad on this page for an example of how organizations publicize their trademarks and service marks.

Public relations practitioners play an important role in protecting the trademarks of their employers. They safeguard trademarks and respect nonorganizational trademarks in the following ways:

- Ensure that company trademarks are capitalized and used properly in all organizational literature and graphics. Lax supervision can cause loss of trademark protection.
- Distribute trademark brochures to editors and reporters and place advertisements in trade publications, designating names to be capitalized.
- Educate employees as to what the organization's trademarks are and how to use them correctly.

FedEx® Is Not Synonymous With Overnight Shipping.

That's why you can't FedEx or Federal Express your package. Neither FedEx® nor Federal Express® are nouns, verbs, adverbs or even participles. They are adjectives and identify our unique brand of shipping services. So if you want to send a package overnight, ask for FedEx® delivery services. When you do, we think you'll know why we say "Why Fool Around With Anyone Else?"® After all, FedEx is "Absolutely, Positively the Best in the Business."® Help us protect our marks. Ask us before you use them, use them correctly, and, most of all, only ask for FedEx® delivery services.

FedEx.

Be absolutely sure.

www.fedex.com

© 1998 Federal Express Corporation

Protection of trademarks requires corporate diligence. Some companies deliver warning messages through advertisements in trade magazines, as in this early FedEx example.

- Monitor the mass media to make certain that trademarks are used correctly. If they are not, send a gentle reminder.
- Check publications to ensure that other organizations are not infringing on a registered trademark. If they are, the company legal department should protest with letters and threats of possible lawsuits.
- Make sure the trademark is actually being used. A 1988 revision of the Trademark Act no longer permits an organization to hold a name in reserve.
- Assure that the trademarks of other organizations are correctly used and properly noted.
- Avoid the use of trademarked symbols or cartoon figures in promotional materials without the explicit permission of the owner. In some cases, to be discussed, a licensing fee is required.

Organizations adamantly insist on the proper use of trademarks in order to avoid the problem of having a name or slogan become generic. Or, to put it another way, a brand name becomes a common noun through general public use. Some trade names that have become generic include *aspirin, thermos, cornflakes, nylon, cellophane,* and *yo-yo.* This means that any company can use these names to describe a product.

The Problem of Trademark Infringement

Today, when there are thousands of businesses and organizations, finding a trademark not already in use is extremely difficult. The task is even more frustrating if a company wants to use a trademark on an international level.

A good example is what happened to Nike at the 1992 Olympic Games in Barcelona. The athletic shoe manufacturer paid millions to be an official sponsor of

PR insights

Accenture: What's in a Name?

A name for a company or organization that isn't already trademarked is getting more difficult to find. As one consultant says, "There isn't a color, a fruit, an animal, or even a prehistoric one that isn't already trademarked by somebody."

Consequently, companies often select new names that sound like something made from leftover Scrabble tiles. A good example is *Accenture,* which is the new name of Arthur Andersen Consulting after a legal dispute with former partner Arthur Andersen, the accounting firm.

According to Jim Murphy, global director of marketing and communications, the company started with a slate of 5000 names. The list was then winnowed down to 500 that met the company's positioning goals. But after checking the list against trademark and other databases, including a Berlitz program designed to spot offensive or adverse translations in 50 countries, Andersen lost all but 29 names. From that list, Accenture, submitted by an employee in Oslo, emerged the winner.

The word, which doesn't exist in any dictionary, is supposed to connote an "accent on the future," according to Murphy. The downside of such coined names, however, is that they don't mean anything in themselves. Companies then have to spend considerable money to assure that employees, customers, and the public identify the name with a particular company. In the case of Accenture, the company spent $175 million on an advertising and marketing communications campaign.

the games, and it planned to introduce a new line of clothes at the event. There was a snag, however. A Spanish high court ruled that the Beaverton, Oregon, firm's trademark infringed on the trademark of a Barcelona sock company that had registered "Nike" more than 60 years ago. The court barred Nike from selling or advertising its sports apparel in Spain, an action that cost the company about $20 million in marketing potential.

The complexity of finding a new name, coupled with the attempts of many to capitalize on an already known trade name, has spawned a number of lawsuits claiming trademark infringement. Here are some examples:

- The Dallas Cowboys and Converse athletic shoes got into a trademark infringement disagreement because both use a five-pointed star as a corporate logo.
- Axiom, Inc., was ordered to change its name after a court found that it infringed on the registered trademark of a competing company, Acxiom Corp.
- Phi Beta Kappa, the academic honor society, filed a $5 million trademark infringement suit against Compaq Computer Corp. after the company launched a "Phi Beta Compaq" promotion to college students.
- An upscale magazine, *Polo,* was ordered by a court to run disclaimers on its cover and table of contents that it was not associated with Polo Ralph Lauren Corp., after the fashion house filed a lawsuit.
- Anheuser-Busch filed a trademark infringement suit against a University of North Carolina student after he designed and sold T-shirts saying "Nag Head, N.C.—King of Beaches." The back of the shirt said, "This beach is for you."

In all these cases organizations claimed that their registered trademarks were being improperly exploited for commercial or organizational purposes. Some guidelines used by courts to determine if there has been trademark infringement are as follows:

- Has the defendant used a name as a way of capitalizing on the reputation of another organization's trademark—and does the defendant benefit from the original organization's investment in popularizing its trademark?
- Is there an intent (real or otherwise) to create confusion in the public mind? Is there an intent to imply a connection between the defendant's product and the item identified by trademark?
- How similar are the two organizations? Are they providing the same kinds of products or services?
- Has the original organization actively protected the trademark by publicizing it and by actually continuing to use it in connection with its products or services?
- Is the trademark unique? A company with a trademark that merely describes a common product might be in trouble.

Misappropriation of Personality

A form of trademark infringement also can result from the unauthorized use of well-known entertainers, professional athletes, and other public figures in an organization's publicity and advertising materials. A photo of Tom Cruise may make a company's advertising campaign more interesting, but the courts call it "misappropriation of personality" if permission and licensing fees have not been negotiated.

Airbus Industrie got into trouble, for example, by featuring a photo of Sir Roger Bannister, famous for the four-minute mile, in one of its advertisements without seeking prior permission. As part of the settlement, the company had to run a full-page apology in *Fortune* and other magazines that had used the advertisement, as well as make a substantial donation to a charity approved by Sir Roger.

Deceased celebrities are also protected. In order to use a likeness of a personality such as Elvis Presley, Marilyn Monroe, or even Albert Einstein, the user must pay a licensing fee to an agent representing the family, studio, or estate of the deceased. The estate of Princess Diana also has exclusive rights to approve and license the use of her image for any commercial purpose.

The legal doctrine is "the right of publicity," which gives entertainers, athletes, and other celebrities the sole ability to cash in on their fame. The legal right is loosely akin to a trademark or copyright, and many states have made it a commercial asset that can be inherited by a celebrity's descendents. One California artist, for example, was sued by the heirs of the Three Stooges because he made a charcoal portrait of the famous acting team and reproduced it on T-shirts and lithographs.

Legal protection also extends to the use of "sound-alikes" or "look-alikes." Bette Midler won a $400,000 judgment against Young & Rubicam (later affirmed by the Supreme Court on appeal) after the advertising agency used another singer to do a "sound-alike" of her singing style in a rendition of the song "Do You Wanna Dance?" for a Ford commercial. The court ruled: "When a distinctive voice of a professional singer is widely known and is deliberately imitated in order to sell a product, the sellers have appropriated what is not theirs."

Regulations by Government Agencies

The promotion of products and services, whether through advertising, product publicity, or other techniques, is not protected by the First Amendment. Instead, the courts have traditionally ruled that such activities fall under the doctrine of *commercial speech*. This means that messages can be regulated by the state in the interest of public health, safety, and consumer protection.

Consequently, the states and the federal government have passed legislation that regulates commercial speech and even restricts it if standards of disclosure, truth, and accuracy are violated. One consequence was the banning of cigarette advertising on television in the 1960s. A more difficult legal question is whether government can completely ban the advertising or promotion of a legally sold product such as cigarettes or alcohol.

Public relations personnel involved in product publicity and the distribution of financial information should be aware of guidelines established by such government agencies as the Federal Trade Commission and the Securities and Exchange Commission.

Federal Trade Commission

The Federal Trade Commission (FTC) has jurisdiction to determine that advertisements are not deceptive or misleading. Public relations personnel should also know that the commission has jurisdiction over product news releases and other forms of product publicity such as videos and brochures.

In the eyes of the FTC, both advertisements and product publicity materials are vehicles of commercial trade—and therefore subject to regulation. In fact, Section

43(a) of the Lanham Act makes it clear that anyone, including public relations personnel, is subject to liability if that person participates in the making or dissemination of a false and misleading representation in any advertising or promotional material. This includes advertising and public relations firms, which also can be held liable for writing, producing, and distributing product publicity materials on behalf of clients.

An example of an FTC complaint is one filed against Campbell Soup Company for claiming that its soups were low in fat and cholesterol and thus helpful in fighting heart disease. The commission charged that the claim was deceptive because publicity and advertisements didn't disclose that the soups also were high in sodium, a condition that increases the risk of heart disease.

The Campbell Soup case raises an important aspect of FTC guidelines. Although a publicized fact may be accurate in itself, FTC staff also considers the context or "net impression received by the consumers." In Campbell's case, advertising copywriters and publicists ignored the information about high sodium, which placed an entirely new perspective on the health benefits of the soup.

FTC investigators are usually on the lookout for unsubstantiated claims and various forms of misleading or deceptive information. Some of the words in promotional materials that trigger FTC interest are: *authentic, certified, cure, custom-made, germ-free, natural, unbreakable, perfect, first-class, exclusive,* and *reliable.*

In recent years, the FTC has also established guidelines for "green" marketing because of extensive consumer confusion about the environmental claims of various products. Words such as *recycled content, recyclable, ozone-safe,* and *biodegradable* can now be used only if the product meets specific FTC definitions of these terms.

The following guidelines, adapted from FTC regulations, should be taken into account when writing product publicity materials:

- Make sure the information is accurate and can be substantiated.
- Stick to the facts. Don't "hype" the product or service by using flowery, nonspecific adjectives and ambiguous claims.
- Make sure celebrities or others who endorse the product actually use it. They should not say anything about the product's properties that cannot be substantiated.
- Watch the language. Don't say "independent research study" when the research was done by the organization's staff.
- Provide proper context for statements and statistics attributed to government agencies. They don't endorse products.
- Describe tests and surveys in sufficient detail so the consumer understands what was tested under what conditions.
- Remember that a product is not "new" if only the packaging has been changed or the product is more than six months old.
- When comparing products or services with a competitor's, make certain you can substantiate your claims.
- Avoid misleading and deceptive product demonstrations.

Companies found in violation of FTC guidelines are usually given the opportunity to sign a consent decree. This means that the company admits no wrongdoing but agrees to change its advertising and publicity claims. Companies may also be fined by the FTC or ordered to engage in corrective advertising and publicity.

Securities and Exchange Commission

The megamergers and the IPOs (initial public offerings) of many new companies in the 1990s made the Securities and Exchange Commission (SEC) a household term in the business world. This federal agency closely monitors the financial affairs of publicly traded companies and protects the interests of stockholders.

SEC guidelines on public disclosure and insider trading are particularly relevant to corporate public relations staff members who must meet the requirements. The distribution of misleading information or failure to make a timely disclosure of material information may be the basis of liability under the SEC code. A company may even be liable if, while it satisfies regulations by getting information out, it conveys crucial information in a vague way or buries it deep in the news release.

A good example is Enron, the Houston-based energy company that became a household word overnight when it became the largest corporate failure in U.S. history. The company was charged with a number of SEC violations, including the distribution of misleading news releases about its finances. According to Congressional testimony, the company issued a quarterly earnings news release that falsely led investors to believe that the company was "on track" to meet strong earnings growth in 2002. Three months later, the company was bankrupt.

The SEC has volumes of regulations, but the three concepts most pertinent to public relations personnel are as follows:

1. *Full information must be given on anything that might materially affect the company's stock.* This includes such things as (1) dividends or their deletion, (2) annual and quarterly earnings, (3) stock splits, (4) mergers or takeovers, (5) major management changes, (6) major product developments, (7) expansion plans, (8) change of business purpose, (9) defaults, (10) proxy materials, (11) disposition of major assets, (12) purchase of own stock, and (13) announcements of major contracts or orders.
2. *Timely disclosure is essential.* A company must act promptly (within minutes or a few hours) to dispel or confirm rumors that result in unusual market activity or market variations. The most common ways of dispensing such financial information are through use of electronic news release services, contact with the major international news services (Dow Jones Wire), and bulk faxing.
3. *Insider trading is illegal.* Company officials, including public relations staffs and outside counsel, cannot use inside information to buy and sell company stock. The landmark case on insider trading occurred in 1965, when Texas Gulf Sulphur executives used inside information about an ore strike in Canada to buy stock while at the same time issuing a news release downplaying rumors that a rich find had been made.

The courts are increasingly applying the "mosaic doctrine" to financial information. Maureen Rubin, an attorney writing in *Public Relations Journal*, explains that a court may examine *all* information released by a company, including news releases, to determine whether, taken as a whole, they create an "overall misleading" impression. One such case was *Cytryn* v. *Cook* (1990), in which a U.S. District Court ruled that the proper test of a company's adequate financial disclosure was not the literal truth of each positive statement, but the overall misleading impression that it combined to create in the eyes of potential investors.

PR casebook

Fake News Release Results in Heavy Fine

The Securities Exchange Commission (SEC) takes a very dim view of misleading and even fake news releases regarding financial information.

Mark Jakob, 23, sought to make a killing on the stock market by issuing a fake news release via Internet Wire, a financial news distribution firm. He allegedly wrote a news release stating that the president of Emulex had quit and the company was restating its quarterly earnings from a profit to a loss.

Within minutes of the release becoming public, Emulex's share price dropped until it was halted in the Nasdaq. Jakob covered his short position and bought additional shares which he later sold at a profit of about $240,000 when the hoax was discovered and the stock recovered most of its original value.

Jakob was able to carry off the hoax because he had worked for Internet Wire for more than a year and knew how to format his release so it looked legitimate. The SEC, however, caught up with him and charged him with wire and securities fraud. Jakob pleaded guilty and agreed to turn over all the profits he made trading Emulex stock. In addition, he was fined $102,000 and faced a jail term.

As a result of such cases, investor relations personnel must also avoid such practices as:

- Unrealistic sales and earnings reports
- Glowing descriptions of products in the experimental stage
- Announcements of possible mergers or takeovers that are only in the speculation stage
- Free trips for business reporters and offers of stock to financial analysts and editors of financial newsletters
- Omission of unfavorable news and developments
- Leaks of information to selected outsiders and financial columnists
- Dissemination of false rumors about a competitor's financial health

In 1998, the SEC passed new regulations supporting the use of "plain English" in prospectuses and other financial documents. The new rules are supposed to make information understandable to the average investor by removing sentences littered with lawyerisms such as *aforementioned, hereby, therewith, whereas,* and *hereinafter.* According to SEC Chairman Arthur Levitt, the cover page, summary, and risk factor sections of prospectuses must be clear, concise, and understandable.

The SEC's booklet on "plain English" gives helpful writing hints such as (1) make sentences short; (2) use *we* and *our, you* and *your;* and (3) say it with an active verb. More information about SEC guidelines can be accessed at its website: www.sec.gov/consumer/plaine.htm.

Two years later, in 2000, the SEC issued another regulation regarding Fair Disclosure (FD). Although regulations already existed regarding "material disclosure" of information that could affect the price of stock, the new regulation expanded the concept by requiring publicly traded companies to *broadly disseminate* "material" information via a news release, Webcast, or SEC filing. According to the SEC, the new regulation will assure that all investors will have more equal access to financial infor-

focus on ethics

To Buy or Not to Buy?

One of your clients at a public relations firm is a medium-sized company that has been somewhat successful in the marketplace. One day, while talking to a corporate vice president on another matter, she tells you off-hand that there's a pretty good chance that the company will be acquired by a large, multinational corporation in the next four to six weeks. If that happens, the company's stock will be worth more than the current selling price. Given this tip, would it be a good idea to call your broker immediately and buy some stock?

mation at the same time. In the past, brokerage firms and analysts often received material information before the general public.

Other Regulatory Agencies

Although the FTC and the SEC are the major federal agencies concerned with the content of advertising and publicity materials, the Food and Drug Administration (FDA) and the Bureau of Alcohol, Tobacco and Firearms (ATF) have also established guidelines.

The FDA oversees the advertising and promotion of prescription drugs, over-the-counter medicines, and cosmetics. Under the federal Food, Drug, and Cosmetic Act, any "person" (which includes advertising and public relations firms) who "causes the misbranding" of products through the dissemination of false and misleading information may be liable.

The FDA, for example, has strict guidelines on the production and distribution of video news releases (VNRs) on health care topics. Agency staff reviews the scripts to assure that the information is accurate, doesn't exaggerate the benefits of a particular product, and doesn't mislead the public that a cure has been found.

Prescription drugs, in particular, have major FDA curbs on advertising and promotion, so the drug companies try to sidestep the regulations by publicizing diseases. Eli Lilly & Co., the maker of Prozac, provides a good example. The company sponsors ads and distributes publicity about depression. And the Glaxo Institute for Digestive Health conducts information campaigns about the fact that stomach pains can be an indication of major problems. Of course, Glaxo also makes the ulcer drug Zantac.

The Federal Alcohol Administration Act is also concerned about misbranding and the dissemination of false or misleading information. Wineries have problems with ATF when they imply the health benefits of drinking wine. Geyser Peak winery was ordered to pull advertisements that included the proverb, "As age enhances wine, wine enhances age." The ATF is also modest. It rejected a design for a wine label that featured a bare-breasted mermaid drawn by Art Deco master Erté. The bureau cited a rule barring "any statement, design or representation which is obscene or indecent."

A recent development in state legislation is "food slander" laws. A dozen states have put "agricultural product disparagement" laws on their books, making it a crime to criticize or denigrate food with information that is not based on scientific fact.

The legislation, which resulted from the U.S. apple industry's losing almost $100 million because of the Alar scare, is designed to curtail activist groups that often use scare tactics and faulty information to disparage a particular food product. Millions of Americans learned about such laws when popular television celebrity Oprah Winfrey was sued by several Texas cattlemen for allegedly disparaging beef on her talk show. The trial, held in San Antonio, was a publicity bonanza for Oprah—and the jury acquitted her.

Corporate/Employee Free Speech

Although there are a number of restrictions on "commercial speech" by regulatory agencies, the Supreme Court has also upheld the right of corporations to express their views of public policy and interest.

Some Recent Cases

A series of court cases has supported the concept of corporate free speech. These are some of the landmark cases:

- *First National Bank of Boston (1978).* The Supreme Court struck down a Massachusetts law that prohibited corporations from publicizing their views on issues subject to the ballot box. The ruling essentially gave corporations the same status as an individual under the First Amendment.
- *Consolidated Edison (1980).* The Supreme Court ruled that a New York Public Utilities Commission regulation prohibiting utilities from making statements on matters of public policy and controversy was unconstitutional.
- *Pacific Gas & Electric (1986).* The Supreme Court ruled that the California Public Utilities Commission could not require PG&E to include messages from activist consumer groups in its mailings to customers. The utility argued that inclusion of such messages impaired the company's right to communicate its own messages.
- *Nike (2001).* A California appeals court ruled that a Nike ad campaign in which the company denied using sweatshop labor has First Amendment protection after an activist sued the company for false advertising. The court said consumers were entitled to "access to the free flow of information and ideas . . . for purposes of political decision making in a democracy . . ."

Although corporations can speak out on public issues in the context of First Amendment rights, a 1990 decision by the Supreme Court seems to indicate that this "free speech" right doesn't extend to endorsement of political candidates.

In a six-to-three decision in *Austin* v. *Michigan Chamber of Commerce,* the Court said a Michigan law that prohibits corporations from buying newspaper advertisements on behalf of a political candidate did not violate the chamber's right to free speech. The Michigan legislation, which applies to all incorporated bodies (even the Sierra Club and the American Civil Liberties Union) is part of a campaign finance law.

Employee Free Speech

A modern, progressive organization encourages employee comments and even criticisms. Many employee newspapers carry letters to the editor because they breed a healthy atmosphere of two-way communication and make company publications more credible.

Yet, at the same time, recent developments have indicated that not all is well for employee freedom of expression. A *Time* magazine essay by Barbara Ehrenreich, for example, gives startling examples of organizations denying free speech to employees. A grocery worker in Dallas was fired for wearing a Green Bay Packers T-shirt to work when the Dallas Cowboys were scheduled to play Green Bay in the conference playoffs. A worker at Caterpiller, Inc., was suspended for wearing a T-shirt titled "Defending the American Dream," a slogan of the union that had bitterly fought the company in a strike.

Employee freedom of expression and the issue of privacy have also been raised by court decisions that give employers the right to read employees' e-mail. Pillsbury, for example, fired a worker who posted an e-mail message to a colleague calling management "back-stabbing bastards." The employee sued, but the court sided with the company. In another case, Intel got a court injunction against a former employee who complained about the company in e-mails sent to thousands of employees. The Electronic Frontier Foundation, a group devoted to civil liberties in cyberspace, worried about violation of First Amendment rights. The company, however, contended that it wasn't a matter of free speech, but trespassing on company property.

Companies say internal e-mail systems are company property and can be used only for official company business. Kmart Corporation even has a policy stating, "Misuse of the e-mail system could result in denial of access to the Kmart computing environment, or dismissal."

Two other aspects of employee free speech are "whistle-blowing" and protection of an organization's trade secrets. State and federal laws generally protect the right of employees to "blow the whistle" if an organization is guilty of illegal activity.

It also is well established that an organization has a legal right to fire employees or sue former employees if they reveal proprietary information to the competition. Public relations firms, for example, usually have employees sign agreements that they will not divulge proprietary information about clients to outsiders or, if they leave the firm, to their new employers.

Liability for Sponsored Events

Public relations personnel often focus on the planning and logistics of an event; they must also take steps to protect the organization from liability and possible lawsuits.

Plant Tours and Open Houses

Plant tours should not be undertaken lightly. They require detailed planning by the public relations staff to guarantee the safety and comfort of visitors. Consideration must be given to such factors as (1) logistics, (2) possible work disruptions as groups pass through the plant, (3) safety, and (4) amount of staffing required.

A well-marked tour route is essential; it is equally important to have trained escort staff and tour guides. Guides should be well versed in company history and operations, and their comments should be somewhat standardized to make sure that key facts are conveyed. In addition, guides should be trained in first aid and thoroughly briefed on what to do in case of an accident or heart attack. At the beginning the guide should outline to the visitors what they will see, the amount of walking involved, the time required, and the number of stairs. This warning tells visitors with heart conditions or other physical handicaps what they can expect.

Many of the points about plant tours are applicable to open houses. The additional problem is having large numbers of people on the plant site at the same time. Such an event calls for special logistical planning by the public relations staff, possibly including the following measures: (1) arranging for extra liability insurance, (2) hiring off-duty police for security and traffic control, (3) arranging to have paramedics and an ambulance on site, and (4) making contractual agreements with vendors selling food or souvenirs.

Such precautions will generate goodwill and limit the company's liability. It should be noted, however, that a plaintiff can still collect if negligence on the part of the company can be proved.

Promotional Events

These events are planned primarily to promote product sales, increase organizational visibility, or raise money for charitable causes.

Events that attract crowds require the same kind of planning as does an open house. The public relations person should be concerned about traffic flow, adequate restroom facilities, signage, and security. Off-duty police officers are often hired to handle crowd control, protect celebrities or government officials, and make sure no disruptions occur.

Liability insurance is a necessity. Any public event sponsored by an organization should be insured against accidents that might result in lawsuits charging negligence. Organizations can purchase comprehensive insurance to cover a variety of events or a specific event.

The need for liability insurance also applies to charitable organizations if they sponsor a 10-K run, a bicycle race, or a hot-air balloon race. Participants should sign a release form that protects the organization against liability in case of a heart attack or an accident. An organization that sponsored a 5-K "fun run" had the participants sign a statement that stated in part, " . . . I assume all risk associated with running in this event, including, but not limited to, falls, contact with other participants, the effects of the weather, including high heat/or humidity, traffic, and other conditions of the road."

Promotional events that use public streets and parks also need permits from the appropriate city departments. A 10-K run or a parade, for example, requires permits from the police or the public safety department to block streets. Sponsors frequently hire off-duty police to control traffic.

A music store in one California city found out about these needs the hard way. It allowed a popular rock group to give an informal concert in front of the store as part of a promotion. Radio DJs spread the word and, as a result, a crowd of 8000 converged on the shopping center, causing a massive traffic jam. The city attorney filed charges against the store for creating a public disturbance and billed it $80,000 for police overtime pay to untangle the mess.

A food event, such as a chili cookoff or a German fest, requires a permit from the public health department and, if liquor is served, a permit from the state alcohol board. If the event is held inside a building not usually used for this purpose, a permit is often required from the fire inspector. In addition, a major deposit may be required as insurance that the organization will clean up a public space after the event.

Working with Lawyers

This chapter has outlined a number of areas in which the release of information (or the lack of release) raises legal issues for an organization. Public relations personnel must be aware of legal pitfalls, but they are not lawyers. By the same token, lawyers aren't experts in public relations and often have a poor understanding of how important the court of public opinion is in determining the reputation and credibility of an organization.

In today's business environment, with its high potential for litigation, it is essential for public relations professionals and lawyers to have cooperative relationships. Although much is written about the tug-of-war between public relations people and lawyers concerning the release of information, a survey by Kathy R. Fitzpatrick, a public relations professor now at the University of Florida, found that almost 85 percent of the public relations respondents said their relationship with legal counsel was either "excellent" or "good."

A number of steps can be taken by an organization to ensure that the public relations and legal staffs have a cordial, mutually supportive relationship:

- The public relations and legal staffs should report to the same top executive, who can listen to both sides and decide on a course of action.
- Public relations personnel should know basic legal concepts and regulatory guidelines in order to build trust and credibility with the legal department.
- Both functions should be represented on key committees.
- The organization should have a clearly defined statement of responsibilities for each staff and its relationship to the other. Neither should dominate.

PR insights

Working with Lawyers: What PR People Should Know

Public relations practitioners increasingly find themselves working with attorneys on a variety of issues that may include community relations, crisis communications, product safety and recalls, investor relations, and even mergers. This often is a difficult partnership because public relations professionals and lawyers have different perspectives. One deals with the court of public opinion, and the other is focused on the court of law.

Public relations professional Lynn Doll and lawyer Coby King, both from Rogers & Associates in Los Angeles, compiled a list of items that showed the difference between the two perspectives:

What Attorneys Do That Drives Public Relations Pros Crazy

- Focus almost exclusively inward—on the judge and jury versus the outside world
- Withhold information from the PR team
- Use legalese when acting as spokespersons
- Try to wordsmith the PR work product
- Take too long to review documents
- Try to muzzle the organization so important messages can't be delivered

What Public Relations Pros Do That Drives Attorneys Crazy

- Disclose too much information
- Mistakenly cross boundaries of privileged information
- Oversimplify
- Overstate
- Inadvertently impact litigation negatively by sharing inappropriate information

Source: *PR Reporter,* November 15, 1999.

- Periodic consultations should be held during which materials and programs are reviewed.
- The legal staff, as part of its duties, should brief public relations personnel on impending developments in litigation, so press inquiries can be answered in an appropriate manner.

Summary

A Sampling of Legal Problems

There are a number of ways that a public relations practitioner may get caught up in a lawsuit or a case with a government regulatory agency. Practitioners may also be held legally liable if they provide advice or support the illegal activity of a client.

Libel and Defamation

There is now practically little difference between libel and slander; the two are often collectively referred to as defamation. The concept of defamation involves a false and malicious (or at least negligent) communication with an identifiable subject who is injured either financially or by loss of reputation or mental suffering. Libel suits can be avoided through the careful use of language. Some offensive communications will fall under the "fair comment" defense; an example of this would be a negative review by a theater critic.

Invasion of Privacy

Companies canot assume when publishing newsletters that a person waives his or her right to privacy due to status as an employee. It is important to get written permission to publish photos or use employees in advertising materials, and to be cautious in releasing personal information about employees to the media.

Copyright Law

Copyright is the protection of creative work from unauthorized use. It is assumed that published works are copyrighted, and permission must be obtained to reprint such material. The "fair use" doctrine allows limited quotation, as in a book review. Unless a company has a specific contract with a freelance writer, photographer, or artist to produce work that will be exclusively owned by that company (a situation called "work for hire"), the freelancer owns his or her work. New copyright issues have been raised by the popularity of the Internet and the ease of downloading, uploading, and disseminating images and information.

Trademark Law

A trademark is a word, symbol, or slogan that identifies a product's origin. These can be registered with the U.S. Patent and Trademark Office. Trademarks are always capitalized and used as adjectives rather than nouns or verbs. Companies vigorously protect trademarks to prevent their becoming common nouns. One form of trademark infringement may be "misappropriation of personality," the use of a celebrity's name or image for advertising purposes without permission.

Regulations by Government Agencies

Commercial speech is regulated by the government in the interest of public health, safety, and consumer protection. Among the agencies involved in this regulation are the Federal Trade Commission, the Securities and Exchange Commission, the Food and Drug Administration, and the Bureau of Alcohol, Tobacco and Firearms.

Corporate/Employee Free Speech

In spite of restrictions imposed by regulatory agencies, corporations do have the First Amendment right to express opinion publicly. Employees may, however, have some limits in expressing opinions within the corporate environment. E-mail, for example, is company property and may be monitored, and employees can be fired (or former employees sued) for revealing trade secrets. At the same time, "whistle-blowers" are protected from retaliation.

Liability for Sponsored Events

Plant tours, open houses, and other promotional events raise liability issues concerning safety and security. Liability insurance is a necessity. Permits may also be required for the use of public streets and parks and for serving food and liquor.

Working with Lawyers

Because of all the issues discussed in this chapter, a cooperative relationship must exist between public relations personnel and legal counsel. It helps if both groups report to the same top executive and both are represented on key committees. Public relations practitioners should also be aware of legal concepts and regulatory guidelines and receive briefings from the legal staff on impending developments.

Case Activity: What Would You Do?

Expresso Unlimited, a chain of coffee shops, hires you as director of public relations and marketing. Some of your ideas include (1) a series of advertisements showing pictures and quotes from satisfied customers; (2) hiring a freelance photographer to build up a photo file for use in possible magazine articles, brochures, newsletters, and advertising; (3) reprinting and distributing various magazine articles that have been written about the company; (4) starting an employee newsletter with emphasis on employee features and "personals"; (5) including in the newsletter and advertisements cartoons about coffee drinking from various publications, including the *New Yorker;* (6) citing a government study that rates the quality of coffee beans from around the world, and pointing out that Expresso Unlimited uses only the highest-quality beans; (7) writing a news release that quotes a survey showing that eight out of 10 serious coffee drinkers prefer Expresso Unlimited; and (8) creating a home page on the Internet that would include pictures of famous people drinking a cup of coffee.

Prepare a memo outlining the legal and regulatory factors that should be considered in implementing the above activities.

Questions for Review and Discussion

1. Why do public relations staff and firms need to know the legal aspects of creating and distributing messages?
2. How can a public relations person take precautions to avoid libel suits?
3. What is the concept of fair comment and criticism? Are there any limitations?
4. What precautions should a public relations person take to avoid invasion-of-privacy suits?
5. If an organization wants to use the photo or comments of an employee or a customer in an advertisement, what precautions should be taken?
6. When the media call about an employee, what kinds of information should the public relations person provide? What other approaches can be used?
7. What basic guidelines of copyright law should public relations professionals know about?
8. What rights do photographers and freelance writers have regarding ownership of their works?
9. How do public relations people help an organization protect its trademarks?
10. What is "misappropriation of personality"?
11. What should public relations people know about the regulations of the Federal Trade Commission?
12. What should public relations personnel know about the regulations of the Securities and Exchange Commission?
13. Many companies contend that they have the right to read the e-mail of employees. What do you think? Is this a violation of privacy and employee free speech?
14. If an organization is sponsoring an open house or a promotional event, what legal aspects should be considered?
15. What should be the relationship between public relations staff and legal counsel in an organization?

Suggested Readings

Green, Leanne. "Examining Electronic Press Clips and Copyrights." *Public Relations Tactics,* May 2001, p. 12.

Greenberger, Robert S. "More Courts Are Granting Advertisements First Amendment Protection." *Wall Street Journal,* July 3, 2001, p. B1.

Greenhouse, Linda. "Freelancers Win in Copyright Case: Court Says Writers Keep Right to Their Work in Databases." *New York Times*, June 26, 2001, pp. 1, 14.

Haggerty, James. "Communicating when Clients Are in Court." *PRWeek*, April 9, 2001, p. 20.

Hoger, Elizabeth A., and Swem, Lisa L. "Public Relations and the Law in Crisis Mode: Texaco's Initial Reaction to Incriminating Tapes." *Public Relations Review*, Vol. 26, No. 4, 2000, pp. 425–445.

McGuire, Craig. "Disagreements over Meaning of New SEC Rule Fuel IR Controversy." *PRWeek*, August 21, 2000, p. 5.

McGuire, George. "Intellectual Property Issues for PR Professionals." *PR Tactics*, December 2000, p. 6.

O'Donovan, Cheryl. "Copyright vs. Copywrong." *Communication World*, October/November 2001, pp. 12–15.

Reber, Bryan H., Cropp, Fritz, and Cameron, Glen T. "Mythic Battles: Examining the Lawyer–Public Relations Counselor Dynamic." *Journal of Public Relations Research*, Vol. 13, No. 3, 2001, pp. 187–218.

Stateman, Alison. "A Big Victory for a Small Firm." *Public Relations Tactics*, May 2000, pp. 1, 18. A public relations firm sues a former client for hiring its staff.

Tripoli, Lori. "As Trials Go Public, PR Seats Itself Courtside." *PRWeek*, August 14, 2000, p. 17.

Corporations

preview

The objective of this chapter is to give students a better understanding of public relations in corporations, whose dealings with customers, communities, governments, stockholders, employees, and the financial world heavily influence their reputations with the public.

Topics covered in this chapter include:

- The corporate role
- The human factor and downsizing
- Consumerism
- Community relations
- Corporations and the environment
- Financial information
- Sensitivity to ethnic groups
- Marketing communications
- Employee communications

The Corporate Role

This is an era of giantism in American and, indeed, world business. International conglomerates control subsidiary companies that often produce a grab bag of seemingly unrelated products and services under the same corporate banner. These conglomerates must deal with government at many levels. Their operations affect the environment, control the employment of thousands, and have an impact on the financial and social well-being of millions. Truly, they have a compelling influence on contemporary life.

Bigness brings remoteness. The popular phrase "the faceless corporation" may be a cliché, but it represents a genuine distrust in the public mind—a distrust often based on lack of knowledge about a corporation rather than on actual unfavorable experiences. When U.S. gasoline prices rise rapidly, for example, suspicion spreads that the oil companies have conspired to gouge the public, a distrust that the oil companies never fully allay.

Because a corporation's impact on society is felt at so many levels, those who plan and conduct its public relations face a complex task. Even relatively small corporations need public relations programs that show them conducting their affairs, both external and internal, in a socially responsible manner.

Figure 14.1 presents, in schematic form, the way one company—General Electric—categorizes the various concerns it must take into consideration at every step of executive decision making.

The Human Factor

The fundamental, irreplaceable element in every business is people. A successful company must treat its customers honestly and in a friendly manner. Equally, it must conduct relations with its employees with a responsible, compassionate, even-handed

FIGURE 14.1

General Electric Company sees four factors that must be taken into consideration whenever a management decision is made: (1) Political—How do government regulations and other pressures affect the decision? (2) Technological—Do we have engineering knowledge to accomplish the goal? (3) Social—What is our responsibility to society? (4) Economic—Will we make a profit?

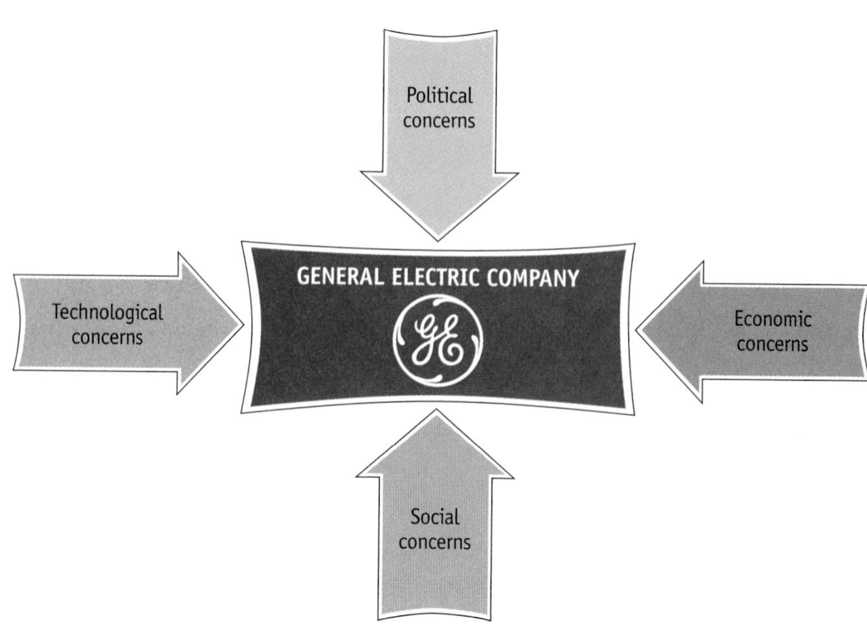

policy. And it must heed the desires and attitudes of people in the communities where it operates.

The Public Perception

What corporations *do* is not enough. The public's *perception* of their conduct also matters. A corporation may operate in a completely legal, technically sound, and financially efficient manner yet find itself viewed by segments of the public as cold, greedy, and heedless of cherished social values. The public relations practitioner's job is to see that this does not happen. According to Dr. Ruth Ann Weaver-Lariscy at the University of Georgia, the practitioner must work within the organization to foster constructive, socially aware behavior, and outside the company to convince the public that the firm is a worthy, caring corporate citizen.

Downsizing Stirs Resentment

The public relations task is especially difficult when a corporation announces large-scale dismissals, as many companies did in 2001.

When corporations engage in "downsizing"—dismissing thousands of employees to increase profits—they magnify the public's distrust.

PR insights

Public Relations Blunders

Fineman Associates of San Francisco, a public relations firm, annually compiles a list of the ten worst public relations blunders. A number of high profile corporations have made the firm's list:

- *Microsoft Corporation*. Among Microsoft's sins: rushing to put a positive spin on each day's trial events and niggling over the meaning of e-mails in court. The software giant also won PR demerits for financially backing a think tank, whose newspaper ads supported Microsoft's position. "Such obvious duplicity is damaging to Microsoft, and it's damaging to public relations," said *Inside PR* newsletter.
- *RealNetworks*. The software company made the list for developing Big Brother-like powers. The Seattle-based company was caught tracking the listening habits of 13 million users of its RealJukebox music-playing software without their consent. But confession is good for the soul—and public relations. "We screwed up," RealNetworks' CEO Rob Glaser told *Time* magazine.
- *Exxon Corp*. The company lobbied and sued to allow the *Exxon Valdez*, which 10 years ago spilled millions of gallons of oil into Prince William Sound, to return to its original Alaska–California route. The tanker had been banned from returning to the sound.
- *Coca-Cola Co*. In Belgium and France, 200 people, including schoolkids, got sick after drinking Coke. Ten days into the crisis, CEO Douglas Ivester flew to Brussels and apologized for the problem. His failure to react quickly may have turned Coca-Cola into "the poster child of ghastly crisis management and bad PR," according to *PR Week* columnist Frank Mankiewicz. Ivester resigned soon after.
- *Great West Casualty Co*. After an 81-year-old woman stepped in front of a grain truck insured by Great West and was killed, the company sued her estate for negligence, seeking $2,800. "I'm not paying them for killing my mom," the woman's daughter told the *Wall Street Journal*. "I'll sit in jail first."

(*Source:* Quinn, Michelle. "PR Blunders of 1999." *Mercury News,* December 1999, www0.mercurycenter.com.)

Most citizens feel vaguely uneasy about the concentration of vast economic power in a few hands when one corporation buys another for more than $10 billion, although they don't understand the financial maneuvers involved. They express strong negative reaction, however, at such news as AT&T's plan to dismiss 40,000 employees, because they sense the plight of their fellow human beings involved.

Once known as Ma Bell, a company offering longtime job security, AT&T came under severe criticism for its dismissal policy. The company had been earning high profits, and almost simultaneously with the staff cutback came news that Chairman Robert E. Allen had received $16 million in salary, bonus, and stock options. This intensified public criticism of the company's conduct.

The public relations challenge in downsizing is twofold:

- To convince top management, before the cuts are announced, that it should think of the employees as individuals, not as statistics—recognize the company loyalty most of them have shown, provide as much financial cushion and insurance protection as possible, and offer retraining and job-placement assistance.
- To make the public understand why the layoffs are justified. The electronic age has caused enormous changes in production and marketing procedures; jobs essential 20 years ago no longer are needed. Changes in the company's line of products, needed to stay competitive, have altered workforce needs. A company that remains static in a fiercely competitive world will not survive. Mergers of corporations and spin-offs of company divisions have created many job duplications.

If a corporation's layoff announcement has shown genuine regard for the employees affected, the public may acknowledge some validity in the dismissals. If the announcement sounds cold and heartless, the justifications will be largely brushed aside.

What Can Happen when Businesses Overlook the Human Factor

Businesses sometimes fail to recognize the human factor. They become so engrossed in computer technology, cash-flow charts, and management techniques that they overlook personal sensitivities. In a public relations blunder, the U.S. Bank of Washington in Spokane did exactly that, to its regret. A man in shabby clothes parked his pickup truck in the bank's parking lot, cashed a check, then asked the teller to validate his 60-cent parking ticket. She refused, claiming that cashing a check wasn't a transaction, as required for validation. When the man protested, she called a supervisor, who looked distastefully at the ragged character and also refused.

"Fine," the man replied. "You don't need me, and I don't need you." Whereupon he closed his account and took the $1 million he had on deposit to a competing bank down the street.

Taco Bell made a costly blunder, too. It fired one of its restaurant managers in Portland, Oregon, because she ran out from her restaurant to aid a teenager wounded in a street fight. In doing so, she broke a company rule requiring employees to remain in the restaurant and call police if trouble occurs.

Public indignation at this harsh treatment for a humanitarian act was so intense that Taco Bell apologized in a full-page newspaper advertisement. It offered the manager her job back, but she refused, taking another job elsewhere.

"Sometimes corporations make mistakes," Taco Bell said. "In this case we did, and we've learned from it."

PR casebook

Starbucks' Response to Tragedy Makes a Profound Statement

The Starbucks Coffee Company reopened seven months after the brutal, after-hours killing of three young employees at the Washington, D.C., area store. Residents welcomed the reopening, stating that business must go on and that criminals cannot "win." But the opening was made special through several extraordinary efforts by the large coffee chain. The company made the store a living memorial, installing a floor-to-ceiling maple wood mural that features three boxes with the initials of the slain employees. Family members placed photos and other mementos in the boxes. Starbucks also immediately offered a $100,000 reward for apprehension of the murderers and paid for funerals of the victims, as well as counseling of family members. And since the store reopened, all net profits have gone to a foundation that promotes nonviolence. The company's efforts have been well received in the community and by many of the 23,000 Starbucks employees who are described as company partners.

The lesson is clear: Before a company takes an action affecting the public, its management should attempt to view the move through the eyes of others. Providing management with these outside perceptions is the job of the public relations specialists. Their antennae must be sensitive to changes in public attitudes.

Similarly, corporate managements should pay heed to how their actions are perceived by their employees. If employees believe that management is treating them unfairly, their work suffers and internal tensions develop. Absenteeism rises.

A disturbing difference in how a company's top management and its employees perceive the workplace atmosphere sometimes develops, with potentially dangerous consequences. The problem can exist, as well, in large nonprofit organizations.

A survey by *Industry Week* and the Wyatt Company points up this conflict in attitudes. It reported that while 69 percent of senior managers responding believed their organizations' management style encouraged treating employees with respect, only 24 percent of their line managers believed this was true. Moreover, 64 percent of the top management respondents believed their firms encouraged freedom of expression, while only 29 percent of the line supervisors thought so. Because line supervisors are in personal contact with most employees, their opinion should be closer to that of the workforce than top management's.

These findings define the challenge for company public relations departments, because they, in conjunction with the human relations department, have the responsibility for communication between management and employees.

Computers versus Humans

As computer wizardry multiplies and increasingly ingenious automated voice equipment comes into service, companies are tempted to substitute this technology for human contact with customers. This should be done with extreme caution. Unwise use of electronic response may alienate the very people the company needs to please. A dissatisfied customer who telephones to protest a billing error or shipping mistake resents being answered by a recording.

Similarly, complaining letter-writers dislike receiving a computerized form-letter reply. Nor are customers placated by the cliché answer, "It was a computer error." They know that mistakes on computers almost always result from indifference to the personal factor in communication. Corporate public relations practitioners should exercise influence with management to maintain the human touch.

According to Maria Len-Rios, too many corporations ignore online opportunities to bind customers to them with small gestures such as thank-you e-mails and appropriately personalized Web site interactions. Although easily offended if they believe they are taken for granted, customers are impressed if someone in a supposedly remote corporation writes a note of appreciation or provides a desired service. Online customer service, like its voicemail counterpart, should also be responsive and trouble free. Following a sinuous trail of Web links through pages of frequently asked questions (FAQs) to either a dead end or a nonfunctioning e-mail complaint system does not build loyalty for a corporation.

Consumerism

The day when business could operate successfully on the Latin precept of *caveat emptor*—"Let the buyer beware"—is long gone. In today's society, sellers are expected to deliver goods and services of safe, acceptable quality on honest terms, without misleading claims and deceptive financing practices. Consumers have rights protected by the federal government and enjoy the assistance of government and private agencies in enforcing those rights. Consumerism is a significant and growing force in the conduct of business. The manner in which public relations practitioners help to guide a company in handling the pressures of consumerism strongly affects the public's attitude toward that company.

Development of the Consumer Movement

The consumer movement developed during the past three decades because far too often business firms were caught either cheating their customers or carelessly giving them inferior products, then making it difficult for them to obtain adjustments. Public trust in business diminished. When the firm of Yankelovich, Skelly and White took a poll in 1967 to measure public trust, the result showed confidence in business at about 70 percent. In a similar poll 14 years later, public confidence had plummeted to 19 percent. Opinion Research Corporation concluded from its 1998 survey findings that companies are *guilty until proven innocent,* suggesting that mistrust of business will persist in the new century.

The high priest of the consumer movement during its growth stages was Ralph Nader, then a youthful attorney in Washington, D.C. His book *Unsafe at Any Speed,* published in 1965, was a searing indictment of automobile safety standards. Nader organized study groups that published generally critical reports on other industries and dwelt heavily upon corporate responsibility to consumers. Nader entered the 2000 presidential race to continue his lifelong advocacy of environmental and consumer safety issues, bringing enough support to his Green Party that it is now eligible for federal campaign funds.

Rising consumer protests coincided with a period of rapid expansion in the "watchdog" role of government. The power of federal regulatory agencies over business expanded in numerous directions. The Food and Drug Administration deter-

focus on ethics

Corporate Campaigns: Righteous Indignation or Unfair Attacks?

In a book provocatively entitled *The Death of a Thousand Cuts: Corporate Campaigns and the Attack on the Corporation,* Jarol B. Manheim describes a corporate campaign as an organized assault on the reputation of a company that has offended some interest group such as a union, an environmental group, or a human rights organization. Jim Lukaszewski states: "Whether we like it or not, there are a handful of special attributes, which are easily recognized and identified, for which appropriate counteractive strategies can be adopted. Four of the most potent current realities are:

- Emotionalism has replaced reason
- Activism has overtaken science and data
- Exaggeration has overwhelmed precision
- Grassroots manipulation is the new realism"

Among the activist tactics cited by Lukaszewski from *Rules for Radicals* (Saul Alinsky, NY: Vintage Books, 1989) are ridicule of corporate leaders by insulting their heritage, attacking their greed, and generally infuriating them. Personalized attacks are recommended through exaggeration, humiliation, excoriation and agitation. (*Strategy,* No. 12/December 18, 2000, a supplement of *pr reporter*).

Corporate public relations professionals consider corporate campaigns—the death of a thousand cuts—to be unfair, destructive, and wrong. Do you agree? Why would there be differences of opinion? What role would one's basic value system, sometimes called worldview, play in how you view the question of corporate campaigns?

mines what medications can be sold to the public. The Federal Trade Commission regulates truth in advertising, and the Securities and Exchange Commission controls the financial conduct of corporations (see Chapter 13). The National Highway Traffic Safety Administration sets standards for automobile manufacture. The Consumer Product Safety Commission examines other manufactured goods. Other federal and state agencies have consumer-oriented policing powers in their domains.

Consumerism Today

The campaign by the conservative Congress elected in 1994 to "get rid of government bureaucracy" by eliminating some federal services found much public support in principle. At the same time, Americans as a whole, in their roles as consumers, appear to want enforcement of rules protecting them from fraud, dangerous food products and medicines, highway perils, toxic wastes, and terrorist threats to their personal well-being—particularly after the September 11 attack on the World Trade Center and the Pentagon.

In a study by Louis Harris and Associates, strong sentiment was expressed favoring continued government regulation of safety, health, and truth in advertising.

Use of Boycotts The *boycott*—refusal to buy the products or services of an offending company—is a widely used tool of the consumer movement, aimed at firms for many different reasons.

Typical boycotts in recent years were those against Kraft Foods and Nabisco for allegedly selling cigarettes to minors, Levi Strauss for moving plants abroad, and Burger King for allegedly promoting sex and violence on TV with its commercials.

Corporations today face a variety of activist publics who are concerned about everything from global warming to exploitation of labor in developing nations. Here, a group protests against Nike's use of overseas labor to manufacture its shoes and clothing. Activist groups on many campuses, in particular, have protested against Nike contracts with university athletic teams.

Consumer Recourse In the private sector, the nationwide network of Better Business Bureaus provides machinery through which wronged consumers may seek satisfaction. Nader's operations in Washington continue to publicize defective products and services. Other consumer organizations do similar work. *Consumer Reports* is widely read.

The Society of Consumer Affairs Professionals in Business (SOCAB) provides an avenue for exchange of information among specialists in the field and a method for increasing corporate awareness of what can be accomplished in building goodwill.

As an example of its work, SOCAB found in a poll that more than two-thirds of American manufacturers now provide toll-free telephone numbers on which customers and critics may complain to company headquarters. Such lines, properly staffed, give companies an opportunity to explain their policies and to disarm complainers by offering apologies when indicated.

Corporate willingness to accept blame when justified softens consumer anger. The PECO Energy Company received favorable reaction when it did so. An explosion

PR casebook

Sometimes You Can't Win

Coors Brewing Company was subjected to a boycott by gay and lesbian activists in retaliation for company actions they believed to be discriminatory against them.

To placate them, Coors announced that it would extend health benefits to the partners of homosexual employees. That policy, in turn, angered groups of anti-gay Christian fundamentalists. They declared a boycott of Coors. The Concerned Women of America also denounced the extension of benefits.

Purview newsletter reported that one opponent of the new Coors policy was Jeffrey Coors, chairman of the Free Congress Foundation. He is a brother of the brewery's chief executive officer, Peter Coors.

caused by a reported but unrepaired gas leak in a company line killed two people. The utility's chief executive quickly apologized publicly, stating, "PECO Energy takes full responsibility."

Product Recalls

Recalls of defective products from the purchasers are the most visible and frequently very expensive aspect of corporate relations with consumers. Hundreds of recalls from major to relatively insignificant are issued every year. In a typical year they ranged from 920,000 pickup trucks by General Motors (GM) for seat and safety-belt problems to 78,000 cases of animal crackers by Consolidated Biscuit Company for improper labeling.

Millions of automobiles have been called back for correction of defects that might endanger the safety of riders. Some recalls have been made voluntarily by manufacturers, others under government pressure.

Ten automobile companies recalled 8.8 million vehicles to replace seat belts, the largest recall ever. Ford called back 8.5 million a year later to replace faulty ignition switches.

When the U.S. Food and Drug Administration found *E. coli* bacteria in a sample of unpasteurized Odwalla apple juice, the maker of the drink responded quickly with a frank, vigorous series of actions. It withdrew all its apple-based products and formed a research council of scientists, industry officials, and health specialists to examine its production process. The company's founder apologized for the outbreak during a news conference in Seattle and offered to pay the medical bills of any person stricken with *E. coli* infection from Odwalla juice.

In a full-page newspaper advertisement, Odwalla corporate officials said that the outbreak "has shaken all of us at Odwalla." They announced creation of a Web site and a 1-800 telephone number to provide information and answer inquiries. "We want to hear from you," their open letter said.

Reaching the owners of defective automobiles is relatively easy because of the state auto registration laws. Reaching the owners of products bought over the counter can be very difficult. Even when informed through direct mail announcements or media publicity, many purchasers fail to respond to the recalls, no matter how serious the problem involved. In an article on product recalls published in *Public Relations Review*, Dirk C. Gibson of the University of New Mexico cites customer response on recalls as low as 10 percent: " . . . there is an undeniable relationship between ineffective recalls and consumer harm," he states. Thus public relations practitioners concerned with recalls need to make strenuous efforts to encourage participation.

Indicative of the tendency by juries to impose heavy penalties against large corporations, a jury in Hayleyville, Alabama, awarded the driver of a Chevrolet Blazer, a General Motors product, $150 million. He claimed that he was thrown from the vehicle and paralyzed because a faulty door latch failed. He contended that GM had known for years that the Blazer latch was deficient but had not recalled the model.

In its defense, GM asserted that the driver had been drinking, fell asleep at the wheel, and was not wearing a seat belt. The verdict was the heaviest product-liability award ever made in the automotive industry. The extensive publicity for such awards sends a compelling message about corporate responsibility, even when the award is later overturned. Years after the Exxon Valdez oil spill, the punitive damages judgment was overturned on the grounds that it was excessive and impractical.

Business Public Affairs

"Corporate citizenship" is a basic tenet of business and industry for several reasons.

First, many business executives have realized that to reduce government regulation they must take the initiative and voluntarily exercise a sense of social responsibility. Historically, business has been regulated in direct proportion to its social abuses.

The so-called robber barons of the late 19th century exploited labor and resources, generating considerable regulation of railway, utility, oil, and other companies (see Chapter 2). More recently, industry's failure to solve many of the environmental problems caused by manufacturing increased demands for government regulation. One result was the creation of the Environmental Protection Agency (EPA).

Second, business and industrial leaders realize that they can survive and prosper only in a stable society that provides safety, security, and economic well-being for its citizens. Business needs to help find solutions to a number of societal problems. Such assistance not only improves the quality of life but creates a reservoir of public support for business.

Third, corporate citizenship enhances a company's reputation and its ability to market goods and services. A survey conducted by Opinion Research Corporation for *Fortune* magazine, for example, showed that 89 percent of adults said a company's reputation often determined what products they bought. *California Business,* commenting on the survey, added, "Companies involved in social issues are considered more sensitive to their customers."

With this thought in mind, companies in recent years have undertaken a variety of projects under the rubric of public affairs and community relations. Some examples:

- Dayton-Hudson Corporation, a Minneapolis-based retailer, conducted a "Child Care Aware" program to help educate parents about quality child care and how to find it. The program included in-store information booths, distribution of 1.7 million brochures, and a toll-free national hotline.
- Liz Claiborne, the apparel manufacturer, commissioned leading American women artists to create works of public art to address issues of concern to women. In San Francisco, for example, six artists developed a public service campaign on the issue of domestic violence. The company also funded a domestic violence hotline.
- Arby's restaurant chain set up a "Neighbors in Need" program with local social service groups to give families down on their luck two meals a day for one month. Through its various franchises, the chain provided more than 670,000 meals.
- Lenscrafters, in association with Lions Clubs International, sponsored a program in England to recycle eye glasses for distribution by its clubs to underprivileged families in developing nations. More than 50,000 pairs of glasses were collected.
- Sempra Energy established an educational support program that helps employees gain knowledge through a seminar series, an On-site College Degree Program, as well as support for completion of college degrees at area educational institutions.

Corporate public affairs specialists engage in a wide range of activities that foster cooperation and interaction at the community and government levels.

Citigroup Asset Management
399 Park Avenue
New York, NY 10022

October 15, 2001

Dear Valued Client:

It is with a deep sense of loss, but also with the certainty of better days ahead, that I write to you in the aftermath of September 11th. A month has passed, and the depth and range of my emotions remain profound. The unfathomable atrocity that occurred that day is sure to be characterized as one of the worst in American history.

As tragic as recent events have been, they have succeeded in unifying us as a people and as a nation, bonding us in common sentiment. The united response, tireless volunteer efforts and the generosity of millions of American citizens are a source of great national pride. The strength of our people and the courage of our convictions will carry us through these most trying times. Like the nation, we at Citigroup Asset Management have come closer as a group.

As you may know, Citigroup Asset Management was located at 7 World Trade Center, a building that was destroyed. We are pleased to report that all of our people were evacuated safely and that we remain committed to assisting them through their recovery. On Monday, September 17th, a day that began with two minutes of silence for the victims, our newly relocated portfolio managers returned to the task of managing your financial assets. While your concern is undoubtedly focused on the healing process and responding to those in need, we can assure you that your investments have been well protected and actively managed.

It is with great pride that I commend our dedicated employees who have risen to the occasion, making numerous sacrifices to ensure uninterrupted service to you and our other valued clients. It is in this same spirit of dedication that I offer you my sincerest gratitude for your unwavering commitment to Citigroup Asset Management, sharing with us the challenges and uncertainties following the reopening of the financial markets. We acknowledge this gesture with gratitude and pride, and restate our commitment to preserving and growing your financial wealth in a tradition that dates back more than 66 years.

Mahatma Gandhi once said, "You must not lose faith in humanity. Humanity is an ocean; if a few drops of the ocean are dirty, the ocean does not become dirty." It is the faith Gandhi describes that will carry us forward; faith grounded in a common cause, enduring freedom. I ask you also to sustain your faith in the economy and in the markets, as they will certainly test our mettle. Our investment professionals, working with your Financial Consultants, will make every attempt to see that your needs are being met as we forge ahead. Welcome their opinions, utilize their knowledge and allow them to advise you regarding your financial affairs as you focus your concern on restoring yourself, your family and our great nation.

Warmest Regards,

Thomas W. Jones

Thomas W. Jones
CEO and Chairman of Citigroup Asset Management

PRIVATE PORTFOLIO GROUP
Citigroup Asset Management

Salomon Brothers
Mutual Funds

Smith Barney
Mutual Funds
Your Serious Money. Professionally Managed.℠

90819

Many corporations, in the aftermath of the September 11 terrorist attack on New York's World Trade Towers and the Pentagon, sought to reassure their customers and the public about their commitment to continued service.

The sponsorship of major events is a common practice among corporations as part of their community relations and branding strategies. Extensive print and television coverage of such events, in addition to the thousands that attend the event, allow the corporate name and logo to be seen by millions. Here, Ludmila Petrova of Russia crosses the finish line of New York City's 2000 marathon, with the record-breaking time of 2.25:45. (Reuters/ Ray Stubblebine.)

A survey by the Public Affairs Research Group at the Boston University School of Management, for example, indicates that the top four activities are (1) community relations, (2) government relations, (3) corporate contributions, and (4) media relations. Government relations is discussed in Chapter 15.

Community Relations

A business slogan says, "Think globally, act locally." Community relations, particularly in those towns and cities where the company maintains an office, retail outlets, or a manufacturing facility, carries out that advice.

Because a corporation relies on local governments for construction permits, changes in zoning laws, even tax concessions, a good working relationship with city hall and community groups is important. A vigorous program also helps in the recruitment of employees and gives the company influence in community affairs.

Public affairs specialists often serve as representatives of their companies on community boards, task forces, and commissions. The purpose is to develop a dialogue between the company and the community. Public affairs personnel presenting the company's viewpoint listen and monitor emerging issues. Thus, they can inform management about any public or governmental concerns that directly or indirectly affect the company.

Corporate Aid to Education

In recent years, many corporations have become involved in supporting schools, in part because their human relations directors are disturbed by the poor education shown by some of their job applicants. Some companies "adopt" schools, supplying needed equipment and company employees to assist teachers. Contributions of computer equipment are one form of assistance. Two examples of corporate aid:

- Westinghouse sponsors an annual Science Talent Search that draws entrants from nearly 2000 high schools. The top prize is a $40,000 scholarship.
- Dow Chemical Company and Ketchum public relations, seeking to spark students' interest in chemistry, created ChemTV, a multimedia show patterned in the MTV-music style, which toured high schools in 16 large cities. Later Dow released a 45-minute video version for other interested schools.

A word of caution: Any company entering the educational field should be certain that its efforts are primarily intended to improve education, not to sell products to students. Otherwise, it can be criticized for crass commercialism. The National Education Association warns teachers not to use ready-made contributed lesson plans if they advance "merely PR purposes." (See Chapter 18.)

Corporate Philanthropy

Company financial contributions to community and national social programs and institutions are closely related to community relations. The campaign to balance the federal budget, with resulting cutbacks in government contributions to many programs, has put pressure on corporations to increase their philanthropy. The Independent Sector, a coalition of nonprofit foundations and charities, estimates that charitable organizations nationwide depend on the government for about 29 percent of their income.

Many corporations follow a policy of "enlightened self-interest" in their giving. That is, they select the charitable institutions they will support and the forms of support to offer that will assist company goals and objectives. (See Focus on Ethics on page 332.)

Hewlett-Packard, for example, is a manufacturer of computers, medical equipment, and test equipment. Product gifts account for most of its philanthropy. The company's philosophy is simply stated: "HP giving to college and universities meets university needs for products while attracting highly skilled workers to the industries we support."

focus on ethics

Corporate Philanthropy Is Really Strategic Communication

Corporate giving is best described as strategic philanthropy, according to *pr reporter* (November 16, 1998). The newsletter offers a definition of strategic philanthropy by Paul Davis Jones and Cary Raymond of IDPR Group: "the long-term socially responsible contribution of dollars, volunteers, products & expertise to a cause *aligned with the strategic business goals of an organization.*" Such giving can reap an array of benefits for the corporation:

- Strengthened reputation and brand recognition
- Increased media opportunities
- Improved community and government relations
- Facilitation of employee recruitment and retention
- Enhanced marketing
- Access to research and development
- Increased corporate profitability

Questions worth asking:

- Do you think that when strategic philanthropy is at work, more giving is made to more worthy organizations than would be true if the corporation ignored the seven benefits of strategic philanthropy?
- Should corporate giving be based in part or entirely on strategic considerations?
- Can the most needy causes be shortchanged because they do not serve strategic interests of corporate givers?
- Why shouldn't a corporation strive "to do good and to do well" at the same time?

On the other hand, Philip Morris uses philanthropy for constituency building and generating favorable perceptions among opinion leaders. The giant beer, tobacco, and food conglomerate donated more than $17 million in one recent year to schools, hospitals, cultural organizations, and charity groups. Many of these funds, activist critics say, were targeted to minority organizations that might help defeat tax and antismoking bills. In other words, corporate giving is based on where there might be political benefit.

American corporations in 2001 contributed $10.86 billion to philanthropic organizations, according to the American Association of Fund-Raising Counsel (AAFRC). This represents 5.3 percent of the total $203.45 billion in contributions reported by the AAFRC. (See Chapter 17.)

Company giving takes many forms—cash, as in the case of Philip Morris; company products, as done by Hewlett-Packard; food and clothing to the needy; loans of company employees to assist fund drives by charitable organizations; and other methods.

A widely used technique is matching funds: A company matches every dollar an employee contributes to a charitable organization. Corporations also encourage employees to do volunteer work, either on company time or after work hours.

Two examples of creative corporate philanthropy:

- Instead of buying its Christmas cards from a commercial printer, the Bank of Boston bought 22,000 cards from the AIDS Action Committee of Massachusetts. This purchase was substantially greater than the total AIDS card sale the previous year.

- Eight companies in Santa Rosa and San Mateo Counties of California competed to see which one could contribute the most food to the Second Harvest Food Bank at Christmas. Winner of the Corporate Food Bowl Challenge was Cisco Systems. Company management vigorously encouraged its approximately 5000 employees to participate. They contributed 914,525 pounds of food to the needy. For convenience, many donated cash, which was used to purchase food.

Corporate philanthropy does have its limitations. Contributions generate a reserve of public support but cannot offset a company performance that the public considers unsatisfactory.

Philanthropy also may come under attack from special-interest groups. This is particularly true regarding extremely emotional issues. Prolife groups, for example, often target companies that give grants to Planned Parenthood and ask supporters to boycott the company's products.

Pioneer Hi-Bred International, a seed corn company headquartered in Iowa, canceled its $25,000 annual gift to Planned Parenthood of Greater Iowa after a prolife group called Rescue the Perishing started distributing leaflets to farmers asking them to boycott the company's products. The company president flatly told the *Wall Street Journal,* "We were blackmailed," but added, "You can't put the corn business at risk."

Prolife groups had originally forced Dayton-Hudson Corporation, a department store chain, to cancel its contribution to Planned Parenthood, but the company reversed its decision after hundreds of irate customers sent in cut-up credit cards.

The Bank of America, headquartered in San Francisco, also was caught in a no-win situation when it decided to stop funding the Boy Scouts of America because of the group's refusal to admit gays. Although gay activists were pleased by the action, a storm of protest arose from other bank customers who supported the Boy Scouts. Many canceled their accounts and encouraged others to do the same.

The bank, caught in the crossfire, first tried to explain that its corporate philanthropy policy was not to give funds to any group that discriminated. However, because of the protest, the bank then reversed itself and decided to support the Boy Scouts.

Patrick Jackson, editor of *PR Reporter,* wonders if this was a wise strategy. He wrote, "The question is first one of ethics—not easily answered on such an issue. Also, one of numbers: are there more Scout supporters . . . and homophobes than there are gays and people who oppose discrimination? More important: who is likely to take action?"

Corporations and the Environment

Public demand for protection of the environment, born of a growing realization that the earth's resources are limited, places a heavy burden on corporations. Much of the world's pollution, but far from all, has been created by their manufacturing processes and use of their products. The public wants those products but protests against the pollution they have created. In earlier decades, smoking factory smokestacks were applauded as a sign of prosperity. Today they are a badge of corporate dishonor, because medical science has established that air pollution damages health.

Social responsibility requires that companies eliminate, to the best of their ability, the sources of environmental damage they have created. At the same time, corporate managements must protect the interests of their stockholders. Corporations face what writer William H. Miller called the green wall, "the towering, though invisible, barrier that separates firms' environmental good intentions from the realities of the bottom line." Activist groups representing many different environmental causes focus the public mood by conducting campaigns against individual companies, sometimes in a highly emotional manner. (Environmental groups are discussed in Chapter 17.)

Even the best-intentioned corporations sometimes have difficulty in eliminating their offenses, because the cost can be extremely high. Nevertheless, companies are increasingly aware that the cost savings of waste reduction, recycling, and elimination of future cleanup efforts can be considerable. The combination of genuine actions to achieve sustainable, low-impact production and effective communication programs can earn goodwill from many of the corporation's stakeholders, including employees, regulators and shareholders.

Alice Rivlin, director of the Office of Management and Budget in the Clinton administration, an environmental activist, summarized the problem many industries face:

> It's sometimes difficult for companies to be as environmentally responsible as they'd like to be, because it's costly in the short run. That's part of the general problem of short-term focus in American companies. But I think if they take a long-range view, especially with the rising concern about the environment in the general public, it's clear that long-term profitability will be aided by environmental responsibility.

The Public Relations Role

Public relations people representing corporations concentrate on three areas concerning the environment:

1. Present to the public the company's environmental accomplishments, its plans for long-term cleanup, and explanations of the company's problems in achieving its goals.
2. Inform top management of the public's perceptions and concerns about the company's environmental record. If management is reluctant to address the problems, public relations experts should persuade senior officials that they should act to protect the company's reputation.
3. Conduct environmental cleanup campaigns within the company urging employees to follow good environmental practices, such as recycling, on and off the job.

Specialists recommend that as a first step a company should take an environmental audit. This involves a detailed investigation of every aspect of the business for its impact on the environment. An audit by a qualified outsider may be more objective than a self-examination. Next, management should create a long-range cleanup program. Some environmental faults may be overcome quickly and cheaply, others only at high cost and retooling.

A company may need to raise prices of its products to remain profitable. Willingness to spend money and take risks is what Alice Rivlin was talking about. Jobs may be in jeopardy because of these decisions, a painful personnel problem.

Bad news always attracts more attention than good news. Public disclosure that a company is committing an environmental sin automatically gets more headlines than the success of a three-year program to reduce waste paper by 25 percent. Two ways in which a public relations practitioner can respond to this psychological fact are:

- Search out all the environmentally positive actions the company has taken and publicize them in a creative manner, such as through videotaped presentations to community groups. This projects a "good citizen" image.
- Have a crisis plan ready in case a company environmental blunder occurs. Be ready to explain how it came about; why it is difficult to correct, if that is true; and the company's plans to correct it. All defensive words fail, of course, if the company does not act vigorously to solve the problem.

Corporate products and methods viewed as dangerous today often were quite acceptable to society when they were created. Pesticides were hailed as a boon to agricultural production; further research has revealed their danger to humans. Asbestos was regarded as valuable fire insulation material; today it is known to cause cancer, yet removing it from buildings is costly and difficult. Lead was used widely in manufactured products; now medical evidence shows the peril of lead poisoning, especially to children. In explaining why a corporation is violating one of today's taboos, the practitioner can make a valid point by emphasizing the historical perspective. Realistic people recognize that complex solutions take time, but they must be convinced that the company is taking action, not just talking.

The "Green" Image

Green has become the symbolic word for being environmentally clean. Many companies try to wrap themselves in mantles of green for image purposes or to sell "green" products. Presenting a "green" corporate image is desirable *if* it is honest. Some companies that have presented themselves in this light, such as by claiming that their products are biodegradable or nontoxic when they aren't, have been publicly embarrassed by having to retract the claims. Others have been caught doing bad things at the same time they were promoting their good acts. Chevron U.S. published a series of advertisements illustrating how its employees try to protect wildlife. Yet it agreed to pay an $8 million fine for violating the federal Clean Water Act by repeatedly dumping excessive amounts of oil, grease, and other toxic wastes from a drilling platform in the Pacific Ocean off California.

When a corporation comes under attack from an activist environmental group, some senior officials instinctively want to fight back in a combative manner. In some instances, that may be a sensible course. Certain protest groups use extremely emotional, even violent, tactics that invite a hard response. Other companies find a policy of conciliation better; they try to work with the environmental group involved in a joint effort to find a solution.

One Company's Program

The 3M Company, operating in 20 countries worldwide, has won numerous awards for its "Pollution Prevention Pays" program. The manufacturing company calculates that the program has saved it $500 million since its inception in 1975.

Company management decided to concentrate on reducing the air pollution created by its production processes. This involved identifying pollution sources, modifying operations, installing control equipment, changing products, recycling, and encouraging suggestions from employees. More than 2500 projects have been put in operation around the world. These have reduced 3M's air pollutants by 120,000 tons. In the early 1990s, 3M decided to invest another $150 million in air pollution control equipment and renamed the project "3P Plus."

Vital to the program is the public relations department, which is responsible for all environmental communications—internal, to stimulate employee understanding and appreciation; and external, to inform the public about what is happening. For employees, the department conducts motivational meetings, shows videotapes, and issues special publications. For external use, it distributes news releases and other material, holds media briefings, and conducts plant tours for community leaders.

The Business–Media Relationship

Reporting by the media is a basic source of public information about the performance and objectives of business. Too frequently it generates misunderstanding and irritation between these two essential segments of society, a situation for which both sides are partially responsible. The trouble arises most frequently when a corporation becomes involved in a communication crisis.

Many business executives regard media stories about their companies as inaccurate, incomplete, and biased, an opinion at odds with the view of many business editors and writers. The pattern emerges in most polls taken on the relationship. A poll by Louis Harris and Associates asked, "Would you rate business journalism positively on being fair, balanced and accurate?" Results showed a striking discrepancy in the percentage of "Yes" responses among the four groups polled:

Business executives	27 percent
Writers and editors	84 percent
Business academics	64 percent
Journalism academics	72 percent

A majority of all four categories agreed, however, that the quality of business reporting had improved substantially during the past 20 years.

Corporate managers' principal complaints against media coverage are inaccuracy, incomplete coverage, inadequate research and preparation for interviews, and antibusiness bias. Business editors and reporters state in response that often they cannot publish or broadcast thorough, evenhanded stories about business because many company executives, uncooperative and wary, erect barriers against them. Writers complain about failing to obtain direct access to decision-making executives and being restricted to using public relations statements that don't contain information they need. Journalists assert, too, that some business leaders don't understand the concept of objectivity and assume that any story involving unfavorable news about their company is intentionally biased.

Public relations practitioners serving business stand in the middle. They must interpret their companies to the media, while showing their chief executive officers and other high officials how open, friendly press relations can serve their interest. And according to *O'Dwyer's PR Services Report,* corporate public relations executives need to spend more time talking to business reporters. "Because many corporate PR pros don't have relationships with reporters, they are terrorized by a press call, regarding it as the 'equivalent of a drive-by shooting,' . . . " (July, 1997, p. 6).

News stories about business leaders and corporations involving deception of the public, fraud, cheating of the government, and theft of funds hit the front pages and newscasts often enough to damage the public's conception of big business. Thus corporate public relations practitioners need to build public confidence in business as a whole as well as represent their own companies.

Financial Information

At a time when corporate mergers, takeovers, and financial scandals make headlines almost daily, the role of investor relations is essential in corporate operations. This falls within the general scope of public relations.

The men and women who handle investor relations work are specialists. In large corporations they may function as a separate unit, in smaller companies as part of the

PR insights

Ethical Guidelines for Business Public Affairs Professionals

a. The Public Affairs Professional maintains professional relationships based on honesty and reliable information, and therefore:

1. Represents accurately his or her organization's policies on economic and political matters to government, employees, shareholders, community interests, and others.
2. Serves always as a source of reliable information, discussing the varied aspects of complex public issues within the context and constraints of the advocacy role.
3. Recognizes diverse viewpoints within the public policy process, knowing that disagreement on issues is both inevitable and healthy.

b. The Public Affairs Professional seeks to protect the integrity of the public policy process and the political system, and therefore:

1. Publicly acknowledges his or her role as a legitimate participant in the public policy process and discloses whatever work-related information the law requires.
2. Knows, respects, and abides by federal and state laws that apply to lobbying and related public affairs activities.
3. Knows and respects the laws governing campaign finance and other political activities, and abides by the letter and intent of those laws.

c. The Public Affairs Professional understands the interrelation of business interests with the larger public interests, and therefore:

1. Endeavors to ensure that responsible and diverse external interests and views concerning the needs of society are considered within the corporate decision-making process.
2. Bears the responsibility for management review of public policies which may bring corporate interests into conflict with other interests.
3. Acknowledges dual obligations—to advocate the interests of his or her employer, and to preserve the openness and integrity of the democratic process.
4. Presents to his or her employer an accurate assessment of the political and social realities that may affect corporate operations.

Source: Public Affairs Council, a Washington-based organization of public affairs executives for major corporations.

public relations department. No matter how the organization chart is designed, cooperation between the general public relations function and this special field should be close.

The two primary targets for a company's financial information are (1) its stockholders and (2) the financial analysts who advise brokers and bankers on the current and probable future financial health of a company. Because large blocks of stock often are held by a single investor, such as a pension fund, special attention must be paid to those investors, as well as to the growing number of foreign stockholders. (Corporate annual reports are discussed in Chapter 20.)

Stockholders

Annual meetings of corporations commonly are routine and dull, with everything going precisely as management has arranged it. Proxy votes obtained in advance assure management solid control of the voting. Management often presents slide and videotaped shows to illustrate achievements, serves light refreshments, and in general tries to create an atmosphere of competence and geniality. Behind the scenes, many hours of public relations department work have been spent in planning the meetings.

At times abrasive moments of controversy may arise if stockholders challenge management policies. This is done through antimanagement resolutions that must be put to a vote of all stockholders. During the 1990s many of these concerned the environment, demanding that the company do something the activists advocate or stop doing something they dislike. Other recent concerns were executive compensation, use of child labor, and job loss through downsizing.

Although antimanagement resolutions rarely pass, they obtain publicity and at times gather enough votes to influence management thinking. Sometimes managements compromise with advocacy groups to obtain withdrawal of their resolutions.

Financial Analysts

Discussion of a company's condition and prospects with financial analysts is important because the advice they give to traders influences the price of a company's stock. In addition to periodic formal presentations to groups of analysts, investor relations people send them information by computer, fax, and video.

Investor relations work has no room for publicity hype and verbal sleight-of-hand. In fact, information must meet legal requirements for accuracy. Financial analysts are experts, and their questions are searching. When a company's chief executive officer makes a presentation, the public relations department is called on to help him prepare. An effective presentation showing a solid growth pattern and sound financing may win "buy" recommendations and make the stock price rise, thus increasing the company's value. Rising stock values are particularly important to top management because much of their compensation is based on significant increases. Therefore, a great deal is riding on the effective communication of financial information, in part explaining why investor relations specialists are among the highest-paid public relations professionals.

Sensitivity to Minority Groups

Swift expansion of the minority population in the United States, bringing with it intensified problems of language and cultural differences, demands heightened sensitivity by corporate management. Traditionally, senior executives have been white males, although female and minority faces are increasingly evident in executive suites. Feedback on attitudes of minority customers and employees collected by public relations departments helps broaden management perspectives.

The racial mixture of workforces sometimes becomes an issue if a large minority group in a community believes that a company fails to hire enough of its members. Communications within a company also can be a problem if some employees speak little or no English. These difficulties can be overcome if management handles them in a sensitive manner. When it fails to do so, the cost in money and public respect can be great.

Texaco, Inc., provides a notorious example. After lingering in federal court more than two years, a suit against the oil company by 1377 employees charging racial discrimination was blown wide open by disclosure of a tape recorded secretly at a meeting of high company executives. They were heard using racial slurs against employees and discussing the destruction of documents the employees might use in their suit.

Eleven days later Texaco agreed to pay $176 million to settle the case, the largest settlement ever in a racial discrimination suit. It agreed to begin intensive sensitivity training, and the corporate chairman apologized publicly. One former executive was charged by the federal government with shredding documents.

Repercussions against Texaco were intense. Black leaders called a boycott but cancelled it after Texaco announced plans to diversify its workforce. Some organizations sold their Texaco stock in protest.

PR casebook

Eddie Bauer's Blunder

The Eddie Bauer, Inc., clothing chain, caught in a racial discrimination crisis, responded so slowly and clumsily that it compounded its problem.

Two black teenage youths were shopping at an Eddie Bauer store in Maryland. As they left, police officers moonlighting as security guards accused one youth of shoplifting the shirt he was wearing. He told them he had purchased the shirt on a previous visit to the store and didn't have with him the sales receipt they demanded. The officers ordered him to take off the shirt and leave it until he brought in the receipt. He returned with the receipt the next day and was given the shirt. A company spokesperson later called the incident "minor" and implied that the company had done the young man a favor by returning it.

Angered at her son's treatment, the youth's mother phoned the Eddie Bauer corporate headquarters to complain. She said she was told someone would call her back. When weeks passed without a return call, she told the story to the *Washington Post,* which published it.

In response to public criticism and a threatened lawsuit, Eddie Bauer hired Hill and Knowlton, the public relations firm, to help. With Hill and Knowlton's guidance, the company president issued a belated apology and went to Washington, where he conferred with NAACP officials. He promised a sensitivity training program for employees. The company donated truckloads of clothing to homeless shelters.

These gestures were insufficient to placate critics. Other black customers told stories of discrimination. The young man's mother pointed out that while the company president was in Washington he spoke with NAACP officials but didn't apologize to the two young men or see them or their families.

Even Bauer's act of hiring Hill and Knowlton drew criticism. *Washington Post* columnist Jonathan Yardley wrote, "Taking on a high-octane public relations firm is *prima facie* evidence of guilt."

The company's delay in response and perceived failure to recognize the personal feelings of the individuals involved made a bad situation even worse.

Other companies have paid in fines and in public opinion for similar cases. Among them: Denny's restaurant chain agreed to pay $54 million to black customers who charged it with racial discrimination; Circuit City, the retail electronics chain, was found guilty of racial discrimination against blacks in promotion and fined; the R.R. Donnelley and Sons, Co., printing firm was sued for $50 million by black employees alleging racial discrimination in layoffs. Avis Rent-A-Car and one of its franchisers were sued by three black women who charged that the franchiser had refused to rent cars to black customers.

Marketing Communications

Many companies use the tools and tactics of public relations extensively to support the marketing and sales objectives of their businesses. This is called *marketing communications* or *marketing public relations.* Personnel who work in this specialty area usually serve in, or work closely with, the marketing, advertising, and promotion departments of the company.

Thomas L. Harris, author of *A Marketer's Guide to Public Relations,* defines marketing public relations (MPR) as "The process of planning, executing, and evaluating programs that encourage purchase and consumer satisfaction through credible communication of information and impressions that identify companies and their products with the needs, wants, concerns, and interests of consumers."

In many cases, marketing public relations also is coordinated with a company's messages in advertising, marketing, direct mail, and promotion. This has led to the concept of *integrated marketing communications* (IMC) in which companies manage all sources of information about a product or service in order to assure maximum message penetration.

In an integrated program, for example, public relations activities are often geared to obtaining early awareness and credibility for a product. Publicity in the form of news stories builds credibility, excitement in the marketplace, and consumer anticipation. These messages make audiences more receptive to advertising and promotions about the product.

The Volkswagen Beetle was introduced in just such a way. Volkswagen won early support of key auto trade and business media by inviting them to participate in background sessions on the car during the preproduction stage. The car was introduced using video news releases and interactive satellite feeds that resulted in 800 individual TV segments, including appearances on *Today* and *Good Morning America.* Such media coverage provided a powerful third-party endorsement that then was merchandised with clever advertising taglines such as "Less flower. More power."

The objectives of marketing public relations, often called marcom in industry jargon, are accomplished in several ways.

Product Publicity

The cost and clutter of advertising and sales promotion have mounted dramatically, and companies have found that product publicity is a cost-effective way of reaching potential consumers. Products, if presented properly, can be newsworthy and catch the eyes of reporters and editors. Clorox, for example, generated many news articles and broadcast mentions for its Combat cockroach killer by sponsoring a contest to find America's five worst cockroach-infested homes.

Other forms of product publicity are found on the food, auto, real estate, business, travel, and sports pages of newspapers and magazines as news and feature stories. Radio and television talk shows and consumer programs contain large amounts of publicity.

A company also can generate product publicity by sponsoring a poll. The Clor-Trimeton Allergy Season Index has measured pollen counts since 1984. Even the Gallup Poll, which newspapers run regularly, is a product publicity technique for the company to promote its polling services to business and industry.

Joan Aho Ryan and George H. Lemmond, writing in the *Public Relations Journal,* make the case for product publicity: "Cynical consumers, zapping commercials and ignoring print ads, are more receptive to the editorial message. The 'third party endorsement' allows advertisers to sell a new product while enveloping the commercial message in a credible environment."

Information Bureaus

Several companies operate information bureaus that help position their products in the marketplace. Quaker's Gatorade has its Sports Science Institute, Reebok has an Aerobic Information Bureau, and Nutri/System operates a Health and Fitness Information Bureau. One primary function of these "information bureaus" is the distribution of news releases and press kits that report research results and give consumer tips on keeping healthy and fit. Of course, the sponsor of the research and the source of the "tips" are mentioned in the resulting news stories.

School Promotions

Companies try to instill brand loyalty and corporate identity early by sponsoring programs and lesson plans in the classroom. AT&T has an Adventure Club that fosters an understanding of communications. Exxon provides science lessons with such titles as "Scientists and the Alaskan Oil Spill." And Domino's Pizza supplies a learning tool to help kids count by tabulating the number of pepperoni wheels.

Although parents and consumer groups dislike having school children made the target of corporate marketing programs, teachers in financially strapped school districts often welcome business support.

Cause-Related Marketing

Companies in highly competitive fields often strive to stand out by supporting causes that appeal to various market segments. Dannon yogurt brand, for example, donates 1.5 percent of its sales to the National Wildlife Federation. This method is used to accomplish several objectives. It can increase sales and brand loyalty and is effective in communicating a company's values and philosophy. It is a form of reputation management.

Corporate Sponsorships

Companies spend about $6.8 billion annually sponsoring activities ranging from the Olympic Games, the Indianapolis 500-mile race, and the Kentucky Derby to the Three Tenors Opera Tour. Experts say that corporate sponsorship is a growth industry averaging a 30 to 40 percent increase annually.

PR insights

Selection Criteria for Corporate Sponsorships

Corporations are inundated with requests from organizations to sponsor everything from rock concerts to museum exhibits and sporting events. Consequently, each corporation selects sponsorships that best support its marketing and public relations objectives. A company considering a sponsorship should ask these questions:

- Can the company afford to fulfill the obligation? The sponsorship fee is just the starting point. Count on doubling it to have an adequate total event budget.
- Is the event or organization compatible with the company's values and mission statement?
- Does the event reach the corporation's target audience?
- Is there enough time before the event to maximize the company's use of the sponsorship?
- Are the event organizers experienced and professional?
- Is the event newsworthy enough to provide the company with opportunities for publicity?
- Will the event be televised?
- Will the sales force support the event and use it to leverage sales?
- Does the event give the company a chance to develop new contacts and business opportunities?
- Can the company live with the event on a long-term basis while its value builds?
- Is there an opportunity for employee involvement? Corporate sponsorships can be used to build employee morale and teamwork.
- Is the event compatible with the "personality" of the company's products?
- Can the company reduce the cash outlay and enhance the marketing appeal by trading off products and in-kind services?
- Will management support the event? If the answer is yes to the previous questions, the likelihood of management support of the sponsorship is fairly high.

Source: Barr, John M. "Maximizing the Value of Sponsorships." *Public Relations Journal.* April 1993, p. 30.

The popularity of sponsored events is due to several reasons. These events: (1) enhance the reputation and image of the sponsoring company through association, (2) give product brands high visibility among key purchasing publics, (3) provide a focal point for marketing efforts and sales campaigns, and (4) generate publicity and media coverage.

Sponsorships can be more cost effective than advertising. Visa International, for example, spends about $200,000 a year sponsoring the USA–Visa Decathlon Team, or about the price of a 30-second prime-time TV commercial. However, Visa also paid $40 million to be an official worldwide sponsor of the 1996 Olympic Games.

The prestige and worldwide audience of the Olympics is the pinnacle of corporate sponsorship, but companies also sponsor any number of other events on a local, regional, or national level. The array of sponsorship activity and opportunities is so great that the International Events Group publishes the 8-page *IEG Sponsorship Report* every two weeks. Nevertheless, sports sponsorships predominate, accounting for 67 percent of the $7.5 billion spent on sponsorships in 1999.

Local stadiums almost everywhere now have corporate names. An obscure high-technology company, 3COM, got reams of national publicity when Candlestick Park in San Francisco became 3COM Park. The Orange Bowl is now officially the Federal Express Orange Bowl.

The demographic characteristics of potential customers determine for the most part what events a company will sponsor. Manufacturers of expensive products sponsor events that draw the interest of affluent consumers. That's why Lexus, a luxury car, sponsors polo championships. General Motors GMC division, however, is interested in selling pickup trucks, so it sponsors a 15-city country-western music tour.

On occasion, a company will sponsor an event for the primary purpose of enhancing its image. Ford Motor Company, seeking to polish its corporate image among the affluent and well-educated, once sponsored an exhibition of Impressionist paintings in Pittsburgh. Intel Corporation works on its corporate image as a patron of the arts by sponsoring traveling museum exhibitions.

Employee Communications

The Internal Audience

The employees of a company form a crucial audience for its public relations department. The department, often working with or within the human resources department, must concentrate on communicating with employees just as vigorously as it does on delivering the corporate story to the outside world. A workforce that respects its management, has pride in its products, and believes that it is being treated fairly is a key factor in corporate success.

In these days of corporate turmoil, unrest and uncertainty among employees create a greater need than ever for effective employee communications. Surveys indicate a dropoff in employees' loyalty to their companies, based in part on their belief that remote corporate managements feel no loyalty to them.

Job security and financial protection against illness are two principal concerns among employees. As much as the facts justify, they need to be reassured. Company magazines, brochures, newsletters, and policy manuals written for employees are a fundamental form of internal communication. These are discussed in detail in Chapter 20.

Much employee communication work is relatively standard—distribution of information about working conditions, retirement benefits, new company products, changes in management and supervisory personnel, and corporate plans for expansion or alterations in operating procedures. *The better informed employees are, the less likely they are to spread erroneous and possibly damaging misinformation.* Gossip flourishes in an information vacuum. Accurate information from management can make the always-present company grapevine a positive rather than a negative force.

Health and Social Issues

Communication with employees involves much more than the nuts and bolts items just described. Critical health and social issues are involved, in which the company must steer a cautious course.

The skyrocketing cost of health insurance for employees has become a heavy and still growing burden on employers. Yet with personal medical and hospital bills so high, employees regard medical insurance for themselves and their families as extremely important. Company attempts to trim benefits have encountered fervent resistance.

Circle K, which operates convenience stores nationwide, found that out when, with little preparation, it denied new employees coverage for illnesses and accidents related to "personal lifestyle decisions."

This meant no coverage for new employees if they became ill with acquired immune deficiency syndrome (AIDS) or had drug or alcohol problems. Circle K was accused, among other things, of making a thinly veiled attack on homosexuality. The dispute was covered on national television and the front pages. Reaction was so severe that Circle K suspended implementation of the plan.

Other social issues in the workplace:

- *Use of drugs on the job.* How much on-the-job drug testing, if any, should a company do? When does a company's right to maintain strong, safe production levels intrude on the individual rights of employees?
- *Smoking by employees.* Evidence that exposure to smoke from others may injure nonsmokers has increased pressure for no-smoking rules in company work and recreation areas. Yet some smokers vehemently insist that they have rights, too.
- *Sexual harassment.* This worries both employees and management, the latter for legal as well as ethical reasons. The U.S. Supreme Court ruled in *Monitor Savings Bank* v. *Vinson* (1986) that a company may be held liable in sexual harassment suits even if management is unaware of the problem and has a general policy against discrimination.

  One major corporation, the DuPont Company, meets the problem of sexual harassment thus, as reported in *Public Relations Journal:* a travel safety seminar for female employees, a personal safety program that includes a rape-prevention workshop, a managers' workshop to define their role in helping employees who have been assaulted, legal assistance, liability coverage, and public relations assistance in handling publicity that might result from a rape trial. The company promotes the program in internal publications, on the company news hotline, and in monthly safety meetings.
- *Child care.* With so many parents of young children working and the cost of private day care so high, should companies provide day-care facilities? Some companies do. To what extent should a company offer general education programs beyond direct job-training education? Is there a danger that companies, in trying to keep employees happy, will do too much and assume a Big Brother role that causes resentment?

Employee attitudes toward these and similar issues should be closely considered by managements as they make decisions. The public relations department's role in gathering employee opinion, and in providing employees with management's thinking, thus becomes vital.

Summary

The Corporate Role

Large corporations have a compelling influence on contemporary life at many levels, making public relations a complex task.

The Human Factor

People are the basic element in every business. Corporations must develop a positive public perception of their conduct. One difficult situation will be downsizing, where the challenge will be in communications with both management and the public. Overlooking the human factor can lead to costly public relations blunders. An example of this would be substituting technology for human contact, with elaborate voicemail systems or computer-generated form letters.

Consumerism

The days of *caveat emptor* are long gone, with tremendous growth in the consumer-rights movement since the 1960s. This has led both to greater consumer awareness and an expansion of regulatory agencies. Boycotts may be among the tools used by consumers today.

Product Recalls

Recalls of defective products are a highly visible and expensive aspect of corporate–consumer relations. Such recalls can be voluntary or done under government pressure.

Business Public Affairs

Responsible "corporate citizenship" is a basic issue in the relationship between businesses and the public, to create not only support for corporations in the community but also improve the quality of life for society. These both can enhance a company's reputation in the community and therefore its bottom line.

Community Relations

Community relations are based on the slogan, "Think globally, act locally." Public relations programs are developed to create a dialogue between a company and the community in which it maintains an office, retail outlet, or manufacturing facility.

Corporate Aid to Education

One goal in supporting schools is to improve the quality of job applicants through a better-educated public. For example, corporations can provide scholarships or donate equipment to schools.

Corporate Philanthropy

A policy of "enlightened self-interest" in corporate giving means that the company targets charitable institutions that will assist company goals and objectives. Company giving can include cash, food and clothing to the needy, or the loan of employees' time. Corporations can also encourage volunteer work among their staff. However, some philanthropy may come under attack from special-interest groups.

Corporations and the Environment

Corporations must balance the need for environmental responsibility with the financial interests of their stockholders, although long-term profitability is clearly aided by protecting the environment. Presenting a "green" corporate image is desirable *if* it is honest.

The Business–Media Relationship

The media are the major source of information about corporations, and the quality of business information has improved substantially during the past quarter-century. Public relations practitioners must foster positive interactions between the businesses they represent and the media.

Financial Information

Investor relations work is a specialty in public relations that may be part of the public relations department or, in large corporations, form a separate unit. Two primary audiences for financial information are stockholders and financial analysts. Such information must meet legal requirements for accuracy.

Sensitivity to Minority Groups

Among the public relations issues in dealing with minority groups are the racial/ethnic mix in the workforce. Sensitivity to minority groups will affect both community and consumer relations, and insensitivity can lead to both high direct financial costs and loss of public respect.

Marketing Communications

Marketing communications supports the marketing and sales objectives of a business. The coordination of marketing public relations with a company's advertising, marketing, direct mail, and promotion communications leads to the concept of integrated marketing communications. This can involve product publicity, information bureaus, school promotions, cause-related marketing, and corporate sponsorships.

Employee Communications

An important audience for public relations practitioners is a corporation's own workforce. Their respect for management, pride in the company's products, and confidence in their fair treatment are key factors in corporate success that can be developed through good communication. However, companies must steer a cautious course in dealing with many health and social issues, such as drug use, smoking, sexual harassment, and child care.

Case Activity: What Would You Do?

Women's sports, both amateur and professional, have attracted an increasing number of women participants in recent years. Nike, recognizing this trend, has developed a new shoe designed for women basketball players. Develop a marketing public relations program for this product that also would be coordinated with an advertising and promotion program. Provide the unique perspective and value of your public relations expertise. Include a response plan for critics of Nike's use of cheaper overseas labor to make shoes. This plan could range from steps to remedy injustices to a defense of open labor markets, depending upon your view.

Questions for Review and Discussion

1. Why is the public perception of a corporation so important to its success?
2. What caused the growth of the consumer movement between 1960 and 1980 in the United States? Who was its best-known leader?
3. Have you ever participated in a boycott? If so, do you believe the boycott achieved its goal? If it failed, why did it?
4. As a corporate public relations director, what actions might you recommend to top management in order to establish your company's image as a socially responsible organization?
5. What are some of the methods government relations specialists use to obtain favorable treatment for their companies?
6. Why are investor relations specialists so important to the financial well-being of a corporation?
7. What mistakes did Texaco make in handling a discrimination suit against it?
8. What is marketing public relations? What primary audience is involved? What kind of activities does it include?
9. Why are corporate sponsorships so popular?
10. What two primary concerns of employees need to be addressed by public relations and human relations departments of companies?

Suggested Readings

Boyle, Matthew. "New Cash-Reputation Results Impact Clients." *PR Week,* June 28, 1999, p. 15.

Caywood, Clarke, (ed). *The Handbook of Strategic Public Relations & Integrated Communications.* New York: McGraw-Hill, 1997.

Howard, Elizabeth. "Swooshed! What Activists Are Teaching Nike." *Public Relations Strategist,* Fall 1998, pp. 38–41.

Ledingham, John A., and Bruning, Stephen D. "Building Loyalty through Community Relations." *Public Relations Strategist,* Summer 1997, pp. 27–29.

Lukaszewski, Jim. "Activism: Preparing Counteractive Strategies." *Strategy,* No. 12/December 18, 2000, a supplement of *pr reporter,* pp. 1–4.

Maccabee, Paul. "How to Survive a Boycott." *PR Tactics,* February 1997, pp. 1, 10–11.

Manheim, Jarol B. *The Death of a Thousand Cuts: Corporate Campaigns and the Attack on the Corporation.* Mahwah, NJ: Lawrence Erlbaum Associates, 2001.

Randall, Karen. "Anatomy of a Nightmare: Denny's Discovers Diversity." *Public Relations Strategist,* Winter 1998, pp. 14–19.

Reber, Bryan, Cropp, Fritz, and Cameron, Glen T. "Impossible Odds." *Journal of Public Relations Research,* Vol. 14, No. 3, 2002.

Seitel, Fraser. "Defending an Embattled Industry." *Public Relations Strategist,* Summer 1999, pp. 7–13.

"Strategic Philanthropy Is More Than Giving $$ to Good Causes." *pr reporter,* November 16, 1998, pp. 2–3.

Thorson, Esther, and Moore, Jeri (eds). *Integrated Communication: Synergy of Persuasive Voices.* Mahwah, NJ: Lawrence Erlbaum Associates, 1996.

Politics and Government

preview

In this chapter, the objective is to provide an understanding of the work performed by governmental relations specialists, lobbyists, and political fund-raisers.

Topics covered in the chapter include:

- Corporate government relations
- Lobbying
- The problem of "influence peddling"
- Grassroots lobbying efforts
- Political action committees (PACs)
- Fund-raising by candidates
- Political campaigns
- Public affairs in government
- Attacks on government information services

Government Relations

A major component of corporate public affairs is government relations. This activity is so important that many companies, particularly in highly regulated industries, have separate departments of government relations. The reason is simple. The actions of governmental bodies at the local, state, and federal level have a major impact on how a business operates.

Government relations specialists have a number of functions: They gather information, disseminate management's views, cooperate with government on projects of mutual benefit, and motivate employees to participate in the political process.

As the eyes and ears of a business or industry, practitioners spend much time gathering and processing information. They monitor the activities of many legislative bodies and regulatory agencies to keep track of issues coming up for debate and possible vote. Such intelligence gathering enables a corporation or an industry to plan ahead and, if necessary, adjust policies or provide information that may influence the nature of government decision making.

Monitoring government takes many forms. Probably the most active presence in Washington, D.C., and many state capitals is the trade association that represents a particular industry. A Boston University survey showed that 67 percent of the responding companies monitored government activity in Washington through their trade associations. Second on the list were frequent trips to Washington by senior public affairs officers and corporate executives; 58 percent of the respondents said they engaged in this activity. Almost 45 percent of the responding firms reported that they also had a company office in the nation's capital.

Government relations specialists spend a great amount of time disseminating information about the company's position to a variety of key publics. Spoken tactics may include an informal office visit to a government official or testimony at a public

John McCain, U.S. Senator from Arizona, uses Congressional hearings to generate publicity and public support for many of his pet projects, including campaign finance reform.

hearing. In addition, public affairs people are often called upon to give a speech or write one for a senior executive.

Written tactics may include writing letters and op-ed articles, preparing position papers, producing newsletters, and placing advocacy advertising. Although legislators are a primary audience, the Foundation for Public Affairs reports that nine of 10 companies also communicate with employees on public policy issues, while another 40 percent communicate with retirees, customers, and other publics such as taxpayers and government employees.

The importance of effective governmental relations to the economic well-being of a company is best summarized by a *New York Times* writer thus:

> Public relations executives can rightly point out that, with the cacophony of interests clamoring for attention in Washington, there is a role for professional advice on how to insure that one's message is heard. With the expanding role of Congress and the increasing complexity of government, this probably is true now more than ever. There are undoubtedly times that public relations firms can help journalists, politicians and clients.

Corporations are also actively engaged in lobbying and making campaign contributions, which are discussed next.

Lobbying

Lobbying is closely aligned with governmental relations or public affairs, and the distinction between the two often blurs. This is because most campaigns to influence impending legislation have multiple levels. One level is informing and convincing the public about the correctness of the organization's viewpoint, which the public affairs specialist does.

Lobbying, on the other hand, is a more specific activity. *Webster's New World Dictionary* defines a *lobbyist* as "a person . . . who tries to influence the voting on legislation or the decisions of government administrators." In other words, a lobbyist directs his or her energies to the defeat, passage, or amendment of proposed legislation and regulatory agency policies.

A good example of how the two functions work in tandem is how Arthur Andersen, the accounting firm, responded when it was accused of massive negligence in covering up the financial problems of Enron, the energy company, just before it went bankrupt.

Public affairs specialists for the accounting firm had the major job of reassuring the public and influential financial leaders that the company had the scandal under control and was taking steps to maintain the credibility of the brand name. One approach was a series of issue advertisements titled "Andersen will do what is right."

At the same time, Andersen hired a number of high-powered lobbyists with good connections to the Bush administration and the House Commerce Committee to assure that the U.S. Congress would not pass legislation that would place more restrictions on the accounting firm and the industry.

Andersen's ability to reach key legislators was assisted by its long-term program of political contributions. Since 1991, the company had contributed corporate "soft money" to national party committees. In a ten-year period, the Republican Party received $2.5 million and the Democratic Party had received $859,000. The accounting firm, through its political action committees (PACs), also contributed $146,000 to the presidential campaign of George W. Bush.

PR casebook

Microsoft's Lobbying Effort Pays Off

Microsoft, after nearly four years, won a victory in the fall of 2001 when the U.S. government announced that it would no longer seek a breakup of the company. The government also abandoned the contention that Microsoft had violated federal antitrust law by integrating its Internet Explorer browser software into its Windows operating system.

A healthy share of the credit, according to Microsoft's critics, was the corporation's major lobbying effort over a period of almost four years. In 2000 alone, Microsoft and its employees donated $4.66 million to federal political candidates and parties, with more than two-thirds of the amount given to Republicans. In addition, the company paid at least $6 million more to lobbyists, who were charged with persuading elected officials to accept Microsoft's point of view.

At the state level, Microsoft also engaged in extensive political contributions to candidates and political parties. According to a lobbying organization working for Microsoft's adversaries, the company donated $6.1 million overall, with about $3.2 million of that to Republicans. Edward J. Black, president of the Computer and Communications Industry Association, told the *New York Times,* "One would be hard pressed to say that all the money and the lobbying was not intended to get a positive result—to get a huge back-off on the case. And they got a huge back-off on the case."

Microsoft, in its effort to influence public opinion and elected officials, hired a number of high-powered lobbyists who had connections to Congress and the Bush administration. One such person was Ralph Reed, former head of the Christian Coalition and a former senior advisor to the Bush campaign. Others included the former chairman of the Republican National Committee, several White House counsel to former Presidents George Bush and Bill Clinton, and several former members of Congress.

The lobbyists delivered a number of position papers to influential Washington opinion-makers, wrote op-ed pieces for major daily newspapers, and even cited national surveys showing that the public was opposed to the government's antitrust suit. The surveys were sponsored by two other Microsoft-financed groups, the Citizens Against Government Waste and the Technology Access Action Coalition.

But not all lobbying occurred at the federal level. Microsoft executives also visited state attorneys general who were part of the broad antitrust suit against the company. Often times, the executives were accompanied by close friends or local colleagues of the attorneys general. Such visits apparently paid off. Texas, South Carolina, and New Mexico dropped out of the federal lawsuit.

Microsoft, until the federal antitrust lawsuit, was relatively inactive as a lobbying force. According to reporter Joel Brinkley in the *New York Times,* "When the Clinton administration's Justice Department filed its first suit against Microsoft, in the fall of 1997, the company had a one-man lobbying shop with an office above a suburban-Washington shopping mall. The company's political donations of all types to federal candidates that year totaled $100,000. Microsoft then, company executives said at the time, considered Washington a distant and largely irrelevant dot on the map, far removed both physically and spiritually from its headquarters just outside Seattle."

What a difference a lawsuit can make in a company's perspective about the importance of lobbying!

Lobbyists can be found at the local, state, and federal levels of government. California, for example, has about 900 registered lobbyists who represent more than 1600 special-interest groups. The interests represented in Sacramento include large corporations, business and trade groups, unions, environmental groups, local governments, nonprofit groups, school districts, and members of various professional groups.

The number and variety of special interests multiply at the federal level. One directory of Washington lobbyists lists 20,000 individuals and organizations. The interests represented include virtually the entire spectrum of U.S. business, educational, religious, local, national, and international pursuits.

The diversity of those groups can be illustrated with the debate about managed health care and patient rights. Opposing new regulations are (1) insurance companies, (2) HMO trade groups, (3) the United States Chamber of Commerce, (4) the National Federation of Independent Business, and (5) the American Association of Health Plans. Groups supporting patient rights include (1) a broad coalition of consumer groups (2) the American Medical Association, and (3) the Trial Lawyers of America.

The groups opposed to patient rights legislation are concerned about higher costs to employers, increased government control of health care delivery systems, and more litigation and lawsuits. As a result, the health industry has spent millions of dollars to lobby against any legislation. According to the Federal Election Commission, the industry's contributions to federal candidates and political parties totaled $90 million in the two-year election cycle, 1999–2000.

This amount doesn't include extensive television advertising, Internet "broadcasts" for doctors, and a variety of other public affairs efforts to reach the voting public. The American Association of Health Plans, for example, planned to spend $5 million in 2001 just on television advertising. Mark Merritt, a spokesperson for the group, told the *New York Times,* "We'll spend whatever it takes."

The Nature of Lobbying

Although the public perceives that only big business lobbies, a variety of special interests do it. *Fortune* magazine, for example, ranked the top 25 lobbying groups in Washington in terms of influence, and the American Association of Retired Persons (AARP) was first on the list. The next four rankings, in descending order, were (1) the American Israel Public Affairs Committee, (2) the National Federation of Independent Business, (3) the National Rifle Association, and (4) the AFL-CIO.

Collectively, interest groups spent $1.45 billion on lobbying in 1999, according to the nonprofit Center for Responsive Politics (CPR). For perspective, the center noted that this amount was enough to cover the entire budget of the Food and Drug Administration (FDA). Businesses involved in real estate, insurance, and finance spent the most money in 1998—$203 million. Tobacco companies spent $67.4 million on lobbying, almost double what they spent in 1997. Leading the pack was Philip Morris Companies, spending the most—$3.62 million.

Competing lobbying efforts often cancel each other out. All this leaves legislators and regulatory personnel the responsibility to weigh the pros and cons of an issue before voting. Indeed, *Time* magazine notes that lobbyists representing all sides of an issue "do serve a useful purpose by showing busy legislators the virtues and pitfalls of complex legislation." A classic conflict is the debate between saving jobs and improving the environment. A coalition of environmental groups constantly lobbies Congress for tougher legislation to clean up industrial pollution or protect endangered species. Simultaneously, local communities and unions often argue that the proposed legislation would mean the loss of jobs and economic chaos.

Environmental groups argue the "public interest"; so do opposing groups. Is it in the "public interest," they ask, to throw thousands of people out of work or to legislate so many restrictions on the manufacture of a product that it becomes more expensive to the average consumer? The answer, quite often, depends on whether the person is a steel worker, a logger, a consumer, or a member of the World Wildlife Federation.

President George W. Bush (L) waves as Texas Attorney General John Cornyn prepares to speak at a Republican Party of Texas-Victory 2002 luncheon, March 28, 2002, in Dallas. Cornyn is running for the U.S. Senate, and the luncheon is expected to raise well over $1 million in donations. Bush is being criticized for signing the campaign finance bill with no fanfare and then immediately embarking on two days of fundraising that will put nearly $4 million into GOP warchests. (Reuters/Mike Theiler)

The Problem of Influence Peddling

Although a case can be made for lobbying as a legitimate activity, deep public suspicion exists about former legislators and officials who capitalize on their connections and charge large fees for doing what is commonly described as *influence peddling.*

Indeed, the roster of registered lobbyists in Washington includes a virtual "who's who" of former legislators and government officials from both Democratic and Republican parties. A good example is Powell Tate, a major public affairs firm in Washington, D.C. The president is Sheila Tate, who served as Nancy Reagan's press secretary and the former President Bush's transition press secretary. Tate's partner is Jody Powell, the former press secretary of President Carter. Together, they know on a first-name basis key Republican and Democratic lawmakers as well as the major journalists covering the Capitol.

"Influence peddling," always an issue in Washington, came into sharp public focus when Michael Deaver quit his job as White House deputy chief of staff for President Reagan and promptly became a public affairs consultant. In short order, he had a list of corporations and foreign governments as clients, including a $1-million contract with South Korean interests. Although he claimed to be doing "strategic planning," Deaver was found guilty of perjury and violation of the Ethics in Government Act.

focus on ethics

Beer Lobbyists Keep the Suds Flowing

The outcry over tobacco as a public-health menace has raised the inevitable question. Is booze next?

Beer producers and wholesalers are taking no chances. The National Beer Wholesalers Association (NBWA), for example, has increased its PAC donations to political candidates from $430,000 to $1.5 million per two-year cycle, an amount more than the powerful AFL-CIO gives through its various PAC groups. The group also makes major contributions to political candidates at the local and state level.

The industry is concerned that its product will make it the next "tobacco wars" because much public concern exists about such issues as (1) underage drinking, (2) binge drinking on college campuses, (3) drunken driving, and (4) how beer is marketed and advertised.

George Hacker, a nationally recognized alcohol-control activist, says, "Like tobacco, alcohol imposes enormous costs on society because this is an addictive substance. And because it can be purchased 24 hours a day and is sold in colorfully packaged containers that appeal to kids."

The Ethics in Government Act forbids government officials from actively lobbying their former agencies for one year after leaving office. Critics say it has little or no impact. Mike McCurry, former press secretary to President Clinton, became a lobbyist shortly after leaving office. Although the law prevented him from lobbying the White House for a year, it placed no such restriction on lobbying members of Congress.

Members of Congress can also become lobbyists immediately upon leaving office. Congress has passed no legislation restricting the lobbying efforts of former legislators and their chief aides. A good example is former Senator Bob Packard, who resigned in the face of ethics charges of sexual and official misconduct. Within three months, he opened a Capitol Hill consulting firm to give clients "... advice on legislation and how they ought to lobby Congress."

Opportunities also are available for congressional staff members who know intimately the structure and operations of key committees. Ann Eppard, an administrative assistant for 22 years to Congressman Bud Shuster, a Republican from Pennsylvania, set up shop after her boss became chair of the House Transportation and Infrastructure Committee. In short order, she had clients such as Federal Express, the American Road and Transportation Builders Association, and other transportation companies—all with vital interests before the committee.

Such connections give the press and the public an uneasy feeling that "influence peddling" flourishes in the nation's capitol. It also gives credence to the cliché, "It's not what you know, but who you know."

A Lobbying Reform Bill

Politicians of both parties have regularly decried the influence of lobbyists, but reform has taken a half-century. At least ten times since the first loophole-riddled lobbying regulations were passed in 1946, efforts to update the law failed to get past the legislative obstacles.

PR insights

Enron—Big Spender on Capitol Hill

Enron, before its financial collapse, was one of the biggest spenders in Washington. In the first six months of 2001, the Houston-based energy trader spent $2.5 million lobbying the Bush administration and Congress.

The company originally reported that it had spent only $825,000 on lobbying, but the Center for Responsive Politics challenged this amount after outside lobbying firms reported income from Enron totaling $1.8 million. It was also disclosed that Enron spent another $2 million during 1999 in an effort to influence legislation that would benefit the energy trading company.

Advocates of stricter lobbying regulation and campaign finance laws used Enron as the "poster child" to illustrate the need for reform. Indeed, the Enron scandal had a major influence in the passing of campaign finance reform in 2002 after a seven-year struggle to get such legislation passed.

Do you have a tough legislative battle ahead?

Grassroots support can help you win!

For you to win a tough legislative battle, it is not enough to just tell elected officials their voters care about an issue. You must prove they care.

Bonner & Associates specializes in producing effective grassroots support.

We have achieved a winning track record on behalf of Fortune 500 corporations, trade associations and coalitions, in Washington and state capitals.

To help you win at the federal and state levels, Bonner & Associates' unique grassroots system proves you have in-depth constituent support by:

- Personally educating and recruiting the precise number of on-record constituent supporters (10-10,000 per targeted legislator) you feel you need to win.
- Enlisting constituents who have no direct vested interest but who strongly and actively support your position.
- Organizing local coalitions of groups which politically count with their legislators to show your position has potent broad-based support.
- Arranging face-to-face meetings between constituent supporters and legislators which prove support is deeply felt and goes far beyond any slick mail campaign.
- Generating on very short notice (24 hours) effective grassroots contacts for critical amendments and floor votes

Bonner & Associates' **unique "pay for results only"** policy ensures you get the most for your investment.

Call today and find out how Bonner & Associates can help you win at the federal and state levels.

Bonner & Associates

1625 K Street N.W. Suite 300 • Washington, D.C. 20006 • 202-463-8880

Stimulating public opinion for or against a pending piece of legislation is a specialized form of public relations work. This advertisement by a Washington, D.C., consulting firm lists ways in which the company generates grassroots responses to impress lawmakers.

In 1995, however, Congress did pass a measure designed to reform lobbying, and President Clinton signed it. Part of the impetus, no doubt, was the impact of polls indicating that the public believed lobbyists had runaway influence in Washington.

One key provision was an expanded definition of what is considered to be a "lobbyist." The new law defines a lobbyist as "someone hired to influence lawmakers, government officials or their aides, and who spends at least 20 percent of his or her time representing any client in a six-month period."

Another key provision requires lobbyists to register with Congress and disclose their clients, the issue areas in which lobbying is being done, and roughly how much is being paid for it. Violators face civil fines of up to $50,000.

The tougher restrictions on lobbyists also apply to eating and drinking. Under the new law, lobbyist-paid lavish lunches and drawn-out dinners are forbidden. Receptions at which finger food is served are allowed. Lobbyists call this the *toothpick rule.* The law also prohibits a lobbyist from buying a meal for a lawmaker unless at least 25 people from an organization attend. That is considered a "widely attended event" at which a lobbyist could not monopolize a lawmaker's time.

New rules also exist for gifts and travel. Senators, their aides, and other Senate officers are barred from accepting gifts worth more than $50 and from accepting privately paid travel to "recreational events." Similar rules about gift giving govern the executive branch of government.

Although there are still loopholes, individuals and organizations violating the law face stiff fines. One case concerns Michael Espy, former Agriculture Secretary in the Clinton Administration. Although he was eventually acquitted of criminal activity in accepting $33,000 in gifts and travel from companies he regulated, some of the companies were not so fortunate. In civil actions, the Smith Barney brokerage firm was fined $1 million for giving Espy a $2,200 Super Bowl ticket, while Robert Mondavi Corp. had to pay $120,000 for giving him six $31 bottles of wine and a $207 dinner at a Washington restaurant.

One area exempted from the lobby reform bill was financial disclosures for so-called "grassroots" lobbying. In many respects, it is the fastest growing area in the political persuasion business.

Grassroots Lobbying

Grassroots lobbying is now an $800 million industry, according to *Campaigns and Elections,* a bimonthly magazine for "political professionals." What makes it so attractive to various groups is that there are virtually no rules or regulations.

The tools of such lobbying are advocacy advertising, toll-free phone lines, bulk faxing, Web sites, and computerized direct mail aimed at generating phone calls and letters from the public to Congress, the White House, and governmental regulatory agencies.

One major firm, Bonner & Associates, has a highly sophisticated communications system that includes banks of telephones and computers that can call or send letters to thousands of citizens within hours. For example, the American Bankers Association hired Bonner to kill a Congressional bill that would lower credit card interest rates. The firm orchestrated 10,000 phone calls from citizens and community leaders to ten members of the House Banking Committee. The bill died in committee.

PR insights

Guidelines for Grassroots Lobbying

Legitimate coalitions of companies, associations, and citizens are effective grassroots tools, but "misleading front groups and sneak attacks are recipes for trouble," says Jay Lawrence, senior vice president of Fleishman-Hillard public relations.

Lawrence gives these tips for effective grassroots lobbying:

- *Target the effort.* Few campaigns need to reach every congressman or state legislator.
- *Go after "persuadables."* Narrow the audience by concentrating on fence-sitters.
- *Build coalitions on economic self-interest.* Go after individuals and organizations who would be financially affected.
- *Think politically.* Find people who know legislative decision-makers or have some connection with them.
- *Letters are best.* Personal letters are the most effective—far better than postcards, mailgrams, and petitions. The best letters are short and simple.
- *Make it easy.* Provide sample drafts of letters, as well as pens, paper, and even stamps.
- *Arrange meetings.* The best single communication is a meeting in the official's home district with a group of interested constituents.
- *Avoid stealth tactics.* If you can't say up front whose interest you are promoting and why, it is a good idea to take another look at the effort

Source: O'Dwyer's PR Services Report, June 1996, p. 12.

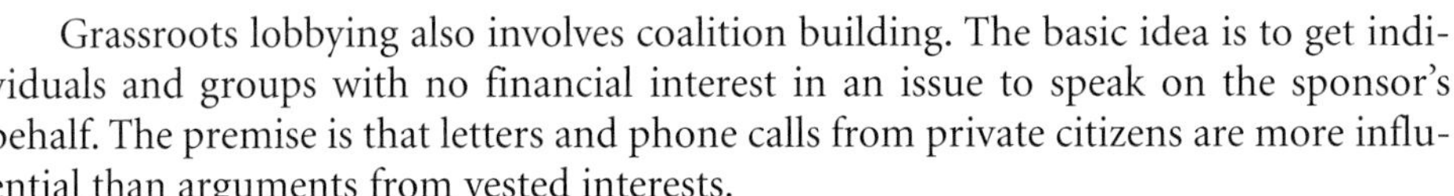

Grassroots lobbying also involves coalition building. The basic idea is to get individuals and groups with no financial interest in an issue to speak on the sponsor's behalf. The premise is that letters and phone calls from private citizens are more influential than arguments from vested interests.

A good example comes from another Bonner campaign. In this case, Congress was considering an auto pollution bill opposed by car manufacturers. The auto companies sought opposition to the bill from beyond the auto industry. Key legislators soon began hearing from disabled and elderly people who were convinced the bill would force the industry to build cars too small to hold walkers and wheelchairs, and from Little League parents worried that fuel-efficient station wagons would not accommodate a whole team. The bill was defeated.

Although public involvement in legislative issues is admirable, critics say grassroots lobbying, with its orchestration of public feedback, often slips into the category of unethical behavior.

Another problem involves doing grassroots lobbying under the cover of front groups (see Chapter 3). This is called *stealth lobbying,* because the public isn't told what vested interests are behind a particular campaign.

In one example, APCO Associates, a unit of GCI public relations, organized the Mississippians for a Fair Legal System (M-Fair) to solicit public support for tort reform. What the public didn't know was that the sponsoring organization, the American Tort Reform Association, included large tobacco and chemical companies, which wanted legislation limiting liability for dangerous or defective products.

Such "grassroots" campaigns make public interest groups wonder if they really shouldn't be called "Astroturf" campaigns, since the "grass" is artificial. Michael Pertschuk, codirector of the Advocacy Institute in Washington, D.C., told *O'Dwyer's PR*

Services Report, "Astroturf groups are usually founded with corporate seed money that is funneled through PR firms." An example is the group National Smokers Alliance, organized by Burson-Marsteller with seed money from Philip Morris.

Political Action Committees

A specialized area of lobbying, unaffected by the reform bill, is the organization and administration of political action committees, commonly known as PACs. They were created as a labor union mechanism during the 1930s, but campaign finance reforms in the 1970s, which prohibited corporate contributions to candidates for federal elections, made PACs an effective alternative.

Today, there are more than 4000 PACs organized by labor unions, business, trade groups, professional societies, and single-issue groups. Under the law, a PAC can give a maximum of $5000 to a federal candidate in a primary election and another $5000 for the general election, a maximum of $10,000 total. This doesn't sound like much, but a corporation with multiple plant sites and operations may have a score of individual PACs. In addition, each local of a national labor union may have its own PAC.

PAC funds come from employees or members of organizations. Corporations encourage employees (particularly managers) to contribute through payroll deduction or by writing an annual check. Union members usually contribute through their local unions as part of their membership, and professionals in medicine and law use PACs organized by their membership societies.

The most PAC money flows to the majority party in the Congress. After years of favoring Democrats 60 to 40 percent or better, corporate PACs flip-flopped when the Republicans took control of the Congress in 1995. When it appeared that Republican House members were in some reelection trouble and the Democrats might retain the White House in 1996, there was some shift back to funding incumbent Democrats.

Another common practice is that chairmen and members of key committees get the most PAC money, primarily because they can exert the most influence on legislation. Commerce committee chairman Larry Pressler, a Republican from South Dakota, for example, led the Senate in fund-raising during 1995 with $1.7 million while his committee was considering the Telecommunications Reform Act of 1996. A large percentage of the contributions came from corporate PACs in the telecommunications, broadcast, and entertainment industries.

Such dependence on PAC money has stirred controversy and prompted calls for campaign finance reform. Many citizen groups believe that vested interests exercise undue influence on legislation by buying "access." Defenders of PACs, however, call the threat of undue influence overrated. They contend that with so many PACs, each pushing its special interest, they cancel out each other. They also say that no PAC sector is big enough to have a major impact on Congress. Health industry PACs, for example, give less than 10 percent of all PAC funding. And finally, defenders say PAC contributions insure that a group or industry can express its free speech rights by presenting its case to legislators.

PAC monies, however, are only one method used in funding incumbents and election campaigns. Corporations and other special interest groups also give unrestricted funds (called "soft" money) directly to local, state, and national political committees for "party-building" activities such as registration drives, getting-out-the-vote efforts, and issue advertising. For the 2000 elections, the national parties and their congressional fund-raising organizations raised nearly $500 million.

Political parties and independent organizations, such as trade unions and the National Rifle Association, also have increased their expenditures on "issue advertising," which is not subject to federal limits on campaign contributions made directly to candidates. Such advertising does not directly urge the election or defeat of a particular individual, but it can be effective in raising a point of view or philosophy held by a particular candidate.

Fund-Raising by Candidates

American-style campaigning is the most expensive in the world. It is estimated that between $3 billion and $4 billion were spent on campaigning at the local, state, and federal level during the 2000 elections. This was considerably more than the $2 billion that was spent on the 1996 elections.

Even the presidential nominating conventions are expensive. Together the Republican and Democratic nominating conventions for the 2000 election cost the equivalent of two months of the national budget of Mali (population 11 million). At the Congressional level, candidates for the November 1998 general election spent a total of $740 million to get elected. In New Jersey, U.S. Senate candidate Jon Corzine (Democrat) spent $61 million of his own money to get elected in 2000.

On a higher level, Al Gore and George W. Bush were raising millions of dollars even before the first primary was held. Experts believe that a serious candidate for the presidency would need a minimum of $22 million before the selection of delegates to the national party convention.

The high cost of running for office in the United States has made fund-raising virtually a full-time, year-round job for every incumbent and aspirant to office.

Incumbent lawmakers utilize professionals to organize fund-raising activities. A popular activity in Washington, D.C., is the luncheon, reception, or dinner on behalf of a legislator's reelection campaign. *The Wall Street Journal*, for example, reported that 14 such events were held on a single day in one October, raising $650,000.

Attending such events are individual donors and lobbyists. Although a chicken dinner is not exactly worth $5000 per plate, the contact with legislators is. No business is actually discussed, but the occasion gives lobbyists an opportunity to say, "Don't forget us in the markup"—the drafting of a bill.

Professional fund-raisers recruit lobbyists to hawk tickets; decide whom to invite; design and mail invitations; employ people to make follow-up calls; rent the room; hire the caterer; make name tags; tell the legislator who came and didn't; and hound attendees to make good on their pledges.

Some consultants specialize in direct mail and telemarketing. They are helped by firms that specialize in computer databases and mailing lists. Aristole Publishers, for example, claims to have records on 128 million people. A political candidate can get a tailored list of prospects using any number of demographic variables, including party affiliation, voting record, contribution record, age, geographic location, and opinions on various issues.

Other firms in the Washington, D.C., area handle mass mailings on behalf of the candidates. Kiplinger Computer and Mailing Services is capable of running envelopes at 10,000 per hour and printing personalized letters at 120 pages per minute.

Public Relations and Campaigning

The tools of today's political campaign are many and varied. Constant focus groups and polls continually test messages and determine the "hot" buttons of the voter. Extensive use of modern communications technology such as satellite media tours and video news releases, bulk faxing of background material, and the use of the Internet have greatly expanded message delivery.

According to James Perry, writing in *The Wall Street Journal:*

> The new media label covers a broad band of new technologies. With satellites, candidates can, and do, hold rallies in several places at once; strategists in different parts of the country meet in teleconference, direct mail gives way to videocassettes delivered door to door; voters with personal computers log on to candidate bulletin boards and call up vast amounts of information. It's an explosion of technology.

Helping the candidates use these tools is another group of consultants and technicians who work to advance the election of their clients—writers of position papers, speech writers, graphic artists, computer experts, photographers, and media strategists. Advance people spend many hours trying to organize events and generate crowds in an age when most people would rather stay home and watch television.

Indeed, even in this age of the Internet and interactive media, television remains the major tool for reaching the American public. But prime time television is increasingly expensive and is cited as one of the major reasons that campaigns cost so much. In the 2000 elections, for example, local television stations made about $1 billion on political ads.

A report prepared by the Alliance for Better Campaigns, a not-for-profit Washington group, concluded that 484 stations in the top 75 media markets took in at least $771 million from the sale of air time for more than 1.2 million political commercials from January 1 through November 7, 2000. This was a 76 percent increase over the

PR insights

New Campaign Reform Legislation

In 2002, after a seven-year battle, Congress passed legislation to ban the large, unlimited donations to political parties known as "soft money." The Shays-Meehan legislation has these major provisions:

- *Soft money.* National political parties are banned from accepting or spending any soft money (large, unlimited contributions by corporations, unions, and individuals). State and local parties can accept up to $10,000 each year per individual for getting out the vote and for voter registration efforts in federal elections.
- *Hard money.* Individuals can make contributions of up to $37,500 each year to all federal candidates, political parties, and political action committees. The previous limit was $25,000.
- *Issue advertising.* Unions, corporations, and nonprofit groups are prohibited from paying for broadcast advertisements if the ads refer to a specific candidate and run within 60 days before a general election or 30 days before a primary. Such ads can be paid for only with regulated hard money through political action committees (PACs).

$436 million that these stations received in 1996. The report, which was titled "Gouging Democracy," noted that the $771 million figure did not reflect the total advertising dollars that candidates and advocacy groups spent on about 800 other stations in the nation's 135 smaller markets. Thus, said the report, the estimated total for political advertising spent in all markets was closer to $1 billion.

Indeed, when campaign reform is discussed, various groups question the traditional system of candidates' having to purchase commercials on TV to reach prospective voters. Not only is it expensive, but the system favors candidates with the most money. President Clinton appointed an Advisory Committee on Public Interest Obligations of Digital Television Broadcasters, and one of its recommendations was to "abolish all forms of the current system of political contributions" by airing all political advertising free. Although the idea was thought provoking, the powerful National Association of Broadcasters (NAB) strongly opposed such reforms on two grounds: (1) loss of profits, and (2) government mandates would violate their First Amendment Rights.

Ethical Guidelines for Political Public Relations

Here are several ethical guidelines for people working in political public relations formulated by the Public Relations Society of America:

1. It is the responsibility of professionals practicing political public relations to be conversant with the various local, state, and federal statutes governing such activities and to adhere to them strictly. This includes laws and regulations gov-

Presidential spokesman Ari Fleischer responds to a question from reporters concerning American efforts to wage war on terrorists during a White House news briefing.

erning lobbying, political contributions, disclosure, elections, libel, slander, and the like.

2. Members shall represent clients or employers in good faith, and while partisan advocacy on behalf of a candidate or public issue is expected, members shall act in accord with the public interest and adhere to truth and accuracy and to generally accepted standards of good taste.
3. Members shall not issue descriptive material or any advertising or publicity information or participate in the preparation or use thereof which is not signed by responsible persons or is false, misleading, or unlabeled as to its source, and are obligated to use care to avoid dissemination of any such material.
4. In avoiding practices which might tend to corrupt the processes of government, members shall not make undisclosed gifts of cash or other valuables which are designed to influence specific decisions of voters, legislators, or public officials.
5. Members shall not, through the use of information known to be false or misleading, conveyed directly or through a third party, intentionally injure the public reputation of an opposing candidate.

Such principles, however, get trampled on in every presidential election. As campaign consultant Mark Goodin once said, "Getting people elected, whether we like it or not, isn't pretty. It, unfortunately, has a lot to do with dividing, setting up bases of support and fracturing off those that—you know, it's like busting a big rock."

Public Affairs in Government

Since the time of the ancient Egyptians 5000 years ago, governments have always engaged in what is known in the 21st century as public information, public relations, and public affairs.

The Rosetta Stone, discovered by Napoleon's troops and used by scholars as the key to understanding Egyptian hieroglyphics, turned out to be a publicity release for the reign of Ptolemy V. Julius Caesar was known in his day as a master of staged events in which his army's entrances into Rome after successful battles were highly orchestrated.

There has always been a need for government communications, if for no other reason than to inform citizens of the services available and the manner in which they may be used. In a democracy, public information is crucial if citizens are to make intelligent judgments about the policies and activities of their elected representatives. Through information it is hoped that citizens will have the necessary background to participate fully in the formation of government policies.

The objectives of government information efforts have been summarized by William Ragan, former director of public affairs for the United States Civil Service Commission:

1. Inform the public about the public's business. In other words, communicate the work of government agencies.
2. Improve the effectiveness of agency operations through appropriate public information techniques. In other words, explain agency programs so that citizens understand and can take actions necessary to benefit from them.

PR insights

The Pentagon: Coming Soon to Your Local Theater

Need a tank or howitzer for a movie you're making? How about 1000 soldiers for a battle scene? Or maybe a nuclear-powered aircraft carrier? If so, the U.S. Department of Defense can often lend a hand.

The Pentagon employs more than 20 public information specialists whose primary duty is to work with moviemakers and producers of TV shows. They review scripts and proposals and decide how much assistance, if any, should be given. One criterion is whether the proposed project portrays the military accurately and in a somewhat positive light.

The movie *Pearl Harbor* got considerable military assistance in terms of technical advice, military hardware, and location shots. In addition, the U.S. Navy also provided the aircraft carrier *USS John C. Stennis* as the location of the movie's premier. Most of the $5 million premier party was paid for by Disney, the producer of the movie, but the carrier was provided at the Navy's expense. It was moored at Pearl Harbor after a six-day voyage from San Diego.

More than 2000 people attended the premier on the flight deck of the ship. A grandstand was erected in front of a giant open-air theater, and the Navy also provided a sunset paratrooper jump and an F-15 fighter jet fly-over as part of the festivities. The Navy said it cooperated on the movie premier because news coverage of the event was good for morale and recruiting. Critics complained that the cost of keeping an aircraft carrier at sea is about a half million dollars a day, and supporting a commercial movie was not a good use of money.

On the other hand, some films don't get any military assistance. *Independence Day* was denied assistance because it featured an alcoholic cropduster flying a fighter jet. *Broken Arrow* was rejected because it featured John Travolta as a deluded Air Force pilot who steals two nuclear missiles with ease.

Military assistance comes in all forms. It may be advice on a proper Navy salute or lending a fleet of Apache helicopters. If you want the helicopter, however, the daily rental rate is $8439, including the pilot. The loan of a Howitzer cannon, however, is only $582 per day, ammunition not included.

3. Provide feedback to government administrators so that programs and policies can be modified, amended, or continued.
4. Advise management on how best to communicate a decision or a program to the widest number of citizens.
5. Serve as an ombudsman. Represent the public and listen to its representatives. Make sure that individual problems of the taxpayer are satisfactorily solved.
6. Educate administrators and bureaucrats about the role of the mass media and how to work with media representatives.

"Public Information" versus "Public Relations"

Although many of the objectives described by Ragan would be considered appropriate goals in almost any field of public relations, in government such activities are never referred to as "public relations." Instead, various euphemisms are used. The most common titles are (1) public information officer, (2) director of public affairs, (3) press secretary, (4) administrative aide, and (5) government program analyst.

In addition, government agencies do not have departments of public relations. Instead, the FBI has an External Affairs Division; the Interstate Commerce Commission has an Office of Communications and Consumer Affairs; and the Environmental Protection Agency has an Office of Public Awareness. The military services usually have Offices of Public Affairs.

Such euphemisms serve to reconcile two essentially contradictory facts: (1) The government needs to inform its citizens, and (2) it is against the law to use appropriated money for the employment of "publicity experts."

Congress as early as 1913 saw a potential danger in executive branch agencies' spending taxpayer dollars to sway the American public to support programs of various administrations. Consequently, the Gillett Amendment (Section 3107 of Title V of the United States Code) was passed: It stated, "Appropriated funds may not be used to pay a publicity expert unless specifically appropriated for that purpose." The law was reinforced in 1919 with prohibition of the use of any appropriations for services, messages, or publications designed to influence a member of Congress. Another law that year required executive agencies to utilize the U.S. Government Printing Office so that publications could be more closely monitored than in the past. Restrictions also prohibit executive departments from mailing any material to the public without a specific request.

Congress was clearly attempting to limit the authority of the executive branch to spend taxpayer money on public relations efforts to gain support for pet projects of the president. Some presidents chafed at this, but others thought it was entirely proper that the government should not be in the business of propagandizing the taxpayers. President Eisenhower, for example, ordered all executive branch agencies to dispense with field office information activity. The only problem was the great number of public and press requests for information. Consequently, information offices lost their titles but continued their dissemination functions under such titles as "technical liaison officers" for the Corps of Engineers and "assistant to the director" in the Bureau of Reclamation.

In 1972, alarmed by Richard Nixon's expansion of the White House communications staff, Congress reaffirmed prior legislation by stating that no part of any appropriation bill could be used for publicity or propaganda purposes designed to support or defeat legislation before Congress.

Although most citizens would agree that government should not use tax money to persuade the public of the merits or demerits of a particular bill or program, there is a thin line between merely providing information and using information as a lobbying tool.

If a public affairs officer for the Pentagon testifies about the number of surface-to-air missiles deployed by Iraq or North Korea, does this constitute information or an attempt to influence congressional appropriations? Or, to use another example, is a speech by the Surgeon General about the dangers of passive smoking only information or support of legislation that would ban cigarette smoking from all federal buildings?

While ascertaining the difference between "public relations" and "public information" may be an interesting semantic game, the fact remains that the terms *public relations* and *publicity* are seldom used by a government agency.

Scope of Federal Government Information

The U.S. government is said to be the world's premier collector of information. It also is maintained, without much disagreement, that the government is one of the world's greatest disseminators of information.

Ascertaining the exact size of the government's "public relations" effort, however, is like trying to guess the number of jelly beans in a large jar. One of the major difficulties is forming a standard definition of what constitutes "public affairs" activity.

The General Accounting Office (GAO) once estimated that probably $2.3 billion was spent each year by federal agencies and the White House on "public relations" activity. Others, often critics of government public relations, have estimated that between 10,000 and 12,000 federal employees are involved in what might be called "public relations" work. It is said, for example, that the Department of Defense has about 1000 people working in public affairs/information jobs.

Such figures, however, give a false impression of government agencies in general. At the Commerce Department, for example, there are 25 public affairs people out of 36,000 employees. The Immigration and Naturalization Service has eight public affairs officers in a staff of 24,000. The Customs Department has 15 public affairs officers in a staff of 18,000. *O'Dwyer's PR Services Report* says, "That translates to 1/10 of one percent of its workforce . . . ."

The size and scope of governmental information efforts are given in other ways. At last count, there were about 12,000 government publications ranging from a monthly law enforcement magazine published by the FBI to a Department of Agriculture pamphlet titled "Making Pickles and Relishes at Home." The armed services have so many magazines, newsletters, and pamphlets that, says one media reporter, it would take a truck to deliver everything on the list. Another writer, probably on a slow news day, estimated that the federal government's production of everything from news releases to magazines would fill four Washington Monuments every year.

This mass of paper, of course, does not include the films and videos the government produces every year. The government's output makes the efforts of Hollywood studios puny by comparison, but few government films are blockbusters. Most are produced by the Department of Defense and used in training. Other films and videos are shown primarily to school and civic groups.

Advertising is another governmental activity. Federal agencies spend several hundred million dollars a year on public service advertising, primarily to promote military recruitment, government health services, and the U.S. Postal Service. In a new approach to recruiting, the U.S. Navy purchased advertising spots on the MTV cable

global PR

Danish Post Office Races to a New Image

After 350 years as the Royal Danish Mail, the national postal service had been privatized and had become Post Denmark. The public, however, still perceived it as out of touch and bureaucratic.

Post Denmark wanted to position itself in the public mind as a modern, dynamic organization with a new logo, so it sponsored a Round Denmark bicycle race under the auspices of the Danish Cycle Union.

The race covered 860 kilometers through 30 cities. Sixteen teams from 14 countries competed, and the race was watched on the roadside by more than 1.2 million spectators. Besides press briefings and regular news releases, TV spots extolled the post office during the five-day event.

About 77 percent of the population saw or read about the race, and all of the Post's 1254 offices conducted special promotions. Awareness of Post Denmark as a new, dynamic entity increased dramatically, and the logo became widely recognized.

TV music channel. The following sections discuss the public affairs efforts of federal agencies, Congress, and the White House.

Government Agencies Public information specialists and public affairs officers engage in tasks common to the public relations department of a nongovernmental organization. They typically answer press and public inquiries, write news releases, work on newsletters, prepare speeches for top officials, and oversee the production of brochures. Senior-level public affairs specialists also counsel top management about communication strategies.

One of the longest-running public relations efforts has been the preparation and distribution of "hometown" releases by the military. The Fleet Home Town News Center, established during World War II, sends approximately a million news releases

PR casebook

Naval PR Strategy Sinks Fishing Boat

A standard public relations strategy of the U.S. military is to invite "influential" civilians and elected officials to tour bases and even ride along in ships, aircraft, and helicopters. It's an effort to build public support for the military and also to win friends in high places.

The U.S. Navy has such a "distinguished visitors" program, and so it was considered somewhat routine to have 16 visitors aboard the nuclear submarine *USS Greenville* on a sunny Hawaiian day. What wasn't routine was a major accident when the submarine surfaced abruptly and collided with a Japanese fishing boat. The vessel immediately sank with the loss of nine lives, including four Japanese high school students on a field trip.

Investigators with the National Transportation Safety Board found that the presence of civilians, including two who occupied control positions when the *Greenville* surfaced, was a distraction to the crew and perhaps prevented the crew from performing their duties in determining whether any ships were in the area.

The accident caused considerable anger in Japan, and the news accounts referred to the *Greenville's* mission as a "public relations demonstration" and a "joy ride." It also caused President Bush to make a personal apology to the Japanese prime minister. The incident ended the submarine captain's career, but the Navy also continued to play host to civilians abroad its ships—arguing that the practice remains one of the most effective ways for the service to enhance its image. What do you think?

—copyright 2001 by Herblock in The Washington Post

Governmental agencies regularly inform citizens of various resources through the distribution of brochures and placement of advertisements in the mass media.

annually about the promotions and transfers of U.S. Navy personnel (including the Marine Corps and Coast Guard) to their hometown media.

Another long-term effort has been the FBI's legendary list of the ten most-wanted fugitives. Initiated in 1950, the list immediately captured the attention of the public and the media. Over the years, the list has led to the apprehension of more than 500 fugitives.

Other federal agencies also conduct public relations to inform citizens. In many cases, a public relations firm is selected through a bidding process to execute the campaign. Some examples include these: (1) the Federal Highway Administration conducted a campaign to promote safety and reduce the number of truck and bus accidents, (2) the Centers for Disease Control and Prevention informed teenagers about the dangers of sunburn and skin cancer, (3) the Library of Congress launched a campaign to raise its profile as a tourist attraction, (4) the Environmental Protection Agency promoted the reduction of greenhouse gases and other pollutants through reduced energy consumption, (5) and the U.S. Mint promoted the use of its golden $1 coins through a marketing effort with Safeway Stores. Every year, at income tax time, the Internal Revenue Service (IRS) distributes news releases loaded with graphics to help people fill out their tax forms. Two other government agencies, the Voice of America and the former United States Information Agency (USIA), are discussed in Chapter 16.

Congressional Efforts The House of Representatives and the Senate are great disseminators of information. Members regularly produce a barrage of news releases, newsletters, recordings, brochures, taped radio interviews, and videotapes—all designed to inform voters back home about Congress.

Critics complain that most materials are self-promotional and have little value. The franking privilege (free postage) is singled out for the most criticism. The late Senator John Heinz, a Republican from Pennsylvania, once distributed 15 million pieces of mail, financed by taxpayers, during one election year. Obviously, the franking privilege is a real advantage for an incumbent.

All members of Congress also employ a press secretary. According to Edward Downes of Boston University, "Capitol Hill's press secretaries play a significant role in the shaping of America's messages and consequent public policies. In their role as proxy for individual members, the press secretaries act as gatekeepers, determining what information to share with, and hold from, the media; thus, they have command over news shared with the citizenry."

■ White House Efforts At the apex of government public relations efforts is the White House. The president receives more media attention than all the federal agencies and Congress combined. It is duly reported when the president visits a neighborhood school, tours a housing development, meets a head of state, or even chokes on a pretzel while watching a football game.

All presidents have taken advantage of the intense media interest to implement public relations strategies that would improve their popularity, generate support for programs, and explain embarrassing policy decisions. And each president has had his own communication style.

Ronald Reagan, by most accounts, was considered the master communicator. He was extremely effective on television and could read a teleprompter with perfect inflection. He understood the importance of using symbolism and giving simple, down-to-earth speeches that often ended with "God bless you." Reagan's approach was the use of the carefully packaged sound bite and staged event.

George H. W. Bush was no Ronald Reagan as a public speaker, but he did project enthusiasm for his job and had a friendly, but formal, working relationship with the White House press corps. While Bush came across as somewhat reserved, Bill Clinton's communication style was more populist. He was at home with today's information technology, analysts say, and made effective use of television. Clinton was most effective when he talked on a one-to-one basis with an interviewer or a member of the audience.

George W. Bush's style is more like his father's approach, with a mixture of Ronald Reagan's "down-home" style. Analysts say he is plainspoken, shows confidence, and does a very good job of staying "on message." After the September 11 terrorist attack on the World Trade Center and the Pentagon, he was able to rally the nation with several stirring speeches to Congress and the American people when he announced his "war on terrorism."

All presidents, of course, have assistance in their constant quest to be popular, sell their policies, and be perceived as effective leaders. On every White House staff are experts in communications strategy, media relations, speech writing, and staging the perfect event. In addition, advance people plan every presidential appearance and trip in meticulous detail. They confirm that the person who heads the receiving line is politically correct and that the sound system works. They make arrangements for the press, organize the cheering crowds, select the best symbolic photo opportunity, decide where the television cameras will be positioned, and plan the president's entrance and exit down to the last second.

The top public relations person in the White House is the Director of Communications. In the first year and a half of the George W. Bush administration, however, the person with the most power was Karen Hughes, special counselor to the president. Her job was to advise the president on communications strategy. It was her decision, for example, to have President Bush visit a local mosque to show support for Muslims just days after the September 11 terrorist attack. The event was a symbolic attempt to assure Muslims in America and around the world that the "war on terrorism" was not a war on the Muslim religion.

Hughes also helped Bush set the tone for his speeches. She, for example, was instrumental in formulating the President's speech to the joint session of Congress about America's planned reaction to terrorist attack. Some aides pressed for a bellicose declaration of war on terrorists, but Hughes intervened and shaped the "reassurance theme" that he ultimately used to great effect. In fact, many analysts said it was the most stirring speech of his presidency to date.

The most visible person, on a daily basis, is the president's press secretary who has the high-pressure duty of briefing reporters. The chief spokesperson for President Bush is Ari Fleischer, another veteran of the Bush presidential campaign. He has to communicate the president's thoughts and opinions on a daily basis to the press that one reporter has called a " . . . ravenous beast, forever hungry."

Fleischer, describing his job in a *New York Times* article, said, "You serve the president of the United States, and you speak for him. And you serve the press, which means you have a duty to provide them accurate information, and to be helpful to them in the daily collection of news. In other words, you're paid every day to walk a tightrope without a safety net."

He also expressed admiration for Michael D. McCurry, who was the public face of the Clinton administration during the impeachment ordeal. McCurry had the unenviable job of facing the media daily during most of 1998 when his boss was under the microscope during the Kenneth Starr inquiry into President Clinton's activities. To retain his credibility, McCurry had to be honest with the press, but he was often hard-pressed to choose his words in walking the fine line between loyalty and the media's incessant need for more revelations about Clinton's relationship with Monica Lewinsky.

Despite the pressure-cooker environment, former George H. W. Bush and Reagan press secretary Marlin Fitzwater says, "It's the greatest job in the world and worth taking no matter how much trouble your President is in. Now, you may die in the job, it may ruin your life and reputation. But it still will have been the greatest experience in your life." Most former press secretaries also give the advice, "keep a sense of humor."

PR casebook

The Clinton Impeachment: An Epic Public Relations Battle

President Clinton became only the second president in U.S. history to be impeached by the U.S. House of Representatives, and he was ultimately acquitted by the U.S. Senate.

Throughout most of 1998, the media world was almost totally saturated by the Clinton/Lewinsky scandal as the President waged a legal and public relations defense while major events unfolded: (1) Independent Counsel Kenneth Starr conducted grand jury proceedings and filed a 445-page report with Congress; (2) the House Judiciary Committee conducted hearings; and (3) the House of Representatives, in a highly emotional and partisan debate, approved two of four articles of impeachment—charging the President with lying under oath and obstructing justice.

The saga began when President Clinton on January 17 testified under oath in the Paula Jones sexual harassment case that he never had an affair with Monica Lewinsky, a former White House intern. In August, after Lewinsky admitted to Starr's grand jury that she did have an affair, and DNA analysis disclosed Clinton's semen on one of her dresses, the President admitted in a nationally televised speech an "improper relationship" and expressed regret about misleading the American public.

Throughout the year, White House legal and public relations advisers were often at odds on how to handle the legal aspects and shape public opinion. Legal advisers cautioned President Clinton to remain silent as much as possible because any admission of guilt could be used by the prosecutor in an impeachment proceeding or could subject the President to further criminal liability after he left office. Clinton's public relations advisers, however, argued that "stonewalling" and failing to admit guilt would just drag out the issue—and that the American people could more easily forgive his sexual transgressions than his lying about them.

Indeed, many public relations professionals said that Clinton committed a public relations error by not admitting an affair until August. Lynn Morgen, principal of Morgen-Walke Associates said: "Clinton should have admitted the affair ages ago and gotten to other things." And Betsy Nichols, principal of Nichols & Co., said: "The people wanted to forgive him but his address (in August) about Monica Lewinsky was not forthright."

Aviva Diamond, president of Blue Streak, Inc., a Los Angeles firm specializing in media and speech training, expressed the opinion that Clinton had violated at least four public relations axioms: (1) Be honest, (2) don't be defensive, (3) don't destroy public trust, and (4) apologize quickly, sincerely, and fully. In an article in *Public Relations Tactics,* Diamond concluded: "What really sticks in the public's collective craw is the lying, the sense that they are being manipulated, the feeling that they cannot trust their top elected official. It's an object lesson for corporate executives as well as politicians."

But Carole Gorney, a professor at Lehigh University and an expert on litigation public relations, was less convinced. In an article in PRSA's *Strategist,* she observed that Clinton's relative silence may indeed have been the best course of action—from a legal as well as public relations standpoint. She cited the fact that, given the President's high approval ratings throughout the scandal (one poll showed the President's job approval rating skyrocketed to 73 percent immediately after the House impeachment vote), it was good politics to have remained silent about his relationship with Lewinsky as long as he did.

The White House, however, did use a number of public relations strategies throughout the year in an attempt to marshal public support for the President. Here are some of the strategies and tactics that were used.

Kenneth Starr as Villain

White House spokespersons, as well as the President and Hillary Clinton, criticized Starr as a right-wing zealot whose single mission in life was to get Clinton out of office. Early in the year, Hillary Clinton went on national TV morning talk shows to defend her husband and lambaste Starr for conducting what she described as a highly partisan "witch-hunt." Clinton, in his August speech admitting "an improper relationship," also berated Starr for "prying into personal lives," and spending more than $40 million in a four-year period on an effort to discredit him. The idea was to focus public attention on the flaws of the judicial process, not the President's transgressions.

GOP as Villain

As with Starr, Clinton focused on the Republican-dominated Congress as the source of his troubles. The White House positioned the Starr inquiry as simply another partisan battle pitting the Democratic White House against the Republican Congress. Polls showed that Newt Gingrich, the Republican Speaker of the House, was not highly popular with the public and was perceived as an ideologue.

President Clinton, although under the shadow of impeachment and having an affair with a White House intern, continued to receive a high public approval rating as President.

(continued)

Acting Presidential

Clinton continued to act "presidential" and as the military's commander-in-chief. He gave talks about the robust economy and offered new initiatives in health, education, and welfare. He took immediate military action when the U.S. embassies in Kenya and Tanzania were bombed and even ordered the bombing of Iraq on the eve of his impeachment. Often, his statements were made in settings with the American flag behind him and the presidential seal prominently displayed on the podium—a visual appeal to patriotism.

Legal Hairsplitting

Clinton continued to argue that he hadn't lied to attorneys for Paula Jones because he had not had "sexual relations" with Lewinsky, defined in most dictionaries as "sexual intercourse."

Grassroots Support

White House operatives encouraged citizens to write their congressional representatives opposing impeachment. One California online organization called "Censure and Move On" delivered 300,000 anti-impeachment signatures to Congress that had been collected at the group's Web site. Another group, liberal People for the American Way, aired radio spots to counter conservative groups and talk-show hosts fueling grassroots support for impeachment.

Lobbying

Democratic legislators were lobbied by the White House to stand united against impeachment. In addition, labor union leaders and black leaders were asked to lobby Republican lawmakers in swing districts.

Media Editorial Support

Sympathetic columnists and editorial writers were enlisted as third-party support. Lars-Erik Nelson, columnist for the *New York Daily News,* for example, wrote: "Most revolting of all is Starr's prissy piousness, insisting that he had to dump this pornography into our history books because Clinton drove him to it."

Leaked Information about Grand Jury Testimony

Washington is famous for leaks, and all sides released details about Clinton's grand jury testimony before it was aired in full on American television. The White House moaned about how degrading the questions were and how terrible it was for the Republicans to release the videotape. By the time the videotape was aired, most Americans were prepared for the worst and, although two of three Americans were convinced that Clinton had lied under oath, most also concluded that it was "no big deal" because the tapes did not live up to their advance billing.

Quick Response to Starr Report

The White House issued a massive rebuttal to the Starr report; it was published in daily newspapers on the same day as the lengthy Starr report. This action helped mute the impact of Starr's allegations.

Election as Referendum

President Clinton's fortunes rose considerably, particularly in solidifying the support of the Democratic Party, when the GOP, predicting advances, lost seats in the House, and the Democrats gained. Traditionally, the President's party loses seats in midterm elections. Although the gains were minor, pundits still saw the election as a major public refutation of the GOP's strategy to proceed with impeachment, and Newt Gingrich even resigned as Speaker of the House. President Clinton also touted the election as a manifestation of the public's opposition to impeachment.

Use of Respected Leaders

In a joint letter to the *New York Times,* former Presidents Jimmy Carter and Gerald Ford proposed that Clinton be censured by a bipartisan vote in the U.S. Senate to avoid a lengthy trial that would further divide the country.

In sum, President Clinton's fate was perhaps just as dependent on effective public relations strategies and public opinion as it was on points of law. Media coverage was also a strong factor. As one headline in a major daily newspaper proclaimed: "Clinton saga is benumbing the public, media: To pundits, drama has been bled dry." According to the article, the sheer volume of coverage caused the public to say "no more" and conclude that the whole issue was nothing more than partisan politics as usual.

MSNBC's Keith Olbermann, moving from White House to sports coverage, said: "One of the sad truths for me is that this is the equivalent of talking about the same ballgame for 300 consecutive days. Rarely has there been such an abuse of the public's time. There have been eight or nine days of real news, and the rest of it has been fill."

focus on ethics

What Shall a Spokesperson Say?

Being a press spokesperson for a member of Congress or even the CEO of a corporation has its occupational hazards. You are supposed to be loyal to your employer and accurately reflect his or her points of view to the press. Often you know more inside information than you can tell the press.

Suppose you are a press secretary to a legislator, and several former female employees claim that he made unwelcome sexual advances. You know that your boss is somewhat of a lecher, but he tells you to deny strongly the women's charges when the media pick up the story. What would you do?

State Information Services

Every state provides public information services. In California, for example, there are about 175 public information officers (PIOs) in about 70 state agencies. On a daily basis, PIOs provide routine information to the public and the press on the policies and activities of the various agencies.

Various state agencies also conduct extensive public relations and advertising campaigns on specific issues. In recent years, there has been a major emphasis on antismoking and tobacco campaigns thanks, in large part, to funds generated from the national tobacco settlement and state-imposed cigarette taxes.

California, for example, generates about $114 million annually in funding from tobacco taxes and about 10 percent of that is devoted to antismoking advertising and public relations. In Massachusetts, roughly $1.5 million of the $13 million that the state spends on antitobacco marketing is devoted to public relations. Minnesota spends about $11 million annually on antismoking advertising and public relations—with teenagers as a major target audience. Indiana spends about $30 million annually on campaigns to reduce smoking, and Virginia spends almost the same amount.

State agencies also conduct other campaigns to inform and motivate citizens regarding other issues. The California Department of Conservation, for example, spent about $10 million on a social marketing campaign designed to raise the state's beverage container recycling rate. In another campaign, the California Office of Family Planning spent $37 million that focused on preventing teen pregnancy and promoting responsible parenting.

Various states also conduct campaigns to boost tourism. Ohio, for example, spent $225,000 on public relations activities to convince people from out-of-state that there were a lot of interesting places to visit. Pennsylvania, on the other hand, spends between $8 and $12 million annually promoting tourism. States also use public relations and advertising campaigns to attract new business. Illinois, for example, spends about $2 million annually to promote the state as a good place to locate a manufacturing plant and other kinds of business.

City Information Services

Cities employ information specialists to disseminate news and information from numerous municipal departments. Such agencies may include the airport, transit district, redevelopment office, parks and recreation, convention and visitors bureau, police and fire, city council, and the mayor's office.

The information flow occurs in many ways, but all have the objective of informing citizens and helping them take full advantage of opportunities. The city council holds neighborhood meetings; an airport commission sets up an exhibit showing the growth needs of the airport; the recreation department promotes summer swimming lessons; and the city's human rights commission sponsors a festival promoting multiculturalism.

Cities also promote themselves to attract new business. *PRWeek* reports "The competition for cities and wider regions to attract businesses is as intense as ever, experts say, with an estimated 12,000 economic development organizations vying for the roughly 500 annual corporate moves/expansions that involve 250 or more jobs each."

Bob Marcusse, President of the Kansas City Area Development Council, told *PRWeek*, "The stakes are so high because success means millions of dollars in taxes, it means wealth creation, it means jobs. It is the lifeblood of the community."

Consequently, many cities pump millions of dollars into attracting new business through a variety of communication tools that include elaborate brochures, placement of favorable "success" stories in the nation's press, direct mail, telemarketing, trade fairs, special events, and meetings with business executives.

Some cities even operate a news bureau to inform local and national media of their success stories. The Kansas City Area Development Council, for example, worked for weeks to get a mention in the *Wall Street Journal* that the city had 20 million square feet of underground warehousing available. In Columbus, Ohio, the Chamber of Commerce distributed a news release about The Gap opening an e-commerce fulfillment center that created 2500 jobs. It was hoped that such news would encourage other companies to also consider Columbus as a location for their e-commerce business.

Cities also promote themselves in an effort to increase tourism, which is further discussed in Chapter 19. An example of city information efforts is the campaign by the Panama City (Florida) Convention and Visitors Bureau to position itself as a prime destination for college students during spring break. According to *PRWeek,* the bureau spent about $300,000 promoting the city through posters, news releases, brochures, advertising, and special events to let students know that they were welcome. Indeed, the "spring breakers," as they are called, pumped about $135 million into the local economy.

Improving the image of a city is also an objective. Gary, Indiana, long a city in decline because of steel mill closings, bid $1.2 million to play host to the Miss U.S.A. beauty pageant. It was hoped that the pageant, televised nationally, would bring recognition and some degree of prestige to the city. The mayor told a *New York Times* reporter that the pageant "has the ability to build local pride in the city and the psychology of the public in a positive way. If you don't have that, nothing else you do is going to work." A local restaurant owner put it more succinctly. She said, "Gary is like dead. So with the Miss USA pageant, it's a whole different atmosphere."

While beauty pageants are a good "hook" for creating national visibility and tourism for a city, extensive information efforts are also needed when a natural disaster strikes. When Des Moines, Iowa, was flooded several years ago and the city's water supply became contaminated, the city conducted an aggressive information campaign to keep the public informed of flood developments and hold anxiety to a minimum.

The importance of public information and public relations at the municipal level is best described by the International City Management Association:

> Public relations is one of many important variables which affect the ability of an administrator to accomplish program objectives. It involves cooperation between the agency (its personnel, decisions and programs) and the attitudes and desires of persons and groups in the agency's external environment. It imposes on administrators the necessity for dealing with public relations as an inherent and continuing element in the managerial process. The administrator must be mindful of public relations considerations at every stage of the administrative process, from making the decision to the final point of its execution.

Attacks on Government Information Services

Although the need for government to inform citizens and publicize programs is accepted in principle, many critics still express skepticism about the activity, as mentioned earlier.

To some, such as book authors James Bennett and Thomas DiLorenzo (*Official Lies: How Washington Misleads Us*), the federal government operates a huge self-serving propaganda machine with tens of thousands of employees paid by taxpayers.

Indeed, taxpayer groups often oppose the employment of information officers as costly and unnecessary. Others, including journalists, criticize public information activities in general because legislators send reams of useless news releases that often merely promote the senders. Such abuse, coupled with snide news stories about the cost of maintaining government "public relations" experts, rankles dedicated public information officials (PIOs) who work very hard to keep the public informed and the press supplied with a daily diet of news stories.

One PIO for a California agency said, "I'd like to see the press find out what's going on in state government without us." Her comment is echoed by another PIO in the Department of Water Resources. He is now called a "government analyst" but says the news media and the public still want and demand information about the state's water supply.

Indeed, a major source of press hostility seems to stem from the fact that reporters are heavily dependent on handouts. In one study Professors Lynne Masel Walters (Texas A&M) and Timothy Walters (Stephen F. Austin State University) found that 86 percent of a state government's news releases were used by daily and weekly newspapers.

One text, *Media: An Introductory Analysis of American Mass Communications*, by Peter M. Sandman, David M. Rubin, and David B. Sachsman, puts it bluntly: "If a newspaper were to quit relying on press releases, but continued covering the news it now covers, it would need at least two or three times as many reporters."

News releases, however, are only one aspect of helping the media do their job. The city of Homestead, Florida, spent $70,000 on facilities and staff just to handle the deluge of reporters who descended on the city in the aftermath of Hurricane Andrew. Congress also subsidizes the media by spending millions of dollars annually on press facilities and services for working reporters.

And although there is much congressional and media criticism of the government's extensive publications, these are defended on the basis of cost efficiency. A deputy director of the Department of Agriculture publications branch, for example, reported that his office alone receives about 350,000 inquiries a year. Two-thirds of the requests, he says, can be answered with pamphlets that cost between half a cent and 12 cents each, whereas individual responses could cost up to $20 each when personnel costs are included. In other words, the sheer volume of public requests requires a large array of printed materials.

Preventative public relations can bring savings. The taxpayers of California spend about $7 billion annually to deal with the associated costs of teenage pregnancy, so $5.7 million spent on a successful education campaign could save the state considerably more in reduced welfare costs. Michigan's $100,000 expenditure to educate citizens about recycling steel aerosol cans does much to reduce the costs of opening more landfills.

An Associated Press reporter acknowledged in a story that government information does have value. He wrote:

> While some of the money and manpower goes for self-promotion, by far the greater amount is committed to an indispensable function of a democratic government—informing the people.
>
> What good would it serve for the Consumer Product Safety Commission to recall a faulty kerosene heater and not go to the expense of alerting the public to its action? An informed citizenry needs the government to distribute its economic statistics, announce its antitrust suits, tell about the health of the president, give crop forecasts.

Summary

Government Relations

In highly regulated industries, corporations may have separate departments for government relations to gather information, disseminate management's views, cooperate with governmental bodies, and motivate employee participation in the political process.

Lobbying

Lobbying is the attempt to influence the defeat, passage, or amendment of legislation and the policies of regulatory agencies. Lobbyists work closely with government relations or public affairs practitioners and can be found at all levels of government. There is a strong public perception of influence peddling among lobbyists, and legislation has been passed promoting lobbying reform. Grassroots lobbying has grown to an $800 million industry, but critics worry about its potentially unethical orchestration of public feedback.

Political Action Committees

Political action committees, or PACs, were first created by unions in the 1930s and have grown into a major source of funding for political candidates. "Soft" money is funding given not directly to candidates but to political parties.

Fund-Raising by Candidates

The expenses of campaigning have made fund-raising a major issue in any election. Professionals organize fund-raising activities, in the form of events, direct mail campaigns, and telemarketing.

Public Relations and Campaigning

Public relations activities for political campaigns may include focus groups and polls, satellite media tours, and bulk faxing of background material. An important aspect of the practitioner's work will be helping the candidates use these tools effectively. Television will be a major tool—and a major expense—for any campaign.

Ethical Guidelines for Political Public Relations

The Public Relations Society of America has published guidelines for those working in political public relations, advising that such practitioners be well informed of the law; that they represent clients in good faith; that their communications not be false, misleading, or unlabeled as to source; that they not make gifts to influence voters, legislators, or public officials; and that they not use false or misleading information to injure opposing candidates.

Public Affairs in Government

Government public relations has a long history, especially in the area of providing public information, although these activities are almost never called "public relations" in a government setting. This is partly because there are legal limits on using government funding to influence the public's support of political programs and projects. However, the government must respond to requests for information, and agencies publish newsletters, write press releases, and produce brochures, and these activities go on in all branches and at all levels of government.

Case Activity: What Would You Do?

The city council of Lakewood (population 150,000), in cooperation with a citizens' commission, has decided that there is a need to improve citizen participation in the city's curbside recycling program. Such a program is environmentally sound, and there are other reasons to increase participation. The city's only landfill is rapidly filling up, and there are new state mandates for recycling.

Recycling is still a relatively new concept for the majority of Lakewood households—only 45 percent of them are separating their trash for recycling. The percentage is even lower among residents in the middle- to lower-income brackets. The objective is to get 80 percent of the households to use the curbside recycling program.

What kind of public information would you recommend to accomplish this objective? Develop a list of program strategies and communication tactics.

Questions for Review and Discussion

1. What is the difference between someone working in governmental relations and a lobbyist?
2. The public, in general, has low esteem for lobbyists. Do you think the perception is justified? Why or why not?
3. Many lobbyists are former legislators and government officials. Do you think they exercise undue influence in the shaping of legislation? Why or why not?
4. What are the major points of the lobbying reform act? Do you think the law will curtail excessive "influence peddling"? Why or why not?
5. The issue is raised about the use of "front groups" in grassroots lobbying efforts. Do you think such approaches are unethical? Should there be laws prohibiting the use of such groups?
6. Name at least five guidelines for effective grassroots lobbying.
7. Explain how a political action committee (PAC) works. What are the pros and cons?
8. How do political candidates raise money? Would you like to be a political fund-raiser? Why or why not?
9. Do you think other nations should adopt American methods of political campaigning? Why or why not?
10. In what ways are reporters dependent on government information efforts?
11. Explain the various laws that regulate government "public relations" efforts.
12. How is "public information" used by states and cities?
13. Do you think attacks on governmental informational efforts are justified? Why or why not?

Suggested Readings

Allan, Marc D. "The Million Dollar Sell: Cities Reel in Companies with PR." *PRWeek,* July 24, 2000, p. 16.

Deatherage, Sherri. "Spinning in Space." *PRWeek,* December 4, 2000, pp. 27, 29. Public relations at NASA.

Edwards, Jim. "Navy Unwavering in Its PR Strategy after Greenville." *PRWeek,* June 18, 2001, p. 12.

Frank, John. "The War on Smoking." *PRWeek,* March 5, 2001, p. 22–23.

Ledingham, John A. "Government–Community Relationships: Extending the Relational Theory of Public Relations." *Public Relations Review,* Vol. 27, 2001, pp. 285–295.

Lee, Mordecai. "The Image of the Government Flack: Movie Depictions of Public Relations in Public Administration." *Public Relations Review,* Vol. 27, 2001, pp. 297–315.

Lilienthal, Steve. "A War of Words for the White House." *PRWeek,* July 17, 2000, pp. 20–21.

Miller, D. W. "Free Speech or Vote-Buying? Money's Role in Politics Is Overstated, Scholars Say." *Chronicle of Higher Education,* March 23, 2001, pp. 14–15.

Mnookin, Seth. "Advice to Ari." *Brill's Content,* March 2001, pp. 94–97, 149–150. Article about Ari Fleischer, press secretary to President Bush.

Paven, Andy, and Murphy, Ann. "PR Lessons from Election 2000." *PR Tactics,* February 2001, pp. 18–19.

Quenqua, Douglas. "Working with Lobbyists." *PRWeek,* April 2, 2001, pp. 18–19.

Stateman, Allison. "Media Relations from Sea to Shining Sea." *PR Tactics,* September 2001, pp. 1, 22–23. Coast Guard public relations.

Straughan, Dulcie. "Women's Work: Public Relations Efforts of the U.S. Children's Bureau to Reduce Infant and Maternal Mortality, 1912–1921." *Public Relations Review,* Vol. 27, 2001, pp. 337–351.

Terry, Valerie. "Lobbyists and Their Secrets: Classic PR Practitioner Role Models as Functions of Burkean Human Motivations." *Journal of Public Relations Research,* Vol. 13, No. 3, 2001, pp. 235–263.

Toner, Robin. "Senate's Debate on Patient Rights Renews Lobby War." *New York Times,* June 20, 2001, p. 1, 16.

International Public Relations

preview

The objective of this chapter is to provide students with an understanding of international public relations and the complications and benefits of working in this cross-cultural area.

Topics covered in the chapter include:

- Global marketing
- Language, culture, and other issues
- Representing foreign corporations in the United States
- Representing U.S. corporations in other countries
- International government public relations
- Public relations by international groups
- Foreign public relations organizations
- Opportunities in international work

What Is International Public Relations?

International public relations may be defined as the planned and organized effort of a company, institution, or government to establish mutually beneficial relations with the publics of other nations. These publics, in turn, may be defined as the various groups of people who are affected by, or who can affect, the operations of a particular firm, institution, or government.

International public relations may also be viewed from the standpoint of its practice in individual countries. Although public relations is commonly regarded as a concept developed in the United States at the beginning of the 20th century, some of its elements, such as countering unfavorable public attitudes by means of disclosure of operations through publicity and annual reports, were practiced by railroad companies and at least one shareholding corporation in Germany as far back as the mid-19th century, to mention only one such country. (See Chapter 2.)

Even so, it is largely American techniques that have been adapted to national and regional public relations practices throughout the world, including many totalitarian nations. Today, although in some languages there is no term comparable to *public relations*, the practice has spread to most countries, especially those with industrial bases and large urban populations. This is primarily the result of worldwide technological, social, economic, and political changes and the growing understanding that public relations is an essential component of advertising, marketing, and diplomacy.

International Corporate Public Relations

In this section we explore the new age of global marketing and point out that differences in language, laws, and cultural mores must be overcome when companies conduct business in foreign countries. We also discuss how U.S. public relations firms represent foreign interests in this country as well as U.S. corporations in other parts of the world. Aspects of public relations practice in some other countries are delineated.

The New Age of Global Marketing

For decades, hundreds of corporations based in the United States have been engaged in international business operations, including marketing, advertising, and public relations. These activities swelled to unprecedented proportions during the 1990s, largely because of new communications technologies, development of 24-hour financial markets almost worldwide, the lowering of trade barriers, growth of sophisticated foreign competition in traditionally "American" markets, and shrinking cultural differences bringing the "global village" ever closer to reality.

Today almost one-third of all U.S. corporate profits are generated through international business. In the case of Coca-Cola, probably the best-known brand name in the world, international sales account for 80 percent of the company's operating profit.

At the same time, overseas investors are moving into American industry. It is not uncommon for 15 to 20 percent of a U.S. company's stock to be held abroad. The United Kingdom, for example, has a direct foreign investment in the United States exceeding $122 billion, followed by Japan and the Netherlands with nearly half that sum each, according to the U.S. Department of Commerce.

Public relations is an essential ingredient in the global megamarketing mix being created. The 15 largest public relations organizations now generate between 30 and 40 percent of their fees outside the United States. Because of fax machines, e-mail, online services, and the Internet, boutique firms are challenging the big agencies for international business. (See Chapter 5.)

Fueling the new age of global marketing are satellite television, computer networks, electronic mail, fax, fiber optics, cellular telephone systems, and emerging technologies such as integrated services digital networks (ISDN) allowing users to send voice, data, graphics, and video over existing copper cables. For example, Hill and Knowlton has its own satellite transmission facilities, and the General Electric Company has formed an international telecommunications network enabling employees to communicate worldwide, using voice, video, and computer data, simply by dialing seven digits on a telephone. Using three satellite systems, Cable News Network (CNN) is viewed by more than 200 million people in more than 140 countries. A number of newspapers and magazines are reaching millions with international editions. *Reader's Digest,* to cite one example, distributes about 11.5 million copies abroad—44 national editions in more than a dozen languages.

Differences in language, laws, and cultural mores among countries (to be discussed shortly) pose serious problems. There also is a need for both managers and employees to learn to think and act in global terms as quickly as possible. Already, Burson-Marsteller, with offices in many countries, has been spending more than $1 million a year on training tapes and traveling teams of trainers and seminars to foster a uniform approach to client projects.

Much of the new business jousting takes place on West European terrain, where a recently unified European Community (EC) attracts enormous attention. Although

global PR

Ronald McDonald and Mickey Team Up for Global Campaign

McDonald's Corporation, in partnership with the Walt Disney Company, marked the millennium by celebrating the achievements of 2000 young people around the globe.

The objective behind the program was to increase awareness of McDonald's and Disney on the part of kids and families around the world. It involved McDonald's operations in almost 90 nations, and the idea was to find children ages 8 to 15 who would be recognized for their achievements.

The concept of a "Millennium Dreamers" award program was first announced on a satellite news conference featuring McDonald's CEO Jack Greenberg, Disney CEO Michael Eisner, and UNESCO's director-general Federico Mayor. The next step was to contact schools and youth organizations in more than 90 nations (where McDonald's had operations) and solicit nominations. Forms were also available on the McDonald's and Disney Web sites, as well as at locations of the restaurant chain.

The names of 2000 "Millennium Dreamers" were announced in a special event at UN headquarters in New York. Featured at the news conference was the first public appearance together of corporate icons Ronald McDonald and Mickey Mouse. The final phase was a Global Summit at Walt Disney World Resort in Florida, to which the 2000 finalists and their parents or guardians were invited. Each child received a medal for outstanding contributions.

The campaign, which received *PRWeek's* "International Campaign of the Year 2001" award, generated massive media coverage (about 2 billion impressions worldwide) and even was the subject of a one-hour episode of Oprah's television show.

Trade is now a global enterprise, but not everyone is happy about it. Here, protestors demonstrate against the World Trade Organization (WTO) and its policies advocating the elimination of trade barriers. Today, as never before, international organizations and corporations must pay attention to public opinion on a global basis.

hampered by recession in 2000–2001, public relations expenditures increased significantly. The growth was precipitated in part by expansion of commercial television resulting from widespread privatization, the desire of viewers for more varied programming, satellite technology, and slowly developing EC business patterns. Satellite TV reached well over 30 million people, mostly through cable systems; direct transmission of programming to homes by high-powered satellites bypassed conventional networks, local stations, and cable systems. On the print side, the business press was growing about 20 percent every year, and there were about 15,000 trade publications in Western Europe.

Although the EC promoted the phrase "a single Europe," corporations and public relations firms still face the complex task of communicating effectively to 320 million people in 12 countries speaking nine languages.

Language, Cultural Differences, and Other Issues

Fundamentally, companies operating in foreign countries are confronted with essentially the same public relations challenges as those in the United States. These include: (1) the formation and maintenance of favorable climates for their operations, involving relationships with local and national government officials, consumer groups, the financial community, and employees; (2) the monitoring and assessment of potentially adverse situations and the establishment of ways to counteract them; and (3) the containment of crises before serious damage is done.

These problems, however, may be aggravated by conditions such as the following:

- Differences in languages and the multiplicity of languages in some countries
- Longer chains of command, stretching back to the home country
- Evident and subtle differences in customs
- The varying levels of development of the media and public relations
- Antipathy expressed toward "multinationals," a pejorative word in many countries
- A dislike grounded in such factors as national pride, past relationships, envy, and apprehension, especially in regard to the United States, concerning foreign cultural, economic, political, and military influence

focus on ethics

Got a News Release? Please Include Cash

Paying a reporter or an editor to publish or broadcast a news release has long been a common practice in many parts of the world, especially in emerging nations where salaries are low.

In Russia, the practice of paying for placement is called *zakazukhi* (bought articles), and the International Public Relations Association (IPRA) has announced the formation of an international committee to eliminate the practice. According to IPRA president Alasdair Sutherland, "The credibility of any publication can only be based on its independent objectivity. As long as the practice of illicit paid-for-editorial continues in any marketplace, the local public can never have confidence in what they read."

The issue of *zakazukhi* in Russia was brought into the open when a public relations firm in Moscow, Promaco, issued a fictitious news release to see how much various publications would charge to publish it as a news item. According to the *Economist,* "Of the 21 publications tested, one published the news release for free (but without checking its accuracy). Four asked for more information, and did not run stories. Three said they would run the article as an advertisement. But 13 papers and magazines offered to run it as an article, for fees ranging from around $135 at *Tribuna,* a paper backed by Gazprom, the national gas company, to more than $2,000 in the official government newspaper, *Rossiskaya Gazeta*. . . . "

IPRA President Sutherland, who is an executive at Manning, Selvage & Lee public relations, said "IPRA has long been aware of this unethical practice in a number of marketplaces around the world, especially in some where the concept of a free press is comparatively 'new'. . . . We urge both Russian and international public relations clients not to support this illegal practice in the future. According to our code, no IPRA member is permitted to use such methods."

Russian editors were less than embarrassed. According to the *Economist,* "The editor of *Noviye Izvestiya* said it made no difference to readers whether articles were paid or not." Another editor suggested that public relations firms were really to blame. When the newspaper wants to run the news release as an advertisement, the PR firms just take their business elsewhere.

What do you think? If you were doing public relations for an American or European firm in Moscow, would you go along with the local custom of *zakazukhi?* Or would you refuse to pay the media for using your news release? How about the common practice in China of giving reporters "transportation" money for attending a news conference?

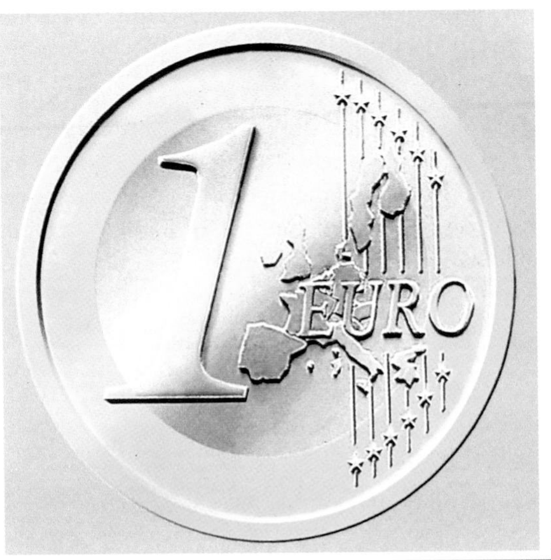

Adoption of the Euro in 2002 as the common currency of 11 countries of the European Union created an uncertain factor in international trade. An extensive public relations campaign helped citizens of the participating countries to change from their traditional national currencies to the new form. Pictured here is a unit of the Euro currency.

The following are some examples of the types of language problems encountered:

- The style of communication is important to the French, who tend to be dramatic and even emotional. Germans, on the other hand, rely heavily on facts and the written word.
- In Asian and African countries, communication often is vague; nonnatives must learn to "read between the lines."
- In communicating, Arabs emphasize form over function, effect over accuracy, and image over meaning. Seeking mainly to convey information, Americans emphasize function and, by extension, substance, meaning, and accuracy.
- Words translate differently in different countries. Chevrolet executives could not figure out why the Chevy Nova was not selling well in Latin America. Then they learned that, although *Nova* means "new" in Latin, *No va* means "It doesn't go" in Spanish.

Cultural differences provide additional pitfalls, as shown by the following examples:

- In the United States white signifies purity; in most Asian countries, white is the color of death. An Asian bride in one of these countries would never wear a white dress; she would wear red, the color of luck and happiness in China. In Latin America, though, red is the color of passion and love.
- In China, tables at a banquet are never numbered. The Chinese think such tables appear to rank guests, so it is better to direct a guest to the "primrose" or "hollyhock" table.
- German and Swiss executives think a person is uncouth if he or she uses first names, particularly at public events.
- The proper etiquette for drinking in Korea is to fill your neighbor's glass as well as your own.
- News releases in Malaysia should be distributed in four languages to avoid alienating any segment of the press.
- Americans, perhaps because of their strong freedom-of-expression tradition, tend to be perceived throughout the world as extremely vocal and opinionated.
- When Japanese executives suck in air through their teeth and exclaim, "*Sa!* That will be *very* difficult," they really mean just plain "no." The Japanese consider an absolute "no" offensive and try to respond euphemistically.

All of these illustrations indicate that Americans not only must learn the customs of the country to which they are assigned but should rely on native professionals to guide their paths. And, although they should study the language both before and after their arrival, they must realize that only by residing in the country for many years will they be free—if ever—of language problems.

Representing Foreign Corporations in the United States

Industries in other countries frequently employ American public relations firms to advance their needs in this country. Carl Levin, vice president and senior consultant, Burson-Marsteller, Washington, D.C., tells why:

- To hold off protectionist moves threatening their company or industry
- To defeat legislation affecting the sale of a client's product

- To support expansion of the client's markets in the United States
- To provide ongoing information on political, sociological, and commercial developments in the United States that could bear on the client's business interests, not only here but worldwide. In the well-organized foreign company, this information is factored into day-to-day policy decisions as well as periodic strategic plans.

A fourth reason might be crisis communications. Bridgestone, a Japanese company, found itself on the defensive when its American company, Firestone, had to recall millions of tires for safety reasons. Japanese management, unfamiliar with American expectations of open communications, stumbled badly in the initial stages of the recall because the Japanese CEO didn't issue an apology or offer to fix the problem. Only after Bridgestone hired an American public relations firm did the company combat Ford Motor Company's assertions that the tire company was completely at fault. See Chapter 1 for the background on this.

Representing U.S. Corporations in Other Countries

On a global basis, public relations as an occupation has achieved highest development in the industrialized nations of the world—United States, Canada, Western Europe, and parts of Asia. It emerges more readily in nations that have multiple-party systems, considerable private ownership of business and industry, large-scale urbanization, and relatively high per-capita income levels—which also relate to literacy and educational opportunities. By the same token, public relations as a specialized activity is less developed in Third World nations in which the vast majority of the citizens are still rural villagers.

U.S. and other Western public relations firms began exporting their expertise to the People's Republic of China during the mid-1980s. Hill & Knowlton, then active in Asia for about 30 years, began its Beijing operation in a hotel room with three U.S. expatriates and a locally hired employee. Today, almost every global public relations firm has a Beijing office, and it is estimated that China has about 1200 public relations firms employing between 30,000 and 40,000 people. In 2000, revenues totaled $180 million, which represented a 50 percent increase over 1999.

INTERNATIONAL PUBLIC AFFAIRS

c.£60k plus car, bonus and excellent benefits

Based in London, this is a truly global opportunity for a person who has worked with or within major international institutions to join a leading company with operations in 100 countries.

You will have worked successfully in one of the key multilateral centres: Geneva, New York, Washington, or Brussels. We are looking for a confident and diplomatic government relations professional with a sound knowledge of international regulatory and current affairs.

You are likely to have around 8 - 10 years' relevant experience building relationships with international organisations, governments and NGOs. You will have demonstrated the ability to manage effective global public affairs campaigns, particularly on social policy issues. You will also have shown a talent for dealing with sensitive regulatory issues and for developing policies, practices and industry codes of conduct.

This is an excellent opportunity to develop a rewarding career in a challenging environment, with plenty of scope to progress.

Please contact Ros Kindersley at JFL.
Email: ros@jflrecruit.com Website: www.jflrecruit.com
47 New Bond Street, London W1S 1DJ
Tel: 020 7493 8824 Fax: 020 7493 7161

This advertisement in the *Economist* is a good description of a job opportunity in international public relations.

global PR

Israel Worried about Its Image

The Israeli–Palestinian conflict has produced any number of news stories and photos showing Israeli soldiers, tanks, helicopters, and guided missiles being used against a relatively unarmed Palestinian population. As Israeli's minister of information, Nachman Shai, says, "We looked like Goliath and they looked like David."

This has caused some concern for the Israeli government, particularly as it affects opinion in the United States, because it is important to have the continuing support of the American population and the government. That support is in danger if public opinion shifts to increased sympathy for the Palestinian cause.

The Palestinians are also beginning to realize how decisive the battle for public opinion is, and various Arab groups, such as the Arab-American Anti-Discrimination Committee (ADC), have stepped up publicity efforts to inform Americans about the Palestinian side of the conflict. The group has taken full-page ads in daily newspapers across the country and written op-ed articles.

Israel has also been active, encouraging the Jewish community in the United States to be more proactive in explaining the Israeli side of the conflict. In addition, a New York public relations firm has been hired to place Israel's representatives in various media outlets. According to Steve Rubenstein, from Rubenstein Associates, "We felt people were missing the whole truth and that if we could show a fuller picture visually, it would be easier to make the Israeli case."

The major area of public relations business in China is information technology, and public relations firms are growing in staff and revenues about 15 percent a year. Local public relations firms are growing even faster—about 30 percent annually—because they can provide cost effective and flexible services, according to a survey by the China International Public Relations Association (CIPRA). In 2001, public relations experienced a major surge of growth with China's admission to the World Trade Organization. More than 30 universities and 300 institutes and colleges offer public relations courses.

In the Republic of China on Taiwan, public relations experienced rapid growth in recent years, paralleling the economic growth of the country.

Australia and New Zealand have public relations industries that are among the most active and developed in the Western world, according to David Potts, a senior public relations counselor in Sydney, Australia. Global public relations firms, as well as many small and medium-sized companies, operate in the two countries. "Some overseas corporations, however, make the mistake of assuming that public relations styles and campaigns which have worked overseas, especially in the U.S.A., will work in [these countries]," said Potts. "They don't always."

Potts has additional observations about public relations in other Pacific Rim countries:

- Hong Kong, because of its international financial, trading, and tourist links and the fact that Western management techniques are widely used, exhibits a widespread understanding of public relations. There are more advertising and public relations practitioners in Hong Kong than in any other Asian country. Their

global PR

Avoiding PR Pitfalls in China

Practicing public relations in the People's Republic of China requires a good understanding of the nation's history and political sensitivities. A California public relations firm, the Hoffman Agency, has an office in Beijing and issues a newsletter about doing business there. Here are some tips:

- It is important to be politically correct. Although Taiwan is considered by the outside world as a separate country, China considers it a renegade province of China. Consequently, companies should not refer to Taiwan as a separate country in their news releases or product specification sheets.
- The Chinese language is different in China and Taiwan. The difference is not only in the form of writing, but in vocabulary and grammar as well. A company will need two translations of the same news release.
- Successful branding for Western companies entering the Chinese market starts with a well-chosen Chinese name. A name that is culturally adept goes a long way in obtaining goodwill from government officials, business partners, and potential customers. Lucent's Chinese name, for example, is "Lang3 Xun4." Lang3 means "bright," and Xun4 means "communications."
- Chinese media need all written and audiovisual materials in Chinese, which means translation and localization of all press materials, such as news releases, backgrounders, and even PowerPoint presentations. Although a new generation of Chinese reporters know English in varying degrees, an on-site interpreter is a must at any media event.
- Advertising is closely tied in with media coverage. If a company does not advertise in a certain publication, it is usually difficult to get coverage.
- Chinese society is built on relationships, and people do exchange favors and gifts. Companies should also have occasional media parties, which are primarily social. Once relationships are established with reporters, it is much easier to work with them.

expertise, however, underwent its greatest test after Britain relinquished the country to China in 1997.

- Singapore and Malaysia enjoy well-developed public relations practices, both local and global. Singapore operations are heavily oriented to visual public relations, and many firms have strong graphics capabilities.
- In Indonesia, public relations consultancies and advertising agencies must be domestically owned.
- Thailand has a great deal of foreign investment and international tourism. The public relations industry is handicapped by a lack of skilled practitioners.
- Unlike most major Asian countries, no global public relations firm operates in the Philippines; instead, outside companies work through local firms on a referral basis. P. A. Chanco III, of the Orientations firm in Manila, advises public relations representatives of foreign corporations to "know the Filipino culture and how it works before anything else."
- In Japan, public relations practice is centered on reaching the media through one or more of the 400-plus reporters' "clubs," with about 12,000 members representing 160 newsgathering organizations.

International Government Public Relations

In this section we explore how and why the governments of most nations seek to influence the opinions and actions of governments and people in other countries. Many employ U.S. public relations firms for this purpose.

Influencing Other Countries

The governments of virtually every country have one or more departments involved in communicating with other nations. Much effort and millions of dollars are spent on the tourism industry, attracting visitors whose expenditures aid their hosts' economies. Even larger sums are devoted to lobbying efforts to obtain favorable legislation for a country's products; for example, Costa Rica urged the U.S. Congress to let its sugar into the nation at favorable rates, and the Department of State threatened to enact trade sanctions against countries such as Korea and China that persisted in "pirating" U.S. products such as computers and books without payment.

Many countries send shortwave broadcasts worldwide to foster their national interests and prestige, keep in touch with nationals abroad, disseminate news, and influence the internal affairs of other nations.

Information Efforts by the United States The American government is a major disseminator of information around the world. This is called "public diplomacy" because it is an open communications process primarily intended to present American society in all its complexity so that the citizens and governments of other nations can understand the context of U.S. actions and policies. Another function is to promote the American values of democracy, free trade, and open communication around the world.

The United States Information Agency (USIA), created in 1953 by President Dwight Eisenhower, was the primary agency involved in shaping America's image abroad. It informed citizens in other nations with a variety of activities. Some of them included (1) the stationing of a public affairs officer (PAO) at every American embassy to work with the local media, (2) publication of books and magazines, (3) distribution of American films and TV programs, (4) sponsorship of tours by American dance and musical groups, (5) art exhibitions, (6) student exchange programs, and (7) sponsorship of lecture tours by American authors and intellectuals.

At its height during the Cold War with the Soviet Union, the USIA had a budget of about $900 million and 12,000 employees. It had 275 posts in more than 100 nations. Once the Cold War was won, however, its fortunes began to fall in the 1990s as Congress and other critics decided that the United States didn't need such a large public profile in the world. As a result, the agency was abolished in 1999, and most of its functions were transferred to the U.S. Department of State. (See the PR Casebook box on how the U.S. government has renewed its commitment to public diplomacy since the September 11 terrorist attack.)

Broadcast Efforts The Voice of America (VOA), created in 1948, was part of USIA for several decades. In 1995, VOA's governing board was constituted as a firewall between the agency and the administration to assure that it would be an objective news service with credibility around the world. Article One of the VOA charter, for example,

PR casebook

War on Terrorism Requires PR Efforts

Perhaps the easiest part of the War on Terrorism was the toppling of the Taliban regime in Afghanistan and the disruption of Osama bin Laden's terrorist network. Most experts agree, however, that the toughest part will be winning the war of public opinion.

The U.S. government has a war of ideas to fight. As the *Economist* points out, "It has to persuade America, its allies and Muslims around the world that its fight is against terror, not Islam." Many experts are less optimistic about winning this part of the war. One Arab expert told the Associated Press, "The U.S. point of view is not unknown to the Arab people, they just don't buy it."

Nevertheless, the United States launched one of the most extensive programs in public diplomacy since the end of the Cold War. It was a highly orchestrated effort by the Pentagon, the White House, and the State Department to get the message out that the United States is, as President George W. Bush says, "a freedom-loving nation, a compassionate nation, a nation that understands values of life."

One immediate effort, with the bombing of Afghanistan, was the dropping of 400,000 leaflets to the civilian population to assure them that they were not targets of American military action. One leaflet showed a picture of an American soldier, in fatigues and a helmet, shaking hands with a man in traditional Afghan garb. The text read: "The Partnership of Nations Is Here to Help." The leaflet was printed in Dari and Pashto, the most common languages in the country.

Another leaflet displayed a radio tower sending out signals and listed the times and frequencies of radio broadcasts being beamed into Afghanistan by two EC-130 aircraft flying daily and broadcasting for five hours at a time. The broadcasts included local music, information about the September 11 terrorist attack on the World Trade Center and the Pentagon, and messages restating that the U.S. bombing isn't "against Muslims or the people of Afghanistan. . . . it is aimed at destroying terrorist threats and those that aid terrorism."

In addition, the U.S. State Department's Voice of America (VOA) stepped up its programming to Afghanistan and other nations in the Middle East. As well as doubling its service to Afghanistan to two hours a day, VOA also increased its service in Urdu, spoken in Pakistan; Farsi, spoken in Iran; and Arabic, spoken in other Middle Eastern nations.

The public diplomacy division of the U.S. State Department also issued reams of news releases about the War on Terrorism. One program was to use the Internet to translate and distribute statements of support from Muslim leaders to U.S. embassies around the world and then distribute them to local reporters. The Bush Administration also dispatched a number of officials for international television interviews, particularly on the widely watched Arab station Al-Jazera. One such official was Condoleezza Rice, Bush's national security advisor.

The Pentagon also hired a well-known Washington public relations firm, the Rendon Group, to monitor news media in 79 nations, conduct focus groups, create a counterterrorism Web site that provided information on terrorist groups and the U.S. campaign against terrorism, and recommend ways the U.S. military can counter disinformation and improve its own public communications.

Leading the U.S. government's efforts in public diplomacy, also called propaganda, were four women who worked together to formulate a consistent message. They were Karen Hughes, special counselor to the president; Charlotte Beers, under secretary of state for public diplomacy; Mary Matalin, chief political advisor to Vice President Dick Cheney; and Victoria Clarke, chief spokesperson for the Pentagon.

According to reporter Peter Marks, writing in the *New York Times*, "In the male-dominated machinery of war, it is a rarity, even in enlightened times, to find so many women in highly visible roles with the responsibility for trying to influence public opinion about military operations and other aspects of a conflict."

It is also noteworthy that the American government, as a result of the War on Terrorism, has placed a new emphasis on public diplomacy and international information efforts. Such efforts were considerably cut back in the 1990s after the end of the Cold War. Budgets were slashed by Congress, and even the United States Information Agency (USIA) was eliminated. The Voice of America (VOA) was also downsized and broadcasts to the Middle East were drastically curtailed.

states that it should be a "reliable and authoritative source of news," and the news should be "accurate, objective, and comprehensive."

Its core work has traditionally been broadcasting news, sports, and entertainment around the world via shortwave. Some VOA broadcasts are in English, but most of its 800 journalists work for the service that broadcasts to tens of millions of people in 53 languages. At the height of the Cold War, VOA's various broadcasts to various world regions totaled almost 2500 hours a week. It's estimated that VOA reaches about 86 million people worldwide via shortwave, and millions more listen to VOA programs placed on local AM and FM stations around the world. The VOA also has audio streaming on World Wide Web sites.

VOA's independence and objectivity, however, is often under threat as members of Congress and even the White House demand that it be more proactive in supporting the government. This debate was brought to a head after the Bush Administration started its War on Terrorism and replacing the Taliban regime in Afghanistan. VOA reporters sought to air an interview with Mullah Mohammad Omar, the Taliban leader, only to raise the ire of anti-Taliban émigrés and some members of Congress. One Republican member of Congress noted, "If we turn this into a PBS documentary—seesawing on every side and being balanced—that's not promoting democracy." By the same token, VOA supporters say the agency cannot afford to squander its credibility among millions of listeners by becoming a mouthpiece of the U.S. government.

The campaign against AIDS has many international ramifications. The Vanatu government distributed this poster in Pidgin English urging precautions against the disease. If you read it carefully, you can probably decipher the message.

global PR

Modifying Attitudes in South Africa

As a way to protest apartheid, some residents of Durban, South Africa, refused to pay taxes. With the coming of democracy, however, the Inner West City Council asked a marketing and public relations firm, Langa Shangase, Vulindleia, to devise an attitude modification campaign. The objective: to bring more than 17,500 homeowners to an understanding of how cities are financed and to expand the base of taxpayers.

The African concept of "ubuntu" was adopted to convey the benefits of developing a sense of communal belonging. "One City, One Tax Base" was a theme. Because of low literacy levels, campaign leaders focused on radio and face-to-face community meetings for message delivery.

Three months of research and development of trainers was followed by six months of implementation, during which the council received monthly feedback on key issues. In all, 22,600 people attended 630 community meetings. Leaders hailed not only the increase in tax payments but also the spirit of consultation and tolerance that pervaded the community.

The International Public Relations Association gave the campaign a Golden World Award for Excellence in Public Relations.

In addition to VOA, the U.S. government has also operated several other broadcast services that have been more proactive in advancing U.S. interests. Radio Free Europe was started in 1949 to reach the nations of Eastern Europe under the thumb of the Soviet Union. Radio Liberty was also started, under CIA funding, to broadcast directly to the citizens of Russia. The Russian response was a major effort to jam the broadcasts during the Cold War. Now that the Soviet Union is no more, both Radio Free Europe and Radio Liberty have significantly fewer staff people and do less broadcasting. More recently, Congress has funded Radio Free Iraq in an effort to weaken President Saddam Hussein's grip on his people. Congress is also establishing a Radio Free Afghanistan. Since 1994, the United States has also operated Radio Free Asia, beaming broadcasts to the Chinese mainland, Burma, Cambodia, Laos, North Korea, Tibet, and Vietnam.

It should be noted that VOA and other broadcasting services, such as Radio Free Europe, are not directed to citizens of the United States. By design, under the United States Information and Educational Exchange Act of 1948, Congress prohibits the government from directing its public diplomacy efforts toward its own citizens.

U.S. Firms Working for Foreign Governments

For fees ranging upward of $1 million per year, more than 150 American public relations firms work in this country for other nations. In recent years, for example, Hill and Knowlton has represented Indonesia and Morocco; Burson-Marsteller has represented Argentina, Costa Rica, Hungary, and Russia (the latter mainly in trade fairs); and Ruder, Finn & Rotman has represented El Salvador, Israel, and Japan. Especially active in representing other nations is Doremus & Company, whose clients have included Egypt, Iran, Jordan, the Philippines, Saudi Arabia, and Tunisia.

In many cases, the objective is to influence U.S. foreign policy, generate tourism, create favorable public opinion about the country, or encourage trade. Table 16.1 shows a sampling of accounts reported by *O'Dwyers Newsletter.*

TABLE 16.1

International Accounts Handled by U.S. Firms

CLIENT	PUBLIC RELATION FIRM	CONTRACT
South Africa	Patrice Tanaka & Co.	$1,100,000
Philippines	Weber Shandwick	$ 480,000
Ecuador	Burson-Marsteller	$ 180,000
Democratic Republic of the Congo	EAW Group	$ 500,000
Saudi Arabia	Powell Tate	$ 320,000
India	Washington Group	$ 300,000

The Countries' Goals What do these countries seek to accomplish? Burson-Marsteller's Carl Levin says that they pursue several goals, including:

- To advance political objectives
- To be counseled on the United States' probable reaction to the client government's projected action
- To advance the country's commercial interests—for example, sales in the United States, increased U.S. private investment, and tourism
- To assist in communications in English
- To counsel and help win understanding and support on a specific issue undermining the client's standing in the United States and the world community
- To help modify laws and regulations inhibiting the client's activities in the United States

Under the Foreign Agents Registration Act of 1938, all legal, political, fundraising, public relations, and lobbying consultants hired by foreign governments to work in the United States must register with the Department of Justice. They are required to file reports with the Attorney General listing all activities on behalf of a foreign principal, compensation received, and expenses incurred.

Action Programs Normally hired by an embassy after open bidding for the account, the firm first gathers detailed information about the client country, including past media coverage. Attitudes toward the country are ascertained both informally and through surveys.

The action program decided on will likely include the establishment of a national information bureau to provide facts and published statements of favorable opinion about the country. Appointments are made with key media people and other influential citizens, including educators, business leaders, and government officials. These people are often invited to visit the client country on expense-paid trips, although some news media people decline on ethical grounds. (Ethical questions will be discussed in more detail shortly.)

Gradually, through expert and persistent methods of persuasion and the expenditure of what may run into millions of dollars, critical public attitudes may be changed or reinforced. Success is difficult to judge.

Public relations firms have played a major role in the worldwide sales of state-owned enterprises (a process known as privatization) during the last decade. More than 2700 such enterprises were transferred into private hands in more than 95 countries in a five-year period, according to the International Finance Corporation. Tens of thousands of companies were privatized in Eastern Europe. For example, Burson-Marsteller designed and implemented public education campaigns in Russia, Kazakstan, and Ukraine in support of market reform and privatization.

■ Problems and Rewards The toughest problems confronting the firm are often as follows:

- Deciding to represent a country, such as Zimbabwe or China, whose human rights violations may reflect adversely on the agency itself
- Persuading the heads of such a nation to alter some of its practices so that the favorable public image sought may reflect reality
- Convincing officials of a client country, which may totally control the flow of news internally, that the American press is independent from government control and that they should never expect coverage that is 100 percent favorable
- Deciding whether to represent an autocratic head of state, such as Mobutu Sese Seko of Zaire, whose lavish living and large Swiss bank accounts stood in stark contrast to an average family income among the lowest in the world

Amnesty International, the Nobel Prize–winning human rights monitor, picketed Burson-Marsteller's offices because of its Argentine account. The Council on Hemispheric Affairs criticized Ruder, Finn & Rotman for working for the government of El Salvador. Norman Wolfson, chairman of Norman, Lawrence, Patterson & Farrell, fled Nicaragua with would-be assassins close on his heels after serving during most of 1978 as the public relations counselor for the late dictator General Anastasio Somoza. A Doremus & Company executive working for the economic development of the Philippines, whose government, headed by Ferdinand Marcos, had placed the country under military law, was also threatened with death.

Why, then, do these firms work for unpopular governments? Said Burson-Marsteller's Carl Levin: "I do not think it is overreaching to state that in helping friendly foreign clients we also advance our national interests. And we help in ways that our government cannot." Black, Manafort, Stone & Kelly felt the same way, but dropped its $950,000 contract with an agency close to the Philippines president when President Reagan called on Marcos to resign. And, of course, retainers are large: Wolfson earned $20,000 to $30,000 per month, including expenses, for example.

■ Intervention Tactics Placing full-page advertisements in major papers such as *The Washington Post* and *The New York Times* is almost invariably the first action taken by agents of foreign governments in seeking to influence American public opinion during a crisis. Surveys have shown that a high percentage of the nation's lawmakers and administrators read the *Post* before or soon after arriving in their offices. The *Times*, in particular, is read by opinion leaders throughout the country, and the advertisements gain important visibility, influencing editorial writers and others. Members of Congress often use these political statements in addresses to their colleagues and obtain permission to insert their remarks in the *Congressional Record*. The advertisements are generally followed by personal visits and telephone calls by foreign government agency people and their key supporters. Arrangements are made to place representatives on broadcast network and cable programs. Press conferences are arranged, and newsletters are hastily dispatched to media, government, and other leaders.

Some examples of recent campaigns include:

- The American–Arab Anti-Discrimination Committee placed full-page advertisements in daily newspapers showing a Palestinian youth throwing a rock at an Israeli tank. The copy stated: "Stones vs. Tanks: Freedom Now. Stop the Aggression Against The Palestinians, End the Israeli Occupation." It also gave a body count: "Since September 29, 2000, 258 dead, 9765 wounded."
- The Arab Intellectual Foundation announced plans for a $2 million media campaign to counter "negative images" of Arabs and Islam that were presented in the Western press in the aftermath of the September 11 terror attacks.
- "The Time Has Come to End the Embargo Against Cuba." So proclaimed the headline of an appeal that Americans urge Congress and the President to pass H.R. 2229, the Free Trade with Cuba Act. The appeal was made by the Faculty Committee for Human Rights in the Americas (FACHRAS), whose names and addresses filled the page.
- An advertisement by Japan's Save the Ozone Network took that country to task for failing to take steps to keep tons of ozone-destroying chlorofluorocarbons (CFCs) from escaping into the atmosphere. Readers were asked to petition Japan's Prime Minister and its Minister of International Trade & Industry.

The successful fight for ratification of the North American Free Trade Agreement (NAFTA) by the U.S. Congress was one of the most expensive lobbying campaigns ever seen in Washington. Mexico assembled a high-powered team of public relations specialists, lobbyists, lawyers, and consultants to promote passage of the agreement at an annual cost of about $15 million, according to Justice Department records.

U.S. public relations firms helped line up speaking engagements for Mexican officials; former U.S. high government officials mapped strategy; and congressional lobbyists worked Capitol Hill. Many members of Congress and their staffs took trips to

focus on ethics

"Sweatshop" Labor Practices under Fire

The University of North Carolina has signed a new contract under which Nike, the athletic shoe maker, will pay $7.1 million to outfit the institution's sports team, the Tar Heels, with Nike apparel. The university signed its original contract with Nike for $4.5 million.

Student protesters at a rally argued that the university should not do business with a company accused of allowing sweatshop labor practices at its Southeast Asia factories. According to the Associated Press, Chancellor Michael K. Hooker responded that it would be hard to find "a consumer good in the United States right now that is not made in a low-wage factory somewhere."

In your opinion, should the university (1) seek to cancel its contract or (2) keep it in effect but urge that Nike improve its labor practices?

global PR

Prince Charles Gets New Image

A public relations makeover for Prince Charles?

The *Economist* magazine says "the most audacious rebranding attempt yet attempted" is under way to transform the image of the heir to the British throne.

"The prince had employed public relations professionals before the death of Diana," the magazine confided in its November 1998 issue. "But, in the aftermath of her death, they came to the fore," led by Mark Bolland, an assistant private secretary to the prince, "who is said to be close to Peter Mandelson, the man who rebranded the Labour Party." Another assistant private secretary, Elizabeth Buchanan, was recruited from the Bell Pottinger public relations agency.

The goals: (1) "to take a leaf out of Diana's book, and to emphasize Charles's role as a parent and as a man with a populist streak"; (2) "to play down those of the prince's interests that might get him labeled as a fuddy-duddy, or a weirdo. He is talking a lot less about architecture and spiritualism these days"; (3) "to cultivate informal contacts with the press" [as Diana did]; and (4) "to get out the good news about their man, in particular the great success of the Prince's Trust, which works with young people in difficult circumstances to set up small businesses, and which is now running part of the government's 'New Deal' programme." All that, and more.

A major public relations problem was the future of the prince's relationship with Camilla Parker Bowles. In 1998, a poll showed that only 53 percent of the public thought the prince should be allowed to become king if he married Camilla. In recent years, however, the widowed prince has successfully introduced her to society as his consort. He also has improved his image as a devoted father to his two sons.

Mexico provided by the campaign. Lobbying expenditures by Mexico and U.S. corporations in one year alone were estimated at $100 million.

Burston-Marsteller public relations was paid $4.5 million to develop brochures, organize a speakers bureau, monitor media coverage, produce speeches, and supervise the work of several lobbying firms. In a separate contract, the Office of the President of Mexico paid the firm $1.5 million in fees and expenses to develop a series of television and newspaper ads that promoted Mexico's efforts to combat drug trafficking.

The Rise of NGOs

Hundreds of nongovernmental organizations (NGOs) depend on international support for their programs and causes. Such organizations as Greenpeace, Amnesty International, Doctors Without Borders, Oxfam, and a large number of groups opposed to globalization have been effective in getting their message out via the World Wide Web, e-mail, and demonstrations.

One study by StrategyOne, the research arm of Edelman Worldwide, showed that media coverage of such organizations more than doubled over a four-year period, and NGOs were perceived by the public to be more credible than the news media or corporations when it came to issues such as labor, health, and the environment.

Thought leaders, for example, trust NGOs more than government or corporations because they consider their motivation to be based on "morals" rather than "profit."

Public Affairs Council president Doug Pinkham said the StrategyOne report should be taken as a "wake-up call" by large corporations that have failed to embrace greater social responsibility and transparency. Pinkham told *PRWeek*, "The next five to ten years will be challenging for companies that operate on a world stage with the rise of technologically enabled activism."

There are, of course, many mainstream NGOs that have been around for decades. Such organizations as the International Red Cross, World Council of Churches, Oxfam, and Christian Aid often administer social services and medical care in many nations that have experienced civil war and other strife. Often, they adminster foreign aid given by major governments.

Foreign Public Relations Organizations

In virtually every country where public relations has become an economic and social force, practitioners have organized to exchange information, maintain and improve standards of professional performance, and aid in the development of international public relations. Codes of conduct are commonplace, and many organizations seek to enhance the standing of their members through certification and accreditation programs. Journals or newsletters are published, awards recognize outstanding performance, and scholarships and other assistance are provided to educational centers.

Public relations associations have been formed in about 70 countries. Many are comparable to the Public Relations Society of America; a smaller number relate exclusively to the business world, such as the International Association of Business Communicators. There is also the International Public Relations Association (IPRA) that

People at a shopping center in Shanghai walk past a giant billboard showing actress Gong Li advertising French cosmetics with a message in Chinese—a vivid example of how world trade crosses national boundaries.

has more than 900 members in 90 nations. Its code of ethics is on the following page, and its Web site is www.ipranet.org.

Opportunities in International Work

The 1990s, according to many experts, represented a new golden age of global marketing and public relations. The opening of the European Market, coupled with economic and social reforms in East European countries and the former Soviet Union hastened the reality of a global economy.

All of these developments led Jerry Dalton, past president of the Public Relations Society of America, to say: "I think more and more American firms are going to become part of those overseas markets, and I expect a lot of Americans in public relations will be living overseas." Indeed, Dalton believes that the fastest-growing career field for practitioners is international public relations. He adds: "Students who can communicate well and are fluent in a foreign language may be able to write their own ticket." But the coming of the "global village," as Marshall McLuhan once described it, still means that there will be a multiplicity of languages, customs, and values that public relations professionals will have to understand.

Many transnational corporations, putting an increased emphasis on international customer relations, are hiring "corporate protocol" officers to be responsible for doing everything from booking hotels, planning banquets, and hiring limousines, to scheduling plant tours, arranging security, and selecting gifts for foreign officials and major customers. They even brief company executives on current events, advise on the correct protocol for greeting royalty, and "hand out sheet music for sing-alongs at Korean banquets," according to a *New York Times* article.

Its author, Paul Finney, says: "Corporations tend to fill their protocol jobs with people who have backgrounds in public relations, marketing, [and] meeting planning and who have a knowledge of the industry." Although knowledge of foreign languages is a plus, it is not a prerequisite. One protocol officer is quoted as saying, "At AT&T, we're dealing with over 100 countries. You can rent language skills—interpreters, translators—if you need them."

Gavin Anderson, chairman of Gavin Anderson & Company, which has several offices abroad, is an expert in international public relations. He writes:

> Practitioners of either global or international public relations are cultural interpreters. They must understand the business and general culture of both their clients (or employers) and the country or countries in which they hope to do business. Whether as an outside or inhouse consultant, the first task is to tell a U.S. company going abroad (or a foreign party coming to the United States) how to get things done. How does the market work? What are the business habits? What is the infrastructure? The consultant also needs to understand how things work in the host country, to recognize what will need translation and adaptation . . .
>
> The field needs practitioners with an interest in and knowledge of foreign cultures on top of top-notch public relations skills. They need a good sense of working environments, and while they may not have answers for every country, they should know what questions to ask and where to get the information needed. They need to know where the potential dangers are, so as to not replenish the business bloopers book.

The decision to seek an international career should be made during the early academic years, so that a student can take multiple courses in international relations, global marketing techniques, the basics of strategic public relations planning, foreign languages, social and economic geography, and cross-cultural communication. Graduate study is an asset. Many students serve internships with international corporations as a desirable starting point.

Taking the U.S. Foreign Service Officers' examination is the first requirement for international government careers. Foreign service work with the innumerable federal agencies often requires a substantial period of government, mass media, or public relations service in this country before foreign assignments are made.

PR insights

Code of Ethics—International Public Relations Association (IPRA)

The following code of professional conduct, based on the charter of the United Nations, has been published in 20 languages:

IPRA Members Shall Endeavor:

1. To contribute to the achievement of the moral and cultural conditions enabling human beings to reach their full stature and enjoy the indefeasible rights to which they are entitled under the "Universal Declaration of Human Rights."
2. To establish communication patterns and channels which, by fostering the free flow of essential information, will make each member of the group feel that he/she is being kept informed, and also gives him/her an awareness of his/her own personal involvement and responsibility, and of his/her solidarity with other members.
3. To conduct himself/herself always and in all circumstances in such a manner as to deserve and secure the confidence of those with whom he/she comes in contact.
4. To bear in mind that, because of the relationship between his/her profession and the public, his/her conduct—even in private—will have an impact on the way in which the profession as a whole is appraised.

IPRA Members Shall Undertake:

5. To observe, in the course of his/her professional duties, the moral principles and rules of the "Universal Declaration of Human Rights."
6. To pay due regard to, and uphold, human dignity, and recognize the right of each individual to judge for himself/herself.
7. To establish the moral, psychological, and intellectual conditions for dialogue in its true sense, and to recognize the right of the parties involved to state their case and express their views.
8. To act, in all circumstances, in such a manner as to take account of the respective interests of the parties involved: both the interests of the organization which he/she serves and the interests of the publics involved.
9. To carry out his/her undertakings and commitments, which shall always be so worded as to avoid any misunderstanding, and to show loyalty and integrity in all circumstances so as to keep the confidence of his/her employers, past or present, and of all the publics that are affected by his/her actions.

IPRA Members Shall Refrain From:

10. Subordinating the truth to other requirements.
11. Circulating information which is not based on established and ascertainable facts.
12. Taking part in any venture or undertaking which is unethical or dishonest or capable of impairing human dignity or integrity.
13. Using any manipulative methods or techniques designed to create subconscious motivation which the individual cannot control of his/her own free will and so cannot be held accountable for the action taken on them.

A rooftop advertisement for Philips, the international electronic firm, stands out above a billboard for a downtown Moscow bank, indicative of the extensive entry of foreign companies into Russia.

global PR

Historic Flight to Japan Commemorated

What would you do if asked to develop a public relations program to celebrate, on two continents, the 50th anniversary of the first commercial flight along the Great Circle Route from the United States to Asia?

Northwest Airlines and Shandwick public relations people faced that mammoth task in 1997. Northwest had become the dominant U.S. carrier in Asia after the flight from Minneapolis–St. Paul to Tokyo, followed by nonstop flights to Beijing and other U.S.–Asia markets. Here's what they did.

Research

Northwest marketing staff helped identify 19 markets strategically important to the past and future of the airline's

Pacific business. Researchers unearthed details about the original flight and collected memorabilia. Northwest and Shandwick employees in the 19 cities were consulted and charged with handling the anniversary activities.

Planning

Planning for the year-long celebration, Bridging the Pacific, was handled by Asian and American communications, marketing, and advertising staffs and agencies, and was designed to involve whole communities. A Northwest Boeing 747-400, dubbed WorldPlane, became the portable, visually appealing focal point for the entire trans-Pacific marketplace. Target audiences were current and potential Northwest Airlines employees and customers in those markets. A children's art contest was planned. The total budget of $750,000 included nearly $125,000 in cash and in-kind WorldPlane charity donations.

Execution

The celebration began with a WorldPlane launch event honoring the child artists. During the month of the original 1947 flight, Northwest produced a week-long celebration. Included were a commemorative exhibit created jointly by the airline and the Minnesota Historical Society, a salute to the original crew members, and a dramatic tarmac event at the airport. Similar events took place in Tokyo and Osaka.

The children's art contest was conducted in 10 Asian and nine North American communities, with school and media assistance. Winners and two adults from each city were flown to Minneapolis–St. Paul for a weekend party. Fourteen news conferences exposed many members of the target audiences to the artists, as each presented a $5000 check to his or her designated charity.

Almost $100,000 was donated to nonprofit organizations in target communities as a part of the WorldPlane community support program. All Northwest international travelers viewed commemorative videos and/or images of the children's art on seat placards and menus. Major newspapers commemorated the historic flight, along with Northwest's employee newspaper and on-board magazines.

Evaluation

Objective No. 1—raising awareness of the airline's 50-year trans-Pacific history—was achieved. An estimated several million people were exposed to knowledge of the activities. For Asia and North America combined, there were 54 confirmed broadcasts and 260 print articles in large target markets. Also achieved was objective No. 2, raising awareness among trans-Pacific communities and the people Northwest serves.

The Public Relations Society of America gave the initiative its coveted Silver Anvil award.

Summary

What Is International Public Relations?

Public relations now takes place on a global scale, with relationships being built with the publics of all nations. Although some elements of public relations were being practiced in Europe over a hundred years ago, American techniques are those most commonly adapted to use throughout the world.

International Corporate Public Relations

In the new age of global marketing, public relations firms represent foreign interests in the United States as well as the interests of American corporations around the world. This means that the practitioner must deal with issues of language and cultural differences, including subtle differences in customs and etiquette and even ethical dilemmas involving bribery.

International Government Public Relations

Most governments seek to influence the international policies of other countries as well as the opinions and actions of the public. These communications can range from promoting tourism to attempts to influence trade policies. The U.S. government refers to its international information effort as "public diplomacy," the attempt to enhance understanding of our culture and promote our foreign policy objectives. The Voice of America radio broadcasts are part of this program. There are also U.S. public relations firms working for foreign governments, helping them advance their political objectives and commercial interests, counseling them on probable U.S. reactions to their proposed actions, and assisting in communications in English.

The Rise of NGOs

Among nongovernmental organizations depending on international support for their causes are Greenpeace, Amnesty International, Doctors Without Borders, Oxfam, and the International Red Cross. Such organizations are widely believed to be more credible than the news media on such issues as labor, health, and the environment, partly because they are perceived to lack the self-interest ascribed to governments and corporations.

Foreign Public Relations Organizations

Public relations practitioners have formed organizations wherever their work has flourished, hoping to exchange information, maintain and improve professional and ethical standards, and aid in the development of their work.

Opportunities in International Work

As global marketing and communications have expanded in recent years, so too have opportunities for international public relations work. Fluency in foreign language is a valued skill but not a prerequisite; also important are backgrounds in international relations, global marketing techniques, social and economic geography, and cross-cultural communication.

Case Activity: What Would You Do?

The Baltic nation of Estonia has a problem. Noone seems to know much about it. A TV reporter asked New Yorkers what they thought of when the word "Estonia" was mentioned, and most of them thought it was a soccer team.

The reality is that Estonia is a leader in market reforms since the collapse of the Soviet Union, and it is a strong contender to join the European Union. So how should Estonia position itself to convince foreign investors (corporations and governments) that it's a good candidate for investment?

Estonia formed a committee of citizens to think about "rebranding" itself. But the suggestions were pretty diverse. Environmentalists suggested an ecotourism approach; a journalist thought a great selling point was ethnic diversity; a fashion photographer liked the idea of using Estonian fashion models as goodwill ambassadors.

Do some research on Estonia to become familiar with its history, culture, people, and economy. What major themes do you think the government should emphasize to generate more foreign investment and tourism?

Questions for Review and Discussion

1. What is meant by international public relations? What are some of the reasons for its growth in recent decades?
2. How does public relations fit into the mix of global marketing operations?
3. What are some of the difficulties that a corporation is likely to encounter when it conducts business in another country?
4. What objectives do foreign nations seek to accomplish by hiring Ü.S. public relations firms to represent them in America?
5. Describe the efforts of the U.S. government to win the "hearts and minds" of citizens in other nations.
6. The U.S. government mounted an extensive program of "public diplomacy" as part of the War on Terrorism. Describe some of the activities that were undertaken.
7. What is the Russian practice of *zakazukhi?* Why does the International Public Relations Association (IPRA) consider it a bad practice?
8. Why is Israel worried about its image in the United States and other nations?
9. International public relations requires knowledge of a nation's history and political sensitivities. What kinds of things should you know if you were going to practice public relations in the People's Republic of China?
10. What kinds of ethical dilemmas do public relations firms face when they are asked to do work for a particular nation?
11. What does the abbreviation "NGO" mean? How has the new information technology enabled NGOs to expand their influence?
12. What opportunities exist for someone who wants to specialize in international public relations as a career?
13. What are some of the components of the code of ethics for the International Public Relations Association (IPRA)?

Suggested Readings

Becker, Elizabeth. "In the War on Terrorism, a Battle to Shape Opinion." *New York Times,* November 11, 2001, p. 1, B4–6.

Benoit, William L., and Brinson, Susan L. "Queen Elizabeth's Image Repair Discourse: Insensitive Royal or Compassionate Queen?" *Public Relations Review,* Vol. 25, No. 2 (1999), pp. 145–156.

"Global Rankings," *PRWeek,* July 30, 2001, pp. 17–41.

Hackley, Carol Ann, and Dong, Quingwen. "American Public Relations Networking Encounters China's Guanxi." *Public Relations Quarterly,* Summer 2001, pp. 16–19.

Ihator, Augustine. "Understanding the Cultural Patterns of the World—An Imperative in Implementing Strategic International PR Programs."*Public Relations Quarterly,* Winter 2000, pp. 38–44.

Jaffe, Greg. "Spreading the Word: An Elite Army Team Opens a New Front: The Afghan Mind." *Wall Street Journal,* November 8, 2001, p. 1, 6.

Kent, Michael L., and Taylor, Maureen. "When Public Relations Becomes Government Relations." *Public Relations Quarterly,* Fall 1999, pp. 18–23.

Murphy, Dean E. "A War Fought without Guns: Appealing to the Hearts and Minds of Muslims." *New York Times,* October 14, 2001, p. 14.

Ritchey, David. "The Changing Face of Public Relations in China and Hong Kong." *Public Relations Quarterly,* Winter 2000, pp. 27–32.

Singh, Raveena. "Public Relations in Contemporary India: Current Demands and Strategy." *Public Relations Review,* Vol. 26, No. 3 (2000), pp. 295–313.

Singh, Raveena, and Smyth, Rosaleen. "Australian Public Relations: Status at the Turn of the 21st Century." *Public Relation Review,* Vol. 26, No. 4 (2000), pp. 387–401.

Taylor, Maureen. "Cultural Variance as a Challenge to Global Public Relations: A Case Study of the Coca-Cola Scare in Europe." *Public Relations Review,* Vol. 26, No. 3 (2000), pp. 277–293.

Wu, Ming-Yi, Taylor, Maureen, and Chen, Mong-Ju. "Exploring Societal and Cultural Influences on Taiwanese Public Relations." *Public Relations Review,* Vol. 27, 2001, pp. 317–336.

Zaharna, R. S. "An Awareness Approach to International Public Relations." *Public Relations Review,* Vol. 27 (2001), pp. 135–148.

Zaharna, R. S., and Villabos, Juan Christobal. "A Public Relations Tour of Embassy Row: The Latin American Experience." *Public Relations Quarterly,* Winter 2000, pp. 33–37.

Nonprofit Organizations

preview

The purpose of this chapter is to explain how public relations serves nonprofit organizations, as compared to work for business and government, and to identify the types of organizations recognized as nonprofit.

Topics covered in the chapter include:

- Membership organizations
- Advocacy groups
- Social, cultural, and health agencies
- Importance of volunteer workers
- Fund-raising
- Health care public relations

The Role of Public Relations

A broad area of public relations work, and the source of many jobs, is the nonprofit organization. The range of nonprofit institutions is astounding, from small city historical societies to gigantic international foundations that disperse million-dollar grants.

The crucial point about nonprofit organizations is that they are tax-exempt. The federal government grants them this status because they enhance the well-being of their members, as in trade associations, or enhance the human condition in some way, such as environmental work or medical research. Many nonprofit organizations could not survive if they were taxed as they face the unending public relations task of raising money to pay their expenses and finance their projects.

Basic Needs of Nonprofits

Mothers Against Drunk Driving seems to have little in common with the American Red Cross or the National Academy of Songwriters, yet they share three fundamental actions for success:

- All three create communication campaigns and programs such as special events, Internet Web sites, brochures, and radio and television appearances that stimulate public interest in organizational goals and invite public participation.
- They develop a strong staff to handle the work. Recruiting volunteers and keeping them enthusiastic are essential.
- These organizations establish a realistic fund-raising goal and a plan to attain it.

The significance of these factors will be evident as we examine the various types of nonprofit organizations. For convenience, these can be grouped roughly as membership groups, advocacy agencies promoting causes, and social organizations.

Membership Organizations

A membership organization consists of people with a common interest, in either business or social life. Their purpose is mutual help and self-improvement. They often use the strength of their common bond to improve community welfare, endorse legislation, and support socially valuable causes.

Trade Associations

At last count, there were about 6000 trade and professional associations in the United States. Because federal laws and regulations often can affect the fortunes of an entire industry, about one-third of these groups are based in the Washington, D.C., area. There, association staffs can monitor congressional activity, lobby for or against legislation, communicate late-breaking developments to the membership, and see government officials on a regular basis.

The membership of a trade association usually consists of manufacturers, wholesalers, retailers, or distributors in the same field. Memberships are held by corporate entities, not individuals. The following are a few examples:

- Electronic Industries Association
- National Soft Drink Association
- National Association of Home Builders

Although individual members may be direct rivals in the marketplace, they work together to promote the entire industry, generate public support, and share information of general interest to the entire membership.

By representing its entire industry, an association often is more effective as a news source than is an individual company. When a news situation develops involving a particular field, reporters often turn to the spokesperson of its association for comment.

Labor Unions

Since the mid-1970s, labor unions in the United States have suffered serious losses in membership and consequently in political clout. The United Auto Workers, for example, saw membership fall from 1.5 million in 1979 to 671,853 in 2000. A perception of unions as money-hungry, inflexible, lacking in concern for the public interest, and at times arrogant created a severe image problem. Media coverage often showed union members in negative, adversarial positions that sometimes inconvenienced the public.

Today total union membership amounts to less than 15 percent of all American workers, with the figure dropping to about 10 percent in the private sector.

Nevertheless, labor unions still are very much a part of the American scene, from players in the National Basketball Association to employees of UPS scurrying with deliveries in each of our communities. The union movement relies on public relations tools in an attempt to regain strength and influence. The unions must seek to build new memberships, protect the job security of members, and improve their public images.

In every national political campaign, the unions spend millions of dollars in support of candidates they regard as friendly. Some of this money goes directly to candidates, while significant amounts are devoted to "issue ads" that do not explicitly endorse an individual. This questionable practice enables support of candidates beyond individual campaign spending limits; probusiness organizations counter with their own issue ads. Significant sums of union money are also spent on lobbying efforts. In one six-month period, the AFL-CIO spent $1.4 million on lobbying.

Like corporations, union managements need to employ public relations extensively with their internal audiences. They must keep their memberships informed about what they receive in return for their dues, including social and recreational programs and the representation to company management that the union leadership supplies.

Professional Associations

Members of a profession or skilled craft organize for mutual benefit. In many ways, their goals resemble those of labor unions in that they seek improved earning power, better working conditions, and public acceptance of their role in society. Because professional organizations do not engage in collective bargaining between employers and employees as labor unions do, they instead place their major emphasis on setting standards for professional performance, establishing codes of ethics, determining requirements for admission to the field, and encouraging members to upgrade skills through continuing education. In some cases, professional organizations have quasi-legal power to license and censure members. In most cases, however, professional groups use the techniques of peer pressure and persuasion to police their membership.

In general, professional associations are national in scope with district, state, or local chapters. Many scientific and scholarly associations, however, are international, with chapters in many nations. Organizations such as the Public Relations Society of America (PRSA) and the International Association of Business Communicators (IABC) are classified as professional associations.

Public relations specialists for professional organizations use the same techniques as their colleagues in other branches of practice. And like their counterparts in trade groups and labor unions, many professional associations maintain a Washington office or one in the state capital and employ lobbyists to advocate positions. One of the most politically active groups is the American Medical Association (AMA).

The lobbying power exercised in Washington by major professional associations was especially evident during one of the most noteworthy political battles of the 1990s, the Clinton administration's unsuccessful promotion of its health care reform plan. The American Medical Association, with 220,000 physician members, applied both public and backstage pressures in an effort to shape the plan to its advantage. So did other health organizations. A barrage of full-page advocacy advertisements by health organizations appeared in Washington newspapers and magazines and in national magazines with strong congressional readership. They contained such lines as "Price controls on health care would be a costly mistake" (AMA) and "What we're doing to hold down the high cost of cancer" (pharmaceutical companies).

Public relations activity on behalf of individual professionals is a relatively new development. Traditionally, lawyers and medical doctors did not advertise or seek to publicize themselves in any way. The taboo arose in part from the rules and regulations of the professional societies. Until recently, many medical societies prohibited their members from hiring public relations firms. The Supreme Court, in several cases, however, said that such regulations infringed on free speech. And the Federal Trade Commission ruled in 1980 that the American Medical Association couldn't tell its members not to advertise.

Many attorneys and physicians still feel uncomfortable about advertising their services, but competition for clients and patients is breaking down the traditional taboos. A survey by *Attorneys Marketing Report,* for example, shows the majority of lawyers using Yellow Pages advertising. In descending order of frequency, they also use (1) entertainment of clients, (2) brochures, (3) seminars, and (4) newsletters.

The *Wall Street Journal* observed another trend: "Medical associations are also hiring public relations firms to publicize new or controversial techniques. 'Fat suctioning' was the focus of a press briefing publicized by Doremus & Co. for the American Society of Plastic and Reconstructive Surgeons."

Chambers of Commerce

A *chamber* is an association of businesspersons, often joined by professionals, who work to improve their city's commercial climate and to publicize its attractions. State chambers of commerce and, nationally, the Chamber of Commerce of the United

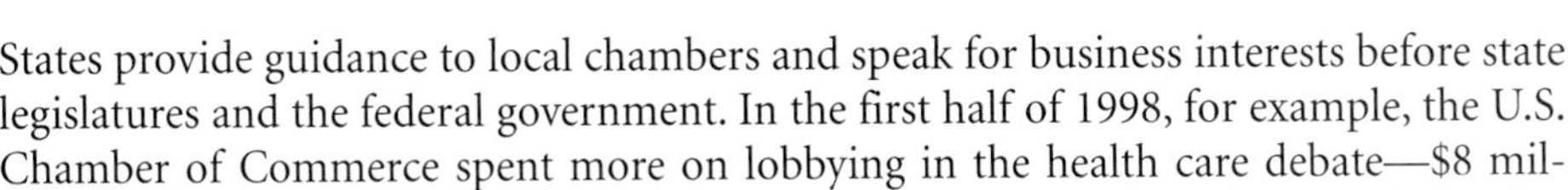

PR insights

Web-Based Techniques for Grassroots Campaigns

Advocacy groups often operate on limited budgets and volunteer effort. Here are some of the ways that the Web can be a powerful tool to leverage limited resources in public relations:

- Facilitate communication among members through online notices, instant messaging, and chat rooms
- Educate the general audience about an issue and the advocacy group's stance
- Generate letters to officials by providing downloadable text, mail and e-mail addresses, and fax numbers
- Provide a more automated method in five mouse clicks for sending a form letter to officials
- Solicit feedback, volunteer support, and campaign ideas
- Identify frequent questions to refine message strategies for greater clarity

States provide guidance to local chambers and speak for business interests before state legislatures and the federal government. In the first half of 1998, for example, the U.S. Chamber of Commerce spent more on lobbying in the health care debate—$8 million—than any other group. The primary focus of most members, however, is local.

Often, the chamber of commerce is the public relations arm of city government. The chamber staff often produces the brochures and maps sent to individuals who seek information about visiting the city or are considering moving to the area. Chambers also conduct polls and compile statistics about the economic health of the city, including data on major industries, employment rates, availability of schools and hospitals, housing costs, and so on. Attracting conventions and new businesses to the city also is an important part of chamber work.

Chambers of commerce play the role of community booster: They spotlight the unique characteristics of a city and sing its praises to anyone who will listen. Chambers often coin a slogan for a city, such as "Furniture Capital of Indiana." Chambers tend to be boosters of business growth.

Advocacy Groups

Environmental cleanup holds a high place on the public agenda, primarily because of vigorous campaigns by environmental organizations. By promoting recycling, elimination of toxic waste sites, purification of air and water, and preservation of natural resources, they strongly influence our collective conscience. Organizations that fight for social causes also achieve significant impact, both positive and negative.

Some of these organizations work relatively quietly through lobbying, litigation, and public education. Others are stridently confrontational.

Environmental Groups

Greenpeace, an organization that operates in 30 countries, including the United States, with 5 million members, is perhaps the best known of the confrontational groups. Television viewers are familiar with the daredevil efforts of some members in small boats to stop nuclear warships and other vessels they regard as harmful to the public.

global PR

Environmental Issues Prompt Planetary Perspective

Because environmental issues often take on global implications, groups such as Greenpeace enjoy global membership and operate in many countries. Although most ecosystems span national boundaries, and pollution of the environment respects no border, some issues are naturally defined as truly global concerns. Greenpeace took on Atlantic Richfield for its oil exploration in the Arctic National Wildlife Refuge. A Greenpeace advocacy advertisement in the *New York Times* depicted an offshore oil rig, citing it as a threat to life in the refuge. The ad maintained that the "real problem" was global warming, pointing out that exploration for new oil reserves postpones the shift from fossil fuels to renewable energy sources. The ad ended on a global note: "If you plan to live on this planet for the foreseeable future, it's your fight, too."

Plant Trees For Wildlife

Our trees make our town a great place to live. For generations people in our neighborhoods have planted trees. Along stream banks, on hillsides, in our yards, and along our streets. These trees shade our homes and increase property values. And they make songbirds and other wildlife a part of our daily lives.

10 Free Trees for Wildlife

You can make a difference in your town, too. Join The National Arbor Day Foundation and receive 10 Free Trees for Wildlife—Red Oak, Hawthorn, Bur Oak, Viburnum, Crabapple, Gray Dogwood, 2 Canadian Hemlock and 2 Redcedar, or other trees selected for your area.

Your trees will protect the environment, shelter wildlife, and provide food for more than 100 species of songbirds. They will be shipped postpaid at the right time for planting in your area, February through May in the spring or October through mid December in the fall. The six to twelve inch trees are guaranteed to grow, or they will be replaced free.

Send your $10 contribution to 10 Trees for Wildlife, The National Arbor Day Foundation, 100 Arbor Avenue, Nebraska City, NE 68410.

The National Arbor Day Foundation promoted its campaign, Plant Trees for Wildlife, with this advertisement offering 10 free trees for each new $10 membership in the organization. Those who join thus get a sense of personal participation in environmental work.

Recently contributions to Greenpeace have declined; so has its political influence. In total membership, Greenpeace is second to the much less flamboyant National Wildlife Foundation, followed by the Sierra Club and Nature Conservancy.

The principal ways that environmental organizations work to achieve their goals are lobbying, litigation, mass demonstrations, boycotts, and reconciliation.

Other Activist Groups

The work of major organizations that receive frequent national attention is illustrative of intense efforts by relatively less prominent associations as well. The National Rifle Association influences Congress and state legislatures by lobbying and campaign contributions. The American Tobacco Institute fights hard to defeat laws limiting smoking by adults. The Christian Coalition fights abortion with public statements, mailings, and telephone calls, and works through the right wing of the Republican Party. Christian church denominations sometimes adopt an activist role. The Southern Baptist Convention mounted a boycott of Disney corporation and all of its subsidiaries in protest of sex and violence in Disney entertainment productions. The Convention was also motivated by "gay days" at Disney's theme parks.

Methods of Operation

The principal ways in which advocacy groups work to achieve their goals include:

- *Lobbying.* Much of this is done at state and local government levels, because environmental problems often can be resolved there. For example, approximately 150 organizations campaigned for laws to forbid smoking in public places and restrict the sale of tobacco. The campaign has had numerous successes.
- *Litigation.* Through litigation, organizations file suits seeking court rulings favorable to their projects or attempting to block unfavorable projects. The Sierra Club did so in a years-long action that resulted in a decision by the U.S. Fish and Wildlife Service declaring the northern spotted owl a threatened species. The American Horse Council contends against changes in insurance laws that would discourage many horse enthusiasts who would not be covered in the event of a horse-related accident.
- *Mass demonstrations.* Designed to demonstrate public support for a cause and in some cases to harass the operators of projects to which the groups object, mass demonstrations require intricate public relations organizational work. Organizers must obtain permits, inform the media, and arrange transportation, housing, programs, and crowd control. A mass demonstration of farmers dependent upon irrigation water from drought-threatened rivers in Klamath Falls, Oregon, culminated with the arrival on a truck trailer of a gigantic metal pail, the symbol of the grassroots movement.
- *Boycotts.* "Hit them in the pocketbook" is the principle underlying use of the boycott to achieve a goal. Some boycotts achieve easily identifiable results. Others stay in effect for years with little evident success. One environmental success story occurred when the Rainforest Action Network boycotted Burger King for buying Central American beef raised in cleared rain forests. The fast-food chain agreed to stop such purchases.

focus on ethics

Working within the System or Selling Out?

Since the 1950s, Americans have joined in events organized by the environmental group Keep America Beautiful (KAB) to clean up neighborhoods and towns. Many also may recall the evocative image of the Native American chief who cries over the abuse of our land. The ad continues to appear as a classic public service announcement.

But the group has its detractors. According to *O'Dwyer's PR Services Report,* KAB includes among its major donors both Anheuser-Busch and Coca-Cola, "whose bottles and cans most clutter parks and waterfronts in the first place." KAB's antigraffiti campaign is sponsored by the Sherwin-Williams paint company. Competing environmental groups say KAB was formed to oppose bottle bill legislation to require recycling of beverage containers, with KAB favoring individual responsibility and community initiative over mandatory recycling.

KAB responds that there is nothing wrong with corporations acting in their own enlightened self-interest by supporting the quiet, constructive work of environmental groups. A KAB spokesperson dismisses the critics this way: " . . . if you're not jumping off a smokestack or lying in front of a bulldozer, then you're part of a crooked establishment."

Where do you stand regarding KAB?

Should KAB take sponsorship money from companies that could be part of the problem in the first place?

Do you think a proactive approach that minimizes protest is the way to go for environmental groups?

- *Reconciliation.* Some environmental organizations find good results by cooperating with corporations to solve pollution problems. The Environmental Defense Fund joined a task force with McDonald's to deal with the fast-food chain's solid waste problem, leading to a company decision to phase out its polystyrene packaging.

Fund-Raising

Direct mail fund-raising and publicity campaigns are basic tools of advocacy groups. Raising money to conduct their programs is an unending and costly problem for them. In the 1990s Greenpeace sent out 4.5 million pieces of mail a month for this purpose. With so many groups in the field, competition for donations is intense. Some professional fund-raisers believe that as a whole the groups depend too much on direct mail and should place more emphasis on face-to-face solicitation. Ironically, while some environmental groups advocate preservation of forests, they also create mountains of waste paper by sending millions of "junk mail" letters to raise funds for their organization.

Social Issue Organizations

Several other widely known organizations are similar to the environmental groups in structure, but with social and behavioral goals. They use public relations methods such as those just described.

Mothers Against Drunk Driving (MADD) urges people who have been drinking to call a friend or a cab to take them home. This poster, with its succinct headline, delivers the message in a graphic manner.

Mothers Against Drunk Driving (MADD) is one such group. The antiabortion Right to Life movement and the prochoice National Organization for Women (NOW), bitter enemies, frequently clash in rival public demonstrations. Animal rights groups such as People for the Ethical Treatment of Animals (PETA) resort at times to extreme confrontational tactics such as raiding animal research laboratories and seeking to shame the wearers of fur. The group's campaign against the dairy industry takes a different tack—humor and parody—on the Web site at www.milksucks.com.

Other groups, such as the American Family Association, pressure advertisers to drop sponsorship of television shows that they consider contrary to family values. As a result of massive letter campaigns by this group, Coca-Cola and Procter & Gamble decided to cancel commercials on *Married . . . with Children.* Members of the AFA also pressured Pepsi into canceling its Madonna ads after seeing the star's video clip for her song "Like a Prayer." Kansas Action for Children, a child advocacy group in Topeka, Kansas, provides an exhaustive databook as well as a report card to assess child well-being in the state. The grades and the data influence policy and legislation concerning children and teens.

Social Organizations

The term "social" includes social service, health, cultural, philanthropic, and religious groups serving the public in their various ways. Because communication is essential for their success, they require active, creative public relations programs.

Because these organizations are not profit-oriented, the practice of public relations on their behalf differs somewhat from that in the business world. Traditionally, nonprofit social agencies have been seen as the "good guys" of society—high-minded, compassionate organizations whose members work to help people achieve a better life. Recently, that perception has changed in some cases.

Numerous agencies have been caught by the recent American urge to scrutinize all aspects of the governmental and social establishment. Famous organizations usually regarded as sacrosanct have found themselves in trouble. The Girl Scouts of America were accused of having such heavy overhead expense for their annual national cookie sale that the girls themselves received little direct benefit. The Boy Scouts of America ran into difficulty for barring homosexuals from membership. Nevertheless, a national survey by the D.C.-based Independent Sector of 2553 U.S. citizens found high confidence in the efficiency and effectiveness of charitable organizations.

These controversies and disclosures were coupled with deep cuts in federal spending on social programs by the 1995 Republican Congress, pursuing its Contract with America. Scandal and economic changes put additional fund-raising pressure on private charities, emphasizing the need for public relations representatives to tell the charity's story more effectively. Like their colleagues in the corporate world, agency communicators feel the need to put crisis management plans in place.

For many nonprofit groups, obtaining operating funds is a necessity that dominates much of their effort. Without generous contributions from companies and individuals whose money is earned in the marketplace, nonprofit organizations could not exist. As an indication of the scope of philanthropy in the United States, and of the money needed to keep voluntary service agencies operating, American contributions to charity were $203 billion in 2001, according to the American Association of Fund-Raising Counsel (see Figure 17.1). Additional funds are donated to specialized nonprofit organizations that do not fall under the "charity" mantle, and still more are contributed by federal, state, and local governments. Competition among nonprofit agencies for their share of donations is intense.

In general terms, nonprofit social organizations are of two types—*service,* typified nationally by the Visiting Nurse Association and the Boys Clubs of America; and *cause,* whose advocacy role is exemplified by the National Safety Council and the National Association for the Advancement of Colored People (NAACP). Frequently organizations have dual roles, both service and advocacy.

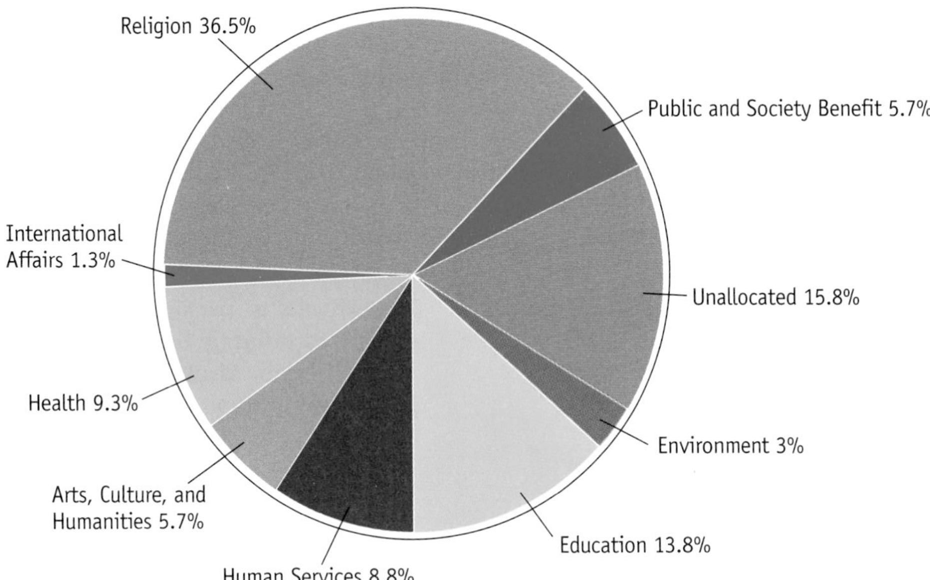

FIGURE 17.1

This pie chart shows how the $203.45 billion given to charity in 2001 was allocated. Individual gifts accounted for $152.07 billion of the total, while foundations gave $24.50 billion and corporations $10.86 billion. Bequests accounted for $16.02 billion.

Categories of Social Agencies

For purposes of identification, nonprofit social organizations and their functions may be grouped into seven categories:

1. *Social service agencies.* Serving the social needs of individuals and families in many forms are social service agencies. Among prominent national organizations of this type are Goodwill Industries, the American Red Cross, Boy Scouts and Girl Scouts of America, and the YMCA. Local chapters carry out national programs. Service clubs such as Rotary, Kiwanis, Lions, and the Exchange Club also raise significant amounts of money for charitable projects.
2. *Health agencies.* Many health agencies combat a specific illness through education, research, and treatment, while others deliver generalized health services in communities. Typical national organizations include the American Heart Association, the American Cancer Society, and the National Multiple Sclerosis Society.
3. *Hospitals.* Public relations work for hospitals is a large and expanding field. The role of a hospital has taken on new dimensions. In addition to caring for ill and injured patients, hospitals conduct preventive health programs and provide other health-related social services that go well beyond the traditional institutional concept. Hospitals may be tax-supported institutions, nonprofit organizations, or profit-making corporations
4. *Religious organizations.* The mission of organized religion, as perceived by many faiths today, includes much more than holding weekly worship services and underwriting parochial schools. Churches distribute charity, conduct personal guidance programs, provide leadership on moral and ethical issues in their communities, and operate social centers where diverse groups gather. Some denominations operate retirement homes and nursing facilities for the

elderly. At times, religious organizations assume political roles to further their goals. The nondenominational Salvation Army provides the needy with shelter, food, and clothing. It has a vigorous public relations program to earn its place at the top of fund-raising ranks.

A recent study by the Brookings Institution, *Fiscal Capacity of the Voluntary Sector,* stated in this regard: "Because religion occupies a stable, central role in American life, religious institutions will be looked to as a backup finance and delivery mechanism by other subsectors . . . particularly . . . in the human service field."

5. *Welfare agencies.* Most continuing welfare payments to persons in need are made by government agencies, using tax-generated funds. Public information officers of these agencies have an important function, to make certain that those entitled to the services know about them and to improve public understanding of how the services function.
6. *Cultural organizations.* Development of interest and participation in the cultural aspects of life falls heavily into the hands of nonprofit organizations. So, in many instances, does operation of libraries, musical organizations such as

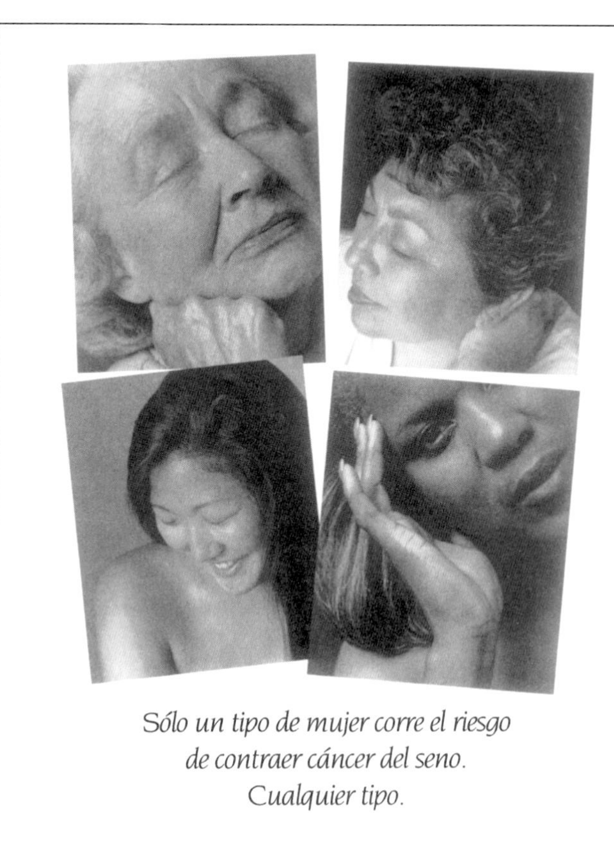

Social service and health care agencies reach out to various publics through public service messages in various languages.

symphony orchestras, and museums of art, history, and natural science. Such institutions frequently receive at least part of their income from government sources; many are operated by governments. Even government-operated cultural institutions depend upon private-support organizations such as Friends of the Museum to raise supplementary funds.

7. *Foundations.* The hundreds of tax-free foundations in the United States constitute about 9 percent of total charitable giving. Money to establish a foundation is provided by a wealthy individual or family, a group of contributors, an organization, or a corporation. The foundation's capital is invested, and earnings from the investments are distributed as grants to qualified applicants.

The public knows about such mammoth national organizations as the Ford Foundation, the Rockefeller Foundation, and the National Science Foundation. It is probably

The Advertising Council often produces ads as a public service for national groups such as the American Cancer Society. This ad raises public awareness of colon cancer.

Social service agencies often provide the logistics and the volunteers when there is a community disaster. Here, a rescue worker works in a bucket line in New York to remove rubble from ground zero at the World Trade Center.

not aware, however, of many smaller foundations, some of them extremely important in their specialized fields, that distribute funds for research, education, public performances, displays, and similar purposes.

Giving away money constructively is more difficult than most people realize. Again, public relations representation has a significant role. The requirements of a foundation must be made known to potential applicants for grants. Inquiries must be handled and announcements of grants made.

From this summary, the student can see what diverse, personally satisfying opportunities are available to public relations practitioners in the social agency fields.

Public Relations Goals

Every voluntary agency should establish a set of public relations goals. In doing so, its management should heed the advice of its public relations staff members, for they are trained to sense public moods and are responsible for achieving the goals. Emphasis on goals will vary, depending on the purpose of each organization. In general, however, nonprofit organizations should design their public relations to achieve these objectives:

- Develop public awareness of the organization's purpose and activities
- Induce individuals to use the services the organization provides
- Create educational materials—especially important for health-oriented agencies
- Recruit and train volunteer workers
- Obtain funds to operate the organization

The sections that follow discuss ways in which each of these goals can be pursued.

■ Public Awareness The news media provide well-organized channels for stimulating public interest in nonprofit organizations and are receptive to newsworthy material from them. Newspapers usually publish advance stories about meetings, training sessions, and similar routine activities. Beyond that, much depends upon the ingenuity of the public relations practitioner in proposing feature articles and photographs. Television and radio stations will broadcast important news items about organizations and are receptive to feature stories and guest appearances by organization representatives. *Stories about activities are best told in terms of individuals, rather than in high-flown abstractions.* Practitioners should look for unusual or appealing personal stories, such as a retired teacher helping Asian refugee children to learn English.

Creation of events that make news and attract crowds is another way to increase public awareness. Such activities might include an open house in a new hospital wing or a concert by members of the local symphony orchestra for an audience of blind children.

Novelty stunts sometimes draw attention to a cause greater than their intrinsic value seems to justify. For example, a bed race around the parking lot of a shopping center by teams of students at the local university who are conducting a campus fund drive for the March of Dimes could be fun. It would draw almost certain local television coverage and raise money too.

Very serious, dramatic messages can also be widely dispersed by staging an event made for television coverage. A North Carolina sheriff was saddened and frustrated by the number of unwanted animals put to death in his county animal shelter. He arranged for telecast of the euthanasia death of a 35-pound collie mix during his local public affairs show, *Sheriff's Beat.* Response was tremendous in the area, with adoptions up 300 percent and markedly increased spaying/neutering by local veterinarians. The story garnered national coverage as well, raising awareness across the nation of the need to control dog and cat reproduction.

Publication and distribution of brochures explaining an organization's objectives, operation of a speaker's bureau, showings of films provided by general headquarters of national nonprofit organizations, and periodic news bulletins distributed to opinion leaders are quiet but effective ways of telling an organization's story.

■ Use of Services Closely tied to creation of public awareness is the problem of inducing individuals and families to use an organization's services. Free medical examinations, free clothing and food to the urgently needy, family counseling, nursing service for shut-ins, cultural programs at museums and libraries, offers of scholarships—all these and many other services provided by nonprofit organizations cannot achieve their full value unless potential users know about them.

Because of shyness or embarrassment, persons who would benefit from available services sometimes hesitate to use them. Written and spoken material designed to attract these persons should emphasize the ease of participation and, in matters of health, family, and financial aid, the privacy of the consultations. The American Cancer Society's widely publicized warning list of cancer danger signals is an example of this approach.

Creation of Educational Materials Public relations representatives of nonprofit organizations spend a substantial portion of their time preparing written and audiovisual materials. These are basic to almost any organization's program.

The quickest way to inform a person about an organization is to hand out a brochure. Brochures provide a first impression. They should be visually appealing and contain basic information, simply written. The writer should answer a reader's obvious questions: What does the organization do? What are its facilities? What services does it offer me? How do I go about participating in its activities and services? The brochure should contain a concise history of the organization and attractive illustrations. When appropriate, it may include a membership application form or a coupon to accompany a donation. Videotapes also are very effective as introductory tools.

Organizations may design logos, or symbols, that help them keep their activities in the public eye. Another basic piece of printed material is a news bulletin, usually monthly or quarterly, mailed to members, the news media, and perhaps to a carefully composed list of other interested parties. This bulletin may range from a single duplicated sheet to an elaborately printed magazine.

A source of public relations support for national philanthropic organizations is the Advertising Council. This is a not-for-profit association of advertising professionals who volunteer their creative and technical skills for organizations. The Council handles more than 30 public service campaigns a year for nonsectarian, nonpartisan organizations, chosen from 300 to 500 annual requests. Newspapers and radio and television stations publish or broadcast free of charge the advertisements the council sends them.

One of the best ways to tell an organization's story succinctly and impressively is with an audiovisual package. This may be a slide show or a video, usually lasting about 20 minutes, to be shown to community audiences and/or on a continuing basis in the organization's building.

Volunteer Workers A corps of volunteer workers is essential to the success of almost every philanthropic enterprise. Far more work needs to be done than a necessarily small professional staff can accomplish. Recruiting and training volunteers, and maintaining their enthusiasm so they will be dependable long-term workers, are important public relations functions. Organizations usually have a chairperson of volunteers, who works with the public relations (often called community relations) director.

The statistics are impressive. One in five American adults volunteers time for charitable causes, according to a Bureau of Labor Statistics survey. The median weekly time volunteers contribute is slightly more than four hours. Yet the demand for more volunteers is intense.

What motivates men and women to volunteer? The sense of making a personal contribution to society is a primary factor. Volunteer work can fill a void in the life of an individual who no longer has business or family responsibilities. It also provides social contacts. Why does a former business leader living in a retirement community join a squad of former corporate executives who patrol its streets and public places each Monday, picking up wastepaper? The answer is twofold: pride in making a contribution to local well-being and satisfaction in having a structured activity that partially replaces a former business routine. For the same reasons, the retired executive spends another day each week as a hospital volunteer. These motives are basic to such volunteerism.

Social prestige plays a role, too. Appearing as a model in a fashion show that raises funds for scholarships carries a social cachet. So does selling tickets for a debutante ball, the profits from which go to the American Cancer Society. Serving as a docent, or guide, at a historical museum also attracts individuals who enjoy being seen in a prestigious setting. Yet persons who do well at these valuable jobs might be unwilling to stuff envelopes for a charity solicitation or spend hours in a back room sorting and mending used clothing for resale in a community thrift shop—jobs that are equally important. Such tasks can be assigned to those volunteers who enjoy working

Senior volunteers have the experience to work wonders.

For 40 years, Jon Ramer engineered ways to get aerospace projects off the ground. Today, he is an RSVP volunteer at a science center. And the exhibits he invents launch kids' imaginations into the wonders of science.

Jon was an aerospace engineer. Now he makes imaginations fly.

Jon is one of nearly half a million RSVP volunteers across the country. **RSVP** stands for **Retired and Senior Volunteer Program**. It's part of the Senior Corps, the national network for senior service. RSVP volunteers are men and women, age 55 and over from all walks of life, who put their life experience to work for their communities.

Through RSVP, volunteers match their talent, creativity and wisdom to community needs. Volunteers like Jon choose how and where they want to serve. They ease over-stressed education systems. They help with health concerns. And RSVP volunteers tackle public safety and environmental issues. The needs and the opportunities are vast. So are the rewards.

Join us. To learn more about volunteer opportunities with **RSVP** and the **Senior Corps** call 800-424-8867, TDD: 800-833-3722.

Senior Corps. The Experience of a Lifetime.

Older citizens make excellent volunteers for many organizations. They have available time, often are looking for an activity, and can draw upon long experience in many fields.

Former President Jimmy Carter generates a great deal of publicity and public support for the organization Habitat for Humanity. He regularly volunteers his time to build houses for the poor and the homeless.

inconspicuously and dread meeting the public. Religious commitment is another powerful motivating force for volunteers.

Retirees Make Excellent Volunteers Retired men and women, who are increasing in number, form an excellent source of volunteers. The Retired Senior Volunteers Program (RSVP) operates 750 projects nationwide, staffing them from its membership of 365,000. The largest organization of seniors, American Association of Retired Persons (AARP), directs its members into volunteer work through its AARP Volunteer Talent Bank.

How to Recruit Volunteers Recruiters of volunteers should make clear to potential workers what the proposed jobs entail and, if possible, offer a selection of tasks suitable to differing tastes. A volunteer who has been fast-talked into undertaking an assignment he or she dislikes will probably quit after a short time.

The public relations practitioner can help in recruiting by providing information resources to explain the organization's purpose, to show the essential role its volunteers play, and to stress the sense of achievement and social satisfaction that volunteers find in their work. Testimony from successful, satisfied volunteers is an excellent recruiting tool.

Like all persons, volunteers enjoy recognition, and they should receive it. Certificates of commendation and luncheons at which their work is praised are just two ways of expressing appreciation. Hospital auxiliaries in particular keep charts showing how many hours of service each volunteer has contributed. Service pins or similar tokens are awarded for certain high totals of hours worked. Every organization that uses volunteers should be sure to say, "Thank you!"

Fund-Raising

At board meetings of voluntary agencies, large and small, from coast to coast, the most frequently asked question is, "Where will we get the money?" Discussion of ways to maintain present programs and to add new ones revolves around that inevitable query.

President Bush addresses Habitat for Humanity volunteers in Tampa, Florida, as part of his campaign to involve more citizens and nongovernmental organizations in charitable work. Having a president visit a charitable agency generates extensive media coverage about the organization.

Finding ways to pay the bills is a critical problem for virtually all nonprofit organizations, even those that receive government grants to finance part of their work. Fund-raising has been elevated to a highly developed art and science.

Although the largest, most publicized donations are made by corporations and foundations, the total of individual contributions far exceeds combined corporate and foundation giving, amounting to about 75 percent of the more than $203-billion annual U.S. philanthropic donations. Depending on their needs, voluntary organizations may try to catch minnows—hundreds of small contributions—or angle for the huge marlin—large gifts from big-money sources. Some national organizations raise massive sums. The Salvation Army, Catholic Charities USA, and the United Jewish Appeal are among the largest recipients.

Public relations representatives may participate directly in fund-raising by organizing and conducting solicitation programs, or they may serve as consultants to specialized development departments of their organizations. Organizations often employ professional firms to conduct their campaigns on a fee basis. In that case, the organization's public relations representatives usually have a liaison function.

Fund-raising on a major scale requires high-level planning and organization. An organizational chart for a typical fund-raising campaign is shown in Figure 17.2.

■ The Risks of Fund-Raising Fund-raising involves risks as well as benefits. Adherence to high ethical standards of solicitation and close control of money-raising costs, so that expenses constitute only a reasonable percentage of the funds collected, are essential if an organization is to maintain public credibility. Numerous groups have suffered severe damage to their reputations from disclosures that only a small portion

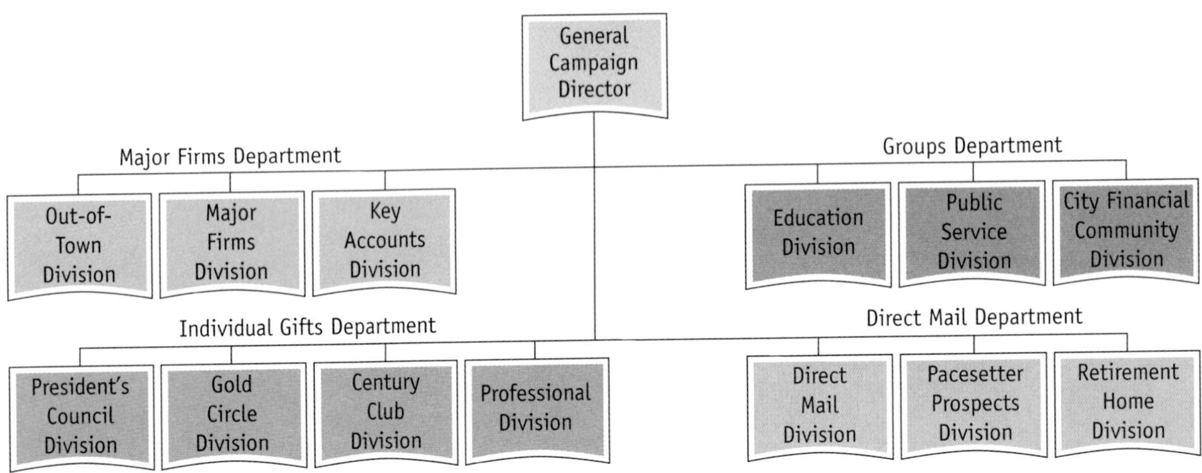

FIGURE 17.2

This chart shows the basic structure of a fund drive. Specialized groups should be added in each division as necessary to meet local organizational and geographical needs.

of the money they raised was applied to the cause they advocated. The rest was consumed in solicitation expenses and administrative overhead.

These fund-raising and administrative costs fluctuate widely among organizations, depending on circumstances, and it is difficult to establish absolute percentage standards for acceptable costs. New organizations, for example, have special start-up expenses. In general, an organization is in trouble if its fund-raising costs are more than 25 percent of what it takes in, or if fund-raising and "administrative overhead" exceed 40 to 50 percent.

Some examples among respected national organizations include the following: The American Cancer Society applies 78.2 cents of every dollar it raises to its anticancer work; solicitation costs are 12.1 cents and administrative overhead 9.7 cents. The American Heart Association applies 75 cents to its work, with 14 cents for solicitation and 11 cents for administration. The National Charities Information Bureau sets a standard that 70 percent of funds raised by a charity should go into programs.

The United Way scandal, in which the national president was forced from office after disclosures of his excessive expenditures of the charity's funds, and later convicted of embezzlement, caused a severe drop in contributions to that organization. It needed years to recover.

Motivations for Giving An understanding of what motivates individuals and companies to give money is important to anyone involved in fund-raising. An *intrinsic desire to share* a portion of one's resources, however small, with the needy and others served by philanthropic agencies is a primary factor—the inherent generosity possessed in some degree by almost everyone. Another urge, also very human if less laudable, is *ego satisfaction.* Those who are motivated by it range from donors to large institutions who insist that the buildings they give be named for them, down to the individuals who are influenced to help a cause by the knowledge that their names will be published in a list of contributors. *Peer pressure* is a third factor; saying "no" to a request from a friend is difficult. The cliché about "keeping up with the Joneses" applies here, openly or subtly.

While many companies truly desire to contribute a share of their profits to the community well-being, they also are aware that news of their generosity improves their images as good corporate citizens. Individuals and corporations alike may receive income tax deductions from their donations, a fact that is less of a motivating factor in many instances than the cynical believe.

Independent Sector commissioned the Gallup Poll to do a survey on volunteerism and giving. The survey found that 53 percent of those responding cited "assisting those who are less fortunate" as their personal motive for volunteering and giving. The second most frequently cited reason was gaining a feeling of personal satisfaction; religion was third. Only 6 percent cited tax considerations as a major reason for giving.

Fund-raisers know that while many contributors desire nothing more than the personal satisfaction of giving, others like to receive something tangible—a plastic poppy from a veterans' organization, for example. This fact influences the sale of items for philanthropic purposes. When a neighbor high school girl rings the doorbell, selling candy to raise a fund for a stricken classmate, multiple forces are at work—instinctive generosity, peer pressure (not to be known in the neighborhood as a tightwad), and the desire to receive something for the money given. Even when householders are on a strict diet, they almost always will accept the candy in return for their contribution rather than merely give the money.

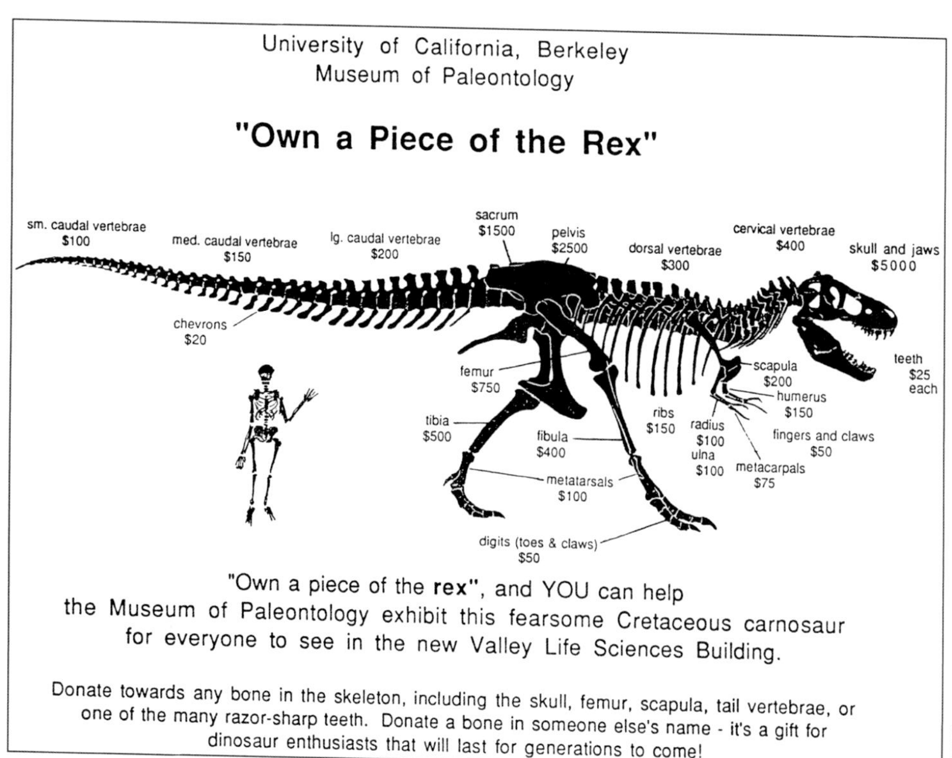

In a unique fund-raising drive, the University of California, Berkeley, Museum of Paleontology requested donations toward any bone in the dinosaur's skeleton—from the skull for $5000 to toes and claws for $500. Contributions helped the museum to display the skeleton in its new Valley Life Sciences Building.

The Competitive Factor The soliciting organization also should analyze the competition it faces from other fund-raising efforts. The competitive factor is important. The public becomes resentful and uncooperative if approached too frequently for contributions. That is why the United Way of America exists, to consolidate solicitations of numerous important local service agencies into a single unified annual campaign.

The voluntary United Way management in a community, with professional guidance, announces a campaign goal. The money collected in the drive is distributed among participating agencies according to a percentage formula determined by the United Way budget committee.

Types of Fund-Raising Philanthropic organizations raise funds in several ways:

- Corporate and foundation donations
- Structured capital campaigns
- Direct mail

PR insights

Writing a "Case for Support"

Charitable organizations requesting major funds from wealthy individuals, foundations, and corporations usually prepare a "case for support." The following is an outline of what should be contained in such a document.

Background of the Organization

The background information should include the founding date, purpose and objectives, what distinguishes the organization from similar organizations, and evolution (development) of objectives and services.

Current Status of Organization's Services

The number of paid and volunteer staff, facilities, the number of clients served annually, current budget, a breakdown of how that budget is allocated, and geographical areas served should be included here.

Need for Organization's Services

The report should present factual and statistical evidence, the availability of similar services, evidence showing the seriousness of the problem, and the uniqueness of the program.

Sources of Current Funding

Public donations, foundations and corporations, and government funding should be listed.

Administration of the Organization

The report should discuss the background of the executive director and qualifications of key staff and the board of directors (including names and titles).

Tax Status of Organization

The tax status of the organization should be stated.

Community Support

Letters from satisfied clients, letters from community leaders, and favorable media coverage of programs will demonstrate community support.

Current Needs of the Organization

Specific programs, specific staffing, financial costs, the amount of financial support needed, and sources of possible funding should be discussed.

Benefits to Community with New or Expanded Program

The report should persuasively present the proposed benefits to the community.

Request for Specific Amount of Funds

This portion will explain the need for the donor's participation and benefits to the donor.

- Sponsorship of events
- Telephone solicitations
- Use of telephone numbers with "800" and "900" area codes for contributors
- Commercial enterprises

Corporate and Foundation Donations Organizations seeking donations from major corporations normally should do so through the local corporate offices or sales outlets. Some corporations give local offices a free hand to make donations up to a certain amount. Even when the decisions are made at corporate headquarters, local recommendation is important. Requests to foundations generally should be made to the main office, which will send application forms.

Corporations make donations estimated at more than $9 billion a year to all causes, of which roughly 40 percent goes to education. Much of this is distributed in large sums for major projects, but an increasing amount is going to smaller local programs. A directory, *Guide to Corporate Giving*, published by the American Council for the Arts in New York, describes the contribution programs of 711 leading corporations. Corporations often fix the amount they will contribute each year as a certain percentage of pretax profits. This ranges from less than 1 percent to more than 2.5 percent.

Increasingly, corporations make donations on a matching basis with gifts by their employees. The matching most commonly is done on a dollar-for-dollar basis; if an employee gives $1 to a philanthropic cause, the employer does the same. Some corporations match at a two-to-one rate or higher.

Corporations make contributions to charities in less direct ways, too, some of them quite self-serving. (The practice of cause-related marketing is explained in Chapter 14.) When applying for a charitable donation, an applicant should submit a "case for support" letter that covers these elements: background of the organization, current status of organization's services, need for organization's services, sources of current funding, administration of the organization, community support, current needs of organization, benefits to the community of the donation, and request for specific amount of funds.

Structured Capital Campaigns The effort to raise major amounts of money for a new wing of a hospital, for an engineering building on a campus, or even for the reconstruction and renovation of San Francisco's famed cable car system is often called a capital campaign.

In a capital campaign, emphasis is placed on substantial gifts from corporations and individuals. One key concept of a capital campaign, in fact, is that 90 percent of the total amount raised will come from only 10 percent of the contributors. In a $10 million campaign to add a wing to an art museum, for example, it is not unusual that the lead gift will be $1 or $2 million.

Capital campaigns require considerable expertise and, for this reason, many organizations retain professional fund-raising counsel. There are a number of firms in the country that offer these services, but the most reputable are those belonging to the American Association of Fund-Raising Counsel.

Traditionally, professional fund-raisers were paid by organizations for their work either in salary or by a negotiated fee. In a controversial decision, however, the National Society of Fund-Raising Executives changed its code of ethics in 1989 to permit its members to accept commissions based on the amount of money their drives raise.

PR insights

Steps in Running a Capital Campaign

Robert B. Sharp, a California professional consultant, recommends the following steps in running a capital campaign.

Conduct a Feasibility Study

Commission an objective review of the cause behind the proposed campaign. This should . . . provide a monetary goal for the campaign, as well as a "gift model"—a chart breaking down the goal into individual gift amounts and indicating how many of each are needed. The review should also lead to the development of a clear "case statement."

Get the Board's Approval and Support of the Feasibility Study

The board should take steps to carry out the recommendations. (This often results in delays.) . . .

Enlist Volunteer Leadership

Choose a campaign chairman and a volunteer chairman. These volunteers will carry the campaign through the private phase to achieve a major portion of the goal before soliciting the general public.

Begin Soliciting Gifts

Using the feasibility study's gift model and suggested campaign phases, begin solicitation of prospects, moving from attempts to get larger gifts to efforts to obtain lesser ones.

Stop for a Midpoint Evaluation

This evaluation, taking place well into the campaign, should make needed adjustments in the drive's time line, financial goal, or strategy. It is here that the campaign is usually announced to the public through the media. Announcement of the campaign should be made only when the goal is assured.

Determine Closing Strategies

Decide what changes need to be made to meet or exceed the original goal. Also, determine when and how to begin general public solicitation.

Honor Volunteer Leadership

Plan special events and permanent recognition.

Perform "Administrative Wrap-up"

Because many large gifts may be divided into pledge payments, set up procedures to process these and to encourage timely payments. Review what the campaign has achieved and then consider the campaign's implications for future fund-raising efforts.

Source: Condensed from *Chronicle of Philanthropy,* February 2, 1990.

The preparation for a capital campaign, whether managed by a professional counseling firm or by the institution's own development staff, is almost as important as the campaign itself. The PR Insight box describes the steps to be taken in organizing and conducting a capital campaign.

A fund campaign usually is organized along quasi-military lines, with division leaders and team captains.

Donors often are recognized by the size of their gifts, and terms such as *patron* or *founder* are used. Major donors may be given the opportunity to have rooms or public places in the building named after them. Hospitals, for example, prepare "memorial" brochures that show floor plans and the cost of endowing certain facilities.

Direct Mail Although direct mail can be an expensive form of solicitation because of the costs of developing or renting mailing lists, preparation of the printed matter, and postage, it is increasingly competitive with advertising costs directed at similarly targeted audiences. An organization can reduce costs by conducting an effective local, limited direct mail campaign on its own if it develops an up-to-date mailing list of "good" names known to be potential donors and can provide enough volunteers to stuff and address the solicitation envelopes. Regional and national organizations, and some large local ones, either employ direct mail specialists or rent carefully chosen mailing lists from list brokers.

The old days when direct mailing pieces came addressed to "Occupant" are largely gone, thanks to the wonders of computerized mailing lists. Now the letters arrive individually addressed. Inside, the appeal letter may bear a personalized salutation and include personal allusions within the text.

The abundance and diversity of mailing lists for rent are impressive. One company offers more than 8000 different mailing lists. A common rental price is $40 per thousand names. Other lists cost more, depending on their special value. *Direct Mail List Rates and Data*, updated bimonthly by Standard Rate & Data Service, Inc., is a basic reference book for direct mail lists.

The best lists contain donors to similar causes. Direct Media List Management Group, for example, offered a list of almost 1.5 million "aware" women who have contributed to at least one of 27 causes.

Recently, however, the *Chronicle of Philanthropy* has reported a sharp decline in direct mail contributions received by several large national organizations, such as the Disabled American Veterans and National Easter Seals. The publication asserts, "Americans have become increasingly fed up with direct-mail appeals from charities."

Direct e-mail campaigns can also be arranged at reasonable costs with companies that compile e-mail addresses similar to print mail lists. Such targeting greatly increases the predictable percentage of successful contacts from the mailing. A response of 1 percent on a mailing usually is regarded as satisfactory; 2 percent is excellent.

Take the following steps to make a profitable return on direct mail investments:

1. Make use of an attention-getting headline.
2. Follow with an inspirational lead-in on why and how a donation will benefit clients of the charitable agency.
3. Give a clear definition of the charitable agency's purpose and objectives.
4. Humanize the cause by giving an example of a child or family that benefited.
5. Include testimonials and endorsements from credible individuals.
6. Ask for specific action and provide an easy method for the recipient to respond. Self-addressed stamped envelopes and pledge cards often are included.
7. Close with a postscript that gives the strongest reason for reader response.

One marketing research firm enhanced direct mail precision by identifying 34 human factors such as age, gender, education, and levels of economic well-being. It fed these factors into computers along with a list of 36,000 Zip code markets and produced 40 neighborhood types. An organization interested in reaching one of these types—the supereducated top income level, for example—could use suitable mailing lists broken down to postal area routes.

Attractive, informative mailing pieces that stimulate recipients to donate are keys to successful solicitation. The classic direct mail format consists of a mailing envelope, letter, brochure, and response device, often with a postage-paid return envelope.

Sponsorship of Events The range of events a philanthropic organization can sponsor to raise funds is limited only by the imagination of its members.

Participation contests are a popular method. Walkathons and jogathons appeal to the current American emphasis on using the legs for exercise. Nationally, the March of Dimes holds an annual 32-kilometer WalkAmerica in 1100 cities on the same day. Local organizations do the same in their own communities. Bikeathons are popular, too. The money-raising device is the same in all such events: Each entrant signs up sponsors who promise to pay a specified amount to the fund for each mile or kilometer the entrant walks, jogs, runs, or cycles.

Staging of parties, charity balls, concerts, and similar events in which tickets are sold is another widely used approach. Often, however, big parties create more publicity than profit, with 25 to 50 percent of the money raised going to expenses. Other methods include sponsorship of a motion picture opening, a theater night, or a sporting event. Barbecues flourish as money-raisers in western cities. Seeking to attract donors from the under-30 age group, some organizations use the "fun" approach by raffling off such items as Madonna's sequined brassiere (for $2500) and a T-shirt by artist Felix Gonzalez-Torres with the message "Nobody Owns Me" (for $50).

Sale of a product, in which the organization keeps a portion of the selling price, ranges from the church baked-goods stand, which yields almost 100 percent profit because members contribute homemade products, to the massive national Girl Scout cookie sale, which grosses about $375 million annually. *A key to success in all charity-fund sales is abundant publicity in the local news media.*

Direct solicitation of funds over television by *telethons* is used primarily in large cities. A television station sets aside a block of airtime for the telethon sponsored by a philanthropic organization. Best known of the national telethons is the one conducted annually by comedian Jerry Lewis for muscular dystrophy. Another high-profile event was the celebrity telethon for aid to victims of the terrorist attacks on the World Trade Center and Pentagon in September 2001.

Telephone Solicitations Solicitation of donations by telephone is a relatively inexpensive way to seek funds but of uncertain effectiveness. Many groups hold down their cost of solicitation by using a WATS (Wide Area Telephone Service) line that provides unlimited calls for a flat fee, without individual toll charges. Some people resent receiving telephone solicitations. If the recipient of the call is unfamiliar with the cause, it must be explained clearly and concisely—not always easy for a volunteer solicitor to do. The problem of converting verbal promises by telephone into confirmed written pledges also arises. The normal method is for the sponsoring organization to send a filled-in pledge form to the donor for signature.

Use of "800" or "900" Telephone Numbers Toll-free telephone numbers with area codes of 800, permitting callers to phone an organization long distance without cost to themselves, have been in use for years. A 900 code has been added by the telephone companies that requires users to pay a fee for each call placed. The phone company takes a service charge from this fee, and the remainder goes to the party being called.

Charitable organizations increasingly are using 900 numbers in fund-raising. Although the callers must pay for their calls, they have the convenience of making a pledge without having to read solicitation material and write a response. Public television station WNET in New York used a 900 number in an annual pledge drive and received $235,000 in contributions through it.

Commercial Enterprises Rather than depending entirely on contributions, some nonprofit organizations go into business on their own or make tie-ins with commercial firms from which they earn a profit. Use of this approach is growing, but it entails risks that must be carefully assessed.

Three types of commercial money-raising are the most common:

1. License the use of an organization's name to endorse a product and receive payment for each item sold.
2. Share profits with a corporation to receive a share of its profits from sales of a special product such as Newman's Own salad dressing.
3. Operate a business that generates revenue for the organization.

Advocates describe commercial involvement by nonprofit organizations as creating wealth, not receiving it, but the risks for an organization are obvious. Entrepreneurship requires good business management, not always available in charitable organizations. Businesses can lose money as well as make it. Ill-advised lending of an organization's name to a shoddy product or a high-pressure telemarketing scheme can damage a charity's reputation.

Any nonprofit organization contemplating operation of a business should check the tax laws, which require that the enterprise be "substantially related" to the purpose of the nonprofit group.

Case Study: A Lesson in Fund-Raising

The Old Globe Theater in San Diego's Balboa Park is an integral part of the city's cultural life. It attracts about 300,000 playgoers a year to its 325 evening performances and has a splendid professional reputation.

The theater's board of directors knew that it needed rehearsal space, refurbishing, and a concession area. They also wanted to pay off debt incurred from rebuilding part of the theater damaged by fire and to acquire a $2 million endowment and reserve fund.

The board decided to conduct a $10 million capital fund campaign. An article in *The Chronicle of Philanthropy* tells how they did so successfully despite severe obstacles.

First, the directors conducted a feasibility study. This showed that San Diego's community leaders did not regard the theater's financial needs as compelling; it also showed that the theater's volunteer leadership lacked members who could make large personal contributions and solicit major campaign gifts.

After a delay caused in part by the death of the theater's campaign consultant, Robert B. Sharp took the job, and the campaign was revitalized. New volunteer leaders were recruited. Several events then occurred:

- A four-color brochure was published to be given to donor prospects.
- A few donors made large gifts as a nucleus of the drive.
- At cocktail parties, board members and major donors heard a presentation about the campaign. They were asked to pick names of people they knew from a list of 20,000 season ticket holders. This provided a list for solicitation.
- A precise goal was set for each prospect—2 to 5 percent of the donor's estimated "adjusted gross worth." The campaign hired a researcher to examine various credit and public records to determine what these goals should be.

With this list, the campaign reached full speed. The cochair made a challenge gift of $500,000 that required the theater to raise $1.5 million within seven months.

Prospective donors were invited to dinner and a play, then taken backstage and given a slide presentation before seeing the play. The campaign used slides rather than a videotape because they enabled the speaker to pause during the presentation for questions.

Solicitors went after the largest gifts first, then moved step-by-step to the smaller prospects. They had a gift model showing the various sizes of gifts sought, from a high of $1 million down to $1000, and the number of prospects for each size (three for $1 million, 1500 for $1000). Actual donors in each category proved to be about one-third of the category's prospects.

So far, everything had been done on a personal basis without major publicity. A total of $8.5 million was raised from individuals, corporations, and foundations.

Then the campaign went public with a media blitz to solicit gifts under $10,000 from the general public. The final phase involved sending direct mail pieces to theater constituents who had not contributed.

Large donors were recognized by having their family coats of arms incorporated in the design of the new facilities, and they received framed versions of the coats of arms. An importing company donated research to find coats of arms for families lacking them.

A crucial part of this successful campaign was the identification of potential large donors and the analysis of how much each might donate, so that solicitors could make their calls with specific money targets in mind.

Health Care Public Relations

The $400-billion-a-year health care industry has an impact on all Americans who are concerned about their personal health and the often-burdensome cost of medical service. Because most medical services—primarily treatments by physicians, hospital stays, sale of medicines, and health insurance—function in a competitive environment, public relations and marketing programs are essential in their operations. Medical breakthroughs, high-profile drugs such as Viagra, the graying of 76 million baby boomers, and the ongoing controversies over health costs and claims of excessive profits for doctors and health care companies guarantee robust opportunities to practice sophisticated public relations.

One multifaceted campaign dealt with a serious health scare. The communication program addressing tainted food employed two firms in the implementation of nearly a dozen distinct strategies over more than a year. The issue was bacterial contamination of precut vegetables. Television news producers were particularly avid to produce "buyer beware" segments about precut salad ingredients, citing lists of common, harmless bacteria while suggesting that their presence could mean dangerous bacteria might also appear.

The Londre Group and Fineman Associates undertook communication efforts for the salad suppliers. Tactics included publicity of university food scientists debunking stories about the innocuous bacteria, video news releases to set forth the scientific facts, trade media briefings, face-to-face meetings with food editors, national opinion surveys, and an array of additional actions.

Also indicative of the growing sophistication of health care public relations is the targeting of women as health care consumers because they comprise 60 percent of doctor visits and 59 percent of prescription drug purchases, according to Kym White, Managing Director of Ogilvy PR Worldwide's Health & Medical Practice.

Audience targeting was also the thrust of a study entitled "Femstat 3 Report: American Women and Self Care." It analyzed where women obtain their health care information and found that about 50 percent get information mainly from their primary care doctors: 24 percent cited magazines and newspapers as their main source, 7 percent television and radio, and 5 percent self-help books. Much of the information in these categories is provided by public relations sources.

Health information and advice on the Web has grown exponentially in the past several years. According to *O'Dwyer's PR Services Report,* 55 percent of the adult population has online access and 86 percent of them have inquired about their health using Internet resources. Some experts estimate that nearly 25 percent of all Web searching is health related. Public relations companies now produce video and audio programming on the Web, often called streaming video/audio, for their health care clients, seeking to provide doctors, medical reporters, investors, and patients with medical and pharmaceutical information.

The tension between health care providers and those who pay for services is ongoing. Federally financed Medicaid, which assists low-income patients, has been under recurring political attack. Older Americans sometimes struggle to obtain eligibility for Medicare, a form of government-operated insurance they help finance from their Social

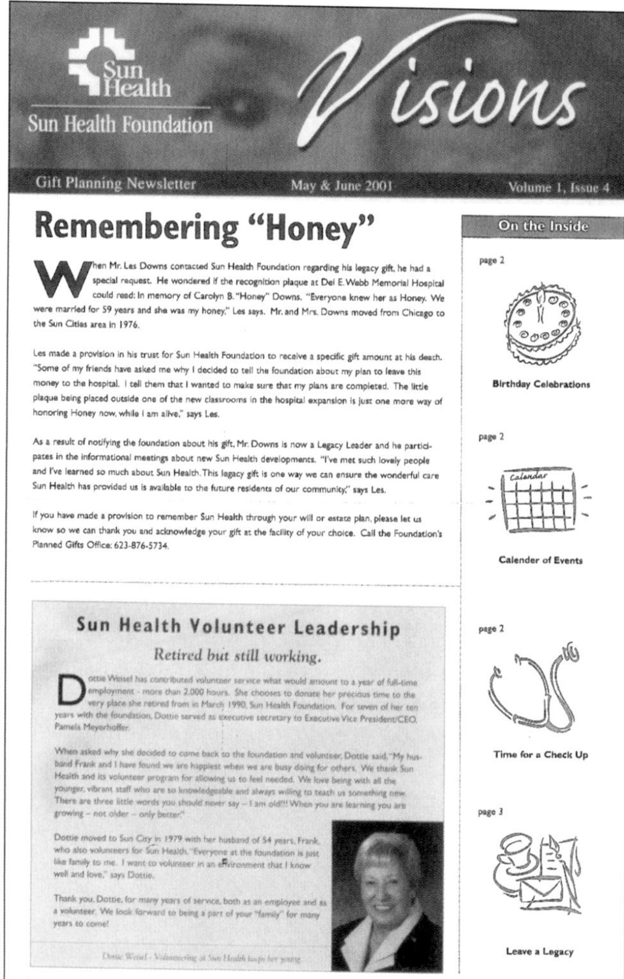

Sun Health
Sun Health Foundation
Visions

Gift Planning Newsletter | May & June 2001 | Volume 1, Issue 4

Remembering "Honey"

When Mr. Les Downs contacted Sun Health Foundation regarding his legacy gift, he had a special request. He wondered if the recognition plaque at Del E. Webb Memorial Hospital could read: In memory of Carolyn B. "Honey" Downs. "Everyone knew her as Honey. We were married for 59 years and she was my honey," Les says. Mr. and Mrs. Downs moved from Chicago to the Sun Cities area in 1976.

Les made a provision in his trust for Sun Health Foundation to receive a specific gift amount at his death. "Some of my friends have asked me why I decided to tell the foundation about my plan to leave this money to the hospital. I tell them that I wanted to make sure that my plans are completed. The little plaque being placed outside one of the new classrooms in the hospital expansion is just one more way of honoring Honey now, while I am alive," says Les.

As a result of notifying the foundation about his gift, Mr. Downs is now a Legacy Leader and he participates in the informational meetings about new Sun Health developments. "I've met such lovely people and I've learned so much about Sun Health. This legacy gift is one way we can ensure the wonderful care Sun Health has provided us is available to the future residents of our community," says Les.

If you have made a provision to remember Sun Health through your will or estate plan, please let us know so we can thank you and acknowledge your gift at the facility of your choice. Call the Foundation's Planned Gifts Office: 623-876-5734.

Sun Health Volunteer Leadership

Retired but still working.

Dottie Weisel has contributed volunteer service what would amount to a year of full-time employment - more than 2,000 hours. She chooses to donate her precious time to the very place she retired from in March 1990, Sun Health Foundation. For seven of her ten years with the foundation, Dottie served as executive secretary to Executive Vice President/CEO, Pamela Meyerhoffer.

When asked why she decided to come back to the foundation and volunteer, Dottie said, "My husband Frank and I have found we are happiest when we are busy doing for others. We thank Sun Health and its volunteer program for allowing us to feel needed. We love being with all the younger, vibrant staff who are so knowledgeable and always willing to teach us something new. There are three little words you should never say – I am old!!! When you are learning you are growing – not older – only better."

Dottie moved to Sun City in 1979 with her husband of 54 years, Frank, who also volunteers for Sun Health. "Everyone at the foundation is just like family to me. I want to volunteer in an environment that I know well and love," says Dottie.

Thank you, Dottie, for many years of service, both as an employee and as a volunteer. We look forward to being a part of your "family" for many years to come!

Dottie Weisel - Volunteering at Sun Health keeps her young

On the Inside

page 2 — Birthday Celebrations

page 2 — Calender of Events

page 2 — Time for a Check Up

page 3 — Leave a Legacy

Most nonprofit organizations publish a regular newsletter to inform citizens about upcoming events and to educate them about such things as health issues. Shown is the newsletter of the Sun Health Foundation in Sun City, Arizona.

global PR

The Web Pushes European Limits on Medical Self-Care

Americans have long enjoyed moderate regulation of medical information, enabling U.S. citizens to make judgments about their own medical care. Now public relations firms are setting their sights on European markets for health care products and prescription pharmaceuticals. Firms in the United States are developing communication programs that offer medical information needed for people to take more initiative in their own well-being. One particularly promising new audience for self-care information will be European nations as they liberalize rules about availability of medical information to all citizens.

What the health communication industry calls direct-to-consumer campaigns have empowered American consumers to make many of their own medical decisions. Although advertising plays a role by announcing availability, it is really the public relations materials that enable education about medical matters. These materials are increasingly available on the World Wide Web, where Europeans may read them, in spite of traditional restrictions by continental governments that are just now changing.

This globalization of medical information probably will accelerate the direct-to-consumer movement in Europe with consequent increases in medical knowledge and self-care, as well as increased commerce for health-related products.

Source: O'Dwyer's PR Services Report, October 1998

Security benefits. Health maintenance organizations (HMOs), in which individuals and families can buy memberships, seek to hold down medical costs by limiting their members' choice of doctors and reserving the right to refuse payment for certain procedures. Although used by millions of Americans, the HMOs face frequent complaints from patients about allegedly insufficient treatment and premature discharge from hospitals. Many American hospitals are operated as commercial enterprises.

Every segment of this complex field, profit-driven or nonprofit, needs public relations support to explain its role, attract patients or customers, and make the ill feel that they are receiving compassionate treatment at a fair price. Work for hospitals is one of the largest areas of health care public relations.

Public Relations for Hospitals

The public relations staff of a hospital has two primary roles: (1) to strengthen and maintain the public's perception of the institution as a place where medical skill, compassion, and efficiency are paramount, and (2) to help market the hospital's proliferating array of services. Many hospitals have sought to redefine themselves as community health centers. Basically, hospitals, like hotels, must have high room-occupancy rates to succeed financially. They supplement this fundamental source of income by creating and marketing supplementary services, an area that offers a challenge to public relations people.

Typical of these supplementary services are alcoholism rehabilitation, childbirth and parenting education, hospices for the terminally ill, pastoral care, and physician referral services.

Hospital Audiences

Because hospitals sell a product (improved health), parallels exist between their public relations objectives and those of other corporations. They focus on diverse audiences, external and internal; involve themselves in public affairs and legislation because they operate under a mass of government regulations; and stress consumer relations. In the case of hospitals, this involves keeping patients and their families satisfied, as well as seeking new clients. Hospitals produce publications for external and internal audiences. They have an additional function that other corporate public relations practitioners don't need to handle—the development and nurturing of volunteer organizations.

Hospital public relations programs have four basic *audiences:* patients, medical and administrative staffs, news media, and the community as a whole. The four audiences overlap, but each needs a special focus. Careful scrutiny can identify significant subaudiences within these four—for example, the elderly; women who have babies or soon will give birth; victims of heart disease, cancer, and stroke who need support groups after hospitalization; potential financial donors to the hospital; and community opinion leaders whose goodwill helps to build the institution's reputation. Each group can be cultivated by public relations techniques discussed in this textbook.

A Sample of Public Relations Efforts

The reputations of some hospitals have been damaged by a public perception of them as cold institutions that don't care enough about individual patients. Complaints by patients about poor food and brusque nurses add to the problem.

Here are a few examples of methods hospitals use to project a positive image:

- Sponsorship of community health fairs, offering free screenings to detect symptoms of certain diseases and low-cost comprehensive blood tests.
- A "direct line" telephone system within the hospital on which patients and visitors can register complaints and suggestions 24 hours a day.
- Bingo games on a closed-circuit television system, for which patients pay a small fee and win cash prizes. This brightens the patients' day.

focus on ethics

Public Relations Faces Tough Calls on Health Care Issues

Doctors and nurses joined forces in the Ad Hoc Committee to Defend Health Care, an activist group opposed to purportedly excessive profits of hospitals. Their Boston Tea Party reenactment, covered in *O'Dwyer's PR Services Report,* won publicity for their claim that $125 billion in corporate health care revenues could be better spent on research and improved patient care. Decrying rushed hospital stays, denial of services, and wasteful bureaucracy, the activists tossed annual reports of for-profit hospitals and HMOs into Boston Harbor.

The other side in the dispute responded that so-called "jungle capitalism" bankrolls research to develop lifesaving techniques and provides a stable health care system best able to serve patients. One could add that competition and profit is what drives innovation and excellence throughout the American system.

Which side in this fight would you most want to help with your developing public relations knowledge and skills?

Would you turn down a good job offer from the opposing side for this issue?

Do you think that you could change the organization's stance with your public relations counsel? In other words, could you take a job with the opposition to shape it up enough to live with yourself every payday?

Summary

The Role of Public Relations
Nonprofit organizations have been given tax-exempt status because their primary goal is to enhance the well-being of their members or the human condition. Fund-raising is a major public relations task in these groups.

Basic Needs of Nonprofits
Although there is a broad range of nonprofit organizations, they all create communications campaigns and programs, need a staff (including volunteers) to handle their work, and are involved in fund-raising.

Membership Organizations
A membership organization is made up of people with a common interest, either business or social. Such groups include trade associations, labor unions, professional associations, and chambers of commerce.

Advocacy Groups
Advocacy groups work for social causes such as the environment, civil rights, gun ownership, or the pro-choice movement. Their efforts include lobbying, litigation, mass demonstrations, boycotts, reconciliation, and public education. As with other nonprofits, fund-raising is an unending issue with these groups.

Social Organizations
Social service groups, health agencies, hospitals, religious organizations, welfare agencies, cultural groups, and foundations all fall into the category of social organizations. Their public relations goals include developing public awareness, getting individuals to use their services, creating educational materials, recruiting volunteers, and fund-raising. Fund-raising can take the form of corporate and foundation donations, structured capital campaigns, direct mail, sponsorship of events, telephone solicitations, the use of toll-free numbers, and commercial enterprises.

Case Study: A Lesson in Fund-Raising
San Diego's Old Globe Theater conducted a successful $10 million capital fund campaign that serves as an interesting case study. After conducting a feasibility study, the board of directors published a brochure for prospective donors. A few large gifts formed a nucleus for the drive; then a list of potential donors was created, each with a precise goal. After raising $8.5 million, the campaign went public to solicit smaller donations. Finally, a direct mail piece was sent out.

Health Care Public Relations
Because of competition among medical services, public relations and marketing programs are essential. Issues can include responding to health scares, targeting new audiences, and establishing a Web presence. Hospitals' public relations campaigns can involve sponsorship of community health fairs, direct lines for consumer suggestions and feedback, and special services for patients.

Case Activity: What Would You Do?

The Vision Council of America is a trade group representing the optical industry. Its three core membership groups are ophthalmologists, opticians, and optometrists.

The group decides to launch a consumer education program after research reveals a reluctance to take children for eye exams because parents rely on free in-school screenings. Additional research shows that 80 percent of learning before age 12 is accomplished through vision, yet traditional in-school vision screenings miss between 70 and 80 percent of children's vision problems.

Your public relations firm is retained to conduct a national consumer education program emphasizing the importance of annual eye exams for children. What would you suggest? Program elements that you should consider include key publics, message themes, time of year, strategies, and innovative communication tactics, especially new technologies such as CD-ROM and the Web.

Questions for Review and Discussion

1. Trade associations, like other membership organizations, often have headquarters in Washington, D.C., or a state capital. Why?
2. What has caused the recent intensified scrutiny of nonprofit organizations?
3. Name the seven categories of social agencies.
4. What challenges do labor unions face today?
5. What are the differences and similarities among trade groups, labor unions, and professional associations?
6. What motivates men and women to serve as volunteer workers?
7. Describe four commonly used types of fund-raising.
8. Chambers of commerce often are described as the public relations arm of city government. Why?
9. Name four methods advocacy groups use to further their causes.
10. What two principal roles does a hospital public relations staff fulfill?

Suggested Readings

Boyle, Matthew. "Quiet NRA Faced with Gun Control PR Crisis." *PR Week,* May 3, 1999, p. 9.

Ciconte, Barbara K., and Jacob, Jeanne G. *Fund-Raising Basics: A Complete Guide.* Gaithersburg, MD: Aspen Publications, 1997.

"Corporate Green Is Beautiful for Keep America Beautiful." *O'Dwyer's PR Services Report,* February 1998, p. 8.

Daspin, Eileen. "Charities Compete for Socialites' Homes." *Wall Street Journal,* February 21, 1997, p. B12.

Feen, Diane. "Doctors Use PR to Create Media Buzz." *O'Dwyer's PR Services Report,* October 2000, pp. 14–18.

"Gospel of Wealth." *Economist,* May 30, 1998, pp. 15, 19–21.

Kaufman, Jonathon. "Black Charities Say Growing Middle Class Isn't Giving Enough." *Wall Street Journal,* January 29, 1996, pp. 1 and 8.

Kelly, Kathleen S. *Effective Fund-Raising Management.* Mahwah, NJ: Lawrence Erlbaum, 1998.

Kinnick, Katherine N., Krugman, Dean M., and Cameron, Glen T. "Compassion Fatigue: Communication and Burnout toward Social Problems." *Journalism and Mass Communication Quarterly,* Vol. 73, No. 3 Autumn 1996, pp. 687–707.

Lilienthal, Steve. "The Cause and Effect: What Makes Non-profits 'Hot' or 'Cold'." *PR Week,* July 19, 1999, p. 23.

Motavalli, Jim. "Tobacco Truths." *Public Relations Strategist,* Summer 1996, pp. 50–53.

"The New Prescription." *PR Week,* December, 1998, pp. 23–26.

Toufexis, Anastasia. "It's Not Easy Being Greenpeace." *Time,* October 16, 1995, p. 86.

18 Education

preview

In this chapter the objective is to explain the role and activities of public relations in educational institutions at the university and secondary school levels and to identify the publics they need to reach.

Topics covered in the chapter include:

- College and university development and public relations offices
- Audiences to be addressed
- Fund-raising from alumni and others
- Student recruitment
- Use of the Internet and World Wide Web
- Contemporary issues in secondary schools
- Public school financial problems

Colleges and Universities

Public relations and development offices fulfill important functions for colleges and universities.

Development and Public Relations Offices

The president (or chancellor) is the chief public relations officer of a college or university; he or she sets policy and is responsible for all operations, under the guidance of the institution's governing board.

In large universities, the vice president for development and university relations (that person may have some other title) supervises the office of development, which includes a division for alumni relations, and also the office of public relations; these functions are combined in smaller institutions. Development and alumni personnel seek to enhance the prestige and financial support of the institution. Among other activities, they conduct meetings and seminars, publish newsletters and magazines, and arrange tours. Their primary responsibilities are to build alumni loyalty and generate funding from private sources.

The public relations director, generally aided by one or more chief assistants, supervises the information news service, publications, and special events. Depending on the size of the institution, perhaps a dozen or more employees will carry out these functions, including writing, photography, graphic design, broadcasting, and computer networking.

Figure 18.1 shows the organization of a public relations staff at a typical university.

In addition, scores of specialists at a large university perform diverse information activities in agricultural, medical, engineering, extension, continuing education, and other such units, including sports.

Public Information Bureau

The most visible aspect of a university public relations program is its public information bureau. Among other activities, an active bureau produces hundreds of news releases, photographs, and special columns and articles for the print media. It prepares programs of news and features about faculty activities and personalities for stations. It provides assistance and information for reporters, editors, and broadcasters affiliated with the state, regional, and national media. The staff responds to hundreds of telephone calls from members of the news media and the public seeking information.

Serving the Publics

In order to carry out their complex functions, top development and public relations specialists must be a part of the management team of the college or university. At some institutions this is not so, and the public relations program suffers. Ideally, these leaders should attend all top-level meetings involving the president and other administrators, learning the whys and wherefores of decisions made and lending counsel. Only then can they satisfactorily develop action programs and respond to questions from the publics those programs concern. They are indeed the arms and voice of the administration.

Vice President for Public Relations and Marketing

St. Bonaventure University invites nominations and applications for the position of Vice President for Public Relations and Marketing. The University's chief communications professional, the Vice President reports directly to the University President and is a member of the senior administrative staff.

The official spokesperson for the University, the Vice President provides executive leadership for all public relations and marketing programs for the University, including promoting its image to alumni, benefactors, friends, current and future students, and all others. The Vice President will also lead the communications and marketing effort for both the University's 150th anniversary in 2008 and the multi-year capital campaign in conjunction with this celebration.

The Vice President for Public Relations and Marketing provides executive oversight for all official University publications, advertisements and publicity, including the official University Web page and the use of its logo. The Vice President is a member of the President's Cabinet and participates in overall planning and direction of institutional affairs.

The University seeks a seasoned communications and marketing professional to lead an independent and motivated full-time staff of five, assisted by part-time assistants and student interns from the Russell J. Jandoli School of Journalism and Mass Communication at the University, whose graduates have won five Pulitzer Prizes.

St. Bonaventure is the nation's first Franciscan university, with approximately 3,000 undergraduate, graduate and continuing education students. Home of the internationally recognized Franciscan Institute, the University serves as the summer home of the National Shakespeare Company and competes in the Atlantic 10 Conference. The campus, spread over 500 acres in a valley surrounded by the Allegheny Mountains, lies between the welcoming communities of Olean and Allegany, which total about 25,000 residents. Shops, restaurants and theaters are nearby, while summer and winter resorts with swimming, golfing, boating, hiking and excellent skiing are just minutes away. For a more in-depth view, visit our Web site at **www.sbu.edu.**

Requirements: Seven years of progressively responsible experience in the public relations, communications and/or marketing fields. Previous experience in higher education is preferred. Master's degree/public relations accreditation is preferred, but not as much as experience.

Compensation will be competitive and commensurate with experience. Candidate review will begin immediately and continue until suitable candidates are identified. Those interested may send a cover letter, résumé and three references to search committee chair **Suzanne Wilcox English, Director of Media Relations, St. Bonaventure University, 224 Hopkins Hall, St. Bonaventure, NY 14778, or fax to (716) 375-2380.** EOE.

This position announcement in the *Chronicle of Higher Education* is an illustration of the duties and responsibilities of a communications executive at a private university.

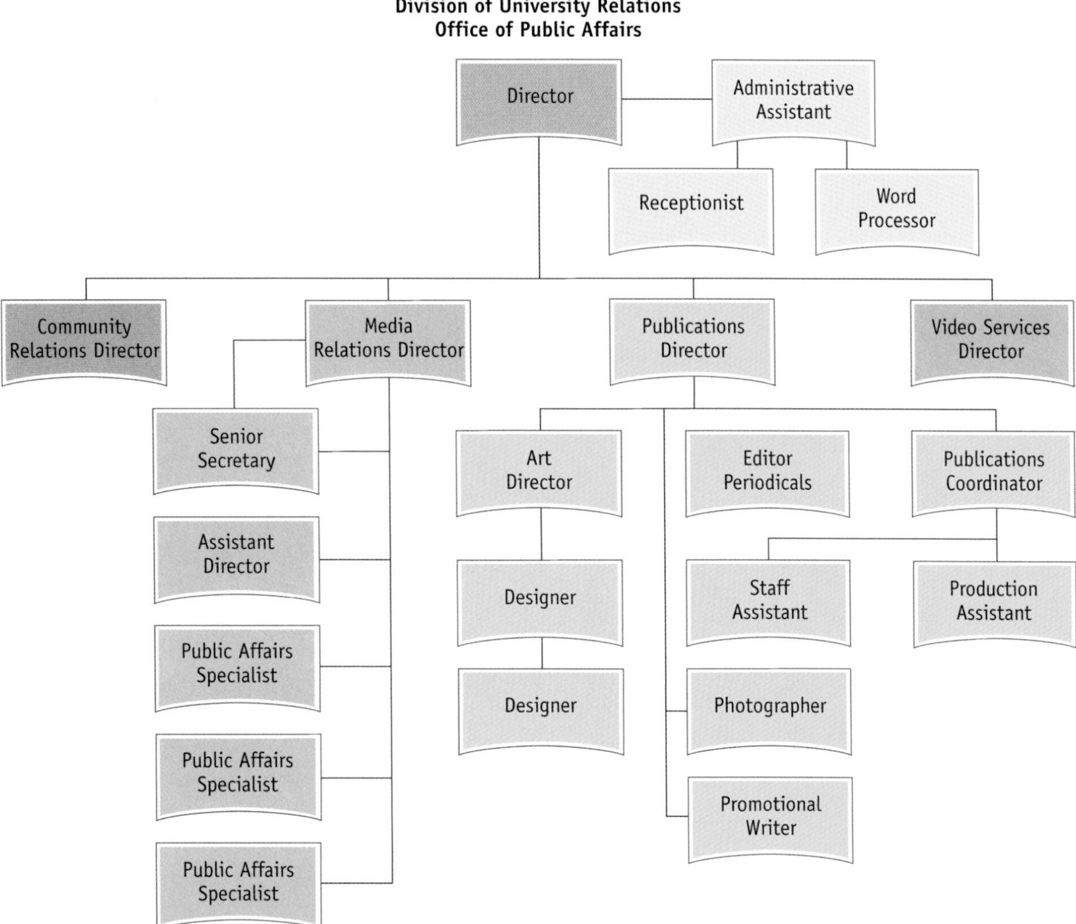

FIGURE 18.1

Organizational chart of the University of Miami's public affairs office, showing the division of responsibility for the various areas of operation.

■ **Faculty and Staff** As noted in previous chapters, every sound public relations program begins with the internal constituency. Able college presidents involve their faculty in decision making to the fullest extent possible, given the complexities of running a major institution. It is a maxim that the employees of a company or institution serve as its major public relations representatives because they come into contact with so many people. Good morale, a necessity, is achieved in large measure through communication.

College administrators communicate with their faculty and staff members through e-mail and in-house newsletters and newspapers; journals describing research, service, and other accomplishments (which also are sent to outside constituencies); periodic meetings at which policies are explained and questions answered; and in numerous other ways.

Faculty and staff members who fully understand the college's philosophy, operations, and needs generally will respond with heightened performance. For example, when the University of Georgia sought to obtain $2.5 million in contributions from its faculty members as part of an $80 million bicentennial enrichment campaign, they responded with a generous outpouring of nearly $6 million—a signal to outside contributors that helped ensure the success of the program.

Students Because of their large numbers and the many families that they represent, students make up the largest public relations arm—for good or bad—that a university has. The quality of the teaching they receive is the greatest determinant of their allegiance to the institution. However, a sound administrative attitude toward students, involving them as much as possible in decisions that affect their campus lives, is extremely important. So are other forms of communication, achieved through support of student publications and broadcast stations and numerous other ways. When, upon graduation, they are inducted en masse into the university's alumni society, chances are good that, if they are pleased with their collegiate experience, many will support the university in its future undertakings. A public relations effort directed at students is thus essential.

Alumni and Other Donors Fund-raising activities have increased dramatically at most colleges and universities in recent years. As a result, private financial support for these institutions rose 13.7 percent over the preceding academic year to an estimated $23.2 billion during 1999–2000, according to the *Chronicle of Higher Education.*

The demand for experienced fund-raisers has created a shortage among those qualified, and salaries in some instances have skyrocketed well beyond $100,000 or more annually, accompanied by elaborate fringe-benefit packages. Women increasingly are holding top positions in the field.

Colleges and universities use the money mainly to attract and pay new faculty, to buy equipment and provide support for faculty research, and to attract and offer financial aid for students. A common complaint is that few grants are provided to repair or replace aged structures, reequip obsolete science laboratories, and provide additional classroom and library space. These pressures are accompanied by a number of complications: societal demands that costs be trimmed and management streamlined; rising costs for salaries and benefits for faculty and staff (particularly in health fields); growing public concern over tuition increases; the cost of serving increasingly diverse student bodies, including remedial programs and provisions for disabled students; and new developments in scholarship, such as the increasing faculty collaboration in combined, expensive research projects across disciplines.

The placement of universities' endowment funds often poses a public relations problem. Groups opposed to South Africa's apartheid system persuaded many universities and other entities to sever financial ties with the nation, but with apartheid at an end in South Africa, most institutions have revoked their bans on investment. Organizations such as the Tobacco Investment Project persuaded Harvard University and the City University of New York to sell their highly profitable stock holdings in the tobacco companies. The movement's spread brought a similar dilemma to other universities: how and if they could withdraw their holdings in tobacco companies without sacrificing the firms' large annual grants.

In addition to annual operating expense drives, universities increasingly conduct long-range capital fund campaigns for very large sums, such as the $1.5 billion goal at Yale University and the $1.15 billion goal at Cornell University.

PR casebook

University Campaign Seeks $1 Billion

The University of Connecticut mounted a campaign to win support for *UConn 2000,* a 10-year, $1 billion program to rebuild the university's infrastructure and to renew and equip academic and research facilities.

As an opening shot, Institutional Advancement leaders persuaded the *Hartford Courant* to examine, editorially, the condition of the university's aging infrastructure. The resulting six-part editorial series set the groundwork for the drive.

Working with the public relations firm of Mintz & Hoke, leaders sought to establish the message that UConn—while maintaining the quality of its academic programs and its faculty and staff—had serious problems with its infrastructure. The message had to be conveyed to as large an audience as possible, yet target key groups such as alumni and other friends as well as key legislators and their constituents. The message had to be conveyed during the most critical time for the recruitment of freshmen for the fall semester of the 23,000-student institution.

Planning/Execution

UConn advancement leaders and public relations firm representatives met to establish messages, through means such as focus groups, and to design the communications plan. Other action:

- University officials met with more than a dozen newspaper editorial boards and the board of a Hartford-based television station that editorialized on the air.
- A direct-mail brochure was sent to 25,000 parents, alumni, and other friends of the university in targeted legislative districts. Included was a postage-paid postal card expressing support for the project. The objective was to establish the level of support and to add names and addresses to a databank of supporters. Additional postal cards were distributed at university sports events and at the Hartford Civic Center.

  Of 40,000 cards distributed, about 10,000 came back, giving a return of 25 percent. In addition, nearly 2000 phone calls of support were made to a special 800-number hotline.
- University President Harry J. Hartley sent letters to faculty, staff, and students as well as to alumni, parents, and other friends of the institution. The objective was to give each constituency an overview of the proposal and urge support.
- A 30-second video spot was aired on local and network broadcasts of men's and women's basketball games. A five-minute video—a minidocumentary—was distributed to key alumni and all legislators. The video also was sent to cable access outlets.
- A news conference at the state capitol building was attended by a bipartisan group of legislators, who announced their support. Large display charts, graphs, and photo blowups portrayed the story.
- Letters to the editor and letters to individual legislators were solicited during the spring as the project, in bill form, made its way through the legislative process. A second direct-mail piece then was sent to targeted UConn friends who were constituents in "swing" legislative districts.
- Upon passage of the bill, President Hartley sent thank-you letters to legislative leaders, Connecticut newspaper editors, and others. Community leaders were among those invited to a closing victory celebration on the steps of the university library.

Budget

The budget was $82,550. Funding was provided primarily by the University of Connecticut Foundation, with additional support from the UConn chapter of the American Association of University Professors, UConn Professional Employees Association, and UConn Alumni Association.

Results

Not only was the legislation approved, but the first bond issue for the reconstruction project was successfully completed.

The University Relations Office of the University of Connecticut won a silver medal in the annual competition sponsored by the Council for the Advancement and Support of Education.

Martin Luther King, Jr.'s, leadership was a prime factor in the civil rights battle. The United Negro College Fund has used him as a role model in its fund-raising based on the slogan, "A mind is a terrible thing to waste." He is shown at a news conference in Atlanta.

Many institutions employ students to participate in fund-raising phonothons. At the University of Michigan students called 970,000 alumni and raised $8.3 million during a nine-month period. Computerized dialing systems are often used.

At most institutions, letters are mailed to specific graduating classes over the names of members who have agreed to be class agents for that purpose.

Sought are not only year-by-year contributions but bequests and annuities as well. In return, the colleges publish honor rolls listing donors, invite contributors to join honorary clubs (the President's Club, for example), and name rooms and buildings for the largest givers. Recently, even admission to the university can be a reward. In an odd twist on the fund-raising and recruitment functions of university public relations, donors to Yonsei University in South Korea can guarantee a student admission to the private institution for a cool $1.5 million contribution. More typically, educational events and tours to foreign countries are arranged to build and sustain alumni interest. Class reunions are said to be the most powerful instruments in getting alumni to give.

Universities often use matching grants to make a donor's contribution go further—and thus make giving more attractive. For instance, a donor in Dallas who wanted to remain anonymous contributed $8 million toward the establishment of faculty enrichment chairs at the University of Texas at Austin. The sum was matched by foundations, and the entire $16 million, in turn, was matched by the university, making possible the establishment of 32 new chairs. Such support is essential in order for good universities to become great universities.

Influential alumni and other important friends of colleges and universities also are encouraged, through personal contact and correspondence, to provide political clout with legislative bodies and boards of regents, in support of the institutions' financial and other objectives. Such support also is important in the recruitment of students with outstanding academic, athletic, or other achievements.

Government State and federal governments often hold the vital key to whether universities receive sufficient monies to maintain facilities, faculty, and programs. Most large institutions have someone who regularly monitors the state legislature on appropriations and issues ranging from laboratory experiments on animals to standardized tests and taxes. Their work includes (1) competing with other state institutions for money, (2) defending proposed increases in higher-education budgets and protecting against cuts, (3) establishing an institution's identity in the minds of legislators, and (4) responding to lawmakers' requests for favors. Said Robert Dickens, coordinator of government relations for the University of Nevada at Reno: "When I say I'm a lobbyist, some people look at me as if I need a shower. It's a new business with the universities, and some people think it's a dirty business. But nothing's dirtier than not having resources."

The declining federal support for higher education since the 1960s also has led to an increase in the number of government relations experts representing universities in Washington, D.C. Their work complements that of the American Council on Education, the National Association of Land-Grant Universities, and the Association of American Universities. They not only lobby members of Congress regarding legislation that might have an adverse or favorable effect on their clients but also seek information from federal agencies about new programs and uncommitted funds.

The Community As in the case of industry, a college or university must maintain a good relationship with the members of the community in which it is situated. The greatest supporters that an institution may have are the people within its immediate sphere of influence, many of whom mingle with its faculty, staff members, and students. Tax dollars also are an immense benefit, although the fact that university property is tax exempt may impose a strain unless the institution voluntarily agrees to some form of compensation for services such as fire and police protection.

In order to bridge the town–gown gap often evident, faculty and staff members are encouraged to achieve community visibility through work with civic and other organizations. Business groups often take the lead. The Chamber of Commerce in Lawrence, Kansas, for example, for many years sponsored an annual barbecue, including various other activities, to give faculty and townspeople an opportunity to get to know each other better.

Prospective Students Suffering from declining revenues, increased costs of operation, and a dwindling pool of prospective students occasioned by lower birthrates, many colleges have turned to highly competitive recruiting methods. Some, in the "hard-sell" classification, use extensive advertising in print and broadcast media and on billboards. Other colleges and universities have replaced their catalogues and brochures with four-color, slick materials that use bright graphics and catchy headlines to lure students. Many use the World Wide Web (see PR Casebook: Universities Open Electronic Doors on page 442).

Various other recruiting devices are used. Vanderbilt University sent personalized videotapes to about 40 highly coveted high school seniors. The College of the Atlantic

PR casebook

Universities Open Electronic Doors

Universities increasingly are opening electronic doors to prospective students, inviting them to tour their World Wide Web campus sites no matter how far away they live. In addition, they are using the Internet to teach courses, provide employment bazaars for those about to graduate, and arrange chat rooms and other specialized services for alumni.

"Students can apply from any part of the globe and take a walking tour of the university by computer," said Joel Stitzel, a computer specialist at the University of Minnesota.

Many students gain college admission via the computer. Penn State University processed at least 80 percent of its applications electronically by 2000. The 22-campus system receives about 50,000 applications a year.

On many campuses, computer job banks allow employers to post openings and students to see the listings almost immediately and to learn more about the companies.

Videoconference hookups permit companies to interview students without going on campus. For example, in 1996 Procter & Gamble held 28 interviews at Case Western Reserve University in Cleveland using Viewnet, a commercial system that shows a résumé on the left of the screen, the student's image on the bottom right, and the corporate interviewer's image at the top right.

Because many in a new generation of college graduates appear to prefer online communication to what they call "snail mail," a growing number of alumni associations are creating online sites. On these sites alumni talk about their families, read the school newspaper and alumni newsletter, share jokes, and discuss innumerable issues.

The Alumni Center for Education on the World Wide Web includes an area with both public and private sections featuring chat rooms, bulletin boards, electronic mail, and a searchable member directory. A security feature allows subscribers to make a pledge or gift by credit card, online.

University Online, Inc., leases about 200 ready-made high school and college courses for extension and corporate training credit purposes. George Washington University and George Mason University are among its first clients.

took prospective students on a 90-foot sailing yacht party. Stanford University was host to 750 high school students who stayed overnight in dormitory rooms, visited classes, attended a musical program, and participated in a campus scavenger hunt. Brown University each spring sponsors a party for up to 250 prospects on an Amtrak train traveling between Washington and Providence, Rhode Island. As competition for students has increased, so have the costs of recruiting them. Expenditures on admissions and recruitment have run about $700,000 or more for private universities and in excess of $600,000 for public universities. This high level of activity creates many opportunities for employment in public relations and development.

The purchase of mailing lists is a common tool of student recruitment. Each of approximately 900 colleges annually buys from 10,000 to 15,000 names and addresses of high school students who have taken College Board Examinations. The most sought-after prospects are National Merit Scholarship winners, and it is not uncommon for competing universities to shower a prospect with such lures as free tuition for four years, a private dorm room, guarantees of priority registration, and so on.

Other Publics Examples of other groups requiring special attention are shown in Figure 18.2.

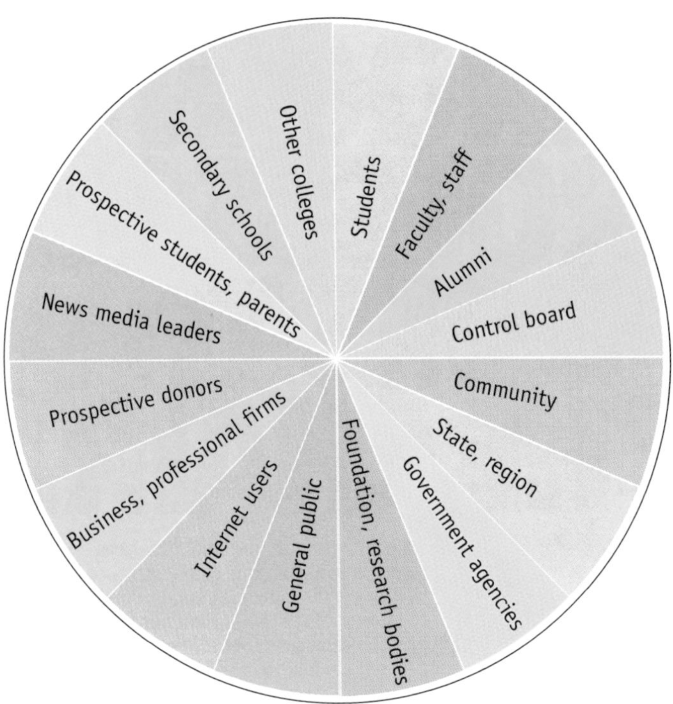

FIGURE 18.2

This wheel shows the variety of publics with which college public relations offices endeavor to maintain communication and feedback.

Support for Advancement Officers

Most public relations, alumni, and development leaders—known euphemistically as *advancement officers*—enjoy the many services of the Council for Advancement and Support of Education (CASE), with headquarters in Washington, D.C. The aims of CASE are described as building public understanding, stepping up the level of alumni involvement and support, strengthening communication with internal and external audiences, improving government relations, and increasing private financial support. Among CASE current objectives are (1) helping leaders at historically black institutions advance in their careers, (2) publicizing a code of ethics, (3) developing gift and expenditure reporting standards, (4) improving the communication of university research to the public, and (5) studying the impact of new technologies.

Representing more than 2400 institutional members, CASE serves nationally as a principal public affairs arm for education, monitoring federal rights legislation and regulations and working with the American Council on Education and other associations on education-related issues. The organization provides district conferences and institutes, evaluation and critique services, a certification program, awards, reference materials, and placement opportunities. Thousands each summer attend its four-day assembly, replete with workshops.

Elementary and Secondary Schools

The strategic planning and skillful execution of public relations programs have materially strengthened many of the nation's elementary and secondary school systems during recent decades.

INNOCENT PROFESSOR GOES TO THE CHAIR.

You'd better sit down for this.

Faced with our worst financial crisis since the Great Depression, we've been forced to start asking professors to retire early. Talk about drastic measures.

Last year alone, one-tenth of our tenured professors left. And with hundreds more eligible this year, Cal will continue to lose many of its most distinguished minds. Frankly, we'd much rather have our faculty members win Nobel Prizes than plant rhododendrons in the backyard. This is where you come in.

Your donations have supported endowed chairs before, and are now helping us to improve facilities and attract a slew of top-ranked faculty recruits. Seeing how it's your alma mater's reputation on the line, we need you this time more than ever. Please, give whatever you can afford.

And help us keep some professors on their feet.

UC BERKELEY

It's not the same without you.

UC Berkeley Foundation, 2440 Bancroft Way, Room 301, Berkeley, CA 94720
To help, call the Development Office at (510) 642-7374.

Faced by a financial crisis that was forcing faculty members into early retirement, the University of California at Berkeley made an unusual public appeal for contributions to help it retain tenured professors. The provocative headline, with its play on words, stimulated much interest.

Response to Contemporary Issues

Should public tax money be used so that parents disaffected with the public schools can send their children to private, often religion-supported, schools?

Should standard courses and programs be offered in non-English languages to accommodate significant numbers of first generation immigrants and children of illegal aliens working in the United States?

Many weighty questions such as these examples confronted the nation and its educational systems as the new century dawned. In fact, education has become one of the crucial planks in political platforms for candidates. Many of these issues are part of two decades of widespread debate spawned by the National Commission on Excellence in Education. Citing "a nation at risk," the commission called for massive educational reform. The resulting nationwide debate represented the most searching public examination that education in America has undergone during the last several decades: integration, busing, accountability, book censorship, sex education, discipline, crime, school violence, and drugs—all these issues and more have commanded continuing public attention.

The 18-member commission proposed increasing requirements in five major areas: content, standards and expectations, time, teaching, and leadership and financial support—all deemed inadequate.

News of the commission's recommendations reached the offices of thousands of school superintendents almost immediately over the Education U.S.A. Newsline and Information Network, an electronic news and advisory service of the National School Public Relations Association (NSPRA). When local media people called shortly thereafter, many of the more alert superintendents and their communication coordinators were prepared to offer reactions.

Governors and business leaders began holding annual two-day National Education Summits to plan school advancement. Corporations throughout the country and smaller businesses formed alliances with schools. Many were year-by-year "Adopt-a-School" arrangements, but some extended for ten years or longer.

Thousands of schools established projects in buying and selling to educate children on the principles of free enterprise. In many classrooms, however, corporate logos and learning went hand in hand. A report by Consumers Union found that many of America's 43 million school-age children were being bombarded by a growing number of blatantly commercial messages. According to the Center for Commercial-Free Public Education, by 1998 at least 24 schools had signed exclusive promotional deals with companies selling soft drinks, sneakers, and telecommunications equipment. Among them was a 10-year contract that the Colorado Springs schools signed with the Coca-Cola Company for $9 million. Pepsi paid $2.1 million to the Jefferson County school district in Colorado. Many found such exclusive contracts troubling because they limit student choice and can require educational institutions to toe the line. At one school, a boy was even suspended for a day for wearing a Pepsi shirt on Coke day.

Overall, however, the partnership with business strengthened the schools. According to the Council on Aid to Education, corporations donate well over $50 million each year to K–12 (kindergarten through 12th grade) schools.

In order to increase public awareness of changing attitudes and their own needs, the largest, most progressive public school systems and independent private schools, as well as thousands of smaller ones, have long maintained public relations programs. But the necessity for sound community relations–at the heart of both management and public relations—was more evident as the new century approached than ever before. If funds were not available or the system too small to warrant a full-fledged public relations program, then a sole information specialist was employed, full- or part-time. School public relations had come into its own.

Reaching the Publics

The primary publics of a school system are teachers, children, parents, staff, and the community. As in all public relations, research, planning, action, and evaluation comprise the essential steps with which to reach these publics. On the desks of information directors, communication coordinators, and school–community relations specialists (or whatever the title may be, and it varies widely) are booklets prepared by national

PR casebook

High School Forms Hall of Fame

A high school Hall of Fame honoring prominent graduates from two Chicago suburbs provides a close tie between the school's administration and the community.

Lyons Township High School, principally serving the towns of La Grange and Western Springs, has an enrollment of nearly 3000 students on two campuses. In more than 100 years of operation it counts nearly 50,000 graduates and former students.

Each year a citizens' committee, administered by the school's community relations coordinator, elects graduates to the Hall of Fame. These men and women are invited to speak to classes for two days and then are honored at a large community banquet. Plaques with the honorees' names are placed on a school wall. The honorees receive individual plaques.

Among the 33 inductees during the Hall's first three years of operation were two admirals, a university president, corporate presidents, a journalist, a major league baseball player, a cancer surgeon, a children's author, and a television star.

"These individuals provide splendid role models for our students," an administrator said, "and show the community the quality of education LTHS provides."

and state offices detailing hundreds of ways in which they may carry out their mission. Perhaps the best way to describe school public relations in its major aspects is to examine some of the outstanding communication programs in elementary and secondary school public relations.

Building Community Support When almost one-third of the elementary schools in the Fort Worth Independent School District tested low in pupils' reading skills, the superintendent asked the public for help. Business leaders, librarians, and teachers, coordinated by the schools' community relations division, developed a year-long awareness campaign with the theme, "Reading Takes You Places."

Communication plans included news releases, bilingual fliers to parents and community leaders, and TV and cable messages, with personal contacts before each activity. Newspapers, the city transportation authority, and advertising companies provided free advertising.

Business firms supported such activities as book donations to libraries and a Reading Rodeo attended by more than 700 children in 69 schools. Community groups such as the Dallas Mavericks and museums also participated. The Reading Summit involving sponsorship by the Governors Business Council drew broad media coverage.

By year's end, only three schools failed to meet state expectations, and a 91-percent improvement rate was recorded in the number of low-performance schools.

Beating the Odds at the Polls Supporters of the Everett (Washington) School District faced a difficult problem: winning a tax levy election that required turning out 40 percent of the voters who voted in the last major election and getting 60 percent of them to vote "yes." The almost 50 percent of voters receiving a permanent absentee ballot were traditionally very negative toward tax measures, and 70 percent of households in the district had no school-age children.

Discarding traditional communication methods, the citizens' committee planned a highly focused campaign. It sought to identify likely "yes" voters and to aim all signs, mailings, brochures, and personal contact at them.

Two campaigns were waged: one for absentee voters and one for election-day voters. About 20 people devoted 25 evenings to phoning targeted voters, getting out mailings, and writing personal messages. On election day, poll watchers looked for "yes" walk-ins; those who had not voted by 4 P.M. were called and reminded to vote.

The levy passed with an almost 64-percent "yes" vote. All project goals were met or exceeded. The committee analyzed every aspect of the election, including the database of 12,000 district supporters, and began a continuing campaign aimed at turning "maybe" voters to "yes" voters in the next election.

Crisis Communication For emergencies such as earthquakes, sudden loss of utilities, severe storms, hazardous material spills, explosions, fires, tornadoes, school shootings, plane crashes, bomb threats—for all such crises, a communication plan should be in readiness. Such plan components were dwarfed by the tragic shooting of 12 students and a teacher at Columbine High School in Colorado. Winner of a Silver Anvil Award from the Public Relations Society of America, the school system's public relations professionals were thrust into the spotlight as the voice of the community as well as the organization. The team managed speculation and rumor flamed by 750 media outlets worldwide; helped the community deal with the unforgettable experience and the heart-rending images; and restored calm and confidence to the school system and thereby to the community. Public relations executive for the school district, Rick Kaufman, drew upon his emergency medical technician experience to help victims at the site, then organized a crisis communication team to handle the onslaught of coverage and inquiries. Symbolic of the eloquence of the communication efforts and the perspective provided by the communication team is this quote by Marilyn Saltzman, manager of communication services: ". . . Columbine is a beautiful flower that blooms in the mountains of Colorado . . . I would hate for it to be a synonym for 'massacre.'" While effectively managing the immediate crisis, the communication department has helped to heal a community and move forward.

Marketing of Public School Education A pioneer in public opinion surveying in education, William J. Banach, administrative director at the Macomb Intermediate School District in Mount Clemens, Michigan, developed a two-year plan designed to discover what the public wants in its schools. The plan also sought ways to respond to those desires and to educate citizens about actions the school could and could not take. Banach based the campaign on what he termed "the 90-7-3 concept of school communication":

> Ninety percent of the school's image is who we are and what we do 24 hours a day. How school people think, act, and appear and what they say are key factors in marketing. This is why staff training is an integral part of a marketing program—to help people understand their communication roles and how important they are.
>
> Seven percent of the marketing effort is listening—tuning in to find out what people like, don't like, want, don't want. Anything we do to know more about our "customers" is worth doing.
>
> Three percent of marketing is outbound communication—publications, posters, news releases, and other visible and tangible items.

focus on ethics

Doctoring Photos to Show Diversity

It was a great photo for the cover of the new University of Wisconsin admissions brochure. It showed a group of happy and cheering students at a football game. The photo, however, was not exactly accurate; it had been doctored.

The original picture contained no black faces, but university officials desperately wanted their admissions materials to reflect a diverse student body. So, using photo-design software, the director of university publications and the director of undergraduate admissions simply asked their staff to add one.

Meanwhile, at the University of Idaho, the school's Web site showed another group of smiling students with two faces—one black and one Asian—that had been digitally pasted onto white bodies.

The digital manipulation of photographs to show diversity raises some ethical questions. The implicit message of a photograph is that it shows something that actually occurred. So, in the interest of political correctness and diversity, should photos be changed?

One defense is that the photograph isn't really a fake; it's entirely reasonable that a crowd at a football game would include blacks and Asians. Another argument is that doctoring a photo is artistic license. If a technician airbrushes a student picking his nose out of a photo, no one seems to mind. Others, however, say it's wrong to lie about who was in a particular photograph.

What do you think? If you were the director of publications for a university, would you use digital techniques to alter a photo for the purpose of showing diversity in the student body?

In successive phases, the marketing plan at Mount Clemens was targeted at (1) elementary parents, with a focus on reading, writing, and arithmetic; (2) secondary students and their parents, emphasizing "the basics and beyond" and beginning with specific objectives based on survey results and meetings with student leaders; and (3) citizens without children in school.

Arrangements were made for teachers to apply "No. 1 apple" stickers to outstanding student papers, and all classroom papers were sent home each Friday. Posters welcoming visitors were placed at each school. The slogan "Your public schools . . . There's no better place to learn" was displayed on billboards, calendars, bookmarks, bumper stickers, T-shirt transfers, and thank-you cards.

A survey made a year after the campaign began revealed enhanced public confidence in the schools. The Macomb Plan, as it is called, has attracted national attention.

Summary

Colleges and Universities

Public relations at colleges and universities involves both development, or fund-raising, and enhancing the prestige of the institution. The office of development and public relations may conduct meetings, publish newsletters, and arrange tours. The audiences for communications will include alumni, students, prospective students, faculty and staff, government, and the general public.

Elementary and Secondary Schools

Public education has received increasing attention in recent years from the media, especially during political campaigns. Issues include school vouchers, curriculum standards, bilingual education, integration, book censorship, sex education, and school violence. Public relations practitioners working with the schools must address all these areas, reaching such publics as teachers, children, parents, staff, and the community. Goals will include building community support for programs and encouraging financial support through taxes. Schools also must have communications plans in readiness for crisis situations, whether these involve earthquakes, power loss, severe weather, fires, bomb threats, or school violence.

Case Activity: What Would You Do?

Southwestern University has a public relations problem. The campus administration, taking the route of many other universities, has signed a contract with Carl's Jr. to open a fast-food franchise on campus. The decision was based on competitive bidding, and campus administrators made the decision that Carl's Jr. was the best choice to answer the needs of hungry students. Remodeling of a space in the student union has already begun to accommodate the new franchise when, much to everyone's surprise, the student/faculty gay and lesbian association of the university publicly denounces the contract.

Representatives of the organization say the university should not let Carl's Jr. operate on campus because the founder of the company, Carl Karcher, is antigay. About 20 years ago, they say, he gave a political donation to a state senator who introduced a bill in the state legislature that would have banned homosexual teachers from the classroom. The bill, however, was never passed. Although Karcher is no longer actively involved in the management of the restaurant chain, the gay and lesbian association says the university should honor its commitment to diversity and equality by denying the franchise. The university president is caught in a bind, since he has been most vocal about campus climate and expressing zero tolerance about any form of "hate" speech.

If you were the vice president of public relations for the university, what would you recommend? Should the university cancel the contract to satisfy the gay/lesbian association? What about the numerous university students who are looking forward to having the fast-food franchise on campus? What steps would you recommend to resolve the issue?

Questions for Review and Discussion

1. Who is the chief public relations officer on a college or university campus? Why?
2. A college news bureau is involved in a vast array of day-to-day public relations operations. Name five or six of these functions.
3. With what primary public does a sound university public relations program begin? Why? List eight other constituencies that must be addressed in such a program.
4. In what ways may powerful alumni and other friends provide support for an institution of higher learning? What is the role of the development office in gaining this support? What is CASE, and what support does it provide for public relations and alumni officers?
5. Describe some of the ways in which universities reach out to their publics electronically.
6. The National Commission on Excellence in Education called for massive educational reform. How did school officials respond?
7. What strategic plan did a citizens committee of the Everett (Washington) School District employ to win its bond-issue election?
8. Do you agree with the marketing concept used by public relations people in the Macomb Intermediate School District in Mount Clemens, Michigan? Describe the key points of this plan in explaining your answer.
9. What public relations problems may be evident when a community turns down a bond issue to improve school financing? What public relations actions do you consider important in building and maintaining strong support of schools?

Suggested Readings

"Affirmative Action: the Next Battlegrounds," *Chronicle of Higher Education,* October 30, 1998, pp. A32–37.

Arenson, Karen R. "More Colleges Plunging into Uncharted Waters of On-Line Courses," *New York Times,* November 3, 1998, p. A14.

Arenson, Karen R. "N.Y.U. Sees Profits in Virtual Classes." *New York Times,* October 7, 1998, p. A20.

"Faceoff: Tying Companies to Schools." *The Strategist,* Spring 2000, pp. 29–33.

Guernsley, Lisa. "Admissions in Cyberspace: Web Sites Bring Complications for Colleges," *Chronicle of Higher Education,* October 9, 1989, pp. A27–29.

Mercer, Joye. "As Elite Universities Increase Spending, Many Others Struggle to Keep Pace," *Chronicle of Higher Education,* October 9, 1998, p. A45.

Mercer, Joye. "The 1990s Bring Colleges a Wealth of Big Gifts," *Chronicle of Higher Education,* October 30, 1998, pp. A44–46.

Stead, Deborah. "Corporations, Classrooms and Commercialism: Some Say Business Has Gone Too Far," *New York Times,* January 5,1997, *Education Life* supplement, pp. A30–34, A41–43.

Zack, Ian. "We Want U! How Madison Avenue Educated the American University," *New York Times,* August 5, 1998, p. A23.

Zoch, Lynn M., Patterson, Beth S., and Olson, Deborah. "The Status of the School Public Relations Practitioner: A Statewide Exploration," *Public Relations Review,* Winter 1997, pp. 361–376.

Entertainment, Sports, and Travel

preview

In this chapter, the objective is to show students how public relations promotes these three vigorous, growing forms of recreation and helps develop the careers of entertainers, public figures, and athletes.

Topics covered in the chapter include:

- Fascination with celebrity and the mystique of personality
- The practitioner's responsibility and ethical problems in handling individual clients
- Operation of a personality campaign
- Promotion of an entertainment event
- Sports publicity
- Goals of travel promotion
- Reaching target travel audiences

Fascination with Celebrity

A dominant factor in today's mass media is the publicizing and glorification of celebrities. Sports heroes and television personalities in particular—along with radio talk-show hosts, members of the British royal family, movie stars, high-profile criminals, and some politicians—are written about, photographed, and discussed almost incessantly.

Such celebrity results in some cases from natural public curiosity about an individual's achievements or position in life. Frequently, however, it is carefully nurtured by publicists for the client's ego satisfaction or commercial gain.

The publicity buildup of individuals is outside the mainstream of public relations work, and some professional practitioners are embarrassed by the exaggerations and tactics used by promoters of so-called "beautiful people." Nevertheless, all students of public relations should learn how the personal publicity trade operates. At some point in their careers they may find a knowledge of its techniques useful.

A Case Study: Princess Diana

Diana, Princess of Wales, for example, was a celebrity worldwide as the divorced wife of Prince Charles, heir to the British throne. Her svelte, gracious manner and high-fashion clothing, plus public interest in the collapse of her once-romantic marriage, created huge media attention to her. She appeared on the cover of *People Weekly* 41 times in a 16-year period and became known to headline writers as Princess Di.

Princess Diana's death in a dramatic, high-speed race to elude press photographers captured world attention. Diana joined a tragic list of celebrities taken all too young from their lives of fame and adulation, including people such as James Dean, Elvis, John Lennon, and John F. Kennedy and his brother Robert. According to Irving Rein, author of *High Visibility,* celebrities exist in one-sided, idealized relationships in which the celebrity demands nothing of us. And, unlike our family and workmates, we get to pick our celebrity idols.

In death, this ideal though distant relationship is severed, and the youthful image is frozen in time. The tragedy and the timeless glamor galvanize us into a mass audience. Princess Diana's funeral was viewed by an estimated 2.5 billion people around the world. An estimated 152,000 visitors to her burial shrine on the family estate paid $24 each to see her childhood home, view family movies in a remodeled stable, and gaze at her island mausoleum. Even in death, both adulation and revenue can follow from celebrity.

The Mystique of Personality

Why is the public so eager to read about and watch personalities it regards as celebrities? What drives individuals to seek such attention?

The abundance of mass media outlets today and their intense competition for audiences has vastly stimulated the natural instinct of humans to know about each other's lives. Appearances on talk shows, often fawning TV interviews, magazine articles whose tone is influenced by publicists, question-and-answer periods on online computer services and the Internet, and ghost-written books contribute to the buildup.

Christine Kelly of *Sassy* magazine writes bluntly, "No-talents become celebrities all the time," a fact that she attributes largely to television. "Once TV started, the whole celeb-creation and worship careened out of control . . . TV gives the false impression that celebrities are talking right to you, and you feel like they're your friends."

Here are some of the motivating factors in the cult of personality.

Fame

Public attention is drawn to some individuals by their accomplishments or positions. The President of the United States is automatically a celebrity. So is the Pope.

Notoriety

Even people who commit major crimes or are involved unfavorably in spectacular trials are treated as celebrities.

Barbara Goldsmith commented on this fact in the *New York Times:*

> The line between fame and notoriety has been erased. Today we are faced with a vast confusing jumble of celebrities: the talented and the untalented, heroes and villains, people of accomplishment and those who have accomplished nothing at all, the criteria of their celebrity being that their images encapsulate some form of the American dream, that they give enough of an appearance of leadership, heroism, wealth, success, danger, glamour and excitement to feed our fantasies. We no longer demand reality, only that which is real-seeming.

Goldsmith adds, "The public appetite for celebrity and pseudo-event has grown to Pantagruelian proportions, and for the first time in history, the machinery of communications is able to keep up with these demands, even to outrun them, creating new needs we never knew existed. To one extent or another, all the branches of the media have become complicitous to this pursuit. . . ."

Self-Glorification

Donald Trump, a New York real-estate high roller with an insatiable desire for publicity, is a striking example of this urge. He put his name on the buildings and casinos he bought and had a personal press agent in addition to the Trump Organization's aggressive public relations department. He even telephoned reporters with stories about himself.

Trump's announcement that he planned to divorce his wife, Ivana, leaving her with a mere \$25 million of his reputed \$1 billion wealth, received major nationwide coverage.

But fame is slippery. Stories revealed that he was in financial trouble. People began to tell jokes, not about his reported sexual prowess, but about his money troubles.

Trump regained the public eye, however, first by announcing that he was the father of a boy born to actress Marla Maples and then marrying her before an audience of 1500 people described by a publicist as "close friends." The cynical tone of media coverage is indicated by the opening sentence of the *Philadelphia Inquirer* story: "Donald Trump finally married Marla Maples on Monday—till death, tabloid scandal or prenuptial agreement do them part." Eventually, the marriage did break up.

Repair of a Bad Image

Public relations counselors who specialize in handling individuals sometimes work to create a positive image for a prominent person who has been cast in an unfavorable light by news stories.

Kathie Lee Gifford, a perky TV personality, suffered a severe blow to her reputation when it was revealed that some of her "Kathie Lee" line of clothing sold by Wal-Mart was made by Honduran child labor and in New York sweatshops.

Gifford hired Howard Rubenstein, a counselor, to help her. She proclaimed her dismay and lack of knowledge that her name was being used in such practices, then sent her husband with a large amount of cash to pay some of the mistreated workers. Under Rubenstein's guidance she sought to reverse her role from apparent offender to righteous crusader against such mistreatment of workers.

The counselor arranged for Gifford to meet the U.S. Secretary of Labor and arrange a conference of national retailers and manufacturers on working conditions. She also held a news conference with Governor George Pataki of New York and another at the New York Fashion Cafe, then met with several unions. She proclaimed her new role in a letter in *USA Today* and a television interview with Larry King.

The climax of Kathie Lee's campaign came when she stood beside President Clinton in the White House Rose Garden as he signed an agreement with ten manufacturers who promised to put labels on their products stating that they had not been made in sweatshops. The combination of constructive actions and celebrity publicity can send a compelling message.

Desire for Money

Sarah Ferguson, Duchess of York and former sister-in-law of Princess Diana, found herself in serious difficulty after her divorce from Prince Andrew. At 36 she was heavily in debt, had two daughters but no job, and was known for her extravagance and flamboyant behavior.

Ferguson too hired Rubenstein. His assignment was a classic job of celebrity public relations: keep "Fergie's" name favorably in magazines and newspapers, obtain television coverage, emphasize her sponsorship of charities, and help her win lucrative endorsements and public appearances. He said he planned to emphasize her "intelligence, devotion to her kids," and respect for the royal family.

When Fergie published a book, she was interviewed on major TV programs, was pictured on two *People's Weekly* covers, and held autographing parties at large bookstores. The book appeared on the *New York Times* best seller list.

Personal publicity can build on itself. A publicist may arrange for an obscure film actress to attend a party as the guest of a well-known performer and issue a news release about the couple. Another party and another news release follow. Soon the news releases refer to the actress as a celebrity. Presto, she is one. No one officially proclaims that status, any more than some mysterious remote Solomon sends down word that a sports "star" has officially become a "superstar."

Indicative of the commercialization of personality is the success of Celebrity Service International, which keeps a 400,000-card databank on well-known persons and publishes daily bulletins in five cities on their comings and goings. It also publishes an annual entertainment-industry contact book that gives the names of managers, lawyers, and publicists who represent celebrities. The daily bulletin, priced at $1250 annually, tips off the media as to what prominent people might be available for a television talk show or a feature interview. The contact book helps business, industry, and charities locate celebrities who might serve as a spokesperson or a charity chairperson or add glamor to a hotel opening.

Psychological Explanations

Psychologists offer varied explanations of why the public becomes impressed—often *fascinated* is the more accurate word—by highly publicized individuals. In pretelevision days, the publicity departments of the motion picture studios promoted their male and female stars as glamour figures who lived in a special world of privilege and wealth. Dreaming of achieving such glory for themselves, young people with and without talent came to Hollywood to crash the magical gates, almost always in vain. Thousands more back home spun fantasies about being Rita Hayworth or Cary Grant. They cherished machine-autographed pictures of their favorites and read with relish inflated stories about the stars in fan magazines, visualizing themselves in the glamor figures' places.

In the earlier days of personality buildup, *wish-fulfillment* was a compelling force. It still is. Exposure on television in the intimacy of the family living room, however, makes personalities seem much closer to admiring viewers today than the remote gods and goddesses were in the glory days of the major motion picture studios. Such is the power of television, in fact, that reporters and news anchors who talk on camera about the activities of celebrities attain celebrity status themselves.

Many ordinary people leading routine lives yearn for heroes. Professional and big-time college sports provide personalities for *hero worship*. Publicists emphasize the performances of certain players, and television game announcers often build up the stars' roles out of proportion to their achievements; this emphasis creates hero figures for youthful sports enthusiasts to emulate. Similar exaggerated treatment is applied to entertainers and politicians. Syndicated gossip columnist Liz Smith once tried to explain the American cult of personality by saying, "Maybe it's because we all want someone to look up to or spit on, and we don't have royalty."

In addition to admiration for individual performers, members of the public develop a *vicarious sense of belonging* that creates support for athletic teams. Sports publicists exploit this feeling in numerous ways. A winning baseball team becomes "our" team in conversations among patrons of a bar. To signify their loyalty, children and adults alike wear baseball caps bearing the insignia of their favorite major league teams. It isn't surprising that alumni of a university gnaw their fingernails while watching their school basketball team in a tight game, but the same intensity of support is found among fans who have no direct tie to the school.

Still another factor is the *desire for entertainment* most people feel. Reading fan magazines, or watching their favorite stars being interviewed, or lining up in front of a box office hours before it opens to be sure of getting a ticket—these are ways to bring variety and a little excitement into the daily routine of life.

A public relations practitioner assigned to build up the public image of an individual should analyze the ways in which these psychological factors can be applied. Since the client's cooperation is vital in promotional work, a wise publicist explains this background and tells the client why various actions are planned.

The Practitioner's Responsibility

A practitioner handling publicity for an individual carries special responsibilities. Often the client turns to the publicist for personal advice, especially for guidance when trouble arises.

Damage Control

A practitioner handling an individual client is responsible for protecting the client from bad publicity as well as generating positive news. When the client appears in a bad light because of misbehavior or an irresponsible public statement, the publicist must try to minimize the harm done to the client's public image. To use a naval term, the objective is *damage control*.

Often politicians who say something controversial in public, then wish later that they hadn't, try to squirm out of the predicament by claiming they were misquoted. This is a foolish defense unless the politician can prove conclusively that he or she was indeed quoted incorrectly. Reporters resent accusations of inaccuracy and may hold a grudge against the accuser. If the accused reporter has the politician's statement on tape, the politician appears even worse. A better defense is for the politician to explain what he or she intended and to express regret for the slip of the tongue.

A similar approach is recommended for Hollywood celebrities who are caught in scandalous acts or unfounded rumor mills. Experts suggest immediate response so that the momentum of subsequent stories is minimized. A brief, honest statement of regret for bad behavior or denial of rumors works well. Television's mass audience enjoys celebrity news. TV lends itself to a short statement that makes a perfect, 20-second sound bite to fit in a brief story. Then the celebrity needs to disappear from sight and take care of personal matters.

Ethical Problems for Publicists

Personal misconduct by a client, or the appearance of misconduct, strains a practitioner's ingenuity and at times his or her ethical principles. Some practitioners will lie outright to protect a client, a dishonest practice that looks even worse if the media show the statement to be a lie. On occasion, a practitioner acting in good faith may be victimized because the client has lied.

Issuing a prepared statement to explain the client's conduct, while leaving reporters and their editors dissatisfied, is regarded as safer than having the client call a news conference, unless the client is a victim of circumstances and is best served by talking fully and openly. The decision about holding a news conference also is influenced by how articulate and self-controlled the client is. Under questioning, a person may say something that compounds the problem. (Defensive news conferences are discussed further in Chapter 21.)

Conducting a Personality Campaign

A campaign to generate public awareness of an individual should be planned just as meticulously as any other public relations project. This is the fundamental process, step by step, for the practitioner to follow.

Interview the Client

The client should answer a detailed personal questionnaire. The practitioner should be a dogged, probing interviewer, digging for interesting and possibly newsworthy facts about the person's life, activities, and beliefs. In talking about themselves, individuals

Publicity, often called "getting ink," is important in the entertainment business. The publicist for the Harlem Globetrotters garnered extensive media coverage by having the team present the Pope with a basketball while they were playing exhibition games in Italy.

frequently fail to realize that certain elements of their experiences have publicity value under the right circumstances.

Perhaps, for example, the client is a little-known actress who has won a role as a midwestern farmer's young wife in a motion picture. During her get-acquainted talks with the publicist, she happens to mention in passing that while growing up in a small town she belonged to the 4-H Club. The feature angle can be the realism she brings to the movie role: When she was a member of the youth organization, she actually did the farm jobs she will perform in the film.

Not only must practitioners draw out such details from their clients, they must also have the ingenuity to develop these facts as story angles. When the actress is placed as a guest on a television talk show, the publicist should prompt her in advance to recall incidents from her 4-H experience. Two or three humorous anecdotes about mishaps with pigs and chickens, tossed into the TV interview, give it verve.

Prepare a Biography of the Client

The basic biography should be limited to four typed pages, perhaps less. News and feature angles should be placed high in the "bio," as it is termed, so an editor or producer can find them quickly. The biography, a portrait and other photographs of the client, and, if possible, additional personal background items should be assembled in a press kit for extensive distribution. Usually the kit is a cardboard folder with inside pockets.

Plan a Marketing Strategy

The practitioner should determine precisely what is to be sold. Is the purpose only to increase public awareness of the individual or also to publicize the client's product, such as a new television series, motion picture, or book? Next, the practitioner should decide which types of audience are the most important to reach. For instance, an interview with a romantic operatic tenor on a rock-'n'-roll radio station would be inadvisable. But an appearance by the singer on a public television station's talk show would be right on target. A politician trying to project herself as a representative of minority groups should be scheduled to speak before audiences in minority neighborhoods and placed on radio stations whose demographic reports show that they attract minority listeners.

Conduct the Campaign

The best course normally is to project the client on multiple media simultaneously. Radio and television appearances create public awareness and often make newspaper feature stories easier to obtain. The process works in reverse as well. Using telephone calls and "pitch" letters to editors and program directors, the publicist should propose print and on-air interviews with the client. Every such approach should include a news or feature angle for the interviewer to develop. Because magazine articles require longer to reach print, the publicist should begin efforts to obtain them as early as feasible.

An interview in an important magazine—a rising female movie star in *Cosmopolitan* or *Ladies' Home Journal,* for example—has major impact among women readers. Backstage maneuvering often takes place before such an interview appears. Agents for entertainers on their way up eagerly seek to obtain such an interview. When a personality is "hot" or at the top of the ladder, however, magazine editors compete for the privilege of publishing the interview. The star's agent plays them off against each other, perhaps offering exclusivity but demanding such rewards as a cover picture of the star, the right to choose the interviewer (friendly, of course), and even approval of the article. Editors of some magazines yield to publicists' demands. Other publications refuse to do so.

News Releases News releases are an important avenue of publicity, but the practitioner should avoid too much puffery. *Bulldog Reporter,* a West Coast public relations newsletter, once gave a "fireplug" award to a press agent who wrote a release about a Frank Sinatra concert in the Dominican Republic. The release said, in part:

> The Sinatra concert represented the first time a legendary star has ever performed for a subscription pay television service. The historical event, in a balmy night that could only rival, not surpass, the audience's decibel level for enthusiasm, should overshadow any in-person star appearance ever offered on subscription television. The Sinatra and Santana/Heart doubleheaders may well be recorded as pay TV milestones.

Photographs Photographs of the client should be submitted to the print media as often as justifiable. Basic in the press kit is the standard head-and-shoulders portrait, often called a "mug shot." Photographs of the client doing something interesting or appearing in a newsworthy group may be published merely with a caption, without accompanying story. If the client seeks national attention, such pictures should be submitted to the news services so that, if newsworthy, they will be distributed to hundreds of newspapers. (Requirements for photographs are discussed in Chapter 22.)

The practitioner and the photographer should be inventive, putting the client into unusual situations. The justification for a successful submission may be thin if the picture is colorful and/or timely.

Sharply increased awareness among editors of women's concern about sexual exploitation has largely eliminated from newspaper pages "cheesecake" pictures—photographs of nubile young women in which the news angle often is as skimpy as their attire. At one time such pictures were published frequently as editors tried to spice up their pages. Occasionally such a picture shows up in print today, blatantly contrived and perhaps in bad taste, such as the one of a smiling man pointing to the replica of a check painted on the bare stomach of a belly dancer. The caption read: "Julian Caruso, an entertainment manager, arrived in court in Stafford, England, yesterday to pay a parking fine. He didn't want to pay the fine, the equivalent of $17, because, he said, Stafford lacks adequate parking. To emphasize his displeasure, he presented the court a check written on the stomach of a belly dancer, Sandrina. Court officials took a look at her—real name, Sandra Audley—and decided they couldn't handle the check in that form."

Stunts like this are a throwback to old-time gimmick press agentry, yet sometimes they succeed. The picture was distributed by the Associated Press and published large size in at least one metropolitan newspaper.

Cheesecake photographs still are printed in the trade press, even though they are seldom seen in daily newspapers in America. Certain British and Australian newspapers, however, continue to publish large photos of skimpily clad young women, often topless.

■ Public Appearances Another way to intensify awareness of individual clients is to arrange for them to appear frequently in public places. Commercial organizations at times invite celebrities of various types or pay them fees to dress up dinner meetings, conventions, and even store openings. A major savings and loan association employed a group of early-day television performers to appear at openings of branch offices. Each day for a week, for two hours, an entertainer stood in a guest booth, signing autographs and chatting with visitors, who received a paperback book of pictures recalling television's pioneer period. Refreshments were served. A company photographer took pictures of the celebrity talking to guests. Visitors who appeared in the pictures received them as a souvenir. These appearances benefited the sponsor by attracting crowds and helped the entertainers stay in the public eye.

■ Awards A much-used device, but still successful, is to have a client receive an award. The practitioner should be alert for news of awards to be given and nominate the client for appropriate ones. Follow-up communications with persuasive material from the practitioner may convince the sponsor to make the award to the client. In some instances, the idea of an award is proposed to an organization by a practitioner, whose client then conveniently is declared the first recipient. The entertainment business generates immense amounts of publicity for individuals and shows with its Oscar and Emmy awards. Winning an Academy Award greatly strengthens a performer's career. Psychologists believe that televised awards ceremonies give viewers a sense of structure in life.This return to normalcy partly explains why the Emmy award ceremony was rescheduled twice after the September 11 attack on the World Trade Center and Pentagon so that the "show could go on."

Nicknames and Labels Creating catchy nicknames for clients, especially sports and entertainment figures, helps the practitioner get their names into print. Celebrity-worshipers like to call their heroes and heroines by nicknames, as though the practice denoted a personal relationship. Thus we see and hear such familiarities for professional basketball players as "Air Jordan" and "Sir Charles" Barkley, and "Old Blue Eyes" and "The Boss" for entertainers.

A questionable variation of the nickname consists of adding a descriptive word to the name of a person being publicized, to create a desirable image or career association. Sometimes this is done to provide a respectable veneer for a person of dubious background. In the Palm Springs resort area, to cite an instance, a socially active figure named Ray Ryan hired a practitioner whose task was to build up the image of Ryan as a well-to-do oilman. In every news release about Ryan and every telegram inviting social, business, and media individuals to Ryan's elaborate parties, the practitioner referred to his client as "oilman Ray Ryan." Publications in the area consistently printed "oilman Ray Ryan," giving the publicist the effect he desired. Actually, Ryan also was involved in big-time professional gambling—an involvement apparently responsible for the fact that when he turned the ignition key of his automobile one day, a bomb planted in the car killed him.

Record the Results

Those who employ practitioners want tangible results in return for their fees. The practitioner also needs to compile and analyze the results of a personality campaign in order to determine the effectiveness of the various methods used. Tearsheets, photographs, copies of news releases, and, when possible, videotape clips of the client's public appearances should be given to the client. Clipping services help the practitioner assemble this material. At the end of the campaign, or at intervals in a long-term program, summaries of what has been accomplished should be submitted.

Promoting an Entertainment Event

Attracting attendance at an event—anything from a theatrical performance to a fund-raising fashion show or a street carnival—requires a well-planned publicity campaign.

Publicity to Stimulate Ticket Sales

The primary goal of any campaign for an entertainment is to sell tickets. An advance publicity buildup informs listeners, readers, and viewers that an event will occur and stimulates their desire to attend it. Rarely, except for community events publicized in smaller cities, do newspaper stories and broadcasts about an entertainment include detailed information on ticket prices and availability. Those facts usually are deemed too commercial by editors and should be announced in paid advertising. However, some newspapers may include prices, times, and so on in tabular listings of scheduled entertainments. Performance dates usually are included in publicity stories.

Stories about a forthcoming theatrical event, motion picture, rock concert, or similar commercial performance should concentrate on the personalities, style, and history of the show. Every time the show is mentioned, public awareness grows. Thus, astute practitioners search for fresh news angles to produce as many stories as possible.

An Example: Publicizing a Play

The methods for publicizing a new play are the same whether the work will be performed on Broadway by professionals or in the local municipal auditorium by a little-theater group.

Stories include an announcement that the play will be presented, followed by releases reporting the casting of lead characters, start of rehearsals, and opening date. Feature stories, or "readers," discuss the play's theme and background, with quotations from the playwright and director inserted to emphasize an important point. In interviews the play's star can tell why he or she finds the role significant or amusing.

Photographs of show scenes, taken in costume during rehearsal, should be distributed to the media, to give potential customers a preview glimpse. As a reminder, a brief "opening tonight" story may be distributed. If a newspaper lists theatrical events in tabular form, the practitioner might submit an entry about the show. In some instances, publicity also can be generated through use of e-mail and World Wide Web pages.

The "Drip-Drip-Drip" Technique of Publicity

Motion picture studios, television production firms, and networks apply the principle of "drip-drip-drip" publicity when a show is being shot. In other words, there is a steady output of information about the production. A public relations specialist, called a unit man or woman, is assigned to a film during production and turns out a flow of stories for the general and trade press and plays host to media visitors to the set. The television networks mail out daily news bulletins about their shows to media television editors. They assemble the editors annually to preview new programs and interview their stars. The heaviest barrage of publicity is released shortly before the show openings.

As an example of the uncertainty and high stakes surrounding television programming, the national television networks—ABC, CBS, NBC, Fox, UPN, and WB—offer dozens of pilot programs, most of which lack staying power. Other such pilots may survive near-death experiences the way *Seinfeld* did in 1989 when ratings were dismal. A year later, the comedy series reappeared to begin a rise in popularity that culminated in the hype surrounding the final episode. An audience estimated as high as 80 million generated advertising revenues at $1.6 million for a 30-second spot. The publicity and suspense surrounding the final episode were so great that Jerry Seinfeld declared, "I'm sick of myself." The comedian's discomfort probably was relieved somewhat by his $1 million salary per episode.

A much-publicized device is to have a star unveil his or her star in the cement of the Hollywood Walk of Fame, just before the star's new film appears. Videotaped recordings of the event turn up on TV stations across the country.

One danger of excessive promotion of an event, however, is that audience expectation may become too high, so that the performance proves to be a disappointment. A skilled practitioner will stay away from "hype" that can lead to a sense of anticlimax.

A Look at the Motion Picture Industry

By market research and interpretation of demographics and psychographics, motion picture public relations departments define target audiences they seek to reach. Most motion picture publicity is aimed at 18- to 24-year olds, where the largest audience lies. Seventy-five percent of the film audience is under age 39, although increased attendance by older moviegoers has become evident recently.

Professional entertainment publicity work is concentrated in New York and Los Angeles, the former as the nation's theatrical center and the latter as the motion picture center. (American television production is divided primarily between the two cities, with the larger portion in Los Angeles.)

A typical Los Angeles–area public relations firm specializing in personalities and entertainment has two staffs: one staff of "planters," who deliver to media offices publicity stories about individual clients and the projects in which they are engaged, and another staff of "bookers," whose job is to place clients on talk shows and in other public appearances. Some publicity stories are for general release; others are prepared especially for a single media outlet such as a syndicated Hollywood columnist or a major newspaper. The latter type is marked "exclusive," permitting the publication or station that uses it to claim credit for "breaking" the story.

Another device is to provide supplies of tickets for a new movie or show to radio stations, whose disc jockeys award them to listeners as prizes in on-the-air contests. In the process, these announcers mention the name of the show dozens of times. Glamorous premieres and trips for media guests to distant points so that they can watch the filming or attend an opening are used occasionally, too.

For such services to individual or corporate entertainment clients, major Hollywood publicists charge at least $3000 a month, with a three-month minimum. The major studios and networks have their own public relations staffs.

Entertainment firms may also specialize in arranging product placement in movies and television programs. Usually the movie or television producers trade visible placement of a product in the show in exchange for free use of the item in the film. For example, Ford Motor Company provided the Explorer sport utility vehicle that was destroyed by a dinosaur in the movie *Jurassic Park*. The vehicle was then marketed with Mattel Toys as the Jurassic Park Explorer.

The fast-food industry also provides excellent opportunities for market-based public relations involving giveaways of film characters with meals. Movies such as *The Lion King* receive huge boosts in visibility and ticket sales. Characters from the film can provide a key incentive to young customers in the highly competitive takeout business, providing a large but transitory advantage in the so-called "burger wars."

Sports Publicity

The sports mania flourishing in the United States and in various forms around the world is stimulated by intense public relations efforts. Programs at both the big-time college and professional levels seek to arouse public interest in teams and players, sell tickets to games, and publicize the corporate sponsors who subsidize many events. Increasingly, too, sports publicists work with marketing specialists to promote the sale of booster souvenirs and clothing, a lucrative sideline for teams.

Sports publicists use the normal tools of public relations—press kits, statistics, interviews, television appearances, and the like—to distribute information. But dealing with facts is only part of their role. They also try to stir emotions. For college publicists, this means creating enthusiasm among alumni and making the school glamorous and exciting in order to recruit high school students. Publicists for professional teams work to make them appear to be hometown representatives of civic pride, not merely athletes playing for high salaries.

Sometimes this effort succeeds spectacularly, if the team is a winner. When a team is an inept loser, however, the sports publicist's life turns grim. He or she must find ways to soothe public displeasure and, through methods such as having players conduct clinics at playgrounds and make sympathetic visits to hospitals, create a mood of patient hopefulness: "Wait 'til next year!"

Emerging sports increasingly compete for prominence and fan loyalty against other, more established sports. Soccer is widely popular among youth in America, leading to hopes among its promoters that the professional game will make inroads where traditional U.S. sports dominate. The Professional Golf Association (PGA) bought an 11-page advertising supplement in *Business Week* magazine to promote the professional golfer as a great athlete, philanthropic leader, and consummate professional in the face of rigorous travel and performance pressures.

Because the public yearns for heroes, publicists focus on building up the images of star players, sometimes to excess. They know that stars sell tickets. The 1998 baseball season featured record-breaking home-run performances by both Mark McGwire and Sammy Sosa. The home-run race may not have been the sole attraction that saved baseball from doldrums that many traced to the baseball strike and shortened season several years earlier. Nevertheless, the two sluggers are credited with bringing baseball "all the way back" as America's sport. By contrast, media treatment of McGwire's successor as home-run king reflects the principle in public relations that building positive relationships over time leads to success. Less attention and adulation was accorded Barry Bonds in 2001 when he broke McGwire's record, partly because of Bonds's diffidence toward the media over the years.

Because sports in America is big business, with $150 billion in gross annual revenue, an unseemly side frequently crops up in sports coverage. The impasse between players and owners in the National Basketball Association (NBA) was only the latest instance that caused fans to lose patience with both the wealthy owners and the highly paid players. A satirical chain letter swept across the Internet calling for donors to

Chris Berman does a National Football League television commentary on ESPN. Sports broadcasting occupies a large portion of TV time, and the commentators become almost as well-known as the major players.

Sports and entertainment celebrities lend their name and fame to multiple products. Here, tennis superstar Venus Williams smiles at a news conference after announcing that she has signed a multiyear contract extension with Reebok International Ltd. The deal, at the time, was the most lucrative endorsement deal ever created for a female athlete.

adopt an NBA player. This grassroots spoof of genuine giving programs for needy children included appeals for a mere $10,000 per month to defray the athlete's car payments or cover his "walking around" money for incidental spending.

Public relations plays a critical role in sports far beyond promotion of celebrities. Two important areas are sports crisis management and sponsorship management. According to John Eckel of Hill and Knowlton Sports, professional communicators must deal with the media focus on issues ranging from player strikes to high ticket and concession costs and boorish athletes who deny that they are role models while they benefit from their visibility as—role models. Jay Rosenstein of Cohn & Wolfe attributes much of sports crisis PR to the "human factor in the sports world, where egos are otherworldly, behavior is reminiscent of the entertainment world, and media focus is unrelenting."

Management of sports sponsorships has become systematic and deliberate. For example, Edelman Event and Sponsorship Marketing uses its "M.U.S.T.S.ystem" to evaluate sponsorships. The acronym means:

Media appeal

User friendliness

Sales appeal

Thematic applications

Special event potential

The advertising agency DDB Needham studied the effectiveness of a very high profile sponsorship, the Summer Olympics. The agency found that the Olympic Games require a huge commitment of $40 million per sponsor plus extensive costs of marketing that sponsorship to the company's benefit in sales and goodwill. Only about half of sponsors successfully linked their names to the Games. The agency recommends an integrated plan that uses the sponsorship as the focal point but includes many opportunities for coverage. Perhaps the best example was the daily auctioning of custom-made, numbered Hanes T-shirts for 500 consecutive days before the 1996 Olympics. The Olympic sponsor donated the million-dollar proceeds to children in war-ravaged Sarajevo, a former Olympic city.

focus on ethics

A Difficult Sports Secret

You are a sports information officer for a university whose high-scoring basketball team hopes to win the national championship. One late evening in the locker room you overhear two top players talking about how they shaved points in two recent games by intentionally missing free throws. Your team won the games, but by a smaller margin than the Las Vegas "oddsmakers" had predicted. Gamblers rewarded them with gifts of expensive sports cars, kept hidden at an off-campus location. You hear that the players are planning to shave points again in the early rounds of the tournament for hefty cash payments.

If you keep the cheating secret, the university might win the national title and obtain generous contributions from enthusiastic alumni. If you report your information to an academic or police authority and a public gambling scandal occurs, the school will suffer disqualification, shame, and financial loss. You will be vilified by many in the university community for "blowing the whistle" when the outcome of games was never put in jeopardy by these players. You consider a constructive approach, because your team did win the previous games. You could tell the players that you know about their scheme and demand that they play competitively from now on or you will report them to the NCAA.

If you don't report the circumstantial evidence you have, will you be guilty of unethical behavior?

What about criminal charges against you for aiding and abetting a criminal act?

If you do report the previous incident, what sort of crisis management approach would you develop?

The Olympic Games are subject to inevitable crises associated with what C. Richard Yarbrough, Director of Communication for the 1996 Atlanta Games, called "the world's largest special event." Salt Lake City was still enjoying the glow of its public relations coup associated with becoming host of the 2002 Winter Olympics when a major crisis broke in national news coverage. Scandalous charges of blackmail and bribery were leveled against the Salt Lake Committee, especially for providing International Olympic Committee (IOC) members and their families with scholarships meant as humanitarian aid to needy athletes. Salt Lake City officials rapidly investigated and then admitted that six relatives of IOC members had benefited from scholarship aid. Resignations of committee directors followed shortly. This rapid and forthright approach may prove to be the most effective single public relations strategy of the 2002 Games.

Travel Promotion

With money in their pockets, people want to go places and see things. Stimulating that desire and then turning it into the purchase of tickets and reservations is the goal of the travel industry. Public relations has an essential role in the process, not only in attracting visitors to destinations but in keeping them happy after they arrive.

Like entertainment and sports, travel draws from the public's recreation dollars. Often its promoters intertwine their projects with those of entertainment and sports entrepreneurs.

Phases of Travel Promotion

Traditionally the practice of travel public relations has involved three steps:

1. Stimulating the public's desire to visit a place
2. Arranging for the travelers to reach it
3. Making certain that visitors are comfortable, well treated, and entertained when they get there

Recently, terrorist actions have forced emphasis on a crucial new element:

4. Protecting the travelers' safety

Stimulation is accomplished by travel articles in magazines and newspapers, alluring brochures distributed by travel agents and by direct mail, travel films and videos, and presentations on the World Wide Web. Solicitation of associations and companies to hold conventions in a given place encourages travel by groups.

Some publications have their own travel writers; others purchase freelance articles and pictures. Well-done articles by public relations practitioners about travel destinations often are published too, if written in an informational manner without resorting to blatant salesmanship and purple prose. Aware of public resistance to such exaggeration, *Condé Nast Traveler* magazine carries the slogan "Truth in Travel" on its cover. In fact, *O'Dwyer's PR Services Report* warns that "PR overkill" results from indiscriminate distribution of news releases, nagging followup calls to editors about releases, ignorance about the publication being pitched with a story, and excessive handling of writers on arranged trips so that the writer finds it difficult to get a complete picture of the travel destination.

An important tool in travel promotion is the familiarization trip, in which tour operators and travel writers are taken as guests to inspect a travel destination. Here, a group organized by Edelman Worldwide public relations samples a host resort's food.

focus on ethics

How Many "Freebies" to Accept?

Creation of newspaper and magazine stories about travel destinations, so essential in tourism promotion, poses a problem for writers and public relations people. Who should pay the writer's expenses in researching them?

Some large newspapers forbid their travel writers to accept free or discounted hotel rooms, meals, and travel tickets. They believe that such subsidies may cause writers to slant their articles too favorably, perhaps subconsciously.

Many smaller publications and most freelance writers cannot afford such an expensive rule, however, and following it would prevent them from preparing travel articles. One freelance travel writer, Jeff Miller, took the publishing industry to task in *Editor & Publisher* magazine for paying $150 per newspaper story and $500–$1000 per magazine story while banning writers from taking subsidized trips. Travel writers claim the hypocritical policy makes the publication look good but has to be regularly ignored by travel writers who simply cannot make a living without subsidized trips. The writers contend that pride in their professional objectivity keeps them from being influenced by their hosts' "freebies." Some point to critical articles they have written on subsidized trips.

For the public relations director of a resort, cruise, or other travel attraction, the situation presents two problems: (1) How much hospitality can be given to the press before the "freebies" become a form of bribery? and (2) How does the director screen requests from self-described travel writers who request free housing or travel?

The Society of American Travel Writers (SATW) sets this guideline:

> Free or reduced-rate transportation and other travel expenses must be offered and accepted only with the mutual understanding that reportorial research is involved and any resultant story will be reported with the same standards of journalistic accuracy as that of comparable coverage and criticism in theater, business and finance, music, sports, and other news sections that provide the public with objective and helpful information.

What do you think of the SATW guidelines? Are they specific enough to guide you in your public relations position for a gorgeous Caribbean resort?

What of the "no sponsored trips" policy at some newspapers and magazines?

Do you believe that heavily discounted trips tend to buy writer loyalty in the same way that free trips do?

Arrangements for travel are made through travel agencies or by direct booking at airlines, airports, and railroad and bus stations. Complicated tours and cruises are arranged most frequently by travel agencies, which charge customers retail prices for accommodations and receive a 10 percent commission from the travel supplier. Wholesalers create package tours that are sold by travel agencies.

To promote sales, the 38,000 U.S. travel agencies distribute literature, sponsor travel fairs, and encourage group travel by showing destination films at invitational meetings. Cities and states operate convention and travel departments to encourage tourism. A widely used method of promoting travel is the *familiarization trip,* commonly called a "fam trip," in which travel writers and/or travel salespeople are invited to a resort, theme park, or other destination for an inspection visit. Fam trips in the past often were loosely structured mass junkets. Today they are smaller and more focused.

Good treatment of travelers is a critical phase of travel promotion. If a couple spends a large sum on a trip, then encounters poor accommodations, rude hotel clerks, misplaced luggage, and inferior sightseeing arrangements, they come home angry. And they will tell their friends vehemently how bad the trip was.

Even the best arrangements go awry at times. Planes are late, tour members miss the bus, and bad weather riles tempers. This is where the personal touch means so much. An attentive, cheerful tour director or hotel manager can soothe guests, and a "make-good" gesture such as a free drink or meal does wonders. *Careful training of travel personnel is essential.* Many travelers, especially in foreign countries, are uneasy in strange surroundings and depend more on others than they would at home.

Fear of Terrorism

The tragic events of September 11 in New York, Washington, D.C., and Pennsylvania created an upsurge of fear and uncertainty about traveling. The Travel Industry Association of America estimates that the impact two months after the terrorist attacks was $43 billion in lost revenue and the disappearance of 527,000 jobs related to tourism. President Bush has taped two public service announcements to encourage travel on behalf of the industry. Nevertheless, Americans were shocked to realize how vulnerable their country was to terrorism.

Security measures were strengthened at airports and aboard airplanes, causing travelers inconvenience and delay. Even so, security experts emphasized the impossibility of a 100 percent guarantee against terrorist attacks.

Travel Business on the Internet Takes Off

Airline tickets, hotel accommodations, and travel packages can readily be shopped and then booked on the World Wide Web. Consumers have found the convenience and the discounted Internet specials to be highly attractive, resulting in a major increase in online travel transactions. Web sites such as Travelocity.com not only offer complete airline booking services but also provide e-mail notification to members of fare changes for itineraries selected by the online user. Airlines and hotels find that last-minute inventory of seats or rooms can be sold effectively online. Because of such online commerce, hotels, resorts, and cruise lines can afford to mount extensive Web sites that provide outstanding information to consumers and journalists alike.

Appeals to Target Audiences

Travel promoters identify target audiences, creating special appeals and trips for them.

Great Britain's skillfully designed publicity in the United States is a successful example. Its basic appeal is an invitation to visit the country's historic places and pageants. It also offers London theatrical tours, golf expeditions to famous courses in Scotland, genealogical research parties seeking family roots, and tours of the cathedrals. Special groups can be arranged for other purposes as well.

Packaging *Packaging* is a key word in travel public relations. Cruises for family reunions or school groups, family skiing vacations, university alumni study groups, archaeological expeditions, even trips to remote Tibet—these and other so-called niche travel packages are offered. A package usually consists of a prepaid arrangement for transportation, housing, most meals, and entertainment, with a professional escort to handle the details. Often supplementary side trips are offered for extra fees.

PR casebook

Viral Marketing—Word-of-Mouth Communication Updated

Long before the rise of the Internet, professional communicators recognized the value of favorable recommendations and "buzz" about a product or service. For public relations programs, the primary objective was often to enhance or maintain the reputation of a company. Today, spreading the word can generate greater traffic to a Web site, where both marketing and public relations objectives can be met. The primary purpose of viral marketing is to stimulate impulse purchases or downloads, but increasingly pass-it-on techniques on the Web serve public relations objectives in reputation management and message dissemination.

Viral marketing has adopted a new terminology and some special techniques that take advantage of the new technology to stimulate a natural inclination to tell others about a good deal, a good service, or a good group. For example, Hotmail began to offer free e-mail in 1997, including a message on each e-mail: "get your free, private e-mail." Within a year and a half, Hotmail garnered 12 million subscribers for a total investment of a half million dollars.

Viral marketing firms devise ways to stimulate the natural spread of recommendations through financial incentives called *cohort communication*. Going beyond the relatively natural spread of information through tactics similar to Hotmail's inviting message, viral marketing specialists orchestrate dissemination of favorable reviews. Software systems track referrals to a Web site or recommendations sent to friends, chalking up cash or merchandise credits for the sender.

Detractors worry that viral marketing is easily recognized as commercial manipulation, except among hardcore enthusiasts. Others say that it is deceptive and unethical to facilitate or reward what should be a natural process of trusted friends exchanging tips and links about great deals or great Web sites. For example, the music industry recruits fans to log onto chat rooms and fan Web sites to hype a band's new album. Some liken this to the questionable old practice of payola in the radio industry—payment to disk jockeys for air time.

Viral marketing companies argue that the technique will work only when the idea, the movement, or the product earns genuine support from the marketplace. Then, Netizens take advantage of the convenience of the Web to forward what they like to others. Jupiter Communications found that over half of online users visit sites based on a recommendation and nearly all have forwarded a recommendation to another friend. Public relations professionals will need to make careful and ethical decisions to decide how best to use the Web to spread a message.

To explore viral marketing on your own and to consider how to adapt the techniques to public relations functions, visit some of these viral marketing companies. (When you do, you will be participating in viral marketing!)

- Caffeine Online Marketing Solutions at www.getcaffeinated.com
- Viralon Corporation at www.viralon.com
- EmailFactory.com at www.emailfactory.com

Appeal to Seniors The biggest special travel audience of all is older citizens. Retired persons have time to travel, and many have ample money to do so. Hotels, motels, and airlines frequently offer discounts to attract them. As a means of keeping old-school loyalties alive, many colleges conduct alumni tours, heavily attended by senior citizens.

A large percentage of cruise passengers, especially on longer voyages, are retirees. Alert travel promoters design trips with them in mind, including such niceties as pairing compatible widows to share cabins and arranging trips ashore that require little walking. Shipboard entertainment and recreational activities with appeal to older persons—nostalgic music for dancing rather than current hits, for example—are important, too.

Ocean cruising, a major aspect of the travel industry, is highly competitive and requires intensive public relations effort. The arrival of the new *Grand Princess,* the world's largest cruise ship, in New York was greeted by a dockside party and heavy national television coverage. Porter Novelli, the public relations firm handling the event, reported that 42 TV crews and 15 radio reporters came aboard to describe the ship's features.

Times of Crisis

Public relations in travel requires crisis management, just as in corporate work. Crises come in many forms, from those of dangerous magnitude to the small but embarrassing varieties.

The spate of attacks against Florida tourists in the early 1990s led to one of the highest-stake crisis management efforts of all time. A multibillion dollar source of revenue, Florida tourism suffered a deluge of damaging international publicity when nine foreign tourists were killed in separate incidents, mostly during robberies. Some victims were exchange students, while others were tourists gunned down only a few days after their arrival from abroad. Attempting to limit the damage, the Florida Division of Tourism sent faxes to 28,000 travel agents in North America, England, and Europe describing steps taken to help travelers and providing an 800 number for inquiries. Travel to Florida from Europe that winter decreased almost 50 percent from normal. Florida's strenuous public relations efforts to repair the damage to its tourism have paid off with a rebound in rates of tourism to Florida.

At a different level, the luxurious liner *Queen Elizabeth II* departed on a high-priced cruise before refurbishing was completed. Many passengers had unpleasant trips because some facilities were in disrepair, leading to one news report describing the ship as a floating construction project. Others had their reservations cancelled because their cabins were not completed. After bad international publicity and a class-action suit by some passengers, the Cunard line offered a settlement. It gave full refunds of cruise fares plus a travel credit for a future cruise.

Sometimes a crisis results from a fluke. The supersonic Concorde flew to Tucson, Arizona, to pick up about 100 tourists who had paid up to $12,000 each for a flight to England, five days in London, and a return cruise. As the Concorde was being pulled out from the gate, a tow bar broke and a flying piece punctured two tires on the plane. Since the Concorde carried only one spare, a second tire had to be flown out from New York. During the anticipated wait of several hours, passengers were entertained by an impromptu champagne breakfast on the taxi strip. Then airline officials realized that because of the Tucson delay the Concorde could not make its necessary refueling stop in New York without violating that city's noise curfew law. The flight had to be postponed until the next day. Passengers who had expected to fly across the Atlantic at twice the speed of sound spent the night instead in a Tucson hotel and lost a day of their London visit.

Travel firms need to make certain that they provide equal facilities and service to all races, and that their facilities are free from environmental pollution, as witness a cruise ship that had to pay a heavy fine after an environmentally aware passenger videotaped its crew members tossing debris overboard.

Summary

Fascination with Celebrity

Today's mass media focus on the publicizing and glorification of celebrities in the fields of sports and entertainment and even high-profile criminals, some politicians, and members of the British royal family. Although the publicity buildup of individuals is not in the mainstream of public relations work, students in the field should learn how the personal publicity trade operates.

A Case Study: Princess Diana

Lady Diana Spencer achieved celebrity status through her marriage to Charles, Prince of Wales and heir to the British throne. The public was obsessed with her clothing, her public appearances, her eating disorder, and the failure of her marriage. Her early death has frozen her youthful image in time, and visitors to her family estate have paid to view the site of her burial.

The Mystique of Personality

Celebrities are motivated by fame (or notoriety), self-glorification, the attempt at positive image creation, and desire for monetary gain. The public is impressed because of wish fulfillment, hero worship, a vicarious sense of belonging, and a desire for entertainment.

The Practitioner's Responsibility

A big factor for the public relations practitioner handling a personality will be damage control from misbehavior or an irresponsible public statement. This may strain the practitioner's ethical principles; it is never wise to lie to protect a client.

Conducting a Personality Campaign

A practitioner planning a campaign to generate public awareness of an individual must interview the client, prepare a biography, plan a marketing strategy, and conduct the campaign through news releases, photographs, and public appearances.

Promoting an Entertainment Event

Publicity campaigns to promote events may include publicity to stimulate ticket sales. The "drip-drip-drip" technique involves a steady output of information as the event is being planned. The motion picture industry defines target audiences.

Sports Publicity

Sports publicists promote both big-time college and professional teams. This effort becomes more difficult when the team isn't winning. Emerging sports must compete for prominence and fan loyalty with more established sports. Some publicity focuses on building images of star players. Publicity efforts will also include both sports crisis and sponsorship management.

Travel Promotion

Travel promotion will involve encouraging the public's desire to visit a place, arranging for them to reach it, making sure they enjoy their trip, and protecting their safety. Campaigns may include a familiarization trip to increase travel agents' awareness.

Case Activity: What Would You Do?

Michael Jackson has decided to return to public life as part of the promotion of his latest album. Your celebrity public relations firm has been hired to develop a strategic communication plan for Michael's attempt to recapture the limelight for his musical talents and for causes such as Heal the Kids that he champions. The overall goal should be to focus attention on Michael's musical talent and not on his rather unusual personal life, including adoption of a chimp named Bubbles, wearing a face mask in public, endless plastic surgeries, marriage and divorce, and the accusation of child molestation that was settled out of court.

The firm is instructed to use traditional celebrity promotion tactics but also to capitalize on the new technologies in the strategic campaign. You have suggested that a crisis communication plan also be implemented. What would be your three main objectives, and what strategies would you showcase to achieve them? For your crisis communication plan, how would you handle subsequent eccentric acts by your star client?

Questions for Review and Discussion

1. Why do public relations students need to understand how the personal publicity trade functions, even if they do not plan to handle theatrical or sports clients?
2. Which of the five motivating factors in the cult of personality (fame, notoriety, self-glorification, repair of bad image, desire for money) make most sense to you and why?
3. Name two psychological factors underlying the American obsession with celebrities.
4. When politicians say something they wish they hadn't and it is published, they often claim that they were misquoted. Why is this poor policy?
5. What is the first step in preparing a campaign to increase the public's awareness of an individual client?
6. What is a "bio"? What should it contain?
7. "Cheesecake" photographs once were commonplace in American newspapers, but few are published now. Why is this so?
8. What does Edelman's MUSTS acronym stand for? Why is each element important, in your opinion?
9. Why do practitioners put emphasis on certain players on sports teams?
10. What are the basic phases of travel promotion?

Suggested Readings

"Access Hollywood: Pat Kingsley Rewrites the Rules of Celebrity PR." *PR Tactics,* July 1999, pp. 26–27.

Bannon, Lisa. "And the Winner Is: Anybody Who Has an Oscar-Night Gig." *Wall Street Journal,* March 21, 1997, pp. 1 and 6.

Gonzalez-Herrero, Alfonso, and Pratt, Cornelius. "Marketing Crises in Tourism: Communication Strategies in the United States and Spain." *Public Relations Review,* Spring, 1998, pp. 83–98.

Klein, Richard. "He's No Jack Sprat: A Scholar's Caloric Book Tour." *Chronicle of Higher Education,* February 28, 1997, p. B7.

McCleneghan, J. Sean. "Sports Information Directors for Colleges." *Public Relations Quarterly,* Summer 1995, pp. 28–32.

Reilly, Patrick M. "Pulling Out All Stops to Push 'Pop'." *Wall Street Journal,* February 13, 1997, pp. B1 and B12.

Sonmez, Sevil F., Apostolopoulos, Yiorgos, and Tarlow, Peter. "Tourism in Crisis: Managing Effects of Terrorism." *Journal of Travel Research,* Vol. 38, Aug. 1999, pp. 13–18.

Tilson, Donn J., and Stacks, Don W. "To Know Us Is to Love Us: The Public Relations Campaign to Sell a 'Business-Tourist Friendly' Miami." *Public Relations Review,* Summer, 1997, pp. 95–115.

Yarbrough, C. Richard, Cameron, Glen T., Sallot, Lynne, and McWilliams, Allison. "Tough Calls to Make: Contingency Theory and the Centennial Olympic Games," *Journal of Communication Management,* 3(1), 1998, pp. 39–56.

Written Tactics

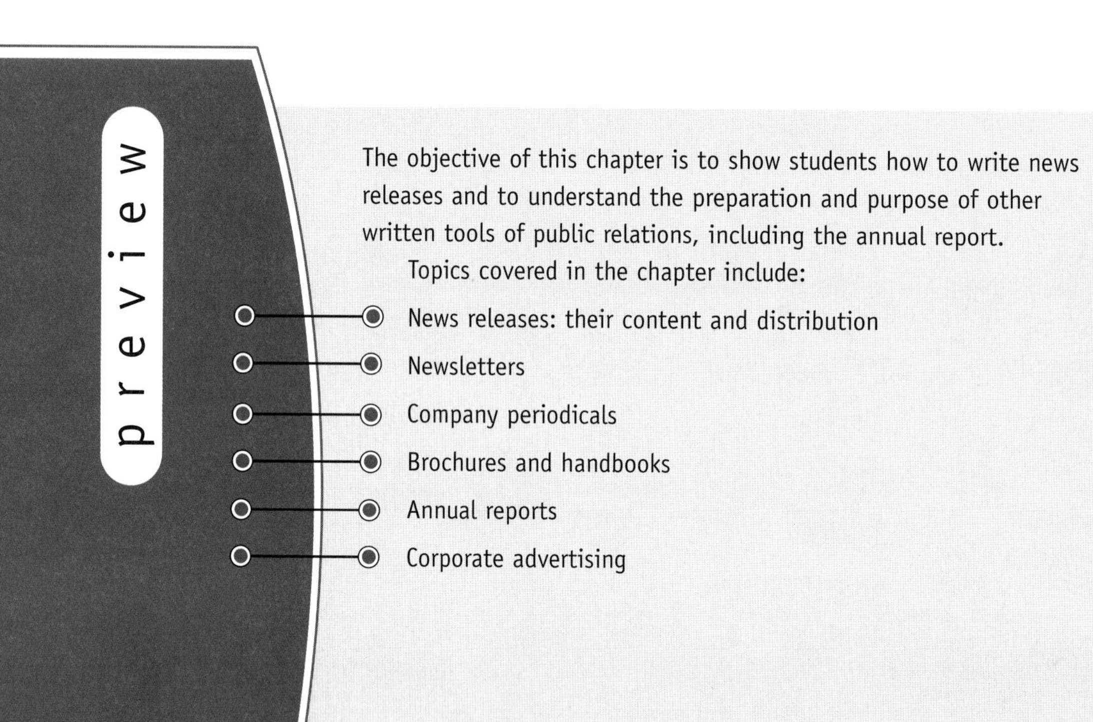

The objective of this chapter is to show students how to write news releases and to understand the preparation and purpose of other written tools of public relations, including the annual report.

Topics covered in the chapter include:

- News releases: their content and distribution
- Newsletters
- Company periodicals
- Brochures and handbooks
- Annual reports
- Corporate advertising

The News Release

Basically, a *news release* is a simple document whose purpose is the dissemination of information in ready-to-publish form. Editors of print and broadcast media to whom news releases are sent judge them on the basis of news interest for their audience and timeliness, and in some instances on their adaptability to the medium's form. No payment is made to the publication or station if the material appears in print or on the air. If an organization or individual purchases space in a publication to present its material, this is a paid advertisement, and the purchaser controls the content.

Releases should be prepared so that the media can relay their news content to audiences easily, with confidence in their accuracy. Editors want the main facts stated succinctly in the opening paragraph of a release, for quick recognition. A news release is a purveyor of information, not an exercise in writing style, except in those cases of longer releases that are clearly intended to be feature stories. The writer of a basic news release should leave the clever writing to staff members of the media.

A news release faces intense competition when it arrives on an editor's desk, against scores or even hundreds of other releases. As they scan the releases, editors make almost instant decisions, assigning each release to one of three categories:

1. *Obvious news.* This would include copy that is certain to be used.
2. *Maybe.* Some stories are possibly worth developing if a reporter has the time. A sharp news angle in a release may put it in the "obvious-news" category instead of the risky "maybe" pile. Potentially good stories placed in the "maybe" pile face the danger of being thrown away after a second reading if the key information is poorly developed.
3. *Discard.* This category includes both releases of insufficient interest to the receiving editor's audience and those of marginal value that would require too much effort to develop. These go into the recycling box or the wastebasket.

News releases that are prepared according to the criteria described in the following sections have the best chance of being accepted for publication, assuming that their content is newsworthy.

PR casebook

"Wedding Kiss Workshop" Makes News

The makers of Moodmatcher lipsticks received prominent media coverage for their products in New York when they invited reporters to a "kissing workshop."

Two stars of an off-Broadway play, *Tony 'n Tina's Wedding,* introduced as kissing experts, demonstrated osculatory styles. Then they judged a "Moodmatcher Best Kiss Technique" contest.

Contestants had been attracted by advance publicity inviting brides-to-be to apply. The winner, an editor of *True Story* magazine, won a free dinner, a wedding make-up makeover, and free lipsticks for up to 500 wedding guests.

After the contest, everyone present shared a wedding cake. Both the *Wall Street Journal* and ABC television covered the event, and lipstick sales rose.

Physical Appearance

There is a standard format for news releases:

- Use plain white 8½-by-11-inch paper.
- Identify the sender in the upper-left-hand corner of the page, listing name, address, and telephone number. Many releases also include a fax number and an e-mail address. Especially if the sender is a large organization, also give the name of an individual within the organization as a point of contact. It is important that the listed phone be answered by an informed person, usually a public relations specialist, not by a recording.
- Below the identification state *For Immediate Release* if the material is intended for immediate publication, as most news releases are. If a time restriction is necessary, as with an advance copy of a speech to be delivered at a specified hour, indicate the desired publication time; for example, *For Release at 6 P.M. EST Feb. 12.* This is called an *embargo.* Media recipients of embargoed material have no legal obligation to obey its restrictions, but they normally do so out of courtesy and mutual convenience unless they believe that the embargo is an obvious effort to manipulate the news. Embargoes should be used only when genuinely necessary.
- Leave 2 inches of space for editing convenience before starting the text.
- Start the text with a clearly stated summary lead containing timely, relevant, important information.
- Leave at least a 1.5-inch margin. Double-space the copy to give editors room in which to edit the material.
- Never split a paragraph from one page to the next. Put *(more)* at the bottom of each unfinished page.
- Place an identifying slugline and page number at the top of each page after the first.

Some public relations practitioners place a summary headline above the text, to tell an editor quickly what the release contains.

Content

There are a few essential rules for the content of news releases:

- Begin the news release with a tightly written summary lead and state the fundamentals—who, what, when, where, and why—early in the copy. The first sentence should state the most important point in the story. *Do not bury the lead.* The opening paragraph should be three to five lines maximum.
- Be concise. Edit the copy to remove excess words and "puff" terminology. A competent editor would cut them out, anyway. Few news releases need to be more than two pages long; most can be written in a single page. A reporter may obtain additional details by telephoning numbers listed or by sending an e-mail. Reporters also routinely access the organization's Web site for additional background information.
- Caution: Avoid clichés and fancy phrases. When editors receive a news release using such terms as "unique," "revolutionary," and "state-of-the-art," they are likely to throw it away.

- Never use excessively technical language in a release for a general audience. The objective is communication, not confusion.
- Be absolutely certain that every fact and title in the release is correct and that every name is spelled properly. Check the copy closely for grammatical errors. Errors can be embarrassing and costly. In a news release announcing a Mexican cruise, distributed nationally, Cunard Lines mistakenly listed the 800 telephone number of a San Francisco optical company instead of its own. The optical company received more than 2000 calls in the first week; its phone lines were tied up and it had to assign personnel to redirect the calls. Cunard compensated for its blunder by giving the optical proprietor and his wife a free cruise to Europe.

For protection against errors and misunderstandings, a public relations counselor is wise to have the client initial a file copy of each news release before its distribution. In company public relations departments, similar initialing by a superior is desirable and in some cases mandatory. Corporate review can become excessive, however. Writing in *Editor & Publisher,* Ron Cantera, a former public relations executive who became a journalism professor, reported: "In one corporate job I held, my news releases were reviewed by at least six different insiders—my boss, his boss, a product manager, the marketing vice president, an agency copyreader and, believe it or not, a word-processing supervisor . . . that led to communication by committee."

Those who issue news releases should welcome follow-up inquiries from reporters and be able to provide additional information. Often reporters complain that the public relations personnel aren't available or don't promptly return phone calls.

To counter this complaint, many public relations people make it a point on news releases to list contact numbers that are direct lines to a real person instead of voice-mail or an answering machine. In addition, many practitioners provide cellular and home phone numbers so that they can be reached after regular business hours.

When a story is controversial, and the organization or individual issuing the news release is in a defensive position, this openness sometimes diminishes or even vanishes. The attitude of some upper-management executives toward the media in controversial situations is, "Tell them only what we want the public to know. Let them find out the rest for themselves, if they can." This attitude on the part of management may persist to the point of having the public relations department omit relatively simple information.

Citing "company policy," Quadrex Corporation refused to answer press inquiries about how many people were being laid off. An editorial in the local newspaper called the company to task. It said, in part: "A public company should be relatively open. There is no reason or excuse—except short-term stonewalling to harbor the company's stock from truth—to withhold such information as the number of persons in a layoff. . . . In the long run, Quadrex would generate a better public image by disclosing rather than withholding information."

This management attitude of playing it close to the vest is a source of mistrust among the media toward companies that follow the practice. A survey by a unit of the J. Walter Thompson advertising agency showed that 55 percent of the business editors who responded criticized corporate press releases for burying important information.

Gradually, many firms are adopting a more forthright approach. A company has no reason to wash its dirty linen in public in a voluntary outburst of confession. Yet greater frankness in news releases and willingness to volunteer answers to reasonable questions that good reporters will ask anyway help to build a company's credibility.

Professors Glen T. Cameron of Missouri, Lynne Sallot of Georgia, and Patricia A. Curtin of North Carolina reviewed several decades of studies of the relationship between reporters and public relations persons. The researchers noted in *Communication Yearbook 20* the increasing respect among reporters for the professionalism of their news sources. Positive experience with ethical and forthright practitioners has improved the standing of public relations in the eyes of the media.

Delivery of News Releases

News releases should be conveyed to the media in a timely and effective manner. As pointed out previously, releases should be addressed to recipients by name whenever possible. Releases may be sent in a broadside manner to large numbers of recipients, in an approach called *macrodistribution*, or to carefully selected target media sources, using the *microdistribution* technique. The high cost of postage and of specialized delivery services causes most public relations practitioners to select recipients of their news releases with care, omitting those unlikely to use the material. Therefore, practitioners should determine the appropriate media sources for their firm or their clients.

Locally, releases can be delivered by first-class mail, fax, messenger, or e-mail if they contain urgent material. Use of bulk mail to save postage is unwise. Delivery is subject to delay, and recipients of bulk mail tend to dismiss it as unimportant.

Delivery of releases regionally or nationally is more complicated because of timing problems and the need to reach the proper outlets and individuals in areas where the sender lacks knowledge of local situations. Accurate, current mailing lists substantially influence the amount of exposure a news release obtains. For this reason, many organizations employ distribution firms to handle their mailings. One of these firms, Media Distribution Services, maintains current lists of more than 150,000 editors and reporters at more than 40,000 print and broadcast media in the United States and Canada and lists the media in 2500 categories of editorial interest.

Distribution of releases by mail still is the cheapest, most common, and least attention-getting method. It is also the first preference of reporters and editors. Overnight delivery by Federal Express, Express Mail, United Parcel Service, or DHL is more expensive but gives the news release an aura of importance. Faxed messages are a popular way of delivering invitations to meetings and events.

Electronic Delivery Newswire companies offer various types of news release delivery, usually aimed at carefully targeted lists of recipients. The public relations practitioner writes a news release and turns over the copy to one of these distribution companies. Depending upon the type of distribution the practitioner chooses, the commercial firm prints and mails it to a selected mailing list, distributes it by high-speed private wire to outlets chosen by the author, or distributes it on the Internet and Web. The release arrives in newsrooms on special public relations printers in the same ready-to-publish form as if it had been mailed. Recognizing the growing dependence on computers in newsrooms, distribution companies also will dispatch news releases from their computers directly into the computers of newsrooms, just as news services send copy to most newspapers.

Business Wire and PR Newswire, the principal distribution firms, handle heavy volume at moderate cost. A 400-word news release distributed nationally costs about $500. They claim better usage of a release sent electronically.

Camera-Ready Feature Services Still another way of distributing news about products, services, and events nationally is through a distribution service that provides newspapers with "camera-ready" copy. A company or firm sends a featurized news release about its project or product to the promotion service. If the service's editors deem the content to be newsworthy and written in competent news story style, they lay out the story in newspaper format and distribute it by mail or in digital form on CD or a Web site. Photographs and appropriate drawings may be included to illustrate the release. Brand names are permitted, although they usually are placed inconspicuously well down in the stories. Smaller newspapers in particular use editorial promotion service copy as textual matter in special advertising sections on such themes as gardening, home repair, Mother's Day, auto repair, and fashions. To win acceptance by an editorial promotion service, copy must be free of hard-sell "puffery."

Localizing a News Release

National corporations realize that when the releases they send out are localized, media use will be substantially higher. The local angle should be placed in the lead if possible. Inclusion of local names or statistics attracts editors; they know it interests readers. For example, a corporation with offices and plants in 20 cities sends out a release reporting that it currently has 30,000 employees systemwide, who last year received total wages and health benefits of stated amounts. The release may be published rather inconspicuously in the newspapers of some company cities but will receive little or no broadcast attention because it is too general. Even company employees will have difficulty relating to it. However, if the releases sent to the media in each company city tell how many employees the company has in that locality, and how much these workers receive in payroll and health benefits each year, likelihood of widespread use will be high.

Lack of localization in the news releases they receive is a major cause of complaint by editors. In a comprehensive study of news releases and their usage, Professor Linda P. Morton of the University of Oklahoma found that fewer than 10 percent of the releases that she reviewed were localized. When they were localized, usage jumped. Of one group she studied, Morton reported, "For instance, of 174 localized releases, 78 were published. Comparably, 1174 general releases resulted in only 87 being used."

Using computer techniques, a corporation can prepare a standard national news release giving general information for use by all recipients. It also can prepare paragraphs containing the local information for each company city. These paragraphs are inserted by computer appropriately into the releases intended for each specific city.

Fact Sheets and Media Advisories

Although fact sheets are distributed by public relations personnel to the same media as news releases are and somewhat resemble releases physically, they are in outline form instead of in news story format.

A *fact sheet* is essentially a quick reference tool for reporters: It summarizes the key points about an event, a product, or a company to help reporters get a quick grasp or overview. Susan Antilla, New York bureau chief of *USA Today*'s money section, said in *Jack O'Dwyer's Newsletter,* "PR people can really help a lot by providing background on companies . . . good factsheets are considered gold and are kept on file."

Summary of Facts

FMD: A Summary of Facts

Background

Foot-and-mouth disease (FMD) is a highly contagious viral disease that does not affect humans but has devastating effects on animals with cloven hooves, such as cattle, swine, sheep, goats and deer. The U.S. has not had a case of foot-and-mouth disease since 1929, an outbreak that was quickly contained and eradicated.

There are seven types of the FMD virus, all of which have similar symptoms. Immunity to one type does not protect animals from other types. The average incubation period for FMD is between three and eight days, but can be up to two weeks in some cases. The disease is rarely fatal but may kill very young animals. Animals that survive are often debilitated and experience severe loss in milk or meat production.

Spread

Foot-and-mouth disease is a highly contagious virus and can be spread by movement of infected animals, movement of contaminated vehicles, and by contaminated facilities used to hold animals. It also can infect animals through contaminated hay or feedstuffs and if susceptible animals drink from a common water source.

While FMD is not considered a threat to human health, people who come in contact with the virus can spread it to animals through clothing, footwear or other equipment/materials. The virus can harbor in the human nasal passages for as long as 28 hours. Wind also can spread the virus through the air.

Economic Effects

If FMD were to occur in the U.S., the degree of economic impact would depend on how quickly the disease was identified and effective control measures put in place. If it was controlled quickly and eradicated, as was the case with the last outbreak in the U.S. in 1929, the damage might be small. However, if the disease became widespread, the economic loss could easily be

http://www.fmdinfo.org/summary_facts.htm 3/11/02

The first page of this fact sheet and the news release (see next page) illustrate the difference between the two types of material distributed by a public relations organization. One is a factual summary, the other a news story in publishable form.

A *media advisory,* also called a media alert, differs from a fact sheet. It gives basic facts about an event, in the hope of attracting media coverage, and it also describes interview prospects as well as photo and video possibilities.

The Pitch Letter

The purpose of the *pitch letter,* an important tool in a public relations campaign, is to obtain coverage of an event in the print and electronic media.

A pitch letter to an editor or producer should be so brisk and bright that it will catch the recipient's attention in the daily stack of mail. These letters offer the writer an opportunity to be clever, even off-beat, but they also must include the basic facts about an event or new product and offer reasons why the editor should assign someone to cover it.

The letter should be addressed personally to an individual, not merely to "Editor." Several directories are available to identify the current editor of a publication as well as its editorial calendar—the planned topics and special issues for the coming year. *Bacon's Directories* is a large set of annual directories in print and CD-ROM format. The *Directories* also include an update service for a fee to the purchaser of the volumes. Frequent updates of the annual directory are provided so that news releases and pitch letters are targeted to the current editor or reporter at a publication. Although reporters and editors move and change positions frequently, they are nonetheless sensitive about receiving mail directed to their predecessor.

News Release

For Immediate Release
Superintendent,
November 1, 2001

Contacts: Dr. Jim Parsley,
Vancouver Public Schools
(360) 313-1200

Tom Hagley, Jr., Community Relations Manager
Vancouver Public Schools
(360) 313-1093

Brad Bass, Public Sector Communications
Hewlett-Packard Company
(301) 258-2366

Vancouver School District and HP Announce Opening of Jim Parsley Center

VANCOUVER, Wash.--- Vancouver School District (VSD) and Hewlett-Packard Company (NYSE:HWP) announced today the completion of a new education, family and community center funded by $6.5 million in private-public contributions.

A grand opening celebration will take place on Friday, November 2. Tours of the center will be given at 12:30 p.m., and a ribbon-cutting ceremony, with remarks by Washington Governor Gary Locke and State Superintendent of Public Instruction Terry Bergeson, will begin at 1:15 p.m.

The Jim Parsley Center (JPC) and the adjacent Eleanor Roosevelt Elementary School will showcase elements of Cooltown, a visionary program within HP aimed at creating information appliances, software and services for a transformed world of diverse, pervasive and mobile computing using the World Wide Web.

HP's technology-supported solutions will assist students, educators, parents and the greater community in pursuing anywhere, anytime access to education and the resources they need to be successful.

The vision for the Cooltown initiative in Vancouver includes the following plans:

- Three fifth-grade classrooms at Eleanor Roosevelt Elementary School will use a web portal to help teachers manage personalized learning programs and monitor the progress of individual students.
- Students in the Communications Academy, a new high school magnet program located within the JPC, will use similar web portal tools.
- The JPC's after-school program, called "Impact," also will benefit from HP and HP partner technology solutions. Each student will have an

News releases are the workhorses of publicity efforts. This news release gives the basic format. It is important to list contact people so reporters can follow up if they have additional questions.

The Press Kit

A *press kit* is often prepared when a company announces a new product or sponsors a major event; frequently elaborate, it gives media representatives a thorough background and provides information in various formats. Press kits may be sent to the media or distributed at a news conference (discussed in the next chapter).

The basic format consists of a large folder cover with pockets inside that contain news releases, fact sheets, backgrounders (background articles), collateral company materials, black-and-white publicity photos, color slides, and even article reprints. The folder usually is visually attractive, incorporating graphic design and color.

Typical of such press kits is one prepared by LMS International, a new company formed as a joint venture of Control Data and Philips corporations. The public relations objective was to announce the new organization and develop a stronger understanding among the electronic trade media of its products; consequently, the press kit contained the following materials:

- Backgrounders on (1) the company/management team, (2) product areas/markets, and (3) major new products
- Separate news releases on each new product

- A six-page, four-color brochure on glossy paper about the new company and its products
- Black-and-white product publicity photos of major products
- Color slides of major products

The budget for the press kit was $10,000. One thousand press kits were distributed to (1) senior editors and reporters of the computer press around the world, (2) business and financial editors covering computer technology, and (3) market researchers and analysts. As a result, articles and photographs about the company appeared in more than 200 publications worldwide. Secondary articles appeared in more than 400 publications; also, the company received more than 100 requests for special features, industry trend/position articles, and technical articles.

Levi Strauss & Co. also prepared a fairly elaborate kit to publicize the results of a national survey about the fashion and lifestyle tastes of today's college students. The survey, conducted on 25 campuses among 7700 undergraduates, was called the Levi's 501 Report.

This kit contained (1) four news releases, (2) a fact sheet on Levi's 501 jeans, (3) a backgrounder on the statistical findings of the survey, and (4) a sampling of fashion publicity photos of college-age models wearing, of course, jeans. A special press kit cover and letterhead also were designed.

The cost to write, produce, and distribute the press kit was $20,000. The cost of the survey was $25,000. The package was distributed to fashion editors at the top 500 newspapers around the United States, the news services, college media news services, and radio syndicates. Within three months, 345 articles appeared.

The Newsletter

Designed as an informal publication to deliver information to a target audience at regular intervals, newsletters are used frequently by corporations to communicate with employees and stockholders, by nonprofit agencies and associations to reach members and friends, and by sales organizations to deliver information and personnel chitchat to representatives in the field. Expert opinion and inside advice in specialized fields also are sold to subscribers in newsletter form by commercial publishing firms.

The typical newsletter is a four-page folder of 8½ -by-11-inch pages, often set in computer type rather than regular printer fonts. This style projects an air of informality and urgency. Ample use of white space increases readability.

The newsletter can be double-folded into a No. 10 business envelope, or it can be a self-mailer—that is, when folded, it has space on an outside surface for the address and stamp. Envelope mailing has greater impact, but the self-mailer is more economical. The choice is a question of budget.

Newsletters for internal audiences typically report to employees on trends in their field of work, forthcoming events, personnel changes and policy announcements within the organization, news from field offices, introduction of new products, unusual achievements by employees, results of surveys, and new publications. The goal is to make employees feel that they are informed about company affairs.

A newsletter aimed at an outside audience, members of an organization, or both, may contain items about political trends that could affect the organization or field of interest, announcements of new programs and policies, brief human interest stories about personnel or recipients of organization services, promotions and retirements—whatever news the editor believes is of interest to readers that can be told succinctly. On complicated stories, the newsletter should give the basic facts and indicate where readers can write or telephone for additional details. A newsletter is a brisk compilation of highlights and tidbits, not a place for contemplative essays or discussion.

Punchiness in writing style is essential for a successful newsletter. Sentences are short and direct. The writing is authoritative and no-nonsense in tone, from a busy writer to a busy reader. Another secret of the successful newsletter is to cover several topics that will appeal to a variety of readers. The single-topic edition should be avoided.

Company Magazines

Hundreds of well-written, well-edited, and attractive periodicals published in the United States never are seen by the general public. They are produced by public relations departments of companies or their public relations firms and distributed free to carefully selected audiences. Whether designed to be read by employees, stockholders, customers, or combinations of these audiences, periodicals are among the most effective channels of continuing communication that a company can use. Like any publication issued at regular intervals, the company magazine or newspaper creates a sense of anticipation of its arrival. This helps to strengthen the ties between management and the groups it seeks to inform and influence.

Although it is commonly accepted that employees with long-term service in a company are the most avid readers of company newsletters and magazines, research has disputed this. Professor John Pavlik, of Columbia University, studied employees of Honeywell, Inc., in Minneapolis and found that an employee's career aspirations are a much better predictor of readership. Quite simply, Pavlik says, "An employee with higher career aspirations tends to place greater importance on reading to keep track of changes in management and to find out what is going on in the company generally."

Experts emphasize the importance of four elements in maintaining a good relationship between management and employees—employee recognition, communication, a sense of belonging, and emotional security. When all of these elements function well, productivity tends to rise. Workers who believe that their jobs are secure and their personal worth recognized will contribute more than disgruntled ones.

Along with other forms of internal communication, company periodicals help substantially in the development of all four elements. The periodicals communicate information and decisions from management to employees. They increase the workers' feeling that they know what is going on in the company, and why. Management can use the periodicals to influence the attitudes of employees. However, this purpose must be accomplished with caution and finesse. If employees sense that management is talking down to them and using the periodical merely as a propaganda vehicle, the publication may become an object of derision. Periodicals also can serve as channels for communication from employees to management through letters to the editor, question-and-answer features, and similar devices.

Major corporations sometimes produce sleek, sophisticated-appearing magazines and colorful newspaper-style publications that are in the forefront of contemporary design. Four-color covers and splashy graphics help attract readers in this age of visual emphasis. Examples of this lavish approach are AT&T's management-oriented *AT&T Magazine* and Transamerica Corporation's *Transamerica.* Some of these, such as the

American Express *Dateline International,* circulate worldwide. Kvaerner, a multinational company founded in Norway centuries ago, distributes tens of thousands of copies of its corporate magazine across the globe in English, Finnish, and Norwegian.

Company publications vary in size, use of color, graphics, photos and frequency of publication, depending on the size of the budget and the target audience management seeks to reach. Some companies have found that their blue-collar employees get more satisfaction from a periodical that is simple in design and presentation than from the elaborate, multicolored, sophisticated-looking magazine that might be intended for stockholders or investment advisors.

Large corporations frequently publish several periodicals, each designed for a different audience. Usually the objective of a publication is stated in small type in its masthead. Typically, *Chevron World,* published quarterly by Standard Oil Company of California, states, "The *Chevron World* is published and distributed by the company's Public Affairs organization for the information of shareholders, employees, and other interested parties." Knowledge of this stated purpose helps a person to scrutinize the content of a periodical and analyze why various elements were included. (*Chevron World* is described in detail later in the chapter.)

Nonprofit organizations publish periodicals for much the same purposes that corporations publish theirs. Instead of trying to please stockholders and customers, nonprofit organizations must seek the support of contributors. Their product is service. Therefore, periodicals aimed at contributors and possible donors emphasize the quality and social value of the service the organization delivers.

Company magazines fall into four major categories, grouped by the audience they serve. To illustrate how the various types function, the following sections analyze the contents of typical magazines in each category: those for employees and retirees, for stockholders and employees, for marketing staff and wholesale customers, and customers and association members.

Magazines for Employees and Retirees

The employee magazine is a means by which management can inject a personal touch into company affairs. As a humanizing tool, it helps offset the feelings of some employees, especially in large corporations, that they have little significance as individuals to management. Through its pages, the company can recognize the achievements and personal milestones of those who work for it. A well-edited employee periodical helps instill an attitude among employees that they are part of the company. At the same time, the magazine offers management an opportunity to report its policies and explain why they were adopted.

Employee publications, like most periodicals, usually have stated objectives. The Clorox Company publishes a quarterly magazine, *The Diamond,* for its 4800 employees. *The Diamond* has the following objectives:

- To assist management in securing employee understanding and support for the company's operations, activities, objectives, and plans
- To recognize employee accomplishments on and off the job, to maintain high morale and develop a sense of participation in the company's affairs and its relationship with local communities
- To educate employees about subjects such as the U.S. economic system, safety, and the obligations of responsible citizenship, to make employees more valuable members of the Clorox family and their communities

The editor of *The Diamond* follows a story mix intended to recognize people in different divisions, departments, and various locations while covering issues important to the company. The magazine exemplifies effective employee communication with a limited staff and budget. In a primarily one-person operation, the editor plans content, interviews people, writes all copy, handles all approvals, takes most of the photographs, and supervises design, production, and printing. The editor also handles all phases of a monthly two- to four-page newsletter.

Company magazines and newsletters for employees normally are distributed to retirees as well. The two groups have similar interests in company affairs. Editors make an effort to include material specifically for retirees, such as pension information and in some instances stories about retiree reunions.

Magazines for Stockholders and Employees

Because a magazine of this type is aimed at two audiences, its approach must be broader. Although stockholders and employees share concern about the success of their company, their interests are not identical. News about the activities and milestones of individual employees does not interest stockholders. The magazine's focus needs to be more on technical and economic developments in the corporation's field and on the company's strategy to take advantage of them. A magazine distributed to stockholders as well as to employees usually is more visibly management-oriented than one for employees only. It must be kept in mind that many employees also are stockholders, often as participants in company-sponsored stock purchase programs.

An example of the company periodical distributed to both stockholders and employees is *Chevron World,* published quarterly by Standard Oil of California as a colorfully printed, 30-page, slick-paper magazine.

One typical issue of *Chevron World* contains a policy statement by the chairman of the board about oil exploration, articles about natural gas reserves and oil taxation, a feature about Chevron's TV school in which the company instructs its executives on how to appear on television programs, and a story about bird life on the company's North Sea oil platforms.

In this publication, employees are given a carefully crafted picture of their company's ambitious search for new energy sources. Their pride in the company's size and ingenuity is stimulated. They receive strong exposure to management's views. Corporate image-building is the dominant theme.

Magazines for Marketing Staff Members and Wholesalers of Company Products

These periodicals are unabashedly promotional, edited to encourage sales through inspirational essays and how-to-do-it articles.

An excellent example of these direct sales-booster periodicals is *Team Talk,* published by Anheuser-Busch of St. Louis to promote its group of beers. Articles contain cheerleader sentences of a type the reader would be unlikely to find in the magazines previously analyzed. Quotations like this one from wholesalers are included in articles about their activities:

> Everybody loves a winner and wants to be associated with a class organization . . . our retailers and the general public know we are proud of our products. Anheuser-Busch is a winner, and we want to be one, too.

In general, the content of *Team Talk* urges marketing people to exploit established events by pushing exposure of their products and to create special events for the same purpose. The publication's goal is motivation of its readers.

Magazines for Customers and Association Members

As a psychological link to their customers, to remind them of company products and services, some firms publish magazines addressed exclusively to this group. Magazines published by national organizations for their members are similar in purpose and character, although in some instances somewhat wider in editorial range. The cost of a membership magazine normally is included in the annual dues.

The customer magazine is not a catalogue, although it may contain pages offering services or products, often packaged in special offers. Primarily its objective is to present a favorable image of the company, rather than direct selling.

A colorful example of the customer magazine is *Silver Circle,* a 48-page quarterly published by Home Savings of America and distributed free to members of its Silver Circle. The Circle is a device designed to increase deposits in this very large savings and loan association. Home Savings depositors who have at least $10,000 in accounts become Silver Circle members. They receive the magazine and a membership card entitling them to discounts on numerous travel and entertainment items.

The editors of *Silver Circle* can make several important assumptions about their audience: (1) Those who receive the magazine have at least a moderate amount of spare money; (2) members may be expected to have substantial interest in travel; (3) all probably have at least a fundamental understanding of financial matters. Relative affluence, money awareness, concern about health, interest in travel—these attributes of the *Silver Circle* audience are the framework on which the magazine is built.

The tie-ins between the magazine and the hotels, restaurants, and amusement parks offering discounts in it illuminate the techniques of entertainment sales promotion. Those who give discounts know they are reaching an audience with money to spend. Home Savings in turn earns goodwill from magazine recipients by offering such bargains.

Brochures and Handbooks

Writing informational publications to fill innumerable needs is among the most common duties of public relations practitioners. Some printed pieces are issued at stated intervals, such as quarterly reports to stockholders and college catalogues. The majority, however, are designed to last for indefinite periods, subject to updating as required. Most of this material is distributed free, although price tags may be placed on more elaborate and expensive items, such as museum catalogs.

Whatever their purpose, these publications share clearly defined writing requirements. Clarity is essential. Frequently the writer must explain technical material or simplify complex issues for a reader who knows little about the topic. This calls for explanations that are straightforward, shorn of jargon, and stated in terms that a casual reader can comprehend quickly. Paired with clarity is conciseness. Informational writing should be tightly done, leaving elaborate literary devices to the novelist. Pare excess verbiage.

Every brochure, handbook, or other form of printed information should be organized on a firm outline that moves the reader forward comfortably through unfamiliar territory. Frequent subheads and typographical breaks are desirable. The writer

PR insights

Guidelines for Writing Brochures and Handbooks

Plain English and basic design enhance the communication effectiveness of any document. These attributes not only increase goodwill with key publics but also reduce complaints and confusion among employees and consumers.

The following are research-based criteria for enhancing readability and comprehension:

- Use 8- to 12-point type. Readers often ignore text that is too small.
- Use plenty of white space. Wide margins, indents, and occasional short pages keep the document from looking crowded and too difficult to read.
- Use ragged right, rather than justified, margins. This gives the document a relaxed contemporary look, and avoids awkward, irregular spacing between words.
- Use short lines. Optimal line length for most text is 50 to 70 characters.
- Use boldface for emphasis. It is easier to read than a word in all capital letters.

Source: Based on material from the Document Design Center of the American Institute for Research, Washington, D.C., as presented in *PR Reporter*.

often operates under budget restrictions that dictate the size of the publication—perhaps a 4-page folder, perhaps a large-format brochure of 30 pages consisting primarily of illustrations with short blocks of type. Space limitations should be regarded as a challenge to the writer's skill at condensation.

The following are the types of publications in this category that a public relations writer is most frequently called upon to create.

Informational Brochures

These describe the purposes, policies, and functions of an organization. Tour-guide folders given out at museums are an example of this form.

Handbooks

More elaborate than basic brochures, handbooks usually include policy statements, statistical information, and listings of significant facts about the issuing organization and its field of operation. Handbooks often are designed for distribution primarily to news media sources as handy references for a writer or broadcaster in a hurry. Trade associations and corporations are frequent users of the handbook as a public relations tool.

Typical examples of the handbook are:

- *"Sharing the Risk," published by the Insurance Information Institute.* Nearly 200 pages describe property and casualty insurance concepts, regulations, and policies, ranging from homeowners' losses to nuclear risks.
- *"Oil & Gas Pocket Reference," published by Phillips Petroleum Company.* This is a 60-page small-format booklet of statistics about the oil industry. Included are such lists as the top 10 U.S. oil-producing states; the top 15 oil-producing nations, with amounts; oil and gas imports by year; and significant reference dates.

Corporate Brochures for External Use

Frequently aimed at specific audiences rather than at the general public, these may be such items as the inserts utility companies include with their bills, financial documents such as quarterly reports to stockholders and proxy statements for potential stock purchasers, owners' manuals, and teaching materials.

Corporate Brochures for Internal Use

To inform and train their employees, companies issue a broad range of brochures and handbooks. These may be distributed at in-plant meetings or to individuals at work or mailed to the employees' homes. In simplest form, information sheets may be posted on company bulletin boards. Readership of these boards is high; anything posted there will be noticed and probably will become a topic of conversation on the job.

Examples of in-company brochures and manuals include:

- *Atlantic Richfield Company's 12-page booklet to assist older employees in making the transition from work to retirement.* It answers questions that concern every employee approaching retirement, such as financial planning, use of leisure time, and health benefits.
- *A manual describing proper telephone techniques, given to employees of Washington Federal Savings and Loan Association in Seattle.* Employees discuss the manual in seminars during which they see a 25-minute film depicting "telephone traps" in which they might find themselves.

Glossaries

Trade associations and corporations in technical fields often issue pamphlets defining terms, including jargon as well as standard words, commonly used in their work. Like handbooks, glossaries are distributed extensively to the news media.

The Annual Report

"The principal purpose of the annual report is to tell the company's story to a multiplicity of audiences," says David F. Hawkins, a professor at the Harvard Business School. "It's a public relations document with a regulatory requirement."

Indeed, preparation of a corporation's annual report is a major function of a company's public relations department or counseling firm and is probably the company's most expensive written contact with its stockholders and the financial community. According to a study by the National Investor Relations Institute, investor relations executives devote about 13 percent of their time to preparing annual reports. The estimated 10,000 public companies in the United States spend an average of $3.52 a copy to produce a glossy publication of abundant color, with striking graphics and impressive photography, averaging 44 pages.

Technically, the corporate annual report is an informational document required by the Securities and Exchange Commission of all publicly traded companies. But there is no legal requirement that annual reports be extravaganzas. Under Rule 14a-3 of the Securities Exchange Act, publicly traded companies are required to include only basic financial information and other material such as a list of directors and the audi-

Corporations issue annual financial reports required by the federal government's Securities and Exchange Commission (SEC). Such reports also serve as a public relations opportunity for the company to tell its stockholders and potential investors about the company's activities and plans for future growth.

tor's opinion letter. Once these requirements are met, the rule states, "the report may be in any form deemed suitable by management."

Companies publish expensive and attractive annual reports for public relations purposes. These include (1) impressing current and potential stockholders that the company is well managed and successful, (2) encouraging potential investors to purchase stock, and (3) using the annual report as a vehicle for recruiting new employees.

Some evidence exists, however, that costly expenditures on such reports don't really influence potential investors. A Hill and Knowlton survey of 501 investors concluded that only 3 percent found annual reports to be the best source of investment information. In that respect, annual reports ranked behind periodicals, stockbrokers, statistical services, friends, and relatives. Some companies recently have reduced the scope of their annual reports, even down to summary size.

Increasingly, large corporations use striking new graphic techniques in their reports to stimulate reader interest and project an image of power.

A corporate annual report is divided into two general sections:

1. *Detailed financial information about the company's condition and performance during the past year.* A consolidated balance sheet and management's discussion of the financial condition are essential elements. A letter from the corporation's auditing firm is included, along with breakdowns of certain aspects. The material in this section, prepared by the financial department and approved by top management, is coldly objective and must be completely accurate, but some companies also use a profusion of numbers that often confuse everyone except specialists in accounting.

   To cite one case, an annual report of Koppers Company had a mass of numbers, charts, and graphs—and even a ten-year financial comparison of 45 items. Yellow lines highlighted the most favorable statistics that the company wanted to emphasize.

   Other relevant information about the corporation is published in this section for reference. This may include lists of key executives and their salaries, names of major stockholders, lists of plant sites, and major subsidiaries. Because specific financial data are required by the Securities and Exchange Commission in an annual report, a specialist in financial public relations should be assigned to compile the reports.

2. *Management's presentation of accomplishments during the past year, its goals and outstanding problems.* This material, appearing in the first portion of the report just after a one-page summary of financial highlights, is designed to give a good impression of management's work. While the prose is restrained, use of striking color photographs and other graphics helps suggest corporate vigor.

   The centerpiece of this front section is a report to stockholders by the board chairperson or the chief executive officer. This is the "message," and it is sometimes used to rail against government regulation or to extol the company's contribution to making America a leader of the "free world."

   When companies have had a bad year financially, or have been involved in an embarrassing episode, they frequently bury that fact in their annual reports, so that only a close reading—not too common among ordinary stockholders—will disclose it. Others discuss their troubles with refreshing candor. In general, recent trends in annual reports have been toward more informality in writing, more focus on employees, and, when a company's operations justify it, emphasis on its roles in the international market and the environmental movement. Many companies also comment on socially responsible efforts to hire more minorities and promote more women.

   On occasion, a company breaks out of the usual mold with a creative approach. BellSouth, for example, used an annual report to focus on the year 2000 by including essays from nationally known authors, commentators, and experts about our lives now and in the future. And First Hawaiian, Inc., a bank-holding group, used color photos of its executives in Hawaiian shirts instead of three-piece suits.

As supplements to printed annual reports, but never as replacements for the financial section, some companies issue videotaped annual reports for showing to employees, stockholders, and financial groups. Teleconferencing an annual meeting is an increasingly common practice. But evidence shows that although a video can provide basic information, comprehension is increased if an executive is present to explain and field questions. Research has shown that recipients don't "reread" video reports as they do printed ones.

Corporate Advertising

Traditionally, *advertising* is defined as purchased space or time used to sell goods or services, while public relations space in the media is obtained free. The line of demarcation becomes fuzzy when a company engages in *corporate advertising,* also called *institutional advertising.* Such advertising is processed and purchased in the regular manner. Its purpose, however, is not to sell the company's products or services directly but to enhance public perception of the company or to advocate a company policy.

A corporate advertisement, as defined by Leading National Advertisers, a checking service, must deal with a company's policies, functions, facilities, objectives, ideas, and standards; build favorable opinions of the company's management, skill, technology, or social contributions; enhance the investment qualities or financial structure of the company; or promote it as a good place to work.

A type of corporate advertising called "advertorial" advertising is used to push products, sometimes rather subtly, to the extent that the distinction between product and corporate advertising becomes blurred. Professor Glen T. Cameron of the Missouri School of Journalism believes this blurring results in information pollution. He and colleagues have found evidence that readers are confused by such practices. He calls for prominent labels to indicate advertising and a statement early in the ad copy declaring the commercial nature of the message.

The largest amounts of corporate advertising appear on television and in magazines. Radio, outdoor advertisements, and newspaper supplements receive much smaller amounts, and daily newspapers receive the least, except for a few with national impact.

Corporate advertising may be divided into three basic types: (1) *general corporate image-building,* (2) *investor and financial relations programs,* and (3) *advocacy.*

Image-Building

Image-building advertising is intended primarily to strengthen a company's identity in the eyes of the public and/or the financial community. Conglomerates whose divisions market unrelated products seek through such advertising to project a unified, readily recognized image. Others use it to correct an unfavorable public impression. Increasingly, corporations use institutional advertising to show their concern for the environment, and by doing so seek to demonstrate what good corporate citizens they are.

Phillips Petroleum, for example, published a full-page magazine advertisement dominated by a photograph of a bird's head and beak, with the headline, "You'd sing too if someone created a sanctuary for you." The text read:

> Thousands of songbirds had no voice. So we gave them one. We helped expand the High Island Sanctuary, a crucial resting place on the Texas coast for migrating songbirds. Originally it was just five acres. But now it spans 170 acres. To make it happen, Phillips Petroleum brought together government agencies, conservation groups, and

> another oil company. Did it make a difference? Just ask the next gray catbird you happen to meet. Respect for wildlife. At Phillips, that's what it means to be The Performance Company.

A warning: Any corporation that strikes a proenvironmental posture, then is caught polluting or otherwise damaging the environment, immediately becomes the object of derision for hypocrisy.

In one instance, Mobil Chemical Company sought to attract environmentalists by advertising that its Hefty brand plastic trash bags are degradable and break down when exposed to the elements. Calling the advertising false, the attorneys general of seven states sued to halt its use and asked civil penalties of at least $500,000 against the company. With its image damaged by the publicity, the company agreed to drop the claim until terminology could be agreed upon among the parties to the suit.

Financial Relations Programs

The second form of corporate advertising is aimed straight at the financial community. The advertiser tries to depict its financial strength and prospects so favorably that securities analysts will advise their clients to purchase its stock. When a corporation has millions of shares outstanding, even a fractional improvement in its price is beneficial. Such advertising is used extensively during proxy fights for control of companies or when a company is undertaking a major reorganization and needs to keep the financial community informed.

Advocacy

The third, sometimes controversial, form of corporate advertising is advocacy. In such advertisements, a corporation or association tries to influence public opinion on a political or social issue. Only a small portion of corporate advertising expenditure goes into advocacy advertising, but, because these advertisements sometimes touch public sensibilities, they receive considerable attention.

Chase Manhattan Bank encountered criticism for some of its advocacy advertising, as it conceded frankly in a full-page newspaper advertisement. This advertisement was dominated by a drawing of several of the Founding Fathers, above the headline:

> In accordance with the wishes of our founding fathers, we'll continue to speak out.

The text stated, in part:

> In the past year, Chase has been running a series of advertisements which expressed our views on some of today's important economic issues. These included the need for greater productivity . . . the need to stimulate research and development . . . tax incentives to spur investment, generate capital and modernize our industrial plant . . . government overregulation . . . inflation. And the spurious rhetoric about "excessive" corporate profits.
>
> Since then, these topics have become central issues in this critical election year. For that we're grateful, because the American public surely deserves a full and open debate as to how best these pressing national problems can be solved.
>
> On the other hand, it's caused us to go through some soul-searching in recent weeks. We've frankly asked ourselves whether an institution such as ours should continue to speak out on important and sometimes sensitive issues in the middle of a national election.

> So we went back to the First Amendment to our Constitution and took a long and thoughtful look. As a result, we've decided to go right on speaking out, even though we obviously risk causing controversy or alienating a constituency....

Evaluating Corporate Advertising

Ogilvy & Mather, a major advertising agency, studied corporate advertising. It announced these conclusions:

> We have learned that good corporate advertising can:
>
> - Build awareness of a company
> - Make a favorable impression on investors and securities analysts
> - Motivate employees and attract recruits
> - Influence public opinion
> - Strengthen relations with dealers
> - Influence legislation
>
> We have learned that corporate advertising cannot:
>
> - Gloss over a poor record or a weak competitive position
> - Boost the price of your stock next month
> - Swiftly turn the tide of public opinion
>
> There are no quick fixes. Advertising can spread the truth about your company but cannot *conceal* it.

Thomas F. Garbett, a recognized authority on the subject, offered this justification for corporate advertising, in an article published in the *Harvard Business Review:*

> Although many companies assume that the safest course is to keep a low profile, this may in fact be a dangerous tack. If some inadvertent disclosure brings high visibility or even incidental exposure, an unknown company maintains little credibility as it moves to counter public criticism . . . When people first get acquainted with a company through an unfortunate disclosure, they often distort what little they know and make generalizations about missing information. The less filled out a company's image is, the more subject that image is to wild distortions.

Summary

The News Release

A news release disseminates information in a ready-to-publish form. It should follow a standard format and must be concise, nontechnical, and factually correct. Delivery must be timely; electronic delivery is increasingly common. It should be targeted to the location of the publication or media outlet to which it is sent.

Fact Sheets and Media Advisories

Fact sheets are quick reference tools for reporters, prepared in outline form. Media advisories or alerts not only give facts but also describe interview prospects as well as photo and video possibilities. A pitch letter is written to attract an editor's attention and obtain coverage. Press kits are usually folders distributed to media representatives with news releases, fact sheets, collateral company materials, photos, and even article reprints.

The Newsletter

A newsletter may be written for employees, stockholders, or members of nonprofit organizations. These tend to be short—usually four pages—with an air of informality and urgency, with a punchy writing style.

Company Magazines

Company magazines are distributed free to carefully selected audiences; the four major categories of these are employees and retirees, stockholders and employees, marketing staff and wholesale customers, and customers and association members. Company periodicals contribute to the mportant elements of employee recognition, communication, a sense of belonging, and emotional security. Sophistication of design may depend on the audience.

Brochures and Handbooks

Many informational publications are created to last for indefinite periods and to be distributed free. Often they must explain technical material or simplify complex issues, clearly and concisely. Such publications include informational brochures, handbooks, corporate brochures for both internal and external use, and glossaries.

The Annual Report

An annual report has been described as "a public relations document with a regulatory requirement." It not only acts to promote public relations with a variety of audiences but is an informational document required by the Securities and Exchange Commission. The report will be divided into two general sections, detailed financial information and management's presentation of the past year's accomplishments as well as its goals and outstanding problems.

Corporate Advertising

Corporate or institutional advertising is not directly intended to sell a company's products or services but for general corporate image-building, investor and financial relations programs, and advocacy.

Case Activity: What Would You Do?

The Cleveland Repertory Theater will move into a new home next month. The $25 million building is part of the city's downtown redevelopment plan. The facility has state-of-the-art lighting and sound, seating for 750, and rooms for drama workshops. The architect is Skinner & Associates, and the contractor is BK Industries. Julie Andrews, star of stage and screen, will be the guest of honor at the official opening.

Write a general news release about the Repertory Theater and its planned grand opening. Second, write a pitch letter to the local media encouraging them to do feature stories about the new facility in advance of the opening. Third, write a media alert or advisory letting the press know that Julie Andrews will be available for interviews on a particular day. Fill in the appropriate quotations and information that you deem necessary.

Questions for Review and Discussion

1. What is an *embargo* on a news release? Does it have any legal standing?
2. What are the physical requirements for an attractive news release?
3. A public relations counselor should have a client initial a file copy of each news release before distribution. Why?
4. Describe the difference between a news release and a fact sheet.
5. To what audiences might a corporate public relations department send a newsletter?
6. As editor of a company magazine intended for employees and retirees, what would be your objectives?
7. Handbooks are issued frequently by corporations and trade associations. What types of material do they usually contain?
8. To what federal agency must corporate annual reports be submitted?
9. Corporate or institutional advertising differs in purpose from ordinary advertising. Explain this difference.
10. What risk does a corporation take when it uses aggressive advocacy advertising?

Suggested Readings

Barmash, Isadore. "The Trouble with Press Releases." *PR Week,* August 23, 1999, pp. 14–15.

Brandon, Michael C. "From Need to Know to Need to Know." *Communication World,* October/November 1997, pp. 18–19.

Cameron, Glen T., and Curtin, Patricia A. "Tracing Sources of Information Pollution: A Survey and Experimental Test of Print Media's Labeling Policy for Feature Advertising." *Journalism and Mass Communication Quarterly,* Spring, 1995.

Cameron, Glen T., Sallot, Lynne, and Curtin, Patricia A. "Public Relations and the Production of News: A Critical Review and a Theoretical Framework." *Communication Yearbook 20,* 1997, pp. 111–155.

Draper, John. "Putting Humanity in Your Newsletter—It's Not Worth It (Or Is It?)" *Communication World,* February/March 1997, pp. 23–25.

Hill, L. N., and White, C. "Public Relations Practitioners' Perception of the World Wide Web as a Communication Tool." *Public Relations Review,* 31 (1) (2000), pp. 68–74.

Larkin, T. J., and Larkin, Sandra M. "Internal Communication: Have We Missed the Mark?" *Communication World,* March 1995, pp. 12–15.

McCleneghan, J. Sean. "The PHD Approach to News Release Writing." *Public Relations Quarterly,* Spring 1999, pp. 42–45.

Minnis, John H., and Pratt, Cornelius B. "Let's Revisit the Newsroom: What Does a Weekly Newspaper Print?" *Public Relations Quarterly,* Fall 1995, pp. 13–18.

Porter, L. V., Sallot, L. M., and Cameron, G. T. "New Technologies and Public Relations: Exploring Practitioners' Use of Online Resources to Earn a Seat at the Management Table," *Journalism & Mass Communication Quarterly,* 78 (1) (2000), pp. 172–190.

Reynolds, Sana. "Editing: The Hidden Management Tool." *Communication World,* October/November 1996, pp. 20–22.

Tixier, Maud. "How Cultural Factors Affect Internal and External Communication." *Communication World,* February/March 1997, pp. 23–25. Writing material for a diverse multicultural audience.

Wilcox, Dennis L., and Nolte, Lawrence W. *Public Relations Writing and Media Techniques.* New York: Addison Wesley Longman, 4th edition, 2001. Various chapters deal with news releases, media advisories, pitch letters, newsletters, magazines, and other organizational publications.

Wylie, Ann. "Cut through the Clutter: How to Make the Next Piece You Write Easier to Read and Understand." *Public Relations Tactics,* September 2001, p. 12. Style tips to improve impact of public relations writing.

Spoken Tactics

preview

The objective of this chapter is to explain spoken tactics in public relations and how such assignments as writing speeches and conducting news conferences are handled. The problem of rumors also is examined.

Topics covered in the chapter include:

- Face-to-face discussion
- Speechwriting techniques
- Staging a speech
- Conducting a news conference
- Press parties and tours
- Interviews
- Conducting meetings
- Word-of-mouth

Face-to-Face Discussion

A recent inductee into the hall of fame sponsored by the Atlanta Chapter of the Public Relations Society of America shared his keys to career success. He stated that the crucial component was personal communication. Speaking to students at his induction, he offered a tip learned decades before from his own mentor: Your highest daily priority should be to return all phone calls in person before any other work is done.

A conversation *face-to-face* between two persons is widely regarded as the most effective form of interpersonal communication. This is certainly true in the world of work. The chemistry of personality that can develop by calling on a client or colleague is not easily defined but can be tremendously valuable.

Telephone or face-to-face conversation also offers immediate clarification and feedback so that misunderstandings are minimized. Although e-mail also offers this immediacy and can emulate some characteristics of conversation, it is no substitute. Because the written word does not convey nuance or emotional tone, it can be easily misconstrued. E-mail messages often appear harsh and curt, leading to communication problems.

Visualize these typical situations: A public relations representative at an editor's desk explaining the reasons for her hospital client's fund drive; a corporate vice president for public affairs calling on a city council member to urge the opening of a new street to reduce traffic congestion outside the company's manufacturing plant. In each case, the logic of the persuader's arguments is reinforced (or undermined) by the impact of the individual's personality. Sincerity impresses the listener. An aggressive, demanding approach arouses irritation. A smile, perhaps a casual quip, and a friendly but respectful manner help immeasurably in getting one's message across.

The personal call is among the most potent methods a public relations practitioner can use. It may fail, however, no matter how good the cause, if the caller arrives ill-prepared and handles the presentation clumsily. Here, from a veteran newspaper editor who has listened to hundreds of across-the-desk public relations presentations, is advice on how to present a case effectively:

1. *Telephone in advance for an appointment.* Then be on time. Don't walk in "cold" and expect a hearing.
2. *Identify yourself and your purpose immediately.* Present a business card if possible, so the recipient has your name and affiliation at hand during the discussion and for filing later.
3. *Be concise.* Editors, program directors, and other opinion-makers on whom you call are busy. Even those who appear relaxed and casual have other work waiting to be done. Make your presentation succinctly. Describe what your client plans to do, explain the purpose of the program, tell how it will help the public, and state specifically what support you hope to receive from the person you are addressing. Respond to your host's questions without meandering up side conversational paths, politely seek a commitment if that seems appropriate, then leave.
4. *Don't oversell.* Don't plead. Persons who receive presentations dislike being pressured and instinctively build defense mechanisms against excessively emotional "pitches." Never say, "You must help us!" Persons whose aid you seek resent being told that they "must" do anything.

5. *Express appreciation for your host's time and for anything he or she can do to assist your cause.*
6. *Leave behind written material—a brochure, a news release, a fact sheet—for your host to study later.* Be certain that the material includes a telephone number at which you can be reached for further information. Asking your host to read the material while you sit there is a poor tactic, unless it is very short; the result may be a hasty, reluctant scanning rather than the thoughtful reading you desire.

   If the presentation can be made at lunch, over coffee or perhaps over a drink, outside the office setting, its impact may be stronger.
7. *Follow up with a note of appreciation for the reception, expressing hope that the recipient can use the information you left.* It subtly reminds the person to read the material, if that hasn't happened, and to do something about it.

   If you are working with an editor or program director in a small community, or with a person you know well, the approach can be more informal.

Face-to-face discussion also is an essential tool for open communication within business organizations. Such conversations between management representatives and supervisors, supervisors and foremen, and management and union officers spread understanding of a company policy or a new product among the employees. Slightly less intimate, but almost as effective if well done, is the small-group discussion directed toward the same goal. Internal communication through staff study meetings, employee training sessions, and department meetings creates a more competent, motivated workforce and identifies areas of employee dissatisfaction. (A discussion on how to conduct an effective meeting appears later in this chapter.)

A blind spot in company management, in small firms as well as large ones, is the too-frequent assumption that employees down the line know the reasons for company policies. The cynical wisecrack "There's no reason for it, it's just company policy" shows a weakness of management. Explaining *why* something is done is just as important as explaining *how* it should be done.

Person-to-person conversations form only one segment of a campaign to inform the public and mold opinion through the spoken word. A public relations campaign usually must reach many persons at the same time. This can be done orally through speeches, news conferences, and appearances of representatives on radio and television. Although the impact of a speaker's personality on individual listeners may be diminished, the sheer abundance of simultaneous contacts speeds up distribution of the message. Repetition in several forms creates greater awareness.

Each of these spoken methods will be discussed in detail. The text will first examine the speech: how to plan it, how to write it, and how to assist the speaker who delivers it.

Assignment: Speechwriting

Public relations practitioners frequently are called on to write speeches for their employers or clients. As speechwriters, their role is a hidden one. They labor silently to produce the words that may sparkle like champagne when poured forth by their employers from the lecterns of convention halls. In the White House, the wraps of anonymity usually are drawn around the writers who churn out speeches and statements for the president of the United States. A president who utters a memorable phrase gets the credit, but some unknown writer in a back office probably created it.

There is nothing discreditable about this. Presidents have more urgent tasks than to think up catchy quotations. Speechwriters find personal satisfaction in creating competent speeches for someone else.

Most of the largest corporations employ speechwriters, some of whom receive annual salaries from $70,000 to $120,000. Freelance writers often command from $1000 to $10,000 for a speech. The writer's copy must be approved by numerous executives, and it sometimes becomes badly mangled in editing battles.

Turning loose a speaker, especially an inexperienced one, before an audience without a text, or at least a careful outline, may be an invitation to boredom. The "and . . . uhs" and "as I was sayings" will proliferate like rabbits. The audience will squirm, inwardly at first and then conspicuously in their chairs, as the speaker stumbles along. The opportunity to deliver a message that informs, persuades, and entertains listeners has been thrown out the window. That is why speakers who lack the time or the skill to do their own preparation need able speechwriters.

Some speakers prefer to work from notes rather than read a text. In that event, the writer should prepare a full speech for the speaker to study, then reduce the main elements of it to note cards arranged in proper sequence. Talking from notes increases the air of spontaneity for an experienced speaker. It also magnifies the risk, however, that the speaker will meander and lose control of the time.

A written speech should reflect the personality and voice patterns of the speaker, not those of the writer, no matter what type of assignment. The writer may be called on to prepare: a light 20-minute talk for the service club luncheon circuit, a provocative 10-minute statement to open a panel discussion, or a scholarly 45-minute lecture to a university audience.

The Basic Points of Speechwriting

Whatever the assignment, here are basic points for the speechwriter to keep in mind:

1. *A speech should say something of lasting value.* Even a talk intended to entertain, full of fluffy humor, should be built around a significant point. A speech needs both content and style; without the former, the latter is empty.

   One veteran speechwriter for a large corporation and an influential trade organization applies what he calls the "door test" to the speeches he writes. After hearing a dinner speaker, the listeners go out the door of the banquet room and on entering the doors of their homes are asked by their spouses what the dinner speaker said. In reply, the listeners give the essence of the speech as they remember it. Was there a message clear and concise enough to remember? Did the speech pass the door test?

2. *A speech should concentrate on one, or at most two, main themes.*

3. *A speech needs facts.* The information must be accurate. The writer's skill as a researcher is put to the test, to dig up information that will illustrate and emphasize the speaker's theme. Before a speaker makes a statement, the information in it should be verified beyond any doubt.

4. *The type of audience should influence the style and content of the speech.* When a company celebrates its 50th anniversary with a reception and dinner dance for its employees, they don't want to hear the president drone on for 30 minutes about the corporate financial structure. The setting calls for some joking, a few nostalgic stories, references to some individuals by name, words of appreciation

for what the employees have contributed, and a few upbeat words about the future. On the other hand, a speech to securities analysts is not the time for droll stories. The audience wants facts on which to base investment decisions, not entertainment.

5. *Clarity in speechwriting is essential.* If the listeners don't understand what the speaker is saying, everyone's time is wasted. This happens when the speech contains complicated sentences, technical information that the speaker fails to explain in terms the audience can comprehend, and excessive jargon or "inside" talk. The speechwriter's challenge is to simplify the message while keeping its significance.

An Example of Speechwriting

To determine how the speechwriting process works, consider how a specific assignment could be handled. The assistant public relations director of a large regional restaurant chain is assigned to prepare a speech for the general manager to deliver at a chamber of commerce banquet in a middle-sized city where the company has recently opened a luxury restaurant. What does the practitioner do?

First, she must know what the speaker desires to emphasize. The management has heard extensive word-of-mouth criticism about the high dinner prices the new restaurant charges. Some business has been lost because of this. The general manager sees the speech invitation as an opportunity to explain why the restaurant must charge these prices and to stress what good values the dinners really are. To do so, he must give the audience a frank look at the restaurant business—an opening for the speechwriter to spice up the necessary financial information with whimsical backstage anecdotes.

Twenty minutes of such material, brightly presented, will entertain and inform this business-oriented audience. It will demonstrate that the restaurant organization is efficiently run and does its best to provide residents with a distinctive place to dine at the lowest feasible cost. Indeed, here is an excellent public relations moment.

The speechwriter must use her speech-planning appointment with the general manager to learn what he wants to say and to study his style. Does he speak intensely or in a casual, wry manner? Is his speech staccato or a bit fulsome? Probably he can provide her with one or two of his favorite restaurant anecdotes. She can talk later with other officials of the company to obtain additional stories.

With this guidance in hand, how does the practitioner organize and write the speech?

A speech is built in blocks, joined by transitions. The following pattern for assembling the blocks provides an all-purpose outline on which most speeches can be built:

1. *Introduction (establishment of contact with audience).*
2. *Statement of main purpose of speech.*
3. *Development of theme—with examples, facts, and anecdotes.* Enumeration of points in 1, 2, 3 order is valuable here. It gives a sense of structure and controlled use of time.
4. *Statement of secondary theme, if there is one.*
5. *Enunciation of principal point to which speaker has been building.* This main point will be the heart of the speech.

6. *A pause at this plateau, with an anecdote or two.* This is a soft place while the audience absorbs the principal point just made.
7. *Restatement of theme in summary form.*
8. *Brief, brisk conclusion.*

This plan of speech organization is *deductive;* that is, the central theme is stated almost at the beginning, and the points that follow support and illustrate the theme. A less common type of organization is *inductive.* In this type of speech, the speaker presents points of information and arguments leading up to a statement of the principal theme near the end.

■ Introduction Following the preceding deductive outline, the speechwriter uses the first two minutes of the allotted 20 to build rapport between the general manager and the audience. The manager explains that when his company first considered coming to this city, he doubted that the area would support the luxury type of restaurant it operates. But the chamber of commerce convinced him that it would, and he is delighted that he had the good sense to listen (a light, slightly self-disparaging touch). He congratulates the chamber on the excellent statistical material it provided.

Then come the building blocks leading up to the conclusion.

■ Statement of Main Purpose The speaker says he wants to tell the audience about how a luxury restaurant operates, what its problems are, and why the customer sees things done a certain way. A summary of purpose in a single theme sentence at this point gives the speech a solid foundation. Almost as an aside he remarks, "Perhaps this will help you understand why our dinners cost as much as they do."

■ Development The manager states his company's total investment in opening this restaurant and reveals the number of people needed to run it . . . mentions kitchen jobs the diner never knows about . . . lists how many potatoes, steaks, heads of lettuce, and pounds of coffee are consumed in a week . . . relates a story about the night when the maitre d' had a full book of reservations and the salad chef walked out in a huff after a quarrel with his waitress girlfriend . . . describes how the chain's bill for pork and beef has soared.

■ Statement of Secondary Theme The speaker explains how the restaurant chooses its menus. He describes research into which entrees sell well or poorly, nutritional factors, and the difficulties in finding reasonable prices for the high-quality foodstuffs that will maintain the restaurant's standards of excellence.

■ Enunciation of Principal Point Operation of a top-flight restaurant in a time of high labor costs and rising food prices is a risky business, subject to the vagaries of weather, the economy, and the largely unpredictable turns of public fancy. By its steady growth, his organization has proved that a significant percentage of the public, "including here in this city," will patronize a restaurant that serves fine food with alert service in a distinctive setting. "Our challenge is to do this at the lowest prices we can."

■ Pause on Plateau The manager relates an anecdote about a diner who tried to steal some silverware, only to have it drop out of his pocket near the front door. The story illustrates problems of operating a restaurant.

Restatement of Theme The speaker's summary emphasizes his pride in the way local diners have patronized the new restaurant, proving his belief that the establishment provides the city with a type of high-quality dining that its citizens want and appreciate.

Brief Conclusion The audience hears a bit of news: The speaker announces that the restaurant has arranged to receive ample supplies of a popular but relatively rare fish. Next week the restaurant will add the fish, prepared in an unusual manner, to the menu at a special low introductory price. He invites everyone to come and try it.

One more step remains to make this a thoroughly successful public relations appearance. The speaker knows that the audience will be invited to ask questions; he has had the speechwriter give him a list of antagonistic queries he may receive. His ability to answer the tough ones will improve the good impression his speech has made.

Speechwriting Techniques

The first principle in writing words to be spoken is to make them flow in the way a person usually talks. Writing intended for the ear must be simpler in construction and more casual in form than writing meant for the eye. Instead of saying, "the Chicago man," make it "the man from Chicago"; it sounds more natural. Contractions such as *don't* and *won't* increase the sense of informality.

Short, straightforward sentences are best. To provide variety, an occasional long sentence is acceptable if its structure is simple. So is a scattering of sentences beginning with brief dependent clauses. Often the ear fails to comprehend as fully and quickly as the eye does because the listener is easily distracted or may not hear clearly. The audio channel becomes clogged. A person can read a complicated sentence again and again until its meaning is clear. A spoken sentence, however, is heard only once. Thus a speaker should repeat key points of the speech, couching them if possible in slightly different form.

Studies indicate that the average person listens four times as rapidly as the average person speaks. Thus the listener may be thinking about other matters while hearing the speaker. Holding the listener's undivided attention is difficult; recapitulation of main points helps the listener retain at least the main thrust of the speech.

Here, for example, is a sentence from a published news story that would be unacceptable in a speech text because of its intricate structure:

> Wright, who has agreed to pay the fine, said she believes the commission's action, which comes three weeks before the Nov. 2 election, will have no effect on her reelection campaign against Democrat C. D. (Dick) Stine.

If the material were written as follows, listeners could comprehend it far more easily:

> Wright has agreed to pay the fine. The commission's action comes only three weeks before the November 2nd election. But Wright believes that it will not affect her campaign for reelection against Democrat Dick Stine.

An excellent way to grasp the concept of writing for speech is to close your eyes and listen to people around you talk. Do the same thing while hearing a radio newscast, which has been written especially for the ear. Visualize how the words you are hearing would appear on paper. Notice how often people use fragments of sentences.

The incomplete sentence is used quite effectively in this excerpt from a speech by John C. Bedrosian, president of the American Federation of Hospitals. His topic, the high cost of medical care, was complex, and he dealt with the problem in depth. A brief text, however, kept the speech from bogging down. Brief sentences, sentence fragments, and short words are used to offset such necessary long ones as *catastrophic* and *ambulatory:*

> Hospital care is expensive. There is no denying that. It is essentially designed to provide care to the critically ill. Catastrophic illnesses. Major surgeries. Serious injuries. Any institution that is equipped and staffed to provide the highest level of care is by its very nature not economically appropriate for low-level care.
>
> That's why we are witnessing the growth of alternative care and treatment sources. Satellite clinics, for example, surgi-centers, and other ambulatory care facilities. Skilled nursing homes for recuperation from illness or surgery. Home health care, a concept that has really only gotten started.
>
> All of these are approaches that match the level of care to the need, and at a significant reduction in cost.

A speaker normally delivers a text at the rate of about 150 words a minute. So, when preparing a 20-minute speech, the writer must produce about 3000 words.

Here are tips on writing from professional speechwriters:

- *Read aloud the words you have written, to be certain that they sound natural to the ear.*
- *Avoid clauses that complicate sentences.*
- *Use smooth transitions to move from one section of the speech to the next.*
- *Use rhetorical questions.*
- *Draw verbal pictures.*
- *Be wary of jokes.*
- *Quote statistics sparingly.*

Visual Aids for a Speech

A speech often can be strengthened by use of visual devices. Graphs and charts, a common kind of visual aid, are only as good as their visibility to the audience. A chart too complicated for easy comprehension or too small to be read from the rear of the room is almost useless. Slides projected onto a screen are frequently used. They must be simple in content; holding a slide on the screen long enough for the audience to study involved information creates restlessness. (Audiovisual aids are discussed in Chapter 22.)

Use of objects is still another form of visual aid for a speaker. The model of a new company product displayed near the lectern is an example. A blown-up reproduction of a United Way fund drive emblem hung behind the head table is another.

Staging a Speech

Effective speeches don't just happen. They have to be rehearsed and prepared—or, in the language of the theater, "staged." Organizations frequently rely upon a practitioner's understanding of potential audiences to ensure that a speaking engagement helps the organization get a positive message across. And to create a pool of talented speakers, some organizations establish training programs.

In some instances, visual effects of staging can be inadvertent and humorous. During a gubernatorial campaign stop in Pennsylvania, a speech meant especially for television coverage was staged in a library where the candidate listed programs he would fund if elected. Unfortunately, he was standing just under the sign for the "Fiction" section.

The Practitioner's Role

Public relations practitioners who write speeches are frequently called on by management to give their opinion about whether the company should accept an invitation to speak and, if so, how the firm should use such a forum to present its views and policies in the most favorable light.

When an invitation arrives, the first decision to be made is whether a speech should be delivered at all. This is where the practitioner's advice may be sought by company management. Thought should be given as to whether the size and significance of the audience justify the time and effort involved. Although this may sound a little arrogant, it is only a matter of practicality.

On the other hand, a public relations representative whose employer desires to make speeches can create ample opportunities. Offers to make a speaker available to organizations without charge may be made discreetly by letter, telephone, or word-of-mouth. The approach is to suggest that the speaker has an unusual message that should be of special interest to the group being solicited. If the speaker is a corporation executive, the hosts should be assured that they will not be subjected to a heavy sales pitch.

Management also is likely to seek out the practitioner's opinion when a speaker must appear before a hostile audience—a real test of public relations skill. While not always pleasant, the experience can pay dividends. A land developer who proposes construction of a shopping center close to a school cannot expect a cordial welcome when addressing an audience of parents. If the speaker can command respect by a pleasant, frank manner, however, some members of the audience may realize that he is not the ogre they had imagined. Having achieved this, the speaker can lay out his arguments and at least make the audience aware of his reasoning. People usually respect frankness.

Members of the external public are not the only audiences an organization's speaker may address. Management representatives—including public relations staff members—frequently make speeches within the organization, as part of an employee relations program. During times of internal hostility such as labor disputes, public relations expertise may be essential.

Speech Training Programs

Even a brilliantly written speech can fail if it is delivered poorly. Upper-echelon executives for whom speeches are a required part of the job should be offered training by professionals in the techniques of public speaking. Progressive organizations also search among their employees for men and women who can be trained to speak effectively.

Employees selected may be assigned to attend on-the-job training sessions in speechmaking. They are instructed in such basics as diction, stage presence, voice projection, reading audience reaction, and handling questions. Videocassette tapes and other teaching aids enhance the instruction.

When a company needs to explain its policy to employees and seek their cooperation, top-echelon officials aren't always the best ones to do it. A well-trained fellow worker in a department may succeed better in convincing his or her colleagues to authorize automatic payroll deduction for United Way contributions than a speaker sent out from the executive offices. When management trains speakers from various work levels, provides them with well-written speeches appropriate for their needs, and gives them a suitable setting, they can fill a valuable role in the internal communication chain. What's more, they can give management enlightening feedback from their colleagues.

Helping the Speaker Polish and Present the Speech

After writing a draft of a speech, the writer should go over it with the speaker, who may request changes. By listening to the speaker read the material aloud, the writer can detect clumsy portions and smooth them out. The more frequently a speaker reads the text aloud in practice, the better the on-stage performance will be. A videotape made of a practice session will show the speaker where improvement is needed.

The finished version of a speech should be word-processed in large type with plenty of spacing.

Writing an introduction and sending it to the person who will present the speaker is a good tactic. This assures that the information about the speaker will be correct. Although the introducer may alter the material, the content probably will be approximately what the public relations representative desires.

At the scene of the speech, the public relations representative should take several actions:

- *The microphone and other apparatus should be tested.* The audiovisual equipment should be set up and checked and the slide projector focused. Charts or flipcards should be numbered and arranged in correct order on an easel. The technician capable of dealing with last-minute equipment failures should be identified to minimize the awkward moments for a speaker seeking assistance at the podium.
- *Extra copies of the speech should be brought along.* Additional copies are for distribution to the news media and to listeners who request a copy.
- *The speech should be recorded.* The tape can be used to settle any disputes over what the speaker said, to provide "actuality" excerpts for local radio stations, and to assemble material for a postmortem session between speaker and writer analyzing the performance.

Two other steps can be taken to obtain additional exposure for an important speech: (1) Copies can be mailed to a selected list of opinion leaders, and (2) the speech can be rewritten as an article for a company publication or submitted to a suitable trade magazine. Robert Dilenschneider, principal of the Dilenschneider Group, delivered an address about "Spin" and public relations at the *Bulldog Reporter*/PR Newswire Media Relations Conference in New York City. Dilenschneider then converted the speech into an op-ed piece for the *Wall Street Journal* (June 1, 1998). The speech achieved far wider exposure for Dilenschneider as a leader in the public relations industry than if it had only been used as an address to industry insiders.

Speakers' Bureaus and Hotlines

Speakers' bureaus operated by trade associations, social agencies, and corporations constitute an important instrument for bringing speakers and audiences together. They function something like a company's pool of internal speakers, but on a more elaborate scale. Speakers developed within an organization are made available by the

EDISON EXPRESSions is Southern California Edison's employee-volunteer speaker organization. Since 1971, our speakers have given thousands of free, multilingual presentations to service clubs, schools, senior and consumer groups, business organizations, and community groups throughout the region on a broad range of electric industry topics. Whether it is a classroom presentation, a luncheon or a community event, we are your one-stop speakers' bureau for all occasions.

An *EDISON INTERNATIONAL*SM Company

www.sce.com

THE POWER BEHIND PEACE OF MIND SM

Recognizing the immense ethnic diversity in its service area, Southern California Edison operates a speakers' bureau, EDISON EXPRESSions. Consisting of company employees, speakers are available in several Asian languages and in Spanish. More than 26 percent of Southern California Edison customers speak Spanish with limited English capability, and 16 percent speak an Asian language.

bureaus upon request. The bureaus also seek to place speakers before influential audiences. Utility companies, which have a constant need to build friendly community relations, are especially heavy users of the speakers' bureau concept. Typically, a telephone company in Illinois has a bureau with 42 trained speakers who talk before all types of clubs and civic organizations. Before being sent out to represent the company, the speakers receive professional training and must pass auditions.

Talent-booking agencies that place professional speakers for a fee sometimes also call themselves speakers' bureaus. The roles of these two types of speakers' bureaus are quite dissimilar: One provides speakers without charge, to promote the sponsor, while the other does so on a direct profit-making basis. For example, a speaker's bureau will book former speaker of the house Newt Gingrich for $50,000 per appearance, while the Montana Committee for the Humanities will provide a historian free of charge to speak in the local library. It is important to distinguish between the two types of speakers' bureaus.

Somewhat related to the organizational speakers' bureau is the telephone hotline service operated by some trade associations and companies to provide quick answers, especially to the news media. This facility generally offers toll-free telephone service using the 800 prefix. The following advertisement by the Edison Electric Institute Information Service in *Editor & Publisher,* the newspaper trade journal, illustrates how the hotline functions:

> You Don't Need a Press Conference to Get the Energy Story
>
> Let's have a conference right now.
>
> And it won't even cost you a dime.
>
> One of our experts is ready to help you with your newsbreak, feature, or editorial.
>
> Ask for facts, background, and the national perspective on electric energy.
>
> Ask about energy sources, economics, and the environment.
>
> Because energy is one of the crucial issues in American life today, there's someone on the hotline, 24 hours a day, 7 days a week.
>
> Just think. By using the phone, you'll be saving energy while writing about it.
>
> Call toll-free 800-424-8897.

Special Types of Speaking Opportunities

A speaker addressing an audience represents one-way communication. Listeners receive the message, either accepting or rejecting it, but do not engage in a dialogue during which they can challenge the speaker's statements. The speaker commands the situation. The only exception occurs when a speaker agrees to accept questions from the floor—a practice that some speakers relish but others avoid, either because they realize that they do not perform well spontaneously or they desire to avoid embarrassing questions.

The News Conference

At a news conference, communication is two-way. The person speaking for a company or a cause submits to questioning by reporters, usually after a brief opening statement. A news conference makes possible quick, widespread dissemination of the sponsor's information and opinions through the news media. It avoids the time-consuming task of presenting the information to the news outlets individually and assures that the

U.N. Secretary General Kofi Annan, second from left, and Hamid Karzai, right, listen to a reporter's question during a joint news conference at the Presidential Palace in Kabul, Afghanistan. Annan was on a visit to review efforts to rebuild the war-ravaged country. Part of the standard procedure is to have a news conference so leaders can answer questions from journalists.

intensely competitive newspapers and electronic media hear the news simultaneously. From a public relations point of view, these are the principal advantages of the news conference. Against these important pluses must be weighed the fact that the person holding the conference is open to severe and potentially antagonistic questioning.

In public relations strategy, the news conference can be either an offensive or a defensive device, depending on the client's need.

Most news conferences—or press conferences, as they frequently are called—are *positive* in intent; they are affirmative actions to project the host's plans or point of view. A corporation may hold a news conference to unveil a new product whose manufacture will create many new jobs, or a civic leader may do so to reveal the goals and plans for a countywide charity fund drive she will head. Such news conferences should be carefully planned and scheduled well in advance under the most favorable circumstances.

Public relations specialists also must deal frequently with unanticipated, controversial situations. A business firm, an association, or a politician becomes embroiled in difficulty that is at best embarrassing, possibly incriminating. Press and public demand an explanation. A barebones printed statement is not enough to satisfy the clamor and may draw greater press scrutiny of the stonewalling organization. A well-prepared spokesperson may be able to achieve a measure of understanding and sympathy by issuing a carefully composed printed statement when the news conference opens. According to experimental research funded by Ketchum PR's SMART Grant program, when the company has a good reputation, audiences will accept a sincere apology. Kennesaw State University professor Lisa Lyon found, however, that organizations with a bad reputation may actually be better off taking a defensive stance.

No matter how trying the circumstances, the person holding the news conference should create an atmosphere of cooperation and project a sincere intent to be helpful. The worst thing he or she can do is to appear resentful of the questioning. The person never should succumb to a display of bad temper. A good posture is to admit that the situation is bad and that the organization is doing everything in its power to correct it, the approach described by Professor Timothy Coombs at Wayne State University as the "mortification" strategy. (Further discussion of crisis public relations appears in Chapter 8.)

Rarely, an organization or public person caught in an embarrassing situation foolishly attempts to quiet public concern by holding a news conference that really isn't a news conference. The host reads a brief, inadequate statement, then refuses to answer questions from reporters. This practice alienates the press.

Two more types of news conferences are held. One is spontaneous, arising out of a news event: the winner of a Nobel Prize meets the press to explain the award-winning work or a runner who has just set a world's record breathlessly describes his feelings. The other type is the regularly scheduled conference held by a public official at stated times, even when there is nothing special to announce. Usually this is called a briefing—the daily State Department briefing, for example.

■ **Planning and Conducting a News Conference** First comes the question, "Should we hold a news conference or not?" Frequently the answer should be "No!" The essential element of a news conference is *news.* If reporters and camera crews summoned to a conference hear propaganda instead of facts, or information of minor interest to a limited group, they go away disgusted. Their valuable time has been wasted—and it *is* valuable. If editors send reporters to a conference that has been called merely to satisfy the host's sense of self-importance, they resent the fact. If the material involved fails to meet the criteria of significant news, a wise public relations representative will distribute it through a press release.

Every news outlet that might be interested in the material should be invited to a news conference. An ignored media outlet may become an enemy, like a person who isn't asked to a party. The invitation should describe the general nature of the material to be discussed so an editor will know what type of reporter to assign.

What hour is best? This depends upon the local media situation. If the city has only an afternoon newspaper, 9:30 or 10 A.M. is good, because this gives a reporter time to write a story before a midday deadline. If the city's newspaper publishes in the morning, 2 P.M. is a suitable hour.

Another prime goal of news conference sponsors is the early evening newscasts on local television stations, or even network TV newscasts if the information is important enough. A conference at 2 P.M. is about the latest that a television crew can cover and still get the material processed at a comfortable pace for inclusion in a dinner-hour show. This time period can be shortened a little in an emergency.

A warning: A public relations representative in a city with only an afternoon newspaper who schedules a news conference after that paper's deadline, yet in time for the news to appear on the early evening television newscasts, makes a grave blunder. Newspaper editors resent such favoritism to television and have long memories. Knowledge of, and sensitivity to, local news media deadlines are necessary.

Deadlines for radio news reporters are less confining than those for newspapers and television, because radio newscasts are aired many times a day. The conference hours suggested for newspapers and television are suitable for radio as well, though.

Here are two pieces of advice from longtime public relations specialists to persons who hold news conferences:

1. *The speaker should never attempt to talk off-the-record at a news conference.* If the information is so secret that it should not be published, then the speaker shouldn't tell it to reporters. Many editors forbid their reporters to honor off-the-record statements, because too often the person making them is merely attempting to prevent publication of material that is legitimate news but might be embarrassing. Any statement made before a group will not stay secret long, anyway.

2. *The speaker should never lie!* If he or she is pushed into a corner and believes that answering a specific question would be unwise, it is far better to say, "No comment" in some form than to answer falsely. A person caught in a lie to the media suffers a critical loss of credibility.

Preparing the Scene At a news conference, public relations representatives resemble producers of a movie or television show. They are responsible for briefing the spokesperson, making arrangements, and assuring that the conference runs smoothly. They stay in the background, however.

Bulldog Reporter, a West Coast public relations newsletter, suggests the following checklist for a practitioner asked to organize a news conference. The time factors given are normal for such events as new product introductions, but conferences concerning spot news developments for the daily press and electronic media often are called on notice of a few days or even a few hours.

- Select a convenient location, one that is fairly easy for news representatives to reach with minimal travel time.
- Set the date and time. Times between midmorning and midafternoon are good. Friday afternoons are deadly, as are days before holidays.
- When possible, issue an invitation to a news conference about six to eight weeks ahead of time, but one month is acceptable. The invitation should include the purpose of the conference, names of spokespersons, and why the event has significant news value. Of course, the date, time, and location must be provided.
- Distribute a media release about the upcoming news conference when appropriate. This depends on the importance of the event.
- Write a statement for the spokesperson to give at the conference and make sure that he or she understands and rehearses it. In addition, rehearse the entire conference.
- Try to anticipate questions so the spokesperson can readily answer difficult queries. Problem/solution rehearsals prepare the spokesperson.
- Prepare printed materials for distribution at the conference. These should include a brief fact sheet with names and titles of participants, a basic news release, and basic support materials. This is sometimes called a press kit.
- Prepare visual materials as necessary. These may include slides, transparencies, posters, or even a short videotape.
- Make advance arrangements for the room. Be sure that there are enough chairs and leave a center aisle for photographers. If a lectern is used, make certain that it is large enough to accommodate multiple microphones.
- Arrive 30 to 60 minutes early to double-check arrangements. Test the microphones, arrange name tags for invited guests, and distribute literature.

Some organizations provide coffee and sweet rolls for their media guests as a courtesy. Others find this gesture unnecessary because most of the newspeople are in a hurry. Liquor should not be served at a regular news conference. Such socializing should be reserved for the press party, discussed in the next section.

At some news conferences, still photographers are given two or three minutes to take their pictures before questioning begins. Some photographers complain that, thus restricted, they cannot obtain candid shots. If free shooting is permitted, as usually is the best practice, the physical arrangements should give the photographers operating space without allowing them to obstruct the view of reporters.

A practitioner should take particular care to arrange the room in such a way that the electronic equipment does not impede the print reporters. Some find it good policy for the speaker to remain after the news conference ends and make brief on-camera statements for individual TV stations, if their reporters request this attention. Such statements should not go beyond anything the speaker has said to the entire body of reporters.

A final problem in managing a news conference is knowing when to end it. The public relations representative serving as backstage watchdog should avoid cutting off the questioning prematurely. To do so creates antagonism from the reporters. Letting a conference run down like a tired clock is almost as bad. A moment comes when reporters run out of fresh questions. A speaker may not recognize this. If not, the practitioner may step forward and say something like, "I'm sorry, but I know some of you have deadlines to make. So we have time for just two more questions."

Presidential press conferences do not have this problem. Long-standing custom limits these conferences to 30 minutes. At that point, the senior news service reporter present calls out, "Thank you, Mr. President!" and the conference ends. Everyone concerned with public relations should study a presidential press conference on television. The kinds of questions asked, the manner in which the president answers them, the nature of any opening announcements, and the physical facilities—all of these provide clues for organizing news conferences of a more mundane nature.

The Press Party and the Press Tour

In the typical news conference, the purpose is to transmit information and opinion from the organization to the news media in a businesslike, time-efficient manner. Often, however, a corporation, an association, or a political figure wishes to deliver a message or build rapport with the media on a more personal basis; then a social setting is desirable. Thus is born the press party or the press trip.

■ The Press Party This gathering may be a luncheon, a dinner, or a reception. Whatever form the party takes, standard practice is for the host to arise at the end of the socializing period and make the "pitch." This may be a hard-news announcement, a brief policy statement followed by a question-and-answer period, or merely a soft-sell thank-you to the guests for coming and giving the host an opportunity to know them better. Guests usually are given press packets of information, either when they arrive or as they leave. Parties giving the press a preview of an art exhibit, a new headquarters building, and so forth are widely used.

The press party is a softening-up process, and both sides know it.

The advantages of a press party to its host can be substantial under the proper circumstances. During chitchat over food or drink, officials of the host organization become acquainted with media people who write, edit, or broadcast material about them. Although the benefit from the host's point of view is difficult to measure immediately, the party opens the channels of communication.

Also, if the host has an important policy position to present, the assumption—not necessarily correct—is that editors and reporters will be more receptive after a social hour. The host who expects that food and drink will buy favorable press coverage may receive an unpleasant surprise. Conscientious reporters and editors will not be swayed by a free drink and a plate of prime rib followed by baked Alaska. In their

PR casebook

"Junket Journalism" at Disney World

Disney World in Florida threw a press party to celebrate its 15th anniversary, and more than 10,000 people came.

The fact that Disney World paid the entire expense of some guests—and offered to do so for all of them—created a debate on media ethics that almost overshadowed the celebration. The party, incidentally, was a classic example of a created news event.

Disney World was well aware of the trend in the media against allowing reporters to accept free trips because the gift might influence the tone of their stories. Its invitations, sent nationwide, offered guests three alternatives:

1. Disney World and its travel-promotion partners would pay a guest's entire travel, lodging, and food costs.
2. The hosts would pay $150 a day of a guest's expense, and the guest's company would pay the balance.
3. A guest's employer would pay his or her entire expense.

Some guests used each method, but Disney World refused to say how many.

In an editorial, the *New York Times* claimed that media guests who accepted the free-trip offer had "debased" journalism and given the impression that the entire press was "on the take." The *St. Petersburg Times* called the party "junket journalism." Rebutting this position, some guests from smaller newspapers and broadcasting stations said that their companies could not afford such expensive travel, so this was the only way they could visit the entertainment center and write about it.

Disney World did not require its expense-paid guests to do anything in return. The park did receive a very large amount of publicity, generally favorable except for the media-ethics dispute. The total cost to Disney World and its cosponsors was estimated at around $7.5 million, according to *Editor & Publisher*.

view, they have already given something to the host by setting aside a part of their day for the party. They accept invitations to press parties because they wish to develop potential news contacts within the host's organization and to learn more about its officials.

Until a few years ago, though, *freeloading* by news people at parties was widespread and accepted as normal practice. Often press guests were given expensive gifts. In large cities, the expectations of certain reporters, especially those covering business and entertainment, became absurdly high. One coauthor of this book recalls attending a new-model announcement dinner for the press given some years ago by the Chevrolet division of General Motors. During dinner, the public relations director announced that there would be gifts for the guests when they went home. Each guest was asked to fill out a color preference card—blue, green, or tan.

One guest at the author's table asked another, quite seriously, "Do you think they are going to give us cars?" The other responded, with equal gravity, that perhaps they might. The actual gift proved to be an expensive blanket of the preferred color, packed in an individualized cedar chest. This type of payoff for attending the presentation became known as "loot." None of the media guests refused to accept the gift. (Present practice concerning gifts will be described shortly.)

Here are two actual examples of press parties:

1. Officials of Blue Cross in a midwestern state regularly hold a series of dinners in major cities for invited members of the local media. The guest lists include

men and women who cover the health field, have a role in editing stories about it, or comment on it editorially. During a cocktail party before dinner, Blue Cross officials mingle with the guests. The public relations consultant accompanying them helps with introductions. During dinner, the host group spreads itself around to sit with guests.

After dinner, the chief executive speaks briefly, explaining what Blue Cross regards as the significant trends and problems in health care. Then he opens the meeting to questions. Inevitably, queries center on why medical costs are so high. The public relations consultant distributes packets of news releases and fact sheets but no gifts.

2. A land developer invited local media guests and civic leaders to a luncheon at which he disclosed plans for a major shopping center at the edge of the city. Arriving guests received paste-on tags imprinted with their names, large folders containing news releases, photographs of the developer and of an artist's rendering of the project's exterior and interior, and a fact sheet giving the developer's biography and a list of projects he had built. The artist's renderings stood on easels around the room; a scale model of the project was displayed on a table. Drinks and luncheon were served. Then the developer spoke about the project and answered questions.

   The normal adjournment hour for luncheon sessions is 1:30 P.M. This one ran a few minutes past that hour because of the number of questions. No press luncheon ever should run past 2 P.M.

■ **The Press Tour** There are three kinds of press tours. The most common is a trip, often disparagingly called a "junket," during which editors and reporters are invited to inspect a company's manufacturing facilities in several cities, ride an inaugural flight of a new air route, or watch previews of the television network programs for the fall season in Hollywood or New York. The host usually picks up the tab for transporting, feeding, and housing the reporters.

A variation of the press tour is the familiarization trip. "Fam trips," as they are called, are offered to travel writers and editors by the tourism industry (see Chapter 19). Convention and visitor bureaus, as well as major resorts, pay all expenses in the hope that the writers will report favorably on their experiences. Travel articles in magazines and newspapers usually result from a reporter's "fam trip."

In the third kind of press tour, widely used in high-technology industries, the organization's executives travel to key cities to talk with selected editors; for example, top Apple Computer executives toured the East Coast to talk with key magazine editors and demonstrate the capabilities of the new Apple iMac computer. Depending on editors' preferences, the executives may visit a publication and give a background briefing to key editors, or a hotel conference room may be set up so that the traveling executives may talk with editors from several publications at the same time.

■ **The Ethics of Who Pays for What** In recent years, severe soul-searching by media members, as well as by professional public relations personnel who feel it is unethical to offer lavish travel and gifts, has led to increased self-regulation by both groups as to when a press tour or "junket" is appropriate and how much should be spent.

The policies of major dailies forbid employees to accept any gifts, housing, or transportation; the newspapers pay all costs associated with a press tour on which a staff member is sent. In contrast, some smaller dailies, weeklies, and trade magazines accept offers for an expense-paid trip. Their managers maintain that they don't have the resources of large dailies to reimburse an organization for expenses and such trips are legitimate for covering a newsworthy activity.

Some newspapers with policies forbidding acceptance of travel and gifts don't extend the restrictions to all departments. Reporters in the "hard news" area, for example, cannot accept gifts or travel, but such policy may not be enforced for reporters who write "soft news" for sports, travel, and lifestyle sections. Few newspapers, for example, pay for the press box seats provided for reporters covering a professional football game, nor does the travel editor usually pay the full rate for rooms at beach resorts that are the focus of travel articles.

Given the mixed and often confusing policies of various media, the public relations professional must use common sense and discretion. He or she, first of all, should not violate the PRSA code of ethics that specifically forbids lavish gifts and free trips that have nothing to do with covering a legitimate news event. Second, the public relations person should be sensitive to the policies of news outlets and should design events to stay within them. A wise alternative is to offer a reporter the option of reimbursing the company for travel and hotel expenses associated with a press tour.

In terms of gift-giving, the sensible approach is a token of remembrance such as a pen, note pad, or a company paperweight. Some large newspapers will not permit even these token gifts. (Ethics are discussed extensively in Chapter 3.)

Organizing a Press Party or Press Tour The key to a successful event is detailed organization. Every step of the process should be checked out meticulously.

In planning the press event, the practitioner has to consider a variety of details. Menus for a luncheon or dinner should be chosen carefully. Do any of the guests have dietary restrictions? Has the exact hour of serving been arranged with the restaurant or caterer, to allow sufficient time for the program? The usual check on microphone and physical facilities is essential.

Even such a seemingly trivial item as a name tag requires the practitioner's careful attention. Paste-on tags written in advance are lined up on a check-in table at the entrance to the room. A host or hostess hands the tags to the arriving guests. A guest who can be welcomed by name, without having to state it, feels subtly flattered. Almost inevitably, though, some name tags will be unclaimed because individuals who accepted fail to show up. In a perfect world, absentees would telephone to cancel their acceptances, but public relations life doesn't work that way. Occasionally, an invited person who failed to answer the invitation will arrive unexpectedly; blank name tags should be kept available for such a situation. Fouled-up transportation is perhaps the worst grief for a person conducting a press tour. For example, buses that failed to arrive at the departure point on time to carry press covering the Centennial Olympics in Atlanta marred the opening days of the Games and dampened coverage by some reporters throughout this highly successful, vast special event. Some guests may be prima donnas who will be dissatisfied with almost any hotel room assigned to them. None of the tour guests should be allowed to feel that others are receiving favored treatment. Maintaining a firm tour schedule is essential. At each stop, the host should round up the strays a few minutes before the departure time.

As much as possible, the tour host should "walk through" the entire route to confirm arrangements and look for possibly embarrassing hidden troubles. When North American Aviation introduced a new jet fighter to the national press at the Palmdale, California, airport in the Mojave desert, it asked the pilot to impress the guests by div-

The news interview, whether formal or informal, attracts a large number of reporters if the news is of high public interest. Here, the spokesperson is practically engulfed by a sea of reporters, photographers, and TV news crews.

ing and creating a sonic boom. He did so—and pieces of glass went flying through the reception area from windows broken by the impact of the boom. The pilot climbed to do it again, but the hosts stopped him in time by yelling into the radio, "Call it off!"

The Interview

Another widely used spoken method of publicizing an individual or a cause is the interview, which may appear in print form in newspapers and magazines or on a television and radio. Online computer interviews are a popular new method. The ability of the person being interviewed to communicate easily is essential to success. Although required to stay in the background, with fingers crossed that all goes well, a public relations specialist can do much to prepare the interviewee.

Andrew D. Gilman, president of CommCore in New York City, emphasizes the need for preparation. Said he: "I would no more think of putting a client on a witness stand or through a deposition without thorough and adequate presentation than I would ask a client to be interviewed by a skillful and well-prepared journalist without a similar thorough and adequate preparation."

Techniques for arranging interview appearances by clients are discussed in Chapter 11. This section will examine the steps the public relations representative can take to increase the odds for an effective performance.

Clear Purpose In all interviews, the person being questioned should say something that will inform or entertain the audience. The practitioner should prepare the interviewee to meet this need. An adroit interviewer attempts to develop a theme in the conversation—to draw out comments that make a discernible point or illuminate the character of the person being interviewed. The latter can help the interviewer—and his or her own cause as well—by being ready to volunteer specific information, personal data, or opinions about the cause under discussion as soon as the conversational opportunity arises.

In setting up an interview, the public relations person should obtain from the interviewer an understanding as to its purpose. Armed with this information, the practitioner can assemble facts and data for the client to use in the discussion. The practitioner also can aid the client by providing tips about the interviewer's style.

Some interviewers on the radio talk shows that have proliferated in recent years ask "cream puff" questions, while others bore in, trying to upset the guest into unplanned admissions or embarrassment. Thus it is especially important to be well acquainted with the interviewer's style, whether it be Larry King before a national audience of millions or a local broadcaster. Short, direct answers delivered without hesitation help a guest project an image of strength and credibility.

Print Differs from Broadcast A significant difference exists between interviews in print and those on radio and television. In a print interview, the information and character impressions the public receives about the interviewee have been filtered through the mind of the writer. The man or woman interviewed is interpreted by the reporter, not projected directly to the audience. On radio and television, however, listeners hear the interviewee's voice without intervention by a third party. During a television interview, where personality has the strongest impact of all, the speaker is both seen and heard. Because of the intimacy of television, a person with a weak message who projects charm or authority may influence an audience more than one with a strong message who does not project well. A charismatic speaker with a strong message can have enormous impact.

Know to Say No When an organization or individual is advocating a particular cause or policy, opportunities to give newspaper interviews are welcomed, indeed sought after. Situations arise, however, when the better part of public relations wisdom is to reject a request for an interview, either print or electronic. Such rejection need not imply that an organization has a sinister secret or fails to understand the need for public contact.

For example, a corporation may be planning a fundamental operational change involving an increase in production at some plants and the closing of another, outdated facility. Details are incomplete, and company employees have not been told. A reporter, either suspecting a change or by sheer chance, requests an interview with the company's chief executive officer.

Normally, the interview request would be welcomed, to give the executive public exposure and an opportunity to enunciate company philosophy. At this moment, however, public relations advisers fear that the reporter's questions might uncover the changes prematurely, or at least force the executive into evasive answers that might hurt the firm's credibility. So the interview request is declined, or delayed until a later date, as politely as possible. The next week, when all is in place, the chief executive announces the changes at a news conference. *Avoiding trouble is a hidden but vital part of a public relations adviser's role.* At a later time, the public relations representative might make a special effort to do the would-be interviewer a favor on a story.

An alternative approach would be for the chief executive officer to grant the interview, with the understanding that only topics specified in advance would be discussed. Very rarely is such an approach acceptable, however, because reporters usually resent any restrictions and try to uncover the reasons for them.

The Print Interview An interview with a newspaper reporter may last about an hour, perhaps at lunch or over coffee in an informal setting. The result of this person-to-person talk may be a published story of perhaps 400 to 600 words. The interviewer weaves bits from the conversation together in direct and indirect quotation form, works in background material, and perhaps injects personal observations about the interviewee. The latter has no control over what is published, beyond the self-control he or she exercises in answering the questions. Neither the person being interviewed nor a public relations representative should ask to approve an interview story before it is published. Such requests are rebuffed automatically as a form of censorship.

A talk with an entertainment personality is among the most common forms of newspaper interview. Many personality interview stories carrying Hollywood or New York datelines are proposed by practitioners endeavoring to build up a performer's image or to publicize a new motion picture or television series.

Excellent promotional results can be achieved in far less popular fields of endeavor than entertainment when the person interviewed has something unusual to offer. The following excerpt from an interview with a grower of kiwis demonstrates the point. Many readers, uncertain what kiwis are, would never guess that a man could become a millionaire by growing them. Notice how well prepared the grower was with quotable comments and pertinent facts about his unusual business. Publication of this *San Francisco Chronicle* interview was timed to the kiwi harvesting season; interest it created could be translated readily into purchases at the food store.

> Kiwi Pioneers Have Last Laugh
>
> When the three Tanimoto brothers planted their first acre of kiwi fruit 17 years ago, "we put it in back of our peach groves so people wouldn't laugh at us," recalled George Tanimoto.
>
> "Everybody laughed anyway, and we laughed too," Tanimoto said last week. "Now they say he's laughing all the way to the bank and it's true."
>
> Year after year, the Tanimoto brothers waited for a crop. Finally—after 5 years of fruitless ridicule—the first fuzzy brown egg-shaped pods of kiwi appeared on their vines.
>
> Tanimoto sold his maiden kiwi crop to Frieda Kaplan, a Los Angeles fruit dealer who happened to be allergic to kiwi. At first, he shipped the fruit south in three wooden boxes that looked suspiciously like coffins, then individually wrapped them in packages called "flats," because kiwis are very sensitive and will shrivel and shrink when exposed to gas fumes or other ripening fruit.
>
> Today, the 56-year-old Tanimoto is a millionaire because he didn't quit on what he affectionately calls the "Ugly Fruit." . . .

This interview is not a direct hard-sell job, nor can it be described as outright "puffery." The purpose from the newspaper's point of view was to tell readers something interesting. From a public relations point of view, the story distributes knowledge of the product involved, with the possibility that this knowledge will stimulate purchases.

Magazine interviews usually explore the subject in greater depth than those in newspapers, because the writer may have more space available. Most magazine interviews have the same format as those in newspapers. Others, such as those published in *Penthouse* and *U.S. News & World Report,* appear in question-and-answer form. These require prolonged taped questioning of the interviewee by one or more writers and editors. During in-depth interviews, the person interviewed must guard against saying something that has unfortunate repercussions.

A famous instance of this occurred when Jimmy Carter was running for president against President Gerald Ford. Carter is a deeply religious man, a fact his public relations advisers emphasized by publicizing his work as a Sunday School teacher and lay preacher in a Southern Baptist church. When they sensed that these pursuits made Carter appear too sanctimonious to voters less religiously inclined, his advisers sought to have him offset this image by being interviewed in *Playboy.*

In the published interview Carter, although happily married, admitted that he had "looked upon a lot of women with lust" and "committed adultery in my heart many times." Angry reactions from his conservative followers were swift. He had besmirched their perceived image of him. Although this frank admission of a common enough male trait made Carter seem more human to some voters, overall the interview statements damaged his campaign. He was, of course, elected anyway.

A third, even more elaborate, form of magazine interview story is the long profile, such as those published in *The New Yorker*. Reporters doing profiles usually travel with the interviewee, observing the subject at close range over extended periods. Before trying to interest a magazine in doing such a profile on a client or employer, the public relations adviser should be satisfied that the intended subject of the profile is willing to accept the interviewer on an intimate basis for long periods and will wear well under close scrutiny. Outbursts of anger, a dictatorial manner toward assistants, excessive drinking, and similar private habits produce a bad effect when revealed in print.

Radio and Television Interviews The possibilities for public relations people to have their clients interviewed on the air are immense. The current popularity of talk shows, both on local stations and syndicated satellite networks, provides many opportunities for on-air appearances in which the guest expresses opinions and answers call-in questions. (See Chapter 11.) A successful radio or television broadcast interview appearance has three principal requirements:

1. *Preparation.* Guests should know what they want to say.
2. *Concise speech.* Guests should answer questions and make statements precisely and briefly. They shouldn't hold forth in excessive detail or drag in extraneous material. Responses should be kept to 30 seconds or less, because seconds count on the air. The interviewer must conduct the program under severe time restrictions.
3. *Relaxation.* "Mike fright" is a common ailment for which no automatic cure exists. It will diminish, however, if the guest concentrates on talking to the interviewer in a casual person-to-person manner, forgetting the audience as much as possible. Guests should speak up firmly; the control room can cut

One spoken tactic that has the potential of reaching millions of people is the appearance on a national talk show. Here, Rudy Giuliani chats with Jay Leno on the *Tonight* show about his selection as "person of the year" by *Time* magazine for his outstanding work as mayor of New York in the aftermath of the September 11 terrorist attack.

down their volume if necessary. (Personal appearances on television are discussed in more detail in Chapter 22).

A public relations adviser can help an interview guest on all of these points. Answers to anticipated questions may be worked out and polished during a mock interview in which the practitioner plays the role of broadcaster. A tape recording or videotape of a practice session will help the prospective guest to correct weaknesses.

All too often, the hosts on talk shows know little about their guests for the day's broadcast. The public relations adviser can overcome this difficulty by sending the host in advance a fact sheet summarizing the important information and listing questions the broadcaster might wish to ask. On network shows such as David Letterman's, nationally syndicated talk shows such as Oprah Winfrey's, and local programs on metropolitan stations, support staffs do the preliminary work with guests. Interviewers on hundreds of smaller local television and radio stations, however, lack such staffs. They may go on the air almost "cold" unless provided with volunteered information.

Conducting a Meeting

Meetings are a major public relations tool in contemporary American life. They can be an extremely effective form of communication, or they can be incredible bores. Speakers who drone on too long and discussions that degenerate into petty quibbling act as soporifics on the audience. The hardness of chairs seems to increase by geometrical progression as the presiding officer introduces speaker after speaker. Collective attempts at mental telepathy by audience members urging the chairperson, "Please, please, let us go home," never seem to work. Far from accomplishing a worthwhile purpose, such meetings alienate their audiences. Everyone's time is wasted.

Plan Ahead to Optimize Meeting Time Meetings held for public relations purposes take many forms and vary greatly in size. Sessions may be informational and friendly, they may be heated and controversial, or they may be largely formalized gatherings such as banquets and dedications. Whatever the size and form of a meeting, good planning and an alert presiding officer can assure that the meeting accomplishes its purpose without leaving participants glassy-eyed with fatigue.

A computer information magazine, *MIS*, estimated after a survey that 12 million meetings are held in North America every business day. The survey also reported that executives spend an average of 16 hours a week in meetings for a total of 21 weeks a year. Many of these meetings, called for informational purposes, could be avoided by distribution of the material in printed form or by e-mail.

Guidelines for Meetings Preparation and firmness discreetly applied can control the dynamics of a meeting. The program should move briskly toward a goal. Few people have ever been heard to complain that a meeting was too short. Participants should have a feeling of movement without the appearance of hurry. By following these 13 guidelines, the organizers and presiding officer can create an effective session:

1. If the meeting is open to the public, an audience should be built through distribution of news releases and through other forms of publicity, such as posters and announcements at clubs.
2. An agenda should be made and followed.
3. The meeting should start promptly at the announced hour.

4. Speakers should be allotted specified amounts of time and urged to cooperate.
5. Physical arrangements of the hall should be checked in advance—acoustics, seating of the audience so that it is centered in front of the speakers, adequate lighting and fresh air, advance placement of visual aids, and the like.
6. If possible, the reading of minutes and reports should be avoided. Distribution of these documents in printed form is one way to solve this time-consuming problem.
7. Printed material should be distributed to an audience at the start or the close of a meeting, not while the session is in progress. The latter is distracting.
8. Discussion should be controlled even-handedly so that the audience has adequate opportunity to express itself but isn't allowed to wander from the theme.
9. In a controversial situation, public involvement techniques become especially valuable. Establish a time limit on each speaker from the floor—5 minutes, perhaps—and enforce it. Sometimes, one or two verbose individuals will dominate a discussion or a string of speakers will repeat similar harangues. Public involvement specialists employ nominal group techniques to defuse anger, to generate meaningful discussion, and to turn the event into a problem-solving session. Groups of four to six persons work on the issue at hand and then report to the plenary session, where their ideas are duly recorded.
10. In a panel discussion, the presiding officer should give all panel members equal opportunity to be heard. The moderator should try to distribute questions from the floor equitably among the panelists.
11. In long meetings such as a seminar or a training session, periodic recesses should be called; the meeting should resume promptly after the allotted time. A recess should be at least 10 minutes, 15 or 20 if the crowd is large. Provide comfortable chairs.
12. The meeting should be brought to a constructive conclusion. If there are several speakers, the best one should be scheduled last, if possible. At the end of a discussion, the presiding officer should summarize for the audience what was said. If a motion for action will be needed, arrangements may be made in advance for someone to offer it.
13. A closing time should be set and enforced.

Audio News Releases

Another form of spoken public relations is the audio news release, sent to radio stations in ready-to-broadcast form. This is commonly called a public service announcement (PSA). The amount of air time required to read a PSA, normally 30 or 60 seconds, is stated in the top of the release—vital information in tightly timed radio programming. PSAs are written in conversational radio style, often employing partial sentences.

Audio news releases often are written in interview form, in which an announcer asks questions and another voice gives responses.

The following 30-second example, distributed by the American Red Cross, illustrates the brisk, short-sentence style commonly used in these releases.

The American Red Cross
"R-Well Received"
Radio: 30
ZDMA-0378

Announcer:
Ever give a gift that didn't go over real big?
One that ended up in the closet the second you left the room?
There *is* a gift that's guaranteed to be well received.
Because it will save someone's life.
The gift is blood, and the need for it is desperate.
Over 20,000 people must choose to give this gift every day.
We need your help.
Please give blood. There's a life to be saved right now.
Call the American Red Cross at 1-800-GIVE LIFE.

Tag:
This public service message brought to you by The Advertising Council and The American Red Cross.

Word of Mouth

Often called "interpersonal communication" by academics, "word of mouth" is an ephemeral form of spoken communication difficult to isolate or measure but which has a major impact on the formation of public opinion. (See Chapters 8 and 10.)

Research shows that people seldom accept new ideas or products unless friends and relatives also endorse them. Studies also show that informal conversations among peers and friends influence our thinking and behavior more than television commercials or newspaper editorials do. The latest buzzword for this phenomenon is viral marketing.

What people tell one another about a political candidate, a product, a play, or a movie often circumvents the multimillion-dollar expenditures of advertising and marketing experts. Word of mouth is instrumental in making or breaking many products. The American automobile industry provides an example. The message traveled by word of mouth that imported cars were more reliable and better crafted than American cars. Despite massive advertising campaigns to change public perception, American automakers lost millions of buyers. Then, subtly, the mood changed, and talk among buyers became far more favorable to American cars.

One study shows that a person dissatisfied with a product tells a minimum of 10 to 15 people about the experience; in turn, these people tell others in an ever-widening ripple effect that condemns the product. On the other hand, if word of mouth designates a product as "trendy," sales soar.

The Insidious Problem of Rumors

Every professional communicator should understand how rumors start and, more important, how to combat them.

Simply stated, rumors are pieces of "information" that cannot be confirmed or verified by personal experience or a highly credible secondary source. They thrive when a combination of uncertainty and anxiety exists and authentic, official information is lacking or incomplete.

PR casebook

Procter & Gamble Fights a Rumor

Despite elaborate efforts to disprove the lie, Procter & Gamble has been plagued for years by a malicious, damaging rumor that it promotes devil worship.

The falsehood is based in part on the soap and food company's circular trademark, which shows a man-in-the-moon face in profile, looking at a field of stars representing the original American colonies. Rumormongers claim that this represents Satan.

Anonymous pamphlets distributed in schools and churches are the chief source of the rumor. They claim that a P & G executive appeared on a nationally televised talk show and pledged the company's profits to the Church of Satan.

The rumor became so intense in 1982 that the company received 15,000 calls in one month about it.

Procter & Gamble struck back with statements from the talk show producers that no P & G executive had ever appeared on their programs, and letters of support from ministers. As a last resort, it filed suits against a dozen persons it identified as rumormongers and won judgments against all of them, ordering them to cease.

In the early 1990s the rumor surfaced again, in the Southeast and Chicago. The company immediately mailed "truth packets" to hundreds of churches, schools, newspapers, and radio stations in those areas. Altogether, P & G has handled much more than 100,000 phone calls concerning the rumor.

The company won its first damage award in 1991—$75,000—from a couple found guilty of spreading the rumor. It also slightly revised the trademark.

Procter & Gamble took an even stronger legal step in 1996 by suing Amway Corporation, a competitor, and five Amway distributors for spreading the devil worship rumor. It charged that one distributor had used Amway's voice-mail system to spread the rumor and alleged that Amway was responsible for its distributors' conduct.

Results of a study commissioned by the Institute for Public Relations suggest that rumors are a common problem faced by public relations professionals. The study authors, Nicholas DiFonzo and Prashant Bordia, suggest that taking a proactive approach and providing formal communication to address the rumor are effective strategies to reduce uncertainty that leads to belief in the rumor. For example, when a company's future is in doubt because of a takeover or merger, employees invariably start rumors about layoffs. The same thing occurs when information is released that the company had a bad fiscal year. The rumors will persist until official information confirms them ("Yes, there will be layoffs") or denies them ("No layoffs are planned"). The key is whether employees trust management to tell the truth.

James Esposito and Ralph Rosnow, writing in *Management Review*, give four strategies for defusing rumors in a company:

1. *Keep employees informed.* Employees are especially sensitive about situations that may affect them directly, such as management–union relations, job advancement, opportunities for relocation, and potential layoffs. Be fully honest, because half-truths encourage additional rumors and destroy the credibility of official spokespersons.
2. *Pay attention to rumors.* If the source of employee anxiety can be determined, the underlying cause of the rumors is obvious. Then, by giving feedback to employees—letting them know how the situation is being dealt with—their fears should be allayed.

3. *Act promptly.* Rumors become more difficult to control as they harden with time. Get the facts out rapidly but don't repeat a false rumor, because repetition may foster belief. If the rumor is true, it must be confirmed.
4. *Educate personnel.* Actually, conducting a workshop on rumors and their destructive potential can help to stop rumors before they get started.

External rumors are more difficult to control, and they can have a devastating effect on a company or its products. Many rumors of this type circulate on the Internet, requiring rapid attention, sometimes called a real-time response. The Internet is also an emerging tool for monitoring chat rooms for rumors or issues that deserve attention.

Plagued by rumors that their company was connected with the Ku Klux Klan, the makers of Snapple ready-made teas decided to attack the problem head-on with an advertising campaign in San Francisco denouncing the tales as "outrageous."

One version of the rumor claimed that the illustration of a sailing ship on a label represented a slave ship. Actually, it depicted the Boston Tea Party. Another rumor charged that the encircled letter K on some labels symbolized the Klan. In fact, it indicated that the product was kosher. The company was unable to discover the source of the rumors.

Rumors that cannot be tracked to any particular cause are more difficult to deal with. McDonald's had to cope with a rumor that its ground beef contained earthworms as a protein supplement, and General Mills had to contend with the rumor that its Pop Rocks candy was explosive.

With a few exceptions, little evidence exists to support the suspicion by many people that rumors are started by commercial competitors. Instead, social psychologist Frederick Koening says, "Rumors validate the world view of those who believe them. If you believe in Satan—and many people do—you're likely to welcome a rumor that he's alive and well in Akron, Ohio."

People spread rumors by word of mouth for a number of reasons: (1) They are advocates of conspiracy theories and distrust all institutions of society; (2) they feel victimized by a complex, uncaring society and have high anxiety; (3) they seek recognition from peers by claiming to have "inside" information; and (4) they find the rumor somewhat plausible.

PR insights

Tips on Combating Rumors

Here are general guidelines for combating rumors:

1. Analyze the nature and impact of the rumor before taking corrective action. Many rumors are relatively harmless and dissipate within a short time.
2. Attempt to track the cause of the rumor and the geographical locations where it is prominent. This will help determine whether the rumor should be dealt with on a local, state, or national level.
3. Compile complete, authentic information that will either refute or confirm the rumor.
4. When denying a rumor, avoid repeating it more than necessary.
5. Use outside experts and credible public agencies to refute the rumor. The public views the U.S. Food and Drug Administration as more trustworthy than the president of a company defending the firm's product. If the rumor is only among certain highly identifiable groups, enlist the support of the groups' leaders.

Another example of environmental context is the continuing recall of products from the American marketplace. People increasingly express anxiety about the general safety of food products they are consuming, and from there it is only a short step to rumors about a particular product.

Measuring the Effects of Word-of-Mouth Communication

Although efforts to measure the specific effects of word-of-mouth communication have been relatively few, and of minor value, the Coca-Cola Company did obtain enlightening information from a study it sponsored concerning public reaction to its handling of consumer complaints.

Questionnaires were sent to hundreds of persons who had filed complaints with Coca-Cola's consumer affairs department. Responses showed that individuals who felt that their complaints had not been resolved satisfactorily told a median of nine to ten persons about their negative experience. Those who were completely satisfied told a median of four to five persons about their good results—a word-of-mouth distribution of bad news over good by a ratio of approximately two to one. Nearly 30 percent of those who felt that their complaints had not been resolved satisfactorily said they no longer bought Coca-Cola products. On the other hand, nearly 10 percent of the satisfied complainers reported that they now bought more Coca-Cola products as a result of the good treatment. Two lessons for companies trying to preserve a favorable image emerge from this survey:

1. The best service possible should be given so that complaints are held to a minimum.
2. Complaints should be handled promptly and thoroughly, so that customers feel the company really cares about them. Not only may unhappy customers become noncustomers, but their word-of-mouth criticism may drive away other potential purchasers—how many, no one ever knows. As an example, an eight-year-old girl sued the makers of Crackerjack because she didn't find a prize in a box she purchased. She had written to the company about the mistake, but it failed to answer the letter. The lawsuit she brought gave the company bad nationwide publicity.

Summary

Face-to-Face Discussion

The most effective form of interpersonal communication is a face-to-face conversation between two people. This is because of its immediacy and the possibility of instant clarification and feedback. However, for a personal call to succeed, the practitioner should: telephone in advance for an appointment; identify him- or herself and the purpose; be concise; avoid overselling; express appreciation for the host's time; leave behind written material; and follow up with a thank-you note.

Assignment: Speechwriting

The speechwriter's role is often a hidden one; the final speech should reflect the personality and voice patterns of the speaker, not the writer. The speech should say something of value; concentrate on one or two main themes; include facts; be influenced by the audience; and be clear. The speech should include an introduction, statement of purpose, development, statement of secondary theme, enunciation of the principal point, pause on plateau, restatement of the theme, and a brief conclusion.

Speechwriting Techniques

Writing for speech must be simpler in construction and more casual than writing meant to be read. Sentences should be simple and transitions smooth. Speechwriters should be careful with jokes and statistics.

Visual Aids for a Speech

Any graphs and charts must be designed for good visibility; they must be large and simple.

Staging a Speech

An effective speech is an opportunity for an organization to promote its image and goals. Those in management positions who may be making speeches as part of their jobs should be trained in delivery techniques.

Helping the Speaker Polish and Present the Speech

The speechwriter should work closely with the speaker to polish both the material and the delivery. To set the stage for success, the public relations practitioner should test the microphone and any other materials being used, bring extra copies of the speech, and record the speech.

Speakers' Bureaus and Hotlines

Speakers are sometimes made available to speakers' bureaus operated by trade associations, social agencies, and corporations, which seek to provide speakers without charge to influential audiences. There are also speakers' bureaus that place professional speakers for a fee. Some trade associations also operate telephone hotlines to provide quick answers, especially to news media.

Special Types of Speaking Opportunities

At news conferences, the speaker usually makes an opening statement and then accepts questions from reporters. Usually news conferences are planned in advance and positive in intent, meant to unveil a new product or promote a new program, although sometimes a news conference may be called as part of crisis management in a difficult situation. Advance planning will involve careful scheduling, preparing the setting, inviting attendees, anticipating questions and preparing answers, and providing printed material for distribution. Press parties or press tours are more informal than news conferences, promoting an organization's goals and enhancing its reputation in a more social setting. With more attention being paid to conflict-of-interest issues, it is important that these events avoid the appearance of attempting to "buy" the media. Interviews are another spoken method of publicizing an individual or cause. There is a distinction between interviews for the broadcast media, where the public gets to see the interviewee directly, and interviews for the print media, where information and character impressions are filtered through the writer. Another form of oral communication takes place in meetings. Effective meetings are carefully planned, with firm agendas, comfortable settings, and adherence to schedule in terms of starting and ending times and the time allotted for each agenda item and/or speaker.

Audio News Releases

Audio news releases are sent to radio stations in ready-to-broadcast form as public service announcements. The amount of air time required should be stated at the top of the release.

Word of Mouth

Word of mouth is an ephemeral form of interpersonal communication that is difficult to measure or control but which has a major impact on public opinion. Such communication can include rumors, which can be defused by paying attention, acting promptly to keep the public informed, and educating personnel. Because dissatisfied customers are more vocal in telling friends and family about their experiences than are those who have happy experiences with a company, it is important to keep complaints to a minimum through good service and handle complaints promptly and thoroughly.

Case Activity: What Would You Do?

Pace Industries, a manufacturer of cordless phones, has a morale problem among its 1200 employees. There is a widespread rumor that the company will lay off from one-third to one-half of its employees. The rumor apparently started because of two environmental factors: (1) Many news stories in recent years have reported the downsizing of corporate America, and (2) the company recently lost the bid on a major contract.

The rumor is false, and Pace executives are worried that it will affect productivity and cause an exodus of valued employees. What steps should the company take to dissipate the rumor and reassure employees that their jobs are secure? What kinds of messages and communication channels should be used?

Questions for Review and Discussion

1. List three tasks a public relations representative should perform when preparing for and making a face-to-face presentation to an editor.
2. How many themes should a speech have?
3. What are some key building blocks a writer uses in constructing a speech?
4. Which type of sentence structure should a speechwriter use? Explain your answer.
5. Why do companies sometimes use fellow workers rather than high executives to address audiences of employees?
6. How should a company executive prepare to hold a news conference?
7. Should a spokesperson speak off the record at a news conference? Why or why not?
8. What might a corporate host hope to accomplish by holding a press luncheon instead of a morning news conference?
9. How can a public relations representative help a client prepare for a television interview?
10. A company may be harassed by malicious rumors about its policies. If it decided to strike back, how might it do so?

Suggested Readings

Bannon, Lisa. "Bazaar Gossip: How a Rumor Spread about Subliminal Sex in Disney's 'Aladdin'." *Wall Street Journal,* October 24, 1995, p. 1.

"Bid to Kill Rumors May Backfire at High-Tech Cos." *O'Dwyer's PR Services Report,* November 1995, pp. 1, 18, and 20.

DeVito, Joseph A. *Messages.* New York: Addison Wesley Longman, 1999.

DiFonzo, Nicholas, and Bordia, Prashant. "How Top PR Professionals Handle Hot Air: Types of Corporate Rumors, Their Effects, and Strategies to Manage Them." A report from The Institute for Public Relations, Gainesville, FL, 1998. Available for $20 from the Institute: (352) 392-0280.

Elsasser, John. "Getting Reporters to Press Conferences." *Public Relations Tactics,* January 1995, p. 4.

Fatt, James. "It's Not What You Say, It's How You Say It." *Communication World,* June/July 1999, pp. 37–39.

Lyon, Lisa, and Cameron, Glen T., "Fess up or Stonewall? An Experimental Test of Prior Reputation and Response Style in the Face of Negative News Coverage," *Web Journal of Mass Communication Research,* January, 1999.

Rabinowitz, Dorothy. "Race and Rumor." *Wall Street Journal,* April 29, 1996, p. A20.

Rizzo, Thomas J. *Speaking with Impact.* Dubuque, IA: Kendall/Hunt Publishing, 1995.

Slater, Wayne. "On Message." *American Journalism Review,* April 2001, pp. 50–54.

Walker, Jerry. "10 Media Myths: How to Get the Best Possible Exposure." *O'Dwyer's PR Services Report,* May 2000, p. 68.

Visual Tactics

preview

The objective of this chapter is to help students understand the advantages and disadvantages of numerous visual and audiovisual techniques, and to explain the visual needs of the various mass media outlets.

Topics covered in the chapter include:

- News delivery to television
- Video news releases (VNRs)
- News on cable television
- Personal appearances on television
- Other uses of videotape
- Motion pictures
- Still images for projection
- Still photography
- Comic books and cartoons
- Outdoor displays
- Corporate design

Television

The human eye is a magnificent channel for communication, carrying messages to the brain at astounding speeds, often so subtly that the recipient is not consciously aware of absorbing them. These images are stored in the brain, combining with the intake of audible and tactile impressions to help form opinions, trigger decisions, and generate actions. Because these are the goals of public relations, the role of visual communication in public relations practice obviously is vital.

Television is the dominant form of visual communication in contemporary life. The Nielsen survey reports that the average American family has its TV set turned on about seven hours a day. During the late 1990s, however, the World Wide Web of the Internet emerged as a visual communicator in competition with television. (See Chapter 12 for a discussion of the World Wide Web.) The Web has increased the average hours that people devote to media use and has caused a definite shift of hours from television viewing to Web browsing.

Chapter 11 examined how the television industry is organized and listed ways in which public relations practitioners can use television to advance their causes. This chapter will look more closely at techniques employed for this purpose and will discuss the growing use of television for internal corporate communication.

News Releases

Practitioners can provide news releases to television stations in several ways, ranging from a simple sheet of paper to an expensively produced videotaped story ready to go on the air. The type of news material, the time factor, and the originator's budget will determine which method is best for each story.

The Printed News Release Identical to that sent to newspapers, the so-called handout frequently is sufficient (see Chapter 21). If the news director or assignment editor at a station judges the material to be newsworthy, a staff member is assigned to handle the story, rewriting it briefly in television style or, if the material justifies, going to the scene with a camera crew to obtain visual support for the facts. Information about coming events also is sent to TV stations in the form of a *media advisory*. When a television reporter and crew come on assignment in response to a news release, the public relations practitioner who sent out the release should do everything possible to assist them, such as providing an authoritative spokesperson to appear on camera and helping to arrange other shots the reporter and photographer may request.

A fundamental difference between a news story on television and one in a newspaper is *motion*. Stories that can be illustrated easily and effectively often will receive more air time than ones that cannot. The rule for a practitioner trying to place a news story on television is: *Think pictures!* The representative never should tell a reporter and photographer what pictures to shoot or what questions to ask, but may discreetly suggest possible picture and story angles.

The other primary factor in television news coverage is *brevity*. A story that runs 400 words in a newspaper may be reported in only two or three sentences in a newscast. If a television crew spends an hour shooting a story with a practitioner's help, and the story then receives 30 seconds or less of air time, the inexperienced public relations representative may feel let down. All that work, with such a brief result! As any veteran will advise, however, there is no reason for disappointment. Even a very brief item on a popular newscast can have a heavy impact on the audience.

The Prepared Script This second, more elaborate, form of television news release is accompanied by one to four slides to illustrate the text. In this method, the public relations representative does most of the television news department's work on the story. Smaller stations with limited news staffs may be especially willing to air such ready-to-use material if it is deemed newsworthy. In preparing scripted news releases, the writer should avoid terminology that sounds like advertising or "puff" publicity. Graphics created by computers can be used effectively in news releases.

For a fee, specialist commercial firms will prepare a news release script with slides from a practitioner's material, send the script to stations, and report on its use.

Videotaped excerpts from local speeches made by the practitioner's client, delivered to a television station along with a written news release explaining the circumstances in which the speech was made, may be used in the station's newscasts if the content is significant or provocative. Prospects for use of the material are improved if it is delivered quickly after the event for same-day use.

The Video News Release The most elaborate and expensive form of news delivery to television stations is the video news release (VNR). This report, prepared by a public relations organization, presents information about a product, a service, or an idea, usually in featurized style.

Delivered to selected stations by satellite feed or by package, the VNR may be a ready-to-use tape of visual and voice material that a TV station may put on the air exactly as received—the use most desired by the supplier. Or, to give the station more editorial control, the release may consist of separate elements an editor can use in preparing the station's own presentation. These may include unedited video pictures, called B-roll footage, any of which the editor may select; brief "sound bites"; a separate voice-over narration by the producer's announcer, which may be aired as-is or instead read by a station announcer; and a script to be used or rewritten.

B-roll footage is especially popular with newscast producers because the journalist maintains greater control over the tone and nature of the story that is broadcast. One study of air checks (news stories derived from a VNR) found that television producers used B-roll almost exclusively and never opted to run the entire packaged story. Material used from the VNR tended to be stock footage of the façade of the organization and sound bites from news conferences and interviews. The authors of the study, David Blount and Glen T. Cameron, concluded that VNRs provide news producers

When some customers claimed they had found syringes in Pepsi cans, the company distributed a video news release (VNR) showing that intrusion into its high-speed bottling process was virtually impossible. The claim proved to be a hoax.

PR casebook

Book Promotions Reach High-Tech Audiences

Recording artist Jewell read poetry from her recent book, *A Night without Armor,* to more than 1000 fans who gathered in the New York Virgin Megastore. The singer-songwriter drew quite a significant crowd for a poetry reading, especially when you consider that the live audience was supplemented by crowds gathered at Virgin Megastore's retail outlets in Orlando, Los Angeles, and San Francisco. Fans in all locations were able to listen and ask questions of the rock star and poet. The event was good for store traffic, book sales, and positioning of Jewell as an artist.

with access to basic visuals for their craft. Although the news producer maintains journalistic integrity by not using the scripted VNR segment, the packaged story probably does influence how the producer develops his or her own story using B-roll footage.

Obviously, preparation and distribution of such VNR packages is expensive—from $5000 to $50,000 for most releases and even higher for elaborate ones. Yet TV stations receive hundreds of VNRs each year, many of inferior technical quality. Several factors should be considered before an organization commits that much money to a news release. Is the story sufficiently newsworthy, so that many stations probably will put it on the air? Can the story be told well visually? Does the producer have sufficient time to prepare the release, perhaps as much as six weeks? If the VNR concerns a legitimate health issue or scientific breakthrough, its chances of being widely used are better than those for introductions of commercial products.

VNRs featuring a celebrity also stand a better chance of garnering airtime. Prince Naseem Hamed was a European professional boxer with several major titles and an undefeated record. Although not well known in the United States, his European fame justified an outlay of $16,000 by sponsor Adidas International for a VNR produced by Medialink. The total audience for news stories based on the VNR exceeded 20 million.

In producing successful video news releases, sponsoring organizations must create a feeling of news or offer an interesting feature idea. Advertising sales pitch techniques should be avoided; so should glorifying adjectives. The benefit to the sponsoring organization is indirect, by making the viewing public aware of the existence of the service, the idea, or the product. A VNR that is clearly an attempt to obtain free advertising goes automatically into a station's wastebasket.

This restriction creates the need for ingenuity. Writing in the *Wall Street Journal,* Michael Klepper described how a company seeking mass exposure for a new talking doll produced a successful VNR about the history of artificial voice synthesis, using the doll as an example of the technology. Not only do such stories downplay commercial messages, they serve the station's need for "evergreen" stories of human interest that do not become immediately dated.

To introduce a new picture book *America Then & Now,* DWJ Television shot part of a video news release from the top of the Brooklyn Bridge, interviewing a still photographer who took a picture from the spot that duplicated one taken from the same place 116 years earlier. The book, published by HarperCollins, compared recent photos of events and locations with pictures taken at the same places many years earlier. Thus the VNR stimulated the viewers' historical interest while promoting the book.

A tie-in satellite media interview was conducted by the author with TV reporters in more than 30 states in which pictures for the book had been taken. (See Chapter 20.) A B-roll containing those pictures was sent in advance to each station, so it could select home state shots for use in its interview, again reflecting the need for video that a station can shape into a story of its own.

Ethical Problems in the Use of VNRs Video news releases are intended to present the sponsoring organization's story in a favorable light, subtly or more obviously. Knowing this, news editors of some television stations refuse to use them, and many stations that use some VNR material refuse to broadcast the ready-to-air versions they receive. That is why the makers of VNRs increasingly supply B-roll footage with their submissions. Small TV stations with limited news staffs are more likely to use the ready-made versions than are their larger colleagues.

Ethical responsibility for the airing of video news releases lies equally with those who produce the VNRs and the television stations that run them. Producers should make clear who is paying for the releases. Stations in turn should tell their viewers the sources of the releases they use (see Chapter 3 for a discussion of this ethical issue). Research on effectiveness of labeling suggests that sources should be credited in the script as well as in the caption on screen.

Infomercials An expanded form of VNR, called an *infomercial* or *program-length commercial,* is a lengthy presentation made to look like an editorial examination of a topic when in reality it is a slightly disguised sales pitch for everything from mops and muscle-strengtheners to children's action figures. Such programs turn up on the screen in the late-evening hours and Saturday mornings, especially on cable systems. Some channels and stations announce that the shows are paid programs; others fail to do so or make announcements so inconspicuous that viewers easily miss them.

Presentation of infomercials in prime-time viewing hours has been undertaken by two small cable networks, Consumer Resources Network and Cable Time Direct. A few mainstream companies, such as Ford and State Farm Insurance, have shown 30-minute infomercials in prime time. Their approach is less hard-pitch salesmanship and more an extended explanation of their products. Infomercials have become so clever at looking like regular TV programs that Disney ran a commercial for its

focus on ethics

Information Pollution or Freedom of the Press?

The FDA has several concerns about VNR use, including labeling and fair balance in stories. Some claim captions that provide the source of a TV story are not effective. The agency worries about medical decisions and self-medication taking place, particularly among older Americans. Some have argued that TV stories should be subject to review in the same way that drug packages and ads must provide counter indications, etc. Others say that freedom of the press precludes this sort of review.

Should TV stories based largely on VNRs sponsored by pharmaceutical companies be prominently labeled so that the audience can judge the merits of the product featured in the story?

Do you think stories on the evening news about prescription drugs can be effectively labeled?

Is the pharmaceutical VNR making an "end run" around proper FDA review?

Duckman cartoon in an infomercial for a music anthology—a commercial within a commercial. Infomercials are sent to the station's advertising department, and airtime must be purchased.

News on Cable Television

An emerging battle in distribution of news by cable television provides new opportunities for public relations exposure. Innovative practitioners will find additional placement possibilities for the cable-viewing audience.

Disturbed by the way Ted Turner's Cable News Network (CNN) has flourished around the world, four over-the-air broadcasting networks struck back in 1996 by forming their own cable news networks. NBC joined with Microsoft to create MSNBC, a 24-hour cable network combined with a World Wide Web news service; the new Fox news service arranged to have its news distributed on the cable systems of huge Tele-Communications, Inc.; and Westinghouse/CBS entered the global cable market by purchasing the Spanish-language cable channel TeleNoticias.

Numerous newspapers have obtained local cable channels on which they produce newscasts, using their own staff-gathered material as resources. Using satellite distribution, nationwide superstations such as WTBS-TV in Atlanta and WGN-TV in Chicago reach large numbers of cable viewers from coast to coast.

Personal Appearances on Television

Anyone invited to appear on television in a talk show or for an interview should prepare for the occasion. The beaming red light of a television camera aimed at a guest, indicating that he or she is on the air, can have a terrifying effect on an inexperienced performer. The throat goes dry. The words won't come out. The guest projects discomfort and uncertainty to thousands of viewers, precisely the opposite of the effect desired. A valuable opportunity is wasted.

Public relations practitioners can help their clients avoid this unpleasantness by coaching them in what to say and how to behave. Playing the role of interviewer in practice sessions, the coach can rehearse the guest by asking anticipated questions. If the subject matter is controversial, the practitioner should fire antagonistic questions to test the guest's mettle. As much as possible, the guest's prepared responses should be honed down to 30 seconds or less. (Preparation for appearances on television is discussed in Chapter 21).

In general, guests on television should dress conservatively. On most shows a business suit is appropriate for men; for women, a suit or dress of simple pattern without conspicuous ornamentation. White clothing, including shirts, should be avoided, as should metallic decorations—all might reflect studio lights. On shows featuring entertainers and sports figures, dress is more informal, to the point of conspicuous casualness. By watching a show in advance or asking production personnel, the public relations person can advise a client how to dress suitably for the appearance.

Professional coaches who prepare guests for television appearances make these suggestions for their personal conduct:

- *Gestures.* The guest should create movement for the camera, even though seated, by changing facial expressions and by moving his or her hands, arms, head, and shoulders to emphasize points. Potential guests can observe these tricks by watching professional actors on talk shows.

- *Eye contact.* The guest should look at the interviewer, as in a private conversation. If the camera is focused directly at the guest, he or she should talk to it. The trick is to think of the camera eye not as an electronic device but as another person whom the speaker is trying to inform or convince.
- *Proper body placement.* Persons being interviewed should not cross their legs; the position is awkward. It is better to sit with one foot in front of the other. Leaning forward in the chair makes a person appear more aggressive. Keeping the hands apart allows the guest to use them for gesturing. Guests should also be coached to mention key points about the event or product several times.

Other Uses of Videotape

Videotape is so flexible and cheap that it is used by public relations people in many ways in addition to video news releases. Commercial firms and nonprofit organizations use it to reach external audiences and to communicate information and instruction to their staffs. Here is a small sample of such uses.

- The state of Nevada aimed a 16-minute video, "What's the Deal with Yucca Mountain?," at school children in its fight against creation of a federal nuclear waste dump there. The video used student interviewers, vivid graphics, and fast music in MTV style to deliver a serious message.
- The Salt Lake City delegation used videos and computer graphics in the presentation that won the 2002 Winter Olympic Games for that city.
- American Express sponsored a video, "It Could Never Happen to Me: Preventing Campus Crime," to be loaned free to colleges nationwide, using actual testimony of campus crime victims.

Videotaped Financial Reports

Corporations increasingly are putting their financial information on videotape for showing to shareholders and securities analysts. Videotaping of annual meetings is one aspect of this trend. Specially prepared reports with graphs and other visual aids are also taped.

Distribution of videotaped material needs as much attention as preparation of the content. Videocassettes may be mailed to brokers and other financial specialists for their individual viewing. Perhaps more effective is a personal showing of the videotaped material by a company executive to groups of invited guests, who can ask questions after viewing the tape. Another method is to invite interested investors and brokers to request a loan copy of the videotape.

Internal Corporate TV News Programs

Large corporations with thousands of employees scattered in many locations keep hunting for ways to give their employees a sense of company pride and common purpose. Among the print media, company newspapers and magazines have that goal. The audiovisual equivalent is the corporate television news program.

Such programs need a strong professional touch in production; hence, they are expensive to create. They should have a well-defined formula for content. Management-oriented material should be presented discreetly in news style. The techniques of brevity, visual storytelling, human interest, and touches of humor that mark a successful commercial television newscast need to be applied to a corporate news program—not an easy task. Television consultant firms may be employed to produce the program or to provide technical assistance.

Showing of these programs to employees on a voluntary basis is done at lunch hours or other convenient times. Videotape cassettes of the shows can be distributed to sales and other employees working in the field. Playing the programs on cable television in cities where corporate plants are located is another possibility.

TV News, a corporate TV magazine for employees of SmithKline Beecham, is an excellent example. A pioneer in the field, it has appeared weekly since 1972. Although some corporations use a TV newscast format with an anchor person, *TV News* has employees do voice-over narrations of stories involving them, such as veterans of the Persian Gulf War and Hurricane Andrew survivors.

Videotaped Training and Marketing Programs

An estimated $3 billion is being spent annually on employee video programs, according to the American Society for Training and Development. The flexibility and economy of videotape makes it ideal for training employees and updating their skills.

Videotaped Sales Messages

A recent development, as the electronic revolution changes publicity methods, is distribution of sales messages on tape to selected potential customers. *Videocassettes* are mailed upon request to prospective buyers who can play these illustrated sales messages on home recorders. A stamped, self-addressed envelope for return of the cassettes to the firm may be included. Because of the costs involved, this method is used primarily for higher-priced items by companies selling direct to the consumer.

Home Video

Most American families now have videocassette recorders (VCRs) with which they record television shows or view rented or purchased movies. A Newspaper Advertising Bureau study showed that VCR owners rented an average of 108 movies a year, while the average American visited a movie theater only five times annually.

Taking advantage of this viewing potential, a growing number of organizations and companies now use videotape to reach key audiences.

In politics, candidates and groups use videotapes as today's "high-tech leaflet." A Massachusetts congressional candidate distributed a 15-minute videotape of himself for campaign workers to show in voters' homes. In Orinda, a community across the bay from San Francisco, proincorporation forces produced a videotape on the advantages of being a city, for showing at neighborhood meetings and in homes. The measure passed, and the city's first mayor credited the videotape as a major factor in the victory.

Increasingly, employees can check out videotapes of company-produced materials ranging from the corporate video news magazine to informational videos such as an explanation of the new health benefits. According to *PR Reporter,* as audiences relinquish time devoted to reading in favor of visual stimulation through television, video games, and the Web, visually oriented strategies must be adopted to convey information. Video production gives organizations an opportunity to communicate with audiences that are increasingly inclined to visual literacy. For example, stockholders are routinely offered videotape cassettes reporting on company affairs. On another level, a corporation may subsidize production of a videotape to be sold to the public at a nominal charge. Political campaigns can send key opinion leaders videotape messages with visual appeal and high emotional impact.

Motion Pictures

Hollywood commercial feature films viewed by millions of customers in theaters constitute only a fraction of the films produced in the United States and Canada every year. Hundreds of motion pictures, often equal in quality to theatrical films, are made annually by sponsors for showing to selected audiences. Only a handful of these ever will appear on commercial theater screens, and then only as supporting films on programs of mass-market entertainment.

Sponsored films have a major role in public relations work, as noted in Chapter 11. Designed to inform, instruct, and persuade, often subtly, they play to a huge cumulative audience. Unlike commercial films, most of them are shown to viewers without charge. The makers of these films, and in some instances the organizations showing them, bear the cost in order to further their purposes directly or indirectly.

Hollywood Entertainment Films

Moviegoers are frequently exposed to publicity projects in the films they watch, although they rarely are aware of it. Public relations specialists who arrange mentions of their clients' products or causes in movies obtain high visibility because Hollywood motion pictures often are seen by millions of viewers (see Chapter 19).

Such mentions dropped into the middle of the story line are not accidental. They are arranged by negotiations between public relations specialists and the film's

Product placements are now a common occurrence in feature films. This scene from "Training Day" prominently features a popular beverage. Increasingly, corporations pay the movie company to feature its products.

producer, in which the filmmaker receives payment in money or services. The show business weekly *Variety* calls the practice "product *pluggola*."

Two examples:

- Oldsmobile arranged for its Silhouette minivan to appear in *Get Shorty,* the MGM film in which John Travolta goes to Hollywood to collect on a debt. He expects to pick up a Cadillac but instead gets "the Cadillac of minivans"—a line repeated several times in the film.
- Internal memos disclosed that Brown & Williamson Tobacco Corporation paid $950,000 in four years to have its cigarette brands shown in more than 20 movies. At least $300,000 of this went to action-film star Sylvester Stallone. The company said that it stopped this activity several years ago.

Benefits of such appearances often are difficult to evaluate in terms of sales, but product exposure, even at high prices, is regarded as a bargain for participants if the film proves to be a hit. When E.T., the lonesome waif from space, ate Reese's Pieces in *E.T., The Extra-Terrestrial,* the makers of that candy, Hershey Food Company, reported a 65 percent increase in sales of the brand. Some companies have paid moviemakers as much as $50,000 for a product placement.

Sponsored Films and Videos

The range of films and videos made to be shown free of charge or to be rented or purchased for showing to external audiences is immense. A well-produced film or video with minimal commercial emphasis is an excellent way for companies and organizations to reach members of school, church, social, cultural, professional, and business groups.

Sponsored films and videos, despite their expense, serve several public relations purposes. They can (1) inform audiences about a topic of educational interest, (2) create understanding of a company or organization's activities, and (3) generate goodwill and name recognition among important audiences. Charms Candy, for example, reached an important audience, schoolchildren, by producing a film on school-bus safety that school administrators often show in school assemblies.

Cable television is another important outlet for sponsored films. Consumer education films and videos in which the company's commercial message is reduced to perhaps just the opening and closing credit lines find widespread acceptance by cable operators, who need to fill broadcast time at minimal expense.

Production of sponsored films and videos, also called *industrial films,* is a substantial industry involving an estimated 600 firms around the world. Their filming techniques and equipment are in many instances highly advanced.

A limiting factor on use of videotape is the projection method. Unless a large group meeting place is equipped with a large television screen or multiple television monitors, viewing is difficult. School-assembly or service-club rooms rarely have large television monitors.

The length of sponsored films and videos varies greatly. A survey by Modern Talking Picture Service, however, shows a strong audience preference for films 21 to 30 minutes in length. But there are exceptions. *Where's the Cap'n?* is a four-minute music video sponsored by the Quaker Oats Company to develop awareness among children six to 12 years old about a cereal promotion. The video was used on nationally and locally produced video music programs, reaching an estimated audience of 7.9 million viewers.

At the other end of the spectrum, Pepsi-Cola sponsored a 40-minute film titled *Amber Lights* that received widespread acclaim as a high school assembly program. It combined popular film clips and music in an MTV format to address the No. 1 killer of teenagers in the United States—drunk drivers. The company estimates that three million teenagers saw the film during one school year.

The Utah Department of Health produced a frank film about a serious social problem. *If You Want to Dance . . .* concerns an unwed teenage couple faced with the consequences of an unplanned pregnancy. Candid but constructive, the 14-minute film opens with a locker-room scene in which three high school boys talk about sex, then shifts to a hospital room where two pregnant unwed teenage girls discuss their problems. Much praised, the film has been widely shown to high school classes, church groups, and community organizations. A discussion guide is distributed with the film, which is available for loan or purchase on both 16-millimeter film and 3/4-inch videocassette.

Still Images for Projection

Slides, filmstrips, and transparencies—all of them methods for projecting still images onto a screen—often are referred to as *audiovisual aids.* Properly, the word *audiovisual* encompasses all forms of sound-and-picture projection, including motion pictures, but in practice it frequently is applied only to these simpler forms. Inclusion of such visual aids in programs stimulates audiences.

Audiovisual aids are much cheaper than motion pictures and videotapes, and have simple projection requirements. All that is needed are a relatively inexpensive slide projector, an electrical outlet, and a small screen. A presentation of still images accompanied by live or recorded narration often is the most efficient method for bringing a message to a small audience. Audiovisual aids are often designed in public relations departments and firms using popular software such as Powerpoint, Harvard Graphics, or Presentations. Several advantages are afforded by the use of presentation software.

PR insights

Visual Aids Improve Meeting Results

Speakers who use visual aids such as slides, filmstrips, and overhead transparencies not only keep their audiences more interested but also accomplish greater results. A study sponsored by the Wharton School of Business at the University of Pennsylvania showed the following percentages:

	With Visuals	*Without Visuals*
Speaker's goal achieved	67%	33%
Group consensus reached	79%	58%
Information retained	50%	10%
Average meeting length	19 minutes	28 minutes

A uniform, stylish look is afforded through the software. Selected portions of the scripts written for the speaker can be turned into bulleted items on the digital slides—with subsequent changes in the script automatically updated on the appropriate slide. Presentations made for printing onto transparencies can also be "mounted" on a Web site. Finally, public relations presentations such as pitches to prospective clients can be projected using machines called LCD Projectors that convert the computer file into images. Quality of image, fluidity of presentation, and the addition of animation, short video clips, and audio are all facilitated. Most top firms now make presentations with this technology.

In spite of the allure of this LCD projection option, however, the rule of thumb is always to make transparency backups; the systems cannot always be trusted to perform at crunch time when the show must go on. Bill Gates's computer, for example, crashed during a demonstration of Windows 98 at the Comdex computer show in Chicago, earning the Microsoft chief a dubious achievement award from *Esquire* magazine.

Slide Shows

Slide presentations now range upward from Uncle Chester showing the dinner guests slides he made during his trip to Europe—usually too many and occasionally upside-down—to the projection of intricate triple-screen, three-dimensional productions issued by some corporations. For his performance before the captive audience in the living room, Uncle Chester selects the slides he likes best and delivers a rambling ad-lib narration about them as they flash on the screen. This is the exact opposite of the way a professional slide show should be constructed.

A slide show should be built on a well-defined theme to tell a story and deliver a message. The script should be written and approved first, then the visual elements should be developed to illustrate and emphasize points in the script. The standard technique is for a visually oriented person to study the script, marking places in it that lend themselves to illustration by photograph or drawing. An artist then creates rough storyboards, indicating the illustration perceived for each point. Photographer and artist go to work, producing 35-millimeter slides that meet the requirements of the storyboards. Slides and motion picture film can be coordinated.

Depending on its purpose, a slide show might consist of photographs, as in a program made by a state tourist board to publicize the scenic attractions of the state. Or, if intended to explain retirement benefits to an internal audience of employees, it might be made entirely with drawings and explanatory text slides. A combination of photographs, drawings, and text also can be effective. Leasing of stock shots of scenery, people, and events from commercial firms such as *Time* that specialize in this work is a convenient way to fill out the picture requirements of a show. Some large picture firms have from two to five million still photos and slides on file to fill requests.

Text-only slides often help to give a presentation cohesion and to emphasize key points. The content of each text slide should be brief, making a single clear statement in a maximum of 25 words, preferably fewer. A slide containing 10 words or fewer can be powerfully effective. Color slides containing text and/or drawings need strong contrast, usually a dark background of blue, black, or brown with letters and pictures in white or yellow. An occasional black-and-white slide may be mixed into a color sequence.

A narrator may deliver the script of a slide show live, or it may be accompanied by a taped voice synchronized with the progression of slides. Slides can be shown on an automatic projector controlled by a button the speaker presses to change them.

If a company or organization has competent writing, photographic, or graphic talent on its staff, it may be able to produce an attractive slide show using its own resources. Outside graphic talent may be hired, or the sponsor may employ a firm specializing in audiovisual work to handle the entire production. Specialist organizations are able to produce elaborate slide shows through use of animation, masking, and multiple screens.

Overhead Transparencies

A simple, economical form of audiovisual aid is a sheet of transparent acetate or similar material on which illustrations and/or lettering have been placed. When this sheet is laid on a flat glass surface in the projector, the images are reproduced on a screen behind the speaker by light transmitted by mirrors and lenses. Overhead transparencies are especially good in classrooms and small discussion groups because of their flexibility. They can be made by running a master on regular paper through a photocopier onto the acetate plastic. Large type (at least 24 point) should be used on overheads, and only about 10 to 12 words of copy.

Masking a transparency permits a speaker to show several steps in a process with only one transparency. If the same series of steps were shown by slides, a separate slide would be necessary for each step.

When a speaker wishes to show the operation of a piece of machinery, for example, masking can be done in the following way: the transparency contains a diagram of the entire machine. A piece of onionskin or white opalescent plastic is laid over each portion of the diagram and taped lightly into place. As the blanked-out transparency appears on the screen, the speaker removes each sectional overlay progressively and explains the revealed portion of the diagram, until the entire diagram is visible. The speaker can draw or write on a transparency while it is being displayed on the screen.

Still Photography

A story in the print media, especially newspapers and magazines, may, and frequently should, be told in pictures as well as words. Still photography is an essential tool for every practitioner who works with publications.

Newspaper Requirements

Newspaper editors like to receive photographs of persons mentioned in news releases. The presence of a photograph with a release sometimes increases the likelihood that the story will be published. Or, as frequently happens, a photograph of a newsworthy individual or group will be published without an accompanying story, the necessary information having been condensed into the photo caption.

The type of photograph most easily placed in a newspaper by a practitioner is the head-and-shoulders portrait of a client. These portraits, known in the trade as *mug shots,* frequently are published in one-column or half-column size to illustrate textual material. Group shots are published less often than individual pictures because they require multiple-column space. Practitioners submitting group photographs should keep the number of persons in a picture small and have them tightly grouped—a maximum of three or four persons unless the picture is a highly unusual one.

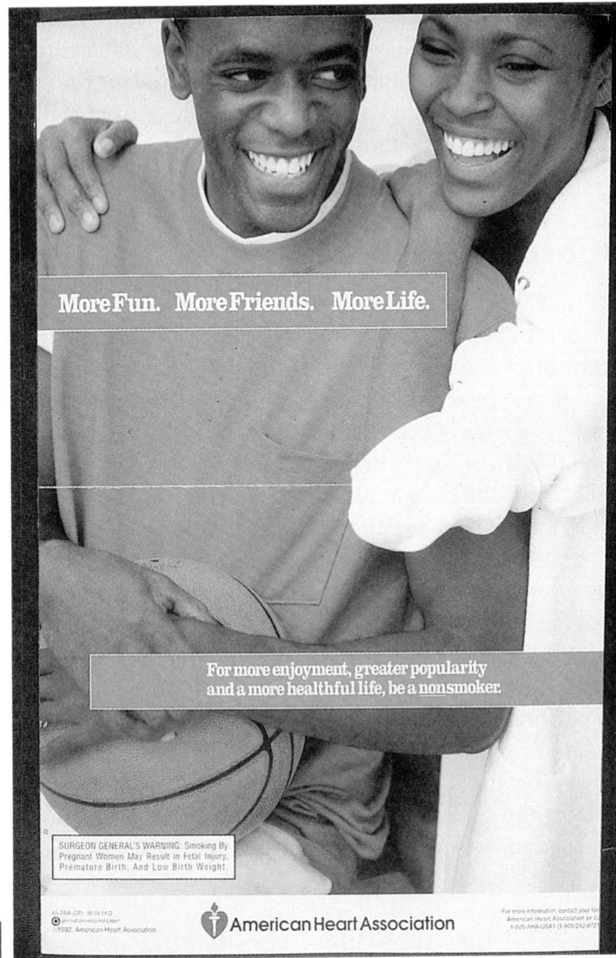

An effective poster delivers a simple message in a few words and includes a striking illustration. This poster by the American Heart Association, urging youths not to smoke, is a good example.

Photographs on the main news pages of a newspaper usually are taken by staff photographers or are provided by the news picture services. They stress action or personality to capture attention. The chances for a public relations practitioner to have a submitted photograph published in these up-front pages are relatively small, except for one-column portraits. When spot news is involved, the practitioner is better advised to telephone the photo editor of a newspaper and call attention to a picture possibility that a staff photographer can cover. Staff photographers know their editors' space limitations and deadlines.

Other sections of a newspaper provide abundant opportunities for publication of photographs submitted by practitioners.

The business pages regularly include photographs of meetings, new products, and individuals appointed to new positions. Sports editors welcome photographs of athletes and coaches in various poses. Entertainment editors need pictures of performers, individually and in groups, and publish still photos taken from scenes in locally playing motion pictures and television shows. Travel editors desire photographs of interesting scenes and modes of transportation.

An especially broad target for the practitioner is the section of a newspaper called "Family Living," "Life Styles," "Today's Scene," or something similar. For many years these sections were referred to as "women's," "society," or, in newspaper jargon, "sock." They concentrated on engagements and weddings, parties and club meetings, food, beauty, and fashion. Now their appeal is greatly enlarged, aimed at men as well as women.

While retaining the traditional elements, these sections have added material about family life and problems, personal finances, careers, and contemporary lifestyles. This broadened appeal has multiplied the photographic possibilities for the public relations practitioner, both to submit photographs and to query editors with ideas for illustrated feature stories by staff members about activities of their clients.

"Family Living" sections often publish pictures of groups planning charity events, civic affairs, and social organization parties. These pictures generate interest in the event, help to sell tickets, and incidentally serve as an ego payoff to workers who appear in them. Unfortunately, far too many such pictures belong to the waxworks school of photography—stilted, self-conscious poses in which the participants appear ramrod-stiff and painfully artificial. A photographer's ingenuity is challenged to invent an interesting piece of business for the participants to do and to coax them to relax.

When shooting a publicity shot, a clever photographer will include, if possible, a prop that helps to carry the message. A picture promoting a Red Cross blood drive, for example, would be strengthened by inclusion of a Red Cross poster or similar symbol.

Publicity shots may be submitted by the practitioner, or arrangements may be made with an editor for a staff photographer to handle the assignment. If a staff photographer is assigned, the practitioner must make certain that all participants in the picture assemble at the appointed place on time, appropriately dressed. The photographer is busy and, in a sense, the editor is doing the organization a favor.

Creativity also should be applied to news pictures submitted for publication. Groundbreakings, installations of officers, delivery of donation checks—routine events for a public relations worker—are notorious sources of clichéd photos. For that reason, some newspapers refuse to publish photographs of these events. A practitioner should use every ounce of innovative skill to find a new camera angle or piece of action.

Photographs submitted to newspapers normally are 8 by 10 inches in black and white, with caption material attached either to the back or bottom of the picture. *The practitioner should be absolutely certain that the names in the caption are spelled correctly and match up in left-to-right sequence with the photograph itself.* An added precaution is to count the number of persons in the picture and the number of names in the caption, to be sure that they correspond. Smaller prints usually are acceptable for head-and-shoulders portraits.

■ **Use of Color** Most newspapers publish color photos on a daily basis, and the practice is growing. Excellent public relations opportunities exist to place color pictures in feature sections. Living sections often run color photos of prepared foods; travel sections show enticing color shots of destinations.

The practitioner should submit color slides, not color prints. To increase the chances that a picture will be used, it is a wise precaution to determine in advance from the picture editor or chief photographer what special technical requirements for color work the newspaper may have. Newspapers now regularly use photographs downloaded from wire services and the Web, so it is also a good idea to ask whether the photo should be submitted in digital form on diskette or as an attachment to an e-mail message.

Keep File Pictures Current Since newspapers maintain large files of published and unpublished photographs, it is not unusual for a mug shot of a newsworthy personality to be published more than once—a bonus for the practitioner who submitted it. Individuals change in appearance as they age, and occasionally an editor will reach into the files in a hurry and publish an obviously outdated picture of a news figure. The public relations person handling a prominent individual can avoid this embarrassment by submitting an up-to-date photograph from time to time. Because journalists also increasingly look to the Web for graphic material, including photographs, it is important to maintain up-to-date photos on the Web site. Doing so serves the interests of the reporter and the public relations person.

The importance of including a selection of photographs in a press kit introducing such projects as a new shopping center, a sales program, a political campaign, or a fund drive is obvious. The kit should contain pictures of the key persons involved and of physical aspects of the projects.

On a national or regional basis, the alert practitioner may obtain space by appealing to newspaper editors' interest in hometown angles. At trade conventions or sales conferences, the public relations staff can run a "production line" in which individual delegates are photographed in company with a celebrity. As with media use of VNRs, the celebrity does enhance chances that a photo will appear in print. At least rudimentary knowledge of photographic techniques is an important asset for everyone working in public relations. The best way to obtain this is to take a college course in news photography. If this cannot be done, courses in photography are available in many adult education programs.

This photograph of Marilyn Monroe is a classic example of the staged photo arranged for publicity purposes. To promote her film *The Seven Year Itch,* she stood over a grating while wind blowers hidden beneath it swirled her skirt upward. Publicists claimed the resulting photo was "accidental."

Magazine Requirements

Magazine requirements resemble those of newspapers, although emphasis is primarily on feature photographs. Some magazines use only color photographs, some only black-and-white, some both. The practitioner should study each magazine before submitting pictures to it.

Trade and professional magazines frequently use submitted photographs of individuals, new products, and industrial installations. When sending in a proposal for a feature story about a client, the practitioner should offer to provide photographs to accompany the text, regardless of whether the story is written by the practitioner, by a freelance writer, or by a magazine staff member. Many magazines do not have photographic staffs or budgets and facilities for acquiring pictures and so depend upon submitted pictures. Attractive photographs accompanying a manuscript enhance the possibility that it will be accepted for publication.

Public relations departments and counseling firms should include in their annual budgets a substantial amount for photographic service. In addition to submitting pictures to the media, representatives often find it effective to send souvenir prints of these pictures to persons appearing in them and to important persons such as dealers and customers. Such small gestures have a flattering effect.

Comic Books and Cartoons

Another eye-catching way to deliver visual messages in print is to use comic books and cartoons. The artwork must be of professional quality, however, or the effect is diminished. Drawings are especially good for illustrating steps in a process, as in an owner's instruction manual. If an artist can create a whimsical cartoon character that symbolizes the service or objective, entire campaigns can be built around it.

A note of warning: published cartoons and comic strips are covered by copyright and may be reproduced only by permission of the owner. Copyright holders often are reluctant to give such permission.

Outdoor Displays

Although billboards, building signs, and other forms of outdoor announcements are erected primarily for advertising and identification, they have potential uses as public relations tools. Billboards may remind motorists and pedestrians of a citywide charity fund drive in progress. A changing electric sign outside a bank showing time and temperature performs a public service and creates goodwill for the bank; so does a signboard on which announcements of forthcoming civic events are placed. An ingenious practitioner working for a nonprofit organization may be able to find numerous outlets of this type to deliver a message, at little or no cost.

A public relations specialist should know the fundamentals of billboard design and economics, in case a situation arises in which outdoor displays will fit into a publicity program. Billboard companies quite fairly maintain that their medium may be the only mass medium remaining in an era of multiple broadcast channels and publications that reach only portions of the total populace. The standard billboard of the type seen along streets and on buildings is 12 by 25 feet. The colorful paper posters

A catchy slogan illustrated by a bright drawing or cartoon draws attention to a product. Readers attracted by the slogan, "The Easy Way to 5 a Day," turn the page to find recipes for serving strawberries.

pasted onto it are slightly smaller, leaving a white frame around them. The standard poster is called a 24-sheet, because at one time 24 sheets of paper were needed to cover the space on a full-sized billboard. Modern printing processes do it with 10 sheets. Small posters called 3-sheets are designed to attract pedestrian readers at sidewalk level. Recent development of computer-controlled painting on vinyl billboards permits use of larger boards.

Outdoor advertising companies rent display space on their billboards on the basis of what they call a *100-showing*—that is, the number of boards in a market area calculated to expose the advertiser's message to approximately 100 percent of the people at some time during the 30 days it is posted. The number of boards that constitute a 100-showing fluctuates from market to market, based on traffic studies.

When messages are painted onto the billboards instead of being pasted on, their effective life is longer and the space rental price higher.

Successful billboard copy must be short and illustrations simple, because the duration of viewing time as motorists pass is brief. Eye-catching impact is the goal. That requires powerful design and strong colors. Two lively examples: "Heaven Can Wait . . . Wellness Works" and "We Don't Do That in Clarke County," an antilittering billboard in Georgia. One message was five words long, the other seven, quickly absorbed. Billboards have reinforcement value in support of a program using other methods as well. Design and preparation of billboard posters are handled by advertising agencies, while physical placement is done by the billboard companies.

Corporate Design

The need to present a unified visual image to the world is becoming increasingly evident to corporations and nonprofit organizations. Especially among corporations that have grown rapidly by acquiring many subsidiaries, the uncoordinated proliferation of letterheads, signs, publication symbols, news release sheets, packages, and other visual public representations of the organization gives a jumbled, unfocused appearance.

Creation of a simple, powerful logotype for use on all printed matter and signs projects an image of the company as a tightly knit contemporary operation. An impressive logo suggests quality and strength.

In the acquisition-minded climate of corporate life today, companies often add so many subsidiaries that the original names of the parent firms become inadequate. So these corporations adopt generalized names, usually of one or two words. United States Steel Corporation changed its name to USX Corporation, and American Machinery & Foundry Company became AMF Incorporated.

Because it no longer makes cans but has moved into such varied fields as life insurance, direct mail, recorded music, and stock brokerage, the American Can Company decided to change its name. It paid Lippincott & Margulies consultants $200,000 to help it choose a new one. The choice was Primerica, a synthetic word intended to reflect the company's "prime" growth prospects and ability to finance them.

Corporate redesign usually involves coordinated effort by the public relations and marketing departments. First, management must define the objectives to be sought in the new design. Should the graphic style be ultramodern, formal and conservative, or perhaps old-fashioned to suggest historical continuity? A counseling firm and graphics specialist are usually brought into the discussion. A detailed audit of existing printed materials and signs is necessary to establish the areas where the new design will be used. In a corporation with numerous divisions, the logotype may be color-coded—a different color for each division, with identification of the division in type below.

As companies enter the international market, they often find that their traditional identifying logotypes are unsuitable in foreign countries because of language complications and cultural differences. So they seek logos that are easily identified around the world. The Fuji Bank of Japan, for example, replaced its symbol using Japanese letters with a simple design consisting of a drawing of Mount Fujiyama and the words Fuji Bank. Corporate designers also must wrestle with the need to create symbols and designs that are effective on computer screens and other electronic outlets.

Creation of a symbolic person to represent a corporate product is another effective graphic method—the Pillsbury Doughboy, for example.

Goodwill Industries formerly had as its symbol a cartoon character, a smiling young man, feather in his hat and a lunch box in his hand, pictured rolling along in a wheelchair. The national help-the-handicapped organization found that the symbol, while clever, did not print well and lacked sales appeal on signs outside its retail outlets. The design consultant Goodwill employed replaced the symbol with a rectangular logo in which a large lowercase g in the upper-left corner looks like half of a smiling face.

Creation of a graphics standards manual helps a large organization to enforce its unified designs throughout all its operations. A consistent use of paper color and texture, print style and size, and standard specifications for ink colors offers a subtle but constant identity for an organization. For example, most consumers of soft drinks can readily recognize the Coca-Cola red.

Summary

Television

Television is the dominant form of visual communication in contemporary life. News releases can be provided to TV stations in printed form, like those submitted to newspapers; as prepared scripts; or as video news releases (VNRs). VNRs can be expanded into infomercials. Cable television news has provided a new outlet for public relations materials.

Other Uses of Videotape

Corporations and nonprofit organizations use videotape to reach external audiences and to communicate information and instruction internally. Such uses include videotaped financial reports, internal corporate TV news programs, videotaped training and marketing programs, videotaped sales messages, and home videos.

Motion Pictures

Most sponsored films are shown to viewers without charge. Public relations opportunities also exist with product placement in commercial films. Sponsored films, or industrial films, can be shown to groups or on cable television.

Still Images for Projection

Slides, filmstrips, and transparencies are cheaper to produce than films and videotapes and also have simpler projection requirements. Text-only slides should have a maximum of 25 words. Color can provide a strong contrast for both visual appeal and readability. Overhead transparencies are especially good in classrooms and small discussion groups because of the flexibility provided by masking out portions of the image to show several steps in a process on one transparency.

Still Photography

Newspaper editors like to have mug shots of people mentioned in press releases. Publicity shots of groups should avoid stiff, self-conscious poses. A press kit should include a selection of photos.

Comic Books and Cartoons

Drawings are good for illustrating steps in a process, but the artwork must be of professional quality. Public relations practitioners must be aware of copyright issues with published cartoons and comic strips.

Outdoor Displays

Billboards and building signs have potential as public relations tools. The practitioner must know the fundamentals of billboard design and economics. Successful billboard copy must be short and illustrations simple.

Corporate Design

Corporations and nonprofit organizations need to present a unified visual image in their letterhead, signs, publication symbols, news release sheets, and packaging. This may involve the use of a logo. With the proliferation of acquisitions and mergers, some corporations have adopted generalized names. Corporate redesign involves coordination between the public relations and marketing departments.

Case Activity: What Would You Do?

The local chapter of the American Lung Association needs to update its ten-minute slide presentation about the activities and services of the organization. Do some research on the American Lung Association and what it does. Then write the script on the right side of the paper. On the left, briefly describe the slides that would be keyed to the basic points of the script.

Questions for Review and Discussion

1. What is the fundamental difference between a news story in a newspaper and one on television?
2. Under what conditions might a public relations adviser recommend distribution of a videotaped news release?
3. In what ways can a corporation make use of videotaped presentations?
4. If you were handling public relations for an airline, what types of publicity tie-ins might you develop with a Hollywood motion picture producer?
5. A food manufacturer plans to produce a sponsored film about a new oat-bran cereal. What elements might it include in the film? To what target audiences might it show the film?
6. Why is it desirable to write the script of a slide show before the pictures are taken?
7. What is a storyboard?
8. Why is a mug shot a useful photographic tool in public relations practice?
9. Billboard companies rent display space on the basis of a *100-showing*. What does this mean?
10. How can graphics design help to strengthen a corporation's public image?

Suggested Readings

Amberg, Alan. "Creating a Visual That's Worth 1,000 Words." *Public Relations Tactics,* January 1995, pp. 14–15.

Blount, David, and Cameron, Glen T. "VNRs and Air Checks: A Content Analysis of On-Air Use of Video News Releases." *Journalism and Mass Communication Quarterly,* Winter, 1997.

Elsasser, John. "More Proof That VNRs Work." *Public Relations Tactics,* November 1995, p. 4.

Frank, Robert. "Seeing Red Abroad, Pepsi Rolls Out a New Blue Can." *Wall Street Journal,* April 2, 1996, pp. B1 and B4.

Harmon, Mark D., and White, Candace. "How Television News Programs Use Video News Releases." *Public Relations Review,* Vol. 27, Summer 2001, pp. 213–222.

Lewis, Peter H. "Home Pages Never Die; You Must Kill Them." *New York Times,* January 2, 1996, p. C15.

Stone, Martha. "Graphics Help Editors Visualize Your Story." *Public Relations Tactics,* October 1995, p. 10.

"VNRs Featuring Celebrities Win Attention of TV News Directors." *O'Dwyer's PR Services Report,* April 1996, pp. 1, 8, 10, and 12–13.

Wilcox, Dennis L. *Public Relations Writing and Media Techniques.* New York: Addison Wesley Longman, 4th edition, 2001.

Directory of Useful Web Sites

General Information/Links

Impulse Research: www.impulse-research.com/prlist.html
PR Watch: www.prwatch.org
PR Network: www.usprnet.com
Public Relations Central: www.publicrelationscentral.com
Public Relations Resources: www.publicrelationsresources.com
Public Relations Navigator: www.prnavigator.com
Online Public Relations: www.online-pr.com
Public Relations Museum: www.prmuseum.com

Publications

Communication Briefings: www.combriefings.com
Communication World: www.iabc.com/cw/index.htm
O'Dwyer's Public Relations Newsletter: www.odwyerpr.com
PR News: www.phillips.com/prnews.htm
PR Reporter: www.prpublishing.com
PR Tactics: www.prsa.org/tactics.html
PRWeek: www.prweekus.com
The Strategist: www.prsa.org/stat.html

Organizations

AEJMC Public Relations Division: www.lamar.colostate.edu/aejmcpr
Council of Public Relations Firms: www.prfirms.org
International Association of Business Communicators: www.iabc.com
International Public Relations Association: www.ipranet.org
Institute for Public Relations (United States): www.instituteforpr.com
Institute for Public Relations (United Kingdom): www.ipr.org.uk
National School Public Relations Association: www.nspra.org
Public Relations Society of America: www.prsa.org
Public Relations Student Society of America: www.prssa.org
Women Executives in Public Relations: www.wepr.org

Services

Business Wire: www.businesswire.com
PRNewswire: www.prnewswire.com
Employment: www.workinpr.com
MediaLink: www.medialink.com

A Public Relations Glossary

Account executive A person in a public relations firm or advertising agency who works with a client on a program.

Accreditation In public relations, the designation APR given to members of the Public Relations Society of America with at least five years of experience who have passed written and oral examinations. The International Association of Business Communicators has a designation, ABC, standing for Accredited Business Communicator, based on experience and testing.

Actuality A brief on-the-scene report, live or on tape, inserted into a radio news show.

Agenda-setter A term often applied to the mass media, whose choice of news stories and headlines suggests to the public what to think about.

Annual report A corporate information document filed each year with the Securities and Exchange Commission. Many companies expand their reports with illustrations and text for distribution to stockholders, employees, and other interested persons.

Backgrounder Slang term for an article giving the background of an organization, individual, or situation.

Benchmark study A measurement of audience attitudes before and after a public relations campaign.

Bill stuffer Company information or sales material placed in an envelope containing a customer's bill.

Bio Slang abbreviation for the detailed biography a practitioner prepares for a client.

Booker Publicist whose assignment is to place clients on talk shows and in other public events.

Bottom line Popular usage indicating the most important fact; derived from the bottom line of a financial statement, showing net profit or loss.

CEO Chief executive officer of a corporation.

Channeling The technique of tapping a group's attitudes with salient messages that propose a course of action.

Cheesecake Photograph of a scantily clad young woman used as a publicity device. Similar photographs of men are called "beefcake."

Communication audit A review to determine what public relations material the target audience is receiving and what it desires to receive.

Copyright The protection of a creative work from unauthorized use.

Copy-testing The technique of trying out material on a small group before distributing it to an entire audience.

Corporate advertising Advertising intended to enhance public conception of a company or to advocate a company policy. (See *Institutional advertising.*)

Corporate communications Term covering all types of communication by a company to both external and internal audiences.

Courtesy bias Tendency of some survey respondents to give a socially "correct" answer rather than one disclosing their true opinions.

Crisis communications Methods and policies a corporation uses in distributing information when its operations become involved in an emergency situation affecting the public.

Database Indexed information held in computer storage, from which a computer user can summon selected material, usually for a fee.

Decoder In communication theory, one who receives a message. (See *Encoder.*)

Demographics The characteristics of a human population, including size, density, growth, distribution, and vital statistics.

Editor Director of a newspaper's news and editorial department; may be subordinate to the publisher or on an equal footing, depending upon the newspaper's organization.

Associate editor Director of the editorial and commentary pages.

City editor Director of the local news staff; the person to whom most news releases are addressed.

Managing editor Manager of news operations, to whom the city editor and other news editors answer.

Electronic mail Textual messages transmitted from one computer terminal to another, rather than delivered by a mail carrier or messenger.

Embargo Statement of the day and hour set by the creator of a news release for use by the news media.

Encoder In communication theory, one who sends a message. (See *Decoder*.)

Facsimile Electronic method of transmitting exact reproductions of printed matter. Often called "fax."

Fact sheet An advisory information sheet about a forthcoming event.

Feedback Reaction from those affected by an activity or public relations material about the situation.

Fiber optics Transmission of signals through highly transparent strands of extremely thin glass, instead of by wire.

Filmstrip Sequence of film frames that, when advanced one by one in a projector, presents a topic on a screen; used as a training tool.

Flack Derogatory term applied primarily to a person who publicizes entertainment events and personalities. (See *Press agentry*.)

Focus group Panel of persons, representative of the audience a public relations practitioner desires to reach, who are asked to give their opinions of proposed programs.

Freeloading The practice of some reporters and editors to accept gifts, entertainment, and travel from organizations seeking to influence them.

Gatekeeper Editor, reporter, news director, or other person who decides what material is printed, broadcast, or otherwise offered to the public.

Gross impressions Total circulation and listening audience of the print and broadcast media that use a news release.

Hierarchy of needs Abraham Maslow's definition of an individual's five levels of needs, a basis for planning appeals to self-interest.

Hit A contact made with a Web site by an Internet user.

Hotline In public relations, a toll-free telephone number set up by a trade association or corporation to provide quick answers, especially to the news media.

Hype The promotion of movie and television stars, books, magazines, and so forth, through shrewd use of the media; used as both noun and verb. (See *Press agentry*.)

Hypodermic needle theory The belief that people receive information directly without any intervening variable, as in a vacuum.

Image-building Protection and enhancement of the reputation of an organization or individual.

Impression Exposure of an individual to a news release through the print or broadcast media. (See *Gross impressions*.)

Information on demand Computerized information on requested topics called up on a television or computer screen by the user.

Information superhighway Popular term to describe the emerging system of transmission that blends television, telephones, and computers to provide vastly expanded two-way communication.

Institutional advertising Advertising intended to strengthen an organization's image rather than to stimulate immediate sales of its products or services. (See *Corporate advertising*.)

Internet Master computer network connecting networks worldwide, enabling computer users to exchange e-mail, hold electronic conversations, obtain information and entertainment, and operate sites on the World Wide Web.

Internship Temporary employment by a student to obtain professional work experience.

Interpersonal communication Exchange between two or more persons in close proximity using conversation and gestures.

Issues management Program of identifying and addressing issues of public concern in which a company is or should be involved.

Libel Defamation mainly by written or printed words; but also, as interpreted by the courts, by broadcast. (See *Slander*.)

Line function Pursuit of management objectives through supervision, delegation of authority, and work assignments. (See *Staff function*.)

Literary agent Person who represents an author in dealings with publishers.

Lobbyist Person who presents an organization's point of view to members of Congress or other government bodies.

Marketing communications Product publicity, promotion, and advertising.

Marketing public relations Use of public relations techniques to support overall advertising and marketing objectives of a company or client.

Message entropy Tendency for a message to dissipate, or lose information, as it is disseminated.

Muckrakers Writers who seek to expose corrupt and immoral conduct by companies, institutions, and governments; specifically, a group of early 1900s writers and publications in America.

Mug shot Slang term for a head-and-shoulders photograph of an individual for newspaper publication.

News conference Meeting at which the spokesperson for an organization or an individual in the news delivers information to reporters and answers their questions; often called a "press conference."

News release Timely information about an activity of a public relations practitioner's client or organization, distributed in ready-to-use form.

Off-the-record Practice of giving reporters confidential information with the demand that it not be published.

100-showing Number of billboards needed to expose a message to approximately 100 percent of the population in a designated area within 30 days.

Online Connection to a computer network through which users exchange e-mail, hold discussions, and call up information from many sources. Customers of commercial online services can enter the Internet.

Pattern speech Basic speech written so that several speakers can deliver it to different audiences with only minor variations.

People meter A device for measuring how much a person watches television, used in determining the size of TV audiences.

Pilot test Tryout of a public relations message and key copy points on a small audience before general distribution.

Planter Publicist who delivers news releases to media offices and urges their use.

Positioning The practice of creating corporate identity programs that establish a place in the market for a company and its products. Also, the effort to get ahead by doing something first.

Press agentry Term applied primarily to the publicizing of entertainers and shows; often used in a derogatory sense. (See *Hype*.)

Press conference See *News conference*.

Press kit Folder containing news releases, photographs, and background information, distributed to media representatives.

Preventive public relations Efforts to maintain goodwill for an organization or individual through reinforcing messages.

Probability sample Survey in which every member of the targeted audience has a chance of being selected for questioning.

Product recall Act of calling back from consumers a company's product found to be defective, for repair or replacement.

Public affairs Term used primarily to describe work in the areas of government and community relations.

Public information Term used primarily by government agencies, social service organizations, and universities to describe their public relations activities.

Publisher Chief official of a newspaper who directs financial, mechanical, and administrative operations, and sometimes news and editorial operations as well.

Purposive sampling Selection of opinion leaders to be interviewed; usually used when approval of the group is necessary for success of a public relations campaign.

Quota sampling Selection of a group to be polled that matches the characteristics of the entire audience.

Royalty fee Amount of money received by an author for each copy of a book sold, usually 10 or 15 percent of the retail price; also money received by program distributors for materials used in broadcasting.

Satellite transmission Method of transmitting text, pictures, and sound by beaming an electronic signal to a transponder on a satellite orbiting 22,300 miles above the earth, from which it bounces back to receiving dishes on the ground.

Semantic noise Inept language usage that impedes the receiver's ability to comprehend a message; for example, use of trade jargon to a general audience.

Semantics Study of words and their use and interpretation.

Slander Oral defamation of character. (See *Libel.*)

Social contract Popular term for a corporation's set of responsibilities to the public.

Source credibility Use of representatives who have expertise, sincerity, and charisma to win acceptance from an audience.

Spam Unsolicited bulk e-mail messages sent on the Internet, widely regarded as junk mail.

Split message Exposure of two or three different appeals to separate audiences, to determine which is most effective.

Sponsored film Motion picture paid for by an organization to deliver information or a message, usually shown without charge.

Staff function Pursuit of management objectives through suggestions, recommendations, and advice. In corporate organization, public relations is a staff function. (See *Line function.*)

Teleconference Presentation or discussion by television involving groups assembled at scattered receiving points, usually with telephone or television channels that permit distant viewers to ask questions or express reactions.

Teletext System of delivering news and other information to a television screen, in which the viewer can select certain portions of the material to watch.

Telethon Fund-raising program on television lasting several hours, in which appeals for donations are mixed with entertainment.

Trade journal Magazine designed and edited for a special-interest commercial or professional group.

Trademark Name, symbol, or other device identifying a product, officially registered and legally restricted to the use of the owner or manufacturer.

Transfer Technique of associating a person, product, or organization with individuals or situations of high or low credibility, depending on the intention of the message.

Transparency Sheet of transparent acetate or similar material on which text or graphic material is placed for showing on an overhead projector.

Videocassette Small container of videotape that can be inserted in a playback machine for projection.

Videoconference See *Teleconference.*

Video news release (VNR) Pictorial news release distributed on videotape, with or without accompanying spoken commentary.

Videotape A recording of moving images and sound on magnetic tape.

Videotex Two-way communication system in which a viewer receives information on a screen and sends messages by keyboard.

World Wide Web Portion of the Internet using color, printed words, illustrations, and sound to deliver information and entertainment. Public relations firms, media, advertisers, and others maintain home pages on the Web.

Bibliography of Selected Books, Directories, and Periodicals

General Books

Baskin, Otis, Aronoff, Craig, and Lattimore, Dan. *Public Relations: The Profession and the Practice,* 4th edition. Dubuque, IA: Brown & Benchmark, 1997.

Caywood, Clarke, editor. *The Handbook of Strategic Public Relations & Integrated Communications.* New York: McGraw Hill, 1997.

Cutlip, Scott M., Center, Allen H., and Broom, Glen M. *Effective Public Relations,* 8th edition. Upper Saddle River, NJ: Prentice Hall, 2000.

Dilenschneider, Robert L., editor. *Dartnell's Public Relations Handbook,* 4th edition. Chicago: Dartnell, 1996.

Dozier, David M., with Grunig, James and Grunig, Larissa. *Manager's Guide to Excellence in Public Relations and Communication Management.* Mahwah, NJ: Lawrence Erlbaum, 1995.

Elwood, William N. *Public Relations Inquiry as Rhetorical Criticism: Case Studies of Corporate Discourse and Social Influence.* Westport, CT: Praeger, 1995.

Grunig, James E., editor. *Excellence in Public Relations and Communication Management.* Hillsdale, NJ: Lawrence Erlbaum, 1991.

Guth, David W., and Marsh, Charles. *Public Relations: A Values-Driven Approach.* Needham Heights, MA: Allyn & Bacon, 2000.

Harris, Thomas L. *Value-Added Public Relations.* Lincolnwood, IL: NTC Contemporary Books, 1998.

Heath, Robert L., editor. *Handbook of Public Relations.* Thousand Oaks, CA: Sage Publications, 2001.

Kendall, Robert. *Public Relations Campaign Strategies: Planning for Implementation,* 2nd edition. New York: HarperCollins, 1996.

Matera, Fran R., and Artique, Ray J. *Public Relations Campaigns and Techniques: Building Bridges to the 21st Century.* Needham Heights, MA: Allyn & Bacon, 2000.

McElreath, Mark. *Managing Systematic and Ethical Public Relations Campaigns,* 2nd edition. Madison, WI: Brown & Benchmark, 1997.

Newsom, Doug, Turk, Judy Vanslyke, and Kruckeberg, Dean. *This Is PR: The Realities of Public Relations,* 7th edition. Belmont, CA: Wadsworth, 2000.

Seitel, Fraser P. *The Practice of Public Relations,* 8th edition. Upper Saddle River, NJ: Prentice Hall, 2001.

Smith, Ronald D. *Strategic Planning for Public Relations.* Mahwah, NJ: Lawrence Erlbaum Associates, 2002.

Stauber, John, and Rampton, Sheldon. *Toxic Sludge Is Good For You: Lies, Damn Lies and the Public Relations Industry.* Monroe, Maine: Common Courage Press, 1996.

Theaker, Alison. *The Public Relations Handbook.* New York: Routledge, 2001.

Toth, Elizabeth L., and Heath, Robert L., editors. *Rhetorical and Critical Approaches to Public Relations.* Hillsdale, NJ: Lawrence Erlbaum, 1991.

Wilcox, Dennis L., Cameron, Glen T., Ault, Phillip H., and Agee, Warren K. *Public Relations: Strategies and Tactics,* 7th edition. Boston: Allyn & Bacon, 2003.

Wilson, Laurie J. *Strategic Program Planning for Effective Public Relations Campaigns.* Dubuque, IA: Kendall-Hunt, 1997.

Special Interest

Business/Management

Austin, Erica W., and Pinkleton, Bruce E. *Strategic Public Relations Management.* Mahwah, NJ: Lawrence Erlbaum Associates, 2001.

Chajet, Clive, and Shachtman, Tom. *Image by Design: From Corporate Vision to Business Reality.* Reading, MA: Addison-Wesley, 1991.

Corrado, Frank M. *Getting the Word Out: How Managers Can Create Value with Communications.* Homewood, IL: Business One-Irwin, 1993.

Ferguson, Sherry D. *Communication Planning: An Integrated Approach.* Thousand Oaks, CA: Sage Publications, 1999.

Green, Peter. *Reputation Is Everything: How to Safeguard Your Company's Image.* Homewood, IL: Irwin, 1994.

Haywood, Roger. *Managing Your Reputation: How to Plan and Run Communications Programs That Win Friends and Build Success.* New York: McGraw-Hill, 1994.

Heath, Robert. *Management of Corporate Communications.* Hillsdale, NJ: Lawrence Erlbaum, 1994.

Ledingham, John A., and Bruning, Stephen D. *Public Relations as Relationship Management.* Mahwah: Lawrence Erlbaum, 1999.

Saffir, Leonard. *Power Public Relations: How to Master the New PR,* 2nd edition. Lincolnwood, IL: NTC/Contemporary Publishing, 2001.

Sobel, Marion. *Shaping the Corporate Image: An Analytical Guide for Executive Decision Makers.* Westport, CT: Greenwood, 1992.

Careers

Helitzer, Melvin. *The Dream Job: Sports Publicity, Promotion and Public Relations.* Athens, OH: University Sports Press, 1992.

Mogel, Leonard. *Creating Your Career in Communications and Entertainment.* Mahwah, NJ: Lawrence Erlbaum Associates, 1998.

Mogel, Leonard. *Making It in Public Relations: An Insider's Guide to Career Opportunities,* 2nd edition. Mahwah, NJ: Lawrence Erlbaum Associates, 2002.

Ross, Billy I., and Johnson, Keith F., editors. *Where Shall I Go to Study Advertising and Public Relations?* Advertising Education Publications, Box 68232, Lubbock, TX 79414–8232. Pamphlet listing college and university programs.

Sequin, James, editor. *Business Communications: The Real World and Your Career.* Belmont, CA: Southwestern College Publishing, 2000.

Case Studies

Center, Allen, and Jackson, Patrick. *Public Relations Practices: Managerial Case Studies and Problems,* 5th edition. Englewood Cliffs, NJ: Prentice Hall, 1995.

Hendrix, Jerry A. *Public Relations Cases,* 5th edition. Belmont, CA: Wadsworth, 2001.

Matera, Fran R., and Artique, Ray J. *Public Relations Campaigns and Techniques: Building Bridges to the 21st Century.* Needham Heights, MA: Allyn & Bacon, 2000.

Moss, Danny, and DeSanto, Barbara. *Public Relations Cases: International Perspectives.* New York: Routledge, 2001.

Peterson, Gary L. *Communicating in Organizations: A Casebook.* Needham Heights, MA: Allyn & Bacon, 2000.

Simon, Raymond, and Wylie, Frank W. *Cases in Public Relations Management.* Homewood, IL: NTC Business Books, 1993.

Communication/Persuasion

Bryant, Jennings, and Zillmann, Dolf. *Media Effects: Advances in Theory and Research.* Hillsdale, NJ: Lawrence Erlbaum, 1994.

Combs, James E., and Nimmo, Dan. *The New Propaganda: The Dictatorship of Palaver in Contemporary Politics.* New York: Longman, 1993.

Crossen, Cynthia. *Tainted Truth: The Manipulation of Fact in America.* New York: Simon and Schuster, 1994.

DeFleur, Melvin L., and Dennis, Everette E. *Understanding Mass Communication.* Boston: Houghton Mifflin, 1994.

Jowett, Garth S., and O'Donnell, Victoria. *Propaganda and Persuasion.* 3rd edition. Thousand Oaks, CA: Sage Publications, 1999.

Larson, Charles U. *Persuasion: Reception and Responsibility,* 8th edition. Belmont, CA: Wadsworth, 1998.

Perloff, Richard M. *The Dynamics of Persuasion.* Hillsdale, NJ: Lawrence Erlbaum, 1993.

Pratkanis, Anthony, and Aronson, Elliott. *Age of Propaganda: The Everyday Use and Abuse of Persuasion.* Salt Lake City, UT: W.H. Freeman, 1992.

Samovar, Larry, and Porter, Richard. *Intercultural Communication: A Reader,* 8th edition. Belmont, CA: Wadsworth, 1997.

Severin, Werner, and Tankard, James. *Communication Theories: Origins, Methods, Uses,* 4th edition. New York: Longman, 1997.

Simons, Herbert W., Morreale, Joanne, and Gronbeck, Bruce. *Persuasion in Society.* Thousand Oaks, CA: Sage Publications, 2000.

Wilke, Jurgen. *Propaganda in the 20th Century.* Creekskill, NJ: Hampton Press, 1998.

Community Relations

Bagin, Don, editor. *The School and Community Relations.* Needham Heights, MA: Allyn and Bacon, 1994.

Kruckeberg, Dean, and Starck, Kenneth. *Public Relations and Community: A Reconstructed Theory.* Westport, CT: Greenwood, 1988.

Pick, Maritza. *How to Save Your Neighborhood, City or Town.* San Francisco: Sierra Club Books, 1993.

Crisis Communications

Adamson, Jim. *The Denny's Story: How a Company in Crisis Resurrected Its Good Name.* New York: John Wiley & Sons, 2001.

Barton, Lawrence. *Crisis in Organizations: Managing and Communicating in the Heat of Crisis.* Cincinnati, OH: South-Western, 1993.

Coombs, W. Timothy. *Ongoing Crisis Communication: Planning, Managing, and Responding.* Thousand Oaks, CA: Sage Publications, 1999.

Fearn-Banks, Kathleen. *Crisis Communications: A Casebook Approach,* 2nd edition. Mahwah, NJ: Lawrence Erlbaum Associates, 2002.

Lerbinger, Otto. *The Crisis Manager: Facing Risk and Responsibility.* Mahwah, NJ: Lawrence Erlbaum, 1997.

Marconi, Joe. *Crisis Marketing: When Bad Things Happen to Good Companies.* Chicago: Probus, 1993.

Mitroff, Ian I. *Managing Crises before They Happen.* New York: AMACOM, 2001.

Ogizek, Michel, and Guilery, Jean-Michel. *Communicating in Crisis: A Theoretical and Practical Guide to Crisis Management.* New York: Aldine De Gruyter Publishers, 1999.

Pauchant, Thierry, and Mitroff, Ian. *Transforming the Crisis-Prone Organization.* San Francisco: Jossey-Bass, 1992.

Vanderford, Marsha, and Smith, David M. *The Silicone Breast Implant Story: Communication and Uncertainty.* Mahwah, NJ: Lawrence Erlbaum, 1996.

Cultural Diversity/Gender

Banks, Stephen P. *Multicultural Public Relations: A Social Interpretive Approach.* Thousand Oaks, CA: Sage, 1995.

Biagi, Shirley, and Kern-Foxworth, Marilyn. *Facing Differences: Race, Gender and Mass Media.* California: Pine Forge Press, 1997.

Certo, Samuel. *Modern Management: Diversity, Quality, Ethics, and the Global Environment,* 6th edition. Needham Heights, MA: Allyn and Bacon, 1994.

Grunig, Larissa A., Toth, Elizabeth L., and Hon, Linda C. *Women in Public Relations: How Gender Influences Practice.* New York: Guilford Publications, 2001.

Henderson, George. *Cultural Diversity in the Workplace: Issues and Strategies.* Westport, CT: Quorum, 1994.

Sonnenschein, William H. *Workforce Diversity.* Lincolnwood, IL: NTC Contemporary Books, 1997.

Trompenaars, Fons. *Riding the Waves of Culture: Understanding Cultural Diversity in Business.* Burr Ridge, IL: Irwin, 1994.

Demographics

Al-Deen, Hana S. Noor. *Cross-Cultural Communication and Aging in the United States.* Mahwah, NJ: Lawrence Erlbaum, 1997.

Crispell, Diane. *The Insider's Guide to Demographic Know-How.* Chicago: Probus, 1992.

Kahle, Lynn R., and Chiagouris, Larry. *Values, Lifestyles and Psychographics.* Mahwah, NJ: Lawrence Erlbaum, 1997.

Desktop Publishing/Design

Baird, Russell N., McDonald, Duncan, and Pittman, Ronald K. *The Graphics of Communication,* 6th edition. Fort Worth, TX: Harcourt Brace, 1993.

Bly, Robert. *Perfect Sales Piece: A Complete Do-It-Yourself Guide to Creating Brochures, Catalogs, Fliers.* New York: Wiley, 1994.

Kostelnick, Charles, and Roberts, David D. *Designing Visual Language: Strategies for Professional Communicators.* Needham Heights, MA: Allyn & Bacon, 1998.

Lichty, Tom. *Design Principles for Desktop Publishers,* 2nd edition. Belmont, CA: Wadsworth, 1994.

Morton, Linda P. *Public Relations Publications: Designing for Target Audiences.* Norman, OK: Sultan Communication Books, 2001.

Education

Barnes, Chris. *Practical Marketing for Schools.* Cambridge, MA: Blackwell, 1993.

Hayes, Thomas J. *New Strategies in Higher Education Marketing.* Binghamton, NY: Haworth, 1991.

Holcomb, John H. *Educational Marketing: A Business Approach to School-Community Relations.* New York: University Press of America, 1993.

Johnson, Kendall. *School Crisis Management: A Hands-On Guide to Training Crisis Response Teams.* Alameda, CA: Hunter House, 1993.

Kowalski, Theodore J. *Public Relations in Schools.* Upper Saddle River, NJ: Prentice Hall, 2000.

Employee Relations

D'Aprix, Roger. *Communicating for Change: Connecting the Workplace with the Marketplace.* San Francisco: Jossey-Bass, 1996.

Holtz, Shel. *Intranets: The Communicator's Guide to Content, Design, and Management.* Chicago: Lawrence Ragan Communications, 1997.

Jablin, Fred M., and Putnam, Linda, editors. *The New Handbook of Organizational Communication.* Thousand Oaks, CA: Sage Publications, 2000.

Marchington, Mick. *Managing the Team: A Guide to Successful Employee Involvement.* Cambridge, MA: Blackwell Business, 1992.

Peterson, Gary L. *Communicating in Organizations,* 2nd edition. Needham Heights, MA: Allyn & Bacon, 2000.

Spicer, Christopher. *Organizational Public Relations: A Political Perspective.* Mahwah, NJ: Lawrence Erlbaum, 1997.

Sypher, Berverly D., editor. *Case Studies in Organizational Communication: Perspectives on Contemporary Work Life.* New York: Guilford Publications, 1997.

Environment

Harrison, E. Bruce. *Going Green: How to Communicate Your Company's Environmental Commitment.* Homewood, IL: Business One-Irwin, 1993.

Ottman, Jacquelyn. *Green Marketing: Challenges and Opportunities for the New Marketing Age.* Lincolnwood, IL: NTC Business, 1994.

Ottman, Jacquelyn. *Green Marketing: Responding to Environmental Consumer Demands.* Lincolnwood, IL: NTC Business, 1993.

Ethics

Baker, Lee W. *The Credibility Factor: Putting Ethics to Work in Public Relations.* Burr Ridge, IL: Irwin, 1993.

Casmir, Fred L. *Ethics in Intercultural and International Communication.* Mahwah, NJ: Lawrence Erlbaum, 1997.

Day, Louis A. *Ethics in Media Communications: Cases and Controversies.* Belmont, CA: Wadsworth, 1997.

McElreath, Mark P. *Managing Systematic and Ethical Public Relations.* Dubuque, IA: Brown and Benchmark, 1997.

Seib, Philip, and Fitzpatrick, Kathy. *Public Relations Ethics.* Fort Worth, TX: Harcourt Brace, 1995.

Sims, Ronald. *Ethics and Organizational Decision Making: A Call for Renewal.* Westport, CT: Quorum, 1994.

Stauber, John, and Rampton, Sheldon. *Toxic Sludge Is Good for You: Damn Lies and the Public Relations Industry.* Monroe, ME: Common Courage Press, 1995. Critical analysis of public relations.

Financial/Investor Relations

Arfin, F. N. *Financial Public Relations.* Philadelphia: Trans-Atlantic, 1994.

Bowman, Pat. *Handbook of Financial Public Relations.* Newton, MA: Butterworth-Heinemann, 1993.

Higgins, Richard B. *Best Practices in Global Investor Relations.* Westport, CT: Greenwood Publishing Company, 2000.

Marcus, Bruce W., and Lee, Wallace Sherwood. *New Dimensions in Investor Relations: Competing for Capital in the 21st Century.* New York: John Wiley & Sons, 1998.

Trautmann, Ted, and Hamilton, James. *Informal Corporate Disclosure under Federal Securities Law: Press Releases, Analyst Calls, and Other Communications.* Riverwoods, IL: CCH Incorporated, 2001.

Fund-Raising/Development

Ciconte, Barbara K., and Jacob, Jeanne G. *Fund Raising Basics: A Complete Guide.* Gaithersburg, MD: Aspen Publications, 1997.

Edles, L. Peter. *Fund-Raising: Hands-on Tactics for Nonprofit Groups.* New York: McGraw-Hill, 1993.

Kelly, Kathleen S. *Effective Fund-Raising Management.* Mahwah, NJ: Lawrence Erlbaum, 1996.

Lindahl, Wesley E. *Strategic Planning for Fund-Raising.* San Francisco: Jossey-Bass, 1992.

Rosso, Henry. *Achieving Excellence in Fund-Raising.* San Francisco: Jossey-Bass, 1991.

Government/Public Affairs

Fitzwater, Marlin. *Call the Briefing! Reagan & Bush, Sam & Helen; a Decade with Presidents and the Press.* New York: New York Times Books, 1995.

Henry, Nicholas. *Public Administration and Public Affairs.* Englewood Cliffs, NJ: Prentice Hall, 1995.

Kurtz, Howard. *Spin Cycle: How the White House and the Media Manipulate the News.* New York: Touchstone, 1998.

Lewis, Michael. *Trail Fever: Spin Doctors, Rented Strangers, and Thumb Wrestling on the Road to the White House.* New York: Vintage Books, 1998.

Rollins, Ed, and DeFrank, Tom. *Bare Knuckles and Back Rooms.* New York: Broadway Books, 1996.

Walsh, Kenneth T. *Feeding the Beast: The White House Versus the Press.* New York: Random House, 1996.

Wittenberg, Ernest, and Wittenberg, Elisabeth. *How to Win in Washington.* Washington, D.C.: Basil Blackwell, 1994.

History

Cutlip, Scott M. *Public Relations History: From the Seventeenth to the Twentieth Century.* Hillsdale, NJ: Lawrence Erlbaum, 1995.

Cutlip, Scott M. *The Unseen Power: Public Relations. A History.* Hillsdale, NJ: Lawrence Erlbaum, 1994.

Ewen, Stuart. *PR! A Social History of Spin.* New York: Basic Books, 1996.

Griese, Noel. *Arthur W. Page: Publisher, Public Relations Pioneer, Patriot.* Atlanta: Anvil Publishers, 2001.

Hill, John. *The Making of a Public Relations Man.* Lincolnwood, IL: NTC Business, 1993.

Miller, Karen S. *The Voice of Business: Hill & Knowlton and Post-War Public Relations.* Chapel Hill: University of North Carolina Press, 1999.

Tye, Larry. *The Father of Spin: Edward L. Bernays and the Birth of Public Relations.* New York: Crown, 1998.

International

Czinkota, Michael. *The Global Marketing Imperative: Positioning Your Company for the World of Business.* Lincolnwood, IL: NTC Business, 1994.

De Mente, Boye. *How to Do Business with the Japanese,* 2nd edition. Lincolnwood, IL: NTC Business, 1993.

Grunig, Larissa A., and Grunig, James E. *Excellent Public Relations and Effective Organizations: A Study of Communication Management in Three Countries.* Mahwah, NJ: Lawrence Erlbaum Associates, 2002.

Hassan, Salah, and Kaynak, Erdener. *Globalization of Consumer Markets: Structures and Strategies.* Binghamton, NY: Haworth, 1994.

Jandt, Fred E. *Intercultural Communication: An Introduction.* Thousand Oaks, CA: Sage Publications, 1998.

Ricks, David. *Blunders in International Business,* 2nd edition. Cambridge, MA: Blackwell Press, 1993.

Samovar, Larry A., and Porter, Richard E. *Intercultural Communication: A Reader,* 9th edition. Belmont, CA: Wadsworth Publishing, 2000.

Internet/World Wide Web

Albarran, Alan B., and Goff, David H. *Understanding the Web: Social, Political and Economic Dimensions of the Internet.* Ames: Iowa State University Press, 2000.

Alexander, Janet E., and Tate, Marsha Ann. *Web Wisdom: How to Evalaute and Create Information Quality on the Web.* Mahwah, NJ: Lawrence Erlbaum Associates, 1999.

DiNucci, Darcy, Gudice, Maria, and Stiles, Lynne. *Elements of Web Design.* Berkeley, CA: Peachpit Press, 1997.

Holtz, Shel. *Public Relations on the Internet: Winning Strategies to Inform and Influence the Media, the Investment Community, the Government, the Public, and More!* New York: AMACOM, 1999.

McGuire, Mary, Stilborne, Linda, McAdams, Melinda, and Hyatt, Laurel. *The Internet Handbook for Writers, Researchers, and Journalists.* New York: Guilford Publications, 2000.

Middleburg, Don. *Winning PR in the Wired World.* New York: McGraw-Hill, 2001.

Reddick, Randy, and King, Elliott. *The Online Journalist: Using the Internet and Other Electronic Resources.* New York: Harcourt Brace, 1995.

Sellers, Don. *Getting Hits: The Definitive Guide to Promoting Your Website.* Berkeley, CA: Peachpit Press, 1997.

Sterne, Jim, and Priore, Anthony. *E-Mail Marketing: Using E-Mail to Reach Your Target Audience and Build Customer Relationships.* New York: John Wiley & Sons, 2001.

Wiggins, Richard. *The Internet for Everyone: A Guide for Users and Providers.* New York: McGraw-Hill, 1995.

Witmer, Diane F. *Spinning the Web: A Handbook for Public Relations on the Internet.* New York: Longman, 2000.

Issues Management

Heath, Robert L. *Strategic Issues Management: Organizations and Public Policy Challenges,* 2nd edition. Thousand Oaks, CA: Sage Publications, 1997.

Law

Lawrence, John, and Timberg, Bernard. *Fair Use and Free Inquiry: Copyright Law and the New Media,* 2nd edition. Norwood, NJ: Ablex, 1989.

Middleton, Kent, and Chamberlin, Bill. *Law of Public Communication,* 4th edition. New York: Longman, 1997.

Moore, Roy L., Farrar, Ronald T., and Collins, Erik L. *Advertising and Public Relations Law.* Mahwah, NJ: Lawrence Erlbaum, 1997.

Roschwalb, Susanne A., and Stack, Richard A. *Litigation Public Relations: Courting Public Opinion.* Washington, DC: Fred B. Rothman, 1995.

Stack, Richard. *Courts, Counselors, and Correspondants: A Media Relations Analysis of the Legal System.* Washington, D.C.: American University Press, 1998.

Marketing

Burnett, John, and Moriarty, Sandra. *Introduction to Marketing Communications: An Integrated Approach.* Upper Saddle River, NJ: Prentice Hall, 1998.

Duncan, Tom, and Moriarty, Sandra. *Driving Brand Value: Using Integrated Marketing to Manage Profitable Stakeholder Relationships.* New York: McGraw Hill, 1997.

Gronstedt, Anders. *The Customer Century: Lessons from World Class Companies in Integrated Marketing and Communications.* New York: Routlege, 2000.

Harris, Thomas L. *Marketer's Guide to Public Relations: How Today's Top Companies Are Using the New PR to Gain a Competitive Edge.* New York: Wiley, 1993.

Henry, Rene A. *Marketing Public Relations: The HOWS That Make It Work.* Ames: Iowa State University Press, 2000.

McCarthy, E. Jerome, and Perreault, William D. *Essentials of Marketing: A Global-Managerial Approach.* Burr Ridge, IL: Irwin, 1993.

Murphy, John H., and Cunningham, Isabella. *Marketing Communications Management.* Lincolnwood, IL: NTC Contemporary Books, 1999.

Percy, Larry. *Strategies for Implementing Integrated Marketing Communications.* Lincolnwood, IL: NTC Contemporary Books, 1997.

Ries, Al, and Trout, Jack. *The Twenty-Two Immutable Laws of Marketing.* New York: Harper Business, 1994.

Schreiber, Alfred. *Multicultural Marketing.* Lincolnwood, IL: NTC/Contemporary Publishing, 2000.

Schultz, Don E., and Barnes, Beth E. *Strategic Brand Communications Campaigns.* Lincolnwood, IL: NTC Contemporary Books, 1999.

Schultz, Don E., Tannenbaum, Stanley I., and Lauterborn, Robert R. *Integrated Marketing Communications: Putting It Together and Making It Work.* Lincolnwood, IL: NTC Contemporary Books, 1993.

Media/Press Relations

Hart, Hal. *Successful Spokespersons Are Made, Not Born.* Bloomington, IN: First Books Library, 2001.

Howard, Carole M., and Mathews, Wilima K. *On Deadline: Managing Media Relations,* 3rd edition. Prospect Heights, IL: Waveland Press, 2002.

Levine, Michael. *Guerilla PR: How to Wage an Effective Publicity Campaign Without Going Broke.* New York: Harper Business, 1994.

Strick, Michael. *Spin: How to Turn the Power of the Press to Your Advantage.* Washington, D.C.: Regnery Publishing, 1998.

Wallack, Katie, Woodruff, Katie, and Diaz, Iris. *News for a Change: An Advocate's Guide to Working with the Media.* Thousand Oaks, CA: Sage Publications, 1999.

Meetings/Seminars

Burleson, Clyde. *Effective Meetings: The Complete Guide.* New York: Wiley, 1990.

Shenson, Howard L. *How to Develop and Promote Successful Seminars and Workshops.* New York: Wiley, 1990.

Simerly, Robert G. *Planning and Marketing Conferences and Workshops: Tips, Tools & Techniques.* San Francisco: Jossey-Bass, 1990.

Nonprofit Groups/Health Agencies

Berkowitz, Eric N., Pol, Louis G., and Thomas, Richard K. *Healthcare Marketing Research: Tools and Techniques for Understanding and Analyzing Today's Healthcare Environment.* New York: McGraw Hill, 1997.

Cooper, Philip. *Health Care Marketing: A Foundation for Managed Quality,* 3rd edition. Gaithersburg, MD: Aspen, 1994.

Elwood, W. N. *Rhetoric in the War on Drugs: The Triumph and Tragedies of Public Relations.* Westport, CT: Greenwood, 1994.

Glaser, John. *An Insider's Account of the United Way Scandal.* New York: Wiley, 1994.

Migliore, R. Henry. *Strategic Planning for Not-for-Profit Organizations.* Binghamton, NY: Haworth, 1994.

Rice, Ronald E., and Atkin, Charles K. *Public Information Campaigns,* 3rd edition. Thousand Oaks, CA: Sage Publications, 2001.

Rungard, John. *Marketing and Public Relations Handbook for Museums, Galleries, and Heritage Attractions.* Blue Ridge Summit, PA: Rowman & Littlefield, 2000.

Publicity/Promotion

See also "Writing in Public Relations" section.

Engel, James. *Promotional Strategy: Managing the Marketing Communication Process.* Burr Ridge, IL: Irwin, 1994.

Gold, G. R., and Ward, S. V. *Place Promotion: The Use of Publicity and Public Relations to Sell Cities and Regions.* New York: Halsted Press, 1994.

Henry, Rene A. *Marketing Public Relations: The Hows That Make It Work.* Ames, IA: Iowa State University Press, 1995.

Kurdrie, Albert, and Sandler, Melvin. *Public Relations for Hospitality Managers: Communicating for Greater Profits.* New York: Wiley, 1995.

Levine, Michael. *Guerilla PR: How to Wage an Effective Publicity Campaign without Going Broke.* New York: Harper Business, 1994.

Yale, David. *Publicity & Media Relations Checklist.* Lincolnwood, IL: NTC Business, 1995.

Yudkin, Marcia. *Six Steps to Free Publicity: And Dozens of Other Ways to Win Free Media Attention for You and Your Business.* New York: NAL-Dutton, 1994.

Research Methods

Berger, Arthur Asa. *Media and Communication Research Methods: An Introduction to Qualitative and Quantitative Research Approaches.* Thousand Oaks, CA: Sage Publications, 2000.

Broom, Glen, and Dozier, David. *Using Research in Public Relations.* Englewood Cliffs, NJ: Prentice Hall, 1989.

Ferguson, Sherry D. *Researching the Public Opinion Environment: Theories and Methods.* Thousand Oaks, CA: Sage Publications, 2000.

Fern, Edward F. *Advanced Focus Group Research.* Thousand Oaks, CA: Sage Publications, 2001.

Frey, Lawrence R., Botan, Carl H., and Kreps, Gary L. *Investigating Communication: An Introduction to Research Methods,* 2nd edition. Needham Heights, MA: Allyn & Bacon, 2000.

Gubrium, Jaber E., and Holstein, James A. *Handbook of Interview Research.* Thousand Oaks, CA: Sage Publications, 2001.

Gunter, Barrie. *Media Research Methods: Measuring Audiences, Reactions, Impact.* Thousand Oaks, CA: Sage Publications, 2000.

Jones, Steve. *Doing Internet Research: Critical Issues and Methods for Examining the Net.* Thousand Oaks, CA: Sage Publications, 1998.

Weisberg, Herbert F., Krosnick, Jon A., and Bowen, Bruce A. *An Introduction to Survey Research, Polling and Data Analysis.* Thousand Oaks, CA: Sage Publications, 1996.

Special Events

Avrich, Barry, and Gill, Len. *Event and Entertainment Marketing: A Must Guide for Corporate Event Sponsors and Entertainment Entrepreneurs.* Chicago: Probus, 1994.

Catherwood, Dwight, and Vankirk, Richard. *The Complete Guide to Special Events.* New York: Wiley, 1992.

Goldblatt, Jeff. *Special Events: The Art and Science of Celebration.* New York: Van Nostrand Reinhold, 1997.

Jasso, Gayle. *Special Events from A to Z.* Thousand Oaks, CA: Sage, 1996.

Speeches/Presentations

Beebe, Steven A., and Beebe, Susan. *Public Speaking: An Audience-Centered Approach,* 4th edition. Needham Heights, MA: Allyn & Bacon, 2000.

Brody, Marjorie. *Speaking Your Way to the Top: Making Powerful Business Presentations.* Needham Heights, MA: Allyn & Bacon, 1998.

Daly, John A., and Engleberg, Isa. *Presentations in Everyday Life.* Boston: Houghton Mifflin, 2001.

DeVito, Joseph A. *The Elements of Public Speaking,* 6th edition. New York: Longman, 1997.

DiSanza, James, and Legge, Nancy. *Business and Professional Communication: Plans, Processes, and Performance.* Needham Heights, MA: Allyn & Bacon, 2000.

Fujishin, Randy. *The Natural Speaker,* 3rd edition. Needham Heights, MA: Allyn & Bacon, 2000.

Gronbeck, Bruce E. *Principles and Types of Speech Communication,* 13th edition. New York: Longman, 1997.

Writing in Public Relations

Aronson, Merry, and Spetner, Donald. *The Public Relations Writer's Handbook.* New York: Free Press, 1993.

Bivins, Thomas H. *Public Relations Writing: The Essentials of Style and Format,* 4th edition. Lincolnwood, IL: NTC Contemporary Books, 1999.

Marlow, Eugene. *Electronic Public Relations.* Belmont CA: Wadsworth, 1996.

Newsom, Doug, and Carrell, Bob. *Public Relations Writing: Form and Style,* 6th edition. Belmont, CA: Wadsworth Publishing, 2001.

Simon, Raymond, and Zappala, Joseph. *The Public Relations Workbook: Writing and Techniques.* Lincolnwood, IL: NTC Business, 1996.

Treadwell, Donald, and Treadwell, Jill B. *Public Relations Writing: Principles in Practice.* Needham Heights, MA: Allyn & Bacon, 2000.

Tucker, Terry, Derelian, Doris, and Rouner, Donna. *Public Relations Writing: An Issue Driven Behavioral Approach,* 3rd edition. Upper Saddle River, NJ: Prentice Hall, 1997.

Wilcox, Dennis L. *Public Relations Writing & Media Techniques,* 4th edition. New York: Addison Wesley Longman, 2001.

■ Directories

Directories are valuable tools for public relations personnel who need to communicate with a variety of specialized audiences. The following is a selected list of the leading national and international directories.

Media Directories

All-In-One Media Directory. Gebbie Press, Box 1000, New Paltz, NY 12561.

American College Media Directory. Vineberg Communications, 6120 Grand Central Parkway, Forest Hills, NY 11375.

Bacon's Media Directories: Newspaper/Magazines, Radio/TV/Cable, Media Calendar, Business Media, International Media Directory, New York Publicity Outlets, Metro California Outlets, Computer & High-Tech Media, and Medical & Health Media. Bacon Information, Inc., 332 S. Michigan Avenue, Chicago, IL 60604.

Broadcasting Cable Yearbook. Broadcasting & Cable Magazine, PO Box 7820, Torrance, CA 90504.

Burrelle's Media Directories: Newspapers and Related Media, Magazines and Newsletters, Radio, Television, and Cable. Burrelle's Media Directory, 75 E. Northfield Rd., Livingston, NJ 07039.

Cable & Station Coverage Atlas. Warren Publications, 2115 Ward Court NW, Washington, D.C. 20037.

College Media Directory. Oxbridge Communications, 150 Fifth Avenue, Suite 302, New York, NY 10011.

Editor & Publisher International YearBook. Editor & Publisher, 11 W. 19th St., New York, NY 10011–4234.

Gale's Directory of Publications. PO Box 9187, Farmington Hills, MI 48333.

Hispanic American Information Directory. 27500 Drake Road, Farmington Hills, MI 48331–3535.

Hudson's Washington News Media Directory. Hudson Associates, PO Box 311, Rhinebeck, NY 12572.

Literary Marketplace. R.R. Bowker Company, 245 W. 17th St., New York, NY 10011.

MediaMap. MediaMap, 130 The Great Road, Bedford, MA 01730.

National Directory of Community Newspapers. American Newspaper Representatives, 1700 W. Beaver Road, Suite 340, Troy, MI 48084.

National Directory of Magazines. Oxbridge Communications, 150 Fifth Avenue, Suite 302, New York, NY 10011.

North American Senior Media Directory. Gem Publishing Group, 250 E. Riverview Circle, Reno, NV 89509.

Publicists Guide to Senior Media. Promo Works, 4165 E. Thousand Oaks Blvd., Suite 335, Westlake Village, CA 91362.

Standard Rate and Data Services: Business Publications, Community Publications, Newspapers, and Spot Radio. SRDS, 3004 Glenview Rd., Wilmette, IL 60091.

The Top 200+ TV New Talk and Magazine Shows. Bradley Communications, PO Box 1206, Lansdowne, PA 19050.

U.S. All Media E-mail Directory. Direct Contact Media Services, PO Box 6726, Kennewick, WA 99336.

International Media Directories

Asia Pacific Media Guide. Asian News Service, 633 West 5th Street, Suite 2020, Los Angeles, CA 90071.

Benn's Media. Benn's Business Information Services, Riverbank House, Angelhare, Tonbridge, Kent TN9 1SE, United Kingdom.

Central American Media Directory. Florida International University School of Journalism, North Miami Campus, 3000 N.E. 151st Street, Miami, FL 33181.

Dun's Europe. Dun & Bradstreet Information Services, 3 Sylvan Way, Persipanny, NJ 07054.

European Media Yearbook: Western and Eastern Europe. CIT Publications, 3 Colleton Crescent, Exeter/Devon EX2 4DG, England.

Hollis PR Annual and Hollis Europe. Harlequin House, 7 High Street, Teddington, England TW11 8EL.

Urlichs International Directory. Reed Elsevier, 121 Chanlon Road, New Providence, NJ 07974.

Willing's Press Guide. Harlequin House, 7 High Street, Teddington, England TW11 8EL.

World Radio/TV Handbook. BPI Communications, 1695 Oak Street, Lakewood, NJ 08701.

Other Selected Directories

Awards, Honors, and Prizes. Gale Research, PO Box 9187, Farmington Hills, MI 48333.

Broadcast Interview Source. 2233 Wisconsin Avenue, Washington, D.C. 20007.

Business Organizations, Agencies, and Publications Directory. Gale Research, PO Box 9187, Farmington Hills, MI 48333.

Celebrity Source: Prime Time Television and Cast Directory. The Celebrity Source, 8033 Sunset Blvd., Suite 1108, Los Angeles, CA 90046.

Congressional Yellow Book. Leadership Directories, 1301 Pennsylvania Avenue NW, Suite 925, Washington, D.C. 20004.

Corporate Directory of Technology Companies. CorpTech, 12 Alfred Street, Suite 200, Woburn, MA 01801–9998.

Directory of Online Databases. Online Information Services, 152 Main Road, Long Hanborough, Oxford OX7 2JY, England.

Hudson's Subscription Newsletter Directory. Hudson Associates, PO Box 311, Rhinebeck, NY 12572.

National Directory of Mailing Lists. Oxbridge Communications, 150 Fifth Avenue, New York, NY 10011.

National PR Pitch Book. Infocom Group, 5900 Hollis Street, Suite R2, Emeryville, CA 94608–20008.

O'Dwyer's Directory of Corporate Communications; Directory of PR Executives; Directory of PR Firms. 271 Madison Avenue, New York, NY 10016.

Professional Freelance Writer's Directory. National Writer's Association, 1450 South Havana Street, Suite 424, Aurora, CO 80012.

The Society of American Travel Writer's Directory. 4101 Lake Boone Trail, Suite 201, Raleigh, NC 27607.

The Sourcebook of Multicultural Experts. Multicultural Marketing Resources, 332 Bleeker Street, Suite G41, New York, NY 10014.

Yearbook of Experts, Authorities, & Spokespersons. Broadcast Interview Source, 2233 Wisconsin Avenue NW, Suite 301, Washington, D.C. 20007.

Periodicals

CASE Currents. Council for the Advancement and Support of Education, 11 Dupont Circle, Washington, DC. 20036. Monthly.

Communication Briefings. 700 Black Horse Pike, Suite 110, Blackwood, NJ 08012. Monthly.

Communication World. International Association of Business Communicators (IABC), One Hallidie Plaza, Suite 600, San Francisco, CA 94102. Monthly.

International Public Relations Review. International Public Relations Association (IPRA). Cardinal House, 7 Woseley Road, East Molesey, Surrey KT8 9EL, United Kingdom. Quarterly.

Investor Relations Update. National Investor Relations Institute (NIRI), 8045 Leesburg Pike, Suite 600, Vienna, VA 22182. Monthly.

Jack O'Dwyer's PR Newsletter. 271 Madison Ave., New York, NY 10016. Weekly.

Journal of Public Relations Research. Lawrence Erlbaum, 10 Industrial Ave., Mahwah, NJ 07430. Quarterly.

O'Dwyer's PR Services Report. 271 Madison Ave., New York, NY 10016. Monthly.

PR Reporter. Box 600, Exeter, NH 03833. Weekly.

PR Week. 220 Fifth Avenue, New York, NY 10001. Weekly.

Public Relations News. 1201 Seven Locks Road, Potomac, MD 20854–3394. Weekly.

Public Relations Quarterly. 44 W. Market St., Rhinebeck, NY 12572. Quarterly.

Public Relations Review. JAI Press, 100 Prospect St., PO Box 811, Stamford, CT 06904–0811. Quarterly.

Public Relations Strategist. Public Relations Society of America (PRSA), 33 Irving Place, New York, NY 10003–2376. Quarterly.

Public Relations Tactics. Public Relations Society of America (PRSA), 33 Irving Place, New York, NY 10003–2376. Monthly.

Ragan Report. 212 West Superior St., Suite 200, Chicago, IL 60605. Weekly.

Special Events Report. 213 W. Institute Pl., Chicago, IL 60605. Biweekly.

Credits

P. 11. Tom Hanson/AP/Wide World Photos; p. 18, Richard Drew/AP/Wide World Photos; p. 22, *(top)* Rick Bowmer/AP/Wide World Photos, *(bottom)* Kim Christensen, The Facts/AP/Wide World Photos; p. 30, © Culver Photos; p. 33, U.S. Library of Congress; p. 35, Used with permission of Union centrale des arts decoratifs/© Musee de la Publicite, Paris, France; p. 39, © UPI/Corbis-Bettmann; p. 42, Marie Hansen/LIFE Magazine; © Time, Inc.; p. 43, AP/World Wide Photos; p. 44, Courtesy Edward L. Bernays; p. 45, Courtesy Edward L. Bernays; p. 86, Jack R. O'Dwyer's Public Relations Service Report; p. 89, Courtesy of workinpr.com; p. 96 *(top left)* Courtesy of Elizabeth Board, The Reader's Digest Association, *(top right)* Courtesy of Diane B. Dixon, Avery Dennison Corporation, *(middle left)* Courtesy of Mary Ellen Kating, Barnes & Noble Booksellers, *(middle right)* Courtesy of Mary Linder/Northwest Airlines, *(bottom left)* Courtesy of Anne M. McCarthy, Polaroid Corporation, *(bottom right)* Courtesy of Judith Muhlberg, The Boeing Company; p. 111 *(top)* Courtesy of Ogilvy Public Relations Worldwide, *(bottom)* Frank Gunn/Canadian Press/AP/Wide World Photos; p. 133, © Forsyth/Monkmeyer; p. 147, © AP/Wide World Photos; p. 154, © Leon Santow/Tony Stone Images; p. 173, Courtesy of the Advertising Council; p. 210, Mark Foley/AP/Wide World Photos; p. 219, PhotoFest; p. 220, Matt Ferguson/AP/Wide World Photos; p. 221, Paul Sakuma/AP/Wide World Photos; p. 225, Courtesy of Defenders of Wildlife; photo credit: © 1998 Tom Soucek/AlaskaStock; p. 256, Rene Macura/AP/Wide World Photos; p. 264, © Bob Child/AP/Wide World Photos; p. 267, Chris Cheadel/Tony Stone Images, courtesy Ford Motor Company; p. 268 *(top)* Courtesy Edelman, *(bottom)* © Morgan/Greenpeace; p. 304, Courtesy of Federal Express Corporation; p. 326, Emile Wamsteker/AP/Wide World Photos; p. 329, Courtesy of Citigroup Asset Management; p. 330, © Reuters NewMedia Inc./CORBIS; p. 348, © Joe Marquette/AP/Wide World Photos; p. 352, © Reuters NewMedia Inc./CORBIS; p. 354, Courtesy of Bonner & Associates; p. 360, Susan Walsh/AP/Wide World Photos; p. 365, © 2001 by Herblock in the *Washington Post*. Used with permission; p. 366, Courtesy of United States Postal Service; p. 369, J. Scott Applewhite/AP/Wide World Photos; p. 380, Ralph Radford/AP/Wide World Photos; p. 381, © Bob Edme/AP/Wide World Photos; p. 394, © Xinhua, Hu Haixing/AP/Wide World Photos; p. 397, © David Brauchi/AP/Wide World Photos; p. 406, the National Arbor Day Foundation; p. 409, Mothers Against Drunk Driving (MADD); p. 412 and 413, Courtesy of American Cancer Society; p. 414, Craig Taylor/AP/Wide World Photos; p. 417, Courtesy Retired and Senior Volunteer Program, Senior Service Corps; p. 418, Ed Reinke/AP/Wide World Photos; p. 419, Chris O'Meara/AP/Wide World Photos; p. 421, Courtesy of UC Museum of Paleontology, Berkeley, CA; p. 429, Courtesy of Sun Health Foundation; p. 436, Courtesy of St. Bonaventure University; p. 440, © Corbis/Bettmann; p. 444, UC Berkeley Foundation; p. 457, Arturo Mari/AP/Wide World Photos; p. 463, © Bob Child/AP/Wide World Photos; p. 464, Kathy Willens/AP/Wide World Photos; p. 466, Courtesy Edelman; p. 470, Courtesy Princess Cruises and Porter Novelli; p. 489, © Johnson & Johnson. Used with permission of the copyright owner; p. 506, Southern California Edison, an Edison International Company; p. 508, Bullit Marquez/AP/Wide World Photos; p. 515, Victor Caivano/AP/Wide World Photos; p. 518, Reed Saxon/AP/Wide World Photos; p. 529, Courtesy Pepsi-Cola Company; p. 535, © 2001 Warner Bros./PhotoFest; p. 540, Reproduced with permission © More Fun. More Friends. More Life. Copyright American Heart Association; p. 542, © UPI/Corbis-Bettmann; p. 544, California Strawberry Association

Index